The NEW ENCYCLOPEDIA *of* SOUTHERN CULTURE

VOLUME 9 : LITERATURE

Volumes to appear in

The New Encyclopedia of Southern Culture

are:

The NEW

ENCYCLOPEDIA *of* SOUTHERN CULTURE

CHARLES REAGAN WILSON General Editor

JAMES G. THOMAS JR. Managing Editor

ANN J. ABADIE Associate Editor

VOLUME 9

Literature

M. THOMAS INGE

Volume Editor

Sponsored by

THE CENTER FOR THE STUDY OF SOUTHERN CULTURE

at the University of Mississippi

THE UNIVERSITY OF NORTH CAROLINA PRESS

Chapel Hill

5/o B/kw/. 4/08 45.10

This book was published with the
assistance of the Anniversary Endowment Fund
of the University of North Carolina Press.

© 2008 The University of North Carolina Press

All rights reserved

Designed by Richard Hendel

Set in Minion types by Tseng Information Systems, Inc.

Manufactured in the United States of America

The paper in this book meets the guidelines for permanence and
durability of the Committee on Production Guidelines for Book
Longevity of the Council on Library Resources.

Library of Congress Cataloging-in-Publication Data

Literature / M. Thomas Inge, volume editor.

p. cm. — (The new encyclopedia of Southern culture ; v. 9)

"Sponsored by The Center for the Study of Southern Culture
at the University of Mississippi."

Includes bibliographical references and index.

ISBN 978-0-8078-3190-8 (alk. paper) —

ISBN 978-0-8078-5875-2 (pbk. : alk. paper)

1. American literature—Southern States—Encyclopedias.
2. Southern States—In literature—Encyclopedias. 3. Southern
States—Intellectual life—Encyclopedias. I. Inge, M. Thomas.
II. University of Mississippi. Center for the Study of
Southern Culture. III. Series.

F209 .N47 2006 vol. 9

[PS261]

975.003 s—dc22

[810.9'97503]   2007049484

The *Encyclopedia of Southern Culture*, sponsored by the Center for
the Study of Southern Culture at the University of Mississippi, was
published by the University of North Carolina Press in 1989.

cloth   12 11 10 09 08   5 4 3 2 1

paper   12 11 10 09 08   5 4 3 2 1

Tell about the South. What's it like there.

What do they do there. Why do they live there.

Why do they live at all.

WILLIAM FAULKNER

Absalom, Absalom!

CONTENTS

In 1989 years of planning and hard work came to fruition when the University of North Carolina Press joined the Center for the Study of Southern Culture at the University of Mississippi to publish the *Encyclopedia of Southern Culture*. While all those involved in writing, reviewing, editing, and producing the volume believed it would be received as a vital contribution to our understanding of the American South, no one could have anticipated fully the widespread acclaim it would receive from reviewers and other commentators. But the *Encyclopedia* was indeed celebrated, not only by scholars but also by popular audiences with a deep, abiding interest in the region. At a time when some people talked of the "vanishing South," the book helped remind a national audience that the region was alive and well, and it has continued to shape national perceptions of the South through the work of its many users—journalists, scholars, teachers, students, and general readers.

As the introduction to the *Encyclopedia* noted, its conceptualization and organization reflected a cultural approach to the South. It highlighted such issues as the core zones and margins of southern culture, the boundaries where "the South" overlapped with other cultures, the role of history in contemporary culture, and the centrality of regional consciousness, symbolism, and mythology. By 1989 scholars had moved beyond the idea of cultures as real, tangible entities, viewing them instead as abstractions. The *Encyclopedia*'s editors and contributors thus included a full range of social indicators, trait groupings, literary concepts, and historical evidence typically used in regional studies, carefully working to address the distinctive and characteristic traits that made the American South a particular place. The introduction to the *Encyclopedia* concluded that the fundamental uniqueness of southern culture was reflected in the volume's composite portrait of the South. We asked contributors to consider aspects that were unique to the region but also those that suggested its internal diversity. The volume was not a reference book of southern history, which explained something of the design of entries. There were fewer essays on colonial and antebellum history than on the postbellum and modern periods, befitting our conception of the volume as one trying not only to chart the cultural landscape of the South but also to illuminate the contemporary era.

When C. Vann Woodward reviewed the *Encyclopedia* in the *New York Review of Books*, he concluded his review by noting "the continued liveliness of interest in the South and its seeming inexhaustibility as a field of study." Research on the South, he wrote, furnishes "proof of the value of the *Encyclopedia* as a scholarly undertaking as well as suggesting future needs for revision or supplement to keep up with ongoing scholarship." The decade and a half since the publication of the *Encyclopedia of Southern Culture* have certainly suggested that Woodward was correct. The American South has undergone significant changes that make for a different context for the study of the region. The South has undergone social, economic, political, intellectual, and literary transformations, creating the need for a new edition of the *Encyclopedia* that will remain relevant to a changing region. Globalization has become a major issue, seen in the South through the appearance of Japanese automobile factories, Hispanic workers who have immigrated from Latin America or Cuba, and a new prominence for Asian and Middle Eastern religions that were hardly present in the 1980s South. The African American return migration to the South, which started in the 1970s, dramatically increased in the 1990s, as countless books simultaneously appeared asserting powerfully the claims of African Americans as formative influences on southern culture. Politically, southerners from both parties have played crucial leadership roles in national politics, and the Republican Party has dominated a near-solid South in national elections. Meanwhile, new forms of music, like hip-hop, have emerged with distinct southern expressions, and the term "dirty South" has taken on new musical meanings not thought of in 1989. New genres of writing by creative southerners, such as gay and lesbian literature and "white trash" writing, extend the southern literary tradition.

Meanwhile, as Woodward foresaw, scholars have continued their engagement with the history and culture of the South since the publication of the *Encyclopedia*, raising new scholarly issues and opening new areas of study. Historians have moved beyond their earlier preoccupation with social history to write new cultural history as well. They have used the categories of race, social class, and gender to illuminate the diversity of the South, rather than a unified "mind of the South." Previously underexplored areas within the field of southern historical studies, such as the colonial era, are now seen as formative periods of the region's character, with the South's positioning within a larger Atlantic world a productive new area of study. Cultural memory has become a major topic in the exploration of how the social construction of "the South" benefited some social groups and exploited others. Scholars in many disciplines have made the southern identity a major topic, and they have used a variety of methodologies to suggest what that identity has meant to different social groups. Literary critics have adapted cultural theories to the South and have raised the issue of postsouthern literature to a major category of concern as well as exploring the links between the literature of the American South and that of the Caribbean. Anthropologists have used different theoretical formulations from literary critics, providing models for their fieldwork in southern communities. In the past 30 years anthropologists have set increasing numbers of their ethnographic studies in the South, with many of them now exploring topics specifically linked to southern cultural issues. Scholars now place the Native American story, from prehistory to the contemporary era, as a central part of southern history. Comparative and interdisciplinary approaches to the South have encouraged scholars to look at such issues as the borders and boundaries of the South, specific places and spaces with distinct identities within the American South, and the global and transnational Souths, linking the American South with many formerly colonial societies around the world.

The first edition of the *Encyclopedia of Southern Culture* anticipated many of these approaches and indeed stimulated the growth of Southern Studies as a distinct interdisciplinary field. The Center for the Study of Southern Culture has worked for more than a quarter century to encourage research and teaching about the American South. Its academic programs have produced graduates who have gone on to write interdisciplinary studies of the South, while others have staffed the cultural institutions of the region and in turn encouraged those institutions to document and present the South's culture to broad public audiences. The center's conferences and publications have continued its long tradition of promoting understanding of the history, literature, and music of the South, with new initiatives focused on southern foodways, the future of the South, and the global Souths, expressing the center's mission to bring the best current scholarship to broad public audiences. Its documentary studies projects build oral and visual archives, and the New Directions in Southern Studies book series, published by the University of North Carolina Press, offers an important venue for innovative scholarship.

Since the *Encyclopedia of Southern Culture* appeared, the field of Southern Studies has dramatically developed, with an extensive network now of academic and research institutions whose projects focus specifically on the interdisciplinary study of the South. The Center for the Study of the American South at the University of North Carolina at Chapel Hill, led by Director Harry Watson and Associate Director and *Encyclopedia* coeditor William Ferris, publishes the lively journal *Southern Cultures* and is now at the organizational center of many other Southern Studies projects. The Institute for Southern Studies at the University of South Carolina, the Southern Intellectual History Circle, the Society for the Study of Southern Literature, the Southern Studies Forum of the European American Studies Association, Emory University's SouthernSpaces.org, and the South Atlantic Humanities Center (at the Virginia Foundation for the Humanities, the University of Virginia, and Virginia Polytechnic Institute and State University) express the recent expansion of interest in regional study.

Observers of the American South have had much to absorb, given the rapid pace of recent change. The institutional framework for studying the South is broader and deeper than ever, yet the relationship between the older verities of regional study and new realities remains unclear. Given the extent of changes in the American South and in Southern Studies since the publication of the *Encyclopedia of Southern Culture*, the need for a new edition of that work is clear. Therefore, the Center for the Study of Southern Culture has once again joined the University of North Carolina Press to produce *The New Encyclopedia of Southern Culture*. As readers of the original edition will quickly see, *The New Encyclopedia* follows many of the scholarly principles and editorial conventions established in the original, but with one key difference; rather than being published in a single hardback volume, *The New Encyclopedia* is presented in a series of shorter individual volumes that build on the 24 original subject categories used in the *Encyclopedia* and adapt them to new scholarly developments. Some earlier *Encyclopedia* categories have been reconceptualized in light of new academic interests. For example, the subject section originally titled "Women's Life" is reconceived as a new volume, *Gender*, and the original "Black Life" section is more broadly interpreted as a volume on race. These changes reflect new analytical concerns that place the study of women and blacks in broader cultural systems, reflecting the emergence of, among other topics, the study of male culture and of whiteness. Both volumes draw as well from the rich recent scholarship on women's life and black life. In addition, topics with some thematic coherence are combined in a volume, such as *Law and Politics* and *Agriculture and Industry*. One new topic, *Foodways*, is the basis of a separate volume, reflecting its new prominence in the interdisciplinary study of southern culture.

Numerous individual topical volumes together make up *The New Encyclopedia of Southern Culture* and extend the reach of the reference work to wider audiences. This approach should enhance the use of the *Encyclopedia* in academic courses and is intended to be convenient for readers with more focused interests within the larger context of southern culture. Readers will have handy access to one-volume, authoritative, and comprehensive scholarly treatments of the major areas of southern culture.

We have been fortunate that, in nearly all cases, subject consultants who offered crucial direction in shaping the topical sections for the original edition have agreed to join us in this new endeavor as volume editors. When new volume editors have been added, we have again looked for respected figures who can provide not only their own expertise but also strong networks of scholars to help develop relevant lists of topics and to serve as contributors in their areas. The reputations of all our volume editors as leading scholars in their areas encouraged the contributions of other scholars and added to *The New Encyclopedia*'s authority as a reference work.

The New Encyclopedia of Southern Culture builds on the strengths of articles in the original edition in several ways. For many existing articles, original authors agreed to update their contributions with new interpretations and theoretical perspectives, current statistics, new bibliographies, or simple factual developments that needed to be included. If the original contributor was unable to update an article, the editorial staff added new material or sent it to another scholar for assessment. In some cases, the general editor and volume editors selected a new contributor if an article seemed particularly dated and new work indicated the need for a fresh perspective. And importantly, where new developments have warranted treatment of topics not addressed in the original edition, volume editors have commissioned entirely new essays and articles that are published here for the first time.

The American South embodies a powerful historical and mythical presence, both a complex environmental and geographic landscape and a place of the imagination. Changes in the region's contemporary socioeconomic realities and new developments in scholarship have been incorporated in the conceptualization and approach of *The New Encyclopedia of Southern Culture*. Anthropologist Clifford Geertz has spoken of culture as context, and this encyclopedia looks at the American South as a complex place that has served as the context for cultural expression. This volume provides information and perspective on the diversity of cultures in a geographic and imaginative place with a long history and distinctive character.

The *Encyclopedia of Southern Culture* was produced through major grants from the Program for Research Tools and Reference Works of the National Endowment for the Humanities, the Ford Foundation, the Atlantic-Richfield Foundation, and the Mary Doyle Trust. We are grateful as well to the College of Liberal Arts at the University of Mississippi for support and to the individual donors to the Center for the Study of Southern Culture who have directly or indirectly supported work on *The New Encyclopedia of Southern Culture*. We thank the volume editors for their ideas in reimagining their subjects and the contributors of articles for their work in extending the usefulness of the book in new ways. We acknowledge the support and contributions of the faculty and staff at the Center for the Study of Southern Culture. Finally, we want especially to honor the work of William Ferris and Mary Hart on the *Encyclopedia of Southern Culture*. Bill, the founding director of the Center for the Study of Southern Culture, was coeditor, and his good work recruiting authors, editing text, selecting images, and publicizing the volume among a wide network of people was, of course, invaluable. Despite the many changes in the new encyclopedia, Bill's influence remains. Mary "Sue" Hart was also an invaluable member of the original encyclopedia team, bringing the careful and precise eye of the librarian, and an iconoclastic spirit, to our work.

Any assessment of the creative contributions of the American South must take its literature into account. Literary historians and critics have written much about the flowering of literary talent in the Southern Literary Renaissance of the early to mid-20th century, and the national culture still recognizes the writings of contemporary southerners. Like Civil War generals and civil rights leaders, the generations of William Faulkner, Eudora Welty, Richard Wright, Thomas Wolfe, Ralph Ellison, Flannery O'Connor, and other 20th-century figures are icons of the South. Literary critics have been key commentators on southern cultural configurations, helping, according to recent scholarship, to "invent" the field of southern literature.

The *Encyclopedia of Southern Culture* provided a thorough overview of literary movements, key topics in the literary study of the South, and a rather modest biographical list of writers generally acknowledged to have been among the "greatest" in their literary achievements. Since the publication of the *Encyclopedia* in 1989, the study of southern literature has undergone seismic shocks representing as substantial a change in outlook as in any field of southern cultural study. Postmodernism was enormously influential in unpacking the criteria agendas that helped formulate the canon of the Southern Renaissance, and postsouthern scholarship questions many of the assumptions for a continuing tradition. Postcolonial and globalization scholars see connections of southern writers with other areas of the world as being more significant than traditional North-South connections within the nation.

The *Literature* volume of *The New Encyclopedia of Southern Culture* responds to these changes with a revised overview essay and a series of new thematic articles that summarize theoretical outlooks on southern literary study, open up thematic and genre issues not considered in the earlier volume, and place southern literature in wider comparative contexts than before. The list of biographical entries has been enormously expanded to reflect the range of writing that now is considered within southern contexts. Critics of the Southern Literary Renaissance at one point privileged the work of novelists and poets. *The New Encyclopedia* has a generous helping of entries in these fields but broadens the scope to include memoirists, mystery writers, humorists, biographers, essayists, dramatists, nature writers, critics, short-story masters, a few seminal historians, and a sociologist. Editors have acknowledged through biographies the work of the "classic" writers of the past, but a major focus has been recognition of contemporary writers. The editors have intentionally included longer entries on contemporary writers (and some earlier ones as well who may not have received adequate reference work attention) than on the well-known figures from southern literary history. So much material is already available on the latter that we chose to highlight the continuing vitality of southern literature today. The list of writers included is the result of input from many literary critics. Writers shape ideas of southern places, and *The New Encyclopedia* has biographies that help document the literary contributions of regions throughout the South. This volume is especially significant in charting topics that cross genres. Music, food, and religion are their own categories in the study of southern culture, but this volume shows how they interact with southern literature as well.

The NEW ENCYCLOPEDIA *of* SOUTHERN CULTURE

VOLUME 9 : LITERATURE

LITERATURE

One could argue that literature in the American South began as early as 1608, when the explorer and adventurer Captain John Smith published his promotional pamphlet, *A True Relation of Occurrences and Accidents in Virginia*, the first of a series of accounts, each of which became more embellished, to include finally the story of his rescue by Pocahontas. Or, to move ahead a hundred years, perhaps southern letters began with the secret diaries, character sketches, poems, and satiric prose of the true renaissance gentleman in residence at Westover, William Byrd II. But because America as an independent nation did not exist until 1776 and neither Smith nor Byrd considered himself other than a British citizen, the most one can say is that they established the traditions of exaggeration, irony, wit, stylistic versatility, and experimentation with form that would characterize southern literature.

Despite general impressions to the contrary, the intellectual life of the colonists in what would become the southern states was rich and varied. In the political and cultural center of Williamsburg citizens attended the theater, gave concerts for each other, built well-designed houses with beautifully patterned gardens, collected selective but impressive libraries, wrote articulate and well-argued letters to friends at home and abroad, read classical authors in the original Greek and Latin, and engaged in political and religious debate. Colonial authors expressed themselves in poetry and prose, satire and invective, essays and pamphlets. Noteworthy published works of the period include the translation into heroic couplets of Ovid's *Metamorphoses* (1626) by George Sandys, Jamestown treasurer and director of industry and agriculture; a humorous prose account of colonial life interspersed with lively poetry, *A Character of the Province of Maryland* (1666), by indentured servant George Alsop; the engaging first history of Virginia, *The History and Present State of Virginia* (1705), written by a plantation owner and member of the House of Burgesses, Robert Beverley; *The Sot-Weed Factor* (1708), a verse satire by poet laureate of early Maryland, Ebenezer Cooke, whose point of view and low-life subject matter were precursors of the southern humor tradition; the two very early novels written by the master of grammar school and professor at William and Mary College, Arthur Blackamore, *The Religious Triumverate* (1720) and *Luck at Last; or, The Happy Unfortunate* (1723); and the works of New Light Presbyterian minister and later president of Princeton University, Samuel Davies, who composed hymns, elegies, sermons, and poems, many of the last of which were collected in *Miscellaneous Poems, Chiefly on Divine Subjects* (1752).

During the revolutionary period, in roles ranging from lawyer, architect, educator, scientist, philosopher, and governor of Virginia to secretary of state, vice president, and president of the United States, Thomas Jefferson served as the intellectual center of a burst of rational and enlightened thought about the American political state, the foundations of society, and the nature of man. The creative energy of Jefferson and his colleagues such as Richard Bland, Patrick Henry, James Madison, and John Taylor of Caroline was invested in political treatises, pamphlets, oratory, and cogent essays rather than belles lettres. Although he wrote only one full-length book, *Notes on the State of Virginia* (1785), perhaps the most significant political and scientific work of its time, it was through his composition of the text of the Declaration of Independence (1776) that Jefferson had a lasting and profound impact on the subsequent history of the political, social, and cultural life of the South and the nation. It is, then, a literary document of the first order. Jefferson continues to arrest our attention as a man of great creative intellect through biographies, histories, plays, poems, and novels about his life and relationships.

Antebellum Era. Political and economic leadership in the South by the end of the 18th century had moved from Virginia to South Carolina, especially Charleston, when it became clear that raw cotton was to be that state's and the region's essential product and that slavery was therefore necessary to the future. For the first 50 years the southernmost outpost of the British empire in America, Charleston became a major commercial center and supported the development of a wealthy merchant and planter class, which in turn encouraged a lively cultural life, including one of two newspapers published in the South, a library society, and bookstores. It was at one of these, Russell's Bookstore, that the members of the "Charleston school" gathered under the leadership of statesman and critic Hugh Swinton Legaré, editor and contributor to the *Southern Review* (1828–32). The group included among its membership romantic poet Paul Hamilton Hayne, editor of *Russell's* magazine (1857–60), and other lyrical sentimental poets of the pro-Confederacy school such as Henry Timrod, "Laureate of the Confederacy."

The most influential member of the group, and probably in his time the best-known southern writer, was William Gilmore Simms, editor during his career of 10 periodicals and author of more than 80 volumes of history, poetry, criticism, biography, drama, essays, stories, and novels, including a series of nationally popular border romances about life on the frontier and historical romances about the American Revolution. He was one of the first to make a profession of writing. Simms's only serious rival as a writer in the South was Baltimore politician John Pendleton Kennedy, whose informal fictional sketches in *Swallow Barn* (1832) helped establish the plantation novel, which in its depiction of a mythic genteel past and an ideal social structure has found hundreds of imitators in American romance fiction.

Less accomplished but talented fiction writers of the time, all of whom wrote historical romances heavily under the influence of Scott, Cooper, and Irving, and all Virginia born, were Nathaniel Beverly Tucker, William Alexander Caruthers, and John Esten Cooke. Two extremely popular southern sentimental novelists of the time were Augusta Jane Evans Wilson and Caroline Lee Hentz, both of whom succeeded where many men had failed—achieving financial independence as professional writers.

The first book published by a black author in the South was *The Hope of Liberty* (1829), which contained poems decrying the slaves' condition, by George Moses Horton of North Carolina. William Wells Brown, a southern-born slave, wrote the first novel by an African American (1853), based on the rumor that Thomas Jefferson had fathered a daughter with one of his slaves. In writing what was, in essence, a novel of social protest, Brown established the mainstream tradition of black fiction in the United States. Another important book of black protest was the *Narrative of the Life of Frederick Douglass* (1845), the work of a former slave who became America's leading abolitionist organizer, orator, newspaper editor, and political figure.

Douglass's book was the epitome of a rich and revealing series of slave narratives, which would become another mainstream tradition of African American literature and culture. Some of the most widely read titles by southern authors included *The Narrative of William Wells Brown* (1847), *The Life of Josiah Henson, Formerly a Slave* (1849), *Narrative of the Life and Adventures of Henry Bibb, an American Slave* (1849), *The Fugitive Blacksmith* (1849) by James W. C. Pennington, and a singular work by a woman, *Incidents in the Life of a Slave Girl* (1861) by Harriett Jacobs. Often mannered and embellished in their style, because of professional and editorial assistance, and formal in their inclusion of certain obligatory scenes (whippings, forced seductions, escape attempts, etc.), they nevertheless exposed the horrors and harsh brutalities of slave life and provided compelling arguments for the abolition of the system. The authors also laid claim to their independence and humanity as individuals of substance and worth in the face of their identification as pieces of property and inferior beings.

The only writer of this period who, with the passage of time, was to rise to a level of national and international prominence was Edgar Allan Poe, whose relationship to his southern heritage may be seen indirectly in his work. Although he was raised in Richmond, attended the University of Virginia, and edited the *Southern Literary Messenger* (1834–64) in Richmond from 1835 to 1837, he turned away from regional materials for the most part in his poetry, fiction, and criticism to devote himself to a form of literary expression that aspired to universality in style and structure. His poetry in which sound and sensuality superseded sense, his fiction in which meaning or message was secondary to emotional impact, and his criticism in which independently and objectively derived standards are used in the evaluation of artistic success would help shape, first in Europe and then in this country, the modern literary sensibility. Creative writing throughout the world was never the same after Poe.

So dazzling was the achievement of Poe from the modern point of view that the work of numerous contemporary southern poets pales in comparison. This includes the sentimental, romantic, lyric poetry of Irish-born Richard Henry Wilde of Georgia, Thomas Holley Chivers of Georgia, British-born Edward Coote Pinkney of Maryland, Philip Pendleton Cooke of Virginia, Theodore O'Hara of Kentucky, and James Matthews Legare of South Carolina.

Outside of Poe, the most influential writing produced by the antebellum South was the work of a group of humorists who had no literary pretensions and therefore were free of the prevailing influences of the literary marketplace. They were lawyers, doctors, editors, politicians, and professional men who set down for the amusement of newspaper readers stories and tales they heard as they traveled through the frontier territories of Georgia, Alabama, Mississippi, Tennessee, or Louisiana—what was then called the Old Southwest. The sketches and fictional pieces they wrote were realistic, bawdy, vulgar, and often brutal, but they were written in a language and style close to the southern idiom and the point of view of everyday people. No one was more surprised than they when their sketches were collected between hard covers and soon constituted an impressive bookshelf of what would prove to be classics of southern humor: Augustus Baldwin Longstreet's *Georgia Scenes* (1835); William Tappan Thompson's *Major Jones's Courtship* (1843); Johnson Jones Hooper's *Some Adventures of Captain Simon Suggs* (1845); Thomas Bangs Thorpe's edition of *The Big Bear of Arkansas* (1845), which included his famous title story originally published in an 1841 issue of the *Spirit of the Times*, where much of this humor first appeared; Henry Clay Lewis's *Odd Leaves from the Life of a Louisiana Swamp Doctor* (1850); Joseph Glover Baldwin's *The Flush Times of Alabama and Mississippi* (1853); and Charles Henry Smith's *Bill Arp, So Called* (1866). Related to this tradition in its uses of comic exaggeration and oral folklore was *A Narrative of the Life of David Crockett* (1834), in which the part Crockett played as an author is uncertain.

The most accomplished of the humorists of the Old Southwest was Tennessean George Washington Harris, creator of the irascible Sut Lovingood, the liveliest comic figure to emerge from American literature before Huckleberry Finn. His first sketches were contributed to the *New York Spirit of the Times* and to Tennessee newspapers in the 1840s; however, the Lovingood stories were not collected until after the Civil War as *Sut Lovingood, Yarns Spun by a "Nat'ral Born Durn'd Fool"* (1867). In masterful use of dialect, striking control of metaphor and imagery, and kinetic creation of explosive action, Harris was to have no match until Mark Twain and William Faulkner, both of whom read Harris with appreciation.

Through studying Harris and the other southern humorists, Samuel Clemens, or Mark Twain, learned his trade, and his first published sketches, such as "Jim Smiley and His Jumping Frog" (1865), belong to this school of humor. Born of southern parents in Missouri, raised in the slaveholding community of Hannibal on the Mississippi River, employed as a steamboat pilot on the great river from St. Louis and Cairo down to New Orleans from 1857 to 1861, and enlisted briefly in the Confederate army before deserting to go with his brother to Nevada, Clemens and his formative experiences were more southern than western. His masterwork, *Adventures of Huckleberry Finn* (1885), is the most incisive satire ever written of southern attitudes, customs, and mores, aside from its central importance as a pivotal work of American literature. Clemens brought frontier humor to a high level of literary artistry, and his work transmitted this brand of humor to many practicing humorists who followed him. Modern southern writers who have maintained this tradition include Guy Owen of North Carolina; William Price Fox Jr. and Mark Steadman Jr. of South Carolina; Robert Y. Drake Jr. of Tennessee; Roy Blount Jr., Lewis Grizzard, and Jeff Foxworthy of Georgia; and Florence King of Virginia.

Local-Color Era. If frankness and realism were dominant characteristics of frontier humor, the movement that superseded it was devoted to delicacy and romanticism. The development of a number of large-circulation, well-paying magazines in New York after the Civil War and an intense interest in things regional encouraged the local-color movement, which Bret Harte's California stories instigated. Peculiarities of speech, quaint local customs, distinctive modes of thought, and stories about human nature became the primary subject matter of this fictional movement, and because the South had an abundance of all these qualities in the popular American mind, southern authors flourished. Unlike the frontier humorists, these were conscious craftsmen producing a marketable commodity; thus the finished product says more about popular misconceptions of the South in many cases than it says about the reality, and nothing that might upset the sensibilities of a young maiden, to use William Dean Howells's criterion, was allowed to see print. Although once thought to be early realists, many of the local-color writers described a quaint and curious world that may never have existed.

In any case, they came from all parts of the South to vie for space in the popular magazines and described in their fiction the worlds they inhabited— George Washington Cable, Kate Chopin, Grace King, and Ruth McEnery Stuart from Louisiana; Thomas Nelson Page and John Esten Cooke (in his postwar fiction) from Virginia; Richard Malcolm Johnston, Harry Stillwell Edwards, and Will N. Harben from Georgia; James Lane Allen from Kentucky; Sherwood Bonner from Mississippi; and Mary Noailles Murfree from Tennessee. The aesthetic sensibilities of such writers as Cable, Chopin, and Murfree allowed them to achieve a level of psychological sophistication in their characters and a stylistic skill unusual for their times.

Joel Chandler Harris's popularity was also fed by the same interests that fostered the local-color writers, but his was a special achievement. Although the exterior settings and scenes for his stories of Uncle Remus were directly out of a romantic world of a Thomas Nelson Page, the stories themselves are remarkable renderings of Afro-American folktales, in which Brer Rabbit serves as an exemplum for black survival in an Anglo-American world. Harris greatly improved, then, on the legacy of happy "darky" stereotypes that Page and the Mississippi dialect poet Irwin Russell had left. One black writer who spoke for his own race in local-color fiction was Charles Waddell Chesnutt, raised in North Carolina, but he had to begin his literary career by disguising his racial identity because of the prejudice that only whites could understand and explain blacks.

The American reading audience seemed to glory in the tales of southern times "befo' de wah," but some southern writers and leaders began a movement to reject that heritage for a concept of a New South that would be industrialized, modernized, and adapted to the larger pattern of American economic and social development. George Washington Cable and Joel Chandler Harris were supporters of this movement, but the intellectual leaders were journalists Walter Hines Page and Henry W. Grady and, in the black community, educator Booker T. Washington.

Their sentiments were shared by the best postwar poet in the South, Sidney Lanier of Georgia, whose poetry aimed for a musical and tonal beauty that stressed sound over content and whose literary criticism attempted to establish a basis for versification in the principles of music. Less accomplished poets publishing at the end of the 19th century and the beginning of the 20th were John Bannister Tabb of Virginia; former slave Albery Allson Whitman, Madison Cawein, Cale Young Rice, and Olive Tilford Dargan, all of Kentucky; Lizette Woodworth Reese of Maryland; William Alexander Percy of Mississippi; and John Gould Fletcher of Arkansas, at first a member of the imagist school of poets in London and later a member of the Fugitive poets, but overshadowed by more talented writers of both groups.

At the turn of the century, southern literature was dominated by several writers residing in Richmond, Va. Mary Johnston produced a series of popular historical romances set in Virginia, while her friend Ellen Glasgow, much more the insightful and talented artist, wrote a series of distinctive and well-crafted novels designed to constitute a social history of the state. Her critical realism was counterbalanced by the medieval romanticism and fantasy of James Branch Cabell, whose epic biography of Manuel set in Poictesme turns out to be, after all, an ironic, disguised commentary on the manners and mores of his real world. In their attention to historic forces, experimental form, and stylistic virtuosity, these Virginia writers anticipated, if indeed they did not originate, the coming renaissance in southern literature. The following generation of writers in Richmond proved to be eminent journalists and historians—Douglas Southall Freeman, who finally left newspaper work after 34 years to complete his distinguished biography of Robert E. Lee; Clifford Dowdey, who had equal success in magazine editing, publishing historical novels, and writing Civil War histories; and Virginius Dabney, who paralleled a career in journalism with that of a liberal commentator on history, politics, and social change in the South.

Southern Literary Renaissance. In a November 1917 issue of the *New York Evening Mail*, Baltimore journalist H. L. Mencken published his notorious essay "The Sahara of the Bozart," in which he excoriated the South as being culturally backward and "almost as sterile, artistically, intellectually, culturally, as the Sahara Desert." In his usual fashion, Mencken was, of course, exaggerating, but almost as if in response the next two decades witnessed an overwhelming production of literature by southern authors, called the "Southern Literary Renaissance." Some literary historians have not been happy with the term, given the quantity of writing in the South up to that time, but if the term is also used to mean a "flowering," then it is clearly appropriate.

Mencken's attack, of course, had nothing to do with initiating the renaissance, which was the culmination of a number of historical and cultural forces at work in southern society. The region had experienced a military defeat on its own soil and the trying Reconstruction era, which brought about a period of self-analysis and reflection on the values it had fought to preserve and, in some cases, a reaffirmation of those values. Some white southerners assumed a burden of guilt with regard to the treatment of blacks but maintained nonetheless a belief in white superiority. Resistance to cultural reconstruction intensified the traditional regional sense of identity and distinctiveness, and some took pleasure in this tradition, whereas others felt the need to escape it. These tensions stirred the creative sensibilities of writers, who were instructed well by southern history in mortality and the inevitability of death—concerns that would bring their themes to a level of universal relevance.

These matters were treated in the grand and eloquent style of William Faulkner, the major writer to emerge from the renaissance and the greatest American writer of the 20th century. Using local, family, and Mississippi history, Faulkner constructed a fictional world populated by southern figures of tragedy and comedy who acted out his major theme of the human heart in conflict with itself. His stylistic innovations under the influence of James Joyce, his mastery of external and internal landscape, the incredible range of characterization in his fiction, and the affirmative spirit that provides a philosophic base for his work—all these promise to make him a writer for the ages, a Shakespeare in southern homespun.

Major writers contemporary with Faulkner were Thomas Wolfe, who attempted a Herculean transformation of his personal dislocation as a southerner into fiction of bardic proportions; Richard Wright, who achieved a disturbing, razor-sharp portrayal of what growing up black in the South and America meant and forced whites to pay attention; and Robert Penn Warren, whose fiction constitutes a lifelong philosophic discourse on the meaning of history, the nature of man, and the compromises necessary in building a workable political and social system. Though overshadowed by Faulkner's achievement, all three achieved distinctive voices in fiction.

Others worked in Faulkner's shadow but followed their own separate sensibilities with notable results, as evidenced by the stylistically perfect stories of Katherine Anne Porter, the keen sensitivity to adolescence in the fiction of Carson McCullers and James Agee, and the richly textured re-creations in the southern vernacular of myth and metaphor in Eudora Welty's stories and novels. Except for their lack of artistic discipline and willingness to publish too much too fast, Erskine Caldwell and Jesse Stuart might have entered this golden circle; as it is, they remain of interest because of the philosophically opposite variations they offer on some of the same material handled by Faulk-

William Faulkner, c. 1930 (Jack Cofield, photographer, Archives and Special Collections, University of Mississippi Library, Oxford, Mississippi)

ner. The single writer who reached more readers than all these major writers put together and has probably done more to shape the larger public's attitude toward the South was Margaret Mitchell. With more enthusiasm than artistry and less skill than imagination, she wrote one novel, *Gone with the Wind* (1936), which remains an enigma but must be considered a significant event of the renaissance.

A host of other fiction writers should be accounted for in any survey of the renaissance, including Harriette Simpson Arnow, Hamilton Basso, Roark Bradford, Brainard Cheney, Alfred Leland Crabbe, Caroline Gordon, Dubose Heyward, Zora Neale Hurston, Andrew Lytle, William March, Julia Peterkin, Josephine Pinckney, Marjorie Kinnan Rawlings, Elizabeth Madox Roberts, Lyle Saxon, Evelyn Scott, Lillian Smith, James Still, T. S. Stribling, Jean Toomer, and Stark Young.

Although drama was never to be a major mode for southern writers, Paul Green began in the 1920s a 50-year career as the successful author of folk plays and historic symphonic dramas; Lawrence Stallings had a notable success in collaboration with Maxwell Anderson, *What Price Glory?* (1924); Lillian Hellman, beginning with the popular reception of *The Little Foxes* (1939), wrote a series of sensitive treatments of life in southern settings; and Tennessee Williams began in the 1940s a singularly distinctive career as the author of numerous plays that examined in depth and detail southern elements of life and character and gained for himself a reputation as one of America's three most accomplished playwrights (along with Eugene O'Neill and Arthur Miller).

A formidable body of poetry emerged during the renaissance beginning with the publication in 1922 of the first issue of the *Fugitive*, a little magazine edited by a group of young faculty members and students at Vanderbilt University in Nashville. Many would mark the event as the official beginning of the Southern Literary Renaissance. Although they were for the moment in agreement that modern poetry must escape the conventionalism of the past, the major figures were to follow different patterns of development—John Crowe Ransom's finding in irony and paradox the tension necessary to good poetry, Allen Tate's turning to abstract methods as more suitable for treating the dislocations in modern society evident to the traditional sensibility, Robert Penn Warren's preferring narrative forms deeply philosophical in their import, and Donald Davidson's finding more compatible folk narratives incorporating history and the lives of influential southern figures. Merrill Moore, John Gould Fletcher, and, for a brief time, Laura Riding were associated with the Fugitive poets. A young Randall Jarrell would come to Vanderbilt in the early 1930s to study under Ransom, Davidson, and Warren and, under their influence, to begin writing poetry striking in its combination of the erudite with the ordinary and its contrast of desperate violence with the seemingly peaceful surface of daily life. Two black poetic voices of the period who used their southern experiences in ethnically sensitive verse were James Weldon Johnson and Arna Bontemps, the former best known for his political activities with the NAACP and the latter as the author of the lyrics for the musical *St. Louis Woman*.

Reunion in 1956 of the Fugitive poets (left to right, front row) Allen Tate, Merrill Moore, John Crowe Ransom, Donald Davidson, and (back row) Robert Penn Warren (Joe Rudis, photographer, Photographic Archives, Vanderbilt University Library, Nashville, Tennessee)

After the *Fugitive* ceased publication in 1925, the four major forces—Ransom, Davidson, Tate, and Warren—began discussions about the state of the South in political and economic terms and found themselves in agreement that only by resisting modern progress and technology could the region maintain a hold on the virtues of its traditional agrarian past. Joining forces with eight other southern intellectuals, including writers Stark Young, John Gould Fletcher, Andrew Lytle, and John Donald Wade, they published the Agrarian manifesto *I'll Take My Stand* (1930), a major document in the debate between science and humanism in the 20th century. The only other prose volume to generate more controversy during the renaissance was W. J. Cash's effort to interpret *The Mind of the South* (1941), which has proved to be more valuable as a study of the mind of a southerner—Cash himself.

In the exciting intellectual milieu of the Fugitive and Agrarian movements, modern southern literary criticism had its birth. Ransom, Tate, and Warren had already been practicing criticism early on, but Ransom in particular began to encourage the development of a formalist approach called the New Criticism, which assessed a work of art on its own terms apart from its relation to the life of the artist or the times in which it was written. One of Ransom's best students at Vanderbilt, Cleanth Brooks, would develop the system more fully, incorporating it in two highly influential textbooks written in collaboration with Robert Penn Warren, *Understanding Poetry* (1938) and *Understanding Fiction* (1943). The adherents to this critical approach became more single-minded in its application than either Ransom or Brooks ever intended, as demonstrated by the fine biographical and historical criticism practiced by Brooks in his important studies of William Faulkner.

Ransom, Davidson, Tate, Warren, and Brooks also provided another service in establishing a role model for the modern man of letters as teacher, all serving throughout their literary careers as lecturers in American universities and becoming, in effect, some of the first writers in residence. A number of university teachers achieved national distinction as practicing critics, scholars, and historians of southern culture, including Edwin Mims and Richmond Croom Beatty at Vanderbilt; Jay B. Hubbell at Duke; Benjamin Brawley at Morehouse and Howard; Floyd Stovall at the University of Virginia; Randall Stewart at Brown and Vanderbilt; Lewis Leary at Duke and Columbia; Edd Winfield Parks at Georgia; Sterling A. Brown, Saunders Redding, and Arthur P. Davis at Howard; Richard Beale Davis at Tennessee; C. Vann Woodward at Johns Hopkins and Yale University; and John Hope Franklin at Chicago and Duke.

As if the first generation had not been sufficient to leave an indelible mark on American letters, a second generation of renaissance writers flooded the bookstores with their works following World War II. Flannery O'Connor arrested the attention of everyone by producing stories and novels shocking in their use of perversely exaggerated southern characters but orthodox in the Catholicism that informs their meaning. William Styron moved away from the stylistic influence of Faulkner and his early novels to achieve a major mode of fiction based on history and personal experience. Truman Capote published stories of impeccable style, while developing what he would call the "nonfiction novel," and his childhood friend Harper Lee wrote a single novel, *To Kill a Mockingbird* (1960), which remains a classic for its sensitive treatment of adolescence and racism in an Alabama town. Ralph Ellison captured history, folklore, music, and the political significance of the black man in America in *Invisible Man* (1952), which was as much concerned with the existential fate of modern man as with the black experience. Walker Percy's interests in Christian existentialism provided a foundation for his increasingly conservative novels, and John Barth brilliantly played with and reworked all the traditional forms and points of view developed in the entire history of fiction.

A beginning list of other significant practitioners of short fiction and the novel among the second-generation renaissance writers should include Doris Betts, Fred Chappell, Ellen Douglas, Shelby Foote, Jesse Hill Ford, Ernest J. Gaines, George Garrett, William Goyen, Shirley Ann Grau, Chester Himes, Madison Jones, John Oliver Killens, David Madden, Cormac McCarthy, Marion Montgomery, Reynolds Price, Mary Lee Settle, Elizabeth Spencer, Peter Taylor, Margaret Walker, John A. Williams, Calder Willingham, and Frank Yerby.

The leading poet to emerge in the postwar period was James Dickey, trained at Vanderbilt and devoted to the achievement of a careful balance between the formal and the emotional within an intricate poetic structure, and raising the ordinary experience to the level of epiphany. His novel *Deliverance* (1970) is a metaphoric study of man's potential for violence and salvation. Other poets to attract critical praise include A. R. Ammons, Wendell Berry, John William Corrington, Julia Fields, Dabney Stuart, Miller Williams, Fred Chappell, Betty Adcock, Margaret Gibson, Jonathan Williams, and Dave Smith. Pulitzer Prize winners were Donald Justice in 1979, Henry Taylor in 1986, Yusef Komunyakaa in 1994, and Charles Wright in 1997. There never seemed to be a lack of poets in the 20th-century South, and many continue to achieve a national audience for their regional accents in the 21st.

A second generation of university teachers continued the earlier critical explorations of southern literature and scholarship; many of them were trained by members of the first generation: C. Hugh Holman at North Carolina; Arlin Turner at Louisiana State University and Duke; Richard Weaver at Chicago; Lewis Simpson at Louisiana State; Ruel Foster at West Virginia; Thomas Daniel Young and Walter Sullivan at Vanderbilt; Floyd Watkins at Emory; Louis D. Rubin Jr. at Hollins and North Carolina; and Louise Cowan at the University of Dallas. The next generation of critics has challenged the assumptions and methods of the earlier, as seen in the work of Fred Hobson at North Carolina; Robert H. Brinkmeyer Jr. at South Carolina; Michael Kreyling at Vanderbilt; John Lowe at Louisiana State University; Anne Goodwyn Jones at Florida; Susan Donaldson at William and Mary; and Suzanne W. Jones at Richmond.

Southern journalists who established a tradition for crusading liberal journalism in the 1950s and 1960s were Ralph McGill, Hodding Carter, Harry Ashmore, and Willie Morris, but in a class by himself was Virginian Tom Wolfe, a founder of the freewheeling, personal, stylistically fluid school of New Journalism.

Contemporary Era. Some scholars have argued that the Southern Literary Renaissance is over, that contemporary writers share too little in the sense of southern tradition and are swept up in faddish social causes and personal crises, but a third generation of considerable promise emerged. Although they both came to fiction late in their lives, black novelists Robert Dean Pharr and Alex Haley attracted attention in the 1970s, Haley in particular for his re-creation of the history of his family in America, *Roots* (1976). Other writers producing fiction and poetry of note are Lisa Alther, Maya Angelou, Pat Conroy, Nikki Giovanni, Gail Godwin, Barry Hannah, Beverly Lowry, James Alan McPherson, Bobbie Ann Mason, Lee Smith, Anne Tyler, Alice Walker, and Sylvia Wilkinson. Many of them are black and female, perhaps a sign of racial and feminine liberation at work in the South.

A recent critical phenomenon has been the designation of certain contemporary writers as members of a "grit lit" school of southern literature. The originating authors most often mentioned include Cormac McCarthy of Tennessee in his early grim and deterministic portrayals of life in the gutter, as in *Suttree* (1979); Harry Crews of Florida for his tough-minded depictions of violence and abject poverty, as in *Scar Lover* (1993); and Larry Brown of Mississippi for the gritty realism and elemental struggles of his characters clutching small shreds of dignity in the face of defeat, as in *Big Bad Love* (1996), *Joe* (1991), and *Fay* (2000). Other works mentioned in this context include Tim McLaurin's *The Acorn Plan* (1989) and *The Last Great Snake Show* (1997), Dorothy Allison's *Bastard Out of Carolina* (1996), Tom Franklin's *Poachers* (1999) and *Hell at the Breech* (2003), Lewis Nordan's *The Sharpshooter Blues* (1995), William Price Fox's *Ruby Red* (1971), Lee Smith's *Oral History* (1983), and Clyde Edgerton's *Walking across Egypt* (1987). The "grit" or grittiness of real life, stark violence, and economic despair seem to be the general characteristics of these stories of poor white southerners who nevertheless cling to survival through humor and adaptation.

But the term "grit lit" is problematic. In her book of recommended readings, *Book Lust* (2003), Nancy Pearl defines it as "Southern-fried Greek tragedies . . . filled with angry, deranged, and generally desperate characters who are fueled by alcohol and sex." In fact, grit lit may be a derogatory term developed by outsiders to ridicule the excesses of southern literature and not a real movement of any kind. Perhaps it is used by southerners with a degree of self-conscious irony and sarcasm as a way of turning back the criticism. Students on university campuses have long called classes in southern literature "grit lit," by which they mean literature written by people who generally eat grits. And since 2004 the city of Hamilton in Ontario, Canada, has held an annual "gritLIT" literary festival to celebrate new and emerging authors from that country. The title derives from the fact that Hamilton has a reputation of being a dirty, gritty city.

Taking into account the definitions offered of grit lit, it is possible to carry its concerns over the grotesque and the aberrant back to William Faulkner, Erskine Caldwell, Flannery O'Connor, and Carson McCullers, or even before them back to the 19th-century humorists of the Old Southwest. Even earlier were the lazy North Carolina "Lubberlanders" of William Byrd's *History of the Dividing Line Run in the Year 1728*. In other words, the term equally applies to all of southern literature that has frequently focused on the dispossessed and the ugly in life and human behavior.

At the turn of the 21st century, critics and historians began to question the concept of southern exceptionalism and to wonder if those things known as distinctly regional had not disappeared into a national, social, political, and economic homogeneity, given changes in voting patterns and job markets. Novelists and poets, however, have always known that the South was more a matter of the mind and imagination than a tangible reality, and they have continued to produce what clearly seems to be a literature immersed in the history and character of the southern experience. Toni Morrison's *Beloved* (1987), Charles Frazier's *Cold Mountain* (1997), and Edward P. Jones's *The Known World* (2003) are just a few such works widely read in the 21st century as masterful examples of novels that lay claim to the power and influence of the southern narrative tradition. Rather than accept the time-honored clichés of southern culture, however, they interrogate the real meaning in human terms of such things as the Civil War, slavery, and the disenfranchisement of women and blacks, and they worry less about politics than about the human condition. Probably a hundred years from now, the same conversation will be continuing.

The new century has also brought a generation of critics who wish to look beyond the regional concerns of patriarchy, community, and agrarianism, and even beyond race, gender, and ethnicity to position the study of southern literature in hemispheric, global, and transnational contexts. Using postcolonial and poststructuralist perspectives, critics view the South through the tensions between its national and regional identities and through the tensions between global and local influences. How do cultural and economic forces from abroad shape the South, and how does the South compare with similar regions outside the United States? Has globalization made a difference in the culture of a region noted for its insularity?

To a certain extent, this sort of analysis has been long under way in the comparative studies of major southern authors and world-class writers from abroad, and by its very nature, southern literature has nearly always required interdisciplinary approaches to its understanding. As long ago as 1952, C. Vann Woodward said in *The Burden of Southern History*, "the South had undergone an experience that it could share with no other part of America—though it is shared by nearly all the peoples of Europe and Asia—the experience of military defeat, occupation, and reconstruction." Gabriel García Márquez put his finger on a major point of discourse when he said in 1968, "Yoknapatawpha County has banks on the Caribbean Sea, so in some way Faulkner is a writer from the Caribbean, in some way he's a Latin American writer." Only recently, however, have the critics emerged with the ability to move across languages and cultures with the fluency necessary to write such criticism.

Whatever the future may hold for literature in the South, the social changes and the cultural challenges at work in the rapidly changing cities of Atlanta, Charlotte, Birmingham, Nashville, and Richmond, as well as the suburbs and the countryside along interstate routes 95 and 85, create the kinds of intellectual conflict that often stir the imagination and stimulate creative writing. Whether in the form of fiction, poetry, or play; memoir, history, or journalism; docu-drama, screenplay, or criticism, in all likelihood, the last distinctively southern writer, like the last southern gentleman, has not been heard from yet.

M. THOMAS INGE
Randolph-Macon College

Robert Bain, Joseph M. Flora, and Louis D. Rubin Jr., eds., *Southern Writers: A Biographical Dictionary* (1979); Richmond Croom Beatty, Floyd C. Watkins, and Thomas Daniel Young, eds., *The Literature of the South* (1952; rev. ed., 1968); John M. Bradbury, *Renaissance in the South: A Critical History of the Literature, 1920–1960* (1963); Robert H. Brinkmeyer Jr., *Remapping Southern Literature: Contemporary Southern Writers and the West* (2000); Deborah N. Cohn, *History and Memory in the Two Souths: Recent Southern and Spanish American Fiction* (1999); Louise Cowan, *The Fugitive Group: A Literary History* (1959); Donald Davidson, *Southern Writers in the Modern World* (1958); Richard Beale Davis, *Intellectual Life in the Colonial South, 1565–1763* (1978); Joseph M. Flora and Lucinda H. MacKethan, eds., *The Companion to Southern Literature* (2002); Joseph M. Flora and Amber Vogel, eds., *Southern Writers: A New Biographical Directory* (2006); Richard Gray, *The Literature of Memory: Modern Writers of the American South*

(1977); Fred Hobson, *Tell about the South: The Southern Rage to Explain* (1983); C. Hugh Holman, *Three Modes of Southern Fiction* (1966); Jay B. Hubbell, *The South in American Literature* (1954); Jefferson Humphreys and John Lowe, eds., *The Future of Southern Letters* (1996); M. Thomas Inge and Ed Piacentino, eds., *The Humor of the Old South* (2001); Blyden Jackson, *A History of Afro-American Literature* (1989); Anne Goodwyn Jones, *Tomorrow Is Another Day: The Woman Writer in the South, 1859–1936* (1981); Suzanne W. Jones, *Race Mixing: Southern Fiction since the Sixties* (2006); Richard H. King, *A Southern Renaissance: The Cultural Awakening of the American South, 1930–1955* (1980); Michael Kreyling, *Inventing Southern Literature* (1998); Michael O'Brien, *The Idea of the American South, 1920–1941* (1979); Ladell Payne, *Black Novelists and the Southern Literary Tradition* (1981); Joseph V. Ridgely, *Nineteenth-Century Southern Literature* (1980); Louis D. Rubin Jr., ed., *The American South: Portrait of a Culture* (1980), *The Wary Fugitives: Four Poets and the South* (1978), with Robert D. Jacobs, ed. *South: Modern Southern Literature in Its Cultural Setting* (1961), with others, *A History of Southern Literature* (1985); Lewis P. Simpson, *The Dispossessed Garden: Pastoral and History in Southern Fiction* (1975); Edmund Wilson, *Patriotic Gore: Studies in the Literature of the Civil War* (1962); Patricia Yaeger, *Dirt and Desire: Reconstructing Southern Women's Writing* (2000); Thomas Daniel Young, *The Past in the Present: A Thematic Study of Modern Southern Fiction* (1981).

African American Literature

The African American southern literary tradition is rooted in the voices of enslavement. Writers such as Oladuah Equiano, Frederick Douglass, Harriett Jacobs, Henry Box Brown, William Wells Brown, and Sojourner Truth set the foundation for a tradition that analyzes the climate of the South, describes the distinct cultural practices found among African American southerners, and offers deliverance from oppressive southern conditions. While most African American southern literature produced during American enslavement is autobiographical and designed to expose the atrocities of enslavement, Phyllis Wheatley and George Moses Horton choose poetic lyrics to write their visions of the South.

Between 1865 and 1900, African American southern writers describe life in the South while its citizens grapple with the economic and social shadows of enslavement. Frances Ellen Watkins Harper's poetry and her novel *Iola Leroy* (1892) stand as testament to African American women's concerns in the late 19th century, while Charles Chesnutt explores masculine concerns as he masterfully manipulates both the short story and the novel. Paul Laurence Dunbar and Joseph Seamon Cotter excel in poetry, along with post–Civil War poets Albery A. Whitman, George M. McClellan, and Joseph S. Cotter Sr., who wrote skillfully about racial and nonracial topics in conventional poetic forms. The eclectic Alice Dunbar Nelson proves herself as journalist, poet, and short-story craftsperson. Many African American southerners of this period, however, choose to treat the South through autobiographical statements that build on the traditions of the slave narrative: Elizabeth Keckley's *Thirty Years a Slave, and Four Years in the White House* (1868), Booker T. Washington's *Up from Slavery*, William Sanders Scarborough's *An American Journey from Slavery to Scholarship*, and Amanda Berry Smith's *An Autobiography: The Story of the Lord's Dealings with Mrs. Amanda Smith, the Colored Evangelist* (1893).

Also in the 19th century, Anna Julia Cooper's *A Voice from the South* (1892) presents rousing essays challenging women to live without gendered limitations. Journalist Ida B. Wells's *A Red Record* (1895) exposes the gruesome practice of lynching. Joan Sherman's *Invisible Poets* (1976) identifies 130 African American poets of the 19th century, many of whom are rooted in the South.

Southern African Americans emerged as dominant voices in the poetry of the Harlem Renaissance of the 1920s and 1930s and thereafter continued to remain in the vanguard of African American poets in America. One wing of the Harlem Renaissance arts movement looked to the African American South for aesthetic inspiration and artistic direction. Langston Hughes's *The Weary Blues* (1926) and James Weldon Johnson's *God's Trombones: Seven Negro Sermons in*

Verse (1927) drew heavily from southern African American folk culture and the experiences of the African American masses within and outside the South. Hughes tapped an essentially secular component of southern African American life—its music. Grounding his poetic technique in musical forms whose origins were southern and African American and which, to a large extent, had evolved from the religious orientation of southern African Americans, Hughes used blues and jazz to shape the form and meaning of his poetry. Johnson tapped the sacred side of the southern African American experience. Choosing the African American folk sermon as the embodiment of a southern African American world view and as an indigenous art form, Johnson elevated folk art to the level of high art. Poets, novelists, and playwrights after the 1920s (blacks and whites) followed the example of Hughes, Johnson, and others of the Harlem Renaissance by deriving artistic inspiration from the social and cultural life of the African American South.

In the 1920s African American poets' use of dialects became more refined as poetic form merged with content. African American dialect gave way to African American idiom, and poets made even more extensive uses of features from the southern African American oral tradition. Many southern African American poets of the Harlem Renaissance also built their poetic canons with forms and themes not exclusively or predominantly African American or southern. The lyricism of Jean Toomer's poetry and the intricate patterns of imagery drawn from nature by Anne Spencer revealed that a poetic voice originating from the African American South could adopt the European American literary heritage and yet remain relatively free of its constraints.

In the decades following the Harlem Renaissance, southern African Americans continued to be major influences on black American poetry. Southerners Sterling Brown, Arna Bontemps, Margaret Walker, and Melvin B. Tolson were among black America's leading poets between the end of the Harlem Renaissance and the 1960s. A native of the District of Columbia, Sterling Brown in his *Southern Road* (1932) captured the spirit of the southern African American folk character in the language, form, and personae of his poetry. Between the 1930s and the 1960s Walker and Tolson exhibited in their poetry an intricate blending of the Euro-American and African American heritages. Tolson became one of the best American poets of his time.

As the movement toward a black aesthetic gained impetus in the 1960s, southern African American writers, many of them poets, were again among the leaders. During the 1960s and after, the poetry of southern African Americans lost many of its more obvious regional qualities and merged with the larger body of black American poetry. The focus shifted from the rural South to the urban North with southern settings, themes, and female personae being re-placed by northern settings, themes, and male personae. Nikki Giovanni, Ethe-ridge Knight, Don L. Lee, Naomi Madgett, Sterling Plumpp, Lance Jeffers, Yusef Komunyakaa, and Kalamu Ya Salaam are only a few of the widely read poets of the black arts movement whose origins are southern.

Southern African Americans wrote few plays before the 1920s. William Wells Brown's *Escape; or, A Leap for Freedom* (1858) and Joseph S. Cotter, Sr.'s *Caleb, the Degenerate* (1903), both dramatic tracts, are notable now chiefly for their historical value. Before the Harlem Renaissance, southern African Americans wrote minstrel shows, musical comedies, and a few serious social dramas, but the significance of these works in black American theater arts is also mainly historical. As an outgrowth of the renaissance, however, Langston Hughes (*Mulatto, When the Jack Hollers*, and *Little Ham*), Zora Neale Hurston (*Great Day, Color Struck*), Hal Johnson (*Run, Little Children*), Georgia Douglas John-son (*Sunday Morning in the South, Blue Blood*), and Arna Bontemps (*St. Louis Woman*) emerged as successful southern African American playwrights. In the 1930s the Works Progress Administration's support of African American the-ater arts—plays, playwrights, actors, and actresses—provided for the writing and production of several dramas of social realism by and about southern Afri-can Americans.

After 1940 the number of southern African American playwrights and plays about southern black life declined. Randolph Edmonds, Theodore Ward, and Alice Childress have, however, produced works in this period that rank with the best American plays. From the 1930s through the early 1960s, southern African American playwrights, like their northern counterparts, used the music, folk-lore, religion, social history, and other components of southern black life as a major source for their art, but after about 1960 the use of distinctly southern materials decreased sharply in plays by northern and southern African Ameri-cans. Settings, themes, and characters associated with the urban North became predominant. Still, Alice Childress's *Wedding Band* (1966) and Samm-Art Wil-liams's *Home*, distinctly southern African American works, were among the most successful post-1960 plays. Also, at Tougaloo College in Jackson, Miss., Tom Dent founded the Free Southern Theater (1969) to take drama and theater into rural areas where residents had little exposure to theater. The Free South-ern Theater eventually moved to New Orleans and continued its work there for years.

In another genre, southerners were among the earliest (if not the first) black short-fiction writers in America. Until well past 1900 southern black short fic-tion in the main was thematically about the slave experience and its aftermath and conformed largely to changes and developments in the short story as an American art form. William Wells Brown, Frederick Douglass, Frances Harper, and a few other southern African Americans wrote various types of short prose fiction during the 19th century. Near the turn of the century Charles Waddell Chesnutt elevated southern African American short fiction to the level of literary art. Many of Chesnutt's stories incorporated characteristics of the American local-color movement, and several were classified regionally as plantation literature. The tales of white southerner Thomas Nelson Page and those of Chesnutt exemplified the essential differences between black writers and white writers in approaches to the plantation South. Through characterization, theme, and incident African American writers of the South repudiated the romantic image of the plantation. Chesnutt's Uncle Julius, for instance, contradicted the white portrayal of the faithful black servant, epitomized by Page's Sam and Joel Chandler Harris's Uncle Remus. The idyllic portrait of plantation life created by white writers was in stark contrast to the image Chesnutt and other blacks showed of a system infested with greed, inhumanity, deception, and cruelty.

Southern African American writers also embellished conventional short-fiction forms by adding features that reflected black life in the South. One such feature was the double entendre, a characteristic of narrative expression rooted especially in the secular and sacred music of the black South. A part of the trickster motif, it helped shape not only characterization but also plot structure, language, and meaning in the different forms of southern African American short fiction. Chesnutt's *The Conjure Woman* (1899) exemplified the African American writer's skillful use of double entendre.

The Conjure Woman was also an early example of the use of the short-story cycle. The cycle is a fictional narrative that combines techniques of the novel and the short story. Among other collections of short fiction, Langston Hughes's *The Ways of White Folks* (1934) and the Simple series (1950–65), Richard Wright's *Uncle Tom's Children* (1938) and *Eight Men* (1961), Alice Childress's *Like One of the Family* (1956), James A. McPherson's *Hue and Cry* (1969) and *Elbow Room* (1977), and Ernest J. Gaines's *Bloodline* (1975) demonstrated the consistent expertise of southern black writers' use of the cycle. Hal Bennet, Toni Cade Bambara, and Henry Dumas are among the best contemporary African American short-fiction writers of southern origin to have produced superior short-story cycles as well as excellent individual stories.

Between 1900 and the 1970s the novel has been the most widely read and critically acclaimed genre in southern African American literature. The manner in which it has concerned itself with the past distinguished it from the general black American novel, the southern white novel, and the Anglo-American novel. The southern white novel has generally dealt with the effects of a real or an imagined past on a present generation, with characters grappling to come to terms with that past. Typically, the southern black novel made the physical and psychological landscapes of the past a living part of the novel; it re-created, repopulated, and critically examined the past as physical setting. Surprisingly, though, southern African Americans produced few novels that can be strictly defined as historical novels. Arna Bontemps (*Black Thunder*, 1936), Frank Yerby (*The Foxes of Harrow*, 1946), Waters Turpin (*The Rootless*, 1957), and Margaret Walker (*Jubilee*, 1966) are exceptions.

Those novels concerned with the past, particularly the slave past, used a rather distinct thematic structure. Characteristically, the southern African American novel was structurally tripartite—usually beginning in the present, shifting to the recent or remote past, and returning to the present. There were frequent variations: a flight-rejection-return pattern evident in Chesnutt's *The House behind the Cedars* (1900) and in other novels in the "passing" vein; a South-North-South pattern in Jean Toomer's *Cane* (1923) and in a host of novels that concerned the southern black migrant in the North, from James Weldon Johnson's *The Autobiography of an Ex-Colored Man* (1912) to Ralph Ellison's *Invisible Man* (1952); a fear-flight-fate pattern in Richard Wright's *Native Son* (1940), William Attaway's *Blood on the Forge* (1941), and several novels whose settings were almost exclusively northern or whose themes were grounded in the violence of living black in America.

Prior to the mid-1970s southern African American novels characteristically were concerned with blacks' identity and their process of self-definition. This overarching theme remained prominent over the generations: the 19th-century novels often focused on the plight of the mulatto; the early 20th-century novels frequently recount the aborted attempts of black characters to "pass" as white; the Harlem Renaissance novels affirmed blackness as a key to identity; the protest-era novels followed in the tradition of *Native Son*; and post-1960 novels dwelt on the effects of black affirmation in a drastically changed but still white-dominated society.

For its form and its content, the southern African American novel found one of its most influential prose models in the slave narrative, which itself was essentially a southern product. Various features of the southern version of the black American novel have their antecedents in the genre: the concentration on generic black experiences and incidents; the tendency toward representative central characters; the emphasis on the protagonist's process of self-definition; the use of the autobiographical mode and the portrayal of an exemplary life; and the analysis of society by an author (or narrator) removed from that society.

Indeed, the first African American American novelist, William Wells Brown, was himself a fugitive slave, and he cast his first novel, *Clotel* (1853), solidly in the traditions of the slave-narrative genre.

As the southern African American novel evolved, from the 19th into the 20th century, its use of narrative voice blended with other features of southern black narrative prose to produce a particularly (but not exclusively) southern point of view in the African American novel. For more than a century, southern African Americans wrote numerous prose narratives, which in their variety conformed to the autobiographical mode. There have been the fugitive-slave narratives and the ex-slave narratives; the spiritual, social, political, and personal autobiographies; the confessional, exemplary-lives, and diary-type autobiographies; and the autobiographical novel. At times, real-life experiences and incidents were the backdrop for fictional characters; at other times real-life characters become the nucleus around which true-to-life (fictional) experiences and incidents are presented. Southern black prose writers were so attracted to the autobiographical mode that in numerous prose narratives they drew a very thin line between fiction and fact.

One group of prose narratives used the techniques of fiction—a group that includes Richard Wright's *Black Boy* (1945), Will Thomas's *The Seeking* (1953), H. Rap Brown's *Die Nigger Die!* (1970), and Alex Haley's *The Autobiography of Malcolm X* (1965) and *Roots* (1976). In another group, the novels (fictional autobiographies) employed nonfiction techniques—Johnson's *The Autobiography of an Ex-Colored Man* and Ernest J. Gaines's *The Autobiography of Miss Jane Pittman* (1971). Finally, in still another group novels such as Toomer's *Cane* and Ellison's *Invisible Man* contain varying degrees and uses of autobiographical material. John Oliver Killens treats violence and racism in the South in *Sippi* (1967).

Folktales and aphorisms, sacred and secular music, and the religious orientation or world view of southern African Americans all influenced language, undergirded imagery and symbolism, delineated characterization, and motivated plot structure in the southern African American novel. This tendency was evident in the polemical, propagandistic, and apologetic novels that preceded World War I; it increased and became more refined in the novels between World War I and the 1930s; it pervaded such 1930s folk novels as Zora Neale Hurston's *Their Eyes Were Watching God* (1937) and George W. Henderson's *Ollie Miss* (1935); it shaped themes and characterization in the social-protest novels of the 1940s; and it pervaded Ellison's *Invisible Man* and several other novels in the period following World War II. Southern black novelists as a group have thus made wide and varied uses of the cultural traditions of their region.

Between 1980 and 2000, a cadre of African American writers who are consciously influenced by the South emerged. During this era that followed the black arts movement, African American southern writing has become much more diverse. Most, however, continue to explore how land, traditions, family values, and language color the experiences of African American southerners in both urban and rural environments of the South. Many writers who were birthed during the black arts movement have continued to write about the South in more diverse forms, refusing to be limited to one genre: Shay Youngblood (*Big Mama Stories, Shaking the Mess out of Misery*), Pearl Cleage (*Flyin' West, Blues for an Alabama Sky, What Looks Like Crazy*), Randall Kenan (*A Visitation of Spirits, Let the Dead Bury the Dead*), Arthur Flowers (*Mojo Rising, De Mojo Blues*), Clifton Taulbert (*Once upon a Time When We Were Colored, The Last Train North*), Alice Walker (*The Color Purple*), Albert Murray (*Train Whistle Guitar, The Spyglass Tree*), Ernest Gaines (*Bloodline, Lesson before Dying*), and John Oliver Killens (*Youngblood*). Each of these writers continued advancing interrogations of the political climate following the civil rights era in the South.

At the dawn of the 21st century, the tradition of African American southern writing seems secure as more African American writers question the influence of race and region in their works. The advance guard of this tradition includes Claude Wilkinson, Tayari Jones, Crystal Wilkinson, Natasha Trethewey, Brian Keith Jackson, Honoree Jeffers, Olympia Vernon, Kevin Young, and Ronald Gauthier.

J. LEE GREENE
University of North Carolina at Chapel Hill

ETHEL YOUNG-MINOR
University of Mississippi

Robert A. Bone, *Down Home: Origins of the Afro-American Short Story* (1988); Arthur P. Davis and J. Saunders Redding, eds., *Cavalcade: Negro American Writing from 1760 to the Present* (1971); Frances Smith Foster, *Written by Herself: Literary Production by African American Women, 1746–1892* (1993); Addison Gayle, *The Way of the New World: The Black Novel in America* (1975); J. Lee Greene, *Blacks in Eden: The African American Novel's First Century* (1996); M. Thomas Inge, Maurice Duke, and Jackson R. Bryer, eds., *Black American Writers: Bibliographical Essays*, 2 vols. (1978); Wolfgang Karrer and Barbara Puschlmann-Nolenz, eds., *The African American Short Story, 1970–1990: A Collection of Critical Essays* (1993); Angelyn Mitchell, ed., *Within the Circle: An Anthology of African American Literary Criticism from the Harlem Renaissance to the Present* (1994); Toni Morrison, *Playing in the Dark: Whiteness and the*

Literary Imagination (1992); Craig Hansen Werner, *Playing the Changes: From Afro-Modernism to the Jazz Impulse* (1994).

Agrarianism in Literature

The ideas associated with agrarianism in the 20th century may be stated as an interrelated set of beliefs.

First, the cultivation of the soil is an occupation singularly blessed by God that provides benefits from direct contact with physical nature. It is the mother of all the arts and instills in the cultivator such spiritual and social virtues as honor, courage, self-reliance, integrity, and hospitality.

Second, the standard by which an economic system is judged is not the amount of prosperity it produces but the degree to which it encourages independence and morality. Because the farmer's basic needs of food and shelter are always met through a cooperative relationship with nature, only farming offers complete self-sufficiency regardless of the state of the national economy.

Third, the life of the farmer is harmonious, orderly, and whole, and it counteracts the tendencies toward abstraction, fragmentation, and alienation that have come with modern urban existence. The farmer belongs to a specific family, place, and region; participates in a historic and religious tradition; and has, in other words, a sense of identity that is psychologically and culturally beneficial.

Fourth, because nature is the primary source of inspiration, all the arts, music, literature, and other forms of creativity are better fostered and sustained in an agrarian society. The mass-produced culture of the industrial society lacks the individuality, humanity, and simple beauty of folk culture.

Fifth, the thriving cities created by industry, technology, and capitalism are destructive of independence and dignity and encourage crime and corruption. The agricultural community, on the other hand, which depends on friendly cooperation and neighborliness, provides a possible model for an ideal social order.

These ideas are the culmination of a philosophical development that is a part of the mainstream of Western civilization. In classical literature, Hesiod, Aristotle, Cicero, Vergil, and Horace are among those who reiterated the advantages of country life and husbandry over the other modes of existence and occupations. From the Middle Ages through the Renaissance and down to the 18th century, most major and minor writers praised the pastoral and rural life over city life and cursed the materialism and decadence fostered by the new spirits of commercialism and progress. When the European settlers arrived in

North America, they brought with them these ideas as a part of their cultural heritage.

The land of the New Englanders was hard and stony and poorly suited to farming. The fertile soil and amenable climate of the South, however, naturally encouraged agriculture as the primary economic pursuit of the entire region. Among his contemporaries, Virginian Thomas Jefferson did more to advance experimentation and technique in agriculture than anyone else by introducing his own innovations and inventions and including agricultural science in the curriculum of the University of Virginia. Of greater importance to southern thought was his early formulation of the agrarian ideal in query 19 of his *Notes on the State of Virginia* (1785), where he states, "Those who labour in the earth are the chosen people of God, if he ever had a chosen people, whose breasts he has made his peculiar deposit for substantial and genuine virtue." Jefferson's concise statement of fewer than 400 words has inspired almost two centuries of literary, social, and political debate.

The place of agriculture in the wealth of the new nation was contested in the early party battle between the Federalist and Republican forces, led respectively by Alexander Hamilton and Jefferson. The Federalists favored a centralized federal government, controlled by a propertied few, supported by commercial and industrial expansion. The Republicans, however, favored reliance on local government, under the leadership of a natural aristocracy of talent and virtue, with a primarily agrarian national economy based on independent farmers and landholders. The tensions of this debate were to reverberate down to and beyond the Civil War, which some have contended was basically a struggle between the two competing economies. While Jefferson's democratic theories largely prevailed in politics, Hamilton's industrial program prevailed in the economic sphere as America realized the extent of its natural resources and looked to capitalism to exploit them.

Southern literature offers a wide variety of novels, poems, and stories that deal in imaginative ways with the theories and realities of agrarianism. The virtues of agrarian life were celebrated in the 19th century in the works of John Esten Cook, Joel Chandler Harris, Richard Malcolm Johnston, John Pendleton Kennedy, Sidney Lanier, Mary Noailles Murfree, Thomas Nelson Page, William Gilmore Simms, Henry Timrod, and Mark Twain. In 1930 agrarianism was the unifying force for a group of writers led by John Crowe Ransom, Donald Davidson, Allen Tate, and Robert Penn Warren of Vanderbilt University in Nashville, which resulted in the publication of a symposium *I'll Take My Stand: The South and the Agrarian Tradition*. To one degree or another, these ideas were to remain the subject matter of much of their later poetry, fiction, and criticism, especially in Davidson's work.

Along with the portraits of the husbandman as an honest champion of individualism, southern literature also contains obverse portraits of poor white farmers as lazy, shiftless, uncouth members of a mongrel race. William Byrd of Westover initiated this brutish characterization with his colonial sketches of the idle lubberlanders observed in North Carolina during his survey of the boundary line between that state and Virginia. Reacting partly out of his upper-class sensitivities and partly out of the tradition that North Carolina was a refuge for criminals and malcontents, Byrd fathered a long-continuing series of descriptions of poor white degenerates, extending through 19th-century southern writing, the humor of the Old Southwest, and local-color fiction, down to Erskine Caldwell's lustful and depraved sharecroppers. H. L. Mencken also had little sympathy for the romance of agrarianism and called the farmer "a tedious brand of ignoramus, a cheap rogue and hypocrite, the eternal Jack of the human pack."

In the 20th century the writers whose fiction and poetry were reflective of agrarian problems and principles included Ransom, Davidson, Tate, Warren, Wendell Berry, Ellen Glasgow, Caroline Gordon, Andrew Lytle, Margaret Mitchell, Flannery O'Connor, Elizabeth Madox Roberts, Mary Lee Settle, Jesse Stuart, Alice Walker, Eudora Welty, Thomas Wolfe, and Stark Young.

Agrarian themes are particularly important in William Faulkner's fictional saga of Yoknapatawpha County. The passing away of the wilderness in the face of industrialism and commercialism is the theme of his story "The Bear," and in the Snopes trilogy (*The Hamlet, The Town,* and *The Mansion*) Faulkner projected on a broad canvas the conflict between agrarianism and materialism, the principles of the first embodied in the defeated chivalry of the Sartoris family, and the valueless animalism of the second embodied in the successful Snopes breed. The independent, small-farm families, such as the McCallums and the McCaslins, are always favorably treated. Faulkner was concerned in much of his work with the transformation of the idyllic agrarian society into the modern urban industrial world. Popeye of *Sanctuary,* described as a mechanical creature with a face of stamped tin, grows hysterical at the sight of fields and trees, and thus stands as Faulkner's ultimate symbol of the machine and its effects on society.

Many southern writers continue to hold onto the humanism inherent in agrarianism, and some of its concerns have found a voice in the modern ecology, environmental, and back-to-the-land movements. Kentuckian Wendell Berry is especially associated with a contemporary agrarianism that includes sustainable agriculture, vital community life, and connection to local places. However, as farming ceases to be a way of life in the South and elsewhere, the coherent philosophy it once represented will likely lose much of its impact or find a new mode of expression.

M. THOMAS INGE
Randolph-Macon College

M. Thomas Inge, ed., *Agrarianism in American Literature* (1969); Mark G. Malvasi, *The Unregenerate South: The Agrarian Thought of John Crowe Ransom, Allen Tate, and Donald Davidson* (1997); Leo Marx, *The Machine in the Garden: Technology and the Pastoral Idea in America* (1964); Henry Bamford Parkes, *The American Experience* (1947); Twelve Southerners, *I'll Take My Stand: The South and the Agrarian Tradition* (1930).

Appalachian Literature

The Appalachian region is loosely defined as a generally rural, moderately urbanized, and partly industrialized region in and around the Appalachian Mountains in the eastern United States. More than 20 million people live in Appalachia, a heavily forested area roughly the size of the United Kingdom, covering largely mountainous, often isolated areas from the borders of Alabama and Georgia in the south to Pennsylvania and New York in the north. Between lie large areas of South Carolina, North Carolina, Tennessee, Virginia, Kentucky, West Virginia, Maryland, and Ohio. The ethnic makeup is diverse, initially including immigrants from the British Isles and later eastern European ethnics, who followed industrialization of the region by timber and coal interests.

The literature of Appalachia has coincided with distinct historical developments including early exploration by Native Americans, hunters, trappers, and adventurers; a pioneer period characterized by scattered settlement and an agrarian life-style (barely interrupted by the Civil War); and a period of exploitation of coal and wood beginning slightly before the 20th century, spawning rapid in-migration; and a postindustrial period characterized by economic fluctuation prompting significant out-migration. Robert J. Higgs and Ambrose Manning in their landmark anthology *Voices from the Hills: Selected Readings of Southern Appalachia* (1975) make a very important distinction between the themes of Appalachian writing and those of the South by suggesting that instead of focusing on the relationship of aristocrats, blacks, and poor whites, Appalachian literature centers upon the mountaineer and his struggles with himself, nature, and the outside world.

Cratis Williams, in his classic dissertation on Appalachian literature (New York University, 1961), divided the literary-historical periods into three: early exploration to 1880, 1880–1930, and 1930 to the present. Scholars have since added a fourth period beginning in the 1960s and continuing to the present. In an updated anthology, the two-volume *Appalachia Inside Out* (1995), Robert J. Higgs, Ambrose Manning, and Jim Wayne Miller parse Appalachian literary history into two broad categories—"Conflict and Change" and "Culture and Custom."

The earliest recorded period of Appalachian literature began in the late 1600s and is identified as journal and diary entries by explorers, trappers, traders, adventurers, and those who were looking for settlement lands or had some investment interests in the area. Many were matriculating from more populated areas in the Northeast. Several of these writings are honest, straightforward accounts of encounters with Native Americans and pioneer life in the region; others have a distinct, romanticized, James Fennimore Cooper–like flavor, and still others are written from the perspective of the supposed more "civilized" outsider. In their 1975 anthology, Higgs and Manning include works from John Lederer, who began to write about the region in 1669; John Fontaine, whose journal published in 1838 included accounts of his travels into the Blue Ridge and the Shenandoah Valley; Timothy Flint, whose *Biographical Memoir of Daniel Boone* (1833) was perhaps the most widely read biography of the early 19th century; James Kirk Paulding, whose *Letters from the South* (1816) demonstrated the captivating qualities of the Appalachian Mountains; and Anne Newport Royal, called America's first hitchhiker, who wrote of the unspoiled region in her *Sketches of History, Life, and Manners in the United States* (1826). Examples from other sources often include portions of William Byrd's *History of the Dividing Line Run in the Year 1728* (1728) and *A Progress to the Mines* (1732) and John Muir's "Crossing the Cumberland Mountains" (an excerpt from his memoir *A Thousand Mile Walk to the Gulf* [1916]).

The second period of Appalachian literature began about 1885 and lasted well into the 1930s. These "local-color" writers were of the Mark Twain or Bret Harte tradition. Their signature was the marketing to urban populations of odd characters and stories found in the somewhat isolated Appalachian Mountains. John Fox Jr. was perhaps the most accomplished of these. His *Little Shepherd of Kingdom Come* (1903) explored the theme of the Appalachian placed in the "foreign" environment of a Kentucky Bluegrass plantation, and *Trail of the Lonesome Pine* (1908) explored the "foreigner" coal company engineer placed in the Appalachian Mountains in southwest Virginia. Other notables include Mary Noailles Murfree (*In the Tennessee Mountains* [1884] and 25 other works, mostly fiction set in the southern mountain area); Elizabeth Madox Roberts (*The Time of Man* [1926] and *The Great Meadow* [1930]); and Lucy Furman, who wrote realistic and positive sketches about the culture near Hindman Settlement School at Hindman, Ky., in her *Mothering on Perilous* (1913), *Sight to the Blind* (1914), *The Quare Women* (1923), and *The Glass Window* (1925). Many of these works were largely romantic and were often written in dialect. Sentimentality and neoromanticism merged with Appalachian stereotypes and motifs to set the tone until the 1930s. Feuding, the Civil War in Appalachia, moonshining, religious fundamentalism, and historical romance became common topics.

The post-1930 period spawned a vital group of writers who dominated the Appalachian literary scene well into the 1980s and 1990s, overlapping the next period that began in the 1960s. Among the outstanding members of the post-1930 group were Kentuckian Jesse Stuart, with his more than 40 books covering biography, autobiography, novel, short story, poetry, essay, and journalism; Kentuckian Harriette Simpson Arnow, whose powerful novel about out-migration to the steel mills of Detroit, Mich., titled *The Dollmaker* (1954) received national acclaim; adopted Kentuckian James Still, with his highly respected attention to art and craft in fiction, short story, and poetry in *River of Earth* (1940), *On Troublesome Creek* (1941), and *Hounds on the Mountain* (1937); North Carolinian Thomas Wolfe, the famed author of *Look Homeward, Angel* (1929), *Of Time and the River* (1935), *The Web and the Rock* (1939), *You Can't Go Home Again* (1940), and *The Hills Beyond* (1941); West Virginia writer and 1977 National Book Award recipient Mary Lee Settle's Beulah Quintet, including *O Beulah Land* (1956), *Know Nothing* (1960), *Prisons* (1973), and *The Scapegoat* (1980); West Virginian Pearl Buck's *The Good Earth* (1931 winner of the Pulitzer Prize and the William Dean Howells Medal), *Sons* (1932), and *A House Divided* (1935); and Tennessean James Agee, who was posthumously awarded the Pulitzer Prize in 1958 for *A Death in the Family* (1957). Dominant themes of this period included politics, religion, rural mountain life customs and traditions, industrialized mountain life, and economic displacement of Appalachians.

In the 1960s the torch was being passed to another set of regional writers such as Wilma Dykeman, whose novel *Tall Woman* (1962) is the quintessential portrait of an Appalachian pioneer woman and the enduring role she has played in American history, and the hard-hitting, frank Harry Caudill, whose *Night Comes to the Cumberlands: A Biography of a Depressed Area* (1963) grabbed the attention of John F. Kennedy and Lyndon Baines Johnson and is credited with having planted the seeds for the antipoverty programs of the 1960s. Others in this era included such notables as Jim Wayne Miller, Cormac McCarthy, Lillie D. Chaffin, Billy Edd Wheeler, Loyal Jones, and Jack Weller. Although the themes of this period are as varied as the number of substantial writers, many of these works began to focus upon the postindustrial malaise brought on by environmental, economic, and social effects of the timber and coal industry.

Beginning in the mid-1970s, a new set of writers who included quality work in the genres of poetry, fiction, creative nonfiction, and essay emerged. Prominent are novelist Charles Frazier, who won the 1997 National Book Award for Fiction for *Cold Mountain* (1997), a novel set in the Blue Ridge Mountains during the Civil War; North Carolinian Robert Morgan, whose acclaimed novel *Gap Creek* (1999) follows a young couple through their lives in their new home in the Appalachian high country at the turn of the 20th century; and southwest Virginia native Lee Smith, who has published 11 works of fiction including *Oral History*, the tale of a mountain family who lives in Hoot Owl Holler. In addition, West Virginian Denise Giardina has written eloquently about the injustices committed by coal companies in Appalachia in her novels *Storming Heaven* (1987) and *The Unquiet Earth* (1992). A new Appalachian writer with great promise is Kentuckian Silas House, whose trilogy of novels *Clay's Quilt* (2001), *A Parchment of Leaves* (2002), and *Coal Tattoo* (2004) has received high praise. East Kentucky native and retired University of Kentucky professor James B. Goode has published three books of coal mining poetry, including *The Whistle and the Wind* (1972), *Poets of Darkness* (1981), and *Up From the Mines* (1993), which James Still declared "the best book of poetry on coal mining ever written." Harlan County, Ky., native George Ella Lyon has published four novels, two books of poetry, and 18 picture books. Southwest Virginia native and University of Kentucky professor Gurney Norman's *Divine Right's Trip* (1971), which originally appeared in the acclaimed *Last Whole Earth Catalog*, and *Kinfolks* (1997) have garnered national attention. Two of Norman's stories, "Fat Monroe" and "Night Ride," have been adapted for film. North Carolinian Fred Chappell has published 22 major works of poetry and fiction, including *World between the Eyes (1972)*, *River: A Poem* (1978), *Bloodfire* (1979), and *I Am One of Yours Forever* (1985). West Virginian Homer Hickam's *Rocket Boys* (1998) was selected by the *New York Times* as one of the "Best Books of 1998," and his *The Coalwood Way* (2000) and *Sky of Stone* (2001) have also received national attention.

Another Appalachian writer of national prominence is North Carolinian mystery/historical fiction novelist Sharyn McCrumb, who is best known for her seven-novel Ballad series beginning with *Lovely in Her Bones* (1990). She also has written satirical and comic novels as well as short stories. Another Tennessean, William Gay, uses the rural mountain landscape for Gothic tales reminiscent of William Faulkner. Gay has published three novels and the collection of short stories *I Hate to See That Evening Sun Go Down*.

Substantial anthologies on the region are rare, but a few good ones exist. Sandra L. Ballard and Patricia L. Hudson's *Women Writing in Appalachia* (2003), Ambrose Manning and Robert J. Higgs's *Voices from the Hills* (1975), Ambrose Manning, Robert J. Higgs, and Jim Wayne Miller's two-volume *Appalachia Inside Out: A Sequel to Voices from the Hills* (1995), Cecille Haddix's *Who Speaks for Appalachia?* (1975), and Ruel Foster's *Appalachian Literature: Critical Essays* (1976) are among the most notable. Two recent Kentucky anthologies are important as resources: Wade Hall's *The Kentucky Anthology: Two Hundred Years of Writing in the Bluegrass State* (2005) and William S. Ward's *The Literary History of Kentucky* (1988).

There are also several good bibliographies. The important ones include Appalachian Studies Association's *A Selected Bibliography of Scholarship on Appalachia* (2004); Morgantown University's *Appalachian Outlook, 1982–2003* (a yearly bibliography of scholarship and articles on Appalachia); Appalachian State University's Carol Grotnes Belk Library's *Appalachian Studies Bibliography, 1994*; and Charlotte T. Ross's *Bibliography of Southern Appalachia* (1976). Others include Louise Boger's *The Southern Mountaineer in Literature* (1976), Robert Munn's *Appalachian Bibliography* (1968), and appendices A–G of "A Guide to Appalachian Studies" (Autumn 1977 issue of *Appalachian Journal*). A few small-shelf lists and other bibliographies are also helpful: the fiction and poetry list of the Berea College Weatherford-Hammond Collection, the former Appalachian Book Record Shop's *Appalachian Literature and Music: A Comprehensive Catalogue* (1981), the Council of Southern Mountains' *Bibliography of the Appalachian South* (1963), and West Virginia Library's *Bibliography and Guide to Appalachian Studies* (1961).

Numerous good literary magazines are located within the region and have consistently published excellent Appalachian poetry, fiction, and essays. Among the most prominent are *Appalachian Journal: A Regional Studies Review* (Appalachian State University, Boone, N.C.), *Appalachian Heritage* (Berea College, Berea, Ky.), the *Sewanee Review* (University of the South, Sewanee, Tenn.), the *Virginia Quarterly Review* (Charlottesville), *Now and Then: The Appalachian Magazine* (East Tennessee State University, Johnson City), *South Carolina Review* (Clemson University, Clemson, S.C.), and *Asheville Poetry Review* (Asheville, N.C.). The *Carolina Quarterly* (University of North Carolina at Chapel Hill) and *North Carolina Literary Review* (East Carolina University, Greenville) also publish Appalachian literature.

Appalachian literary history includes a remarkably skilled number of writers and an extraordinary variety of writing that has immeasurably added to the evolving body of American letters. A part of that literature unmistakably has some kinship with the South but also has a strong, unique identity found in the central character and life of the mountaineer. The rural agrarian mind-set, the mass immigration from nearby southern states, the fierce independence as evidenced by the bloody union movements (which may parallel the ideas reflected in the Civil War), the emphasis upon folk tradition and culture, the history of oral tradition, the inclination to use literature to express sociological or anthropological concerns, and the struggle by Appalachians to bridge the gulf between traditional Appalachian culture and contemporary America are all characteristics that prove both a link to southern literature and the separateness of its place. Appalachian writing remains an independent body of letters with an important place in American literature.

JAMES B. GOODE
University of Kentucky

Sandra L. Ballard and Patricia L. Hudson, eds., *Listen Here: Women Writing in Appalachia* (2003); Dwight B. Billings, Gurney Norman, and Katherine Ledford, eds., *Confronting Stereotypes: Back Talk from an American Region* (1999); George Brosi, ed., *Appalachian Literature and Music: A Comprehensive Catalogue* (1981); Rodger Cunningham, *Apples on the Flood* (1988); Ruel Foster, ed., *Appalachian Literature: Critical Essays* (1976); Cecille Haddix, ed., *Who Speaks for Appalachia?: Prose, Poetry, and Songs from the Mountain Heritage* (1975); Wade Hall, ed., *The Kentucky Anthology* (2005); Robert J. Higgs and Ambrose Manning, eds., *Voices from the Hills* (1975); Robert J. Higgs, Ambrose Manning, and Jim Wayne Miller, eds., *Appalachia Inside Out: A Sequel to Voices from the Hills*, vols. 1 and 2 (1995); Jim Wayne Miller, *Appalachian Journal* (Autumn 1977); William S. Ward, ed., *A Literary History of Kentucky* (1988); Cratis Williams, "The Southern Mountaineer in Fact and Fiction" (Ph.D. dissertation, New York University, 1961).

Autobiography and Memoir

From the colonial period to the present, southerners and visitors to the region have created a rich body of autobiographical writing, whether in diaries and journals, slave narratives, family memoirs or formal autobiographies, revealing a remarkable diversity of experiences, backgrounds, and perspectives. Using the persuasive authority of first-person testimonial, many of these writers have defended the region's social practices, while others have criticized them. Many have shown no hesitation in reinforcing stereotypes of southerners, whereas others have used the autobiographical occasion to resist demeaning stereotypes and assert their self-worth. Collectively, they constitute a significant contribution to American letters and a composite portrait of the South, and some have become recognized as classics of American literature.

In the colonial era through the early years of the republic, when their New England counterparts were writing narratives of spiritual self-examination, southern authors focused their personal narratives on the external world, mostly in the form of exploration narratives and natural histories. From Captain John Smith's *A True Relation of Such Occurrences and Accidents of Noate as Hath Hapned in Virginia* . . . (1608), which contains the now-mythic account of Pocahontas's intervention on behalf of the captive Smith, to William Byrd of Westover's *History of the Dividing Line* (1729), an account of the 1728 survey expedition to map the boundary between North Carolina and Byrd's native Virginia, to Philadelphian William Bartram's *Travels through North and South Carolina, Georgia, East and West Florida* (1794), whose lush descriptions of the flora and fauna of the South entranced and inspired the British romantic poets, these authors helped to shape early impressions of the region's landscapes and of the people who dwelled there.

Although these early narratives were all written by white men of privilege, by the mid-19th century, autobiographical writing in the South began to reflect the egalitarianism of the new nation as well as the emergence of sectional conflict and a distinctive regional identity. The most important and widely read of these are the narratives of former slaves who escaped to freedom in the North, but the diaries and memoirs of white women and nonaristocrat white men offer an intimate glimpse into the hardships and occasional joys of life in the region's most tumultuous era, as well. In *Mary Chesnut's Civil War* (edited by C. Vann Woodward, 1982), the author, who was the wife of a prominent member of the Confederate government, chronicles the decline of the white South's fortunes, from the first shots of the war (she was in Charleston during the siege of Fort Sumter), through the deprivations of civilian life behind the battle lines, to the fall of the Confederacy. Along the way she expresses her ambivalence concerning the South's attitudes toward slavery and her impatience with the largely ornamental role assigned to women in her sphere. Countering the reflective tone of Chesnut's behind-the-lines account, Sam R. Watkins's *"Co. Aytch"; or, A Side Show of the Big Show* (1882) presents the war from a foot soldiers' frank, often irreverent perspective, capturing the frenetic confusion of headlong combat as well as the tedium of the infantryman's life between battles, the naive excitement of the enlistees at the beginning of the conflict as well as the jaded bitterness of those few who survived to see the Confederacy's defeat.

Slave narratives constitute the most distinct subgenre of autobiography to be created by southern-born authors (they were all written and published in the North). *Narrative of the Life of Frederick Douglass, an American Slave* (1845), the first and most highly regarded of three autobiographies written by Douglass, follows the basic pattern of the antebellum slave narrative by tracing the author's path from bondage to the acquisition of literacy to escape and, finally, to freedom in the North. His sophisticated analyses of the mechanisms of oppression used by slaveholders results in a convincing glimpse into the power dynamics of the master-slave relationship. Although not as widely read in its day, Harriett Jacobs's *Incidents in the Life of a Slave Girl* (1861) is now ranked with Douglass's 1845 account as one of the most powerful of all slave narratives. Written for a female readership, *Incidents* exposes the effects of human bondage upon the domestic sphere, recounting Jacobs's sexual harassment by her master, her failed attempts to form an alliance with her master's wife, her subsequent stratagems for avoiding her master's advances (which include taking another white slaveholder as her lover and protector), and her struggles to gain freedom for her children and herself. These works and other antebellum slave narratives, including those by William Wells Brown (1847), Henry Bibb (1849), and Solomon Northup (1853), became a highly effective weapon in the campaign to change public opinion in the North on slavery; the antebellum slave narrative also became a template for subsequent African American literature, providing a set of themes and narrative patterns that can be found in such disparate works as *The Autobiography of Malcolm X*, Ralph Ellison's *Invisible Man*, Richard Wright's *Black Boy*, and Toni Morrison's *Beloved*.

Although the antebellum slave narrative garners more critical attention than its postemancipation counterpart, the larger share of slave narratives was produced after the end of the Civil War. Lacking much of the suspense and drama found in the earlier slave narratives (few of these later authors escaped slavery), they nevertheless remain important sources of information about how the typical slave was treated in the last decades of the South's peculiar institution. The most famous of these is Booker T. Washington's *Up from Slavery* (1901), which, like Douglass's *Narrative*, evokes Franklin's rags-to-riches story, framing Washington's rise to fame and founding of Tuskegee Institute as a series of personal lessons in the virtues of thrift, personal responsibility, self-education, and industry. In the late 1930s the federal Works Project Administration (WPA) funded a project to collect the stories of former slaves, resulting in the recording of over 2,000 oral histories. While these narratives can seem scripted and lacking candor and spontaneity because of the methods used by the interviewers, collectively they represent the most detailed record we have today of American slavery.

The Mississippi River provides the backdrop for two of the most important southern autobiographies in the years between Reconstruction and World War II. In *Life on the Mississippi* (1883), Mark Twain reminisces about his youth in Hannibal, Mo. (which he had popularized in *Tom Sawyer* seven years earlier and to which he would soon return in *The Adventures of Huckleberry Finn*), but the most memorable sections of the narrative depict his apprenticeship as a steamboat captain in the years immediately before the Civil War. Though less widely read, William Alexander Percy's *Lanterns on the Levee: Recollections of a Planter's Son* (1941) offers an equally engaging portrait of a life on the Mississippi (in this case the Delta town of Greenville, Miss., and the Percys' 3,000-acre cotton plantation). Percy captures the charm and beauty of the Delta in lyrical prose (a minor poet, he had published three collections of verse before *Lanterns*) and then uses his powerful evocation of place to ground his defense of the aristocratic class to which he was born, the paternalistic leadership and genteel manners he associates with that tradition, and the racial and class status quo that made such a tradition possible.

By the mid-20th century, most southern autobiographers took a more critical view of the South's racial practices, gender roles, and class hierarchies, typically authorizing their critiques by demonstrating their intimate familiarity with the manners and social codes of their respective communities. Fred Hobson has argued convincingly that white southern autobiographers of the late Jim Crow era adopted the conventions of New England's spiritual autobiography, which they had heretofore eschewed in favor of less confessional modes of personal narrative, in order to describe their "conversion" to racial liberalism, confessing their earlier sins of racism as a means of expiating their guilt and initiating reform. Notable examples of this branch of southern autobiography include Katherine Du Pre Lumpkin's *The Making of a Southerner* (1941), Lillian Smith's *Killers of the Dream* (1947), Willie Morris's *North toward Home* (1968), and Melton McLaurin's *Separate Pasts: Growing Up White in the Segregated South* (1987). It is worth noting, though, that none of these narratives came close to achieving the level of popular success or critical acclaim accorded to two important autobiographical works by southern African Americans published in the same era. Richard Wright's *Black Boy: A Record of Childhood and Youth* (originally titled *American Hunger*) depicts the segregated South in even darker tones than those found in Douglass's and Jacobs's work. Wright paints a psychologically complex, nightmarish portrait of the author's coming of age in

Mississippi and Memphis as he resists the lessons—taught by African Americans as well as whites—of subservience to whites. Maya Angelou's *I Know Why the Caged Bird Sings* (1970) paints a similarly grim picture of the realities of racism in the Jim Crow South, but whereas Wright consistently portrays other African Americans as antagonists who are threatened by his failure to adopt the submissive role expected of him, Angelou depicts most—though not all—family members and individuals in the larger African American community as sources of strength and comfort.

Recent decades have borne witness to a proliferation of autobiographical writing in the South. Many of these works are by established fiction writers interested in examining the ways in which their southern childhoods helped to shape their artistic sensibilities. Noteworthy recent examples of this type include Harry Crews's *A Childhood: The Biography of a Place* (1978), Eudora Welty's *One Writer's Beginnings* (1984), Reynolds Price's *Clear Pictures: First Loves, First Guides* (1989), and Bobbie Ann Mason's *Clear Springs* (1999). Works such as Rosemary Daniell's *Fatal Flowers: On Sex, Sin, and Suicide in the Deep South* (1980, 1999), Susan Abbott's *Womenfolks: Growing Up Down South* (1987), Deborah McDowell's *Leaving Pipe Shop: Memories of Kin* (1996), and Minrose Gwin's *Wishing for Snow: A Memoir* (2003) reflect strong feminist concerns as the authors affirm matrilineal ties in their sympathetic portraits of mothers and grandmothers. The autobiographies of rural working-class whites, notable examples of which include Will D. Campbell's *Brother to a Dragonfly* (1978), Crews's *A Childhood*, Rick Bragg's *All Over But the Shoutin'* (1998), and Janisse Ray's *Ecology of a Cracker Childhood* (1999), uniformly show a strong concern with rehabilitating the image of the oft-maligned "redneck" and exposing the social injustices that contribute to working-class whites' economic exploitation. These works, which represent but a small portion of the wealth of autobiographies coming out of the region in recent years, take their place in a tradition of life writing whose roots extend deep into southern soil, a tradition that shows every sign of continued vitality in the foreseeable future.

JAMES H. WATKINS
Berry College

Ruth A. Banes, in *Perspectives on the American South*, vol. 3, ed. James C. Cobb and Charles Reagan Wilson (1985); J. Bill Berry, ed., *Located Lives: Place and Idea in Southern Autobiography* (1990), *Home Ground: Southern Autobiography* (1991); Will Brantley, *Feminine Sense in Southern Memoir: Smith, Glasgow, Welty, Hellman, Porter, and Hurston* (1993); Cleanth Brooks, *Journal of Southern History* (February 1960); Fred Hobson, *But Now I See: The White Southern Racial Conversion Narrative*

(1999); John Shelton Reed, *One South: An Ethnic Approach to Regional Culture* (1982); C. Vann Woodward, *The Burden of Southern History* (1960).

Biography

Almost 60 years ago, in his own study of Leonardo da Vinci, Sigmund Freud warned that biographers, for personal reasons, often choose their own heroes for their subjects. Out of "special affection," Freud wrote, "they then devote themselves to a work of idealization." Intolerant of anything in their subject's inner or outer life that smacks of human weakness or imperfection, biographers "then give us a cold, strange, ideal form instead of a man to whom we could feel distinctly related." Freud might have added that because the majority of biographers have traditionally been white men, so are the subjects of most American biographies, South and North.

Two of the best examples of this kind of deification in southern biography are Thomas Jefferson and Robert E. Lee, both of whom have been the subjects of numerous biographies. The "Sage of Monticello" was truly an eloquent, erudite scholar and a brilliant statesman, but his chief biographers—James Parton, Douglas Southall Freeman, Merrill Peterson, and Dumas Malone—have glorified his accomplishments, minimized or denied his flaws, and canonized his name so that a demigod, not a man, emerges from the pages of their biographies. Not until 1974 and the appearance of Fawn Brodie's eye-opening psychobiography, *Thomas Jefferson: An Intimate History* (1974), did someone finally put flesh and bone on Jefferson. Brodie's Jefferson was ambivalent about love and power, slavery and revolution. Brodie's Jefferson was extremely virile and passionate and at the same time compulsively controlled. Most controversial of all, Brodie insisted that rumors of Jefferson's longtime love affair with Sally Hemmings, one of his slaves, were indeed true. The vehemence with which Jefferson's white male biographers, particularly Peterson and Malone, have leaped to their subject's defense in this sensitive matter is evidence of a continued refusal to admit that Jefferson had even a particle of human frailty. Jefferson's relationship with Hemmings is now a key to how biographers interpret Jefferson's complex character. Annettee Gordon Reed's *Thomas Jefferson and Sally Hemmings: An American Controversy* (1997) brings the two life stories together directly. Joseph J. Ellis's *American Sphinx: The Character of Thomas Jefferson* (1997) aims to get at the "living, breathing person" behind the icon. R. B. Bernstein's *Thomas Jefferson* (2003) is an evenhanded and judicious life story.

Jefferson's sanctified image has been matched only by that of Robert E. Lee.

Of the two Virginians, Lee is the one who, for most white southerners, long evoked the lump in the throat, the tearful faraway gaze. This is partly because Lee's biographers purposely created and perpetuated the Lee myth: the man of flawless character; the perfect son, husband, and father; the noble officer torn between love for Union and loyalty to Virginia; the gallant general and brilliant militarist defeated only by overwhelming odds. He exemplified all that was best in the Old South, in the vanquished Confederacy. For the white South, Lee was a saint.

Thomas Connelly, in *The Marble Man: Robert E. Lee and His Image in American Society* (1977), traces the fascinating history behind the creation of the Lee legend. During and immediately after the Civil War, Lee was only one of several celebrated Confederate military leaders. Others, like Thomas "Stonewall" Jackson, Joe Johnston, and P. G. T. Beauregard, were rivals for southern popularity. Lee even received criticism from his earliest biographers for his alleged mistakes at Gettysburg. But in the mid-1870s, shortly after Lee died, a group of Virginians led by General Jubal Early, one of Lee's corps commanders, took control of the Southern Historical Society and its influential papers. For personal reasons, their image of the Civil War centered upon Lee and the Virginia military theater. So they decided to raise Lee far above the other war heroes, silence any critics, and downplay or discredit the exploits of other Confederate generals. Connelly shows how every subsequent biography of Lee, including Douglas Southall Freeman's prizewinning four-volume work, has taken its cues from these far-from-disinterested Virginia men.

Connelly suggests that none of Lee's biographers tell much about the inner man or the drives that shaped his life. Like Freeman, they paint a superficial portrait of Lee, leaving out his humanity, giving readers a man more marble than flesh. The real Lee, the essential Lee, says Connelly, has been buried under the hero symbol. And though his own book is a history of Lee biographies, not a biography of Lee, Connelly's "Epilogue" raised the kind of questions about Lee—his troubled marriage, his ambivalence over slavery and secession, his morbidity and haunting sense of failure, his parochial vision of war—that soon provided the meat for new biographies. Emory M. Thomas's 1995 biography of Lee explores the general's inner life, suggesting he knew little happiness but lived an honorable life. Thomas's book reflected the knowledge of one of the leading contemporary historians of the Confederacy. Michael Fellman's *The Making of Robert E. Lee* (2000) also focuses on Lee's psychology.

Jefferson was a statesman, Lee a military leader; politics and the military were traditional avenues to male power. Not surprisingly then, much of southern biography focuses on politicians and generals. Southerners, active in the

American Revolution, dominated presidential politics for the first quarter of a century of the new nation and dominated federal politics until secession in 1861. So there has been no dearth of biographies about southern statesmen like George Washington, Jefferson, James Madison, James Monroe—all from Virginia—John C. Calhoun, and Andrew Jackson. Civil War leaders Jefferson Davis and Alexander Stephens have also had their biographers, although in the case of these two political foes, early biographies were acts of justification with the biographers carrying old fights into print. William C. Davis's 1991 biography of Davis is a critical assessment. Southern fire-eaters like Robert Barnwell Rhett, William Lowndes Yancey, Edmund Ruffin, and James Henry Hammond have received less attention, although several biographies have appeared, among them Drew Gilpin Faust's *James Henry Hammond and the Old South* (1982) and Betty L. Mitchell's *Edmund Ruffin: A Biography* (1981). And, of course, Robert E. Lee's comrades in arms—Longstreet, "Jeb" Stuart, Beauregard, Johnston—have all been the subjects of essentially military biographies. James I. Robertson Jr.'s *Thomas J. Stonewall Jackson: The Man, the Soldier, the Legend* (1997) presents Jackson in the context of his time, offering a full portrait of his childhood and stressing the importance of his religious attitudes.

The usual subjects for southern biography have been white and male, and they have come, almost exclusively, from the upper classes. Those men not blessed with wealth and/or family position at birth, like Washington, Lee, and Hammond, had the good sense to marry wives who had been. But politics sometimes makes for strange bedfellows, so biographers have studied the lives of important working-class heroes like populist rebel Tom Watson and "Kingfish" Huey Long (who liked to masquerade as a redneck despite his respectable yeoman background). C. Vann Woodward's *Tom Watson: Agrarian Rebel* (1938) and T. Harry Williams's Pulitzer Prize–winning *Huey Long* (1969) are fine examples of this kind of southern biography.

Whether biographers are discussing Jefferson's paradoxical feelings about slavery, Ruffin's unapologetic defense of the peculiar institution, or Watson's vicious race baiting, race itself has been a constant theme in southern biography. Until recently, distressingly few biographies were written about blacks. Those that did exist have usually treated men working in one way or another toward black liberation and racial justice. Thus, in Stephen B. Oates's *The Fires of Jubilee: Nat Turner's Fierce Rebellion* (1935), readers witness the re-creation of the dramatic but short life of a black revolutionary, a slave convinced he is God's violent instrument for the salvation of his people. Benjamin Quarles and Nathan Huggins, biographers of runaway slave and abolitionist Frederick Douglass, reveal a man just as dedicated to black freedom but convinced, at first, that this freedom could be won through nonviolence. Booker T. Washington's biographers, Louis Harlan and Bernard Weisberger, demonstrated his commitment to racial self-improvement through accommodation to segregation. Oates's *Let the Trumpet Sound: The Life of Martin Luther King, Jr.* (1982) vividly connects the line of history that exists among these four black leaders. Like Turner, King was nurtured by his family and encouraged to feel he was somebody special, a Moses for his people. Like Washington, he was committed to improvement for his race, but unlike the great founder of Tuskegee, he was not satisfied with segregated "racial uplift" programs. With Douglass, he believed in peaceful means to conquer racism and thus embraced Gandhian techniques of nonviolent resistance in order to combat racial oppression and social injustice. David J. Garrow won the Pulitzer Prize for Biography for *Bearing the Cross: Martin Luther King Jr. and the Southern Christian Leadership Conference* (1987). Taylor Branch's three-volume *America in the King Years* (1988, 1998, 2006) places King in the context of his times.

Even fewer biographies exist on southern black women than on black men. Mildred I. Thompson's 1990 biography of activist Ida B. Wells-Barnett is an exception. Southern white women have fared better with the recent emphasis on women's history, but not much. Biographies of southern white women, like those of white men, usually deal with the concept of honor, because, as historian Bertram Wyatt-Brown argues in *Southern Honor: Ethics and Behavior in the Old South* (1982), honor was the psychological and social linchpin of the antebellum South. For southern white men, honor required "both riches and a body of menials"; for white women, honor required sexual innocence and a childlike meekness. This "cult of true womanhood" touched women North and South, but southern men made a fetish out of extolling the purity and excellence of southern womanhood and, by extension, southern civilization. Biographers of southern women show how their subjects accept, reject, or modify this feminine domestic ideal.

Gerda Lerner's *The Grimké Sisters from South Carolina* (1970) recounts the lives of Sarah and Angelina Grimké, daughters of a South Carolina planter, who refused to accept meekly the South's peculiar institution of slavery and moved to the North to become the first salaried female abolitionists and the first American women to speak in public. These two women, who were the epitome of piety and purity—both were Quakers—violated the sacred cannons of southern honor to perform what they believed was God's own work.

Elizabeth Muhlenfeld's portrait of Mary Boykin Chesnut reveals a South Carolina woman much like the Grimkés in class background and wealth. She, too, hated slavery, calling it a "monstrous institution," not out of any sympathy for the slaves, but because of the plight of white women whose honor depended on ignoring evidence of miscegenation in their own families. Unlike the Grimké sisters, Chesnut never left the South, and she became an ardent Confederate. Yet she, too, spurned the southern feminine ideal. In antebellum days, this educated, intelligent, but childless woman often felt like a useless ornament; in the postwar period, she took charge of the family plantation.

Nancy Milford's biography *Zelda* (1970), the tragic story of Zelda Sayre Fitzgerald, gives the reader a 20th-century twist on the 19th-century feminine ideal of southern white womanhood. Zelda Sayre, a Montgomery, Ala., belle who lived life in the fast lane, rejected the innocent passivity of the "true woman" to boldly embrace the modern "New Woman": the flapper who used her good looks and sexual allure to get what she wanted from men. But this new brand of femininity was equally perverse, even schizophrenic, and Zelda finally succumbed. Jacquelyn Dowd Hall's *Revolt against Chivalry: Jessie David Ames and the Women's Campaign against Lynching* (1979) was a pioneering work of new women's history. Martha Swain authored a 1995 biography of New Deal reformer Ellen S. Woodward.

Literature, music, and religion are among the other aspects of southern culture that have produced major biographies, still often dealing with white men but now with more balanced critical interpretations. Joseph Blotner's two-volume *William Faulkner* (1974) was a detailed study of the Nobel Prize winner's life, combining plot summaries with his life story. Blotner did the same type of study for another icon of southern literature, Robert Penn Warren, in 1997. Blotner's study of Faulkner was followed by others on the Mississippian, including Michael Millgate, David Minter, Frederick Karl, Judith Bryant Wittenberg, Richard Gray, Joel Williamson, and Daniel Singal. Suzanne Marrs's *Eudora Welty: A Biography* (2005) got past the conventional wisdom of Welty's isolated life, stressing her travel, political interests, and romantic engagements. Flannery O'Connor has attracted extensive critical studies, but Jean W. Cash's *Flannery O'Connor: A Life* (2002) is one of the few full biographies of this seminal southern writer. Robert Hemenway's *Zora Neal Hurston: A Biography* (1977) was unusually timely in helping focus new attention on Hurston's significance. Leading biographies of Richard Wright are by Michel Fabre (1973) and Hazel Rowley (2001).

Given the emergence of the blues, country music, ragtime, jazz, bluegrass, gospel, and early rock 'n' roll in the South, entertainers have been the subject of many biographers. These figures were mostly working class, often rural, and many times from families poor in worldly goods. Music offered them a means to success. They were "great men and women" but differed from the political leaders who have sometimes been the subject of hero-worshiping biographies. One of the most prolific and accomplished biographers of southern music is Peter Guralnick. Through essay profiles, he has chronicled the lives of performers in virtually every genre of southern music. His two-volume life of Elvis Presley (1994, 1999) gets past the King's celebrity and mythology to offer a thorough picture of Elvis's rise to fame and his later decline. Guralnick also authored *Dream Boogie: The Triumph of Sam Cooke* (2005).

The South has produced some of the most prominent of American ministers, and biographers increasingly are offering studies on leaders of many denominations. One of the best-known preachers, Billy Graham, has naturally attracted the most attention from biographers. Marshall Frady's *Billy Graham: A Parable of American Righteousness* (1979) was a critical study, while sociologist William Martin's *A Prophet with Honor: The Billy Graham Story* (1991) was a sympathetic but objective story. David Edwin Harrell Jr. offers biographies of two other leading southern ministers, Oral Roberts (1985) and Pat Robertson (1988).

BETTY L. MITCHELL
Southeastern Massachusetts University

Blues Literature

When wandering black songsters—also called "musicianeers" and "musical physicianeers"—first began drawing notice across the South at the dawn of the 20th century as the purveyors of what composer W. C. Handy called "the weirdest music I'd ever heard," nobody could have predicted that their unassuming little song form and its bittersweet tonalities would, by century's end, become arguably the world's best-known musical idiom, thanks to "St. Louis Blues," the Blues Brothers, and B. B. King. Just as unlikely was the impact that blues music and culture would ultimately have on African American literature, southern literature, and American literature as a whole. The blues, it has become clear, are a kind of vernacular taproot within contemporary American culture, at once infinitely malleable and instantly recognizable, hardened with laughter, and inflated with an epic braggadocio that owes something to the tall-tale telling of the American West in its Mississippi Delta variant. "I'm the hoochie-coochie man," Muddy Waters proclaimed in words penned by Willie Dixon. "*Everybody* knows I'm here." The tales the blues tell—tales of restlessness and sexual pursuit, heartbreak and survival, abject poverty and willful self-creation—have proved irresistible to American writers, as has the double-voiced signifying language through which they work their seductions.

To speak of "blues literature" is to court confusion. Many assume that the subject under discussion is folkoric and biographical studies that have long shaped popular and academic understandings: Paul Oliver's *Blues Fell This Morning: Meaning in the Blues* (1959), Peter Guralnick's *Searching for Robert Johnson* (1998), or Alan Lomax's monumental *The Land Where the Blues Began* (1993). Worthy books, all, but off topic. Blues literature is simply the range of genres—including poems, short stories, novels, plays, and autobiographies—through which creative writers and blues musicians themselves have attempted to tell blues-based stories in blue-toned language. Three key elements frame the tradition: blues form, blues portraiture, and blues power.

Blues form includes all those structural and linguistic elements of blues songs that blues writers seek to translate into their literary equivalents. Chief among these is the three-line AAB stanza, with its signature repetition—a stanza that W. C. Handy's hit composition "St. Louis Blues" (1914) helped make the reference standard among blues singers, and that Langston Hughes in turn shaped into a six-line poetic stanza with his equally influential paean to a Harlem piano man, "The Weary Blues" (1925). Blues form includes vernacular language, much of it drawn from the life experience of working-class black southerners, some of which takes the form of sexual signifying. "Look here, sugar," says Levee, a Mississippi-born trumpeter flirting up a girl named Dussie Mae in August Wilson's *Ma Rainey's Black Bottom* (1984), ". . . what I wanna know is . . . can I introduce my red rooster to your brown hen?" Blues form also encompasses a range of expressive techniques, including wordless cries, apostrophes (overt pleas to the Lord or one's Baby), and repeated words or phrases, that Sherley Anne Williams has collectively labeled "worrying the line." A banjo-plunking lover in Hughes's poem "Ma Man" who "plays good when he's sober / An' better, better, better when he's drunk" is described in language that exemplifies both sexual signifying and worrying, evidencing Hughes's debt to the blues music he absorbed in Kansas City, Harlem, and Washington, D.C.

Blues portraiture, the second constitutive element of the blues literary tradition, speaks to content rather than form: the fact that blues literature is heavily invested in the project of representing the larger-than-life personae that bluesmen and blueswomen, most of them southern-born, have evolved within the diversified world of black show business. Historical icons such as Ma Rainey, Bessie Smith, Robert Johnson, Muddy Waters, Howlin' Wolf, Lightnin' Hopkins, Big Joe Williams, and Sterling "Mr. Satan" Magee have all been the subject of literary portraits, as have fictional bluesmen such as Tea Cake (in Zora Neale Hurston's *Their Eyes Were Watching God*), Luzanna Cholly (in Albert Murray's *Train Whistle Guitar*), and Mississippi Ham Rider (in Toni Cade Bambara's story by that name). Blues autobiographers have also contributed evocative self-portraits as the tellers of their own tales (often assembled with the help of white ghostwriters): W. C. Handy, Mezz Mezzrow, Big Bill Broonzy, Mike Bloomfield, Mance Lipscomb, Willie Dixon, B. B. King, David "Honeyboy" Edwards, Yank Rachell, and Henry Townsend.

Blues literature seeks to portray not just the charismatic performer but also his or her typical surroundings, what French literary critic Hippolyte Taine called "milieu": juke joints, concert halls, recording studios, urban sidewalks, back porches, cotton fields, bedrooms. The audience, too, is a crucial part of the literary blues portrait: the effete African American narrator of "The Weary Blues" who is overcome by emotion as he watches a "Negro play" a "sad raggy tune like a musical fool" in a Harlem dive; or the "Folks from anyplace / Miles aroun'" who "Flocks in to hear / Ma do her stuff" in Sterling Brown's poem "Ma Rainey" (1932); or the good-timing black folk of Raleigh, N.C., in J. J. Phillips's novel *Mojo Hand: An Orphic Tale* (1966), who serve as a foil for the guitar-driven wizardry of Blacksnake Brown, a fictionalized version of Texas bluesman Lightnin' Hopkins: "The music began by straining against itself, each note deceiving the other into existence. Blacksnake was seated at the front of the bar, hunched over his guitar. He stroked the box, argued with it, caressed it, beat it, then made a grand reconciliation. And the music kept on gathering intensity like the shaft of a tornado, and carried everyone down with it, down to their knees and crying for mercy as the blues spun around them. Driving them on, he whirled them to the same mind as himself and, whatever he said, they became, as he beat them down with the blues."

As these examples from Hughes, Brown, and Phillips suggest, blues power— the power wielded by charismatic performers and registered by audiences in their bodies and souls—is a third vital element of the blues literary tradition. Both blues musicians and blues-literary conjurors work a kind of mojo; they cast healing spells, issue calls that provoke life-affirming responses, and conduct collective needs into rollicking good times. On occasion, as with Blacksnake Brown, blues conjurors exert power to uncertain effect—cursing or beating down the audience as a way of purging something troublesome and deep-rooted, like a trickster god mounting a supplicant and riding hard. Sometimes, of course, the power flow is reversed and the audience (or a particularly provocative audience member) holds all the cards. When Muddy Waters sings "She moves me, man . . . honey and I don't see how it's done," he's configuring blues power as the power of a woman to incite the bluesman's desirous song—a song that a blues poet such as Sterling Plumpp, also a native Mississippian, reconfigures yet again as the morale boost it was for the men of his father's Jim Crowed but unbowed generation. "He / put a moving in my father," writes

Plumpp in "Muddy Waters," "I / saw it ripe as liver /. hung / up / on hog / killing day. / And they made / the image they dreamed from it. / I / saw gods in their strides, / feisty bold, desires tilted / like derby hats."

A brief history of blues literature would begin with Langston Hughes's poetic experiments in the mid-1920s: first *The Weary Blues* (1925), which made him famous as the so-called busboy poet of the New Negro Renaissance; then the considerably racier poems of *Fine Clothes to the Jew* (1927), whose southern-tongued vernacular directness ("Shall I carve ma self or / That man that done me wrong?") got him condemned by the black intelligentsia as the "poet low-rate" of Harlem. Claude McKay's novel *Home to Harlem* (1928), similarly panned, featured a plucky young black protagonist adventuring in Harlem's cabarets, partying to the blues—McKay salts his text with lots of AAB verses—and re-solving *not* to kill his braggadocious rival when guns and knives are pulled at the novel's climax.

White writers were quick to jump on the blues literary train piloted by Hughes and McKay. Chapel Hill sociologist Howard Odum, whose pioneering folkloric studies *The Negro and His Songs* (1925) and *Negro Workaday Songs* (1926) had made an early case for the academic importance of black southern music, fic-tionalized the reminiscences of John "Left Wing" Gordon, a well-traveled black southern roustabout, to create the first as-told-to blues autobiography, *Rainbow Round My Shoulder: The Blue Trail of Black Ulysses* (1928). In *Sweet Man* (1930), West Coast writer Gilmore Millen told the story of John Henry, a fictional Mis-sissippi bluesman, offering a somewhat sensationalized view of blues life in Memphis and L.A.'s Central Avenue. Not surprisingly, Mississippian William Faulkner occasionally touched on blues themes: his first novel, *Soldiers' Pay* (1926), features an extended dance sequence in which a bandleader modeled on W. C. Handy (whose concerts Faulkner had attended at Ole Miss) helps incite a ballroom filled with disillusioned young southerners into a libidinous display of slow-dragging. A blind, street corner bluesman and a serenading black jug-band trio make cameo appearances in *Sartoris* (1929).

Several southerners contributed classics to the emergent blues literary tra-dition during the 1930s. In his essay "The Blues as Folk Poetry" (1930), Wash-ington, D.C., native Sterling Brown brought the mind of a trained literary critic to the blues for the first time; his volume *Southern Road* (1932) included "Ma Rainey," "Tin Roof Blues," and other dialect poems that drew heavily on black folk culture. Zora Neale Hurston translated her participant-observer relation-ship with the piney-woods blues people of her native Florida into two land-marks: *Mules and Men* (1935) and *Their Eyes Were Watching God* (1937). In the former, a folkloristic travelogue, she describes her innocent flirtations with the men of the Loughman Lumber Camp from whom she was "collecting material" and her near-fatal encounter with Lucy, the jealous knife-wielding denizen of the Pine Mill, a Polk County jook; in the latter novel, she returns to the jooking life-style in the person of her questing protagonist Janie Crawford and finds her horizons thrillingly expanded thanks to Tea Cake, a playful but violent young bluesman who takes her down on "de muck" of Lake Okeechobee where "the blues are made and used right on the spot."

The 1940s are marked by two foundational blues autobiographies: W. C. Handy's *Father of the Blues* (1941), in which the author argues for his origi-nality as a blues composer on the heels of Jelly Roll Morton's angry denun-ciations in a 1938 article in *Down Beat*; and Mezz Mezzrow's *Really the Blues* (1946), ghostwritten by Bernard Wolfe, which offers an indelible portrait of the Chicago-born Jewish protagonist as a race-changing hipster, convinced, after a transformative prison concert, that the blues-drenched spirit of New Orleans jazz is speaking through his horn and vanquishing Jim Crow segregation in the process. The vivid and sometimes deadly blues life of Memphis, perched at the northern terminus of the Mississippi Delta, is evoked not just by Handy but by black Tennessean George Washington Lee in *Beale Street Sundown* (1942).

Although Richard Wright's Mississippi-based work of the 1930s and 1940s had deliberately avoided overt representations of blues culture out of a desire to show the destructive effects of Jim Crow on black southern life, Ralph Ellison argued in an influential essay entitled "Richard Wright's Blues" that Wright's aggrieved and forthright autobiography *Black Boy* (1945) "represent[s] the flowering—cross-fertilized by pollen blown by the winds of strange cultures—of the humble blues lyric." A few years later, with *Invisible Man* (1952), Elli-son would offer his own novelistic blues portrait of Alabama sharecropper Jim Trueblood, a man who accidentally rapes and impregnates his own daughter, is badly beaten by his wife, and manages to find grace by embracing his shat-tered life: an enactment of the blues ethos par excellence. As so-called country blues—prewar rural southern blues—slowly found its way toward a white folk audience in the course of the decade, blues literature reflected this growing interest. Big Bill Broonzy's autobiography, *Big Bill Blues* (1955), assembled from interviews by Belgian journalist Yannick Bruynoghe, painted the Mississippi-born Broonzy not as the urbane, commercially savvy recording star he would become in 1930s Chicago, but as the overalls-wearing repository of down-home wit that the European concert audience demanded he be. Toni Cade Bambara's short story "Mississippi Ham Rider" (1959), set in Mississippi on the cusp of the civil rights movement, depicts a cantankerous old bluesman's refusal to allow two Yankee record scouts—an Irish American male and an African American female—to play him for a fool. "Black Water Blues" (1951), a story by Monte Culver, dramatizes the tensions within an integrated swing band when their tour takes them south into a confrontation with Jim Crow violence. James Baldwin's much-anthologized "Sonny's Blues" (1957), set in Harlem and Greenwich Village, explores the relationship between two African American brothers, one of whom, a jazz pianist, triumphs over heroin addiction and heals his deep blues with the help of his fellow musicians, teaching his brother something essential about the meaning of community.

As the folk revival of the late 1950s and early 1960s (which featured Mississippi bluesmen such as Son House, Skip James, and Mississippi John Hurt) gave way to the amped-up British blues invasion (Eric Clapton, John Mayall) and the subsequent white blues revival (Paul Butterfield, Charlie Musselwhite, Janis Joplin), African American writers associated with the black arts movement debated the cultural meaning of the blues and, in the process, produced an unprecedented outpouring of blues-toned literature. One contingent, led by political theorist Ron Karenga, claimed that the blues were "invalid," a retrograde holdover from southern plantation days that encouraged "resignation" rather than fostering black revolutionary action. "[W]e ain't blue, we are black," insisted poet Haki Madhubuti (Don L. Lee), in "Don't Cry, Scream" (1969), "/ (all the blues did was / make me cry." In "liberation / poem" (1970), Sonia Sanchez agreed: "no mo / blue / trains running on this track. / they all be de / railed." But another and much larger group of black arts writers, led by Georgia native Larry Neal and Kalamu ya Salaam (born Val Ferdinand in New Orleans), was determined to reclaim the blues as an irrevocably black cultural inheritance, the distilled wit and wisdom of generations of black southern survivors and their northward-migrating descendants. "To write a blues song," wrote Mississippian Etheridge Knight in "Haiku" (1968), "is to regiment riots / and pluck gems from graves." These are the blues and blues people celebrated by Jayne Cortez ("Lead," "Dinah's Back in Town," "You Know"), Stanley Crouch ("Howlin' Wolf: A Blues Lesson Book"), James Cone (*The Spirituals and the Blues*), Al Young ("A Dance for Ma Rainey"), Quincy Troupe ("Impressions / of Chicago; for Howlin Wolf"), Eugene Redmond ("Double Clutch Lover"), Ben Caldwell (*Birth of a Blues!*), Raymond Patterson (*Elemental Blues*), Tom Dent ("For Walter Washington"), Salaam ("The Blues [in two parts]"), Nikki Giovanni ("Poem for Aretha," "Master Charge Blues"), and critic Stephen Henderson ("Blues, Soul, and Black Identity: The Forms of Things Unknown").

Although the black arts movement per se dissolved in the mid-1970s, the movement's long-term effects on the blues literary tradition—a fundamental revaluation of a race's cultural inheritance—have been profound. Coming of age during the mid-1960s, his life's purpose revealed by the chance hearing of a Bessie Smith record, Pittsburgh-born playwright August Wilson has dramatized migrant southern blues lives with pitch-perfect authenticity in *Ma Rainey's Black Bottom* (1984), *The Piano Lesson* (1990), and *Seven Guitars* (1995). In *Blues: The Story Always Untold* (1989), *Blues Narratives* (1999), and other volumes of fractured, incantory poetry, Mississippian Sterling Plumpp sings praise songs for the Delta legends of his youth (Robert Johnson, Muddy Waters, B. B. King, Bessie Smith), retells the post-Reconstruction trials of his grandparents, and honors his role as a self-appointed *griot*. Memphis-born Arthur Flowers revises Hurston's *Their Eyes Were Watching God* in his novel *Another Good Loving Blues* (1993), the story of a bluesy romance between Delta bluesman Luke Bodeen and hoodoo practitioner Melvira Dupree; in *Mojo Rising: Confessions of a 21st-Century Conjureman* (2001), Flowers fuses autobiography with manifesto and performance art. Ishmael Reed's "Neo-Hoodoo Manifesto" (1970), like Flowers's work, finds a black-magical core, African sourced and blues-toned, at the heart of African American literature. In the contrarian critical writings of Albert Murray, above all, the blues have found their paradigmatic organic intellectual: Alabama-born, Harlem-bred, brimming with mother wit and nimble dialectics. Murray's essential works include *Train Whistle Guitar* (1974), *Stomping the Blues* (1976), and *The Blue Devils of Nada* (1997).

Zora Neale Hurston's influence on blues-based writing by contemporary African American women has been considerable. Alice Walker, whose early partisanship helped reignite Hurston's reputation in the mid 1970s, made her own literary ancestry explicit in an essay entitled "In Search of Our Mothers' Gardens" (1974). *The Color Purple* (1982), a novel of womanly friendship and self-transformation grounded in the healing power of blues music, echoed *Their Eyes* in these and other respects. Set primarily in Brazil, New York, and various southern states, Gayl Jones's novels *Corregidora* (1975) and *Eva's Man* (1976) invoke blues performance in darker, more troubling ways; rather than tears hardened with laughter, they are grim stories of violence and compulsion, blues in a distinctly minor key. In her collection entitled *Some One Sweet Angel Chile* (1982), poet Sherley Anne Williams envisions the sisterly intersubjectivity and survivor's pride that binds Ma Rainey and Bessie Smith; her essay "The Blues Roots of Contemporary Afro-American Poetry" (1979) is an essential contribution to the critical dialogue. In poems such as "Bottom Out Blues," "Variations on a Blues Motif," and "Identifying Marks," Wanda Coleman mines traditional blues forms and invents new ones. Although Toni Morrison is not normally thought of as a blues writer, her first novel, *The Bluest Eye* (1970), fuses a black arts critique of ideologies of whiteness with an explicit invocation of blues materials in the form of Mama McTeer, who sings "St. Louis Blues" in her nourishing, "greens and blues"–filled kitchen, and a prostitute named Poland, who knows many blues songs and chants them in a "sweet strawberry voice."

During the last several decades, the blues literary tradition has consolidated its position as a vital and distinctive subset of American and African American literature. Some of this vitality is a by-product of the second wave of the blues revival, one that began with the first Blues Brothers movie in 1979, grew to encompass a black southern audience with Z. Z. Hill's "Down Home Blues" (1982) and Little Milton's "The Blues Is Alright" (1984), and caught fire in 1990 when the CD boxed set *The Complete Recordings of Robert Johnson* sold more than a million copies. Blues autobiography, in particular, has flowered, as southern-born elder statesmen (and their younger white apprentices) have committed their life stories to print: Michael Bloomfield's "Me and Big Joe" (1980), Willie Dixon's *I Am the Blues* (1989), Mance Lipscomb's *I Say Me for a Parable* (1993), B. B. King's *Blues All around Me* (1996), David "Honeyboy" Edwards's *The World Don't Owe Me Nothing* (1997), my own *Mister Satan's Apprentice* (1998), Henry Townsend's *A Blues Life* (1999), Taj Mahal's *Taj Mahal* (2001), and Yank Rachell's *Blues Mandolin Man* (2001). Not surprisingly, the myth of Robert Johnson's selling his soul to the devil at a Mississippi crossroads has proved irresistible to writers in search of local color and/or racial melodrama: fictional and dramatic treatments of the Delta bluesman's life include T. C. Boyle's "Stones in My Passway, Hellhound on My Trail" (1977), Alan Greenberg's *Love in Vain: A Vision of Robert Johnson* (1983), Walter Mosley's *RL's Dream* (1995), Sherman Alexie's *Reservation Blues* (1996), and Ace Atkins's *Crossroad Blues* (2000). By any measure, literature is a place in which the blues are alive and well—brash, intimate, southern-born, and northern-yearning, sounding their bittersweet song.

ADAM GUSSOW
University of Mississippi

Barbara Baker, *The Blues Aesthetic and the Making of American Identity in the Literature of the South* (2003); Houston A. Baker Jr., *Blues, Ideology, and Afro-American Literature: A Vernacular Theory* (1984); Tony Bolden, *Afro-Blue: Improvisations in African American Poetry and Culture* (2004); Adam Gussow, *Seems Like Murder Here: Southern Violence and the Blues Tradition* (2002); A. Yemisi Jismoh, *Spiritual, Blues, and Jazz People in African American Fiction: Living in Paradox* (2002); Valerie Sweeney Prince, *Burnin' Down the House: Home in African American Literature* (2005); Patricia R. Schroeder, *Robert Johnson, Mythmaking, and Contemporary American Culture* (2004); Steven C. Tracy, *Langston Hughes and the Blues* (1988), in *The Cambridge Companion to the African American Novel* (2004).

Civil Rights in Literature

From 1954 (*Brown v. Board of Education of Topeka, Kansas*) until 1968 (assassination of Martin Luther King Jr.), the American South was clearly a major focal point in the struggle for freedom and justice as black citizens organized and actively demonstrated for basic rights too long denied them by an inherently racist white southern tradition. Literary artists began using the civil rights movement in their creative responses during the movement and, up until the present day, continue to do so. During the movement, those who wrote about this racism that manifested itself in psychological, physical, and societal violence consciously chose to take a stand. These creative responses were bold political statements, born of the movement and responding to a time when black-white professional, romantic, and social relationships could not function normally or freely in society.

More than 50 novels and memoirs, hundreds of poems, and a dozen plays and movies have responded to the news events of this time. Some literary responses prepare the way for readers to think about the movement; they consciously depict the days leading up to the passage of *Brown*, and linger around what new possibilities will be forthcoming. Other pieces of literature incorporate fictional characters into the activities of historical people, places, and events. A third category includes those writers who publish their work after the fact, showing the results of the movement on the lives of the now damaged characters. On the periphery are those writers who simply use the civil rights movement as backdrop to a story; in these cases, the movement itself is little more than setting or happenstance.

GETTING READY FOR THE CIVIL RIGHTS MOVEMENT. In 1949 Lillian Smith first published what she knew would be a controversial collection of essays, *Killers of the Dream*. In her foreword, she asks a question that propels the whole book: "Why has the white man dreamed so fabulous a dream of freedom and human dignity and again and again tried to kill his own dream?" Smith was ahead of her time in her advocacy of an integrated South. Yet southern history does not exist apart from the history of entanglements between the races. When *Brown* was unanimously passed on 17 May 1954, a new era began. This is the watershed. Since that time, novelists have tried to make literary sense of racial connections and separations: in the dependency of white women on their black women domestic helpers depicted in *Almost Family* and *Can't Quit You, Baby*; in the forbidden love of a black man for a white woman in *Five Smooth Stones*; in the childhood interracial friendships of both boys and girls in *Halfway Home*; in the completely black, all segregated worlds of *I Been in Sorrow's*

Kitchen and Licked Out All the Pots; in the gradual awakening of a new day for protected white girls in *Heartbreak Hotel* and for black adults in *1959*; in the violence of "parent killing child" in *Caleb, My Son* and *A Cry of Absence*; in the lynching of black men by white men in the stories of James Baldwin. These works show how dreams are killed and who may be responsible.

SCHOOL DESEGREGATION. Does the segregation of children in public schools solely on the basis of race deprive the minority children of the equal protection of the laws guaranteed by the 14th Amendment? This is the question symbolically posed by *Brown* to which the Supreme Court answered, with a fair amount of urging, a unanimous "yes." The lynching of Emmett Till in Money, Miss., in August 1955, has been seen by some as a response to this court action: "Well, it kind of puts the whole United States of America on notice. . . . The Supreme Court ain't gon' ram no integration down our throats." *Your Blues Ain't Like Mine*, *Wolf Whistle*, *Blues for Mister Charlie*, and *A Killing in This Town* offer new ways to imagine the story of Emmett Till.

At Central High School, the situation is presented up close and personal from a woman who was a key player in the political maneuvering in *The Long Shadow of Little Rock* and from one of the nine black students who attended the school during the dangerous and chaotic school year 1957–58 in *Warriors Don't Cry*.

County Woman and *The Last Gentleman* comment, in part, on James Meredith's integration of Ole Miss in the fall of 1962. The hyped anticipation of the coming of integration is the subject of *1959*, *Birthright*, and *Betsey Brown*. The fear in the black households and the sacrifices black parents are willing to make are clear in short stories by James Thompson, R. V. Cassill, and Diane Oliver; for white children there is a hesitancy among their parents, a fear more disembodied, more distant and denied, such as in *The Last of the Whitfields*, and in short stories by Joan Williams. Emmett Till and Little Rock raise their heads in fictional texts, and television and newspaper reports suggest, in earnest, a reality worth fearing.

SIT-INS AND DEMONSTRATIONS. On 1 February 1960 four young black male students at North Carolina A&T College walked to the downtown Woolworth's and sat at the counter to order some coffee. Thus began what was to become known as the sit-in. Students in Nashville had been getting ready all fall to launch their own slate of activities, but Greensboro stole their thunder. Within weeks, throughout the major cities of the South, sit-ins spread quickly.

Sit-ins are depicted as a symbol of freedom in *The Autobiography of Miss Jane*

Pittman. In *A Walk through Fire*, the same activities appear slight and silly and white people even more so for invoking stringent requirements. Short stories by Joanne Leedom-Ackerman and Lee Martin use the events in Nashville to depict both clashes and sympathy between blacks and whites.

Birmingham was the site in the spring of a massive effort called Project Confrontation, encouraged by Fred Shuttlesworth and led by Martin Luther King Jr. It involved demonstrators, many of them children, on one side, and police dogs and fire hoses aimed at the demonstrators, on the other side. In the fall, Klansmen blew up the 16th Street Baptist Church and killed four young girls. In creative responses, revenge against white people occurs in *Song of Solomon*. A murder mystery unfolds against this backdrop in *Streets of Fire*. The church bombers are imagined in *Four Spirits*, and another child killed on that same day is the inspiration for a major character in *Bombingham*. In "Negro Progress," the hosing of Birmingham's black children is the focus of the story.

VOTING RIGHTS ACTIVITIES. Singing and the movement are of a piece; the latter could not have existed without the former. When demonstrators and activists went to jail, they sang; when they heard that somebody in the movement was dead, they sang; when they prepared for the work that lay ahead of them, they sang. The words of old spirituals and gospel tunes were changed to fit their pursuits of freedom: "Who's that yonder dressed in red? / Let my people go. / Look like the children Bob Moses led. / Let my people go." From such a line comes a depiction of Freedom Summer, *The Children Bob Moses Led*. During the summer of 1964 hundreds of college-aged students—white and black—gathered in Oxford, Ohio, for orientation before heading off to Mississippi for direct action in getting out the vote. Some would be assigned to Freedom Schools; others were to canvass the neighborhoods and speak with people about registering to vote. The Mississippi Freedom Democratic Party would make its presence felt in August in Atlantic City at the National Democratic Convention. What happened that summer or what might have happened is explored in *And Do Remember Me* and *Freshwater Road*, the poems of Margaret Walker and Sam Cornish.

Some of the most violent short stories about the movement depict those who participated in helping disenfranchised black citizens obtain their voting rights: "Liars Don't Qualify," "Advancing Luna—and Ida B. Wells," "Means and Ends," and "Going to Meet the Man."

LOOKING BACK. In Mark Childress's *Crazy in Alabama*, Peter Joseph is 40 years old when the book opens, but quickly a phone call from his Aunt Lucille takes him instantly back to 1965, "the deepest summer of [his] life . . . when everybody went crazy in Alabama." When fictional characters, sometimes thinly veiled real-life participants, look back on their days in the movement they appear to get stuck. For all those protagonists this has been the "deepest" experience of their lives: for Teddy in *Civil Wars*, who loses his whole family over his not being able to move forward; for Meridian in Alice Walker's book of that title; for Velma Henry in *The Salt Eaters*, who is not ready to be healed because she still lingers in those days when life was its most pulsating. In *And All Our Wounds Forgiven*, Lisa Adams lives again and again the seven years she spent with John Calvin Marshall, a Martin Luther King–like leader, who has been dead for decades. In *Boats against the Current*, Jack Harris returns to Montgomery at the summons of his old friend, now governor Jesse Stuart, a George Wallace–like character with a Lurleen-like wife. Alice Walker's auto-biographical offering, *The Way Forward Is with a Broken Heart*, reflects on her 1960s life in Mississippi. Some must tell their stories over and over as though, if the story can be told just one more time, the civil rights movement will eventually exorcise itself. Maybe for some a new self will emerge, but the shadows of former times cast a huge net over all the survivors.

As a genre, civil rights in literature is a time capsule, an intense look at the violent, unvarnished reality of those times. It demands a close study with and through the historical documents of the time; especially enlightening is the Public Broadcasting System video series *Eyes on the Prize: America's Civil Rights Years, 1954–1965* and its companion text. Through such an approach, this important decade in America's history comes into sharper focus.

MARGARET WHITT
University of Denver

James Baldwin, *Going to Meet the Man* (1965), *Blues for Mister Charlie* (1964); Toni Cade Bambara, *The Salt Eaters* (1980); Daisy Bates, *The Long Shadow of Little Rock* (1962; repr. 1986); Melba Pattillo Beals, *Warriors Don't Cry* (1994); Rosellen Brown, *Civil Wars* (1984); Bebe Moore Campbell, *Your Blues Ain't Like Mine* (1992); Mark Childress, *Crazy in Alabama* (1993); William Cobb, *A Walk through Fire* (1992); Julia Duncan Coley, *Halfway Home* (1979); Thomas H. Cook, *Streets of Fire* (1989); Lucy Daniels, *Caleb, My Son* (1956; repr. 2001); Thulani Davis, *1959* (1992); Ellen Douglas, *Can't Quit You, Baby* (1988); Ann Fairbairn, *Five Smooth Stones* (1966); Ernest Gaines, *The Autobiography of Miss Jane Pittman* (1972); Marita Golden, *And Do Remember Me* (1992); Anthony Grooms, *Bombingham* (2001); William Heath, *The Children Bob Moses Led* (1995); Roy Hoffman, *Almost Family* (1983); Madison Jones, *A Cry of Absence* (1971); Julius Lester, *And All Our Wounds Forgiven* (1994); John Logue, *Boats against the Current* (1987); Toni Morrison, *Song of Solomon* (1977); Sena Jeter Naslund, *Four Spirits* (2003); Denise Nicholas, *Freshwater Road* (2005); Lewis Nordan, *Wolf Whistle* (1993); Lettie Hamlett Rogers, *Birthright* (1957); Elise Sanguinetti, *The Last of the Whitfields* (1962; repr. 1986); Ntozake Shange, *Betsey Brown* (1985); Anne Rivers Siddons, *Heartbreak Hotel* (1976); Lillian Smith, *Killers of the Dream* (1949; repr. 1961, 1994); Susan Straight, *I Been in Sorrow's Kitchen and Licked Out All the Pots* (1992); Alice Walker, *Meridian* (1976), *The Way Forward Is with a Broken Heart* (2000); Walker Percy, *The Last Gentleman* (1966); Olympia Vernon, *A Killing in This Town* (2006); Margaret Earley Whitt, ed., *Short Stories of the Civil Rights Movement: An Anthology* (2006); Joan Williams, *County Woman* (1982); Juan Williams, *Eyes on the Prize: America's Civil Rights Years, 1954–1965* (1987).

Civil War in Literature

Southern literature related to the Civil War has long been considered an enigma. While periodically struggling with an unwieldy tension between memory and the bonds of regionalism, critics have suggested an almost pathological inability to produce an American *Iliad,* or any type of literary work that defines the war experience for the ages. Yet the events of those days, in the full bloom of their emotion and complexity, largely define the region and the ideas that have become the New South, and the literature born during and after the conflict, when crafted in its highest forms—in the hands of a master like a William Faulkner, or a Robert Penn Warren, for example—remains a palpable fabric in the culture of the New South that cannot be separated from the universal American experience.

American writers, both North and South, wielded their pens from the moment the first shots were fired at Fort Sumter. Throughout the war, poems, lyrics to songs, novels, stories, and essays were circulated within both sections of the country in publications such as *Harper's Weekly*, the *Southern Illustrated News*, and the *Southern Literary Messenger*. The volume of surviving letters and diaries from the time period has still not been adequately grasped. Nonetheless, any close scrutiny of Civil War literature encounters an apparent contradiction: although much was written, less has remained cogent or significant over time.

The best-known contemporary literary treatments of the war were inked from the pens of northern writers such as Herman Melville in *Battle-Pieces and Aspects of the War* (1866), Walt Whitman in *Drum-Taps* (1865), and Louisa May Alcott in *Hospital Sketches* (1863). The apparent lack of important southern offerings stems in part from the one-sided outcome of the military conflict; part of this may also stem from the human carnage the conflict wrought on the

South. The wholesale destruction of a generation of southern youth eliminated countless poets, novelists, and philosophers on a scale proportionate to that suffered by a hitherto literate German intelligentsia during the First World War. Is it really any surprise there was a significant drop in literary production? Not only did many of the South's greatest writers take up the sword, but those who didn't were often struck with a curious case of wartime writer's block. "I can't compose, I can't think of anything," novelist John Esten Cooke wrote in 1861. Many other authors, North and South, suffered regularly from this curious wartime phenomenon. Cooke recovered from his writer's block and contributed to the *Southern Illustrated News* and later added a successful Civil War novel, *Surry of Eagle's Nest* (1866), along with other works.

In spite of the upheaval of war, the life of the mind did not disappear in the South. Henry Timrod became in essence "Poet Laureate of the Confederacy," crafting poems that optimized the early widespread commitment to the southern cause, typified by *Ethnogenesis* (1861), *Carolina*, and *Ode*. Francis Orray Ticknor, physician and writer, dramatically recounted the plight of a wounded Confederate soldier in the poem *Little Giffen*. Augusta Evans's best-selling novel *Macaria; or, Altars of Sacrifice* (1863) made a challenging statement about gender roles during the wartime crisis, a notable accomplishment for a female author in a particularly male-dominated culture. Countless men and women including Sarah Morgan Dawson (1841–99) and Mary Boykin Chestnut (1823–86) filled their diaries with poems, prayers, vignettes, and stories. Much of this wartime literature was lost, or remains relatively obscure.

Later, military defeat and wartime destruction turned southern authors toward fictional interpretation *and* reinterpretation of the sweeping and often tragic events they had witnessed. Their collective writing, typified by books like *Marse Chan: A Tale of Old Virginia* (1884) by Thomas Nelson Page, *The Reign of Law* (1900) by James Lane Allen, and the writings of Cooke, was a direct contribution to a collective southern reframing of antebellum culture and the war itself that critics referred to as glamorization of the "Lost Cause." Romantic, idealized, and occasionally insincere in view of modern sensibilities, these efforts represented a bridge between the unfathomable destruction of war and the reality of a reunited and powerful industrial United States.

Innovative authors around the turn of the century, perhaps following the lead of John William DeForest, who in *Miss Ravenel's Conversion from Secession to Loyalty* (1867) clearly diverged from the early romanticists, focused more on the reality of war and social issues. Anticipating Faulkner's realism, *The Cavalier* (1901) and other works by George Washington Cable also strayed from the path of romanticism and often conveyed positive messages about civil rights for

African Americans. Cable was close friends with another Civil War–era writer of note, Mark Twain, who toured the country with him on speaking engagements. Unlike Cable, Twain tended to eschew the Civil War as primary subject material, and his most notable works are largely devoid of war-related material. Stephen Crane's *Red Badge of Courage* (1895) portrayed combat in harsh detail, but with notable literary aplomb and tact. Ambrose Bierce, in stories such as "Occurrence at Owl Creek Bridge" in *Tales of Soldiers and Civilians* (1891), also rendered compelling and sometime gory war narratives, albeit without the smoothness of Crane.

In the 1920s the southern Agrarians captured conservative populism and used the Civil War as a dramatic stage to hearken back to more traditional and simple forms of existence. Prominent among the Agrarians were two writers who engaged in important Civil War narrative discourse for almost 50 years. Robert Penn Warren tapped deeply into the Civil War and the pathos of the South throughout his long literary career. Much of his early Agrarian writing set the stage for important later works. In *Legacy of the Civil War* (1961) he captured with the eloquence of a novelist and the mind of the historian a number of unresolved and misunderstood elements of the war, a book that was "brilliant," according to the *New Yorker*. He wrote novels haunted by the specter of the war, including his best-known work, *All the King's Men* (1946), and novels that were set during the war, such as *Wilderness: A Tale of the Civil War* (1961). His Agrarian colleague Allen Tate also made notable use of the war, penning such well-known works as the poem "Ode to the Confederate Dead" (1928) and writing important biographies of Stonewall Jackson (1928) and Jefferson Davis (1929). *The Wave* (1929) by Evelyn Scott is also from this period, a novel that attempted in a relatively unique fashion to paint the war in more universal terms.

The shift from romanticism to realism set the stage for arguably the most significant Civil War literary luminary. William Faulkner remains in a class by himself. Faulkner brought modernism into Civil War literature, weaving complicated narrative threads through the jumbled and depressed postwar South that still demand contemporary attention. The width and breadth of his art are perhaps most apparent in *Absalom, Absalom!* (1936) and *The Unvanquished* (1938), stories that ultimately led to a Nobel Prize in Literature in 1949. His contribution to Civil War literature challenged all who followed.

At the end of this period came one of the most beloved and criticized Civil War novels, *Gone with the Wind* (1936) by Margaret Mitchell. Little needs to be said about a novel so popularized by the cinematic adaptation that the images and themes have become part of popular culture. While arguably an "epic" work in the popular sense, the novel fails at the highest levels to convince serious readers. Shelby Foote, best known for his historical narratives, also contributed a noteworthy Civil War novel in *Shiloh* (1952) in this period.

In the last 25 years or so, the Civil War has defied postmodern novelists. The most notable works of the late 20th century were generally variations on previous themes. *The Killer Angels* (1974) by Michael Shaara was a knowledgeable and sweeping fictionalization of Lee's Pennsylvania campaign and the critical battle at Gettysburg. While the novel was commercially successful and the winner of a Pulitzer Prize, many endorsements of the novel are by military historians rather than literary critics. Another commercial success of note was the novel *Cold Mountain* (1997) by Charles Frazier, winner of the 1997 National Book Award. While a compelling and well-crafted story, *Cold Mountain* was not crowned an immediate classic; instead, reviewers called it "a promising but overlong, uneven debut" (*Kirkus Reviews*, 1997). More recently, *Confederates in the Attic: Dispatches from the Unfinished Civil War* (1998) by Tony Horwitz enjoyed mainstream literary attention. In stark contrast to either Shaara or Frazier, Horowitz examined the aftermath of the war with a frank appreciation for the complexities of the American and southern experience. None of these books, however, aspired for, or achieved, anything approaching universality in illuminating the American *Odyssey* of the Civil War.

Several important investigations of Civil War literature have been undertaken. Among these are *Patriotic Gore: Studies in the Literature of the American Civil War* (1962) by Edmund Wilson; *The Unwritten War: American Writers and the Civil War* (1973) by Daniel Aaron; and ". . . the Real War Will Never Get in the Books": Selections from Writers during the Civil War* (1993), edited by Louis P. Masur. All three books directly investigate the literary impact of the war, confirming what many have long seen as a dearth of Civil War literature. The authors and editors also puzzle over instances of collective writer's block, highlighting the great irony that "whenever these [Civil War] authors lamented their inability to compose they did so in some of their finest prose."

In the 21st century, the enigma remains. Many books have been written; many words have been printed and circulated; many critics have temporized or championed a noteworthy work. Where is the American *Iliad* or *the* novel that defines the Civil War experience? While some literary lights shine brighter than others, something critical in the American Civil War experience still appears to be defying narrative illumination. Perhaps, quoting Whitman, "The real war never will get in the books."

JACK TRAMMELL
Randolph-Macon College

Daniel Aaron, *The Unwritten War: American Writers and the Civil War* (1962); Louis P. Masur, ed., *". . . the Real War Will Never Get in the Books": Selections from Writers during the Civil War* (1993); Edmund Wilson, *Patriotic Gore: Studies in the Literature of the American Civil War* (1962).

Detective Fiction

The American mystery story begins with a southerner by upbringing—Edgar Allan Poe, born in Boston but raised in Richmond. The first of the three stories with C. Auguste Dupin as detective, "The Murders in the Rue Morgue," was published in 1841, usually being considered the first detective story. It certainly begins the popular genre. That story and the two Dupins that followed were set in France, unfortunately for present purposes—but "The Gold Bug" appeared in 1843, and it is set in South Carolina. The "detective," so to speak—actually an amateur cryptographer—is William Legrand, born in New Orleans but living on Sullivan's Island, near Charleston. The main part of the action, the finding of treasure, takes place on the mainland, northwest from the island—in the early 19th century, says the story, "a tract of country excessively wild and desolate, where no trace of a human footstep was to be seen."

The second writer of importance chronologically is Melville Davisson Post, author of 22 stories about a detective named Abner, narrated by his nephew Martin, that were published between 1911 and 1928. The stories are laid before the Civil War in what is now West Virginia but was then just Virginia. "Abner pulled up his horse and looked down at the sweep of country that fell away from the range of the Alleghenies westward toward the Ohio. [T]he country sloped over long, steep, sodded fields to the river and meadow beyond. It is the oldest cattle country in America. For a hundred years it has been fence and pastured" (the opening of "The Mystery at Hillhouse"). Abner is a staunch Christian, believing in God's justice. A few of the stories may be too religious (and too supernatural) for modern taste; however, as a depiction of mid-19th-century culture the stories are highly enjoyable. Abner probably was based on Post's father.

After the Uncle Abner stories of (mainly) the 1910s, a pause took place—not in the writing of detective stories, but in the merging of the mystery and regionalism. Marvin Lachman, whose *The American Regional Mystery* (2002) is the basic study of the topic, says that the modern movement began around 1940. Lachman uses "mystery" in the broad sense of crime fiction, so he mentions William Faulkner's *Sanctuary* (1931) in his Mississippi survey and Robert Penn Warren's *All the King's Men* (1946) in Louisiana. (Surprisingly, Harper

Lee's trial novel, *To Kill a Mockingbird* [1960], is not mentioned in his survey of Alabama.)

Faulkner's two books that reflect the genre conventions are notable. *Knight's Gambit* (1949) has six stories with lawyer Gavin Stephens. Several critics in the mystery field have suggested that the nephew-uncle pattern with the nephew narrator in *Knight's Gambit* was suggested to Faulkner by Post's Uncle Abner stories. Faulkner's mystery novel, *Intruder in the Dust* (1948), involving racial politics, is also a Gavin Stephens story, but, as Lachman observes, "the detective work is done by two teenagers and an old woman, using clues provided by . . . a black man." The mystery plot is the first eight chapters; a discussion of the South follows, for the last three.

A survey of the other states that made up the Confederacy, with one or two mystery writers mentioned connected to each, indicates the scope of the genre. For the most part racial themes and Civil War tie-ins have been omitted here, to avoid repetition. Lachman gives many examples.

Virginia has many locales—Williamsburg, Monticello, the Shenandoah Valley, among them—that have been used in mysteries. The most successful modern mystery writer is Patricia Cornwell, especially in her series of novels about a medical examiner, Dr. Kay Scarpetta, beginning with *Postmortem* (1990). The early setting was Richmond, although Scarpetta later shifted jobs and moved to Florida. Cornwell's work is noted for its accurate details.

North Carolina has what Lachman calls "one of the best American regional series" in Margaret Maron's fiction about Judge Deborah Knott, starting with *Bootlegger's Daughter* (1992). The setting is usually Johnson County (near Raleigh), fictionalized as "Colleton County." Here is one of Knott's comments on race, from *Home Fires* (1998): "God knows life would be a lot simpler if we could all wake up one morning color-blind, but we're nowhere close to it on either side. Not by a long shot. We continue to lead separate, parallel personal lives, seldom connecting without self-consciousness, at genuine ease only at points of old familiarity such as Maidie [a black housekeeper] and me here in my mother's kitchen."

South Carolina has been mentioned for Poe's "Gold Bug." Carolyn G. Hart sets her Annie Laurence (later Annie Darling) bookstore series on Broward Rock Island, a fictionalized version of Hilton Head Island. Hart's series, beginning with *Death on Demand* (1987), is lightweight—the books are "cozies" in the field's jargon—but she does bring much state history into them.

Georgia, of course, has a number of mysteries that allude to Margaret Mitchell's *Gone with the Wind* (1936), including Patricia Sprinkle's *A Mystery*

Bred in Buckhead (1994). Name authors who have set crime fiction in Georgia include Tom Wolfe, with *A Man in Full* (1998), and, among genre writers, Phyllis A. Whitney, with *Lost Island* (1970)—the island is St. Simon's, although she calls it "Hampton Island."

Florida inspired what Lachman calls "probably the first ecological crime novel," John D. MacDonald's *A Flash of Green* (1962), about developers wanting "to create landfill in [a] bay." Lachman says, by the 1970s "most Florida [crime] writers" were "environmentally concerned." The state is also culturally varied, with (to mention nothing else) the Cuban influence—with reflections in mysteries. John D. MacDonald is also the best-known Florida mystery novelist, with his colorfully titled novels about Travis McGee on his houseboat *The Busted Flush*, starting with *The Deep Blue Good-by* (1964). McGee was not exactly a detective, but a solver of problems or, as his card says, a "salvage expert."

Tennessee has two particularly notable mystery writers. T. S. Stribling was born in the state, and the second volume in his southern trilogy, *The Store* (1932), won him a Pulitzer. But Stribling supported himself by popular writing throughout his life. His series of 37 short stories about Professor Henry Poggioli, all but eight collected in three volumes, are his contributions to detective fiction. Several of the later stories—in *Best Dr. Poggioli Detective Stories* (1975)— are set in Tennessee. Sharyn McCrumb's Ballad series of mystery novels are laid in the Appalachian Mountains in the eastern part of the state, beginning with *If Ever I Return Pretty Peggy-O* (1990). Sheriff Spencer Arrowood is the "detective," but the emphasis is not on him but on the culture, the people, and the traditional folksongs. In *The Rosewood Casket* (1996), in a passage from 1824, "The old woman . . . had risen before dawn, as she had all her life, mindful of the Hunters, who waited with their arrows to take the souls of Cherokees they found sleeping after daybreak. Perhaps they watched her more carefully now that she was old, but she would disappoint them."

Alabama does not seem to have many culturally descriptive mysteries set in its borders. Lachman mentions 23 only. He finds Alabama's first detective to be a black man—Octavus Roy Cohen's Florian Slappey—with stories about the Alabama-born detective collected in *Florian Slappey Goes Abroad* (1928) and *Florian Slappey* (1938). Unfortunately, Slappey is a stereotyped humorous black, however good at solving the crimes. Revealingly about the approach, Cohen (who was born in South Carolina) was a writer for the radio's *Amos 'n' Andy* show in 1945–46.

Arkansas's most popular mystery writer is Joan Hess, primarily for her series about a small town, Maggody, with its population of 755. The first of the series, with Sheriff Arly Hanks, was *Malice in Maggody* (1987). But Lachman points out that the local color in Hess's books is "negative Arkansas stereotypes" used for humor. More serious, and with some reflection of the state's culture, is a brief 1990s series about attorney Gideon Page by Grif Stockley, beginning with *Expert Testimony* (1991).

Louisiana is one of the areas rich in mystery novels, with New Orleans, its French Quarter, Mardi Gras, jazz, food, and sexual attractions, overweighing the rest of the state. But the best current mystery writer about Louisiana is James Lee Burke, with his Dave Robicheaux series, beginning with *The Neon Rain* (1987). Robicheaux is a Cajun, and by the fourth novel, *A Morning for Flamingoes* (1990), he has joined the New Iberian police force. In *Jolie Blon's Bounce* (2002), Robicheaux's opening description is of New Iberia when he was growing up in the 1940s—from "the antebellum homes along East Main" to Hopkins and Railroad avenues with their "paintless cribs . . . [and] blowsy women." A writer using the New Orleans setting in an interesting way is Barbara Hambly, with a series about Benjamin January, a free black man in the city in the 1830s, beginning with *A Free Man of Color* (1997). In addition to the novels, a short story, "Libre," appears in the New Orleans issue of *Ellery Queen's Mystery Magazine* (November 2006). January's mother is the *placée* of a white man who brought and freed her, January, and her older daughter. January's half sister is also a *placée*, while his older, full sister has turned to the voodoo belief and trade. The culture of New Orleans of the time proves very exotic.

Texas is also a mystery-rich state. All the major cities have their novels, as do the Mexican border and the dry west Texas. The problem is that—despite some Civil War battles between Texas and New Mexico—the southern culture is really on the eastern edge of the state. Probably the best depictions of east Texas are in Joe R. Lansdale's mysteries, especially *The Bottoms* (2000), a nonseries book. It is told in the present about events in 1933–34. "The wind had blown away most of North and West Texas, along with Oklahoma, but the eastern part of Texas was lush with greenery and the soil was rich and there was enough rain so that things grew quick and hardy." In this setting and amid a growing-up plot occur racial hatred and a serial killer.

C. S. Lewis wrote in an essay "On Stories" (1947) that a plot was a mesh in which something other was sometimes caught. In realistic stories, one "other" is a feeling for culture and setting—in these stories, southern culture.

JOE R. CHRISTOPHER
Tarleton State University

Allen J. Hubin, *Crime Fiction IV: 1749–2000* (2003); Marvin Lachman, *The American Regional Mystery* (2002); Charles A. Norton, *Melville Davisson Post: Man of Many Mysteries* (1873); Melville Davisson Post, *The Complete Uncle Abner*, introduction and annotated bibliography by Allen J. Hubin (1977); Kenneth W. Vickers, *T. S. Stribling: A Life of the Tennessee Novelist* (2004).

Folklore in Literature

With the exception of Native American lore, folklore, like language and literature, came to this country as part of the cultural baggage of the various waves of its settlers. In the South, its sources are mainly British, African, and French, with important admixtures of Spanish and German and touches of almost everything else.

From the beginning, new experiences and a new environment eroded this imported lore and reshaped it to new purposes. Erosion and adaptation may be rapid, but the emergence of a new folklore, like the development of a distinctive and significant literature, is always slow. It was slowed further in the United States by increasing literacy, mobility, urbanization, homogenization, and the influence of the mass media. Forces at work in the South, however, and not alone its geography and history, reduced the effect of such inhibiting factors while encouraging the evolution of a southern folklore and easing its incorporation into its literature. The result was to enhance the regional flavor of southern letters.

If the Puritans of New England were a people of the book, then southerners harkened enthusiastically to pentecostal tongues—and to the silvery words of their politicians at the hustings, the tall tales of their hunters and riverboatmen, the animal stories of their slaves, the brags, songs, and sayings that were part of the life of what came to be folk communities. Mark Twain charmed audiences all over the world because he knew from his memories of folklife that the way the tale is told is as important as the tale itself. Style, the manner in which things are said and done, was prized, whether on a bear hunt in the backwoods or at a Mardi Gras ball. In short, the living word and the performance, the marrow of folklore, were likewise the marrow of southern culture.

The most obvious feature distinguishing the South from the rest of the United States was its racial composition and the resulting historical developments provoked by profound sectional difference. Like others who crossed the Atlantic, Africans brought with them their myths and their music, their beliefs and their words. Folklore travels in the heart of humankind and therefore had the power to survive even the horrors of the middle passage and the merciless process of annihilation of African traditions that took place upon arrival. The archsurvivor, Brer Rabbit, was born in Africa.

People forget their victories and virtues but never their defeats and sins. Thus, southerners were hypersensitive to the past, for it included racial repression and the loss, on their own precious soil, of the bloodiest war in American history, followed by a decade of military occupation. Original sins and lost causes can be the cement of a culture and the germ of its folklore and literature.

As the North raced into the Industrial Age, the South seemed to stand still. Its folk traditions remained in place. Such southern writers as George Washington Cable, Joel Chandler Harris, Mary Noailles Murfree, and Charles Chesnutt—local colorists for whom folklore was a vital element—won national recognition. From the viewpoint of the Gilded Age, the postbellum South was backward. It valued old ways more than new dollars. The South's literary success may be attributed to its reluctance to deny its past. It refused to run away from its history, traditions, and reverence for form.

Folklore in literature is not folklore in the raw. Certainly a folktale told in its natural habitat is art of its own kind, but literary art is another kind of performance. The explorer John Lawson, who included folk materials in his descriptions of the interior of Carolina, was a sophisticated writer using what he found to render his account vivid or incorporating what he saw and heard because it was too good to pass up. The contributors of frontier sketches to the *Spirit of the Times*, a popular sportsman's journal in the antebellum period, were mostly lettered men—doctors, lawyers, college presidents, army officers—with a taste for the earthiness and oddities of folklore, and a talent, not untrained, for storytelling. Professional writers who employed folklore, such as William Gilmore Simms, bent it to an immediate purpose. Even the classic American writers, such as Edgar Allan Poe, Mark Twain, and William Faulkner, were less concerned with folklore as such than with the ways it could serve their art.

John Lawson's *New Voyage to Carolina* (1709) exemplifies one of the earliest genres of southern literature, the travel account. He describes a journey from Charleston to the foothills of the Blue Ridge Mountains with a ready eye for the inhabitants' customs and lore, which he sets down with gusto and exploits with literary skill. Thus, he provides a lively description of Indian deer hunters who disguise themselves so perfectly with antlers and skins that they sometimes shoot each other. Lawson's method here is to record a curious hunting practice and then dramatize it with a folk story. Or, he brings a gritty account of starved and abused Indian dogs to a climax with a literary application of a folk remedy:

"It is an infalliable Cure for Sore Eyes, even to see an *Indian's* Dog fat." Or, he illustrates the prodigious power of rattlesnakes by citing their ability "to charm Squirrels . . . in such a way that they run directly into their Mouths." Lawson also contributes to the emergence of indigenous southern legend as he moves from an authentic history of the Lost Colony and speculation about its fate to a local folktale: "I cannot forbear inserting here a pleasant story that passes for an uncontested Truth among the Inhabitants of this Place; which is, that the Ship, which brought the first colonies, does often appear among them, under sail, which they call Sir Walter Raleigh's Ship." Paul Green, whose plays drew upon southern lore and legend, would use this material for his historical drama *The Lost Colony* (1937).

Edgar Allan Poe and William Gilmore Simms, the major professional writers of the antebellum period, each used folklore in a different, though characteristic, way. Poe saw himself as an alienated poet, ideally the resident of a dreamland "Out of space—Out of time," and his settings and sources are usually consistent with this vision. "The Gold Bug" is a notable exception. His source is the folk motif of the buried treasure, particularized in the widespread legends of Captain Kidd. His locale is Sullivan's Island, which he knew well from his military service at Fort Moultrie on the South Carolina coast. His characters, if not southern folk types, are southern stereotypes—William Legrand, the withdrawn, decayed aristocrat, and Jupiter, the faithful, comic, superstitious black servant. Even his narrator is familiar, a rational man doubting the sanity of the friend whose summons he answers. (There is much here reminiscent of the timeless "The Fall of the House of Usher." Is this, too, within the context of southern folklore?) For the black servant, the gold bug that he and his master find is an object of superstitious dread, and Poe uses it for minstrel-show effects. "I'm berry sartain dat Massa Will bin bit somewhere about de head by dat goole-bug," Jupiter tells the narrator. The rational faculties of Legrand, an amateur scientist, have been superseded by his fancies—his mind, as the narrator comes to believe, "infected with some of the innumerable Southern superstitions about money buried." These "Southern superstitions" are validated by the recovery of the pirate treasure. Poe's concern is the balance between rational method, epitomized in Legrand's solution of a cryptogram, and the irrational, here represented by a romantic legend and the inexplicable force of superstition. In "The Gold Bug," folklore is associated with poetry and reverie and is a way of knowing what surpasses rational methodologies and precedes their application.

In *The Yemassee* (1835), one of his romances of the southern frontier, William Gilmore Simms expands Lawson's account of the rattlesnake's fabulous powers into a flamboyant set piece. The heroine, a "peerless forest flower," goes into the wilderness to met her lover, an English officer. Entranced by the beauties of nature, she is captivated "by a star-like shining glance—a subtle ray, that shot out from the circle of green leaves." She is dazzled by its "dreadful beauty" and then transfixed with terror when she realizes that what she sees is the "fascinating gleam" in the eyes of a rattlesnake. As the snake slithers toward her and coils to strike, it is shot through the head by the arrow of her lover's Indian ally. Simms, in a footnote, doubts the rattler's "power over persons" but claims to have heard of "numberless instances," a sufficient number, in any case, "for the romancer." Not given to subtleties, the sexual implications of his serpent in Eden would have surely surprised him. Simms's end was melodrama, and a folk belief was his means.

In 1870, the year he died, Simms wrote a North Carolina mountain sketch for *Harper's*, "How Sharp Snaffles Got His Wife and His Capital." It is essentially a tall tale, told at a hunting camp by a backwoods trickster whose nickname, "Big Lie," indicates his qualities as a hunter, sharp operator, and storyteller. His performance, much appreciated by his backwoods peers and the gentleman hunters who compose his audience, is presented within a descriptive frame by one of the latter. Such separation between the genteel observer who transcribes the tale and the folk artist who tells it may be a way of maintaining a distance of generation, caste, race, or political persuasion, but always a factor for the southern writer is the art of the performance itself. This was not entirely an aesthetic matter. In southern culture, the way a thing is done is significant. Simms himself, in this story, was reaching back to the frontier humor of the Old Southwest, with its folkloric situations, in order to recover his own literary capital, the northern readership he had lost during the sectional conflict; and he reached forward toward the emerging local-color movement, likewise seamed with folklore.

In Mark Twain's *Adventures of Huckleberry Finn* (1885), identifiable elements of folklore give this masterpiece its flavor as they serve complex purposes, and the folklife of the Mississippi Valley, broadly speaking, provides physical and moral texture. The role of the runaway slave, Jim, is evidence of this. Poe's Jupiter, with his superstitious gibberish about the gold bug, is little more than a comic stereotype. But Mark Twain's Jim, a comparable character at the outset, becomes in the end not simply a rounded character, a stereotype humanized, but the spiritual center of the book. To accomplish this transformation (as well as to move his plot, enhance verisimilitude, and add humorous touches), Mark Twain uses superstition.

Superstitions, by definition, are the supernatural beliefs that some disdain

Scene from **The Reivers**, the 1969 film made from William Faulkner's novel
(Film Stills Archives, Museum of Modern Art, New York)

but others accept. At the beginning of the novel, Tom Sawyer and Huck to
amuse themselves play upon Jim's belief in witches. Jim also believes in ghosts,
weather signs, omens, and dreams. On the river with Huck, he becomes a free
and living man, and when he puts his superstitions to work, they become ef-
fectual. This natural world has a place for the supernatural, and Jim's superstitions save his own life and Huck's and ultimately make possible Huck's spiritual
salvation as well. In two other great books, *Adventures of Tom Sawyer* (1876)
and *Life on the Mississippi* (1883), southern folklife also functions memorably.
Seeking a cure for warts in a graveyard at midnight, as the folk remedy requires,
is the occasion that initiates the plot of *Tom Sawyer*. *Life on the Mississippi* contains the classic description of the folklife of raftsmen, including their songs
and dances, brags and fights, beliefs and stories. It is a genre painting, both
realistic and idealized.

Like Mark Twain, William Faulkner embodied within his southern particularity a moral depth and artistry that brought him the acclaim of the world. Faulkner's novella *The Bear* (1942) is a capstone to a series of earlier, major works that emerged from his response to the southern cultural experience. Its motif, a ceremonial hunt of a totemic animal, is universal, but the version he adopts derives from American Indian lore and, more immediately, from countless stories of bear hunts in backwoods oral tradition. Stories of this kind had already made their way into antebellum popular culture through the media of the Davy Crockett almanacs and the sporting journals. Thomas Bangs Thorpe's "The Big Bear of Arkansas" (1841), a case in point, is essentially a literary creation originating in southern hunting lore. So is *The Bear*.

The Bear, like *Huckleberry Finn*, is an initiation story in a pristine natural setting. Sam Fathers, "son of a negro slave and a Chickasaw chief," is teacher and surrogate parent of young Ike McCaslin, in an analogue to the relationship of Huck and Jim. His knowledge of woodcraft, which he imparts to Ike, has moral validity, like Jim's old beliefs. In the end, Ike learns how to hunt Old Ben, the legendary bear, and how to "relinquish" his quarry and his heritage. Though it contains specific folk elements (e.g., the hunt motif), *The Bear* transcends them and emphasizes folklife, the totality of the culture, rather than its details. This transcendence and extension, even as they detach *The Bear* from its folkloric detail, bring folklore and literature into closer proximity and make their southernness universal.

Faulkner moved beyond folklore at a pivotal time for both folklore and southern tradition generally. There are ironies in this, southern style: the irony of lost causes won and regrets for the loss of old ways assuaged. Ironically, southern literature has attained its greatest eminence at a time when the South becomes more and more like the rest of the country, and its folklore, a prime source of its distinction, withers under the increasing pressure of literacy. Ultimately, at its best, literature absorbs folklore, and in this way assures its survival.

HENNIG COHEN
University of Pennsylvania

Gene Bluestein, *The Voice of the Folk: Folklore and American Literary Theory* (1972); Shelley Fishkin, *Was Huck Black?: Mark Twain and African-American Voices* (1993); Henry Louis Gates Jr., *The Signifying Monkey: A Theory of African-American Literary Criticism* (1988); Daniel Hoffman, *Form and Fable in American Fiction* (1965); Gavin Jones, *Strange Talk: The Politics of Dialect Literature in Gilded Age America* (1999); Gayl Jones, *Liberating Voices: Oral Tradition in African-American Literature* (1991); Bruce A. Rosenberg, in *Interrelations of Literature*, ed. Jean-Pierre Barricelli and

Joseph Gibaldi (1982); Constance Rourke, *American Humor: A Study of the National Character* (1931).

Food in Literature

In the section of *Killers of the Dream* called "The Women," Lillian Smith tells the story of the middle-class Georgia white women in the 1930s who come together as the Association of Southern Women for the Prevention of Lynching. These women believe that it is meaningless for them to take communion, that central ritual of the Christian church, a foretaste of the heavenly banquet that all believers are promised, unless "they break bread with fellow men of color." They gather in small groups to eat with African American women, deliberately breaking one of the strongest taboos of southern culture. The well-meaning attempt does not go smoothly. After these early attempts at sharing a table, both black and white women become physically ill. What the women attribute to "food poisoning," Smith describes as a symptom of "how this eating taboo in childhood is woven into the mesh of things that are 'wrong,' how it becomes tangled with God and sex, pulling anxieties from stronger prohibitions and attaching them to itself."

Food and cooking have been since the earliest days of southern literature one of the primary ways by which southern culture has been defined and celebrated. In this telling episode, Smith sums up many of the food-related themes that run through the literature of the South: images of plenty, feasting, the banquet, hospitality, all of them qualified by questions of which races, gender, and classes are entitled to places at the table. The South's religious and political conservatism, racial segregation, and class consciousness have given southern writers the myth of a stable society with conventions that they can make use of or rebel against.

Images of plenty and feasting characterize southern literature from its earliest days. Captain John Smith in *The Generall Historie of Virginia* (1624) pauses in his recounting of his capture by Powhatan and deliverance by Pocahontas to mention the hospitality of the king's brother Opitchapam, who invited him into his house and presented him with "many platters of bread, foule, and wild beasts" and gave him the leftovers to take home to the settlers. William Byrd II, writing in about 1738 in a journal that was published in 1844 as *The History of the Dividing Line*, described the ease of life in North Carolina, where "the easiness of raising provisions" led to a great "Disposition to Laziness" on the part of the men.

For Thomas Jefferson, accused in his own time of "abjuring his native victuals," good food and good eating were an integral part of his vision of a nation of independent yeoman farmers. Even though Thomas Jefferson's commitment to the rational ideas he espoused has been called into question by his relation to the enslaved African Americans at Monticello, it was Thomas Jefferson in the gardens and kitchens of Monticello and the White House who fused native plenty to European traditions of fine dining that he found in France and Italy. Damon Fowler eloquently sums up Jefferson's contribution to American food history: "He embraced the relationship between garden and table; he sought out quality ingredients both from home and abroad; he understood both the simplicity of classic dishes and the adventure of new foods; he preserved his own food roots and reached out to the cuisines of other cultures; he encouraged the connection between food and sociability and cherished lingering conversation over fine wine . . . in this brilliant and complex man is a timeless articulation of the role and value of food in our lives."

John Pendleton Kennedy's novel *Swallow Barn* was the model for a whole genre of novels glorifying the myth of plantation life in the South. Central to the idealized plantation life of Virginia is a vision of hospitality and shared plenty: "They frequently meet in the interchanges of a large and thriftless hospitality. . . . Their halls are large, and the boards ample; and surrounding the great family hearth, with its immense burthen of blazing wood casting a broad and merry glare over the congregated household and the numerous retainers, a social winter party in Virginia affords a tolerable picture of feudal munificence."

This benevolent feudal munificence of plantation life, however, is often undercut by the narratives of the enslaved people who raised and cooked the food that made plantation hospitality possible. Frederick Douglass in *My Bondage and My Freedom* (1855) sees the heavy, elaborate dinners consumed by the Lloyd family as physically and spiritually poisonous: "Lurking beneath all their dishes, are invisible spirits of evil, ready to feed the self-deluded gormandizers with aches, pains, fierce temper, uncontrolled passions." Harriett Ann Jacobs's *Incidents in the Life of a Slave Girl* (1861) shows the travesty of the generosity of the plantation system in her recounting of her mistress's habit of spitting in the pots after Sunday dinner was dished up in order to prevent the slaves from eating the leftover food. "The Lord's Supper," Jacobs muses, "did not seem to put [her mistress] in a Christian frame of mind."

The problems posed by questions of race in defining the food traditions of the South are further complicated by questions of gender. Many white southern women have the reputation of being great cooks when the actual cooking was done for them and their families by African American servants. The stereotyped image of the mammy has played a large part in southern fiction, most notably Mammy in Margaret Mitchell's *Gone with the Wind* (1936), Dilsey in

William Faulkner's *The Sound and the Fury* (1929), Berenice in Carson McCuller's *The Member of the Wedding* (1946), and Calpurnia in Harper Lee's *To Kill a Mockingbird* (1960). Trudier Harris has perceptively explored the Mammy stereotype in the works of African American writers such as Kristin Hunter, Toni Morrison, Richard Wright, and others.

The elaborate meals of *Swallow Barn* and of the Lloyd family are a way of asserting class as well as racial superiority. "Eating together," Mary Titus has pointed out, "signifies community and social equality." Descriptions of meals have given generations of southern writers a shorthand for describing the social class to which characters belong and for talking about class conflict in the changing South. In *I'll Take My Stand*, the agrarian manifesto (1930), Andrew Lytle and other writers see the midday dinner as symbolic of the family values that characterize life in the upper- and middle-class South, a world in which "everybody has had something to do with the long and intricate procession from the ground to the table." The meals in Kate Chopin's *The Awakening* (1899) show the dissatisfaction of Edna Pontellier with the strictures of the Creole society in which she lives. In Harper Lee's *To Kill a Mockingbird*, the class difference of the visiting Walter Cunningham is immediately apparent to the Finch family when he pours syrup on his dinner.

Eudora Welty is the master at using food as a shorthand for class differences and to show class conflict. The five family meals around which *Delta Wedding* (1946) is structured allow Welty to show the family conflict created by two disapproved-of marriages and their final resolution and acceptance. In *Losing Battles* (1970), the dinner assembled for the family reunion on the occasion of Granny Vaughn's 90th birthday provides a rich background for this comic portrait of family life and conversation.

Restaurants are also important in southern literature, and it is no accident that a significant part of the civil rights movement was fought over lunch counters. Only equals share a table and eat together, and while those who would restrict access to the table to those like themselves have not entirely disappeared from the South, most southerners now realize that any banquet is richer if shared.

THOMAS HEAD
The Washingtonian

Damon Lee Fowler, ed., *Dining at Monticello* (2005); Peggy Prenshaw, ed., *Southern Quarterly* 30 (1992); Mary Titus, in *Companion to Southern Literature*, ed. Joseph M. Flora and Lucinda H. MacKethan (2002).

Fugitives and Agrarians

Literary historians and critics have frequently confused the two related but different groups known as the Fugitives and the Agrarians. Although both were composed of writers coming to terms with their individual and regional identities, and attempting to find suitable artistic means to express their concerns, they had quite different members, intentions, and agendas.

The Fugitives were a group of 16 young poets who began to gather informally in Nashville in 1915 with no purpose in mind other than to read, share, and discuss their own work. The main organizers were Vanderbilt faculty members John Crowe Ransom and Donald Davidson and students Allen Tate and Robert Penn Warren. The others were young men on their way to diverse careers in education, the arts, and business. The list of participants included the Chaucer scholar Walter Clyde Curry, the French literature scholar William Frierson, novelists Ridley Wills and Stanley Johnson, psychiatrist and poet Merrill Moore, Harvard professor of political science William Yandell Elliott, and the dilettante Jewish mystic Sidney M. Hirsch, whose main claim to fame was that he thought of the name "The Fugitives." The remainder would go into business: James Frank produced custom-made shirts, Alec Stevenson became an investment banker, Alfred Starr opened motion picture theaters, and Jesse Wills became chairman of the board of the National Life and Accident Insurance Company in Nashville, as well as a world-class iris breeder. Between 1922 and 1925 they published 19 issues of a little magazine called the *Fugitive*, almost entirely devoted to poetry.

Given their diverse interests and backgrounds, and connected primarily by their proximity and devotion to poetry, they had no common cause or program, except for artistic freedom, individuality, and a lack of social commitment. This is set forth in the opening statement in the first issue of their magazine:

> Official exception having been taken by the sovereign people of the mint julep, a literary phrase known rather euphemistically as Southern Literature has expired, like any other stream whose source is stopped up. The demise was not untimely: among other advantages, THE FUGITIVE is enabled to come to birth in Nashville, Tennessee, under a star not entirely unsympathetic. THE FUGITIVE flees from nothing faster than from the high-caste Brahmins of the Old South. Without raising the question of whether the blood in the veins of its editors runs red, they at any rate are not advertising it as blue; indeed, as to pedigree, they cheerfully invite the most unfavorable inference from the circumstances of their anonymity.

Thus the Fugitives did not want to be associated with southern notions of aristocracy, or postbellum literature of the romantic moonlight-and-magnolias school, and they even invite their readers to make the startling inference that they are bastards, out of the mainstream of southern culture and without legitimate pedigree. By adopting pseudonyms in the first two issues, each tried to achieve a distinctive poetic voice to be judged entirely on the basis of aesthetic quality.

The Fugitives were conscious of their regional identity only insofar as they understood that gaining a national audience out of provincial Nashville was difficult, and that they were flying in the face of a national prejudice that the South was uncultured. Their intent to orient themselves toward a larger culture was expressed by Davidson only a year after the *Fugitive* began: "If there is a significance in the title of this magazine, it lies perhaps in the sentiments of the editors (on this point I am sure we all agree) to flee from the extremes of conventionalism, whether old or new. They hope to keep in touch with and utilize in their work the best qualities of modern poetry, without at the same time casting aside as unworthy all that is established as good in the past."

Not only were the Fugitives early on fascinated with modernism in poetry, but they fell heavily under its influence through their reading of T. S. Eliot, William Butler Yeats, Ezra Pound, and Conrad Aiken. Tate was the first in the group to champion Eliot and his "Waste Land" poems and to write work obviously under his influence. Tate became such an ardent defender of Eliot, and so aggressive was his admiration, that he provoked a long-running argument among the members about the relations of traditional material to modern poetry and the relative importance of conventional aesthetics to modernist experimentation. Even Davidson, who would prove to be the most devoted exponent of regionalism and tradition, could not escape the Eliot manner. Encouraged by Tate, Davidson wrote several poems in 1922 affecting the satiric tone of the moderns and the abstract images of Eliot, but it soon became clear that his heart was not in them.

The *Fugitive* itself attracted contributors from outside the South, and among them were several prominent modernist poets, such as Hart Crane, Robert Graves, and Laura Riding. Riding became so excited about their work that she visited Nashville to meet them, and in a moment of enthusiasm, they adopted her as a member of the group, making her the 16th Fugitive poet. The debate over traditionalism versus modernism was far from being settled when the magazine came to an end in December 1925. In the final paragraph of a review by Davidson on the last page of the last issue, he concluded, "Nothing in the history of poetry is so remarkable as its variety and flexibility. Yet while new forms are always being added, few disappear, and thus literature is constantly being enriched. The strangest thing in contemporary poetry is that innovation and conservatism exist side by side. It will probably always be so!"

The Agrarian movement came about around three years later in 1928 when four of the former Fugitives who remained friends—Ransom, Davidson, Tate, and Warren—began to debate what they saw as the harmful influence of industrialism and technology on life in the South and their lack of belief in secular progress as a route to the perfectibility of man. They wrote and gathered essays by like-minded intellectuals who were making a name for themselves in literary and academic circles for an anthology published under the title *I'll Take My Stand: The South and the Agrarian Tradition* in 1930. These kindred minds in addition to the four organizers included imagist poet John Gould Fletcher, economist and journalist Henry Blue Kline, psychologist and educator Lyle Hicks Lanier, former actor and novelist Andrew Lytle, political scientist and professor Herman Clarence Nixon, historian Frank Lawrence Owsley, biographer John Donald Wade, and the best known of the group, drama critic and novelist Stark Young.

What brought these people together was clearly stated in the opening sentences of their common statement of principles: "The authors contributing to this book are Southerners, well acquainted with one another and of similar tastes, though not necessarily living in the same physical community, and perhaps only at this moment aware of themselves as a single group of men. By conversation and exchange of letters over a number of years it has developed that they entertain many convictions in common, and it was decided to make a volume in which each one should furnish his views upon a chosen topic." These were men with a program, a commitment of shared opinion, and a manifesto for action that would attempt to reclaim the agrarian past of the South in the face of the encroachments of the industrial way of life.

For the four former Fugitive poets turned ideologues, the Agrarian movement was not a desertion of art and poetry for politics and social change. In both contexts they saw themselves as men of letters, as poets who attempted to discover in the material world, through imagery and metaphor, those values that inform nature and give life meaning. For all but Davidson, Agrarianism proved to be but one stage in the development of maturing literary artists, and Ransom would even repudiate it. The movements were indeed separate, but the social concerns of the Agrarians for a better way of life in the face of industrialism and progress were inspired by the concerns of the Fugitive poets for the life of the imagination.

M. THOMAS INGE
Randolph-Macon College

Charlotte H. Beck, *The Fugitive Legacy: A Critical History* (2001); John M. Bradbury, *The Fugitives: A Critical Account* (1958); Paul K. Conkin, *The Southern Agrarians* (1988); Louise Cowan, *The Fugitive Group: A Literary History* (1959); Louis D. Rubin Jr., *The Wary Fugitives: Four Poets and the South* (1978); John L. Stewart, *The Burden of Time: The Fugitives and Agrarians* (1965); Twelve Southerners, *I'll Take My Stand: The South and the Agrarian Tradition* (1930).

Gender and Sexuality in Literature

The heritage of a strong class and caste system in the South narrows the range of roles for men and women in southern literature. Within that range the most prominent writers of the modern South—Ellen Glasgow, William Faulkner, Robert Penn Warren, and Eudora Welty—explore the depths of a variety of individual characters. In southern fiction, as in most American writing, a confused identity is often attributed to failure to deal with sexuality directly and responsibly, whereas healthy sexuality becomes the basis for self-awareness.

The southern white male appears in fiction most frequently as either the gentleman-father or his cavalier son. The prototype of the gentleman-father appears in John Pendleton Kennedy's *Swallow Barn* (1832). Frank Meriwether had dominion over all, white and black; his wife's control of daily plantation life frees him for leisure and contemplation. Meriwether's fictional descendants include the ineffectual Gerald O'Hara in Margaret Mitchell's *Gone with the Wind* (1936) and Battle Fairchild, continuing Meriwether's life into the 1920s in Welty's *Delta Wedding* (1946). Faulkner shows the deterioration of the southern aristocrat in alcoholic Mr. Compson in *The Sound and the Fury* (1929), portrays Sutpen ironically attempting to become a gentleman and found a dynasty in *Absalom, Absalom!* (1936), and further mocks the tradition in Flem Snopes's journey to his mansion-mausoleum. Warren satirizes the figure of the southern gentleman in Bogan Murdock, with his bogus sense of honor, in *At Heaven's Gate* (1943) and even has Jed Tewksbury, a redneck-scholar in *A Place to Come To* (1977), jokingly refuse to become an "S. G."

The fictional cavalier frequently dies young; if not, he may become a gentleman-father, a rake (like Rhett Butler), or a true southern bachelor. Thomas Nelson Page's hero in "Marse Chan" (1885), the ideal cavalier, dies in the war. Faulkner's cavaliers, often confused about sexual roles, are likely to destroy themselves early, like young Bayard in *Sartoris* (1929) and Quentin Compson. In *All the King's Men* (1946) Warren details Jack Burden's rebellion against his aristocratic heritage in his long journey toward becoming a true gentleman. Will Barrett, Walker Percy's protagonist in *The Last Gentleman* (1966), is haunted by his past, particularly his gentleman-father's suicide. In *The Second*

Coming (1980), Will finally frees himself from the past and achieves a sensitive relationship with a sexually free younger woman. Faulkner excels in his depictions of true southern bachelors, especially Ike McCaslin, whose obsession with the past destroys his marriage. Peter Taylor's *A Summons to Memphis* (1986) interrogates the dying breeds of the southern cavalier and gentleman-father when southerner Phillip Carver temporarily abandons his New York life to confront his father and his continuing patriarchal control. In contemporary fiction, like that of Barry Hannah, Harry Crews, and Larry Brown, the southern gentleman is often supplanted by lower-class southern heroes and troublemakers.

The prevailing roles in fiction for the southern white female are the lady-mother and the belle. Kennedy's Lucretia Meriwether, controlling domestic life in spite of her physical weakness, is followed by fictional lady-mothers like Ellen O'Hara and Ellen Fairchild. Augusta Jane Evans [Wilson] gives characters like Edna Earl in *St. Elmo* (1866) the education and opportunity to choose nontraditional roles, but they usually marry gentleman-fathers. In *The Awakening* (1900) Kate Chopin focuses on the unfolding sexual identity of Edna Pontellier, who marries and bears children, then realizes she is unsuited for the role of "mother-woman" in her Creole society. Glasgow's protagonist in *Virginia* (1913) rigidly follows the pattern of her lady-mother's life but loses her husband to an unconventional New York actress. Faulkner's Granny Millard in *The Unvanquished* (1938) is strong, but she relies on the conventions of society to the point of destruction; Mrs. Compson is lady-mother evolved into controlling matriarch. In recent southern fiction, white women grapple with balancing their creative talents and careers with the lady-mother role—for instance, in Lee Smith's depictions of women like Ivy Rowe in *Fair and Tender Ladies* (1988) or Katie Cocker in *The Devil's Dream* (1992).

The life of a fictional belle is short, for she is most often portrayed as moving toward the goal of marrying a cavalier, as Kennedy's Bel Tracy does, and settling down as a lady-mother. The refusal to play the role of belle can have grave consequences, as seen in Faulkner's Drusilla Hawk and Caddy Compson. Katherine Anne Porter's Miranda, in "The Old Order" and other stories, must reject the legacy of the belle with her destructive sexuality before she can live as an independent woman. Glasgow's incisive portrait of Eva Birdsong in *The Sheltered Life* (1932) shows that marriage does not always offer the belle a new role; Scarlett O'Hara, rebelling at the prospect of becoming a lady-mother, finds new options in the chaos of the Reconstruction. However, in *The Moviegoer* (1961) Percy gives hope for stability in the comfortable role of the southern lady, while her cousin-husband Binx Bolling assumes the role of gentleman-father.

The fictional South of the 1920s produces a variation on the role of belle with the flapper, most notably Temple Drake in *Sanctuary* (1931) and Sue Murdock in *At Heaven's Gate*, who both illustrate the dangers of irresponsible sexual freedom. Depictions of the belle often disappear as young southern women struggle with understanding their place in the postmodern world of malls and consumer culture. Characters like Bobbie Ann Mason's Sam Hughes in *In Country* (1985) or Josephine Humphreys's Lucille Odom in *Rich in Love* (1987) exemplify the independent woman of the contemporary South.

Although the fictional southern woman's sexuality may destroy her or imprison her in a prescribed role, it may also free her from tradition. Glasgow's lower-class rural protagonist in *Barren Ground* (1925) is saved from the entrapment of an illegitimate pregnancy by miscarrying. Faulkner's mythic Eula Varner Snopes is imprisoned by her sexuality, but Lena Grove in *Light in August* (1932) placidly bears her illegitimate child. In *The Reivers* (1962), Corrie rejects her life as a prostitute and is rewarded with an optimistic future with Boon Hogganbeck. Welty's Gloria in *Losing Battles* (1970) rejects the opportunity for freedom through education, but gains a strong sexual identity in her relationship with Jack Renfro; and Laurel McKelva Hand in *The Optimist's Daughter* (1972) finds hope for an independent future in understanding her parents' marriage and her own. Doris Betts portrays, in *The River to Pickle Beach* (1972), the healthy sexuality and strong marriage of Bebe and Jack Sellars, contrasted with the destructive perversion of Mickey McCane. Betts also confronts the complexity of woman's struggle for independence through librarian Nancy Finch in *Heading West* (1981). Percy's Allison is freed from a conventional role in society by mental illness, which allows her to find a positive relationship with Will Barrett.

Demeaning roles for black men and women, especially as the child and the brute, haunt the pages of southern fiction from *Swallow Barn* through *Gone with the Wind* and after. Less demeaning but still lacking individuality and dignity are the tragic mulatto, male or female, and the faithful uncle or mammy. However, a few black characters, mostly in recent fiction, are freed from these roles and given autonomy as human beings. In *Clotel* (1853) William Wells Brown traces the suffering of three generations of mulatto women under the domination of insensitive southern gentlemen who perceive them as the lowest of human beings—black and female. George Washington Cable focuses on the Creole society of Louisiana for his moving story of Honoré Grandissime, a free man of color in *The Grandissimes* (1880). In *The House behind the Cedars* (1900), Charles W. Chesnutt allows Rena Walden to question her role in society as a black woman who appears white; her brother John can live with dignity only by assuming the identity of a southern cavalier. Faulkner portrays mulatto characters, especially Joe Christmas and Charles Bon, as individuals in their quests for identity; likewise, Warren's Amantha Starr in *Band of Angels* (1955) and Margaret Walker's Vyry in *Jubilee* (1966) transcend the limitations of stereotyping.

The stereotype of the black uncle, such as the narrator of "Marse Chan," has occasionally been displaced by the role of the autonomous black male. In spite of the ending of *The Adventures of Huckleberry Finn* (1885), Mark Twain gives the character of Jim dignity and wisdom in his quest for identity as a free man. Tea Cake, in Zora Neale Hurston's *Their Eyes Were Watching God* (1937), is an independent man who is strong enough to think of Janie's happiness as well as his own. Faulkner gives Rider in "Pantaloon in Black" (1940) the sensitivity to be destroyed by the real human emotion of grief. Through the struggles of Bigger Thomas in *Native Son* (1940), Richard Wright emphasizes the significance of race and sex in attaining self-identity, even in defeat. Black leaders Ned and Jimmy, although destroyed by the white society in Ernest J. Gaines's *The Autobiography of Miss Jane Pittman* (1971), are autonomous. Gaines's *A Lesson before Dying* (1993) extends depictions of the independent black male in the characters of Grant Wiggins and his jail-bound protégé Jefferson.

The fictional black mammy, often seen in contrast to the aloof white lady, may have originated in the local-color fiction of Sherwood Bonner; Mitchell and others strengthened the stereotype. Occasional black women characters are more complex, like Twain's Roxy in *Pudd'nhead Wilson* (1894), strong and passionate, or like Faulkner's Dilsey, superior to the white Compsons in her patience, her love, her wisdom, her endurance. Rather than portraying Janie in *Their Eyes Were Watching God* as a tragic mulatto or turning her into a mammy, Hurston develops her as an independent woman with love for and commitment to a strong black man. Gaines's Miss Jane, old and wise, is in no sense a stereotyped mammy; in fact, like Janie, she is not even a biological mother. Rather, Gaines gives her identity as a strong, brave, loving, free black woman. In Alice Walker's *Meridian* (1976), the title character emerges as an independent woman fighting for the rights of African Americans after the dissolution of the civil rights movement. In her neo-slave narrative *Dessa Rose* (1986), Sherley Anne Williams creates the feisty, enduring Dessa as a direct challenge to the wench or mammy.

While southern race and class systems supported images of the gentlemen, belle, uncle, and mammy, these systems also assigned heterosexual identities to such images. The southern man and woman were expected to marry and produce children. Southern writers challenge the heterosexual norm through depictions of "queer" characters. Often, these writers critique southern society as offering either acceptance or intolerance of homosexuality.

Truman Capote interrogates white, male, heterosexual norms in his first novel, *Other Voices, Other Rooms* (1948). The youth, Joel, uncovers the secret past of his cousin, Randolph, and his love affair with an abusive boxer, Pepe Alvarez. When Joel falls in love with Randolph, Joel's individual identity evolves as he connects with a "queer" southern community. In much of her fiction, Carson McCullers interrogates homosocial and homosexual relationships. In *The Heart Is a Lonely Hunter* (1940), McCullers depicts John Singer's undying devotion to his companion, Spiros Antonapoulos. In *The Ballad of the Sad Café* (1951), McCullers creates a love triangle between Amelia, Lymon Willis, and Marvin Macy, blurring the boundaries between heterosexual and homosexual love.

In Tennessee Williams's plays, white male characters suffer the consequences of their attractions to other men. In *Cat on a Hot Tin Roof* (1955), Brick's prejudices against homosexuality lead his best friend, Skipper, to commit suicide. As Brick tries to come to terms with his own sexual confusion, he turns to alcohol, mistreats his wife, Margaret, and generally abuses his family. In *Suddenly, Last Summer* (1958), Catherine Holly battles against her aunt, Violet Venables, who wants her lobotomized so that Catherine cannot reveal the homosexual desires responsible for her cousin Sebastian's death. While on vacation, Sebastian is literally torn apart and consumed by a mob of local boys, whom he previously used for sexual favors. Williams's plays expose the destruction caused by an intolerant southern society that views heterosexuality as the norm.

From the 1970s to the present day, southern authors write about homosexuality with more frequency and openness. Often homosexual characters are shunned by the larger southern community. Rita Mae Brown's novel *Rubyfruit Jungle* (1975) charts Molly Bolt's coming of age as a lesbian in a South that refuses to accept her. When Molly's lesbian relationship with her college roommate is discovered, she loses her scholarship and leaves the South for New York. In *A Visitation of Spirits* (1989), Randall Kenan exposes the conflicts between black masculinity and homosexuality. Sexual discrimination intersects with racial conflict when Horace becomes friends with white boys who accept him as "queer" when his own zealously religious family will not. Horace eventually commits suicide. In Harlan Greene's novel *What the Dead Remember* (1991), the narrator describes growing up gay in Charleston, S.C. After escaping the South for a time, the narrator returns to a homophobic South dealing with the AIDS crisis of the 1980s. Similarly, Allan Gurganus's *Plays Well with Others* (1997) reveals the struggles of gay southerner Hartley Mims Jr. as he searches for a tolerant society in New York and ends up caring for his friends who contract AIDS. Like Williams's plays, these novels critique the persistence of an intolerant southern society (even in the face of a national epidemic).

As in the works of Capote, homosexuality often creates strong southern communities. In Alice Walker's novel *The Color Purple* (1982), Celie learns to value herself outside of her abusive husband's expectations through her relationship with the bisexual Shug Avery. Walker subverts portrayals of black women as sexual objects through the women's mutual love for one another. Fannie Flagg's popular novel *Fried Green Tomatoes at the Whistlestop Café* (1987) alludes to a love relationship between Idgie Threadgood and Ruth Jamison that engenders a tolerant community as the women indiscriminately serve all customers at their café. In her novel *Bastard out of Carolina* (1992), Dorothy Allison explores the sex roles of "white trash" women through characters Bone Boatwright and her aunts. In Bone's Aunt Raylene, Allison posits a queer woman free from men and their patriarchal conscriptions (such as the lady-mother). John Berendt's best seller *Midnight in the Garden of Good and Evil* (1994) celebrates "queer" characters like Jim Williams and the Lady Chablis. In *The Promise of Rest* (1995), Reynolds Price shows how the AIDS crisis reunites a family when Hutchins Mayfield nurses his dying son, Wade. Jim Wilcox's comic novel *Plain and Normal* (1999) tells the tale of Lloyd Norris, whose wife outs him in order to divorce him. Although Wilcox's portrait of Lloyd's struggle with aging and romance inspire laughter, it also depicts the prejudice and stereotyping that can occur in Lloyd's community. While southern writers sometimes uphold southern sex roles, such authors also faithfully test the bounds of women's and men's assigned places. Depictions of these mutable roles reflect not only the ever-changing southern literary canon but also the evolution of southern social norms.

MARTHA E. COOK
Longwood College

COURTNEY GEORGE
Louisiana State University

Francis Pendleton Gaines, *The Southern Plantation: A Study in the Development and the Accuracy of a Tradition* (1924); Anne Goodwyn Jones, *Tomorrow Is Another Day: The Woman Writer in the South, 1859–1936* (1981); Richard H. King, *A Southern Renaissance: The Cultural Awakening of the American South, 1930–1955* (1980); Gary Richards, *Lovers and Beloveds: Sexual Otherness in Southern Fiction, 1936–1961* (2005); Anne Firor Scott, *The Southern Lady: From Pedestal to Politics, 1830–1930* (1970); Mab Segrest, *My Mama's Dead Squirrel: Lesbian Essays on Southern Culture*

(1985); William R. Taylor, *Cavalier and Yankee: The Old South and American National Character* (1961); Patricia Yaeger, *Dirt and Desire: Reconstructing Southern Women's Writing, 1930–1990* (2000).

Globalization and Southern Literature

In the past 20 years, southern studies has evolved from an inaugural effort to document things particularly and peculiarly southern—food, song, demographic patterns, voting habits, religious practices, and, of course, literary styles and preoccupations—all within a largely American context that confirmed the South's status as a region successfully maintaining, for good or ill, an identity and a way of life distinctive from the national whole. The region's literature has alternately embraced and rejected that sense of difference. Scholars including Cleanth Brooks, Hugh Holman, and later Louis D. Rubin Jr. offer a vocabulary for describing what was particular to the region's literary production, emphasizing a powerful overlapping of the past and the present, a persistent sense of southern place rooted in the land and its specific history, and a white ambivalence toward the historic South that buffeted the writers of the 1920s and 1930s into creating a Southern Literary Renaissance, the shadow of which stretches even into contemporary writing.

By the 1980s, critics were aware that the South's self-sponsored narrative of whiteness—white power, white guilt, white place—was an incomplete story told by only a portion of the region's population. Texts that critics had formerly considered the exclusive province of African American literature (and thus less often discussed as southern literature), for example, gained new interest as they began applying the questions of southernness to them. How did concepts including "the past in the present," "a sense of place," and "southern distinctiveness" work when discussing Ernest Gaines, Richard Wright, or Zora Neale Hurston? How did the writing of southern women engage issues that were equally important but different from the work of male authors, particularly in terms of white southern womanhood and its famed role as the centerpiece of the Lost Cause? By the turn into the 21st century, studies including Michael Kreyling's *Inventing Southern Literature* (1998) and Patricia Yaeger's *Dirt and Desire: Reconstructing Southern Women's Writing, 1930–1990* (2000) began changing the very questions scholars ask and redrawing the shape of southern literary study as a result, paying attention to the processes by which canons have been shaped and the very notion of southernness defined.

An even more recent paradigm shift in southern studies joins the field to the transnational turn in literary and cultural studies more generally by recognizing the region as significant not only within a national context but within a global one as well. A tendency to frame "the North" and "the South" only in terms of U.S. borders led to a kind of narcissism that has, in fact, thwarted a broader vision of the nation as a global resident and the region as affected by the forces of globalization. Innovative phenomena including I-pods, cell phones, and the Internet shrink the globe into the virtual excursion of a few moments, and economic border crossings in the form of the Euro or NAFTA or transnational corporations are intended to facilitate the monetary health of multiple nation-states, although such measures have not, obviously, minimized national affiliations. Literature from and about the U.S. South has reflected the region's implication in the world's broader landscape, in part by tracking the movement of people in and out of the South. Robert Olen Butler's short-story collection *A Good Scent from a Strange Mountain* (1992), for instance, focuses primarily on Vietnamese residents of Louisiana and the hauntings of a different war. Susan Choi's recent novel *The Foreign Student* (1998) interweaves one main character's memories of his youth in war-torn Korea with seemingly idyllic life in Sewanee, the campus of a small liberal arts college nestled in the mountains of Tennessee. Cynthia Shearer's *The Celestial Jukebox* (2005) similarly takes up the Mississippi Delta and reveals it to be a crossroads of all humanity, an inter-section of Asian, Latino, African, African American, and white characters who, Shearer importantly signals, have always already been there but not given a voice in any official story of the South.

Suzanne W. Jones and Sharon Monteith's recent invaluable essay collection, *South to a New Place: Region, Literature, Culture*, registers the multiple interests of a postmodern, globally conscious southern studies with essays titled "Where Is Southern Literature?" and "Dismantling the Monolith," ecocritical treatments of Toni Morrison and Linda Hogan, a chapter about Vietnamese fiction in the contemporary South, and a section headed "Making Global Connections" in which scholars link U.S. southern literature to Italy, Germany, Latin America, and Britain.

A second related, but distinctively different, concept is that of the "Global South," a term still in considerable flux within literary circles. This approach encourages the scholarly imagination to pierce the boundaries of nation and imagine space as differently configured. In the most basic terms of weather (U. B. Phillips's starting point for his 1929 discussion of a self-absorbed South), the hurricane-vulnerable coastal South has much in common with the Carib-bean, for instance; in a study of 19th-century plantation life, the antebellum Deep South has much in common with Brazil—perhaps as much as it does with Massachusetts. A global southern studies reads for such connections and locates the U.S. South squarely within its hemispheric citizenship, recognizing it, in the words of Jon Smith and Deborah Cohn in *Look Away! The U.S. South in New World Studies*, as "a space simultaneously (or alternately) center and margin, victor and defeated, empire and colony, essentialist and hybrid, northern and southern (both in the global sense)." Out of this liminal space grow new questions about the U.S. South's relation to locations around the world and an obligation to see the region famed for its isolation as always deeply embedded in global crosscurrents of money, labor, and power. From the time it was shifting among British, French, and Spanish ownership, the yet-to-be U.S. South was a multicultural space that would soon be home to a significant African presence. Making that fact central to any study alters readings of its infamous "sense of place" by setting aside the literary compass that insists on pointing North and allowing examination of the U.S. South relative to points further south or east or west.

More broadly, and more interdisciplinarily construed, "Global South" connotes a system of power relations in which "South" conjures markers of the Third World poverty, disenfranchisement, environmental degradation, and inequity rooted in racism, sexism, and inflexible economic structures—while "North" evokes the power of First World privilege, dependent on the labor of "the South" to guarantee the staying power of capitalism and its consumers. Plotting the U.S. South on this rubric is an enterprise that obviously requires caution. Physically a part of the world's only widely acknowledged superpower, the South's residents enjoy the protective umbrella of U.S. dollars and, in fact, work in some of the nation's major corporate centers—Atlanta, Charlotte, Houston, Memphis—that in turn offer global links of extraordinary power in the form of Coca-Cola, CNN, and FedEx, as James Peacock has argued. Yet undeniable parallels to other "Souths" emerge from even cursory study, and it is just this delicate position of "betweenness" that Smith and Cohn so effectively underscore as central to any reassessment of the region within a global framework. Patterns of labor practice, ongoing poverty, and inadequate educational opportunities and health care facilities, for example, align significant portions of the U.S. South with the distributions of power Americans more familiarly associate with other parts of the world. Reading across the artificially constructed but very real political boundaries of governments, scholars of the Global South find particularly useful the perspectives of postcolonial theory that allow them to recognize similar hierarchies of power in seemingly dissimilar places. Global South studies, then, might examine racial practices in the Deep South and in South Africa; it might study agricultural practices in river deltas across the globe; it might consider how religious fundamentalism varies by location. The goal of focusing on a "Global South," then, is not to erase the U.S. South's claim to a distinctive sort of Americanness but rather to understand that persistent sense of difference as a means of connection to globally articulated patterns of human behavior and the resulting arrangements of power.

The academic consequences of situating the U.S. South globally are not yet precisely clear. What does seem clear, however, is that locating the region in this way will alter much about the practice of southern literary and cultural scholarship as it has been carried out until recently. Scholars may, for instance, prepare differently to enter the field, and they will read differently than they have in the past. They will pay attention not so much to differences in accent between New Hampshire and Georgia but to the ways in which Spanish is taught in local school systems. They will train their attention on the means by which southern writers from Korea and Mexico and Africa make the place of the South their own and take the South into their places. This transnational focus signals a U.S. South and a southern studies that understand themselves as important participants in an international dialogue, not just about tensions between the region and the nation but, just as importantly, about tensions between the local and the global.

KATHRYN MCKEE
University of Mississippi

James C. Cobb and William Stueck, eds., *Globalization and the American South* (2005); Deborah Cohn, *History and Memory in the Two Souths: Recent Southern and Spanish American Fiction* (1999); Leigh Anne Duck, *The Nation's Region: Southern Modernism, Segregation, and U.S. Nationalism* (2006); George Handley, *Postslavery Literatures in the Americas: Family Portraits in Black and White* (2000); Suzanne W. Jones and Sharon Monteith, *South to a New Place: Region, Literature, Culture* (2002); James L. Peacock, Harry Watson, and Carrie R. Matthews, eds., *The American South in a Global World* (2005); Jon Smith and Deborah Cohn, eds., *Look Away!: The U.S. South in New World Studies* (2004); Charles Reagan Wilson, *Southern Missions: The Religion of the American South in Global Perspective* (2006).

Humor

From its inception in the 18th century, southern humor has favored the extravagant, eccentric, outlandish, and the physically and/or psychologically grotesque; its principal focus has involved encounters between characters of different cultures and social classes, with marginalized local characters as the principal players; and its prevalent mode has typically been the earthy, unrestrained, and hyperbolic.

Ebenezer Cooke's satiric poem "The Sot-Weed Factor; or, a Voyage to Maryland" (1708) exhibits most of these features. In it, the narrator, a naive sophisticate and urban outcast from England, travels to Maryland, confidently hoping for a second chance to prosper, to gain his fortune, this time as a tobacco merchant in New World society, which he views as uncouth and inferior. In scripting this lively and amusing encounter between different cultures, Cooke accomplishes two purposes: he burlesques British notions of the New World as well as the customs and manners of tobacco planters on Maryland's frontier, with the greater share of his satire directed against the naiveté, ignorance, and stupidity of the English factor. William Byrd II's *History of the Dividing Line* (1841) and a second "Secret History" (written to entertain his close friends) were based on his experiences as the leader of the Virginia contingent that, along with a similar group from North Carolina, was commissioned in 1728 to establish the boundary line between the two colonies. A landed aristocrat, wealthy planter, expert on colonial flora and fauna whose scientific reports were published by the Royal Society, a bibliophile, colonial official, and man of many other talents, Byrd hyperbolically ridiculed the region on the North Carolina side of the line as "Lubberland." Byrd depicted this region as an environment of ease and fertility, degeneracy, and religious indifference and inhabited by ignorant, lazy, irresponsible, uncivilized, immoral lower-class whites, pork eaters whose overindulgent dietary habits caused them to be afflicted with unsightly "cadaverous complexions." Though not exactly an equal-opportunity satirical humorist, Byrd nevertheless directed some of his condescending barbs against Native American males, whom he perceived as lazier than North Carolina poor whites, and, in his livelier "Secret History," against the licentious behavior of his fellow dividing-line commissioners to whom he gives amusingly degrading names like Meanwell, Firebrand, Jumble, and Shoebrush.

In that Cooke's "The Sot-Weed Factor" and Byrd's *Dividing Line* histories are amusing social commentaries showcasing in an exaggerated comical manner eccentricities and outrageous antics reflecting cultural and social differences between the frontier backwoods and sophisticated and refined societies, they provided a usable scenario that would be treated more extensively and popularly in antebellum southern newspaper humor. The so-called humor of the Old Southwest, which flourished between the 1830s to the end of the Civil War, in an area encompassing the sparsely settled frontier regions of Georgia, the Carolinas, Alabama, Mississippi, Louisiana, Arkansas, Missouri, and Tennessee, was the work of amateurs who often wrote anonymously or pseudonymously. To the comical recipe of Cooke and Byrd, most of the southwestern humorists added the vernacular dialect of the southern common folk, often giving them extended voice and space in their sketches, tall tales, almanac pieces, mock sermons, humorous letters, and dramatic speeches and often in juxtaposition to the formal and standard English spoken by the gentleman-author who also sometimes functioned as frame narrator.

Frequently, the usually genteel frame narrator introduced the embedded vernacular character and described circumstances prompting the humorous anecdote or tale the rustic would recount. Tales and sketches featuring hunts, fights, horse races and horse trading, frolics, camp meetings, sermons, militia drills, courtship, courtroom antics, gambling, roguery and deception, and other subjects befitting their masculine brand of humor and early form of literary realism first appeared in newspapers such as the *Augusta States Rights Sentinel*, *New Orleans Picayune*, *St. Louis Reveille*, *La Fayette East Alabamian*, and *Columbia South Carolinian*. Many others were published in William T. Porter's New York sporting weekly, the *Spirit of the Times*. During Porter's 25 years as editor of the *Spirit*, he encouraged and promoted numerous southern correspondents to contribute original humorous sketches, tales, and sporting epistles or to allow him to reprint their previous published pieces, giving these amateur humorists exposure to a national audience. While admittedly most antebellum southern humorists feature marginalized white males at the center of the action, sometimes a few, such as, Henry Clay Lewis, John S. Robb, Hardin Taliaferro, Francis James Robinson, James Edward Henry, Sol Smith, William Tappan Thompson, Orlando Benedict Mayer, and George Washington Harris shift the focus to African Americans and/or women who transgress the narrow roles mandated by a patriarchal culture, giving them a broader range of experiences and more liberal voices than they were customarily allowed by the circumscribed race and gender restraints in antebellum society.

In treating the contrast-of-cultures paradigm common in much humor of the Old South, Kenneth Lynn in *Mark Twain and Southwestern Humor* (1959) oversimplified the role of the gentlemanly narrators in these sketches and tales, designating them as "self-controlled" and "outside and above the comic action," and as such functioning as critics of the foibles of the common folk characters. Yet with rare exception is Lynn's claim representative of what actually occurs in southwestern humor texts; instead, most of the rustic characters who dominate the action are, while often uncouth and uninhibited, affable and offer readers an amusing and liberating alternative to the stuffy order and formality of the "morally irreproachable [g]entleman."

The works of about 50 humorists of the Old Southwest, including a few who wrote under pseudonyms but whose identities are not verified, have been recovered from antebellum newspapers and literary journals. Among those in the first rank are Augustus Baldwin Longstreet, the author of *Georgia Scenes*

(1835), the first book-length collection of humorous frontier sketches; William Tappan Thompson, the author of *Major Jones's Courtship* (1843), a popular collection of mock letters of a vernacular rustic; Johnson Jones Hooper, who created one of the most memorable backwoods rogues in American literature and who authored *Some Adventures of Captain Suggs* (1845); Thomas Bangs Thorpe, who wrote "The Big Bear of Arkansas," commonly regarded as southwestern humor's best-known sketch, and a collection *Mysteries of the Backwoods* (1847); Henry Clay Lewis, who, under the pseudonym of Madison Tensas, chronicled the experiences of frontier medical practice in *Odd Leaves of a the Life of a Louisiana "Swamp Doctor"* (1850); Joseph Glover Baldwin, who wrote *Flush Times of Alabama and Mississippi* (1853), a series of essays and sketches treating the legal profession on the lower southern frontier; and George Washington Harris, the best of the southwestern humorists, creator of fun-loving east Tennessee mountaineer prankster Sut Lovingood, and author of *Sut Lovingood: Yarns* (1867).

Young Samuel L. Clemens, who became Mark Twain, the main beneficiary of the brand of humor popularized by the southwestern humorists, reflected this influence in some of his apprenticeship sketches and in *Adventures of Huckleberry Finn*. In his first published work, "The Dandy Frightening the Squatter" (1852), Twain employed the clash of civilized and backwoods cultures, the conflict resolved with the triumph of the offended backwoodsman. Also, in three humorous letters, published in the *Keokuk (Iowa) Post* in 1856 and 1857, he employed the epistolary form, chronicling in the dialect discourse of a naif from the country, Thomas Jefferson Snodgrass, and his misadventures in the city. "A Washoe Joke" (1862), a tall-tale anecdote about the discovery of a petrified man and parody of sensationally incredible scientific discoveries; "Jim Smiley and His Jumping Frog" (1865), a frame story in which a naive eastern sophisticate is duped by an old miner's stories about a compulsive bettor; the sketches of *Roughing It* (1872), which chronicles a tenderfoot's encounters with the eccentricities of western life, also demonstrate Twain's use of conventions and subject matter of southwestern humor. Yet Twain's great achievement, *Huckleberry Finn* (1884), which likewise involves culture clashes and gives extensive voice to an ingenuous, vernacular-speaking, poor-white boy, employs many of the subjects and humorous conventions of his southern humorous predecessors, though in his capable hands Twain transforms the genre into a higher level of literary art.

Some of Twain's contemporaries also drew from the rich mine of materials of the humorists of the Old Southwest but used them for different purposes. Several southern women writers—Mary Noailles Murfree, Idora Mc-

Clellan Moore, Sherwood Bonner, and Ruth McEnery Stuart—whom Kathryn B. McKee has aptly dubbed "female local humorists," employed regional subject matter and comic style similar to that of antebellum humorists but in a women-centered fictional milieu. Joel Chandler Harris's Uncle Remus stories and African American Charles Waddell Chesnutt's conjure stories, collected in *The Conjure Woman* (1899), draw on the trickster figure popularized by the southwestern humorist. Both Harris and Chesnutt feature former black slaves as embedded dialect-speaking narrators who, in donning masks of anti-intellectuality and assuming a humorous demeanor to disguise their sometimes transgressive intentions and the inferior associations such poses imply, function simultaneously as entertaining raconteurs of tall tales and tricksters who regain some sense of their humanity through the stories they recount. Heavily steeped in folklore, these tales subtly display instances of African American empowerment, albeit without offending their listeners within their narratives or the outside readers. The anonymous John and Old Master tales, which, like Harris's and Chesnutt's stories, often contest the racial status quo of white supremacy and which are a product of the African American oral folklore, treat humorously direct interactions involving conflict and struggle between a slave (often named John and a transgressor and sometimes a trickster) and his master. In them, whether John triumphs and is heroic or is victimized and is a fool in his attempts to transgress inhumanity and exploitation, there is always a sense that race conflict under the system of bondage will be ongoing.

The viability of the South's quintessential humorous tradition continues in many southern writers of the 20th century. While Faulkner's principal métier was not the comic mode, there is much evidence of the extent to which he assimilated and reconfigured some of the themes, character types, and folk materials popularized by his southwestern predecessors to serve a higher and more complex artistic purpose than his humorist forebears, amateur entertainers, ever envisioned or achieved. In the "Spotted Horses" segment of *The Hamlet* (1940), the hyperbolic descriptions and foolish antics of the victims of Flem Snopes's horse-selling scam; in *Sanctuary* (1931), the script of simple and vulnerable country naifs coming to town; in *As I Lay Dying* (1930), the comically bizarre Bundrens and their amusing but outrageous behavior; in *The Reivers* (1961), the comic misadventures and roguery of Lucius Priest, Boon Hogganbeck, and Ned McCaslin; and in "Afternoon of a Cow," the tall-tale self-parody and calculated stretcher—all attest to Faulkner's using materials of this 19th-century tradition.

Some of Faulkner's southern contemporaries and successors likewise exploited the subject matter, character types, and humorous stylistics similar to those of the antebellum humorists. Erskine Caldwell, in using comic caricaturing to create a grotesque portraiture of the Lesters in *Tobacco Road* (1932), the Waldens in *God's Little Acre* (1933), and Semon Dye, the hypocritical backwoods preacher and con man in *Journeyman* (1935), has adapted the method of comic exaggeration of the Southwest humorists for social indictment. Evidence of their influence appears in the physical and psychological grotesques of Flannery O'Connor in stories such as "Good Country People," "The Artificial Nigger," "A Good Man Is Hard to Find," "A Stroke of Good Fortune," and "A Late Encounter with the Enemy" and in her novel *Wise Blood* (1952). Other examples occur in the psychologically warped, physically deformed, and sometimes obsessively violent characters of Harry Crews, who, as literary descendant of George Washington Harris, effectively combines comedy, horror, and pain and who sympathetically portrays his poor whites in novels such as *A Feast of Snakes* (1976) and in *Body* (1990). The comic liars, con men, braggarts, and practical jokers in William Price Fox's story collection, *Southern Fried* (1962), and the comically grotesque primitive fundamentalists and religious zealots in his novels *Moonshine Light, Moonshine Bright* (1967) and *Dixiana Moon* (1981), and the incongruous characters and ludicrously grotesque violence in Barry Hannah's "Quo Vadis, Smut?," *Ray* (1980), and *The Tennis Handsome* (1983) likewise exhibit connections to Old Southwest humor. Cormac McCarthy in *The Orchard Keeper* (1965), *Suttree* (1979), and *Outer Dark* (1993); Eudora Welty in "Petrified Man," "Keela, the Outcast Indian Maiden," "Why I Live at the P.O.," *The Robber Bridegroom* (1942), and *Losing Battles* (1970); and Ralph Ellison in *Invisible Man* (1952)—writers not principally noted for their comic muse—likewise are beneficiaries of the southern frontier humor tradition.

The sometimes comic portrayal of marginalized characters in contemporary southern fiction—African Americans and women—also shows signs of intersection with this 19th-century frontier tradition. Strong and assertive female characters, such as Flannery O'Connor's Mary Grace in "Revelation"; Fannie Flagg's Idgie Threadgoode in *Fried Green Tomatoes at the Whistle Stop Café* (1987); Sofia in Alice Walker's *The Color Purple* (1983); and the lampoons, character sketches, and autobiographical pieces of Florence King, demonstrating her unrestrained iconoclasm and acerbic and shocking wit, using brash and outspoken female personae, represent this particular strain. And African American Ishmael Reed's creative dual use of the trickster figure in his role as author and as a vehicle and subversive force in his central character Quickskill, a runaway slave in his parodic, iconoclastic, and freewheeling comic novel *Flight to Canada* (1976), further exemplifies how a minority southern writer continues to attack and transgress barriers as did some of the marginalized characters featured in southwestern humor.

Among contemporary southern writers who are professional humorists and who work in the still vibrant strain of comedy popularized by the South's antebellum humorists, Lewis Grizzard, Jeff Foxworthy, and Roy Blount Jr. prominently stand out. Grizzard, first in his widely syndicated newspaper columns and then in best-selling book collections, typically fictionalized autobiography with zany titles, such as *If I Were Oil, I'd Be about a Quart Low* (1983), *Elvis Is Dead and I Don't Feel So Good Myself* (1984), *My Daddy Was a Pistol and I'm a Son of a Gun* (1986), and *Don't Bend over in the Garden, Granny, You Know Them Taters Got Eyes* (1988), often assumed a conservative "good old boy" persona, an anachronistic pose standing in stark contrast to the changing South in which he lived. As a humorist whose homespun anecdotes and tales appealed to ordinary folks, Grizzard's forte was his witty and incongruous depiction of southern characters, places, folkways, idiosyncrasies, preferences, and foibles. Jeff Foxworthy, the most popular contemporary southern humorist, is known for his stand-up comic routines, particularly his redneck jokes, the latter subsequently published in book-length collections such as *You Might Be a Redneck If . . .* (1989), *Red Ain't Dead* (1991), and *Check Your Neck: More of You Might Be a Redneck If . . .* (1992). His comic autobiography *No Shirt, No Shoes . . . No Problem!* (1996) accentuates southern stereotypes, and in his comic depiction of the subculture of lower-class whites, Foxworthy features vernacular speech and uses an informal method of storytelling reminiscent of that of the South's antebellum yarn spinners.

Roy Blount, the author of books of humor and the editor of a popular trade anthology, *Roy Blount's Book of Southern Humor* (1994), in which he has included a significant number of the writers from the Old Southwest tradition as well as moderns and contemporaries whose featured writing exhibits traits harkening back to this tradition, has also appeared on National Public Radio on Garrison Keillor's *Prairie Home Companion* and as a panelist on various quiz shows and has authored a one-man off-Broadway play, *Roy Blount's Happy Hour and a Half.* Lauded by John Shelton Reed as "arguably the funniest southerner alive," Blount employs comic techniques that indicate he is in a line of descent from the southern frontier tradition, if not directly, then through Mark Twain, the American writer whom he admires the most. As a writer who appreciates southern oral humor of a rollicking and unrestrained kind, the brand popularized by the South's backwoods humorists, Blount employs dialect (though usually of a readable variety). His fascination for the vernacular, likely influenced through his reading of Twain and Joel Chandler Harris's Uncle Remus tales; use of a variation of the frame device of dual voices through his juxtaposition of the rhythms and sounds of conversational speech and formal English; hilarious portraits of common folk in some of the fictitious relatives of President Jimmy Carter he creates in *Crackers: This Whole Many-Angled Thing of Jimmy, More Carters, Ominous Little Animals, Sad Singing Women, My Daddy, and Me* (1980); and use of the tall tale in his novel *First Hubby* (1996) and in "Unseen Rock City" are further indications of his connection with the earlier humorists.

If the southern tradition of humor continues to be adapted and reconfigured, the seeds of which were germinated first in Cook and Byrd, developed into a popular form by the antebellum Southwest humorists, permanently rooted and elevated to literary distinction in Mark Twain, and brought to the levels of the highest literary art in William Faulkner and in other modern and contemporary southern writers, and if it continues to be expressive of southern and American life, particularly in the mass media and on the Internet, its durability seems assured.

EDWARD J. PIACENTINO
High Point University

Barbara Bennett, *Comic Visions, Female Voices: Contemporary Women Novelists and Southern Humor* (1998); M. Thomas Inge, in *The Companion to Southern Literature: Themes, Genres, Places, People, Movements, and Motifs*, ed. Joseph M. Flora and Lucinda H. MacKethan (2001), in *Frontier Humorists: Critical Views*, ed. Inge (1975); M. Thomas Inge and Edward J. Piacentino, eds., *The Humor of the Old South* (2001); James H. Justus, *Fetching the Old Southwest: Humorous Writing from Longstreet to Twain* (2004); J. A. Leo Lemay, *Men of Letters in Colonial Maryland* (1972); Kenneth S. Lynn, *Mark Twain and Southwestern Humor* (1959); Kathryn Burgess McKee, "Writing in a Different Direction: Women Authors and the Tradition of Southwestern Humor, 1875–1920" (Ph.D. dissertation, University of North Carolina at Chapel Hill, 1996); Ed Piacentino, ed., *The Enduring Legacy of Old Southwest Humor* (2006); John Shelton Reed, *Southern Cultures* (Summer 1995).

Indian Literature

All southern literature begins with American Indian literature of the South. It is perplexing that many literary histories of "southern literature" to this day do not take into consideration the historical presence of American Indian literature and culture. It is even more startling given the fact that the South as a place is a crucial point of origin for many native people who lived and continue to live here. For the Choctaws, for instance, the remains of Nanih Waiya, their sacred mound of origin located in Winston County, Miss., continue to play a powerful role in the origin stories and oral traditions of both Mississippi and Oklahoma Choctaws. The Choctaws, Cherokees, Creeks, Seminoles, Chickasaws, and many smaller tribal groups lived on their homelands in the South for hundreds of years. Their stories, histories, and self-definitions are tightly meshed with southern landscapes.

Southern literature then begins with the Native American oral tradition, rich in stories and rooted in southern settings. Many of these stories, like the Cherokee emergence story that begins with Selu, the Corn Woman, are about the origin of the earth and its people, gender roles, social organization, and life-styles. Other oral stories can be characterized as historical narratives that explain the movements of various tribes, how they came to live in a particular place, or why different tribes speak many different languages (e.g., the Caddo's story of Moon). These ancient oral stories endure to this day, and many of them have been transcribed, recorded, and written down.

Despite the processes of transcription and preservation, such Native American cultural materials are often left out of the canon of southern literature. A major reason for this omission may be the Indian Removal Act of 1830 that forced Indians from their homelands in the Southeast to a designated Indian territory west of the Mississippi River. This physical removal of Indians—first by "voluntary" emigration and later at gun point in a forced and violent ordeal that is known as the "Trail of Tears"—resulted in their discursive removal as well and in a reductive view of the South's racial and ethnic makeup as primarily "black and white." But many of the Indian writers, both those who remained in the South and those who left, continued to tell and write about the South.

In fact, in the early half of the 19th century, many Native Americans started writing in English, and some of the most significant literary production occurred in the South by two Cherokee writers from Georgia: Elias Boudinot (1802–39) and John Rollin Ridge (1827–67). Boudinot initially protested the removal, and as editor of the *Cherokee Phoenix* he put his pen to work so that white readers, including his southern neighbors, could recognize the Cherokee's progress toward social, political, and religious acculturation. Sadly, Boudinot later succumbed to state and federal pressures and signed the removal treaty, the Treaty of New Echota, in 1835, and he was killed for it by some of his own people who opposed the removal. Like Boudinot, John Rollin Ridge argued for the assimilation and "civilization" of Indians as the best strategy for Native American survival. As a young boy, Ridge witnessed how members of his family who supported the treaty were also killed, an experience that sent him into flight first to Arkansas and later to California, where he published poetry, prose, and his novel *The Life and Adventures of Joaquin Murieta, the Celebrated California Bandit* (1854). Though the setting of this novel concerns the U.S. colonization of California and the Mexican-American War, some critics have argued that Ridge transposes his own traumatic southern experience as a Cherokee onto the California landscape where Native Americans had also been violently displaced from their ancestral lands.

When the southern canon opens up to acknowledge and include the literature of Native American writers, several things occur. The historical signposts around which southern literary history usually gathers take on different forms. Native Americans were certainly influenced by the Civil War, and many of them fought in the war—some even for the Confederacy, like the Cherokee General Stand Watie, who is credited with the last surrender of the war at Doaksville in the Choctaw Nation, 23 June 1864. The Civil War is, however, only one of the decisive historical moments that help to structure southern literary history. In the 19th century alone, the dates of the removal period (1830–38), the Mexican-American War (1846–48), and the Allotment Act (also known as the Dawes Act [1887]) must be considered significant. The latter legislation proved to be disastrous for many homesteading Indians, such as the Catawba of South Carolina, whose lands were cut up into small plots and sold for bottom dollar. Daniel Littlefield and James Parins argue that the period between 1875 and 1935 provides its own historical integrity and importance for Native American writing, marking, on one end, the "close of the treaty-making period" and, on the other, the beginning of the Indian's New Deal.

If the first consequence of including Native American writing in a study of southern literature is an expanding sense of history, a second one expands the idea of place itself. Southern literature is primarily a place-based concept, however shifting our understanding of that place. If we define "the South" to mean the southeastern United States, we are including the artistic and literary productions of Cherokees, Choctaws, Chickasaws, Creeks, and Seminoles, just to name some of the larger tribal groups that were and are located here. Littlefield and Parins's anthology *Native American Writing in the Southeast* (1995) takes this geographical approach, showcasing work by Choctaw authors Israel Folsom, David McCurtain, and Muriel Hazel Wright; Chickasaw authors James Harris Guy, Ben Colbert, and Charles David Carter; Muscogee writers Alexander Lawrence Posey, Charles Gibson, and Jesse McDermott; Cherokee writers John Milton Oskison and Will Rogers, among many others. But, as the example of John Rollin Ridge shows, many Native American writers who were displaced continue to create literature influenced by or responding to the South. Southern American Indian literature then also includes works by Native American authors living outside the traditional regional boundaries of "the South." These writers, no matter where they are located, can be said to (re)occupy southern territory discursively and imaginatively—that is, in their ways of writing and talking about the region.

Contemporary Native American writers whose tribal affiliations are southeastern but who do not live and work in the South, such as Louis Owens (Choctaw/Cherokee), Joy Harjo (Muscogee Creek), Diane Glancy (Cherokee/German/English), Linda Hogan (Chickasaw), and LeAnne Howe (Choctaw), productively complicate notions of literary regionalism.

What precisely counts as southern American Indian literature? Is it writing produced in the South by Native American writers? Or is it writing about the South by native writers who live outside of it? And is such writing in any way recognizably "southern," in the way that work by William Faulkner or Eudora Welty, for instance, can be said to be "southern"? Or, rather, in what ways are southern writers sharing characteristics of Native American traditions of writing? We may think of the shared reliance on the oral tradition, on storytelling and myth; or of the interest in tribal and family stories that Faulkner, for instance, shares with N. Scott Momaday (Kiowa) and Louise Erdrich (Anishaabe). Understanding the land as a crucial aspect of identity and heritage is certainly a compelling theme for writers of the South, and so is the preoccupation with conquest and defeat, racial struggle, and cultural sovereignty. In addition to shared thematic concerns, experimentation with different viewpoints, styles, and genres characterizes both canonical southern writing and southern American Indian literature. Diane Glancy's novel about the Cherokee removal, *Pushing the Bear* (1996), for instance, is presented by multiple narrators in fragments of dialogue, history, songs, prayers, stories, and inventories. The English text is strategically interspersed with words and phrases from Sequoyah's alphabet, a strategy that, according to the author, creates "holes in the text so the original can show through." Southern American Indian literature, however, not only addresses problems of cultural translation and loss; there is also humor, irony, and the Gothic. What Gothic vision did Barry Hannah inherit from John Rollin Ridge? What sense of humorous irony does Faulkner share with Oskison? What common bond is there between Zora Neale Hurston and Leslie Marmon Silko? Our willingness to investigate such questions depends on a larger question about the possibility for a productive exchange between the disciplines of Native American studies and southern studies.

The study of southern American Indian literature necessitates dialogue and intellectual interchange between Native American and southern studies not in the sense of a colonizing incorporation of one into the other, but in a much needed recognition of the way native contributions to the southern canon— many of them predating European contact and inspiring "southern" writers— can creatively and productively reshape our understanding of the South's geography, history, and literature.

ANNETTE TREFZER
University of Mississippi

Eric Gary Anderson, in *South to a New Place: Region, Literature, Culture*, ed. Suzanne W. Jones and Sharon Monteith (2002); Cecile E. Carter, *The Caddo Indians: Where We Come From* (1995); Louise Erdrich, in *Louise Erdrich's* Love Medicine: *A Casebook*, ed. and intro. Hertha D. Sweet (2000); Diane Glancy, *Pushing the Bear* (1996); Charles Hudson, *The Southeastern Indians* (1999); Daniel F. Littlefield Jr. and James W. Parins, eds., *Native American Writing in the Southeast: An Anthology, 1875– 1935* (1995); *Mississippi Quarterly* (Spring 2007), special issue on American Indian Literatures and Cultures in the South; Alfonso Ortiz, *American Indian Myths and Legends* (1984); Theda Purdue and Michael D. Green, *The Cherokee Removal: A Brief History with Documents* (2005); John L. Purdy and James Ruppert, eds., *Nothing but the Truth: An Anthology of Native American Literature* (2001); John Carlos Rowe, Novel: *A Forum on Fiction* (Spring 1998).

Nature Writing and Writers

In the 16 March entry of his *Journal of 1820–21*, John James Audubon described the annual migration of American golden plovers down the Mississippi Flyway. Their numbers were prodigious, "a passage of millions" as he estimated it, yet that was not the pressing thought that Audubon was moved to record. It was "the destruction of innocent fugitives from a winter storm" by a collection of shooters and market hunters that preoccupied the ornithologist. As the hunters called the birds into range, Audubon marveled at the efficiency of the marksmen: "I saw several times a flock of 100 or more plovers destroyed at the exception of 5 or 6," he added. In an attempt to estimate the afternoon's carnage, Audubon continued, "A man near where I was seated had killed 63 dozens—from the firing before and behind us I suppose that 400 gunners were out. Suppose each man to have killed 30 dozen that day, 144,000 must have been destroyed."

Audubon's experience of witnessing not only the exuberance of southern nature but also its decimation seems a point of departure for those who would follow. Certainly, the primary topic of southern nature writers has been the sheer fecundity of the lush southern states and its multiplicity of forms and numbers, and the great theme of our nature writing has been an exploration of our reactions to this richness: subsumed by its potency or scarred by our destruction of it or, as in the case of Audubon, the simultaneous moment of the two.

Writers and scholars lament that the tradition of southern nature writing is not as easily delineated as other subgenres of the same subject. Whereas other U.S. regions had writers who devoted entire careers to the exploration and meditation of nature in print—Henry David Thoreau and John Burroughs in New England, Aldo Leopold in the Upper Midwest, John Muir in the West— southern readers can point to no monolithic figure from literary history whose books establish a clear type. Instead, the attempt to recognize and describe such a tradition must not only include native writers but also borrow from a variety of visiting writers of different topics, whose careers, interests, and even regional identities are far removed from the South itself.

The reader interested in early southern nature writing is faced with sparse but potent offerings. William Bartram's classic account *Travels through North and South Carolina, Georgia, East and West Florida* (1791) describes the young botanist's adventures among the Indians, planters, and wilderness creatures of the late 18th-century southern landscape. Son of the eminent botanist John Bartram, William Bartram was a New England Quaker primarily traveling alone and often overwhelmed with a nature outsized and frighteningly primitive. His lonely wandering in the Blue Ridge Mountains and close encounters with American alligators often provoked him to experiences of the sublime. In a representative passage from *Travels*, surrounded by alligators in a Florida swamp, Bartram finds himself in a battle with that mythic southern animal: "I was attacked on all sides, several endeavouring to overset the canoe. My situation now became precarious to the last degree: two very large ones attacked me closely, at the same instant, rushing up with their heads and part of their bodies above the water, roaring terribly and belching bloods of water over me. They stuck their jaws together so close to my ears, as almost to stun me, and I expected every moment to be dragged out of the boat and instantly devoured." Descriptions such as these in Bartram's *Travels* would have an enduring effect in both American and English literature as scholars have uncovered his influence on the English romantic writers Wordsworth and Coleridge, the American novelist James Fenimore Cooper, and even the transcendentalists Emerson and Thoreau.

Also worth noting are sections of Thomas Jefferson's *Notes on the State of Virginia* (1781–82) and the aforementioned journals of John James Audubon, but possibly greater than both are Audubon's vignettes of American life and wildlife first written for his *Ornithological Biography* and later unified in an edition entitled *Delineations of American Scenery and Character* (1926). Like its author, *Delineations* has a distinctly American rather than regional character; however, the presence of the South is primary in essays such as "Improvements in the Navigation of the Mississippi," "The Cougar," "The Earthquake," "The Hurricane," "Kentucky Sports," and many others. A diverse collection, some essays are straight natural history, others focus on regional folkways, some utilize the conventions of the tall tale and southern humor, and a few border on conservation advocacy.

Finally, early southern nature writing appears in the humor of the Old Southwest, especially in tales such as Thomas Bangs Thorpe's "The Big Bear of Arkansas" and David Crockett's "Bear Hunting in Tennessee." Thorpe's tall tale about a prodigious "unhuntable bear" utilizes the same theme of coexisting with extreme superabundance where plants and animals are overgrown. In an attempt to explain these environmental conditions to a stranger complaining of the big mosquitoes of the Arkansas country, the storyteller replies, "But mosquitoes is natur, and I never find fault with her. If they ar large, Arkansaw is large, her varmints ar large, her trees ar large, her rivers ar large, and a small mosquito would be of no more use in Arkansaw than preaching in a cane-brake."

The post–Civil War South saw a renewal of visitors interested in the southern condition and environment—many completing legendary journeys. Just after the close of the war, America's most renowned naturalist and wilderness preservation advocate John Muir hiked the back country of Kentucky, Tennessee, Georgia, and Florida—a southern landscape in which the war's devastation was still evident. Though unpublished until 1916, his account, *A Thousand-Mile Walk to the Gulf,* was fashioned from his diary entries during a botanical trek through the southern states in 1867. Instead of by foot, many travelers came to the South to embark down the Mississippi River, and of those accounts, Mark Twain's *Life on the Mississippi* (1883) bears mentioning because of his accurate descriptions of the lower Mississippi and his meditations on man's fraught relationships with the nation's primary waterway. A native southerner instead of a tourist, the poet, musician, author, and scholar Sidney Lanier contributed a wonderful guidebook for visitors in *Florida: Its Scenery, Climate, and History* (1875). His introductory remarks on climate, though, demonstrate that his book was not reserved for mere tourists: "The ignorance of intelligent men and women about the atmospheric conditions amid which they live is as amazing to one who first comes bump against it as it is droll to one who has grown familiar with its solid enormity."

The 20th century would provide what many believe is the central text in the tradition of southern nature writing in the form of William Faulkner's *Go Down, Moses* (1942), specifically the short novella *The Bear*. While *The Bear* recounts the central character Ike McCaslin's struggle to understand his relationship with the Mississippi wilderness and his family's involvement in slavery, the larger work explores the intersection between the social and environmental history of north Mississippi as expressed through the story of the extended McCaslin clan over a period of a century. Though Faulkner is not primarily considered a nature writer, *Go Down, Moses* marks the environmental changes that took place during the late 19th and early 20th centuries: the growth of agriculture, the transition of dominance from railroad to automobile, the destruction of wildlife and habitat, the loss of a spiritual connection to the landscape.

Contemporaneous with Faulkner, other southern writers were making valuable contributions in the area of nature writing. The Rivers of America series originally published by Farrar and Rinehart and lasting for 37 years and 65 titles featured a variety of authors often writing about their native rivers. Two volumes should be of particular interest to those reading southern nature writing: Hodding Carter's *Lower Mississippi* (1942), a traditional cultural history of place; and Marjorie Stoneman Douglas's *The Everglades: River of Grass* (1947), a description of and plea for the preservation of the Florida Everglades.

During the last half of the 20th century, American nature writing blossomed, and with it southern nature writing flourished. Of particular note is Annie Dillard's Pulitzer Prize–winning *Pilgrim at Tinker Creek* (1974), set in the Blue Ridge Mountains of Virginia, which, as some critics have noted, probably finds its inheritance in New England transcendentalism rather than that of southern nature writing. Although the theological aspects of Dillard's writing have been emphasized as much as the environmental, *Pilgrim at Tinker Creek* still stands as the example of the type of nature writing predominantly sought and read today: the solitary author whose rambles now matter in regard to how far they deliver the author to a mediation of the human relationship with nature.

A farmer and writer who has dedicated his life's work to both the reinhabitation of his Kentucky homeland and an examination of American attitudes toward the environment, Wendell Berry's five-decade career includes works in poetry, fiction, and nonfiction. While Berry's prose often receives the most acclaim—books such as *A Continuous Harmony* (1972), *The Unsettling of America* (1977), *Home Economics* (1987), and *Sex, Economy, Freedom, and Community* (1992)—his poetry often displays the link with previous southern nature writers. Berry's familiar themes are inheritance, destruction, and repair, whether spoken by a "Mad Farmer" who plows cemeteries and the parson's wife or the poet-farmer who burns down an old farmhouse in "The Supplanting." In "The Sycamore," Berry finds "a great sycamore that is a wondrous healer of itself," which could very easily become a symbol of his Kentucky homeplace and of southern nature, for "[f]ences have been tied to it, nails driven into it, / hacks and whittles cut in it." In fact, "There is no year it has flourished in / that has not harmed it," but by the end of the poem, the poet understands that the great tree is "a fact, sublime, mystical and unassailable."

Two other southern writers from the last two decades of the 20th century have produced works considered nature writing. A beekeeper in the Missouri Ozarks, Sue Hubbell, recorded her thoughts on her vocation and rural life in *A Country Year* (1983). Montana writer Rick Bass's first two works of nonfiction also bear mention. *The Deer Pasture* (1985) chronicles his family's connection to hunting land in the Texas Hill Country, and *Wild to the Heart* (1987) describes his brief stay in Jackson, Miss., before ultimately removing to the West. His literary endeavor since leaving the South has been partially dedicated to saving the Yaak Valley of Montana, where he now makes his home.

Like Bass, contemporary southern nature writers have incorporated an activist approach to saving their subjects. Writers and poets Janisse Ray, Jim Kilgo, Bill Belleville, Jan DeBlieu, Christopher Camuto, Franklin Burroughs, Ann Fisher-Wirth, John Lane, Melissa Walker, Thomas Rain Crowe, and others have come together under the name of the Southern Nature Project to educate and advocate concerning the preservation of the southern wild landscape. Two anthologies of present-day southern nature writing have been produced from their association: *The Woods Stretched for Miles* (1999) and *Elemental South* (2004). In addition, many of these authors have produced books of distinction, including southern Georgia writer Janisse Ray's *Ecology of a Cracker Childhood* (1999), Christopher Camuto's *Another Country: Journeying Toward the Chero-kee Mountains* (2000), and South Carolina writer John Lane's *Waist Deep in Black Water* (2002).

DIXON BYNUM
Northwest Mississippi Community College

Lorraine Anderson and Thomas S. Edwards, eds., *At Home on This Earth: Two Centuries of U.S. Women's Nature Writing* (2002); Robert Finch and John Elder, eds., *The Norton Book of Nature Writing* (1990); Peter Fritzell, *Nature Writing and America* (1990); Thomas J. Lyon, ed., *This Incomperable Lande: A Book of American Nature Writing* (1989).

New Critics

John Crowe Ransom long ago complained that no one had defined what the critic's responsibilities were. Criticism, he said in 1937, was in the hands of amateurs who had insufficient instruction to prepare them to perform the important function for which they were responsible. The 20th century, Ransom believed, had produced some of the most important poetry in the history of English literature, but it was difficult verse and no one made it available to the general reader. The poets and the philosophers should be culture's critics, but the modern poet's understanding of his craft was "intuitive rather than dialectical" and the philosopher's "theory is very general and his acquaintance with the particular work of art is not persistent and intimate." Only the college teachers of literature were left, and "they are learned but not critical men." They "spend a lifetime compiling the data of literature" and yet rarely "commit themselves" to a literary judgment. Criticism, Ransom concluded, must be precise and systematic; it must be "the collective and sustained effort of learned persons"; adequately trained persons in the universities should do it.

Almost as if on cue, the year following Ransom's challenge two of his former students, Cleanth Brooks and Robert Penn Warren, who had become university teachers of literature, published a new approach to the teaching and reading of poetry, one that they had been using in mimeograph form in their classes. It was *Understanding Poetry* (1938), which in the subsequent 20 years went through four editions and left a lasting impression on the way poetry is taught and read. Rather than disseminating facts of the authors' lives or historical and cultural information about the times in which they lived, it demonstrated that if a poem is to reveal its unique quality, it must be read purely as poetry and not as history, biography, philosophy, or anything else. Rather than dealing with the kind of questions that lead to vague, impressionistic interpretations of a poem—the kind included in most textbooks of the time—*Understanding Poetry* offered concrete, inductive analyses of some 200 poems, demonstrations of how poems should be read, and questions that stated explicitly and exactly the "approach" to literature upon which the book was based. This approach is explained in a lengthy and detailed "Letter to the Teacher": "(1) Emphasis should be focused on the poem as poem; (2) Discussion of all poems should be specific, concrete and inductive; (3) A poem, if it is to be fully understood, must always be treated as an organic system of relationships and never thought to be included in one or more isolated lines or parts."

This book, followed by *Understanding Fiction*, also by Brooks and Warren (1943), and *Understanding Drama*, by Brooks and Robert B. Heilman (1945), surely contributed to the improved audiences for creative writers to which Ransom referred. The critical principles in these books came from the theoretical criticism of Ransom, as well as from that of his friends, associates, and former students. "Poetry," Ransom explained in *The World's Body* (1938), "is the kind of knowledge by which we must know that which we cannot know otherwise." Its intent is not to "idealize" the world, but to help its readers to "realize" it, to know its "common actuals," its "concrete particularities" (what he calls "the world's body"), which science, social science, and philosophy have attempted to reduce to abstract principles. The world that poetry reveals is not one of absolute innocence, one in which a reader should expect "to receive the fragrance of the roses on the world's first morning." The poetic world is a postscientific world, one that is revealed through both intellect and emotion. Only poetry can show the "body and solid substance of the world, that which has retired into the fullness of memory." With a combination, however, of image and idea, figure and statement, the poet can "construct the fullness of poetry, which is counterpart to the world's fullness."

In *The New Critics* (1941), the book that gave the movement under discussion its name, Ransom sought to identify the cognitive function of poetry by examining the way in which it differs from prose discourse. Allen Tate, like Ransom, was concerned with the unique nature of poetic discourse and the specific order of knowledge it contains. He agreed with Ransom that the poet attempts to reconstitute reality, not to make some comment about it. One of the first betrayers of literature, Tate said, was Matthew Arnold, who "extended the hand of fellowship to the scientist" and tried to make literature and religion synonymous. I. A. Richards followed Arnold's lead by suggesting that the significance of poetry resides in a "mere readiness for action." He could not find in poetic thought "action" itself. Readers of poetry are, therefore, merely passive recipients; they do not expect poetry to move them to significant action or reveal to them a fundamental truth.

In their attempt to restore literature to its rightful place in the center of human life, Ransom and Tate were joined by Cleanth Brooks and Robert Penn Warren. Soon after *The World's Body* (1938) appeared, Brooks published *Modern Poetry and the Tradition* (1939), in which he hoped to assist those readers—whose "conception of poetry is . . . primarily defined . . . by the achievements of the Romantic poets"—to appreciate the poetry of their own age. One must go back beyond the 18th century, Ransom and Brooks both insist, to find poets who do not attempt to oversimplify human experience by removing all discordant elements from it.

Although Warren is well known for the essays in which he introduced readers to important modern writers—William Faulkner, Peter Taylor, Katherine Anne

Robert Penn Warren, American man of letters, 1979 (William R. Ferris Collection, Southern Folklife Collection, Wilson Library, University of North Carolina at Chapel Hill)

Porter, Eudora Welty, John Crowe Ransom, and many others—he did write at least one basically theoretical essay. In "Pure and Impure Poetry," he argues that one finds in poetry many points of resistance: there is tension between the rhythm of the poem and the rhythm of speech, between the formality of the rhythm and the informality of the language, between the general and the abstract, between the beautiful and the ugly. This statement of tension among the various elements of a poem is very similar to Ransom's theory of the discord between its structure and texture. Both critics believed the poem is achieved through this tension.

The southerners who developed the New Criticism did so as a collective effort. Two earlier movements served as background for this collective literary endeavor. The Fugitives of the 1920s, including Ransom, were interested in a new poetry that would depart from traditional romantic, sentimental, south-ern verse. The Nashville Agrarians, including Ransom, Tate, Brooks, and War-ren, were social critics, concerned with social and economic ideas; their ideas appeared in the symposia *I'll Take My Stand* (1930) and *Who Owns America?* (1936). As an organized movement, Agrarianism was over by 1937, though, and New Criticism had already begun to assume central importance. The New Critics made a number of periodicals into organs for disseminating their views. Brooks and Warren edited *Southern Review* from 1935 to 1942, Ransom founded the *Kenyon Review* in 1940 and remained its editor for more than two decades, and Tate made the venerable *Sewanee Review* into a quarterly for literary and critical studies reflecting his theories. In addition to their textbooks and quarterlies, the influence of the New Critics was also felt through teaching, as they shaped a generation of students at Vanderbilt, Louisiana State University, Kenyon College, the University of Minnesota, Bread Loaf, and Yale. One can chart the changing geography of New Criticism, as its leaders moved from Nashville to Baton Rouge to Gambier, Ohio, and finally to New Haven, Conn. The peak of the New Criticism was in the 1940s and 1950s, but its influence continues to be felt.

The effect of the New Critics upon the understanding of what a poem is and how it works has been profound. One of their most enduring achievements is to make available the material essential to exploring the cognitive function of literature. Surely every student who has had an introductory course in literature in this country since World War II has been affected by the concerns of Ransom, Tate, Brooks, and Warren, even in the unlikely event that he has never heard the name of any one of them.

THOMAS DANIEL YOUNG
Vanderbilt University

Charlotte H. Beck, *The Fugitive Legacy: A Critical History* (2001); Louise Cowan, *The Southern Critics* (1972); Richard Foster, *The New Romantics: A Reappraisal of the New Criticism* (1962); William J. Handy, *Kant and the Southern New Critics* (1963); Mark Jancovich, *The Cultural Politics of the New Criticism* (1993); Murray Krieger, *The New Apologists for Poetry* (1968); Robert Wooster Stallman, in *A Southern Vanguard*, ed. Allen Tate (1947); Walter Sutton, *Modern American Criticism* (1963); Mark Royden Winchell, *Cleanth Brooks and the Rise of Modern Criticism* (1996); Thomas Daniel Young, ed., *The New Criticism and After* (1976).

North in Literature

Flannery O'Connor's first published story, "The Geranium," opens with an old man, come up from the South to stay with his daughter in New York, looking "out the window fifteen feet away into another window framed by blackened red brick." He is waiting for the people across the way to put a potted geranium on the sill, even though "those people across the alley had no business with one. They set it out and let the hot sun bake it all day and they put it so near the ledge the wind could almost knock it over. They had no business with it, no business with it." In "Judgment Day," her final story and retelling of the matter of "The Geranium," O'Connor's displaced old southerner stares through a window looking "out a brick wall and down into an alley full of New York air, the kind fit for cats and garbage. A few snowflakes drifted past the window but they were too thin and scattered for his failing vision." "The Geranium" ends with a man across the alley telling the old southerner to mind his own business; "Judgment Day" ends with old Tanner grotesquely dead, his feet dangling over the apartment house stairwell "like those of a man in the stocks."

O'Connor's images of New York as a sterile desert and New York as a freezing prison almost too neatly epitomize the North as it figures in southern literature. Sometimes it is a wasteland awaiting apocalypse, even at times an infernal region of horror. In Alice Walker's *Meridian*, "The subway train rushed through the tunnel screeching and sending out sparks like a meteor. . . . Ninety-sixth street flashed by, then 125th, then there was a screaming halt, a jolt as the car resisted the sudden stop, and the doors slid back with a rubbery thump. The graffiti, streaked on the walls in glowing reds and yellows, did not brighten at all the dark damp cavern of the station." Sometimes the North as viewed by southerners is a region of freezing cold, lacking in human warmth and community. The hero of Robert Penn Warren's *A Place to Come To*, a southern-bred academic who spends most of his life in Chicago, a city he thinks of as a "benign and *fourmillante* hive of de-selfedness," toward the end of the novel goes walking along the shore of Lake Michigan, "watching the sparse flakes ride in over the darkening water, out of the infiniteness of the north," toying with the idea he is "some lost man with nothing before him but the snow-blind lake and nothing behind but the tundra, and only one obligation, or doom—that of survival."

The image of the North as a dark region of cold finds its classic expression in the closing words of William Faulkner's *Absalom, Absalom!*, when Shreve McCannon, the Canadian, asks Quentin Compson, the Mississippian who soon afterward kills himself in Cambridge, Mass.: "'Why do you hate the South?'" Quentin's reply, "quickly, at once, immediately," is "'I dont hate it, . . . I dont,' he said. *I dont hate it* he thought, panting in the cold air, the iron New England dark; *I dont. I dont! I dont hate it! I dont hate it!*" Faulkner's New England is a region of cold, iron, darkness; it is not a good place. And such is the case with the North as depicted in southern literature in general, particularly in southern literature of the 20th century.

Such was not always the case, however. As John Hope Franklin has pointed out, southerners who traveled to and wrote about the North in the early decades of the 19th century found the region "invariably interesting and frequently attractive and admirable." In 1836 John H. Hammond wrote from Philadelphia to his wife in South Carolina: "I never was in so delightful a city. Chestnut Street is worth all I ever saw before in the way of commercial elegance. You must see it." Two years earlier, William Carruthers, in the novel *The Kentuckian in*

New-York, had advised: "Every southerner should visit New York. It would allay provincial prejudices, and calm his excitement against his northern country-men. The people here are warm-hearted, generous, and enthusiastic, in a degree scarcely inferior to our own southerners." Even while Carruthers was testifying to the warmth and generosity of the "northerns," however, the southern penchant for looking favorably, even enviously, upon the North was weakening, and the land of the Yankees was increasingly viewed as a spawning ground of evil and corruption. A negative view of the North was prompted in part by the South's growing defensiveness with regard to the matter of slavery, its sense of being beleaguered in the expanding American union. It may also have been part of the South's emerging sense of itself as, in Lewis Simpson's words, "a special redemptive community fulfilling a divinely appointed role in the drama of history." Perhaps more importantly, the unfavorable view of the North taking shape in southern literature was congruent with criticisms of northern society being formulated by northerners themselves.

William R. Taylor's *Cavalier and Yankee: The Old South and American National Character* notes that early in the 19th century Americans of the North and the South began to worry about the direction their democracy seemed to be taking, "about the kind of aggressive, mercenary self-made man who was making his way in their society. . . . In the face of the threat posed by this new man, Americans—genteel and would-be genteel—began to develop pronounced longings for some form of aristocracy. . . . They sought, they would frankly have conceded, for something a little old-fashioned." The democratic-egalitarian, commercial-industrial North was not a region in which such a fantasy could take root, but the agrarian-hierarchical South did lend itself to such mythologizing. By the 1930s, Taylor points out, the "legendary Southern planter, despite reservations of one kind or another, began to seem almost perfectly suited to fill the need" for a hero who could be invested with admirably aristocratic virtues. Concomitantly, "the acquisitive man, the man on the make, became inseparably associated with the North." In elaborating the myth of Cavalier and Yankee, northern writers, such as Sarah Hale, James K. Paulding, and Harriet Beecher Stowe, were probably more influential than writers from the South.

The image of the North in southern literature is, then, to some extent, a curious legacy *from* the North. That image, at any rate, which has persisted since before the Civil War, unmodified except during those years when evangelists for the New South were wooing northern capital and good feeling, is not very different from the harshly critical portrait of the urban and industrial North to be found in northern writers. O'Connor's brick walls are not as frighteningly alienating as those confronting Melville's Bartleby; Faulkner's Cambridge is almost idyllic if compared to the muddy suburb of James's *The Bostonians*.

It is no surprise, then, that images of the North provided by black southerners, such as Walker and Ellison and Wright, agree with those projected by white southerners. Blyden Jackson has argued that "all negro fiction tends to conceive of its physical world as a sharp dichotomy, with the ghetto as its central figure and its symbolic truth," but such a vision—of the North as a confining and dehumanizing prison—is not alien to the imagination of white southerners (at the beginning of *Sophie's Choice*, William Styron's narrator describes himself "self-exiled to Flatbush," as "another lean and lonesome young Southerner wandering amid the Kingdom of the Jews"). Faulkner would have felt himself in sympathy with the words that begin Richard Wright's *American Hunger* (later retitled *Black Boy*), the account, published only in 1977, of what happened to "black boy" after he had escaped to the North: "My first glimpse of the flat black stretches of Chicago seemed an unreal city whose mythical houses were built of slabs of black coal wreathe in palls of gray smoke." And Faulkner would have sympathized with the ending of his fellow southerner's account of his sojourn in the North. Sitting alone in his narrow room, "watching the sun sink slowly in the chilly May sky," he is nevertheless determined to "hurl words into this darkness and wait for an echo." Alone in the cold dark of the North, he is yet determined "to tell, to march, to fight, to create a sense of the hunger for the life that gnaws in us all, to keep alive in our hearts a sense of the inexpressibly human." Willie Morris, in his memoir *North toward Home* (1967), finds the North a land of opportunity but finds himself drawn toward other expatriate southerners, black and white.

ROBERT WHITE
York University

John Hope Franklin, *A Southern Odyssey: Travelers in the Antebellum North* (1976);
Jay B. Hubbell, *The South in American Literature, 1607–1900* (1954); Blyden Jackson,
The Waiting Years: Essays on American Negro Literature (1976); Lewis P. Simpson, *The
Man of Letters in New England and the South: Essays on the History of the Literary
Vocation in America* (1973); Robert B. Stepto, *From Behind the Veil: A Study of Afro-
American Narrative* (1979); William R. Taylor, *Cavalier and Yankee: The Old South
and American National Character* (1961).

Periodicals

The southern periodicals of paramount cultural importance have been the literary magazines, the most impressive of which were the antebellum *Southern*

Review (Charleston) (1828–32), the *Southern Literary Messenger* (1834–64), the *Southern Quarterly Review* (1842–57), and the *Magnolia* (1840–43). Twentieth-century titles of note include the *Sewanee Review* (1892–), the *Southern Review* (Baton Rouge) (1935–42; n.s., 1965–), the *South Atlantic Quarterly* (1902–), and the *Virginia Quarterly Review* (1925–). The problems that beset the antebellum editor were given a definitive summary in two letters from William Gilmore Simms, printed January and February of 1841 in the *Magnolia*, which Simms, against his better judgment, would soon edit. Literary magazines were begun with "confident hope and bold assurance" but ended in "early abandonment" because two essentials were lacking in the South—contributors who possessed literary talent and subscribers who could pay when promised. The task of the 20th-century southern editor has been easier because he often has the support of a college or university as well as having contributors with literary talent.

Although most literary magazines in the 19th century floundered and failed, agricultural magazines, such as the *American Farmer* (1819–97) and the *Southern Planter* (1841–1973), survived and even prospered modestly by reaching the planter class, from whom the literary magazines could never entice much-needed subscriptions. Religious magazines also outlived literary magazines; but their flowering was not until the 1850s, after southern churches had broken away from the North and were providing financial support for their own magazines. At least two political and economic magazines, *Niles' Weekly Register* (1811–49) and *DeBow's Review* (1847–61), persisted and apparently thrived for a reason Simms knew too well: the real passion of the southern male reader was for politics. It was, therefore, essential that historical and political articles have a prominent place in each issue of a literary magazine. A strictly belles-lettres magazine had no chance of survival in the South. The *Orion* (1842–44) was founded by William Richards, a scholarly minister, and his artist brother, Thomas Addison Richards, with the intention of publishing southern literature and featuring etchings of southern scenes. Political articles were added too late. The *Orion* was the handsomest antebellum magazine, but it perished in less than two years.

Although the *South Carolina Weekly Museum* (1797–98) is credited as being the pioneer southern magazine, the first with tangible influence on the character of subsequent magazines was the *Southern Review*, edited in Charleston by William and Stephen Elliott and the scholarly lawyer Hugh Swinton Legaré. Legaré, with his impressive classical learning, his devotion to neoclassical tenets, his rational political conservatism, and his judicial fairness as critic, contributed notably to the self-image of southern editors. Southern magazines have been edited, usually briefly, by men of letters (Poe, Simms, Hayne, Tate); but most of the work has been done by professionals like Legaré, Daniel K. Whitaker, and John Reuben Thompson, all of whom had a strong ulterior motive of promoting a southern literature to rival the best efforts in the North.

These editors of antebellum southern literary magazines were consistently conservative in their political and social views and in their literary tastes. New ideas (such as transcendentalism, positivism, and unitarianism) and new literary movements (including romanticism, and, later, naturalism) were regarded with suspicion. The editors were professedly traditional in their views of what should be said about literature. Henry Timrod, writing in *Russell's* in 1857, complained of the lingering influence of the Scottish rhetoricians. Lord Kames was still the model for a literary critic in Charleston, and Hugh Blair was the author of what continued to be the most widely used rhetoric in the South. Until Timrod and Paul Hamilton Hayne started writing for *Russell's*, there was little interest in sympathetic or reproductive criticism, advocated for indigenous American works in the North as early as the 1830s and 1840s. Southern editors were apparently convinced that they were judicious in contrast to many northern editors, who were seen as unfair to southern writers and as advocates of northern writers. By the 1850s, however, sectional tensions had made it almost impossible for editors like Thompson of the *Southern Literary Messenger* and Paul Hamilton Hayne of *Russell's Magazine* to maintain any pretense of objectivity about northern literature and magazines.

There was an attempt to revive southern magazines immediately after the Civil War and to continue the traditions of maintaining critical standards against the intrusions of popular taste and of promoting a proper southern literature. Editors of the new magazines of the 1860s, *Southern Opinion*, *Southern Magazine*, and the *Land We Love*, tended to be "unreconstructed," idealizing the Old South and showing less sympathy toward new trends in literature than the antebellum editors had. New writers, including Sidney Lanier and Thomas Nelson Page, were introduced; but southern magazines still faced the old problem of few contributors and subscribers. There was a new problem as well: southern magazines lacked the resources to compete with a new type of periodical, the pictorial magazine, most successfully exemplified by *Harper's Weekly*. The best literary magazine before the 1890s was the *Southern Bivouac* (1882–87), which published some of the best work of Paul Hamilton Hayne.

The renaissance of southern magazines began in the 1890s with the *Sewanee Review* in 1892, published by the University of the South, and the *South Atlantic Quarterly*, started 10 years later in 1902 at Trinity College, now Duke University. The *Sewanee Review* continued the tradition of promoting southern literature without being provincial; the *South Atlantic Quarterly*, founded by historian

John Spencer Bassett, began with an emphasis on social and political issues, earning a reputation for controversy, and gradually became more literary. By the time these two magazines were joined in 1925 by the *Virginia Quarterly Review* and in 1935 by a new *Southern Review*, the dream of the antebellum editors was being realized. The Southern Literary Renaissance, sparked by the writings of William Faulkner, Robert Penn Warren, Katherine Anne Porter, John Crowe Ransom, Allen Tate, Thomas Wolfe, and others, was well under way.

Twentieth-century southern magazines had two important advantages over their predecessors—the flowering of southern literature and, in some cases, a dependable means of financial support, the southern college or university. Editors could at long last pay contributors and more nearly compete with northern magazines. Southern magazines could retain their southern identity but become truly national and even international. Modernism in literature and in literary criticism could be supported. The avant-garde, however, was not pushed. With few exceptions—the *Fugitive* (1922–25) in Nashville and the *Double Dealer* (1921–26) in New Orleans—the South did not develop the true home of the avant-garde, the little magazines, and those that did appear were not experimental. Conservatism and traditionalism still prevailed. There were conservative social and political essays. The criticism of industrialization and of positivism in philosophy begun by George Fitzhugh in *DeBow's Review* in the 1850s and 1860s was renewed in the Agrarian essays of Donald Davidson, Allen Tate, John Crowe Ransom, and other contributors to the 1930 Agrarian manifesto *I'll Take My Stand*. Literary criticism and formalist analysis were practiced in the *Southern Review* in the 1930s under Robert Penn Warren and Cleanth Brooks; in southern critic John Crowe Ransom's *Kenyon Review*, a bastion of the New Criticism; and in the *Sewanee Review* under Allen Tate in the 1940s.

The day of the southern literary magazine had come. Some magazines were as influential as northern magazines. Circulation of the *Sewanee Review* and the *Southern Review* even exceeded 3,000. And yet a proper perspective on these literary magazines must be maintained. As far as a mass southern audience is concerned, the situation has not changed greatly. In 1860 *Southern Field and Fireside* (1859–65) could afford the luxury of hiring the discouraged John Reuben Thompson away from the *Southern Literary Messenger* for the handsome salary of $2,000 a year. Today's *Field and Fireside* equivalent, *Southern Living* (1966–), is the most widely read southern magazine, with a reported total readership of more than 16 million.

The latest southern-based periodical to make an almost successful bid for a national audience, entirely on its own without institutional support, is the *Oxford American* (1992–), subtitled "The Southern Magazine of Good Writing."

Founded by editor Marc Smirnoff in Oxford, Miss., as a monthly, it became noted for its smart graphics, effective use of photographs, and good fiction by the latest writers of note. It became especially well known for its annual Music Issue featuring largely overlooked southern musicians and including a compact disc of selected songs to accompany the articles. Never fully gaining its financial footing, the *Oxford American* moved to less frequent publication and ceased publication at one point until best-selling author John Grisham purchased the magazine in 1994. Although the magazine was livelier than ever, the investment never paid off, so publishing ceased again in 2001. In 2003 the University of Central Arkansas in Conway revived the publication with a substantial investment, and it continues there as a quarterly to maintain its mission "to explore the American South through good writing."

RICHARD J. CALHOUN
Clemson University

Richard J. Calhoun, *Southern Literary Journal* (Fall 1970); John C. Guilds, *Southern Literary Journal* (Spring 1972); Jay B. Hubbell, in *Culture in the South*, ed. W. T. Couch (1934), *The South in American Literature* (1954); Robert D. Jacobs, *Southern Literary Journal* (Fall 1969); Frank L. Mott, *A History of American Magazines*, 5 vols. (1930–68); Marc Smirnoff, ed., *Best of the Oxford American: Ten Years from the Southern Magazine of Good Writing* (2002); John R. Welsh, *Southern Literary Journal* (April 1971).

Poetry

Despite widespread assumptions to the contrary, poetry was common in the colonial South. While relatively little poetry by colonial "southern" poets has previously been incorporated into anthologies of American poetry that purport to represent that historical era, the composition of poems was an everyday aspect of life among white southerners from various socioeconomic backgrounds. People across the South recited poems at social gatherings and incorporated original poems (as well as poems by English poets) into letters, diaries, newspapers, pamphlets, and books. Poetry composed by colonial southerners tended to be highly imitative of the work of the English masters. For example, one important poem written near the fringe of the southern colonies—"The Sot-Weed Factor; or, A Voyage to Maryland, A Satyr" (1708) by Ebenezer Cooke (c. 1670– c. 1732), an emigrant from England to Maryland—was closely modeled upon English poet Samuel Butler's poem of political satire, "Hudibras." Similarly, "A Journey from Patapsko to Annapolis, April 4, 1730" (1732)—the best-known poem by Richard Lewis (c. 1700–1734), a Welsh immigrant to Maryland—was strongly influenced stylistically by the highly formal pastoral poetry of such early 18th-century English poets as Alexander Pope and James Thomson. Indeed, despite the strain of stylistic imitation (particularly regarding form and metrics) among colonial southern poets, the most distinctive poems by Cooke, Lewis, and other poets living and writing in the southern colonies broke thematically from Old World models by imaginatively assessing the New World natural environment and insightfully reflecting colonial experiences (such as the interactions between settlers and Native Americans). Additionally, many poems from the southern colonies responded to the unique religious, political, and social issues of that formative period in American history.

Historically, few 18th- and 19th-century poets from the southern states were included in the American literary canon, an outgrowth of the nation's elitist attitude that the South was culturally retrograde. That attitude was notoriously articulated in journalist H. L. Mencken's 1917 *New York Evening Mail* article entitled "The Sahara of the Bozart." Edgar Allan Poe (1809–49)—the sole "southern" poet associated with the pre–World War I South whose work has been deemed worthy of widespread anthologizing and study—was primarily reared in Virginia, yet Poe's highly imaginative poetry was the antithesis of "regional" writing (in part because Poe spent most of his adulthood living outside of the South). A few 19th-century authors from the South were included in the canon of American literature as "minor" poets, including South Carolina's William Gilmore Simms (1806–70) and Georgia's Sidney Lanier (1842–81).

Few people then or now would attempt to argue that, other than the finest poems of Poe, 19th-century southern poetry was aesthetically the equal of the best poems by numerous 19th century poets from other American regions. Nonetheless, the marginalization of southern poetry in mainstream American culture has unfortunately led to the neglect of poems that not only are interesting in themselves but also serve as fascinating documents revealing the complexities inherent in southern culture. For instance, the poetry of George Moses Horton (1797–c. 1883)—composed orally when Horton was a North Carolina slave and copied down by whites who had commissioned the poems—is illustrative of the role of poetry in alleviating racial tensions between socially segregated people. Also, the poetry by several white wartime poets—most significantly, South Carolinians Henry Timrod (1828–67) and Paul Hamilton Hayne (1830–86)—reflects the unique circumstances of life in the Confederate States of America. Additionally, poems by postwar southern poets often articulated southern attitudes toward the Lost Cause myth or embodied the southern involvement in the national "local-color" literary movement (the latter type of postwar southern poetry, often sold for publication in national periodicals, included poems written in dialect, nature lyrics, and inspirational verses).

Much of the previous disregard for or inattention to the poetry of the South dissipated in the early 1920s with the emergence of the group of southern authors known as the Fugitives (named after a literary journal, the *Fugitive*, that the group produced during the period 1922–25). Associated with Vanderbilt University, the Fugitives included several poets who taught at Vanderbilt, including Tennesseans John Crowe Ransom (1888–1974) and Donald Davidson (1893–1968), as well as Kentuckian Allen Tate (1899–1979); also part of the Fugitives was a Vanderbilt undergraduate student from Kentucky, Robert Penn Warren (1905–89). Ransom soon developed a national reputation for writing well-crafted poems—such as the much-anthologized "Bells for John Whiteside's Daughter" (1924)—that possessed the qualities of verbal economy and understatement. In his best-known poem, "Ode to the Confederate Dead" (1936), Tate, an influential literary and cultural critic, interpreted the legacy of the Civil War from a southern perspective, and yet the poem rejected the tragic sentimentalism toward the defeated South inherent to the Lost Cause myth, opting instead to dispassionately question the direction of the modern South. While less acclaimed than Ransom and Tate, Davidson displayed skill at incorporating traditional narrative techniques and elements of folklore into his otherwise modernist poetry. Warren would eventually become one of the most accomplished and revered figures in southern letters, and poetry was a vital part of his diverse literary legacy.

Wanting to project a more explicitly cultural rather than exclusively literary mission, the Fugitives in the late 1920s reconfigured under the name the Agrarians, and that group, in its 1930 collection of essays entitled *I'll Take My Stand*, championed, among other aspects of the southern cultural heritage, the South's historical ties to a rural, agricultural way of life. Poetry played a less central role among the Agrarians, yet in 1937 Warren and critic Cleanth Brooks published the influential book *Understanding Poetry*, which popularized the mode of close text-based literary analysis that John Crowe Ransom in a 1941 book would term "New Criticism"; that approach to interpreting literature dominated literary studies in the United States for nearly three decades. Given the marginalization of southern culture through World War I, it was ironic that, because of the work of the Fugitives/Agrarians, by World War II the southern intellect had become a significant force in American culture.

Three Vanderbilt students who were working on degrees at the beginning of the Great Depression—James Still (1906–2001), from Alabama; Jesse

Stuart (1907–84), a native of Kentucky; and Georgian Don West (1906–92)—all studied with and were inspired by Fugitive/Agrarian group members. Still, Stuart, and West within the next decade published important books of poetry that would collectively launch a renaissance in Appalachian literature. Several leading participants in a more famous literary movement, the New York City–based Harlem Renaissance of the 1920s, were black poets from the South—the most influential of whom was James Weldon Johnson (1871–1938), originally from Florida. Other poets from the pre–World War II era who were nationally prominent for composing poetry in the modernist style include three white southerners: Georgia native Conrad Aiken (1889–1973); John Peale Bishop (1892–1944), from West Virginia; and Arkansan John Gould Fletcher (1886–1950).

After World War II, with southern perspectives gaining acceptance in American culture, a new generation of poets from the South played central roles in American letters, including Randall Jarrell (1914–65), a native of Tennessee; Floridian Donald Justice (1925–2004); A. R. Ammons (1926–2001), from North Carolina; and Georgia native James Dickey (1923–97). Those poets produced poems that were among the most often studied, anthologized, and honored works of American literature of that era. In the early 1950s the most artistically successful experimental school of poetry in America was based in the South—at the now defunct Black Mountain College, located in western North Carolina. Given the gap between that group's aesthetically radical art and the traditionalism of southern culture, it was perhaps inevitable that only one of the Black Mountain poets was a southerner: North Carolina native Jonathan Williams (b. 1929).

By the 1960s, the South was anything but the cultural wasteland that, 50 years earlier, Mencken and many other nonsouthern critics had perceived the South to be. Indeed, in the past half century, southern poetry has been as recognized as the poetry of any other American region, with poets from the South—Justice, Ammons, Dickey, Virginia natives Ruth Stone (b. 1915), Henry Taylor (b. 1942), and Claudia Emerson (b. 1957), Kentucky's Wendell Berry (b. 1934), North Carolina's Fred Chappell (b. 1936), Tennessean Charles Wright (b. 1935), Louisiana native Yusef Komunyakaa (b. 1947), and Arkansan Miller Williams (b. 1930)—receiving at least one major national poetry award. Three of the most popular poets of the 20th century are African American women with southern connections, including Maya Angelou (b. 1928), who spent key formative years in Arkansas; Nikki Giovanni (b. 1943), who was reared in Tennessee; and Alice Walker (b. 1944), from Georgia. Illustrating the social diversity of southern poetry are the works of three contemporary poets who in their poetry blend southern perspectives with perspectives from other ethnic backgrounds: Texas's Naomi Shihab Nye (b. 1952), whose ancestors were Palestinian; Georgia-based Judith Ortiz Cofer (b. 1952), who is Puerto Rican by birth; and Tennessee's Marilou Awiakta (b. 1936), who is Cherokee.

A full list of other contemporary southern poets who have published excellent poetry in books, chapbooks, periodicals, and via other venues of communication would be quite lengthy. Suffice it to say that poetry in the South is very much a living, ongoing phenomenon, with new perspectives on an ever-changing region being expressed into the 21st century through both long-familiar and recently emerged poetic voices. In a 1997 interview conducted for the *Carolina Quarterly*, poet Robert Morgan, a native of North Carolina, asserted that "the best poetry being written these days is being written by Southerners, white and black, men and women. Because they still have subject matter. They believe that poetry's about something. Not just about language, but about stories, about history, about characters, about nature."

In a region where poetry has historically been created by tight-knit groups of poets (from the Fugitive/Agrarians to the Black Mountain poets), it is hardly surprising that southern poetry has been nurtured within groups founded to address clearly identified and deeply felt social missions. The unifying principles for such groups have included celebrations of gender (e.g., the Appalachian Women's Alliance), explorations of ethnicity (for instance, the Lexington, Ky.–based Affrilachian poets circle), and defenses of subregional identity (one example being the Appalachian Poetry Project of the late 1970s), as well as articulations of protest (such as the collective of writers—several of them poets—from Kentucky who in 2005 embarked on a speaking and reading tour of eastern Kentucky to protest mountaintop-removal coal mining in Appalachia).

In recent decades, as poetry was increasingly associated with degreed writing programs based at both private and public colleges and universities, an increasingly specialized group of people relied heavily upon a time-honored and rather stratified procedure for getting poems to readers: first, the publication of poems by numerous poets in literary periodicals and book anthologies, and, second, the collection of poems by an individual poet into chapbooks or books published by small presses and by nonprofit university presses. Some of the most important and visible periodicals based in the South that have regularly published poetry by southern writers have included the *Georgia Review*, the *Virginia Quarterly Review, Callaloo: A Journal of African Diaspora Arts and Letters, Shenandoah: The Washington and Lee University Review*, the *Sewanee Re-*

view, the *Southern Review*, *Appalachian Journal*, *Appalachian Heritage*, *Southern Poetry Review*, and *CrossRoads: A Southern Culture Annual*. Small presses that have specialized in publishing books containing work by individual southern poets in recent years have included Iris Press, Sow's Ear Press, Sarabande Books, Gnomon Press, and Wind Publications, while the Louisiana State University Press, the University of Georgia Press, and the University of Arkansas Press have been notably committed to publishing collections from southern poets.

Emergent technologies and recent social trends have provided new opportunities by which people in the South can appreciate and disseminate poetry. Online journals, printed books released on compact disc, and file-shared recordings of spoken contemporary poems have gained popularity as the technologies that render them possible are increasingly found in homes, classrooms, and libraries. In recent years, as social mechanisms for celebrating and promoting poetry—from writers' conferences and workshops to poetry book signings, poetry readings, and "slams" (the latter coinage refers to a specific type of poetry reading that involves pronounced performance elements)—have gained popularity across the South, poetry has moved from being viewed as the domain of a relatively few people to being embraced as a populist cultural expression to be enjoyed by many, many people.

TED OLSON
East Tennessee State University

Charlotte H. Beck, *The Fugitive Legacy: A Critical History* (2001); Richard Beale Davis, *Literature and Society in Early Virginia, 1608–1840* (1973); Joseph M. Flora and Lucinda H. MacKethan, eds., *The Companion to Southern Literature: Themes, Genres, Places, People, Movements, and Motifs* (2002); Joseph M. Flora and Amber Vogel, *Southern Writers: A New Biographical Dictionary* (2006); Edward Halsey Foster, *Understanding the Black Mountain Poets* (1995); Maurice G. Fulton, *Southern Life in Southern Literature: Selections of Representative Prose and Poetry* (1917); Addison Hibbard, *The Lyric South, An Anthology of Recent Poetry from the South* (1928); Parks Lanier Jr., *The Poetics of Appalachian Space* (1991); Guy Owen and Mary C. Williams, eds., *Contemporary Southern Poetry: An Anthology* (1979); Edd Winfield Parks, *Southern Poets: Representative Selections, with Introduction, Bibliography, and Notes* (1936); David Rigsbee and Steven Ford Brown, *Invited Guest: An Anthology of Twentieth-Century Southern Poetry* (2001); William Gilmore Simms, ed., *War Poetry of the South* (1867); Leon Stokesbury, *The Made Thing: An Anthology of Contemporary Southern Poetry* (1999).

Popular Literature

The romantic South has been a mainstay of popular fiction in the United States from the beginning of mass-market publishing. John Pendleton Kennedy, the first major novelist to set fiction on southern plantations, achieved early popularity with *Swallow Barn; or, A Sojourn in the Old Dominion* (1832) and *Horse-Shoe Robinson* (1835). These novels were patterned after the works of Sir Walter Scott and painted a picture of the Virginia gentry and romantic plantation life that would become typical in popular fiction during the next decades. Almost immediately, southern settings became the symbol for romance, aristocracy, gallant chivalry, grandeur, and a life-style of elegant leisure.

By the 1850s the "plantation romance" had become moderately successful. Eliza Ann Dupuy set her 1857 novel, *The Planter's Daughter: A Tale of Louisiana*, in Louisiana, and Mary J. Holmes, who published *Meadow Brook* that same year, wrote of plantation life in Kentucky. In general, these works portrayed the South as a region containing only plantations, genteel planters, delicate and beautiful women, and contented slaves.

None of the antebellum novelists portraying southern life and culture, however, was the equal of Emma Dorothy Eliza Nevitte (E. D. E. N.) Southworth. One of the most prolific and popular American novelists of all time, Southworth used plantation settings in her romantic novels. Among her many best-selling works were *Shannondale* (1850) and *Virginia and Magdalene* (1852). Like all of her books, Southworth's novels of the South were contemporary "domestic romances," a form that dominated American best sellers until late in the century. Typically, Southworth's tales offered no truly distinctive southern themes, but they did contribute greatly to popular imagery of the plantation South. Southworth and her contemporaries filled their novels with palatial homes, endless social gaiety, princely and gallant aristocrats, and sentimental belles.

Harriet Beecher Stowe's *Uncle Tom's Cabin* (1852), essentially a domestic novel, not only caused a stir over the slavery issue but also spawned numerous novels in imitation and elicited a healthy number of proslavery novels. In spite of Stowe's didactic, antislavery tone, *Uncle Tom's Cabin* tended to reinforce the image of romance and aristocracy associated with the South. In fact, the true villain of the novel, Simon Legree, was a northerner. Although Stowe's book was intended to condemn and vilify the institution of slavery, the work also contributed to the popular image of the South as a romantic region, an image that has dominated popular fiction since the antebellum era.

The Civil War and the end of the slave system did not weaken the impulse of popular authors to glorify the plantation South. Quite the contrary, the antebellum South took on new romance as a "lost civilization," and popular writers celebrated the Old South with nostalgia. Joel Chandler Harris offered his *Uncle Remus* tales from 1888 through 1906. These "folktales" reflected a world of racial harmony on the South's plantations. Similarly, F. Hopkinson Smith's popular novelette of 1891, *Colonel Carter of Cartersville*, delineated a world of contented servants and genteel masters.

The works of Harris and Smith were typical and widely popular, but their impact was not nearly so great as that of Thomas Nelson Page. More than any other postbellum writer, Page codified the popular image of the Old South rounding out the traditional stereotypes of the beautiful young belle, her chivalrous beau, and the faithful slave. Like almost all of his works, *In Ole Virginia; or, Marse Chan, and Other Stories* (1887) was a collection of short stories, which centered on romance among the southern aristocracy. Narrated by elderly freedmen, the stories recalled the glory and tranquillity of the perfect social order that, in Page's view, prevailed before the war. Most significantly, they depicted loyal and totally devoted slaves who believed that their own happiness was tied to that of their masters.

Later in his career, Page became disillusioned with the state of race relations in the post–Civil War South. In *Red Rock: A Chronicle of Reconstruction* (1898) and *The Red Riders* (1924), Page developed more sinister characterizations of black people. Along with Thomas Dixon Jr., who published *The Clansman: An American Drama* in 1905, Page blamed the South's difficulties, particularly racial and economic problems, on the freedmen and northern interventionists. Implicit in the Page and Dixon novels of the Reconstruction South was the glorification of the Old South as an idyllic Garden of Eden.

From about 1890 and continuing into the 1930s the historical novel was a dominant genre of popular fiction in the United States, and novels of the antebellum South assumed a central position. Most of the Old South best sellers that emerged were of the "moonlight-and-magnolias" variety. Mary Johnston, who wrote more than 20 historical novels, penned significant portrayals of both the antebellum and postbellum South. Her *Miss Delicia Allen* (1933) was a classic story of aristocratic grace and romance on a Virginia plantation, and *The Long Roll* (1911) remains one of the best popular treatments of the impact of the Civil War. Stark Young's widely successful *So Red the Rose* (1934) explored life on a Mississippi plantation. Young continued the tradition developed by Page, and he seemed to argue that the Old South was a highly admirable society and that its demise after the Civil War was a crushing blow to civilization itself. Ellen Glasgow was not only popular but talented as well. Her novel *The Battle-Ground* (1902) demonstrated that the South could be portrayed as a many-faceted society with flaws as well as strengths. Although Glasgow portrayed the southern elite in rather grand and romantic fashion, she also recognized the importance of the yeoman farmer and the poor white in the southern social structure.

By the mid-1930s, popular writers, following Glasgow's lead, seemed to be on the verge of offering a more accurate and realistic treatment of the Old South. But a single event, the publication in 1936 of *Gone with the Wind*, brought popular fiction squarely back into the romantic and sentimental portrayal that had flourished for so long. Margaret Mitchell's incredibly successful novel relied on stock settings and stereotypes to mythologize the Old South more effectively and more popularly than any other book before or since. Moreover, the sections of *Gone with the Wind* that deal with the Reconstruction South clearly portray the antebellum era as a lost and glamorous period of aristocratic gentility and high romance.

Mitchell's immediate successor was Frank Yerby, a black writer whose short fiction exploring racial issues had won literary acclaim. Yerby turned to historical fiction in 1946 with the publication of *The Foxes of Harrow*. He eventually became one of the most popular novelists of all time. Although he worked within a "pot-boiler" formula, Yerby was always careful to research the historical background of his tales in meticulous detail. His works continued the romantic tradition established by Margaret Mitchell, but Yerby was also careful to include details of life in the slave quarters. Additionally, Yerby's portrayal of sexuality among the planter elite was more explicit than earlier writers'.

Yerby's popularity undoubtedly piqued the public's interest in romantic fiction set in the Old South. Kyle Onstott cashed in on the trend with *Mandingo* in 1957, the same year that Yerby issued *Fairoaks*. But the novels were quite different. Yerby's novel provided a wealth of accurate information related to slave life and culture, including a sensitive and painfully detailed passage on the slave trade. On the other hand, *Mandingo* can make no claim to historic accuracy. Onstott's novel and its several sequels are still in print, and total sales for the series are around 30 million copies.

The world of *Mandingo* is a miasmic wasteland of slave-breeding plantations, populated by vicious masters, their drunken wives, generously endowed "breeding studs," and eager and wanton "breeding wenches." *Mandingo* might be passed off as a prurient example of the worst tendencies in popular fiction were it not for its impact on the publishing industry. Onstott's success was so great that hundreds of imitations, mostly paperback originals, were published over the next quarter of a century. All of them relied on sensational portrayals of interracial sexuality, degenerate aristocrats, and black people who found it impossible to control their libidinous desires. The widespread popularity of the post-Onstott "plantation novel" attests to his importance in developing popular imagery of the Old South as a land of "lust in the dust."

Onstott's successors in this genre included Norman Daniels, the author of skillful paperback originals in several genres, who created the Wyndward Plantation series (1969 and after), and Raymond Giles, who wrote the Sabrehill saga (1970–75). Marie de Jourlet offered several novels in the Windhaven series beginning in 1978, and Richard Tresillian initiated his Bondmaster series in 1977, with each novel enjoying an initial print run of roughly 700,000 copies. Although Tresillian's series is set in the West Indies, the novels are clearly modeled on Onstott's work, and the books often use details and portrayals based on United States settings. Finally, Lonnie Coleman's hardback best seller *Beulah Land* (1973) evolved into an influential series, which was eventually adapted as a controversial television miniseries. Coleman's history was somewhat more accurate than that of the other popular novelists, but his concentration on themes of miscegenation, degenerate gentry, and "women on the pedestal" clearly indicated his debt to Onstott's work.

Although the so-called poor white generally has been neglected in popular fiction set in the South, the paperback reprinting of Erskine Caldwell's *Tobacco Road* (1947; hardcover edition 1932) spawned an impressive trend in "backwoods" novels that extended throughout the 1950s and maintained moderate success in the 1960s. *Tobacco Road* was a racy tale of poor sharecroppers and seemed to strike a responsive chord among readers who had tired of the "moonlight-and-magnolias" imagery. The paperback sales of the work far outstripped the publisher's expectations, and soon dozens of authors were rushing to cash in on the trend. Indeed, the paperback publishing revolution seemed to provide the perfect outlet for Caldwell's many imitators. In the words of one publisher, the "backwoods" novels centered on the "earthy humor, the primitive passions and quaint ways of Southern hill folk." These "folk" were libidinous, raucous, and illiterate, and the stories involved cockfighting, moonshining, prostitution, gambling, and general depravity.

Other notable "backwoods" authors included John Faulkner (William's brother), whose *Cabin Road* (1951) was reprinted at least six times; Jack Boone, who offered *Dossie Bell Is Dead* in 1951; and Charles Williams, who published a series of novels using variations on a single theme. Under titles such as *Hill Girl* (1951), *River Girl* (1951), and *Girl Out Back* (1958), Williams penned stories in which a dishonest and somewhat brutish "po' white" meets his match in a tough and ruthless backwoods siren with whom he falls in love. Williams was

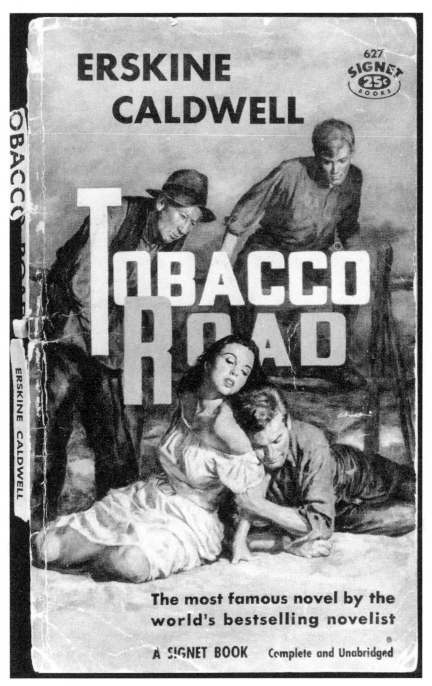

Cover from 1956 paperback edition of Erskine Caldwell's best seller
(Charles Reagan Wilson Collection, University of Mississippi, Oxford)

imitated by many, including Cord Wainer (pseudonym of Thomas B. Dewey) with *Mountain Girl* (1952), Allen O'Quinn with *Swamp Brat* (1953), and Jack Woodford and John B. Thompson with *Swamp Hoyden* (no date).

Although dozens of additional authors might be mentioned, none was able to capture the spirit of the "backwoods" formula and play to the demands of the audience quite so well as Harry Whittington, who also wrote under the pseudonyms of Hallam Whitney and Whit Harrison. His works included *Backwoods Hussy* (1952), *Shack Road* (1953), *Cracker Girl* (1953), *Shanty Road* (1954), and *Backwoods Tramp* (1959). His "backwoods" tales were enormously popular and eventually gave the formula its name. Later in his career, Whittington helped to complete the Falconhurst Series begun by Kyle Onstott, and he created the popular Blackoaks series of plantation novels that were published under his Ashley Carter pseudonym.

Even after the rise of Kyle Onstott and the backwoods formula, both considered male genres, there remained a market for less violent and less racist versions of romantic fiction set in the antebellum South. This genre continued to maintain substantial popularity into the 1980s. Mainly targeted at women, historic romances in an Old South setting were very similar to the traditional historical romance set in any period. By the 1970s the form was referred to as the "bodice ripper" by critics. In these tales the principal focus was on the romantic involvement of the heroine and a rough but handsome hero, a macho figure who often nearly raped the heroine in their first sexual encounter, an act that only served to heighten her desire for him. The setting was essentially a mere backdrop for the romance, but the overall portrayal served to extend and popularize the "moonlight-and-magnolias" image of the Old South, albeit in somewhat unsavory fashion.

Many authors wrote popular novels of this sort, and recent representative titles include *Wild Honey* (1982) by Fern Michaels, Julia Grice's *Emerald Fire* (1978), and *Texas Temptress* (1985) by Jean Haught. Other novelists adapted the Old South setting to closely related genres in the general field of romantic fiction. For example, Jane Aiken Hodge's *Savannah Purchase* (1970) is little more than the traditional "Gothic romance" set in the Old South. Even major figures in feminine romantic fiction, such as Kathleen Woodiwiss, could not resist the temptation to set their sentimental and always passionate tales in the antebellum South. Woodiwiss's romantic *Ashes in the Wind* (1979) is typical of the feminine fiction set in the Old South during the past decades. It recounts the tale of "an impudent, plantation bred beauty" with "reckless bravado" who falls in love with a "ramrod straight Yankee" who renders her "incapable of reason." Such paperback romances, coupled with occasional best-selling historical fiction, such as John Jakes's *North and South* (1982), have helped to maintain the popular romantic image of the "lost civilization" of the antebellum South.

Popular fiction set in the South traditionally provided a consistent and rather limited perspective on the region since the rise of mass fiction during the two decades prior to the Civil War. Geographically the region was depicted either as one great plantation or as an impoverished wasteland of "hill folk" and backwoods hamlets. Only two levels of society were portrayed, the elite planter class (including their slaves) and the extremely poor white class. In the former case, novelists have either presented a highly idealized and romantic image or have depicted a depraved and sadistic society that glorifies violence and justifies racism. In portraying poor whites, writers have contented themselves with simplistic images of illiterate and sexually active bumpkins. Black southerners have most often appeared in fiction set in the antebellum era and have been relegated to one of two categories—wanton, sex-starved slaves or contented, childlike slaves intent on making their masters happy.

More recently, popular writers are critical of parts of the South's culture and less given to use of older southern stereotypes. Pat Conroy, for example, has written several portrayals of the southern family, drawing on autobiographical references to his dysfunctional family and his strict father. The old domestic novel, long dominated by women, is turned on its head, as father-son relationships recur as the central ones in Conroy's work. His popular appeal was witnessed with films made of his novels *The Great Santini*, *The Lords of Discipline*, and *The Prince of Tides*.

John Grisham has penned a long list of best sellers, beginning with *A Time to Kill* (1989), that draw from traditional southern themes of racism and injustice but with the central figures typically, for Grisham, being attorneys. Grisham is the king of suspense thrillers, using southern settings, such as Memphis (*The Firm* [1991]) and New Orleans (*The Pelican Brief* [1992]). Hollywood has spread Grisham's popularity even farther through film versions of his works.

Like Grisham's work, the novels of two other popular southern writers, Anne Rivers Siddons and Jan Karon, focus on the contemporary South and make use of the settings and genres different from early southern popular literature. Siddons sets most of her 18 books in Georgia or in other parts of the South. She especially writes about Atlanta and its surrounding smaller communities. *Peachtree Road* (1989) is her best-selling novel, described by Pat Conroy as "the southern novel for our generation." Her characters are middle class, identifiable modern types living in urban and suburban worlds. Her most recent novels, *Islands* (2004) and *Sweetwater Creek* (2005), are set in the South Carolina Lowcountry.

Jan Karon, from Blowing Rock, N.C., has carved out a best-selling niche, the Mitford series of nine novels set in the fictional town of Mitford, N.C. The first, *At Home in Mitford* (1994), introduced Father Tim, the bachelor Anglican rector who is a central character in the saga. The series has sold more than 25 million books and led to Karon's related children's books, Mitford Christmas gift books, and such spin-offs as *Patches of Godlight: Father Tim's Favorite Quotes* (2001). Karon's South is a hill country—"the green hills" is a recurring phrase to describe Mitford's place of loving people. Old southern issues of the burdens of history, racial tensions, and poverty seem far away in this new popular literature coming from the region.

CHRISTOPHER D. GEIST
Bowling Green State University

James C. Cobb, *Away Down South: A History of Southern Identity* (2005); Bill Crider, *Journal of Popular Culture* (Winter 1982); F. Garvin Davenport Jr., *The Myth of Southern History: Historical Consciousness in Twentieth-Century Southern Literature* (1967); Robert B. Downs, *Books that Changed the South* (1977); Betina Entzminger, in *The Companion to Southern Literature*, ed. Joseph M. Flora and Lucinda H. MacKethan (2002); Francis Pendleton Gaines, *The Southern Plantation: A Study in the Development and the Accuracy of a Tradition* (1925); Christopher D. Geist, *Southern Quarterly* (Spring 1980); Dennis Hall, ed., *Studies in Popular Culture* (October 1996); Anne Goodwyn Jones, *Tomorrow Is Another Day: The Woman Writer in the South, 1859–1936* (1981); Jack Temple Kirby, *Media-Made Dixie: The South in the American Imagination* (1978); James M. Mellard, *Journal of Popular Culture* (Summer 1971); Elizabeth Moss, *Domestic Novelists in the Old South* (1992); C. Michael Smith, *Journal of Popular Culture* (Winter 1982).

Postcolonial Southern Literature

"Postcolonial Southern literature" denotes less a particular group of southern texts than the application to southern literature of postcolonial theory, a set of critical principles originally developed to help understand the hybrid literatures, cultures, and senses of identity of Asian, African, and Caribbean nations during and after their experiences of European colonialism. Over time postcolonial theory has proved much more widely useful, but applying it to the South can still be complicated. Historically, three often-conflicting southern populations have considered themselves colonized, and their various literatures often reflect a sense of oppression as palpable as the more commonly noted senses of community and place. Native southerners were colonized by European settlers; southerners of African descent often presented the struggle for civil rights as part of an anticolonial struggle for freedom by people of color worldwide; and southerners of European descent routinely compared themselves, in the long wake of the Civil War and Reconstruction, to invaded, conquered, and oppressed nations such as Poland. This last view took its most intellectually respectable and influential form in historian C. Vann Woodward's observation that "the South had undergone an experience that it could share with no other part of America—though it is shared by nearly all the peoples of Europe and Asia—the experience of military defeat, occupation, and reconstruction." For nearly half a century, historians and literary critics generally ignored Woodward's intercontinental caveat, almost exclusively emphasizing the region's alleged differences from the northern United States. However, at the same time major Latin American and Caribbean writers such as Carlos Fuentes, Gabriel García Márquez, and V. S. Naipaul—each also working in a postplantation culture of the Americas—drew, often directly, on Woodward's careful qualification to articulate their own cultural and historical *bonds* with the South. Though initially slow to attend to their insights, 21st-century U.S. and European scholars of the South are today less likely to examine the region as unique or aberrant within the U.S. than as a case study in local responses to global processes.

A truly postcolonial approach, however, is more complicated still. The literatures, cultures, and identity politics of the U.S. South are seen as important not simply because they share several traits with those of the global *South*—a history, for example, of colonial plantations, race slavery, race mixing, vibrant African cultural survival, disappeared bodies, poverty, state-sponsored right-wing terrorism, insular communities, the "experience of defeat," and an aesthetic predilection for the baroque—but also because, as part of the neoimperial United States, they share many traits with the metropolitan global *North* from which Woodward, the Nashville Agrarians, and others sought to distance the region. In this view, the South actually *is* special after all: not because it is different from other places, but because it appears *similar* to places often thought very different, with important implications for both postcolonial theory and American studies. By blurring neat boundaries favored by some earlier scholars, the new approaches also draw heavily on concepts from postmodern geography. However, because these models emphasize southerners' similarities with both blue-state Yankees to the North and darker-skinned peoples to the South, they seem unlikely to find favor with many conservative white southerners who traditionally have advocated "southern" identity most vociferously and who continue to define themselves in opposition to precisely these two groups.

Though scholars have not arrived at any set canon of postcolonial southern literature, Faulkner's *Absalom, Absalom!*, which positions the Souths of Virginia, Mississippi, and New Orleans in relation not only to each other but also to Haiti, Alberta, and Massachusetts, is widely considered an essential text. Courses emphasizing this approach tend also to include one or more Caribbean novels that respond to *Absalom, Absalom!*: for example, Alejo Carpentier's *Explosion in a Cathedral* or Rosario Ferré's *The House on the Lagoon*, which deal respectively with Cuba and Puerto Rico. Some courses juxtapose Zora Neale Hurston's *Mules and Men* with her *Tell My Horse*, anthropological works about black U.S. and Haitian culture. The Society for the Study of Southern Literature maintains a syllabus bank on its Web site.

JON SMITH
University of Montevallo

Melanie R. Benson, in *Disturbing Calculations: The Economics of Southern Identity* (2005); Deborah N. Cohn, *History and Memory in the Two Souths* (1999); Demetrius L. Eudell, *The Political Languages of Emancipation in the British Caribbean and the U.S. South* (2002); George Handley, *Postslavery Literatures in the Americas: Family Portraits in Black and White* (2000); Jon Smith, *American Literary History* (Spring 2004); Jon Smith, ed., *Rethinking the United States South*, special issue of *Forum for Modern Language Studies* (April 2004); Jon Smith and Deborah Cohn, eds., *Look Away! The U.S. South in New World Studies* (2004); Jon Smith, Kathryn McKee, and Scott Romine, eds., *Postcolonial Theory, the U.S. South, and New World Studies*, *Mississippi Quarterly* (Fall 2003, Winter 2003–4); Douglass Sullivan-González and Charles Reagan Wilson, eds., *The South and the Caribbean* (2001); C. Vann Woodward, *The Burden of Southern History* (1960; 1993).

Postsouthern Literature

"Postsouthern" is a term that has been widely used in recent years to describe a new literature produced in and about the American South, as well as a new way of *reading* southern literature and talking about the "South" in general. Lewis P. Simpson coined the term in the 1980 essay "The Closure of History in Postsouthern America," in which he observes—as Walter Sullivan, Allen Tate, and other critics had already done—the passing of an agrarian-based southern culture and with it the demise of the Southern Literary Renaissance of the earlier 20th century. Like Sullivan, Simpson identifies Walker Percy's fiction as expressive of the new conditions of southern life in the latter 20th century: one full of anxiety over the production of meaning and the possibility of authenticity. Indeed, although Michael Kreyling makes a convincing case for Faulkner's later work as postsouthern (and post-Faulknerian) parody, Percy's *The Moviegoer*

(1961) makes a good candidate for the first fully self-consciously postsouthern novel. At least it does so if we accept the broadest definition of "postsouthern literature" to mean work that (1) describes a place and culture that is no longer distinctively southern (or that calls into question traditional assumptions about southern culture) and/or (2) exhibits a sensibility fundamentally different from the preceding literature of the Southern Literary Renaissance.

Percy's fiction meets both of these criteria. In *The Moviegoer* the stockbroker protagonist, Binx Bolling, has rejected the burden of his family's genteel past and the old New Orleans neighborhoods of the French Quarter and the Garden District, preferring instead the new nondescript suburb of Gentilly. Through Binx, Percy interrogates the commodification and loss of authenticity in southern spaces, as well as the proliferation of standardization. These results of modernity, which exacerbate Binx's growing preoccupation with life's "everydayness," began in the cities but have infiltrated even "the remotest nooks and corners of the countryside, even the swamps." In *Lancelot* (1977) Percy calls attention to the problems of authentically representing "southernness" when a movie crew chooses to film its absurdly nonreferential southern film at the restored New Orleans mansion of Belle Isle, which, in becoming a tourist trap, has lost any meaningful connection to a historical past.

Percy establishes the model of the postmodern southern writer as seen by Fred Hobson, who distinguishes the generation writing in the 1980s and afterward from earlier generations. In *The Southern Writer in the Postmodern World* (1991), Hobson observes that the radically different and new environment of the post-1970s Sun Belt—distinguished by economic prosperity and racial integration—has made the vision of earlier writers no longer viable. The assumptions of Faulkner's generation and of later writers such as William Styron—that the South was "defeated, failed, poor, guilt-ridden, tragic"—no longer apply to new generations of writers and the South they describe. Instead, these new writers have tended to serve as social critics of a South that has lost its agrarian economic base and historical mind and is caught in the flux of accelerating cultural change along with the rest of the country.

Writers of the Upper South perhaps most typify this trend. Western Kentucky's Bobbie Ann Mason describes a South overwhelmed by new development and popular culture. Like certain characters in her first book, *Shiloh and Other Stories* (1982), the protagonist of her novel *In Country* (1985), Samantha Hughes, is searching for a lost connection to her family's recent history. (Sam's father died in Vietnam before she was born.) Sam's quest is impeded by the fact that, like the rest of her community (and nation), she is immersed in a seemingly eternal present, one dominated by popular culture. Page after page, brand names proliferate. Samantha occupies her time by watching M*A*S*H* on TV, listening to Bruce Springsteen and Michael Jackson on the radio, drinking Coca-Cola, shopping at Kroger's, and eating at McDonald's.

Doris Betts, from the North Carolina Piedmont—one of the areas most affected by Sun Belt prosperity—also focuses on the ways that southerners' historical sensibility is swept away by popular culture and economic and demographic changes. In *The Sharp Teeth of Love* (1997), which begins in the university town of Chapel Hill, at one corner of North Carolina's Research Triangle Park, there are no characters who were born in the town—or even in the South. The only character who speaks with a southern accent is an army major, who in retiring to Virginia affects a drawl. In a 1991 essay entitled "Many Souths and Broadening Scale," Betts addresses the Americanization of Dixie, observing that "in every way, the region is now closer to national norms than it used to be. The satellite dish stands where the outhouse used to lean; after the tobacco curing barn gave way to the sharecropper's cabin, that was replaced by a rusting trailer, and now by an elaborate furnished mobile home that cost $35,000. In North or South, the following look much alike: airports, malls, hotel chains, fast-food restaurants, television programs, most suburbs, highways, billboards, and city outskirts. The drive from New Jersey to Atlanta offers few surprises."

Novelist and short-story writer Lee Smith offers a similar assessment of Appalachia, the region of the South that was once its most geographically and culturally isolated. Like much contemporary Appalachian fiction—by writers such as Robert Morgan and Charles Frazier—Smith engages the postsouthern condition of contemporary Appalachia by restoring a lost sense of the region's history. In novels such as *Oral History* (1983), *Family Linen* (1985), and *The Devil's Dream* (1992), chapters set in contemporary Appalachia (usually western Virginia), which is overcome by shopping malls and theme parks, are juxtaposed with chapters that feature voices from past generations, providing a history of the region and its people.

In his debut novel, *A Visitation of Spirits* (1989), and the story collection *Let the Dead Bury Their Dead* (1992), Randall Kenan engages the loss of agrarian traditions in the African American community of Tims Creek, which is based on Kenan's childhood home of Chinquapin, N.C. In his next major work, *Walking on Water: Black American Lives at the Turn of the Twenty-First Century* (1999), a book that blends the genres of travelogue, oral history, and spiritual autobiography, Kenan extends his concern for the survival of autonomous black communities in the South to a consideration of their cultural survival across the North American continent. Here Kenan demonstrates that the post-South exemplifies the condition of postmodernity throughout the country and, as Betts has asserted, that "the next great [southern] novelists will be international in scope."

Not only novelists but sociologists and journalists have written extensively about the durability of regional boundaries in America. Among those who have debated the question of an enduring South, the Americanization of Dixie, and the Dixification of America are John Shelton Reed, John Egerton, and Peter Applebome. Postcolonial and comparative literary scholars have increasingly begun to consider southern literature within the context of the "Global South," reading William Faulkner and Gabriel García Márquez together or John Barth and Jorge Luis Borges. Recent anthologies of southern literature (e.g., those published by Norton in 1998 and Pearson Longman in 2005) show an absence of immigrant literature in the contemporary canon, an absence all the more glaring when compared to anthologies of contemporary American literature. Nevertheless, the South's rapidly expanding immigrant and migrant worker populations promise the inclusion of multiple ethnic perspectives in its literature, in contrast to the long-standing bifurcation of white and black perspectives. Some of the writers now chronicling the lives of immigrants in the South are Susan Choi, Lan Cao, Robert Olen Butler, Roberto G. Fernández, Mary Gardner, and Gustavo Pérez Firmat.

Richard Ford, born in Jackson, Miss., is a fiction writer who has often been labeled as "postsouthern," although he seems less concerned than most about the state of postsouthernness. Frank Bascombe, the narrator and protagonist of Ford's novel *The Sportswriter* (1986), dismisses the relevance of his southern childhood by saying that "all we really want is to get to the point where the past can explain nothing about us and we can get on with our life." Like so many contemporary southerners (and like the author himself), Frank has lived an itinerate existence—in Mississippi, Illinois, Michigan, and Haddam, N.J., where he resides throughout most of the novel. The novel ends with Frank in Florida, that least southern of southern locales, where he discovers distant relatives, with whom he shares no past. In *The Sportswriter*'s sequel, *Independence Day* (1995), Bascombe attempts to come to terms with the burden of his own history and to develop some sense of roots—not by returning to the southern home of his childhood but by returning to Haddam, N.J., where, after abandoning his former career as a sportswriter, he becomes a "Residential Specialist," or real-estate agent. *The Lay of the Land* (2006) continues the Bascombe saga.

Just as Ford is unconcerned about the durability of southern culture, the scholar Jefferson Humphries is not concerned about the effect of a changing economy and society on the future of southern letters. In his essay "The Discourse of Southernness; or, How We Can Know There Will Still Be Such a

Thing as the South and Southern Literary Culture in the Twenty-First Century" (1996), Humphries uses Edward Said's concept of "Orientalism" to explain how the idea of the "South" was a narrative creation of both northerners and southerners and how invented southern character *types* persist and evolve to help southerners explain their lives, despite changes in southern society. Other postmodern and poststructuralist scholars have similarly emphasized that the "South" and southernness are and have always been narrative creations, rather than an actual entity and a fixed set of characteristics rooted in southern soil and culture. As these postmodern critics point out, this position is one radically different from that of the Agrarian and neo-Agrarian writers and critics who framed the assumptions about the region and its literature that prevailed from the time of the Southern Literary Renaissance until the latter decades of the 20th century.

From this postmodern perspective, stability of *place* is of less importance to the continuing health of southern letters than is the approach of the writer. Julius Raper has called for a self-consciously postmodern literature, one that emphasizes the individual imagination over a fixation on stability of place as evoked in memory. Like Raper, Scott Romine and Michael Kreyling have identified parody as an important component of postmodern southern literature. Maryland's John Barth seems to epitomize this type of postsouthern writer. Lewis Lawson has observed that after Barth's earlier work, place no longer serves to "particularize an existence" but "simply becomes a trifle, like Muzak in the dentist's office—an external which bores but in no other way impinges upon consciousness." This treatment by Barth of place Lawson finds evident even in an ostensibly historical novel like *The Sot-Weed Factor* (1960), which makes use of colonial Maryland only as a backdrop for the existential struggles of individual characters to construct their own lives through narrative.

In *The Postsouthern Sense of Place in Contemporary Fiction* (2005), Martyn Bone expresses both appreciation and concern for the emphasis given to postsouthern parody by scholars such as Kreyling, Romine, and Raper. In particular, Bone is concerned that if southern literature becomes exclusively self-referential and parodic of the southern tradition, it will lose its ability to engage the very real sociopolitical and economic realities of an increasingly changing South. In his treatment of Tom Wolfe's *A Man in Full* (1998), Toni Cade Bambara's posthumous *Those Bones Are Not My Child* (1999), and Anne Rivers Siddons's *Peachtree Road* (1988) and *Downtown* (1994), Bone examines Atlanta, the South's "international city," as a case study of the changes occurring throughout the region in response to the developments accompanying late capitalism.

Other writers often considered in discussions of postsouthern literature include Barry Hannah, James Alan McPherson, Barbara Kingsolver, and Josephine Humphreys. An implicit if typically unspoken problem associated with the term "postsouthern"—as with the terms "postmodern," "New South," and the like—is the word's durability. What comes *after* "postsouthern" literature? And how long can this particular theoretical perspective continue to describe an ever-changing response to a culture in flux?

GEORGE HOVIS
State University of New York at Oneonta

Doris Betts, in *The Future South: A Historical Perspective for the Twenty-first Century*, ed. Joe P. Dunn and Howard L. Preston (1991); Martyn Bone, *The Postsouthern Sense of Place in Contemporary Fiction* (2005); Marti Greene, *Carolina Quarterly* (Spring 2000); Fred Hobson, *The Southern Writer in the Postmodern World* (1991); Jefferson Humphries and John Lowe, eds., *The Future of Southern Letters* (1996); Suzanne W. Jones and Sharon Monteith, eds., *South to a New Place: Region, Literature, Culture* (2002); Michael Kreyling, *Inventing Southern Literature* (1998); Lewis A. Lawson, in *The History of Southern Literature*, ed. Louis D. Rubin Jr. et al. (1985); Julius Raper, *Southern Literary Journal* (Spring 1990); Lewis P. Simpson, *The Brazen Face of History: Studies in the Literary Consciousness of America* (1980); Jon Smith, *Southern Literary Journal* (Fall 2003).

Publishing

Although the migration of big business to the South and the decay of northern urban centers are undisputed, there have been no major book publication centers in the South, with the exception of university presses. In 1981, of the 1,200 publishers in the country issuing five or more titles annually, 83 were located in the South. Of the annual national production of 66,000 titles, southern presses issued 2,200 titles, one-fourth of which bore the imprints of university presses. The South, with over one-fourth of the nation's population, published only 3 percent of its book titles. Why did southern printshops and booksellers not develop into publishing houses prior to 1830, the period of greatest growth in the publishing industry? Why did the balance of activity in publishing shift from localized presses in the late 18th century to centers like New York and Philadelphia at the beginning of the 19th century rather than to Charleston or Richmond? The answers reside in the very nature of the region.

Historically, the establishment of those primal founts of heresy and rebellion, printing presses, was inhibited in the South by royal governors; geographically, the South had only limited access to distribution routes that would enable it to claim interior markets; demographically, the South never developed those large population centers necessary to support major publishing houses; culturally, the South remained dependent on the North and England for too long—moving to create its first publishing centers several decades after the northern publishing houses had established their fortunes by issuing cheap reprint editions of English works; and, traditionally, the southern ideal of cultural isolation created an insular society that, until tensions began to arise between the North and the South prior to the Civil War, felt no need for active regional publishing. By the 1850s when the southern press first called for a regional publishing center, New York and Philadelphia already dominated the American publishing industry, and whatever hopes the South might have had of creating a parallel publishing center in the wake of the regional sentiment that preceded the Civil War were dashed with those of the southern cause during that conflict.

For all this, southern university presses have recorded notable achievements in the 20th century. The titles published by these presses reflect a close identification with their region. The story of publishing in the South falls into five stages: (1) the establishment of the printing industry in the colonial South, (2) the effort to establish a southern publishing center in the antebellum South, (3) the expansion of that industry during the Civil War, (4) the production of southern titles during Reconstruction, and (5) the formation of southern university presses in the 1920s and 1930s.

The desire to establish a press in the South preceded its establishment by close to half a century. The earliest southern printers combined the functions of printer and publisher in their shops. They served at the discretion of royal governors who, like their English monarch, perceived the printer to be promulgator of disobedience and heresy. Thus, in 1682, when William Nuthead attempted to establish the first southern press in Jamestown, the Virginia Council banned printing of any kind in the colony, and Nuthead moved his press to Maryland. Only in 1730, nearly a century after the establishment of the first press in New England, did the Virginia Assembly reconsider its act and, succumbing to a need for a public printer, lure William Parks to Williamsburg. Within succeeding decades, presses were established in Charleston, S.C. (1731), New Bern, N.C. (1749), and Savannah, Ga. (1762), at the behest of colonial assemblies, which, like Virginia's, found the dangers of insurrection posed by the free printer to be less threatening than the need for someone to make clear the confused manuscript copies of the acts of the assembly.

More than one-half of all titles produced in the South during this period were legal (assembly proceedings, executive utterances, and statutes), whereas the titles of New England presses were 46 percent theological and only 17 percent legal. The figures have been misread to imply that southern colonial interests were legal rather than theological. In fact, the number of government publications issued in both regions was about the same. What the figures suggest is that the South never developed interests—beyond those of governmental procedure—that required active regional publication. Whatever regional controversies took place in the South, like the smallpox inoculation controversy of 1738–39 chronicled by Lewis Timothy's Charleston press, were amply treated in pamphlets. The population density of the New England area, its cultural diversity, its trumpeting of rights and launching of crusades—all these resulted in the kind of polemics that supported a functioning regional press; the scattered nature of the southern population, its cultural homogeneity (only 12,320 unnaturalized foreigners were counted in the South in 1820 in contrast to 41,335 in the rest of the nation), its insular nature, and its confidence in traditional values required no such outlet.

Until the end of the 18th century, the book publisher in America was a tradesman, either a bookseller who printed editions for his own shop or a printer who sold the products of his press in a back room. By 1830 this structure had become outmoded. In the publishing centers of New York and Philadelphia, craft and trade functions were abandoned by the publisher who turned his attention to selecting books to be printed and marketed on the basis of popular appeal and potential profits. In the 1830s, for instance, the Philadelphia firm of Carey and Hart boldly purchased all the seats in a mail stage to ship Bulwer-Lytton's *Rienzi* (1836) to New York, beating the New York firm of Harper's in its own market. In contrast, John Russell of Charleston chose William Gilmore Simms's *Areytos* (1846) as his firm's first imprint, basing his decision not on the profit motive but on an idealistic desire to serve the literary needs of his region. Russell's firm (with a stock valued at $20,000) was essentially a bookstore, not a publishing house. In the North publishing had become a competitive business in and of itself, whereas in the South it remained the avocation of printers and booksellers.

The American copyright act of 1790, which provided that the works of English authors could be reprinted in America without payment of royalties, had a great part in encouraging the growth of the northern publishing houses. New York became a trade center after the War of 1812 by developing a triangular trade that carried cotton from the South to England, manufactured goods from England to New York, and northern and foreign goods from New York to the cotton ports. The preference of the average American reader prior to 1840 for English authors was reflected in the publishing industry (only 30 percent of the titles published at this time were written by American authors), so that the publishing industry was largely an import industry. This fact not only contributed to the growth of the New York firms—ideally situated at the center of the American import system—but paradoxically created the very situation in which the early domination of the publishing trade by northern houses would appear least threatening to southern audiences. Literature imported into the South, whether channeled through northern or southern shops, reflected English values rather than the values of either region. Although some important titles were reprinted in the South during this period, the favorite publishers of southern readers were northern houses that "puffed" and promoted their wares. Works published in the South, though technically comparable to their northern counterparts, were simply not promoted. A book published in the North would receive national distribution, but southern-issued books were rarely even read in neighboring states.

By 1840, when approximately half the books printed in the United States were written by American authors, the North with its Protestant work ethic and business acumen had acquired a virtual monopoly on book publishing. Not until the middle of that decade did southern authors, who perceived the increased interest in publishing among their northern counterparts, feel themselves uncomfortable with northern publishing houses; and not until the northern publishing houses began exporting to the South books and texts espousing northern rather than English ideals did the South feel sufficiently besieged by northern culture and propaganda to establish its own publishing houses.

As tensions increased between the North and the South prior to the Civil War, the South came to resent keenly its literary vassalage to the North. One writer complained of textbooks, which were prepared by northern men unfamiliar with the South, that devoted two pages to Connecticut onions and broomcorn and only 10 lines to Louisiana and sugar. Charges of moral laxity made by the abolitionists angered southerners who, because of the limited number of publishing houses established in their region, saw no means of promoting their side of the issue. Southern authors, like William Gilmore Simms, who sought a national audience found that the novels they published in the South sold far less than those that came out of the North. Although a substantial number of Simms's titles were printed by southern presses, of the major works only *The Sword and the Distaff* (published in 1852 by Walker, Richards of Charleston) was of southern issue. By 1858 Simms, who had extensive experience with both northern and southern publishers, could remark that there was "not in all the Southern States a single publisher." Less prestigious writers found themselves in the dilemma of either subsidizing their own works in southern houses that lacked the capital of the northern operations or seeking publication in the North, where southern writers were widely considered to be inferior.

Prior to the Civil War, only three publishing houses of any consequence— Randolph and English in Richmond, West and Johnston in Richmond, and Sigismund H. Goetzel in Mobile—existed in the South. Richmond, New Orleans, and Charleston were the printing centers. The desire for reading matter did not cease with the Civil War, however, although blockades cut off northern book sources. Much that he produced during the war was ephemeral, but the southern publisher, his competition to the North removed, flourished.

Of the 105 book titles published in the Confederacy between 1861 and 1865, nearly one-third were published in Richmond and most of these were by West and Johnston. In the early days of the war, southern publishing houses issued the essential field manuals and military handbooks, but by 1862 the South was forced, in a way that it had never been, to turn to itself for books and authors. West and Johnston, in searching for regional talent, unearthed Augusta Jane Evans [Wilson] whose novel *Macaria* (1864) outsold any other edition in the South. The Richmond firm also issued the Confederacy's first original drama, James Dabney McCabe's *The Guerillas* (1863). In all, the Confederacy produced 49 works of fiction, 29 volumes of verse, 15 songsters, and 5 dramas among other miscellaneous publications.

Had Reconstruction been less agonizing, the Confederate presses might well have developed into a publishing center of some kind. But with the end of the war, the hopes of southern publishers were vanquished. The products of the few Reconstruction presses, most notably Clark and Hofeline of New Orleans, were devoted to embittered defenses of the South and to angry denunciations of the North. Among Clark and Hofeline's imprints were Randell Hunt's *Appeal in Behalf of Louisiana, to the Senate of the United States for the fulfillment of the constitutional guaranty to her of a republican form of government as a state in the union* (1874) and James Dugan's satirical depiction of postwar Louisiana, *Doctor Dispachemquic: A Story of the Great Southern Plague of 1878* (1878). But for all his bravado, the southern publisher working in the Reconstruction era found himself enduring a period of emotional and financial bankruptcy. When in 1922 the first state university press was established at the University of North Carolina, it was the only professionally staffed, continually publishing book publisher in all the states that once composed the Confederacy.

The university presses, which have flourished in the South during the 20th century, have filled a need for serious scholarly southern study that was, prior to their inception, both ignored and misunderstood by northern publishing houses. Most of these presses (Duke University Press, the University of North Carolina Press, the University of Georgia Press, the University of South Carolina Press, the Louisiana State University Press, the Southern Methodist University Press, the University of Tennessee Press, and the University Presses of Florida) were established in the 1920s, 1930s, and 1940s—when their treatment of the social and economic ills of the region was often controversial. Others (the University Press of Mississippi, the University of Texas Press, and the University of Virginia Press) have been established only in the past few decades.

W. T. Couch, who became assistant director of the University of North Carolina Press in 1925 and its director in 1932, sought the kind of regional studies, books on the South written by southerners, that would shake the region out of its complacency. Under his direction the press produced a number of important regional studies, like Howard W. Odum's *Southern Regions of the United States* (1936) and Stella Gentry Sharpe's *Tobe* (1939), as well as critical studies of textile unions, mill villages, child labor, lynching, and race relations. Couch's aggressive attitude toward regional studies filled a vacuum left by northern houses and provided the South with a publishing center, which, as an organ of the region it served, offered a means of defining and molding a "New South" during the days of the New Deal. His leadership set the tone for other southern university presses.

The representation of the southern university presses among the nation's university presses soon became more indicative of the intellectual health of the region than were the figures relating to publishing as a whole. Of the 2,300 titles published by the nation's university presses in 1981, close to 500 were issued by southern university presses. Yet the impact of the university press on the South, especially in the 1920s and 1930s when a modern South was in its early stage of self-definition, has been out of proportion to its productivity. For the first time in their history, southerners read analyses of their region written by southerners and selected for publication by southerners. The impact was enormous.

The number of presses the South should have 100 years from now will depend on how the needs of the industry are met by the region. On 11 February 1982 Harcourt Brace Jovanovich, a major New York publishing house since 1919, announced its decision to move its operations from New York to centers in Florida and California. Although a single move of this kind does not suggest a trend, William Jovanovich's announcement did express a genuine dissatisfaction with New York as a publishing center, and in the future other major publishers may also head South.

In addition to publishing houses moving south, new publishing houses across the region have begun to emerge. For example, in 1982 Louis D. Rubin Jr.

and Shannon Ravenel founded a small independent trade publishing house called Algonquin Books of Chapel Hill. In 1989 Workman Publishing, a successful independent publisher of cookbooks, practical books, and children's books, acquired Algonquin and through its financial backing helped to make Algonquin Books one of the premier publishers of southern fiction and nonfiction. Over the years Algonquin Books has published works by some of the most recognizable names in contemporary southern fiction such as Jill McCorkle, Larry Brown, Ellen Douglas, Clyde Edgerton, Kaye Gibbons, Lewis Nordan, and Lee Smith.

CAROL JOHNSTON
Clemson University

Book Forum, no. 2 (1977); Richard Barksdale Harwell, *Confederate Belles-Lettres* (1941); Jay B. Hubbell, in *American Studies in Honor of William Kenneth Boyd*, ed. David Kelly Jackson (1940); Hellmut Lehmann-Haupt, *The Book in America: A History of the Making and Selling of Books in the United States* (1951); *Literary Market Place 2008: The Directory of the American Book Publishing Industry* (2008); Madeleine B. Stern, *Imprints on History: Book Publishers and American Frontiers* (1956); John Tebbel, ed., *A History of Book Publishing in the United States*, 4 vols. (1972–81).

Regionalism and Local Color

Although the terms regionalism and local color are sometimes used interchangeably, regionalism generally has broader connotations. Whereas local color is often applied to a specific literary mode that flourished in the late 19th century, regionalism implies a recognition from the colonial period to the present of differences among specific areas of the country. Additionally, regionalism refers to an intellectual movement encompassing regional consciousness beginning in the 1930s.

Even though there is evidence of regional awareness in early southern writing—William Byrd's *History of the Dividing Line*, for example, points out southern characteristics—not until well into the 19th century did regional considerations begin to overshadow national ones. In the South the regional concern became more and more evident in essays and fiction exploring and often defending the southern way of life. John Pendleton Kennedy's fictional sketches in *Swallow Barn*, for example, examined southern plantation life at length.

The South played a major role in the local-color movement that followed the Civil War. Although the beginning of the movement is usually dated from the first publication in the *Overland Monthly* in 1868 of Bret Harte's stories of

California mining camps, a disproportionate number of contributors of local-color stories to national magazines were southerners. The genesis of the local-color movement was not surprising. The outcome of the Civil War signified the victory of nationalism over regional interests. With the increasing move toward urbanization and industrialization following the war and the concurrent diminishing of regional differences, it is not surprising that there was a developing nostalgia for remaining regional differences. Local-color writing, which was regionally, and often rurally, based and usually took the form of short stories intended for mass consumption, met a need for stories about simpler times and faraway places.

Although local-color writing encompassed a number of regions, including New England and the Midwest, southern local color had about it a special quality—the mystique of the Lost Cause. In many stories written about life in the antebellum South, there was an idealization of the way things were before the war; the South was often pictured in these stories not as it actually had been but as it "might have been." Representative of this writing is the fiction of Thomas Nelson Page, whose tales of Virginia plantation life in such stories as "Marse Chan" pictured beautiful southern maidens, noble and brave slave owners, and happy, contented slaves. Although not all southern local-color writing depicted the South in such romanticized terms, the exotic and quaint characteristics of this region were dominant motifs.

Southern writers after the Civil War wrote about a variety of places and people, providing a sense of the diversity of the South. Sidney Lanier's poems ("The Marshes of Glynn," 1878; "Sunrise," 1887) offered images from the marshes of south Georgia; Richard Malcolm Johnston's *Georgia Sketches* (1864) and *Dukesboro Tales* (1871) presented stories of the "cracker"; Mississippian Irwin Russell's sketches and *Collected Poems* (1888) popularized the use of black dialect in literature; and Sherwood Bonner's *Dialect Tales* (1884) and her accounts of Tennessee mountain life dealt with the everyday life of plain folk.

Other writers achieved more national fame and literary success in portraying aspects of southern life. George Washington Cable immortalized the Creoles of south Louisiana in the pages of *Scribner's Monthly* and then in such books as *Old Creole Days* (1879) and *The Grandissimes* (1884); Mary Noailles Murfree spent her summers in the Cumberland Mountains of Tennessee and then wrote about the mountaineers, using pen names such as Charles Egbert Craddock and E. Emmett Dembry, in the *Atlantic Monthly* and in a book of stories, *In the Tennessee Mountains* (1884); James Lane Allen created initial literary images of Kentucky life and people with stories in *Harper's Magazine* (April 1885) and in such books as *Flute and Violin, and Other Kentucky Tales and Romances* (1891) and *Kentucky Cardinal* (1894); and Joel Chandler Harris used folklore in his *Uncle Remus: His Songs and Sayings* (1880), which created enduring portraits—some say stereotypes—of black southerners. Other local colorists included Kate Chopin, Ruth McEnery Stuart, Charles E. A. Gayarré, and Grace E. King (Louisiana); Margaret Junkin Preston and Mary Johnston (Virginia); John Fox Jr. (Appalachia); and Lafcadio Hearn (New Orleans).

As a genre, southern local-color writing flourished through the 1890s, after which this genteel mode of writing lost popularity. At the turn of the 20th century regional writing in the South was still evident, as in the Virginia-based novels of Ellen Glasgow, whose work attempted a more realistic depiction of the strength and weaknesses of the South. By the 1930s there was a resurgence of interest in regionalism, this time as an intellectual movement. Writers sought to treat each of the regions of the country as discrete geographical, cultural, and economic entities. Again the South played a major role in the regional movement. In fact, a cornerstone of the movement was the manifesto *I'll Take My Stand: The South and the Agrarian Tradition* by Twelve Southerners, published in 1930. The authors of this work, among them John Crowe Ransom, Donald Davidson, Allen Tate, and Robert Penn Warren, argued that the South, having held on to its agrarian culture longer than the rest of the country, could serve as a model for a society in which man rather than the machine was dominant. Citing the dehumanization brought about by industrialization and the assembly line, the authors posited that, although the South would not remain entirely agriculturally based, the southern way of life was more conducive to a full relationship between man and his surroundings.

Although the regional, agrarian philosophy set forth in *I'll Take My Stand* was to a great degree sociological in its thrust, as was much writing about regionalism at this time, there was in the South a corresponding literary movement, known as the Southern Literary Renaissance, which, although not always parallel to the regional movement in its philosophic principles, also emphasized the importance of regional setting and tradition to individuals' lives. Notable writers of this period who explored the importance of their southern heritage and environment included William Faulkner, Robert Penn Warren, and Thomas Wolfe. Although it may be argued, and rightly so, that their works are universal in their implications, each writer's work is firmly rooted in the southern region.

In the decades after the 1930s, literature and the other arts that grew out of southern culture flourished. Such writers as Flannery O'Connor, Carson McCullers, Eudora Welty, and Walker Percy continued to place characters and action in the South. Although their work is regional, it is universal as well. Each writer, through the exploration of specific characters and places, seeks answers to the questions of life and death that concern all men and women. One can conclude of the work of these late 20th-century southern writers that all art must find its roots in a specific place or region. The best art is not of a region but transcends region.

In the last quarter of the 20th century and on into the 21st, the South seems to have retained many regional distinctions. Although the region has not lived up to its position as the agrarian model so bravely postulated in *I'll Take My Stand*, it has not succumbed entirely to the homogeneous tendencies resulting from mass media and the shift in population toward the Sunbelt. The South continues to assert in its art its distinctive regional qualities.

ANNE E. ROWE
Florida State University

George Core, ed., *Regionalism and Beyond: Essays of Randal Stewart* (1968); Donald Davidson, *The Attack on Leviathan: Regionalism and Nationalism in the United States* (1938); Judith Fetterly and Marjorie Pryse, eds., *American Women Regionalists* (1992); Sherrie A. Innes and Diana Royer, eds., *Breaking Boundaries: New Regional Perspectives on Women's Regional Writing* (1997); Merrill Jensen, ed., *Regionalism in America* (1951); Robert Rhode, *Setting in the American Short Story of Local Color, 1865–1900* (1975); Claude M. Simpson, ed., *The Local Colorists: American Short Stories, 1857–1900* (1960); Robert E. Spiller et al., eds., *Literary History of the United States* (1963); Helen Taylor, *Gender, Race, and Region in the Writings of Grace King, Ruth McEnery Stuart, and Kate Chopin* (1989).

Religion and Literature

Religion has influenced the imagination of southern writers in fundamental ways. Both aesthetically and thematically, religious practice in the region has helped writers render a particular place and time as a target for their satire and as a prism through which they interpret human experience. Often southern writers' debts to the religious beliefs and practices of their region are unacknowledged, perhaps even unconscious. William Faulkner asserts such influences exist, nonetheless: "The writer must write about his background. He must write out of what he knows and the Christian legend is part of any Christian's background, especially the background of a country boy, a Southern country boy. I grew up with that, took that in without even knowing it. It's just there. It has nothing to do with how much of it I might believe or disbelieve—it's just there." Southern writers, whether or not they expressly address religious issues, engage questions that preoccupy southern culture, questions that often arise in the practice of religion.

The South historically has been more homogeneous and orthodox in its beliefs than other regions. Survey data by sociologist John Shelton Reed showed that 90 percent of southerners surveyed identified themselves as Protestant as opposed to 60 percent of nonsoutherners. The same study found more agreement in religious beliefs among these southern Protestants than among nonsouthern Protestants or Catholics. Within this homogeneity, there is, however, individuality—institutionalized in the many Protestant denominations—producing colorful variants in religious behavior. This individuality within an overwhelmingly Protestant culture resulted from the particular emphasis of the southern church as it parted from the pluralistic patterns of the North. The Baptist and Methodist movements that swept across the largely rural South after 1755 often featured preachers who delivered dramatic, emotional pictures of the struggle to escape sin and achieve salvation. With common roots in the New England Calvinism of the Great Awakening, this expressive religion stressed personal piety and the preeminent importance of achieving one's salvation. Appealing to the often-isolated poor, it cared little for abstract theology or issues of ethical responsibility within the society. No church-state was envisioned. In the hospitable, fertile southern landscape, preachers taught that one must struggle inwardly with an inherent sinfulness. This sense of human frailty and limitation combined with the hedonism of a rich, frontier culture led to what Samuel S. Hill has called a pattern of "confession, purgation, and going out to sin again."

As private morality became more exclusively the domain of the church, engagement with issues of public morality became less frequent. The explanation lies with the South's commitment to slavery. Because the southern church avoided confronting the immorality of the institution of slavery, it could not validly address issues of ethical responsibility in the larger society. Instead, spokesmen of the church defended the institution as consistent with God's plan, vilifying its critics as ungodly in motivation and action and reaffirming the position that the church should concern itself only with issues of personal piety and salvation. Also, the southern church undertook elaborate missionary efforts to teach the slave community to share its outlook.

When writers of the Southern Literary Renaissance looked to the social history of the South for reasons behind its 20th-century ills, they blamed the church's preoccupation with matters of personal behavior and its carefully defended historical blindness to slavery. Writers like Faulkner, Allen Tate, Flannery O'Connor, and Erskine Caldwell created communities of self-righteous churchgoers and hypocritical preachers practicing a narrow, spiritless religion insensitive to the moral issues with which these writers were concerned. Mark Twain had earlier laid the ground for satirizing the formal practice of religion in the South as a fountain of intolerance; Faulkner tilled the same soil in his depiction of the good Baptist ladies of Jefferson who close the door to those who violate the standards of personal behavior endorsed formally by the church. Once questioned about his own religious beliefs, Faulkner said what other southern writers seemed to be implying in their portrayal of institutional religion: "I think that the trouble with Christianity is that we've never tried it yet." These writers created worlds where issues of public morality had to be engaged; adherence to strict codes of personal piety was insufficient. As Robert Penn Warren wrote at the end of *All the King's Men*, the challenge was to immerse oneself in "the awful responsibility of time."

Yet even as they attack the self-satisfied attitudes of the southern religious establishment, many of these writers accept views basic to regional religious belief. For example, Flannery O'Connor, a writer who makes this gap between belief and practice the focus of her work, finds in the southerner's belief in the Devil, in the reality of evil, an important article of faith. From the perspective of her own orthodox Roman Catholic beliefs, O'Connor keenly perceives the fundamentalist Protestant experiences of the majority of southerners. She introduces her collection of short stories *A Good Man Is Hard to Find* with a quotation from St. Cyril of Jerusalem: "The dragon is by the side of the road, watching those who pass. Beware lest he devour you. We go to the Father of Souls, but it is necessary to pass by the dragon." O'Connor believes she addresses a modern world in which evil is dismissed as sociological or psychological aberration. In the South, particularly the rural Protestant South, this Roman Catholic writer ironically recognizes another point of view.

Episcopal Bishop Robert R. Brown writes that southerners "believe more in the reality of Satan than in the reality of God," and John Shelton Reed's research shows that by a significant margin (86 percent to 52 percent) southerners are more likely than nonsoutherners to say they believe in the Devil. Southern writers, too, insist upon the reality of evil. They present it as active, powerful, inescapable, irreducible, threatening the individual from within as well as from without. They also criticize ideas of social reform dependent upon a view of mankind as essentially good. Writers such as Faulkner, Warren, Katherine Anne Porter, Carson McCullers, and Truman Capote join O'Connor in representing evil as violence, grotesque psychological distortion, selfish pride, or despair. These storytellers find in the individual's confrontation with evil the conflict from which dramatic fiction arises.

Another common theme that reflects the debt of southern writers to their religious environment is closely allied to this acceptance of the existence of evil: man is flawed, limited, imperfect. "Man is conceived in sin and born in corruption," says Warren's Willie Stark, "and he passeth from the stink of the didie to the stench of the shroud." The viewpoint is essentially conservative, even pessimistic if contrasted with visions of a more idealized human nature. Without explicitly referring to original sin, southern writers create characters more sinning than sinned against. Mr. Thompson of Katherine Anne Porter's "Noon Wine" or Horace Benbow of Faulkner's *Sanctuary* awaken to their own capacity for violence and evil. Individuals resist or succumb to their own selfish pride, their greed, their bestial natures. It is a mistake, however, to label such a vision of man as pessimistic or deterministic. Within the context of the accepted religious beliefs of their culture, southern writers turn their attention to how one conducts life given these imperfections. The measure of the spiritually healthy individual is in his or her ability to recognize limitations and then to involve oneself with the world and its complexities.

In the emotional style of southern evangelical Protestantism lie the clearest connections to the South's creative literature. The southern writer could have turned, and often did turn, to the preacher for models of imaginative, moving uses of language. Faulkner once speculated about the appeal of the Southern Baptist movement: "It came from times of hardship in the South where there was little or no food for the human spirit—where there were no books, no theater, no music, and life was pretty hard and a lot of it happened out in the sun, for very little reward and that was the only escape they had." The southern preacher dramatized the struggles of good and evil in vivid, concrete stories, enlivened by expressive flourishes, which allowed the churchgoers to forget for the moment their day-to-day fight to survive. In the competitive world of the itinerant preacher, he who could touch the imagination as well as the conscience of his congregation thrived. Every writer who grew up in the South, then, breathed in this dramatic, emotional atmosphere.

The preacher offered southern writers literary tools and visions that guided them in confronting central questions about life. Writers worked scenes of camp meetings and revivals into their stories. Johnson Jones Hooper, for example, introduces the character Captain Simon Suggs to a camp meeting, where he becomes the object-lesson sinner for the preacher. Mark Twain presents a camp meeting through Huck Finn's eyes as the duke and the king, Huck's con-artist companions, prey on the gullible there assembled. Flannery O'Connor in "The River" shows the preacher Bevel, who baptizes a small boy so that he will "count now." Lisa Alther has portrayed the modern youth revival and evangelist Brother Buck, who couches his message in extended football metaphors of Christ Jesus Thy Quarterback, the Celestial Coach, and the water boys of life. And Faulkner shows the power of the preacher to raise his audience to new levels of self-recognition in *The Sound and the Fury* with the sermon of the Reverend Shegog.

Faulkner chose to depict a black preacher when he wanted to express a redemptive quality in the religion practiced in the South. Samuel Hill has pointed out that the black church developed along lines different from those of white Protestantism, in that "the theology of black people's Christianity was shifting, not away from glorious heaven, to be sure, but away from the threats of hell. It remained a religion of salvation, but less and less from eternal punishment and more from alienation from Jesus. . . . [Black people] created an authentic folk variant of a traditional religion. It featured expressiveness, joy, fellowship, moral responsibility, pious feelings and the hope of heaven." Yet black southern writers, like their white counterparts, respond with ambivalence when portraying religious practice in the region.

Richard Wright in his autobiographical *Black Boy* depicts the women of his family as threatening him with God's punishment for his transgressions. In *Native Son* religion weakens black rebellion with promises that suffering in this life will be rewarded in the next. But in the short story "Fire and Cloud," Wright presents the Reverend Taylor as a man who lives his religious commitment as social action. In his picture of the Reverend Homer Barbee in *Invisible Man*, Ralph Ellison illustrates the rhetorical power of the black preacher even as he suggests that such power is used to misdirect the attention of the congregation from its exploitation. Alice Walker, however, seems to capture the spirit of what Hill called the joyful folk variant of traditional southern religion in *The Color Purple*. Shug Avery celebrates a personal religion, independent from any formal church, which asks only that one express love for God's creation. It is one of the most positive, albeit unconventional, expressions of religious feeling in southern literature.

H. L. Mencken once characterized the South as the "bunghole of the United States, a cesspool of Baptists, a miasma of Methodism, snake-charmers, phony real-estate operators, and syphilitic evangelists." Southern writers have populated their work with hypocritical preachers, self-righteous congregations, rigid Calvinists, and spiritually twisted fanatics. They have, nevertheless, drawn their vision of human limitation and a world in which good and evil contend from the most basic beliefs of southern religion. Perhaps as the distinctions between the South and other regions fade, the southern writer will become more indistinguishable in his response to his community. In the work of Walker Percy, a southerner and a Catholic, there is attention to philosophical and theological issues that cannot be said to be strictly southern. Contemporary writers continue, though, to explore themes rooted in the religious life of the South. Clyde Edgerton writes humorously of southern preachers and parishioners, Mary Ward Brown explores the psychology of charismatic believers, and Lee Smith tells darkly comic tales of religion in Appalachia. Dennis Covington wrote of serpent handlers in *Salvation on Sand Mountain,* conveying how he became caught up in its drama.

Other recent southern writers who write of religion include James Wilcox, Randall Kenan, and Larry Brown. Steven Stern has carved out a special sacred literary geography, with short stories and novels about the Pinch district of Memphis, peopled by a Jewish community that sees itself isolated in the South and truly a lost tribe.

ROBERT R. MOORE
State University of New York at Oswego

Robert H. Brinkmeyer Jr., *The Art and Vision of Flannery O'Connor* (1989), *Three Catholic Writers of the Modern South* (1985); Doreen Fowler and Ann J. Abadie, eds., *Faulkner and Religion* (1991); Samuel S. Hill, *The South and the North in American Religion* (1980); Fred Hobson, *The Southern Writer in the Postmodern World* (1991); C. Hugh Holman, *The Immoderate Past: The Southern Writer and History* (1977); Susan Ketchin, *The Christ-Haunted Landscape: Faith and Doubt in Southern Fiction* (1994); Rosemary Magee and Robert Detweiler, in *Encyclopedia of Religion in the South,* ed. Samuel S. Hill and Charles Lippy (2005); Perry Miller, *Errand into the Wilderness* (1956); John Shelton Reed, *The Enduring South: Subcultural Persistence in Mass Society* (1972); Louis D. Rubin Jr., in *The Added Dimension: The Art and Mind of Flannery O'Connor,* ed. Melvin J. Friedman and Lewis A. Lawson (1977); Lewis Simpson, in *The Cry of Home: Cultural Nationalism and the Modern Writer,* ed. H. Ernest Lewald (1972).

Southern Gothic

Literary endeavor in the South has repeatedly devolved from, and has been associated with, Gothic tradition. In literary contexts "Gothic" evokes anxieties, fears, terrors, often in tandem with violence, brutality, rampant sexual impulses, and death. All result from persecution, mainly for power, by persons who may be known but untouchable or unknown. In addition, natural, supernatural, or seemingly supernatural forces may cause these negative effects. Singly or collectively they link with issues of identity as they relate to sexuality, marriage, and family. Typically a Gothic work focuses on individuals whose existence highlights the impacts of such persons or forces cited. For many, "southern literature" means only creative work by southern writers published during the 20th and 21st centuries, whereas a sturdy Gothicism had been established much earlier in the South. Thus Gothic writings before 1900, or, perhaps, those that preceded Faulkner should not be relegated as inferior to later works.

Recognizable Gothicism first appeared in *The Mysterious Father: A Tragedy in Five Acts* (1807), by William Bulloch Maxwell (1787–1814), a Savannah, Ga., native. Although this play owes debts to Shakespeare's plays and British Gothic drama of Maxwell's own era—and more particularly to *The Mysterious Monk* (1796), revised as *Ribbemont; or, The Feudal Baron* (1801) by the "Father of American Drama," New Jersey–born William Dunlap—*The Mysterious Father* stands nonetheless as an early specimen of literary Gothicism in the South. It may be ranked with several Dunlap plays of the 1790s as one of the first American Gothic works

Additional pioneer, tentative Gothicism, observable in much early 19th-century southern verse, is presented at its best by poets Edward Coote Pinkney (1802–28) and Richard Henry Wilde (1789–1847). Both poets relished the works of British romantic poets Byron and Thomas Moore, whose verse repeatedly betrays Gothic antecedents. Pinkney's "Melancholy's Curse of Feasts," for example, is brief, but its hanging "shadowy skeletons" and vases that resemble burial urns create a funereal aspect that would be at home in some of the melancholy lyrics of Byron and Moore, whose poems often feature themes of death, drinking, bleak hilarity, and morbidity.

Typically, however, the Gothic impulse is more, or more obviously, at home in fiction, and an early southern novelist, John Pendleton Kennedy (1795–1870), added enlivening Gothic touches to his novels. Episodes of mystery and intrigue, muted by the overarching comic tone, remind us that tragic undertones may enrich comedy, as is certainly the case in *Swallow Barn* (1835). The remote country house in this loosely structured novel supplants the grim castle featured in many British Gothics, though Kennedy eschewed the horrifying torture chambers and instruments, live burials, and supernatural trappings, so popular in that same tradition. The pirates' den, calculated to suggest a haunted house situated in equally terrifying coastal territory, thus to keep the populace at a distance, adds thriller content to Kennedy's third novel, *Rob of the Bowl: A Legend of St. Inigoe's* (1838). Pirates' stratagems may baffle the unwary here, but the eerie frontier lurker in James Hall's brief novel *The Harpe's Head: A Legend of Kentucky* (1833) arouses far more fright than anyone in Kennedy's novels does, what with a monstrous hulk of deformed humanity for a showcase character, whose appearance and savage disposition understandably appall those he encounters.

Far more distinguished Gothicism is evident in the verse and prose fiction of William Gilmore Simms (1806–70) and Edgar Allan Poe (1809–49), the South's two greatest antebellum authors. Many of Simms's poems accrue zest from supernaturalism or other Gothic weirdness, especially in two lengthy verse narratives, "The Hunter of the Calawassee: A Legend of South Carolina" (1838) and "The Cassique of Accabee: A Legend of the Ashley River" (1853). Here we find the finest Gothic poetry in Simms's canon, a blend of the otherworldly element of regional folklore with characterizations and melodrama from Gothic tradition. Simms's fiction reveals a sophisticated Gothicism that rivals work by contemporaries like Hawthorne and Melville. His early novella, *Martin Faber* (1833), is clearly influenced by the Gothic novels of William Godwin and by German literature. Simms's debts to German sources are undeniable, and these origins surface in his many short stories and novels. Sometimes Simms's Gothicism remains close to European tradition, more so in his short fiction than in his novels. A telling example, "Conrade Weickhoff" (1837), carries earmarks of "German" (for which, read "Gothic") luridness in a diabolic cult whose members practice successive suicides. As in many poems, Simms perceptively adapted Gothicism to southern settings and situations. "Grayling; or, Murder Will Out" (1842) is a ghost story set in a frontier locale, in which the ghost of murdered Major Spencer appears to young James Grayling, a character whose imaginative powers were not dulled by a rationality increasingly admired as the basis for modern life. Enlightened by Spencer's ghost, Grayling brings about the trial and execution of the villain.

Simms's novels offer even more artistic adaptations of Gothic tradition to American life. In the first of his Revolutionary War novels, *The Partisan* (1835), and its sequel, *Mellichampe* (1836), the evil "Goggle" Blonay and his witchlike mother resemble the mysterious villains in older Gothic works, though this pair anticipates the river rats found in much later southern fiction. Their own wildness imbues them with an unpredictability inherent in frontier conditions, which characters like Colonel Walton and his associates are trying to transform into more settled ways of life. A move toward more plausible creation of the violence and murderous impulses found in frontier life may be seen in novels like *Guy Rivers* (1834), in which the Byronic villain of volcanic disposition is domesticated in the person of Guy, who, like many other criminals, could have been equally strong for good causes, had his life been different. Although many of his other novels incorporate Gothic elements, Simms perhaps achieves his most artistic Gothicism in *Woodcraft* (1854). In this final novel in the Revolutionary War series, the scheming British are portrayed as villains, replete with characterizations that make them devil figures, as contrasted with the more honest and otherwise moral Americans. The Widow Eveleigh is an American cousin to the legion numbers of persecuted maidens and wives in European Gothics, though, being a three-dimensional character, she is not so cloyingly naive as many of the cardboard heroines in preceding British Gothics were.

Edgar Allan Poe is the antebellum southern writer who composed the most sophisticated Gothic art, which continues to be perennially attractive to current, worldwide reading audiences. He quickly discerned how to transform the weird landscapes within British romantic poetry into exquisite symbols for the human mind, as is unmistakable in poems like "The Lake, To—" (1827), "The Sleeper" (1831), "The Raven" (1845), and "Ulalume" (1847). Interestingly, "The Sleeper," often dismissed as disgusting necrophilia, may be read as a convincing portrayal of a survivor's grief and of funeral customs of the time. In "The Raven" and "Ulalume" respectively, the claustrophobic chamber and the dreary October night landscape constitute adroit transformations of the older haunted castle and the threatening landscape into representations of stressed human minds. In fiction, too, Poe made rapid transitions from what originally read as straight Gothic thrillers—for example, "Metzengerstein" (1832) or "The Assignation" (1834)—to creating outstanding situations of human emotions shattered by traumas from physical torture ("The Pit and the Pendulum" [1843], "The Black Cat" [1843]), to those in which sexual and gender issues were symbolized (*The Narrative of Arthur Gordon Pym* [1838], "Ligeia" [1838], "The Fall of the House of Usher" [1839], "Eleonora" [1843]), sometimes in tandem with dual or multiple personalities ("William Wilson" [1839], "The Masque of the Red Death" [1842], "A Tale of the Ragged Mountains" [1844]). Forbidding and crumbling castle or mansion stones became compelling representations of fragmenting human psyches. Never satisfied with the state of his creative works, Poe revised many poems and tales to center them more firmly in the human mind—instead of merely creating what seemed to be supernatural nightmare narratives—finally revealing that alcohol or opium, not ghosts or demons, had produced the weird effects. For example, in "The Murders in the Rue Morgue" (1841) Poe perpetrates a hoax upon those who desire supernaturalism by creating a detective tale with a psychologically sound conclusion: an ape, not an otherworldly presence, committed the atrocious murders.

Later 19th-century southern authors also produced vestigial Gothicism after the initial craze for lurid works diminished somewhat. Augusta Evans Wilson

(1835–1909) re-created the Byronic hero in the title character in *St. Elmo* (1866). George Washington Cable (1844–1925) presented a New Orleans that seems to harbor mysteries of locale and character, as in *The Grandissimes* (1880), where intricate family and racial relationships seem as intriguing as those in the more obviously Gothic fiction of Thomas Nelson Pages's *Red Rock* (1898). That novel gains dimension from mysterious threats to the protagonists, and violence, execution, and supernaturalism mingle in Page's "No Haid Pawn" (1887). Likewise, Mary Noailles Murfree (1850–1922) produced fiction containing episodes bordering on the supernatural.

A resurgent Gothicism infiltrates much 20th-century southern writing, the chief exemplars being William Faulkner (1897–1962), Andrew Lytle (1902–95), Eudora Welty (1909–2001), and Flannery O'Connor (1925–64). Faulkner's awareness of Gothic tradition is evident in many works, though perhaps the chief representatives are *As I Lay Dying* (1930), *Sanctuary* (1931), *Light in August* (1932), and *Absalom, Absalom!* (1936). The first novel centers on the extended funeral journey of the Bundren family to bury the body of Addie, wife of Anse Bundren and mother his four children and one fathered by the minister Whitfield, though the paternity remains unknown to most family members, Darl excepted (because he has the imaginative insight lacked by the others). The funeral journey itself is fraught with perils, and in dictating that she be buried in her own family's far distant cemetery, Addie becomes a more forceful presence after her death than when she was alive. Faulkner creates in her a modification of the vengeful spirit who wreaks havoc upon the living in supernatural Gothics. Darl's delicate psychic balance, which eventually topples into insanity and incarceration—thus saving Jewel from being revealed as Whitfield's child—also recalls earlier horrific tales of undesirables being consigned to madhouses, a variation on the live burial theme. The shifting narrative point of view in *As I Lay Dying* is reminiscent of the vicissitudes in characters' temperaments so widespread in Gothic fiction, where mercurial ascents or descents in emotions are commonplace.

Sanctuary, which used to be typically dismissed as little more than near-pornographic trash, has been revalued as symbolic of the rape of southern womanhood by outside forces. Thus Popeye's relationship with Temple Drake is rescued from the depths of sleaze. *Light in August* relates the misfortunes of characters who find themselves alienated by the world. The harsh religious ethic in his foster home sends Joe Christmas farther into a miasma of otherness, which, as it links with his ambiguous racial identity, fascinates Joanna Burden, who uses him for her own warped sexual pleasure. The Reverend Gail Hightower in *Light in August* joins company with numbers of false or defrocked clergy in early Gothic fiction. The high-pitched emotions and sensational physical violence combine with pervasive mysteries enshrouding race, sex, and morality, as well as family identities, to make this a true Gothic novel. Several of these motifs recur in *Absalom, Absalom!*, Faulkner's most highly wrought Gothic novel. From Quentin's opening encounter with the (physically and emotionally) weird Rosa Coldfield, on to the burning of the Sutpen mansion, we encounter characters whose curiosity, doubts, sexuality, suicidalness—elements contributing in one way or another to a character's social adjustment—interplay to form one of the finest novels in the American literary canon.

Near Faulkner in theme and technique, Andrew Lytle created several fictions in which Gothic mystery and violence reign supreme. Devolving as it does from the writings of Poe, Lytle's novel *The Velvet Horn* (1957) bears testimony to his excellent employment of Gothic techniques. The paternity of young Jack, the central character, is ambiguous, and the ultimate unraveling of that mystery involves interesting journeys away from home-civilization into near wilderness conditions, sexual awakenings, and eerie night scenes. All these characteristics would, with few revisions, be at home in the fiction of Poe and Simms. Just so, they dovetail with similar questions regarding family issues—those of the protagonist, Jack Burden, and those of the Stanton siblings in another famous southern novel, Robert Penn Warren's *All the King's Men* (1946). Dr. Adam Stanton is driven to distraction, then to murder Governor Willie Stark because of Stark's affair with Adam's sister, Ann. Warren masterfully builds up suspense, low-key and gradual initially, then intensifying to emotional, and sometimes physical, explosiveness.

Flannery O'Connor's fiction makes fitting companion reading for Faulkner's and Lytle's works: the unrelenting death dealing of the Misfit toward his victims in "A Good Man Is Hard to Find" or the grotesque comedy of a girl, seduced, then left, robbed of her artificial leg, in a hayloft, in "Good Country People"— both collected in *A Good Man Is Hard to Find* (1955). There are no supernatural trappings but instead stark realism in the violence, sex, and death in O'Connor's works. Such themes and grotesque, terrifying characters are treated more expansively in her novels, *Wise Blood* (1952) and *The Violent Bear It Away* (1960)

Although she denied the fact, Eudora Welty obviously ranks with Hawthorne, Poe, and others in her Gothicism, albeit her variety is much toned down in comparison with what some readers find overwrought in Poe's Gothics. An overpowering curtain of green (growing plants), which stimulates onlookers to ponder what lies behind, and a chronicle of suspect characters facing off those who are eminently civilized, respectable, and virtuous, may well attest to the Gothic nature of Welty's fiction. Particularly in *The Robber Bridegroom*

(1942), a novella, Gothicism is deftly brought to the fore in characters like the outlaw Harpe brothers, Mike Fink the legendary keelboatman, a stereotypical southern-planter father to the bride, plus the robber groom himself. Welty's use of doublings in this tale are kindred to those found in Poe's works.

Many more southern writers might be analyzed under a Gothic lens, though few of them achieve the artistic Gothicism of Poe, Faulkner, O'Connor, or Welty.

BENJAMIN F. FISHER IV
University of Mississippi

Richard P. Benton, *ESQ: A Journal of the American Renaissance* 18 (1972); Benjamin Franklin Fisher IV, in *The Cambridge Companion to Edgar Allan Poe*, ed. Kevin J. Hayes (2002), *The Gothic's Gothic: Study Aids to the Tradition of the Tale of Terror* (1988); Jay B. Hubbell, *The South in American Literature 1600–1900* (1954); Elizabeth L. Kerr, *William Faulkner's Gothic Domain* (1979); Carolyn Perry and Mary Elizabeth Weaks, eds., *The History of Southern Women's Literature* (2002); *Southern Quarterly* (Winter 2003), special issue on William Gilmore Simms; Ruth D. Weston, *Gothic Tradition and Narrative Techniques in the Fiction of Eudora Welty* (1994).

Theater, Early

A long period of vitality, from the colonial era to the Civil War, marked theater in the South. Virginia, the only colony other than Maryland not to pass legislation against the theater, was a center of American theatrical life during the colonial period. The first known play to be acted in America, *Ye Bare and Ye Cubb*, was performed at Cowle's Tavern, in Accomac County, in 1665, and in the next century the first theater was erected there, at Williamsburg.

Charleston, S.C., was, however, the South's theatrical center for 100 years. The first dramatic season opened in 1735 with Thomas Otway's *The Orphan* performed in the city's courtroom; in a prologue, the actors ridiculed the theatrical censorship of New England. The following year plays were staged at the city's new Dock Street Theater.

In 1790 two pioneers in the Georgia backcountry opened Augusta's first theater. Professional actresses from Baltimore, Ann Robinson and Susannah Wall, established themselves in a converted schoolroom, where they staged performances of *The Beaux Stratagem, Douglas*, and a variety of simplified 18th-century dramas. The final performance of the group coincided with George Washington's postelection trip to Augusta, with a banquet held in the makeshift theater honoring the president.

Touring companies provided audiences in the colonial South with the chance to see many of the best works of English drama. London's Lewis Hallam began his American tour in 1752 at Williamsburg with *The Merchant of Venice*. David Douglass's American Company visited Virginia theaters from 1758 to 1761. Douglass's 1773–74 season in Charleston, according to one chronicler, "the most brilliant" of colonial America, included 58 plays, 20 of which were musicals. Shakespeare, however, was the favorite dramatist, with *Richard III* and *Romeo and Juliet* his most popular works.

Postrevolution conditions helped to encourage the production of native dramatic writing in the South. From 1793 in Charleston, for example, there were strong resident companies, managers who encouraged native playwrights, newspaper critics, and the Federalist-Republican controversy, which often turned the stage into a political platform.

William Ioor (1780–1850), a country doctor living near Charleston and a fervent Jeffersonian, wrote his first play, *Independence* (1805), to praise the small farmer and country life. Although its setting was England, *Independence* dramatized Jefferson's agrarian philosophy. Ioor's *Battle of Eutaw Springs* (1807) commemorated the last Revolutionary War battle in South Carolina and indirectly condemned contemporary impressment by Great Britain. A prototype of the southern gentleman appeared as a humorous, hospitable farmer named Jonathan Slyboots.

John Blake White, also from Charleston, wrote plays advocating American social reform. His *Modern Honor*, presented in 1812, was the first antidueling play given in America. After 1825 novelist William Gilmore Simms continued the tradition of dramatic writing with *Michael Bonham; or, The Fall of Bexar* (written 1844; produced 1852), favoring the annexation of Texas, and *Norman Maurice; or, The Man of the People* (published 1851), a proslavery play set in Missouri.

In Virginia, dramatist Robert Munford (1737–83), a planter and a member of the House of Burgesses, wrote *The Candidates* (published in 1798), which satirized corruption in electioneering, and *The Patriots* (published in 1798), which ridiculed intolerant Tories and Whigs. George Washington Parke Custis (1781–1851) wrote several patriotic plays, including *The Indian Prophecy* (1827) and *Pocohontas* (1836). The fascination with history, state pride, and an agrarian bias—themes that emerge in some of these early regional plays—would continue to be distinctive hallmarks of southern drama.

In the 19th century, architecture testified to the popularity both of serious drama and extravaganza. At the turn of that century, even minor southern towns had their sometimes opulent theaters.

In Richmond, the Marshall Theater (1838), remodeled and named in honor of Chief Justice John Marshall in 1838, was said to rival, in its "pure classical character," with its burnished gold, crimson, and damask, the celebrated New Orleans Caldwell. Destroyed by fire in 1862, the theater was rebuilt in the midst of the Civil War by determined Richmonders.

The elegant North Broadway Opera House, which opened in 1887 in Lexington, Ky., made that already performance-conscious city even more theater oriented. With a seating capacity of 596, illumination provided by 250 gaslights, and a stage large enough to be adapted for the chariot race in the 1904 production of *Ben Hur*, the Opera House attracted touring companies and talents like Lillian Russell, the Barrymores (John, Ethel, and Lionel), Sarah Bernhardt, James O'Neill, and Helen Hayes.

Mobile's splendid Saenger Theater, built at a cost of $750,000 in 1927, was the capstone of a chain of playhouses located throughout the South. The Springer Opera House (1871), of Columbus, Ga., booking such notables as Mme Modyeska, Irene Dunne, and Edwin Booth, continued as a legitimate theater well into the Depression.

Whether performing in opera houses or in rented halls, professional stock and touring companies, vaudeville acts, and minstrel shows enlivened the southern theater scene into the 20th century. Not until the second decade of the century, when live performances were forced to compete with "talkies" and with the radio at home, did the era of decentralized professional theater in the South, and in the nation at large, decline. It would not be revitalized until the modern regional theater movement of the late 1940s and early 1950s.

A new movement in drama did begin, though, at the University of North Carolina in the 20th century with the folk plays of the Carolina Playmakers and later the outdoor dramas of Paul Green. This close associate of the Playmakers started his career with folk plays like *In Abraham's Bosom* (1926), about a black educator in the New South, for which he received the Pulitzer Prize. Disenchanted with the commercial theater of New York, Green advocated taking drama to the people and exploiting regional material. Under the influence of Bertolt Brecht's epic theater, Green began his series of symphonic dramas in 1937 with *The Lost Colony*, celebrating the 350th anniversary of Virginia Dare's birth. It was performed on the historical site, Roanoke Island, N.C., and has been repeated almost every summer since. By "symphonic" Green meant the blending of all the stage arts in one production, including spectacle, music, and acting.

Green's dramas, almost all produced in the South, commemorate historic events of the region. The first category deals with the early explorers' transmission of their culture to a new land. *The Lost Colony* was in this category as were

The Founders (1957, featuring John Rolfe and Pocahontas of the Jamestown settlement, performed at Williamsburg) and *Cross and Sword* (1965, at St. Augustine, Fla.). The second category, the making of America, includes *The Common Glory*, Green's second most popular production. This play about Jefferson and the Revolution exemplifies the glory of democracy through Cephus Sicklemore, a propertyless but patriotic humorist; expresses Jefferson's philosophy of the individual's importance in forming the corporate personality; and presents the battle of Yorktown. It opened in 1947 at the Lake Matoaka Amphitheater, Williamsburg. Among Green's colleagues with productions in the South and elsewhere, Kermit Hunter dramatized Indian history in *Unto These Hills* (published in 1950 and performed at Cherokee, N.C.).

Significant links exist between early and modern drama in the South. The first native plays and outdoor dramas reflect the fascination with history, state pride, and the sense of place found in the region. These affirmative plays reveal also such distinctive southern qualities as an agrarian, antiurban bias and a liking for outdoor, spectacular entertainment. As a balance to urbane plays, epitomized by those of Tennessee Williams, which have also attained wide popularity in the South, the historical dramas have given expression to deep-seated feelings of the people.

CHARLES S. WATSON
University of Alabama

Rodney M. Baine, *Robert Munford: America's First Comic Dramatist* (1967); James H. Dormon Jr., *Theater in the Ante-Bellum South, 1815–1861* (1967); Clarence Gohdes, *Literature and Theater of the States and Regions of the U.S.A.: An Historical Bibliography* (1967); Vincent S. Kenny, *Paul Green* (1971); Hugh S. Rankin, *The Theater in Colonial America* (1965); Charles S. Watson, *Antebellum Charleston Dramatists* (1976), *The History of Southern Drama* (1997).

Theater, Modern and Contemporary

The Barter Theater, one of the oldest professional regional theaters in the nation, was a unique product of the Depression-era economy. Founded in 1932 by Virginia-born actor Robert Porterfield and located in the Town-Hall Opera House of Abingdon, the company in its first season made a profit consisting of $4.30 plus three barrels of jams and jellies and assorted surplus foods, some of which were canned and stored and used to "pay" playwright royalties. Growing slowly but steadily, in 1945 it became the official state theater of Virginia.

The Barter Theater holds a distinctive place in the annals of regional theater, which has generally had a shaky history. At the turn of the 20th century hundreds of legitimate professional theaters could be found throughout the United States, but in the decades before World War II the Barter was one of less than a dozen outside New York City.

Although the Little Theater movement of the 1920s, the Federal Theater Project (founded in 1935 as part of the Works Progress Administration), and the American National Theater and Academy (1935) had sought to counter the influences of motion pictures and the radio and had expressed a commitment to audiences throughout the country, the situation for regional theater remained bleak. Professional theater activity had once been supported even in remote locales, but outside of New York it had all but ceased by 1940.

Not surprisingly, the postwar modern regional theater movement first bore fruit away from the East Coast. A principal concern of those active in it was decentralization, so cities closer to Broadway, despite their artistic traditions, received less initial attention. Modern American regional theater began in the Southwest, however, largely because of one dynamic personality, Margo Jones.

In June 1947 Jones, a native Texan, a teacher, and a director, opened Theater '47 (the date changed annually) in Dallas. Conscious of the need for innovation yet responsive to public taste, she helped develop new talents and popularize important playwrights such as William Inge and Tennessee Williams. Inge's *Farther Off from Heaven*, retitled *Dark at the Top of the Stairs*, was the theater's initial production. Both Williams's production of *Summer and Smoke* and Jerome Lawrence and Robert E. Lee's *Inherit the Wind* debuted in Dallas before moving to Broadway.

In the same year, 1947, another "southern belle with a will of iron," Nina Vance, established the Alley Theater of Houston. Recruiting local support through a postcard campaign (the cards bore two words: "Why Not!"), Vance fostered what has been called the most regional of regional theaters.

A fully professional company by the mid-1950s, the Alley was one of the first professional resident theaters to receive major financial support from the Ford Foundation. From its quarters in an abandoned fan factory (225 seats), the theater moved into Houston's spacious $3.5 million playhouse in 1968. Among the Alley's most notable productions was Paul Zindel's Pulitzer Prize–winning *The Effect of Gamma Rays on Man-in-the Moon Marigolds*, which premiered in 1965. Today, the Houston Theater District is second in the nation in the number of seats available for audiences attending theatrical productions. The Alley commissioned and produced the world premiere of Horton Foote's *The Carpetbagger's Children* in 1997, celebrating the 50th anniversary of its founding.

In 1955 a Richmond theater became the first in the nation to be located in a fine arts museum. With its stable physical setting (audience capacity of 500) and consistent community support, Virginia's Museum Theater was able to develop into a full equity company before the start of its 1972–73 season.

Two years later, actor-producer George Touliatos began his work with an amateur group that performed in the basement of the King Cotton Hotel, and he went on to found the Front Street Theater of Memphis. By 1959 the company moved to a refurnished movie house. Front Street Theater performed a broad range of plays, from *Othello* to *Guys and Dolls*, until financial burdens forced it to close in the late 1960s. More recent Memphis productions have been developed by black playwright Levi Frazier Jr. This native Memphian is cofounder and artistic director of Blues City Cultural Center in Memphis.

Repertory Theater of New Orleans opened in the fall of 1966 under the direction of Stuart Vaughan, but it was a short-lived regional experiment. From the onset, the federally funded company faced strong competition from the very popular Le Petit Theater de Vieux Carré. Failing to establish itself as an integral part of the local scene, Repertory Theater closed its doors after the 1971–72 season.

Established in Jackson, Miss., in 1963, Free Southern Theater was an outgrowth of civil rights activism, especially that of the Student Nonviolent Coordinating Committee. Dedicated to presenting nonstereotypic views of southern blacks, the company had relocated in New Orleans by 1964, alternating tours of rural areas in the South with resident seasonal productions.

Actors Theater of Louisville, founded in 1964 by Richard Black, presented bills featuring the classics, but leavened its fare with bold, often controversial productions such as *End Game* and *Slow Dance on the Killing Ground*. Continuing the theater's tradition of responsiveness to new talent, *Crimes of the Heart* by Beth Henley (1979) and *Getting Out* by Marsha Norman (1979) made their pre-Broadway premieres on its stage.

In 1968 the $13 million Atlanta Memorial Cultural Center opened to house symphony, ballet, and also resident drama produced by Atlanta's Repertory Theater. Reorganized as the Alliance Theater in 1969, it supplemented offerings by that city's already active and innovative Pocket Theater.

Professional resident companies now exist throughout the South, but they are not the only sources of serious, quality drama. Adding to the diverse dramatic scene are community and educational theaters and university-affiliated companies, such as the illustrious Carolina Playmakers; and festival theaters such as the High Point, N.C., and Anniston, Ala., Shakespeare festivals and the Oxford Shakespeare Festival at the University of Mississippi. Lighter fare is offered by ever-popular dinner theaters like Sebastian's in Orlando, Fla., while annual outdoor dramas, staged in unique open-air settings like that of the 2,900-seat Mountainside Theater in Cherokee, N.C., have long attracted regional and national interest. The 1990s saw the appearance of medium-sized professional theater companies, such as the Zachary Scott Theater in Austin, smaller than resident theatrical companies.

The theatrical world of the South rested on the work of southern playwrights who emerged as major figures in the American theater in the early 20th century. Lillian Hellman's *The Little Foxes* (1939) portrayed a patriarchal and aristocratic southern family unable to cope with the transition from an agrarian society into a modern one. Greed and cold calculation characterize the main figure, Regina Hubbard. Hellman's *The Children's Hour* (1934) was an early effort to explore lesbianism on the stage, and *Watch on the Rhine* (1941) reflected her international involvement, exploring fascism in Europe.

Black playwrights examined race relations with predominantly southern expressions. Georgia Johnson's *A Sunday Morning in the South* (1925) revolved around lynching. Alice Childress's first off-Broadway play, *Florence* (1949), took place in a segregated railroad depot. Childress's *Trouble in Mind* (1955) showed African American actors rehearsing a play about lynching. Childress was born in South Carolina but grew up in Harlem, living with her grandmother.

In terms of playwrights, Tennessee Williams has surely been the dominating force in modern and contemporary theater in the South. Influenced by Eugene O'Neill, Williams became a preeminent exponent of expressionistic theatrical techniques, which he combined with a critical attitude toward southern cultural forms he inherited. Although his plays tapped universal feelings, they were rooted in his grappling with southern culture's prescriptions on gender, family, race, and individualism. The society he portrays is often decadent and in decline. Some of the problems of his characters stem from their backward look toward past family glory, while other problems come from corrupt, greedy people on the make. Williams's heroes and heroines are creative, sensitive individuals trapped in places where societal values cannot tolerate their differences. The appeal of fantasy and magic becomes an understandable escape from dysfunctional norms. He portrays strict gender expectations and their stifling effects on repressed women and gay sons of patriarchal fathers.

Among Williams's greatest plays are *The Glass Menagerie* (1946), *A Streetcar Named Desire* (1947), *Summer and Smoke* (1948), *The Rose Tattoo* (1951), *Cat on a Hot Tin Roof* (1955), *Suddenly Last Summer* (1958), *Sweet Bird of Youth* (1959), and *The Night of the Iguana* (1961). Each of these plays became a major Hollywood film, extending Williams's influence and helping to popularize images of a sexually charged, emotionally turbulent American South.

Horton Foote's career as playwright and screenwriter overlapped with Tennessee Williams's creative years; he created a southern world that reflected the same patriarchal ethos of Williams's plays but with a gentler and less turbulent emotional temperature. Foote's imaginative saga is the Orphans' Home cycle of nine plays set in and around Harrison in east Texas. Horace Robedaux Sr. first appeared in *Roots in a Parched Land* (1994), and the saga ended with *The Death of Papa* (1997). Foote finds drama in the small events of everyday life, with much slow storytelling, and spirituality is a recurring theme amid human sufferings. Some of his plays, such as *The Trip to Bountiful* (1953), were made into films, and Foote wrote influential original screenplays (1983's *Tender Mercies*) and screenplays for other films, including Harper Lee's *To Kill a Mockingbird* (1962). Foote earned a Pulitzer Prize in 1995 for *The Young Man from Atlanta*.

Hellman, Williams, and Foote were dominating figures from a southern dramatic renaissance in the 20th century. Beth Henley is among younger playwrights who have continued to explore settings and characters with southern resonances. Raised in Jackson, Miss., Henley aspired to be an actress, but she has become an honored and popular playwright who uses her native state for her stories of eccentric behavior. Henley especially excels at exploring the psychology of women caught upon a world where concern for beauty and purity still exists. Henley won the Pulitzer Prize for *Crimes of the Heart* (1981), which portrays the three McGrath sisters in Hazlehurst, Miss. Gossip, conversations in southern vernacular, and an intense commitment to family appear in not only this play but Henley's other works. *The Miss Firecracker Contest* (1984) and *The Debutante Ball* (1985) examine rituals of performing southern beauty.

African American playwrights continue to look into the southern past to understand the black experience in the United States. Charles Fuller, who was born in Philadelphia and founded the Afro-American Arts Theatre there, won the Pulitzer Prize in drama in 1982 for his play *A Soldier's Story*, which portrayed the search by a black army captain for the murderer of a black sergeant on a Louisiana army base in 1944. Fuller later wrote the screenplay for a film version of his play. Alfred Uhry, who is from Atlanta, writes from a distinctive perspective on Southern race relations as a Jewish southerner. *Driving Miss Daisy* (1986) shows the possibilities and complexities of interracial friendship, seen through the relationship between Miss Daisy, the older matriarch of an Atlanta Jewish family, and Hoke, her longtime black driver. The play was also made into a movie, again illustrating the importance of film in popularizing the stories of modern and contemporary southern playwrights.

University of Mississippi

Elizabeth Brown-Guillory, *Wines in the Wilderness: Plays by African-American Women from the Harlem Renaissance to the Present* (1990); Robert Gard et al., *Theatre in America* (1968); Philip C. Kolin and Colby H. Kullman, eds., *Speaking on Stage: Interviews with Contemporary American Playwrights* (1996); Robert McDonald and Linda Rohrer Paige, *Southern Women Playwrights* (2002); Sandra Schmidt, *Southern Theatre* (1971–); *Tulane Drama Review* (Summer 1963); Charles Watson, *The History of Southern Drama* (1997); Joseph Wesley, *Regional Theatre* (1973).

Travel Writing

Between 1948 and 1962 the University of Oklahoma Press published six bulky volumes devoted to description of and comment upon travel books about the South: E. Merton Coulter's bibliography of travels in the Confederate South and five other volumes, under the general editorship of Thomas D. Clark, dealing with books published between 1527 and 1955. All told, these six bibliographical volumes take into account 2,703 titles. Although they include many books that are perhaps only marginally travel accounts (memoirs, for example, written long after journeys undertaken, or accounts of military campaigns and experiences), the editors are under no illusion that they have ferreted out all the travel books that explore or venture into the South. In the decades since 1955, many more travel books about the South have appeared.

Categorizing and evaluating this welter of writing is difficult. Even if one puts aside the obviously superficial and leaves out of the reckoning all those books that are more strictly "guides-to" than "reports-upon" (guidebooks to southern cities and regions began to circulate prior to the Civil War), and even if it were possible to assess the biases and prejudices all travelers to the South carry in their carpetbags, this most troublesome question would still remain: In "travel writing," is the "travel" of more importance than the "writing"? Does one read a travel book primarily as a more or less reliable *record* of things seen and persons encountered? Or does one read a travel book primarily for the *recording* of the traveler's experiences? Some travel books, of course, inform the historical sense while at the same time appealing to an aesthetic bent, but such books are exceptional. A literary critic can term Henry James's *The American Scene* (1904) "one of the great American documents," but a historian is apt to complain that James, in writing of Charleston, gives "the impression of having visited a state of mind rather than a city." And a historian might find vexing what other readers might find entertaining in the earliest English-language travel writing about the South—John Smith's "unusually vivid imagination."

Smith, whose *True Relation of . . . Virginia* was printed in 1609, was, in his active, roving life if not in his tendency to embroider fact with fiction, a typical early traveler. Of the more than 100 travel books by observers from the British Isles or by English colonials written between 1600 and 1750, 40 were by preachers and missionaries, 30 by government officials, 12 by merchants and fur traders, 10 by doctors and scientists, and others by ship captains, land speculators, and surveyors. Indians and natural history, and the unpleasantness and difficulty of travel, were major concerns of these writers. Perhaps most entertaining among these early writings are William Byrd's 1728 *History of the Dividing Line*, with its Virginian put-down of North Carolina and its inhabitants, and Ebenezer Cooke's *The Sot-Weed Factor* (1708), a virulent verse diatribe against Maryland and its settlers.

The second half of the 18th century in the South was a time of war, new nationhood, and expansion westward across the Appalachians, as well as a period in which slavery and the condition of blacks began to claim the attention of travelers. Most reliable among these reporters were those whose business and professional concerns had prompted their travels, men such as Thomas Jefferson, whose *Notes on the State of Virginia* appeared in 1785; William Bartram, whose *Travels through North Carolina* (1791) recounts his pioneering botanical expeditions; and Philip Vickers Fithian, whose journals deal with his employment as a tutor in the Tidewater and his work as a frontier missionary.

By the turn of the century the corps of travelers in the South had been swelled by numerous Europeans, who came to America sometimes on professional errands but more frequently as observers of the American experiment in democracy. They were drawn to the South by Washington's Mt. Vernon, a mecca for travelers, but they also wished to investigate plantation society and to inquire about the growth and expansion of slavery. Increasingly, the South was viewed as a region distinct from the rest of the new United States, almost as another country. Access to this South was primarily by water—along the coastal shipping lanes and into the interior by way of the Ohio and Mississippi. Notable among travel accounts of the first decades of the 19th century are Thomas Ashe's *Travels in America* (1808), John Melish's *Travels through the United States of America* (1812), J. K. Paulding's *Letters from the South* (1817), and Timothy Flint's *Recollections of the Last Ten Years* (1826).

As the American nation lurched toward civil war in the middle decades of the century, more and more travelers visited the South; Thomas D. Clark observes that never again would there be so many "in so short a time." By the 1830s most travelers moved along segments of what had become an established "grand tour" in America: along the seaboard to Georgia, across Alabama to Mobile and New Orleans, then up the Mississippi and Ohio, with dips into the interiors of

Tennessee and Kentucky. Many of the travelers were distinguished Europeans (Charles Dickens, Harriet Martineau, Charles Lyell, Fredrika Bremer, Alexis de Tocqueville, Frederick Maryatt), but the most important travel writing of the antebellum years (Tocqueville's *Democracy in America* is not really a travel book) was the work of a young New Englander, Frederick Law Olmsted, who published three books detailing his travels through the South, with *A Journey in the Seaboard Slave States* (1856) being perhaps the most readable. After the war, which occasioned a good bit of fortuitous travel, travelers from abroad tended to bypass the South in their eagerness to board transcontinental trains headed west, but Americans, particularly American journalists, flocked to the South to see and report on postwar conditions and Reconstruction efforts. In addition, "promotional" travel writing extolling the attractions of a "New South" began to appear. The booster literature may not have advanced southern prosperity, but books such as Whitelaw Reid's *After the War: A Southern Tour* (1866) may have furthered the efforts of Radical Republican legislators; later, James Pike's *The Prostrate State: South Carolina under Negro Government* (1874) and Edward King's *The Great South* (1875) undoubtedly helped into being a climate of opinion that welcomed the end of Reconstruction efforts. The last decades of the century were notable for several quirky individualistic classics of southern travel writing: Mark Twain's *Life on the Mississippi* (1883); Charles Dudley Warner's *On Horseback* (1888), about a trip into some of the more rugged sections of Appalachia; and Nathaniel Bishop's two books about his small-craft voyages along the seaboard and down the Mississippi—*Voyage of the Paper Canoe* (1878) and *Four Months in a Sneak-Box* (1879).

In the 20th century the South again figured in the "grand tour" of visitors from abroad, and after World War I the automobile and better highways made the region more accessible to visitors of all sorts, who came in search of health, for economic advantage, and out of curiosity about southern social conditions— with race relations the topic of most concern. Attempting to "get at the facts" about black-white relations was the motive for Ray Stannard Baker's *Following the Color Line* (1908); Jay Saunders Redding's *No Day of Triumph* (1942) is about an auto trip undertaken to obtain insight into the lives of southern blacks; and the issue of race is ever present in Jonathan Daniels's *A Southerner Discovers the South* (1938), which Rupert B. Vance characterizes as "the definitive travel account of the South in the depression." Other striking books from the Great Depression era are Erskine Caldwell and Margaret Bourke-White's *You Have Seen Their Faces* (1937) and James Agee and Walker Evans's *Let Us Now Praise Famous Men* (1941), two books that wed prose and photography. Photographs began to be incorporated in southern travel books as early as the first decade of this century, being essential and integral parts of Clifton Johnson's explorations of southern rural life, *Highways and Byways of the South* (1904) and *Highways and Byways of the Mississippi Valley* (1906). Today, the camera—still, motion picture, video—is as ubiquitous an instrument of southern travel "writing" as the word processor.

Since World War II, when technological change and new wealth set in accelerated motion forces that would forever alter the old agrarian order, and since the Supreme Court's *Brown v. Board of Education* decision of 1954, which marked a drastic unsettling of the "color line" in the South, there has been no abatement of the fascination with, and concern about, the land below the Mason-Dixon line. Books continue to appear that undertake to explore and explain what Jonathan Daniels termed the South's "warm dark." Among all these books, among all this travel writing about the contemporary South, three in particular stand out: John Howard Griffin's *Black Like Me* (1961), about the southern encounters of a white man who chemically darkens his skin; Albert Murray's account of his tentative return to the land of his birth and youth, *South to a Very Old Place* (1971); and perhaps the finest of all the reports on voyages in the wake of Huck and Jim's archetypal trip down the Mississippi, the Britisher Jonathan Raban's *Old Glory* (1981).

More recently, race continues to be a motivating factor for travel to the South. Eddy L. Harris's *South of Haunted Dreams: A Ride through Slavery's Old Back Yard* (1993) recounts a northern black's journey in search of African American identity. "Black Americans as a race are essentially southerners," he concludes. Anthony Walton's *Mississippi: An American Journey* (1996) combines a travel account with memoir, Farm Security Administration photographs, blues lyrics, and his own poetry in searching beneath the mystique of Mississippi for the meaning of race in America. V. S. Naipaul, the well-traveled cosmopolitan writer, found the American South an intriguing place and told of his visit in *A Turn in the South* (1989). Naipaul was surprised by the South's functionary biracial culture, with religious values key to understanding it.

ROBERT WHITE
York University

Thomas D. Clark, ed., *Travels in the Old South: A Bibliography*, 3 vols. (1956), *Travels in the New South: A Bibliography*, 2 vols. (1962); E. Merton Coulter, *Travels in the Confederate States: A Bibliography* (1948); C. Brenden Martin, *Tourism in the Mountain South: A Double-Edged Sword* (2007); Eugene Schwaab and Jacqueline Bull, eds., *Travels in the Old South: Selected from Periodicals of the Times* (1973).

Agee, James

(1909–1955) WRITER.

Born in Knoxville, Tenn., in 1909, James Agee was to remain a dedicated southerner until his death in New York City in 1955. His childhood in Knoxville and his adolescence at St. Andrew's School, later evoked in two of his novels, *A Death in the Family* (1957), which won the Pulitzer Prize in 1958, and *The Morning Watch* (1950), shaped his sensibility and his imagination and provided him with crucial and contradictory experiences—that of happiness and bereavement (after his father's death), that of community and solitude (in the religious atmosphere of the school). Leaving the South to study at Exeter and Harvard, and later becoming the most gifted and versatile writer in the Henry Luce empire, Agee nevertheless liked to think of himself as a sort of hillbilly stranded in the sophisticated world of academia.

When asked by *Fortune* to write an article on sharecroppers, with photographer Walker Evans, he welcomed this opportunity of going back to his roots, "all the way home." This assignment also awakened his sympathy for, and sense of commitment to, the southern poor and led to his most striking work, *Let Us Now Praise Famous Men* (1941), which became a book on three tenant farmer families in the 1930s. It contains some of Agee's best writing: as a poet alive to the "cruel radiance of what is," as an ethnographer respectful of "the other," and as an impassioned humanist angry with injustice and pretense.

Wavering between his attraction to worldly intellectuals and his longing for a humbler, more authentic life in the South, he also vacillated between experimental and realistic writing. Intent on improving his art, he was no less concerned for people, and for the events that shook his times—the Depression, the rise of fascism, the war. As an artist he was extremely curious about all aesthetic forms: poetry (*Permit Me Voyage*, 1974), photography, journalism, and moviemaking. His passion for the cinema, born in his early childhood in Knoxville, drove him to become one of the most attentive and witty film critics and a versatile screenwriter, who went to Hollywood and worked with such directors as Charles Laughton (*The Night of the Hunter*) and John Huston (*The African Queen*). As a journalist, he contributed many articles to *Time* and *Fortune*, and Paul Ashdown has collected the best of Agee's articles from those magazines in *James Agee: Selected Journalism* (1985).

Concerned to avoid involvement in any movement, whether literary or ideological, Agee stands as an isolated, original artist who voyaged far but who never forgot his dedication to his real homeland, the South.

GENEVIÈVE FABRE
Université de Paris III
Sorbonne Nouvelle

Alfred Baxson, *A Way of Seeing: A Critical Study of James Agee* (1972); Lawrence Bergreen, *James Agee* (1984); Mark R. Boty, *Tell Me Who I Am: James Agee's Search for Selfhood* (1981); Michael A. Lofaro and Wilma Dykeman, eds., *James Agee: Reconsiderations* (1992); James Lowe, *The Creative Process of James Agee* (1995); David Madden and Jeffrey J. Folks, eds., *Remembering*

James Agee, Tennessee poet, novelist, and critic, 1930s (James Agee Film Project, Knoxville, Tennessee)

James Agee (1997); Peter H. Ohlin, *Agee* (1966); Kenneth Seib, *James Agee: Promise and Fulfillment* (1968); Alan Spiegel, *James Agee and the Legend of Himself: A Critical Study* (1998).

Aiken, Conrad

(1889–1973) WRITER.

Born in Savannah, Ga., in 1889 of pure New England stock, Conrad Aiken was just 11 years old when he discovered the dead bodies of his parents in an upstairs bedroom. His troubled father, enraged by the real or imagined infidelities of his socialite wife, shot her and then himself only yards away from where their four children slept. Aiken, the eldest, organized the family in the immediate aftermath, but was soon separated from his siblings, settling with his mother's relatives in New Bedford, Mass.

In the absence of this horrific event, it might accurately be said that the South's claims on Aiken are slight. Throughout most of his career as a critic, poet, playwright, novelist, and curator of powerful literary friendships, the dispute over Aiken's "place" raged over whether he was more properly understood as a New England writer or a British one. In the 1920s and 1930s (his most productive period) Aiken cut a transatlantic figure, splitting time between Rye, Sussex, and Massachusetts. But, in keeping with the themes outlined in his novel *The Great Circle* (1933), the South loomed as a psychological place to which Aiken would return again and again in search of solace and understanding. Fittingly, this New Englander spent the last decade of his life in the same town in which he had spent the first; he was even named the poet laureate of Georgia in 1973.

Aiken probes the disconnect between these two locations, North and South, to fascinating effect in his best-known short story "Silent Snow, Secret Snow" (*Among the Lost People*, 1934). The story's protagonist, a prepubescent boy named Paul, retreats into an imagined world of ice and snowfall while listening to a teacher's lecture on the tropics. The snow becomes a powerful image of the psychological wall Paul erects between himself and his parents, whose adult world he associates with the sexual humidity of the tropics. However horrifying, the boy's radical self-isolation might be one of the more benign psychological maladies that Aiken envisions for his "lost people."

Aiken's poetry, though of a piece thematically with his fiction, often complements Freudian self-analysis with a dreamlike transcendentalism acquired from the writings of his maternal grandfather, the liberal humanist and Unitarian minister William James Potter. Arvid Schulenberger calls the union of these two influences in Aiken's poetry "a kind of inverted transcendentalism," a poetry that reaches up even as it attempts to burrow down. Although the result is too often obscure or labored, at its best Aiken's poetry manages to unite precise vision with more pervasive questions about knowledge and identity, as in "Senlin: A Biography" (1918) or "Priapus and the Pool" (1925).

For contemporary scholars Aiken remains of most interest as a shrewd critic of his own contemporaries and for his experimental autobiography, *Ushant* (1952), which includes intimate portraits of friends T. S. Eliot and Malcolm Lowry. Aiken was awarded the Pulitzer Prize for *Selected Poems* in 1930, the Bollingen Prize in 1956, and the National Medal for Literature in 1969. He is buried in Bonaventure cemetery in Savannah, a site made famous by John Berendt's *Midnight in the Garden of Good and Evil* (1994).

SETH M. MARTIN
University of North Carolina at Chapel Hill

Edward Butscher, *Conrad Aiken: Poet of White Horse Vale* (1988); Neil Corcoran, in *Reference Guide to American Literature* (1994); Catherine Kirk Harris, *Conrad Aiken: Critical Recognition, 1914–1981* (1983); Catherine Seigel, *The Fictive World of Conrad Aiken: A Celebration of Consciousness* (1992); Ted R. Spivey, *Time's Stop in Savannah: Conrad Aiken's Inner Journey* (1997); Ted R. Spivey and Arthur Waterman, eds., *Conrad Aiken: A Priest of Consciousness* (1989).

Allen, James Lane

(1849–1925) WRITER AND CRITIC.
Interpreter and defender of the genteel
tradition in postbellum Kentucky,
James Lane Allen was born on a farm
near Lexington in 1849. The youngest
of seven children, Allen was tutored at
home until age 16. Not a member of the
gentry himself, Allen's formal education,
reading, and romantic leanings drew
him to the world of the aristocracy.

Allen thrived as a student at Kentucky University (Transylvania University), despite his family's financial
hardships because of the Civil War and
Reconstruction. Allen graduated in
1872 as class valedictorian. Thereafter,
he filled various teaching positions in
Kentucky, Missouri, and West Virginia.
After more than a decade, Allen returned to Kentucky University for the
M.A. program. He pursued writing full
time by the mid-1880s, writing articles
and stories for well-known publications
of the day, including *Atlantic Monthly*,
Harper's, and *Lippincott's*.

Molded by his education, Allen
began his writing career as a literary
critic. His criticism was built upon
18th-century prose, romantic poetry,
and works with didactic, moral, and
sentimental intent. Allen's influences
included Addison, Steele, Keats, Shelley,
Dickens, Irving, and Hawthorne. His
scientific and mathematical studies
inspired his belief that literature could
be judged based on its adherence to set
standards. For Allen, the main purposes
of literature were entertainment and
instruction, rather than realism.

Along with fellow Kentuckian,
John Fox Jr., Allen wrote fiction that
was part of the local-color movement.
Allen began to write about Kentucky
and Kentuckians: depictions of the state
and its people became his primary aim.
His stories often portrayed the glory of
the antebellum period, focusing on the
central Kentucky, or Bluegrass, gentry,
including people, manners, and social
history. Allen's critical piece "Local
Color" (1886) offered systematic rules
for writing such fiction. Local-color
writers should interpret a given environment's moral and ethical effects on
its inhabitants.

Allen's criticism and local-color
writing garnered national attention.
Many of his short stories were collected
in *Flute and Violin* (1891); his articles
were collected in *The Blue-Grass Region
of Kentucky* (1892). Reputation in tow,
Allen moved to New York in 1893, returning to Kentucky only once. He soon
turned his attention and themes to the
novel. His first was *John Gray* (1893),
followed by the commercially successful
A Kentucky Cardinal (1894).

The Choir Invisible (1897)is often
considered Allen's best work. Instantly
successful, second on the best-seller
list in 1897 and top ten of the 1890s,
it earned Allen wide acclaim. In it he
depicts the inner lives of people on the
Kentucky frontier. Schoolmaster John
Gray falls in love with a married woman
but does not act on his feelings due to
moral conviction. Allen's novels include
Summer in Arcady (1896) and *The Reign
of Law* (1900).

Today, James Lane Allen is generally
regarded as a minor southern writer.
His scientific approach, critical stance,
and desire for gentility cast him out of

vogue in the early 20th century. By 1909 he had alienated much of his audience, especially Kentuckians, with *The Mettle of the Pasture* (1903) and *The Bride of the Mistletoe* (1909). His criticism is yet to be collected into a single volume.

Other Allen works include *The Doctor's Christmas Eve* (1910), *The Heroine in Bronze* (1912), *The Sword of Youth* (1915), *A Cathedral Singer* (1916), *The Kentucky Warbler* (1918), *The Emblems of Fidelity* (1919), *The Alabaster Box* (1923), and *The Landmark* (1925).

NICOLE DREWITZ-CROCKETT
University of Tennessee

William K. Bottorff, *James Lane Allen* (1964); Wade Hall, *The Kentucky Anthology* (2005); Grant C. Knight, *James Lane Allen and the Genteel Tradition* (1966); William S. Ward, *A Literary History of Kentucky* (1988).

Allison, Dorothy

(b. 1949) WRITER.
"Writing is a political act," says Dorothy Allison, whose poems, essays, short stories, and novels depict the experiences and desires of poor, rural, white families from the South. Describing herself as a "cross-eyed working-class lesbian," Allison was born in Greenville, S.C., in 1949, and eventually left South Carolina to attend Florida Presbyterian College, graduating with a B.A. and going on to graduate studies in anthropology. During college she became involved with women's groups, and of this period Allison has commented that "feminism for me was a religious conversion experience." During the 1970s and 1980s, Allison worked in women's collectives and for the magazines *Quest* and *Conditions*, often spending more

time writing grants than writing stories, and in 1982 she participated in the landmark "Towards a Politics of Sexuality" conference at Barnard College. It was the political and literary space of feminist and lesbian journals that first published Allison's works, which grapple with issues of sexual and economic violence. Allison has said that writing and speaking out saved her life, making her feel like a "human being instead of a puppet."

Allison's first book-length work, a collection of poems published by Long Haul Press called *The Women Who Hate Me* (1983), was followed by a collection of short stories published by Firebrand Books, a lesbian and feminist press, called *Trash* (1989), which won Lambda Literary Awards for Lesbian Fiction and for Small Press Book. In 1991 Firebrand Books reissued an expanded version of her poems as *The Women Who Hate Me: Poetry, 1980–1990*. Both *The Women Who Hate Me* and *Trash* were written in the aftermath of the protests that emerged during the Barnard Sexuality conference. Of *Trash*, reviewer Patricia Roth Schwartz wrote, "Rarely have I read such unsparing narrative, dense and gritty with realism, crackling with anger, pulsing with uncompromised sexuality."

It is for *Bastard Out of Carolina* (1992) published by Plume, however, that Allison is most widely known. One of five finalists for the 1992 National Book Award for Fiction, *Bastard Out of Carolina* centers on the life of Ruth Anne "Bone" Boatwright, the bastard of the title and the narrator of the story. Here, Allison emphasizes the transformative power of storytelling and the socially constructed, and therefore contestable, nature of various "truths"—the state of South Carolina names Ruth Anne "illegitimate"; neighbors call her family "white trash"; Bone's mother tells stories to explain Bone's bruises; and Bone's fantasies reframe her sexual abuse. *Bastard Out of Carolina* has been widely translated, and in 1996 a movie version directed by Angelica Huston premiered on Showtime.

Following *Bastard Out of Carolina*, Allison published a collection of essays about sex, desire, and economic privilege in *Skin: Talking about Sex, Class, and Literature* (1994), which won the American Library Association Gay and Lesbian Book Award. This was followed by Allison's memoir, *Two or Three Things I Know for Sure* (1995), named Notable Book of the Year by the *New York Times Book Review*, and adapted in 1998 as a Public Broadcasting System documentary called *Two or Three Things and Nothing for Sure*. Allison's second novel, *The Cavedweller* (1998), also features a female protagonist confronting past violence. It won the Lambda Literary Award for Fiction, and in 2004 Lisa Cholodenko directed a film adaptation. Since *Cavedweller*, Allison has contributed to various collections, including an essay in Michelle Tea's *Without a Net: The Female Experience of Growing up Working Class* and a foreword to Amber Hollibaugh's *My Dangerous Desires: A Queer Girl Dreaming Her Way Home*. She wrote introductions to reissues of Carson McCullers's *The Member of the Wedding* and Djuna Barnes's *Nightwood*

and contributed to a book on artist Ida Applebroog.

In 1988 Allison founded the Independent Spirit Award, an annual prize for authors who publish with small presses and work with independent bookstores. Living in California since 1987, Allison is widely sought as a public speaker and as a writer in residence and is currently working on her third novel.

JILLIAN SANDELL
San Francisco State University

Dorothy Allison, *San Francisco Bay Guardian* (1994), *In These Times* (27 April 2004); Christine Blouch and Laurie Vickroy, *Critical Essays on the Works of American Author Dorothy Allison* (2004); Ann Cvetkovich, *GLQ* 2 (1995); E. J. Graff, *Poets and Writers Magazine* (January–February 1995); Gillian Harkins, in *Incest and the Literary Imagination*, ed. Elizabeth Barnes (2002); K. K. Roeder, *San Francisco Review of Books* 16:4 (1991); Patricia Roth Schwartz, *Belles Lettres* (1989).

Ammons, A. R.

(1926–2001) WRITER.
Born 18 February 1926, Archie Randolph Ammons grew up during the Great Depression on his family's small farm near Whiteville, N.C., located not far from the Atlantic Ocean. After graduating from high school, Ammons worked as a mechanic in a shipyard, and in 1944 he joined the U.S. Navy. Stationed in the South Pacific, Ammons composed his earliest poems while serving on a Navy ship. Later, able to afford college on the G.I. Bill, Ammons attended Wake Forest. His childhood interest in the natural world led him to

study the sciences, primarily medicine, biology, and chemistry. Fond of the vocabularies of those disciplines, he would liberally incorporate scientific words into his poetry.

Upon earning a B.S. degree in 1949, Ammons married Northfield, N.J., native Phyllis Plumbo and accepted a position as principal for an elementary school in Hatteras, N.C. As he composed more poems, Ammons saw need for further formal study. Serving as a principal for one year, Ammons attended graduate school the next year at the University of California at Berkeley. Subsequently, he moved to southern New Jersey, where he would live for 12 years; while there, he began to evoke New Jersey's coastal landscape in innovative and eclectic poetry.

Ammons's initial volume of poems— the self-published book *Ommateum* (1955)—went virtually unnoticed, yet the poet was undaunted. His next two books, *Expressions of Sea Level* (1964) and *Corson's Inlet* (1965), contained poems that improved upon the work in *Ommateum* by exhibiting a surer sense of language and form and by revealing a more mature philosophical perspective. Whereas in his first book he had played the role of an isolated prophet, Ammons in his second and third books embodied the more public role of visionary; the newer poems challenged readers to deepen their perceptions of the world of "things" (i.e., of quotidian reality).

In 1964, after giving a poetry reading at Cornell University in Ithaca, N.Y., Ammons was hired to teach for Cor-

nell's English Department. Remaining at that university the rest of his teaching career, he was eventually granted the title Goldwin Smith Professor of Poetry. Ammons's subsequent books include such critically recognized volumes as *Tape for the Turn of the Year* (1965), which contained a single book-length poem; *Collected Poems, 1951–1971* (1972), winner of the National Book Award for Poetry; *The Snow Poems* (1977), which incorporated many of his most overtly autobiographical poems; *A Coast of Trees* (1981), selected for the National Book Critics Circle Award for Poetry; and *Garbage* (1993), which, featuring one long poem that critiqued contemporary culture and reassessed the poet's own life and work, was also a National Book Award winner. Ammons, after enduring illness for several years, died on 25 February 2001. A posthumous volume, *Bosh and Flapdoodle* (2005), collected poems composed by the poet shortly before his death.

Ammons was the recipient of more critical praise than virtually any other American poet during the final decades of the 20th century, garnering support from major literary scholars (such as Harold Bloom and Helen Vendler) and receiving, in addition to the aforementioned accolades, the Bollingen Prize for Poetry, a Guggenheim Fellowship, the Lannan Foundation Award, and a MacArthur fellowship. Many of Ammons's poems reflect his background in eastern North Carolina, and some of his finest poems (such as "Easter Morning") offer sophisticated, eloquent, and original expressions of the meanings of place, community, and the past. Taken as a whole, Ammons's work can be interpreted as being the poet's attempt as an expatriate southerner living in the North to reconcile with and return to his beloved if difficult southern cultural roots.

TED OLSON
East Tennessee State University

Alan Holder, *A. R. Ammons* (1978); Ted Olson, *North Carolina Literary Review* (2006); Donald H. Reiman, *Twentieth-Century Literature* (Spring 1985).

Andrews, Raymond

(1934–1991) WRITER AND ILLUSTRATOR.

Raymond Andrews was born 6 June 1934 in the southern, rural city of Madison in Morgan County, Ga., the fourth child of 10, to sharecroppers. Within this tight-knit African American community, Andrews was first introduced to and fell in love with the oral tradition out of which his writing grew. He often stated that there was nothing he loved more than a good story. He began drawing and reading voraciously at a very young age. Eventually reading became his sole pursuit. Reading, in turn, piqued his desire at a very young age to become a writer; however, his first work was not published until very late in his life.

In 1949 he left the cotton fields of Georgia and joined the great southern migration northward. There he worked a succession of jobs before joining the air force in 1952. After his discharge in 1956, Andrews attended Michigan State University. He did not graduate but continued to labor in various fields. During his stint as an airline employee, he reached an impasse. Frustrated, he abruptly walked away from his job determined to write.

Drawing extensively upon his experience as a youth growing up in the South and determined to portray the complexity of small-town, rural, African American life there prior to the civil rights movement as blacks sought to come to terms with the land as well as their white neighbors, Andrews began his first novel, *Appalachee Red*, in 1968 at age 34. It was not published until 10 years later. *Appalachee Red* began first as a poem, which soon evolved into a short story and then a novella before it assumed its final form.

Appalachee Red was the first, and perhaps most well known, of the trilogy of novels Andrews penned set in the mythical northeastern Georgian milieu of Muskhogean County in the city of Appalachee. The novel earned Andrews the James Baldwin Prize for Fiction (1978). *Rosiebelle Lee Wildcat Tennessee* (1979) and *Baby Sweet's* (1983) round out the trilogy.

Through the trilogy, as well as his subsequent works, Andrews deftly and insightfully examined the complex interracial relationships conditioned by the institution of slavery and the subsequent period of Reconstruction of blacks and whites living in close proximity. The effect of this unequal relationship and the various postures the characters must assume because of the demands of a repressive social system are always in evidence. Not only do African Americans suffer adversely, but whites, too, find themselves veritable prisoners of the social structure they work so hard to maintain.

Against the machinations and violence of a social system that tempers every aspect of their existence, Andrews developed outrageous, larger than life African American characters, both male and female, that are almost Homeric in proportion. In doing so, however, he reveals a reactionary African American community not without its own flaws, complete with its own social divisions based on class and skin color in which the victimized often become victimizers who wreak havoc on the lives of those closest to them.

Following his trilogy, Andrews published his memoir, *The Last Radio Baby: A Memoir* (1990), and the novellas *Jessie and Jesus* and *Cousin Claire* (1991). In addition, he illustrated Lily Mathieu Labraque's *Man from Mono* (1991).

Critics recognized Andrews for his ability to accurately capture the melodic rhythms of the southern dialect, his adeptness in weaving intricate but accessible narratives, as well as his deep understanding of life in a small southern town. Perhaps Andrew's greatest strength was his ability to capture the intricacies and vicissitudes of African American southern existence within this period of virulent racial discrimination and segregation prior to the civil rights movement. He subtly interjects a sense of often boisterous humor in the daily tragedy, violence, and heartbreak that characterized African American life in the South without ever trivializing the situation. He is often depicted as a *griot* of sorts who engaged in the revisionist project of retelling the social history of the South from an African American point of view.

Andrews died in 1991 of self-inflicted gunshot wounds. Emory University currently houses a collection of his papers.

JAMES ARTHUR GENTRY
University of Florida

Keith Byerman, *Remembering the Past in Contemporary African American Fiction* (2005); Jeffrey J. Folks, *Southern Literary Journal* (Spring 1986); Trudier Harris, in *Contemporary Black Men's Fiction and Drama*, ed. Keith Clark (2001); M. Daphne Kutzer, ed., *Writers of Multicultural Fiction for Young Adults* (1996); Susan M. Trosky, *Contemporary Authors, New Revision Series* (1994).

Ansa, Tina McElroy

(b. 1949) WRITER.

Tina McElroy Ansa has enjoyed great popularity with readers and with budding writers. Perhaps her early success as a novelist can be attributed to her daring use of racy scenes and language, sprinklings of pop culture, and even supernatural elements such as ghosts. Indeed, Ansa's fiction has attracted early critical attention. It is fitting, then, that Ansa has also been active as a mentor for new writers at an annual writer's retreat she hosts. In a competitive publishing market, Ansa's literary career remains an inspiration.

Tina McElroy Ansa grew up in Macon, Ga., which she uses as a model for the fictional town of Mulberry in her novels. Ansa graduated from Spelman College in 1971, the same year she became the first black woman to work at the *Atlanta Constitution*. Ansa lives on

St. Simon's Island and, since 2004, has hosted the Sea Island Writer's Retreat held at Sapelo Island, Ga. Ansa's greatest influence was Zora Neale Hurston, who also wrote proudly about women of color.

One unusual aspect of Ansa's fiction is her use of ghosts. *Ugly Ways* (1993) handles the spiritual realm by having "Mudear" remain a powerful influence on her three grown daughters even after her death. In Ansa's other novels, ghosts play leading roles, starting with the introduction of Lena McPherson in *The Baby of the Family* (1989), Ansa's first novel. Based on the author's own childhood as the baby of the family growing up in middle Georgia, the book explains that the protagonist Lena is also special, even magic, because she was "born with a caul over her face," a rare event said to have given the child the ability to communicate with ghosts. Even though Lena's mother destroyed the caul and did not believe in such tales, Lena does have special abilities.

Ansa returns to the character Lena for *The Hand I Fan With* (1996). Lena, now middle-aged, is successful as a business owner and as the proud possessor of a luxuriously appointed home. Lena's problem is that she takes care of everyone else in the community before she takes care of her own needs. She has a beautiful car, home, land, and designer clothes, but she does not have romantic love or passion in her life. Ansa created a lover for Lena who is a ghost—but a ghost capable of doing anything a living man could do and more. Although Lena has always been special and lucky, her new lover finally makes her life com-plete when he teaches her how to enjoy life for herself.

You Know Better (2002) portrays three generations of black women in the same family. The youngest generation is represented by LaShawndra Pines, who is immature and wild, but whose immaturity is the result of her upbringing and therefore provides a comment on society as a whole. Ansa cleverly represents the low but rich phrasing of contemporary youth when her characters talk about "my baby daddy" and being "a little freak." Lily Paine Pines, Ansa's character of the oldest generation, wisely calls much of this brash, youthful talk destructive. Ansa designed a chapter for each woman's perspective on her own life and on the two other generations: mother, daughter, granddaughter. This structure allows Ansa to comment insightfully on contemporary issues of race, gender, and age.

RACHEL G. WALL
Georgia State University

Barbara Bennett, in *The World Is Our Culture: Society and Culture in Contemporary Southern Writing*, ed. Jeffery J. Folks and Nancy Summers Folks (2000); Novella Brooks de Vita, *Griot* (Spring 2005); Warren Nagueyalti, *CLA Journal* (March 2003); Gloria Naylor, *Essence* (May 1995).

Applewhite, James

(b. 1935) POET AND LITERARY CRITIC.

James Applewhite transforms the sounds and sights of his southern experience into honest, often lyric, reflective poetry. The reader who seeks to "understand [his] accent" will learn what it means to be born in Stantonsburg, N.C., in 1935 and carry that time and place with him always. The legacy of Stantonsburg, a rural tobacco-farming town of 700, marks Applewhite's poetic voice as much as the sound of "broom sedge in wind" affects his speech. The influence of Stantonsburg's rural landscape is matched only by the population's racial divide, like many small southern towns, almost equally split between black and white. An awareness of historic separations—town from country, white from black, and tradition from change—carries through Applewhite's 1975 *Statues of Grass* to his 2006 *A Diary of Altered Light*.

This 30-year span of poetic discovery and experience, largely encapsulated in the 2005 *Selected Poems*, follows the poet's move from the tobacco-farming region of Wilson County 80 miles northwest to Durham County and Duke University. Within the period of college education and his early teaching, Applewhite found two of his early poetic influences and two of his major themes. He received a B.A. from Duke under the mentorship of William Blackburn and earned his M.A. there with a thesis on Faulkner's *The Sound and the Fury*. He then worked with Randall Jarrell for three years as an instructor at Woman's College in Greensboro, N.C., after which he returned to Duke for a Ph.D. and completed a dissertation on William Wordsworth.

Blackburn and Jarrell helped bring the younger poet to ideals of the remote, rural life espoused in the 1930s by the Agrarian movement. The works of Faulkner and Wordsworth, furthermore, connected with Applewhite's sense of place in the agrarian South and the beauty of its landscape and people. In a 2006 interview with the North Carolina Arts Council, Applewhite summarizes Wordsworth's influence: "Like the water that fish swim in; assumed. Wordsworth brought the human quest for meaning down out of the mythological clouds and situated it in the landscape, in recognizable characters, traveling through space and time." For Applewhite, this landscape is both rural North Carolina and Durham's Eno River; these characters are the extended Applewhite family as well as new mentors and friends, all traveling from the re-created past into the poetically imagined future. While Faulkner's South is still reflected in agrarian "hierarchical ownership of land" and the persistent injustices of its past, Applewhite notes that those stereotypes are now exaggerated and "beyond ridiculous."

Applewhite seeks to explore the constant changes of southern society and thought against the backdrop of an often changeless natural abundance. The man-made aspects of landscape often decay, as in "State Road 134" and its "Two board shacks with / windowpanes crushed by the heat, / paint bruised off by a weight of deprivation." The promise of nature, however, endures; in "Upstream from the Little River Reservoir," Applewhite writes: "The Little River shivers with times in contrast. / The history I breathe is alive, exists to save. / When we reverence what we shall become, / we walk within the reservoir of time, / inhaling *origin* like oxygen."

STEVE SCHESSLER
Emory University

James Applewhite, *Raleigh News and Observer* (September 2005); George S. Lensing, *Southern Review* (December 1995); Jynne Dilling Martin, *Duke Magazine* (November–December 2002); Sylvia Pfeiffenberger, *Duke University News and Communications* (December 2005); Katharine Walton, North Carolina Arts Council (ncarts.com) (2006).

Armstrong, Anne Wetzell

(1872–1958) WRITER, BUSINESSWOMAN, AND LECTURER. Anne Wetzell Armstrong spent much of her life in the South and wrote about the people of the southern Appalachian region. She was born 20 September 1872 in Grand Rapids, Mich., to Henry B. and Lorinda (Snyder) Wetzell. In 1885 the family moved to Knoxville, Tenn., where her father operated a lumber business. Anne Audubon Wetzell attended Mount Holyoke College, Mass., during the 1889–90 and 1890–91 school years, but did not graduate. On 1 July 1892 she married Leonard T. Waldron and gave birth to a son, Roger Waldron, on 8 September 1893. The marriage ended in divorce in 1894, and for a time Annie Wetzell Waldron taught at Girls' High School in Knoxville. During the summer of 1898, she took courses at the University of Chicago. She married Robert Franklin Armstrong on 14 June 1905, and the couple lived for a few years in Harriman, Tenn. Around 1911 they came to Bristol, Tenn., and in 1916 built a home, "Knobside," near the Holston River in a mountainous part of Sullivan County.

Although Anne Armstrong is best known for her novel *This Day and Time* (1930), which is considered one of the earliest examples of realistic writing about the Appalachian region, she had published an earlier novel, *The Seas of God*, anonymously in 1915. Her identity as the author was revealed the following year when the book was published in Great Britain. *The Seas of God* is the story of a young woman who has grown up in a southern town (patterned after Knoxville, but called "Kingsville" in the novel), which she leaves after the death of her father to seek her fortune. She ends up in New York City and eventually becomes a kept woman. Many passages in the book are highly descriptive of the social conditions, customs, culture, and natural beauty of the South (as remembered by the main character) at that time.

This Day and Time also has as its main character a young woman struggling to eke out a living for herself and her young son. However, this book is set in the hill country of upper east Tennessee and southwest Virginia (although not specifically identified), where Armstrong was living at the time, and the heroine works the land—refusing the advances of lecherous suitors and living a very different life from that of the protagonist in *The Seas of God*.

In addition to these two novels, Armstrong published numerous journal and magazine articles, many based on her experiences as a businesswoman. She began working as personnel director for the National City Company of New York City in 1918, an experience described in her article "A Woman in Wall Street—by One," published in the *Atlantic Monthly* in 1925. From 1919 to 1923, she was assistant manager of

Industrial Relations for Eastman Kodak Company in Rochester, N.Y. During the following 10 to 12 years, Armstrong wrote and lectured on business, labor relations, and issues involving women in the work force. She chaired two sessions at the annual convention of the Industrial Relations Association of America in 1920, was a featured speaker at the annual convention of the National Federation of Business and Professional Women's Clubs in 1928, and is reported to have been the first woman to speak before Tuck School of Business at Dartmouth and the Harvard School of Business Administration.

Sometime during the latter half of the 1920s, Armstrong and her husband returned to Knobside, making it their permanent home. After Robert Armstrong's death in 1931, Anne Armstrong continued living at Knobside until the 1940s when the Tennessee Valley Authority (TVA) built South Holston Dam, creating a lake that took her home. In following years, she lived at various times in Asheville, N.C.; Lafayette, La.; and Abingdon, Va., where she died 17 March 1958. Other articles for which Anne W. Armstrong is known and still cited include "The Southern Mountaineers" (*Yale Review*, 1935) and "As I Saw Thomas Wolfe" (*Arizona Quarterly*, 1946).

LINDA BEHREND
University of Tennessee

Anne W. Armstrong, *This Day and Time*, with a personal reminiscence by David Mc-Clellan (1970); Linda Behrend, in *Encyclopedia of Appalachia*, ed. Rudy Abramson and Jean Haskell (2006); Robert J. Higgs, in *An Encyclopedia of East Tennessee*, ed.

Jim Stokely and Jeff D. Johnson (1981); *Who Was Who among North American Authors, 1921–1939* (1976).

Arnow, Harriette Simpson

(1908–1986) WRITER.

Born at home in Wayne County, Ky., on 7 July 1908, Harriette Simpson spent her early years in the Cumberland Mountains of Kentucky and wrote about the region and its people for the rest of her life. The second oldest of six children, she lived with her family in and around the town of Burnside until graduating from high school in 1924. Although she spent most of her adult years in Michigan, rural Kentucky hill people and landscapes profoundly affected her imagination and her work.

Her early short stories appeared in "little literary magazines" of the 1930s, as well as the *Southern Review, Atlantic Monthly*, and *Esquire* (under the name H. L. Simpson, and with a photo of her brother-in-law, at a time when the magazine did not accept submissions from women). She is best known as a novelist, with five novels published during her lifetime. The first three books—*Mountain Path* (1936), *Hunter's Horn* (1949), and *The Dollmaker* (1954)—provide a compelling chronicle of southern history by illustrating in human terms what happened to Appalachian communities from the 1920s through World War II. Set in the same region of Kentucky where she grew up, these novels include place-names and characters that loosely link them together. She told interviewers that she had envisioned the novels as a trilogy recording what happened to mountain people as roads came in and people left home for northern industrial cities: her working titles were *Path*, *End of the Gravel*, and *Highway*.

In 1939 Harriette L. Simpson married Harold B. Arnow, a fellow writer for the Federal Writers Project in Cincinnati, and bought a 150-acre farm bordering the Cumberland National Forest, where they lived for five years. They had four children, two of whom, a daughter, Marcella, and a son, Thomas, survived to adulthood. The family moved to Detroit in 1945 and lived in wartime housing, where Arnow began writing *Hunter's Horn*, an innovative novel that subverts traditional American male hunting stories by devoting equal time to the dramas of women's lives. *Hunter's Horn* explores the costs—to an individual, a family, a community—of following an obsession. Arnow admitted that this rich, heartbreaking novel was her favorite.

While in Detroit, Arnow got the idea for *The Dollmaker* as she wondered how her rural Kentucky neighbors would have fared there. *The Dollmaker* is an unprecedented account of the lives of rural southerners who stayed in America but were forever changed by World War II. Arnow's character Gertie Nevels is a wife, mother, and artist whose admirable abilities to farm and care for her family in Kentucky are compromised when they move to Detroit for her husband to find work during the war. In urban temporary housing, her family must learn to "adjust" or suffer immeasurable losses, a fate also faced by neighbors relocated from their homeplaces by the war. This remarkable American novel contains some of Arnow's most powerful writing.

Best known for the historical authenticity of her fiction about southern Appalachia, Arnow is the author of three additional novels, three nonfiction books, and a collection of short stories. *The Weedkiller's Daughter* (1970), an environmental novel with an anti-McCarthyism subplot, is her only work set entirely in Michigan, though Gertie Nevels appears here as a character called The Primitive. *The Kentucky Trace: A Novel of the American Revolution* (1974) features a makeshift family of a land surveyor who adopts a child and befriends a Native American boy. *Between the Flowers* (1999), written prior to *Hunter's Horn*, is the story of a marriage between a world-traveling oil man who wants to put down roots and a Kentucky woman who longs to travel the world and break free of deep ties to her rural community. *Seedtime on the Cumberland* (1961) and *Flowering of the Cumberland* (1963) are award-winning social histories, the former focusing on lives of lone frontiersmen, and the latter on daily lives of pioneer families in the Cumberland mountains, from the earliest settlement to the Louisiana Purchase (1780–1803). *Old Burnside* (1976), Arnow's only autobiographical book, describes growing up in her hometown. *The Collected Short Stories of Harriette Simpson Arnow* (2005) includes 25 stories, 15 of which were previously unpublished.

SANDRA L. BALLARD
Appalachian State University

Harriette Simpson Arnow, introduction to
Mountain Path (1963); Thomas L. Arnow,
Appalachian Journal (Summer 2005);
Barbara L. Baer, Sandra L. Ballard, Glenda
Hobbs, Danny L. Miller, and Kathleen Walsh,
in *Harriette Simpson Arnow: Critical Essays
on Her Work*, ed. Haeja K. Chung (1995).

Atkins, Ace

(b. 1970) WRITER.

Though he was born William Ellis
Atkins on 28 June 1970 in Troy, Ala.,
no one has ever called the author anything but "Ace." Before he had reached
30, Atkins had been nominated for a
Pulitzer Prize and published two critically acclaimed crime novels featuring the only fictional detective with a
doctorate in southern studies from the
University of Mississippi.

After the first of his crime novels,
Crossroad Blues (1998), was published,
Kinky Friedman wrote, "If Raymond
Chandler came from the South, his
name would be Ace Atkins." Indeed,
Crossroad Blues and Atkins's subsequent three novels—*Leavin' Trunk Blues*
(2000), *Dark End of the Street* (2002),
and *Dirty South* (2004)—can be enjoyed
simply as traditional detective novels,
written with a keen eye for detail in
language that is, in turn, brutal and
lyrical. They are southern noir spiced
with humor and unexpected plot twists
involving indelible characters who are
often eccentric (like the albino Cracker
and oddly endearing Elvis-wannabe hit
man introduced in *Crossroad Blues*) and
sometimes despicable (like the socio-
path Stagger Lee and butcher-knife-
wielding Annie in *Leavin' Trunk*).

Lovers of the blues and Elvis Presley—as Atkins is—can also appreciate
his first four novels on another level. A
James Bond fan from his youth, Atkins
acknowledges that Ian Fleming's novels
"were one of the reasons I became
a writer," and he admires Chandler,
Ernest Hemingway, and Dashiell
Hammett. However, he also cites the
influence of blues legends Robert Johnson and Muddy Waters on his work.
Atkins describes his novels as "a cross-
pollination of hard-boiled detective
stories with southern music."

His protagonist Nick Travers teaches
blues history at Tulane and hangs out in
the blues bar owned by his best friends,
JoJo Jackson and his blues-singing wife,
Loretta (who are recurring characters
in all the novels). His investigations
take him to the Mississippi Delta in
search of nine lost Robert Johnson
recordings and to Chicago's South Side
to help out an imprisoned blues singer
who migrated there like so many other
Mississippi blacks. In Memphis and at
the Tunica casinos, he encounters the
Dixie Mafia and a forgotten, supposedly
dead soul singer. The final novel of the
series returns to Louisiana and involves
a teen-age Dirty South rapper from the
notorious Calliope housing project.
Readers who go along for the ride end
up sharing Atkins' fascination with the
blues, whether they started out that way
or not.

Travers is also an ex-pro football
player, reflecting Atkins's own background. His father, Billy Atkins, was an
All-Pro football player and later coach
with the Buffalo Bills, and Ace played

defensive end on the 1993 undefeated Auburn football team.

In 2006 Atkins left the popular Nick Travers series behind and began exploring real-life crime with the publication of *White Shadow*, based on the murder of Tampa, Fla., crime boss Charlie Wall in 1955. It grew out of work during Atkins's five years as a crime reporter with the *Tampa Tribune*, preceded by a year with the *St. Petersburg Times*. In 2000 he earned Pulitzer Prize and Livingston Prize nominations for his seven-part series "Tampa Confidential," on the 1956 slaying of socialite Edy Parkhill, the wife of Charlie Wall's attorney. During the voluminous research on the series, Atkins was given the 2,000-page file on Wall's bludgeoning death.

Wall's story and images of the vibrant and violent life in 1950s Tampa stayed with Atkins when he left the *Tribune* in 2001 to move to Oxford, Miss., and write full time. *White Shadow* is the culmination of five years of revisiting court and police records, interviewing surviving observers of the 1950s scene, and even taking a trip to Cuba. Because the crime is still officially unsolved, Atkins wrote the story as fiction. However, he uses the names of many of those involved in real life and makes it plain who he thinks was guilty.

Atkins lives in a century-old farm house in rural Lafayette County with his wife, Angela, and an ever-changing pack of rescued canines led by his beloved mutt Elvis.

JAN HUMBER ROBERTSON
Oxford, Mississippi

Dick Lochte, *Los Angeles Times* (1 July 2006); Kevin Walker, *Tampa Tribune* (7 May 2006).

Baldacci, David

(b. 1960) WRITER.

David Baldacci, a best-selling novelist and a philanthropist, was born in Richmond, Va., where he currently resides. He earned his B.A. degree in political science from Virginia Commonwealth University, completed his law degree at the University of Virginia, and practiced law in Washington, D.C., for nine years as both a trial and a corporate attorney. Throughout his years of education, Baldacci wrote for his private satisfaction in the evenings, but he finally decided to abandon law for literature with the publication of *Absolute Power* in 1996. This novel of murder and corruption in the American presidency and the Secret Service struck a wildly popular chord with the public, and it became a film with Clint Eastwood and Gene Hackman a year later.

Baldacci has continued annually to produce a remarkable series of national and international best sellers translated into more than 37 languages in over 85 countries: *Total Control* (1996), *The Winner* (1997), *The Simple Truth* (1998), *Saving Faith* (1999), *Wish You Well* (2000), *Last Man Standing* (2001), *The Christmas Train* (2002), *Split Second* (2003), *Hour Game* (2004), *The Camel Club* (2005), and *The Collectors* (2006), mostly thrillers reflecting contemporary political and news events in the corridors of power. A clean, clear prose and clever plot development mark his stories often told through the voices of innocents who unintentionally witness dangerous circumstances and seek answers to the questions they raise.

He has authored several screen plays and young adult novels, as well as short stories, essays, and articles published in magazines and periodicals here and abroad. His books attract high profile readers across the political spectrum, from Bill Clinton, Charlie Rose, and Larry King to George H. W. Bush, Rush Limbaugh, and Newt Gingrich. Reading John Irving's *The World according to Garp* made him want to be a novelist, and he counts among his inspirations Mark Twain, Flannery O'Connor, Eudora Welty, Walker Percy, Truman Capote, and Harper Lee.

When not writing, Baldacci spends much of his time working as a philanthropist on behalf of such charities as the National Multiple Sclerosis Society, the American Cancer Society, and the Cystic Fibrosis Foundation, and serving on the boards of the Virginia Foundation for the Humanities, the Virginia Literacy Foundation, and Virginia Commonwealth University.

M. THOMAS INGE
Randolph-Macon College

Barth, John
(b. 1930) WRITER.

Born on 27 May 1930, in Cambridge, Md., on the Eastern Shore—an area one of the characters in the author's 1979 novel LETTERS asserts is "more southern than Virginia"—John Barth is technically a southerner. A southern postmodernist, one of the first of his generation, and the author of ten books of fiction, the best known of which are

The Floating Opera (1956), *The Sot-Weed Factor* (1960), *Giles Goat-Boy* (1966), and *Lost in the Funhouse* (1968), Barth rejects, in his most representative work, traditional notions of storytelling associated with the realistic novel. Instead, he regards reality as based on words, transitory and relativistic; and he focuses self-consciously on the writing process. In so doing, he often reconfigures literature, history, and myth and, in recycling them, creates a fresh imaginative construct, which he intends his reader to view as artifice rather than as an imitation of life. In his experimentation with narrative technique, Barth has discovered new and vital ways of presenting old narratives and new meanings. Thus, storytelling itself is Barth's preeminent concern.

Barth's interest in a sense of place and history—that place and history associated with the Mid-Atlantic South of Maryland's Eastern Shore, both real and imagined—may be the best indication of his connection with traditional southern literature and culture. Maryland's Eastern Shore landscapes, its environs, society, and culture, are prominent ingredients in all his works, except *Giles Goat-Boy*. His story collection, *Lost in the Funhouse*, includes four stories with Maryland place descriptions, particularly East Dorset, Barth's fictional creation based on his Cambridge, Md., birthplace. LETTERS, one of his most ambitious books, is an epistolary novel employing multiple narrative voices to present different perspectives of the same story, as Faulkner does in *Absalom, Absalom!* (1936). An exercise in self-reflexivity, LETTERS features

Barth himself and some of his previous fictional characters and their descendants writing letters to each other. In doing this, he employs a strategy similar to that of Faulkner, who sometimes revived characters with continuing chronicles such as he does with Quentin Compson of *The Sound and the Fury* (1929), whom he resurrected in *Absalom, Absalom!* so readers could view Quentin working through problems that led to his suicide in the earlier novel.

Barth's most southern-based work is *The Sot-Weed Factor*, a novel with a picaresque structure that features ribald parody and that purports to be the life of Ebenezer Cooke, an actual historical personage and author of an 18th-century satirical poem of the same title. In *The Sot-Weed Factor* Barth employs what he has called "historical imitation," a refashioning of history and the creation of pseudohistories, thereby freeing fiction "from all the conventions of realism," and in using these techniques, he debunks colonial Maryland and Virginia. In his comical, freewheeling recasting of spurious tales of history, such as the John Smith–Pocahontas tale and his invention of lively and sometimes bawdry details from fictionalized historical accounts such as *The Privie Journall of Sir Henry Burlingame*, Barth gives a fictional quality to his stories, presenting a comically satirical corrective to the more conventional script of Maryland's and Virginia's early history.

The Sot-Weed Factor, which treats a conflict of cultures, also shares another connection with the southern literary tradition. Ebenezer Cooke, the central character, voyages from England to Maryland to claim an estate, which he discovers to be an opium den and a brothel that he inherited from his father. Naive and impressionable and a victim of many scams, Ebenezer resembles the tenderfoot-outsider found in sketches and tales of the humorists of the Old Southwest. Proclaiming himself to be poet laureate of Maryland, Ebenezer originally intends to compose a celebratory poem, *Marylandiad*, based on his impressions of Maryland, but he is duped by almost everyone whom he meets—aristocrats, prostitutes, barmaids, chimney sweeps, and mostly his tutor, the trickster-hypocrite Henry Burlingame—whose roguishness and amorality suggest a literary kinship with some of the trickster-rascals of southwestern humor.

While John Barth may not have many of the requisites usually associated with the mainstream of southern writing, and while his prevalent themes and subject matter may not be those commonly found in southern literature, he often treats in his work Maryland's Eastern Shore, the region of his origins and the section of the state most discernibly southern. Along with this, his fascination with history, particularly the invention of new and sometimes burlesque historical perspectives, his preoccupation with the storytelling process, and his use of some of the character types, techniques, and naughty and coarse comic fare found in southwestern humor may further justify a modest and secure place for him in the southern literary canon.

EDWARD J. PIACENTINO
High Point University

Zack Bowen, *A Reader's Guide to John Barth* (1994); John J. Enck, *Wisconsin Studies in Contemporary Literature* (1965); Stan Fogel and Gordon Slethaug, *Understanding John Barth* (1990); Alan Prince, *Prism* (Spring 1968); E. P. Walkiewiez, *John Barth* (1986).

Barthelme, Frederick

(b. 1943) WRITER.

Frederick Barthelme has worked as a writer, educator, editor, and artist, although he may be best known for his fiction. He is critically acclaimed as a master of literary minimalism, a title that causes him some discomfort. The American South provides both the setting for his fiction and much of his professional life as writer and professor at the University of Southern Mississippi.

Frederick Barthelme was born 10 October 1943 in Houston, Tex., to Donald Barthelme, an accomplished modernist architect, and Helen Bechtold Barthelme, a teacher. He is one of seven children from a literary family, including brothers Donald and Steven—both respected writers. Barthelme attended Tulane University in 1961–62 and the University of Houston from 1962 to 1965 and in 66–67. In 1965–66 he studied at the Museum of Fine Arts in Houston, Tex., pursuing his initial ambition to become a painter.

Barthelme worked in the art world for several years after receiving his B.A. from the University of Houston. While building a painting career, he worked as an architectural draftsman, an exhibit installer, assistant to the director of the Kornblee Gallery in New York City, and creative director and senior writer at several Houston advertising firms.

During this period, his artwork was featured in many galleries, including the Louisiana Gallery in Houston, Tex., the Museum of Normal Art in New York City, the Seattle Art Museum, and the Museum of Modern Art in New York City.

During his time in New York, Barthelme decided to change artistic direction because, as he later stated, he "didn't want to carry big pieces of lumber through the streets of New York" for the rest of his life. He transitioned from working with found objects to viewing books as "containers" and not as literary entertainment. This transition can be seen in his first two books, after which he became interested explicitly in the craft of fiction. He enrolled at the Johns Hopkins University and earned an M.A. from the Department of Writing Seminars in 1977. At Johns Hopkins, Barthelme's short story "The Storyteller" earned the Eliot Coleman Award for Prose in 1976–77.

In 1977 he took a position as director of the Center for Writers at the University of Southern Mississippi, where he has remained. Early in his career, he received major grants and acted as a leader in writers' organizations. Today, Barthelme continues to direct the Center for Writers at the University of Southern Mississippi and edits *Mississippi Review*, a quarterly publication that includes poetry, fiction, and creative nonfiction pieces. He is a member of PEN, Associated Writing Programs, and the Coordinating Council of Literary Magazines. In 2004 he was nominated for the PEN/Faulkner Award for Fiction for his novel *Elroy Nights*.

Barthelme has written 14 books. His collections of stories are *Rangoon* (1970), *Moon Deluxe* (1983), *Chroma* (1987), and *The Law of Averages: New and Selected Stories* (2000). He has written the novels *War and War* (1971), *Second Marriage* (1984), *Tracer* (1985), *Two against One* (1988), *Natural Selection* (1990), *The Brothers* (1993), *Painted Desert* (1995), *Bob the Gambler* (1997), and *Elroy Nights* (2003). In 1999 Barthelme published the memoir *Double Down: Reflections on Gambling and Loss*, with his brother, Steven. He also wrote the text for a book called *Trip* (1999), with photographs by Susan Lipper. In addition to books, he has authored the screenplays *Second Marriage* (1985) and *Tracer* (1986), and his work appears in numerous periodicals.

Characterized by *Los Angeles Times* reviewer Daniel Akst as the "bard of suburban disconnectedness," Barthelme belongs to what has become known as the minimalist movement of writing. His books and short stories portray a world that critics call the New South, defined by shopping malls and brand names. Through economical use of language and dialogue, and vivid description peppered with buzzwords of contemporary American culture, Barthelme captures modern life in suburban America and thus comments on the changing landscape of the modern South. Barthelme's style indicates he is "not particularly interested in plot or story," as James Kaufmann noted in the *Washington Post Book World* but rather "in scenes, in snapshots which illustrate such fashionable problems as fear of intimacy, loneliness, hostility, and other

sub-clinical manifestations of the modern malaise."

FRANCES ABBOTT
University of Mississippi

John C. Hughes, *The Novels and Short Stories of Frederick Barthelme: A Literary Critical Analysis* (2005), *Frederick Barthelme* (2004); *Contemporary Literary Criticism*, vol. 36, (1986); *Dictionary of Literary Biography Yearbook: 1985* (1986).

Bass, Rick

(b. 1958) WRITER.

The son of a geologist, Rick Bass seemed in the process of following in his father's footsteps, graduating with a degree in geology from Utah State University in 1979 and subsequently moving to Mississippi to work as a petroleum geologist in charge of prospecting for new wells. But shortly after finishing college, he began to write magazine articles about hunting and fishing, work that led to the publication of his first two books of essays, *The Deer Pasture* (1985) and *Wild to the Heart* (1987). Since that time, Bass has published more than a dozen works of fiction and nonfiction.

In 1987 Bass moved with his family to the Yaak Valley in the northwest corner of Montana to dedicate himself to writing full time. Two years later he published a memoir of his time as a geologist in Mississippi, *Oil Notes*, and his first collection of stories, *The Watch*, which won the 1988 PEN/Nelson Algren Award. The title story, set in the piney woods and swamps of central Mississippi, also won a 1989 O. Henry Award. The central theme of the collection is the passage of time and human relations to it, and this concern, with humanity and its connections to the natural world, temporally as well as physically and spiritually, has become the defining characteristic of Bass's work. Bass has called Montana the state of his "rebirth," and often in his writing the wilderness is the source of a revitalizing power. In works such as *Winter: Notes from Montana* (1991), *In the Loyal Mountains* (1995), *The Sky, the Stars, the Wilderness* (1997), *The Hermit's Story*, and *The Diezmo* (2005) Bass explores the nature and potential of this power, and they have solidified his reputation as significant writer and activist.

A founding member of the Yaak Valley Forest Council, which works for conservation and restoration in the area, Bass continues to live and work in northwest Montana.

JACOB SULLINS
Georgia State University

Bonnie Lyons and Bill Oliver, eds., *Passion and Craft* (1998); O. Alan Weltzien, ed., *Literary Art and Activism of Rick Bass* (2001).

Basso, Hamilton

(1904–1964) WRITER AND JOURNALIST.

A prominent journalist and novelist from the 1920s through the 1960s, Hamilton Basso contributed to the liberal and realistic traditions of the Southern Literary Renaissance, in contrast with the conservative, Gothic, and modernist tendencies of many of the age's other authors. Unlike the southern "traditionalists" who idealized the plantation and aristocratic traditions of the antebellum South, Basso and the other "realists" rejected the southern

past in favor of a more veritable new South. Through his novels and newspaper articles, Basso sought to represent the region accurately by addressing the problems of the southern middle class from a realistic, ethical, and objective perspective.

Hamilton Basso was born 5 September 1904 in the heart of the French Quarter in New Orleans, La., where his Italian American father owned and operated a small shoe factory. Basso's experiences in this diverse and cosmopolitan city, particularly with his African American neighbors, may have contributed to his progressive ideas about black civil rights. Moreover, New Orleans served as the backdrop in three of his novels and was the literary and intellectual center that attracted local and visiting writers who were associated with the *Double Dealer*, a "National Magazine of the South" founded in 1921. These writers, including William Faulkner, Sherwood Anderson, Edmund Wilson, and Oliver LaFarge, encouraged and helped Basso to publish his first novel, *Relics and Angels* (1929). The founding principles of *Double Dealer* influenced young Basso to, in his own words, "get rid of all of the old sentimental truck and explain, by using facts instead of poetry, what has happened here in the South and why this romantic conception is so untrue."

A prelaw student at Tulane when he met the *Double Dealer* writers, Basso withdrew three months before graduation in 1926 and became a journalist, his lifelong profession. After a brief stint in New York, Basso returned to New Orleans as a reporter for the *Item* and later worked as an advertising writer and as the night city editor of the *Times-Picayune*. Meanwhile, *Relics and Angels* (1929) garnered little praise, and Basso began writing a historical biography of Confederate general P. G. T. Beauregard entitled *Beauregard: The Great Creole* (1933), which was critically acclaimed but suffered from lack of sales. In the early 1930s, Basso also worked for the *New Republic* as a "southern correspondent" and reviewer of southern novels. Basso's reviews revealed his fervent anti-Agrarianism and resentment for authors who stereotyped blacks and the black experience. In fact, his second and more successful novel, *Cinnamon Seed* (1934), is a straightforward indictment of racism in the South that critics praised for its unusual and realistic treatment of blacks.

In 1935 Basso became the associate editor of the liberal *New Republic*, and his next novel, *In Their Own Image*, was published, notably lacking the now-recognizable "Basso protagonist" who returns to his native South and must confront its societal injustices. The autobiographical protagonist reappears in *Courthouse Square* (1936), Basso's first completely successful novel, which brought him modest fame as a young southern writer. After leaving the *New Republic*, Basso wrote his two intellectual novels, *Days before Lent* (1939) and *Wine of the Country* (1941), the former about a doctor in New Orleans who specializes in tropical diseases, and the latter about a young anthropologist from South Carolina.

Basso returned to journalism and the North in the 1940s, working first at *Time* magazine (1942–43) and later for the *New Yorker* (1944–61), for which he wrote book reviews, short stories, and profiles of well-known artists, including playwright Eugene O'Neill and novelist Somerset Maugham. During the war, Basso published one novel, *Sun in Capricorn* (1942), and one nonfictional piece, *Mainstream* (1943); in 1949 he published *The Greenroom*, his first novel to depict complex feminine personalities.

In the 1950s Basso achieved widespread popular appeal for his travel and general interest articles in *Holiday* and *Life*, as well as his first best-selling novel, *The View from Pompey's Head* (1954). The novel was his second to appear as a film: Gerald Meyer made the movie version of *Days before Lent* (Hollywood title, *Holiday for Sinners*) in 1952. Basso conceived of *The View from Pompey's Head* as the first in a southern trilogy; however, he completed only the second volume, *The Light Infantry Ball* (1959). He published two additional works before his death, a collection of travel sketches called *A Quota of Seaweed* (1960) and a less successful novel, *A Touch of the Dragon* (1964). Basso died 13 May 1964, just two years after he wrote a touching eulogy in the *Saturday Review* for his longtime friend William Faulkner.

ALISON RUTH CAVINESS
University of Virginia

Inez Hollander Lake, *The Road from Pompey's Head: The Life and Work of Hamilton Basso* (1999); Joseph R. Millichap, *Hamilton Basso* (1979); Earl Rovit and Arthur Waldhorn, eds., *Hemingway and Faulkner in Their Time* (2005).

Bausch, Richard

(b. 1945) WRITER.

Although he was born in the military town of Fort Benning, Ga., and teaches in Memphis, Richard Bausch grew up in and around Washington, D.C., and has lived most of his life within a short drive of the capitol. Since publication of his first novels in the early 1980s, he has been a highly regarded fiction writer who has come to be known as one of America's best in the short-story form.

Bausch's identical twin, Robert, also is a fiction writer; between them they can claim 24 books. In person, with their trademark beards, hats, and jovial senses of humor, they can easily be mistaken for one another. Richard has been the more critically acclaimed and prolific with 10 novels, six collections of short stories, and a book of three short novels.

Three years after the twins were born, the Bausches (a staunchly Democratic and Catholic family of eight) moved to Washington, D.C., and later they moved into suburban Silver Spring, Md. The family again moved, this time to Virginia after the brothers finished high school. In 1965 both enrolled in the air force, serving until 1969. Upon being discharged from service, Richard briefly played guitar in a rock band and performed as a stand-up comedian. In 1969 he began studies at Northern Virginia Community College and George Mason University in Fairfax, earning his undergraduate degree from George Mason in 1972. He went on to the prestigious University of Iowa M.F.A. program, finishing in 1975. He returned to teach at George Mason and remained on the faculty there until 2005, when he took the Lillian and Morrie A. Moss Chair of Excellence professorship at the University of Memphis.

Despite his reputation as a master of the short story, his first three books were novels. His second novel, *Take Me Back* (1981), was nominated for the PEN/Faulkner Award, an honor that his first story collection, *Spirits and Other Stories* (1987), also received. His prolific output continued with three novels and a story collection from 1989 through 1993, followed by *Rare and Endangered Species* (1994), a novella accompanied by short stories. His stature as one of the nation's best short-story writers was first realized with the Modern Library edition of *The Selected Stories of Richard Bausch* (1996).

He followed that celebrated story collection with two more novels and a new collection of stories in the latter half of the 1990s, prior to publication of *Hello to the Cannibals* (2002). This inventive novel intertwines the story of a young woman in the 1990s with that of Mary Kingsley, a Victorian explorer in Africa.

The publication of *The Stories of Richard Bausch* (2004), a hefty collection of 42 short fictions, sealed his reputation (and perhaps his fate) as being known best as a writer of short stories. That same year Bausch won the PEN/Malamud Award for Excellence in the Short Story.

Bausch's work, while sometimes set in his fictional small town of Point Royal, Va., is much more about people than of place. His novels and stories are marked by empathy and compassion for the difficulties within families. Bausch told an interviewer in 2005, "I write about love. The word 'relationships' bothers me—it's used too loosely these days." Bausch noted that his novels have focused on such various topics as innocence, child abuse, fear, the civilian cost of war, the loss of faith, the ravages of a dead dream, and old age, among other things. Bausch regrets that he is known to some exclusively for his short fiction, saying, "People who only read my stories are missing a lot, if I may say so."

In 2005 Bausch published *Wives and Lovers: Three Short Novels*, and the fall of 2006 saw the release of *Thanksgiving Night*, another novel set in his fictional burg of Point Royal. As productive and consistent a writer as Bausch has been, turning out 17 books in the last 26 years, readers can certainly expect to see his name on the spines of forthcoming works of fiction.

JOE SAMUEL STARNES
Saint Joseph's University

Art Taylor, *Carolina Quarterly* (Winter 2005); Patrick Meanor and Joseph McNicholas, eds., *American Short-Story Writers since World War II* (1993).

Bell, Madison Smartt

(b. 1957) WRITER.
Madison Smartt Bell is a prolific and versatile writer. Since the appearance of his first short story in 1978, he has published 12 novels, 2 story collections, 2 histories, a book on writing, and dozens of uncollected essays and stories. His novel *Soldier's Joy* (1989) won the Lillian Smith Award, and *All Souls' Rising* (1995) was a finalist for the PEN/ Faulkner Award and the National Book

Award. He received a Guggenheim Fellowship in 1991 and a National Endowment for the Arts fellowship in 1992.

Bell spent his childhood on a 96-acre farm in rural Williamson County, Tenn. His father was a circuit judge in Franklin, the county seat, and his mother raised horses and gave riding lessons. Both his parents attended Vanderbilt University. His mother taught him to read before he entered school, and during his teenage years he read many of the Southern Literary Renaissance writers, including Robert Penn Warren, Andrew Lytle, and Peter Taylor. Bell received his undergraduate degree in literature from Princeton University (B.A., 1979), where he studied under George Garrett, who published Bell's first short story, "Triptych I," in the journal *Intro*. The story is an examination of ritual, race, violence, and death revolving around an annual hog butchering on a family farm.

After graduating from Princeton, Bell enrolled in the Hollins College Creative Writing Program (M.A., 1981). While at Hollins, he continued to write and publish short stories. He also began working on his first published novel, *The Washington Square Ensemble* (1983), the narrative of a group of small-time drug dealers who frequent Washington Square Park in New York City. The plot develops through a series of vignettes told from the perspectives of six characters, and it introduces several themes that remain prominent in Bell's later writings, including urban decadence and religious pilgrimages. In an interview, he explained that *The Washington Square Ensemble* contains an argument between Islam and Santeria, and that subsequent novels, such as *Waiting for the End of the World* (1985) and *Straight Cut* (1986), explore Eastern Orthodox and Kierkegaardian Christianity, while *Dr. Sleep* (1991) deals with Hermetic Gnosticism.

Bell considers himself a southern writer, yet the southern landscape is absent from much of his work. Some of his short stories take place in the South, but *Soldier's Joy*, a tale of Vietnam veterans living in Tennessee, *Anything Goes* (2002), an account of an underground rock band on tour, and *Ten Indians*, a story about a man opening a Tae Kwan Do school in inner-city Baltimore, are the only novels set primarily in the South. His portrayal of the urban and pastoral, however, corresponds to traditional southern modes in which the urban becomes associated with psychological, physical, and spiritual decline while the pastoral offers salvation and renewal. Critics have pointed out that Bell's cityscape in *Waiting for the End of the World* is one "where half-crazed derelicts and condemned buildings wait in torment for final demolition." In *Save Me, Joe Louis* (1993), the novel's protagonist is saved from his life of crime only after fleeing New York City and returning to the Tennessee farm of his childhood.

Bell's short-story collection *Barking Man and Other Stories* (1990) highlights his range as a writer. The collection opens with "Holding Together," a story told from the perspective of a philosophical Chinese mouse that relies on the *I Ching* to guide him through his ordeal of being captured and sold to a laboratory. A young sheriff's deputy narrates "Black and Tan," a tale of loss, isolation, and self-realization set at a Doberman kennel. The collection's title story is a Kafkaesque chronicle of a man's gradual transformation into a dog.

All Souls' Rising, the first in a trilogy of novels set during the Haitian Revolution, is Bell's most critically acclaimed novel. Centered on a fictional portrayal of historical figure Toussaint Louverture, a slave-turned-general of the Revolution, the novel revisits the themes of religion, race, violence, and the pastoral. Bell's Haitian trilogy continues with *Master of the Crossroads* (2000) and concludes with *The Stone that the Builder Refused* (2004).

Bell is currently a creative writing instructor and Director of the Kratz Center for Creative Writing at Goucher College in Baltimore, Md., where he has taught since 1984. He is married to the poet Elizabeth Spires, who also teaches writing at Goucher.

DARIEN CAVANAUGH
University of South Carolina

Wyn Cooper, *Ploughshares* (Winter 1999–2000); Justin Cronin, *Four Quarters* (Spring 1995); Farrell O'Gorman, *Southern Literary Journal* (Spring 2002); William Sharpe and Leonard Wallock, *Visions of the Modern City* (1987).

Berry, Wendell

(b. 1934) POET, NOVELIST, AND ESSAYIST.
Wendell Berry, author of more than 30 books of essays, novels, poems, and short stories, farms and writes in Henry County, Ky., his native ground. Berry

was born on 5 August 1934 in New Castle, Ky. He earned B.A. and M.A. degrees from the University of Kentucky and attended Stanford University as a Wallace Stegner Writing Fellow in 1958–59. In 1960 his first novel, *Nathan Coulter*, was published. Berry taught at New York University for two years before returning to his home state, where he taught at the University of Kentucky from 1964 to 1977. In 1965 Berry and his wife, Tanya, moved to Lanes Landing Farm in Port Royal—a small farming community near the Kentucky River—where they continue to live. In their four decades of permanent dwelling, the Berrys thus model the life-style that Wendell preaches in his prolific literary work.

In his life and writing, Berry advocates sustainable agriculture and the importance of reestablishing healthy local cultures and economies. His cultural criticism, best expressed in his numerous essay collections, challenges the destructive habits of contemporary life-styles, citing as especially problematic the transience of human populations following World War II. The habit of transience fosters an attitude that human beings can avoid responsibility for their actions by moving on to new places and other relationships, therefore abetting a culture of abuse. As a rejoinder to the irresponsibility that can accompany transience, Berry advocates fidelity to places and people. Berry's belief in the value of particular places encompasses the nonhuman world as well as the human, as he expresses in the essay "Health Is Membership": "I believe that the community—in the fullest sense: a place and all its creatures—is the smallest unit of health and that to speak of the health of an isolated individual is a contradiction in terms." We will best care for the world, Berry says, if we love the world; and people are most likely to love places they know intimately. Berry's alternative to the widespread destruction of land and human communities in modern life is, therefore, the regeneration of local cultures and economies. "The real work of planet-saving," he writes, "will be small, humble, and humbling, and (insofar as it involves love) rewarding. Its jobs will be too many to count, too many to report, too many to be publicly noticed or rewarded, too small to make anyone rich and famous."

While Christian values inform Berry's work, Berry's brand of Christianity is not doctrinaire but pragmatic. In an essay "Christianity and the Survival of Creation," Berry writes: "[O]ur destruction of nature is not just bad stewardship, or stupid economics, or a betrayal of family responsibility; it is the most horrid blasphemy. It is flinging God's gifts into His face." Berry criticizes the exploitative American economy, defined by global trade and absentee ownership, and encourages consumers to secede from this destructive economic system by buying good-quality locally made products that honor the materials of Creation. An artist, Berry claims, does "good work" when he uses the materials of the earth in a respectful, sustainable manner.

Berry has remained faithful to his

place and to the central themes of community, land, stewardship, and marriage through his four decades of farming and writing. The title of Berry's essay collection, *Another Turn of the Crank* (1995), is a humorous acknowledgment by the writer that he, the "crank," is taking yet another "turn" on these important themes. Insisting that human communities require wholesome food, water, and air to be healthy, Berry continues to present a vision of "right livelihood"—a moral vision that requires responsibility and restraint in economic life.

WES BERRY
Martinsville, Indiana

Wendell Berry, *Another Turn of the Crank* (1995), *Sex, Economy, Freedom and Community* (1993), *The Unsettling of America: Culture and Agriculture* (1977).

Betts, Doris

(b. 1932) WRITER.
Born in Statesville, N.C., on 4 June 1932, Doris June Waugh was the only child of a mill worker, William, and his wife, Mary Ellen. Before becoming a noted writer of short stories, novels, and literary criticism, Betts earned degrees from the Women's College of the University of North Carolina (now UNC at Greensboro) and the University of North Carolina at Chapel Hill and worked as a journalist for several North Carolina newspapers. She returned to Chapel Hill to teach in 1966 and continued to teach there until her retirement in 2001.

Betts became best known during her early writing career as a master of short-story writing, publishing several collections: *The Gentle Insurrection and Other Stories* (1954), which won the UNC-Putnam Booklength Manuscript Prize; *The Astronomer and Other Stories* (1965); and *Beasts of the Southern Wild and Other Stories* (1973), which was nominated for the National Book Award. During these years Betts also wrote several novels—*Tall Houses in Winter* (1957), *The Scarlet Thread* (1964), and *The River to Pickle Beach* (1972)—but she thought of herself mainly as a short-story writer. Betts claimed in an interview with Jean W. Ross that as her career progressed, her focus and vision changed, as she became more "interested then in longer structures and also in the things that abide." This shift in genre produced three well-received novels: *Heading West* (1981), *Souls Raised from the Dead* (1994), and *The Sharp Teeth of Love* (1997).

Her themes and ideas, however, have remained the same throughout her career. As an early reader of the King James Version of the Bible, both her language and her topics show its influence. Although Betts admits her closest influences came from Anton Chekhov, Walker Percy, and Graham Greene, she is often compared to both William Faulkner and Eudora Welty. Her characters often yearn for religious faith in a modern world where doubt is on the rise, reflecting on a life lived either well or not so well. They ponder inevitable death and the questions implicit in that knowledge. In addition, her characters often find themselves on a quest for self-discovery, love, and connection to other humans—sometimes succeeding and sometimes falling pitifully shy of that goal. And, like another southern writer to whom she is often compared, Flannery O'Connor, Betts shows a bent for the southern Gothic, the grotesque, and black humor.

In addition to various awards for her short stories, Betts received the Guggenheim Fellowship in fiction (1958–59), the John Dos Passos Award (1983), and the Medal of Merit from the American Academy and Institute of Arts and Letters (1989).

BARBARA BENNETT
North Carolina State University

Elizabeth Evans, *Doris Betts* (1997); Mary Anne Heyward Ferguson, in *The History of Southern Women's Literature*, ed. Carolyn Perry and Mary Louis Weaks (2002); Susan Ketchin, *The Christ-Haunted Landscape: Faith and Doubt in Southern Fiction* (1994); Dorothy M. Scura, in *Southern Women Writers: The New Generation*, ed. Tonette Bond Inge (1990).

Blotner, Joseph L.

(b. 1923) WRITER AND SCHOLAR.
Joseph Blotner was born in White Plains, N.J., 21 June 1923. Educated at Drew University, he did graduate work at Northwestern University and earned his Ph.D. at the University of Pennsylvania. He taught English at the University of Idaho, the University of Virginia, and the University of Michigan, and had a distinguished international career as a Fulbright Professor at the University of Copenhagen and as lecturer at international symposiums on William Faulkner and other American writers. He is a member of the Fellowship of Southern Writers and an officer in the French Legion of Honor.

A prolific scholar and author, he is best known for his biographies of William Faulkner (2 volumes, 1974; 1 volume, 1984) and Robert Penn Warren (1997). At the University of Virginia, Blotner met and became friends with William Faulkner, who had come there as writer in residence. That friendship led to him becoming Faulkner's official biographer. With his colleague Frederick L. Gwynn, he edited *Faulkner in the University*. Other books include *The Modern American Political Novel* (1966) and a memoir, *An Unexpected Life* (2005).

NOEL POLK
Mississippi State University

Joseph L. Blotner, *An Unexpected Life* (2005); *Robert Penn Warren: A Biography* (1997); *William Faulkner: A Biography* (1974, 1984).

Blount, Roy, Jr.

(b. 1941) WRITER.
Roy Blount Jr. was born in Indiana, grew up in Georgia, and received a bachelor of arts degree from Vanderbilt in 1963 and a master's degree from Harvard in 1964. After serving in the army for two years, he accepted a position on the *Atlanta Journal*, where he worked first as a general assignment reporter and then with the editorial department. In 1968 he moved from the *Journal* to *Sports Illustrated*. Several years later, the editors of the magazine asked him to live with and cover the Pittsburgh Steelers, an experience that resulted in his first book, *About Three Bricks Shy of a Load* (1980), for which he was praised for his talent and toughness. Although he was promoted to associate editor of

Sports Illustrated in 1974, he was ready to work without magazine constraints. Hence, in 1975 he moved into freelance writing, contributing to *Esquire, Playboy, Parade*, and the *Atlantic*.

Blount's next book, *Crackers* (1982), centers on the presidency of Blount's fellow Georgian, Jimmy Carter. For it, Blount uses a series of essays, some previously published, that alternate with humorous descriptions of fictional people whose surname is Carter. The nation was divided about the Carter presidency, and so was Blount to some degree, but throughout the book Blount attempts to combat images of the president as an ignorant southern redneck.

The books Blount published after *Crackers* lack the unity of that volume because for the most part they are collections of previously written essays. They include *One Fell Soup; or, I'm Just a Bug on the Windshield of Life* (1984), *What Men Don't Tell Women* (1984), *Not Exactly What I Had in Mind* (1985), *Now, Where Were We?* (1991), and *Camels Are Easy, Comedy's Hard* (1991).

Blount has published a biography of Robert E. Lee; the novel *First Hubby* (1990), about a man whose wife is the president of the United States; and a book about New Orleans called *Feet on the Street* (2005). He has also edited a substantial anthology, *Roy Blount's Book of Southern Humor* (1994), containing items from Joel Chandler Harris, Dave Barry, John Kennedy Toole, Tennessee Williams, Fred Chappell, Clyde Edgerton, Zora Neal Hurston, and many others. On the basis of his own substantial comic achievement, he is recognized by writers in the *Chicago Tribune* and the *New York Times* as one of America's foremost humorists.

MARY ANN WIMSATT
University of South Carolina

Jerry Elijah Brown, *Roy Blount, Jr.* (1990); Mel Gussow, *New York Times* (26 January 1988).

Bonner, Sherwood

(1849–1883) WRITER AND
JOURNALIST.

Born Katharine Sherwood Bonner on 26 February 1849 in Holly Springs, Miss., Kate was the eldest of three surviving children of Irish physician Dr. Charles Bonner and local planter's daughter Mary Wilson Bonner. An avid reader in her father's extensive library, Kate was educated locally except for a brief term at Hamner Hall, an Episcopal boarding school in Montgomery, Ala. During the Civil War, she witnessed her father treating wounded soldiers and experienced the federal occupation when General U. S. Grant, on his way to Vicksburg, commandeered the Bonner home Cedarhurst and nearby residences for use by his officers and their families. In 1865 Mary Wilson Bonner died, leaving Kate, with siblings Sam and Ruth, to be cared for by their father, his sister Martha, and the family's black "Grandmammy," Molly Wilson, who had nurtured Kate's maternal family for three generations.

On Valentine's Day, 1871, Kate married Edward McDowell, an attractive suitor. Their only child, Lilian, was born that December. The young family moved to Texas, where Edward had relatives, but by the fall of 1873, mother and daughter returned to Holly Springs.

Leaving the baby with disapproving relatives, Kate traveled alone to Boston, Mass., in search of employment. Secretarial positions with a series of prominent Bostonians—editor Nahum Capen, reformer Dr. Dio Lewis, and renowned poet Henry Wadsworth Longfellow—provided the young southerner entrée to the highest social and literary circles of the self-styled "hub of the universe." In Longfellow, Kate also found a lifelong friend and literary patron.

Southern-slanted reports that Kate wrote from Reconstruction-era Boston (1874–75) for the *Memphis Daily Avalanche* contrast strikingly with ubiquitous commentaries on southern culture published in the postwar North; with her "public letters," Kate discovered a successful journalistic voice and an enduring pen name, Sherwood Bonner. In 1875 her budding literary career gained New England notoriety with "The Radical Club," a poem satirizing Boston literati that was printed (and reprinted) by the *Boston Times*. She was subsequently able to finance in 1876 an extended European tour with a series of travel columns featured in both the *Times* and the *Avalanche*.

Over the next few years, Sherwood Bonner placed short fiction, nonfiction, and poetry in prominent national magazines: *Harper's Monthly*, *Harper's Weekly*, *Lippincott's*, *Youth's Companion*, *Cottage Hearth*, *Harper's Young People*, *St. Nicholas*, and *Our Continent*. In particular, her series of affectionate reminiscences featuring the character and voice of Molly Wilson in her "Grandmammy" sketches, published 1875–80, helped to launch the instantly

popular genre of black dialect literature. Other southern stories in the robust "Southwest" tradition of Mark Twain built Bonner's substantial reputation as an atypical female humorist. Biographical sketches of notable women commissioned by *Cottage Hearth* and reports for the *Avalanche* hint at emerging feminist themes, and two evocative historical essays describe wartime events in Holly Springs and the 1878 yellow fever epidemic that claimed the lives of Bonner's father and brother.

Sherwood Bonner is most often remembered for her pioneering local-color efforts. Several early stories are set on the Texas Gulf Coast, including one involving a hurricane that mirrors the story's melodramatic romantic maelstrom. She continued to mine the profitable vein of dialect fiction with four Tennessee mountain stories and with four later ones, the first published fiction to depict realistic characters and dialects of southern Illinois. In 1878 Harper Brothers published Bonner's unconventional Reconstruction novel *Like unto Like*, set in Yariba, allegedly a fictional blend of Holly Springs and Huntsville, Ala. A lighthearted novella set partly in Hot Springs, Ark.—*The Valcours*—was serialized in *Lippincott's* in 1881.

After Bonner finally obtained an 1881 Illinois divorce from Edward, she moved Lilian and Aunt Martha Bonner with her to Boston. When soon afterward her health declined, she returned to the South and was diagnosed in New Orleans with advanced breast cancer. She died in the family home on Salem Street in Holly Springs on 22 July 1883 and is buried, at her request, in an unmarked grave in the family cemetery plot.

ANNE R. GOWDY
University of Mississippi

Sherwood Bonner, *Dialect Tales* (1883), *Suwanee River Tales* (1884), *A Sherwood Bonner Sampler, 1869–1884*, ed. Anne R. Gowdy (2000); Hubert McAlexander, *The Prodigal Daughter* (1981, 1999); Kathryn McKee, "Writing in a Different Direction: Women Authors and the Tradition of Southwest Humor, 1875–1910" (Ph.D. dissertation, University of North Carolina at Chapel Hill, 1996), *Legacy* (2005).

Bontemps, Arna

(1902–1973) WRITER AND SCHOLAR. Arnaud Wendell Bontemps was three years old when his father decided to move his family from his son's birthplace in Alexandria, La., to California. The elder Bontemps hoped to escape the prejudice and intimidation that tormented his and other black families. Trying to protect his son, he later warned Arna never to act black.

Having read *Harlem Shadows*, a book of poems by black author Claude McKay, Arna Bontemps became aware of the emergence of black voices from Harlem. After he graduated from Union Pacific College in 1923 and with the first publication of one of his own poems, Bontemps moved from Los Angeles to Harlem, where he taught at the Harlem Academy. He continued to write and, subsequently, became identified with the Harlem Renaissance. In 1931 he published his first novel, *God Sends Sunday*, which was later adapted as *St. Louis Woman*, the musical in which Pearl Bailey made her Broadway acting debut.

A few years of teaching and writing in Alabama, a master's degree from the University of Chicago, and work with the Illinois Writers Project marked Bontemps's career until the beginning of his 22-year tenure as librarian at Fisk University in Nashville, Tenn. In 1968 he resumed teaching, first at the University of Illinois and then at Yale, where he served also as curator of the James Weldon Johnson Collection of Negro Arts and Letters. He had moved back to Nashville when he died of a heart attack in 1973.

Bontemps devoted much time to writing about black life, wanting, as he said in *Harper's*, "to write something about the changes I have seen in my lifetime, and about the Negro awakening and regeneration." Short stories portraying southern black life (*The Old South: "A Summer Tragedy" and Other Stories of the Thirties*), historical novels about black uprisings (*Black Thunder*), children's literature about black leaders (*Free at Last: The Life of Frederick Douglass*), and anthologies of works by black authors (*American Negro Poetry*) represent the range of his writings. He also edited W. C. Handy's autobiography, *Father of the Blues*, and collaborated with fellow writers Langston Hughes, Jack Conroy, and Countee Cullen.

Arna Bontemps spent much of his life exploring the culture of his race and his southern black heritage. In doing so, he became a primary force in the development and promotion of black literature in America.

JESSICA FOY
Cooperstown Graduate Program

J. A. Alvarez, *African American Review* (Spring 1998); Robert A. Bone, *Down Home: A History of Afro-American Short Fiction from Its Beginnings to the End of the Harlem Renaissance* (1975); Arthur P. Davis, *From the Dark Tower: Afro-American Writers, 1900–1960* (1974); V. Harris, *The Lion and the Unicorn* (1 June 1990); D. Reagan, *Studies in American Fiction* (Spring 1991).

Bradford, Roark

(1896–1948) WRITER AND JOURNALIST.

Roark Bradford was born on 21 August 1896 in Lauderdale County, Tenn. He was the child of Richard and Patricia Bradford, both descendants of prominent colonial families. Bradford was raised on his family's cotton plantation and from a young age was well acquainted with its black sharecroppers. This plantation and its workers would become the inspiration for his writing career.

Bradford volunteered to serve in World War I and, after being discharged in 1920, began his career as a journalist. He initially worked as a reporter for the *Atlanta Georgian* and *Macon Telegraph*, but then moved to Louisiana, where he continued his reporting career with the *Lafayette Daily Advertiser* and then with the *New Orleans Times-Picayune* in 1924. His career as a journalist ended in 1926, when he dedicated his life to writing fiction.

The encounters Bradford had with the blacks on his family's plantation inspired his fiction. He was particularly interested in the black religious experience and placed this theme at the center of many of his texts. Despite his close encounters with blacks, Bradford chose to represent them as the "happy darky," a 20th-century caricature that depicted blacks as docile, lazy, content with plantation life, and dependent on whites to survive. One work in which this is evident is his essay "Notes on a Negro," published for *Forum* in 1927. In this essay, Bradford classifies blacks into three groups: nigger, colored person, and the Negro. He was also famous for inventing a black vernacular that is used by the characters in his texts.

Bradford began his career in fiction writing short stories. *Ol' Man Adam an' His Chillun* (1928) is a collection of 32 of his short stories. This collection was adapted by Marc Connelly into a play called *The Green Pastures*. The play's success earned Bradford and Connelly the Pulitzer Prize in 1930. Some of his other works include *This Side of Jordan* (1929), *John Henry* (1931), and *The Green Roller* (1949).

Bradford continued his career in the military and served as a lieutenant in the navy during World War II. From 1946 to 1948, he was a visiting lecturer in the English Department of Tulane University. On 13 November 1948 he died from an amoebic infection he contracted in the war. During his lifetime, Bradford's work had a large readership in both the North and the South; however, after his death, his work lost its popularity because of the changing images of blacks in America.

LAKISHA ODLUM
University of Maryland

Roark Bradford, *Forum* (1927); Wade Hall, in *Dictionary of Literary Biography*, vol.

86, ed. Bobby Ellen Kimbel (1989); Martin Seymour-Smith and Andrew C. Kimmens, eds., *World Authors: 1900–1950* (1996).

Bragg, Rick

(b. 1959) JOURNALIST AND
MEMOIRIST.

Rick Bragg's mother went into labor with him on the evening of 29 July 1959 at the Midway Drive-In during a showing of the *Ten Commandments*. Around dawn the following morning, a Sunday, in the Piedmont Hospital in rural northeastern Alabama, she gave birth to a son and named him after Ricky Ricardo. His father was not present for little Rick's birth—he had abandoned the family months earlier.

Bragg grew up in abject poverty in a family that he has frequently referred to as "white trash." He was one of three boys; his youngest brother, the fourth son, never named, died in infancy. His father had served in Korea, and the eventual effects of the war on him culminated in alcoholism and the plague of persistent demons. His father was but a sporadic presence in Bragg's young life, and Bragg was 16 years old when he last saw his father alive.

Bragg grew up listening to storytellers in the foothills of the Appalachians. It was by listening to people tell stories about their everyday lives, filled with "sadness, poverty, cruelty, kindness, hope, hopelessness, faith, anger, and joy," that he became interested in telling and writing stories. While in his junior year of high school at Jacksonville (Ala.) High, Bragg took journalism classes and became the sports editor of the high school newspaper. "I was

probably not very good," he wrote in his memoir *All Over but the Shoutin'*, "but I liked to see my name above the stories. It made me feel important." After high school Bragg entered Jacksonville State University where he began to write sports columns for the *Chanticleer*, the school newspaper. Soon after he began writing for the *Chanticleer*, Bragg began writing sports for the local weekly newspaper, the *Jacksonville News*.

Bragg eventually dropped out of college and went to work writing sports articles for the *Talladega Daily Home*, and then the *Anniston Star*. He wrote his first news story, for the *Anniston Star*, on the accidental shooting deaths of deer hunters by other hunters. Since then Bragg has written for the *Los Angeles Times*, the *St. Petersburg Times*, the *Birmingham News*, and the *New York Times*. In 1991, while working for the *St. Petersburg Times*, Bragg traveled to Haiti as a foreign correspondent and covered the terror of the Tontons Macoutes. He went on to win a nine-month Nieman Fellowship for Journalism to Harvard University in 1992 ("I think I was filling their white trash quota," he wrote) and then a Pulitzer Prize for Feature Writing (1996) and the American Society of Newspaper Editor's Distinguished Writing Award—twice (1991, 1996).

In 1997, while working as a national correspondent for the *New York Times* out of Atlanta, Bragg published his most famous work, *All Over but the Shoutin'*, a memoir reflecting on his growing up poor in rural Alabama, the tragedies of that childhood, the strength and determination of his mother (a woman "who went 18 years without a new dress so

I could have school clothes"), and his meteoric rise into the world of journalism. With the advance paid him by his publisher, he bought his mother the first house she ever owned.

Bragg's other works include *Somebody Told Me* (2000), a collection of his journalistic writings; and *Ava's Man* (2001), a memoir about his mother's childhood during the Great Depression. In 2003 Bragg resigned from the *New York Times* after a two-week suspension as a result of allegations that he had published feature news stories under his own byline that stringers, interns, and freelance reporters had chiefly written.

Today Rick Bragg works in the University of Alabama journalism department in the College of Communication and Information Sciences as a professor of writing. He continues to work as a freelance writer for various magazines and newspapers.

JAMES G. THOMAS JR.
University of Mississippi

Brickell, Henry Hershel

(1889–1952) EDITOR AND CRITIC. Henry Herschel Brickell is best known for his prominent role in the Southern Literary Renaissance, when he promoted unknown southern writers within the New York publishing community and the world. Among them were Eudora Welty, Margaret Mitchell, Stark Young, Langston Hughes, and William Alexander Percy.

Brickell was born in Senatobia, Miss., in 1889, grew up in Yazoo City, and enjoyed literature from an early age. After graduating as valedictorian at Yazoo City High School, where he played in the state's first interscholastic football match, Brickell attended the University of Mississippi, majored in English, and edited the *University of Mississippi Magazine*. He married Norma Long of Jackson in 1918. Between 1910 and 1919, Brickell advanced his career at southern newspapers, from reporter for the *Montgomery Advertiser*, to editor of Pensacola's *Florida News*, to managing editor of the *Jackson Daily News*. He then moved to New York City to join the thriving publishing industry. On the staff of the *New York Evening Post*, Brickell worked as a copyreader from 1919 to 1923 before obtaining his own column, *Books on Our Table*. In 1928 Brickell left the *Evening Post*, becoming general editor of the publishing house Henry Holt and Company. Returning to the *Evening Post* in 1934, he revived his column and served as the paper's literary editor until 1938. During these years, he began to call public attention to many of the best novels and short stories of the Southern Literary Renaissance.

In 1939 Brickell received a Guggenheim Fellowship to study the history of Spain and a Julius Rosenwald Fund Fellowship to study the history of Natchez, Miss. Brickell's numerous articles and essays were published by a variety of newspapers and magazines. He was on the faculty of various writers' conferences, including those at Blowing Rock, N.C., and Bread Loaf, Vt., where he taught with Robert Frost. He had great influence as editor of the *O. Henry Memorial Award Prize Short Stories*, a position he held from 1940 to 1952.

After 1940 his diplomatic roles overlapped with his literary work. Between 1941 and 1943, Brickell served as the senior cultural relations assistant to the U.S. Embassy in Bogota, Columbia, and became assistant chief of the State Department's Division of Cultural Cooperation in charge of Latin America for two years (1944–46). He also lectured for the State Department on American literature between 1951 and 1952. In 1952, with his car motor running, he died of asphyxiation in the garage of Acorn Cottage, his Ridgefield, Conn., home.

Brickell's lasting contribution to southern culture was his introduction of southern writers to the world. He was the first reviewer to call attention to Julia Peterkin and T. S. Stribling. Both went on to win Pulitzer Prizes. He was also the first journalist to interview Margaret Mitchell. As editor of the *O. Henry Prize Memorial Short Stories*, Brickell chaired a committee that selected many stories written by southerners, and Eudora Welty was the first to win first prize two years in a row. Years later Welty remarked that "[he was a] good man. Herschel was so kind and so abundantly helpful to people."

Brickell's Mississippi roots gave him a clear understanding of the region and its culture, enabling him to comprehend and evaluate the work of southern authors. He favored truthful depictions of southern regions and events and strong characterization, but the stories he admired most contained universal themes that resonated beyond the South.

Those who knew him describe Brickell as a southern gentleman, but a modern one who lived in New York City and traveled extensively in Europe and Latin America. Arthur Palmer Hudson, an Ole Miss classmate and friend who became a professor at the University of North Carolina at Chapel Hill, describes his achievements best: "That [the] hitherto obscure, backward state [of Mississippi] had produced writers of the English language . . . more likely to endure than the best that New England and the Middle West and the Far West . . . [is] in some part [to] Brick's credit." Consequently, Hudson concludes, "Herschel Brickell deserves a place in the history of the 'Southern Renaissance.'"

AMANDA JARMIN BRICKELL
Middlebury College

David Bain, *Whose Woods These Are: A History of Bread Loaf Writers' Conference, 1926–1992* (1993); John M. Bradbury, *Renaissance in the South* (1963); Herschel Brickell, *Saturday Review of Literature* (3 November 1928); William Ferris, interviewed with Eudora Welty, *Southern Cultures* (Fall 2003); James B. Lloyd, ed., *Lives of Mississippi Authors, 1817–1967* (1981).

Brooks, Cleanth

(1906–1994) CRITIC.

The son of a Methodist minister, Cleanth Brooks was born in Murray, Ky., and grew up in the villages and small towns of that state and of west Tennessee in which his father served as pastor. After graduating from the McTyeire School in McKenzie, Tenn. (1920–24), he attended Vanderbilt University, from which he received a bachelor's degree in 1928. The following year he earned a master of arts degree from Tulane University and enrolled as a Rhodes scholar in Exeter College,

Oxford University, from which he earned a B.A. (Honors) in 1931 and a B.A. Litt. the following year.

After leaving Oxford, he accepted a position in the English department of Louisiana State University. On 12 September 1934 he married Edith Ann Blanchard. The following year he and Robert Penn Warren, who had recently joined the faculty, and a small group of scholars and critics from the university founded the *Southern Review*, which, before it ceased publication in 1942, was one of the most distinguished literary quarterlies ever published in America. Many of the writers, later called the "New Critics," were regular contributors.

Brooks's reputation as one of the most respected modern American critics is based primarily on three books: *Modern Poetry and the Tradition* (1939), *The Well Wrought Urn: Studies in the Structure of Poetry* (1947), and *William Faulkner: The Yoknapatawpha Country* (1963). Some of the other books he has written are *Literary Criticism: A Short History*, with W. K. Wimsatt (1957); *The Hidden God: Studies in Hemingway, Faulkner, Yeats, Eliot, and Warren* (1963); *American Literature: A Mirror, Lens, or Prism?* (1967); *A Shaping Joy: Studies in the Writer's Craft* (1971); and *William Faulkner: Toward Yoknapatawpha and Beyond* (1978).

In addition to the influential books of criticism he wrote, Brooks coedited four textbooks that brought the principles of the New Criticism into the classroom and virtually revolutionized the way literature is taught and read: *An Approach to Literature*, with John T.

Purser and Robert Penn Warren (1936, 1939, 1952, 1964, 1975); *Understanding Poetry*, with Robert Penn Warren (1938, 1950, 1956, 1960); *Understanding Fiction*, with Robert Penn Warren (1943, 1959); and *Understanding Drama*, with Robert B. Heilman (1945).

THOMAS DANIEL YOUNG
Vanderbilt University

John N. Duvall, *Mississippi Quarterly* (Winter 1992); James A. Grimshaw, ed., *Cleanth Brooks and Robert Penn Warren: A Literary Correspondence* (1998); John Edward Hardy, in *Southern Renascence: The Literature of the Modern South*, ed. Louis D. Rubin Jr. et al. (1953); Lewis P. Simpson, ed., *The Possibilities of Order: Cleanth Brooks and His Work* (1976); Thomas Daniel Young, *Tennessee Writers* (1981); Alphonse Vinh, ed., *Cleanth Brooks and Allen Tate: Collected Letters, 1993–1976* (1998); Mark Royden Winchell, *Cleanth Brooks and the Rise of Modern Criticism* (1996).

Brown, Larry

(1951–2004) WRITER.

When Oxford, Miss., native, Larry Brown died on 24 November 2004, the South, in particular, and the United States, in general, lost one of its most outstanding new authors. In 1988, when he published his first collection of short stories, *Facing the Music*, Harry Crews, whose work Brown had read and admired since 1980, announced "talent has struck." From this propitious beginning, Larry Brown emerged as one of the leading new talents in southern fiction. After that collection, Brown wrote five novels—*Dirty Work* (1989), *Joe* (1992), *Father and Son* (1996), *Fay* (2000), *The Rabbit Factory* (2003); a second collection of stories, *Big Bad Love* (1990); and two collections of nonfiction, *On Fire* (1993) and *Billy Ray's Farm* (2001). Just before his death, he was completing a sixth novel, *The Miracle of Catfish* (2007).

Following in the tradition of Crews, arguably the first contemporary southern writer to produce vivid portrayals of members of the working class, Brown produced a body of work that both portrays and humanizes such characters. Carefully written, hard-packed, realistic, and heavily fraught with emotion, Brown's work first drew readers from throughout the South and later from elsewhere in the country. Honors also followed. Brown received the Mississippi Institute of Arts and Letters Award in 1989 for *Dirty Work* and twice won the Southern Book Critics Award for Fiction (for *Joe* in 1992 and *Father and Son* in 1997). In 1998 Brown also received the Lila Wallace-Reader's Digest Fund Writers' Award. Brown was posthumously inducted into the Fellowship of Southern Writers in 2005. In a 2001 review of *Billy Ray's Farm*, Jonathan Yardley evaluated Brown and his work: "Brown is the real thing: a self-taught country boy who may now make the rounds of the writing conferences but whose heart is obviously, and wholly, in the country he loves."

Because he was born in Oxford and lived in the area for all but about 12 years of his life, Brown faced constant comparison with William Faulkner; however, except for their mutual reverence for north Mississippi, the two writers are quite different, especially in social focus. Faulkner personally represented the upper-middle class of Oxford, with roots strongly entrenched in the town. His grandfather was president of the First National Bank in the town and his father, Maury, served as bursar at the University of Mississippi. Brown's family was of the yeoman class, like the Varners, Armisteds, and Tulls of Faulkner's fiction. Knox Brown was a sharecropper in Tula when Larry Brown was born on 9 July 1951. Family members on both sides were country people who worked hard, hunted the land, and fished the waters for both food and pleasure.

Although as a youngster Larry Brown had no dreams of becoming a writer—he told Dorie LaRue "It never crossed my mind"—he was an inveterate reader. He revealed to Kay Bonneti that his love of books and reading came "[m]ainly from my mother. One of my earliest memories is of seeing her reading. There were always books in our house." Brown told Susan Ketchin, "When I read the *Iliad* and the *Odyssey* when I was little, on my own, it got me thinking in terms of myths and dreams; I was really into Greek mythology, all the battles and gods. . . . They formed the core of my belief about storytelling."

Upon his discharge from the Marines in 1972, Brown returned to Lafayette County, and he married Mary Annie Coleman in 1974. The marriage produced four children, including a daughter, Delinah, who died in infancy. In 1973 Larry Brown became a paid fireman for the Oxford Fire Department; not able to support his growing family with just the money he earned there, Brown, for six years, held a wide

Larry Brown in Oxford, Miss., 1997 (Tom Rankin, photographer)

variety of part-time jobs: bagging gro-
ceries, working with molds in a local
pottery, setting out pine trees, helping
build houses, cleaning carpets, cutting pulpwood and deadening timber,
building chain-link fences for Sears and
Roebuck, painting houses, and hauling
hay. In "A Late Start" Brown described
his decision to become a writer: "When
I was twenty-nine, I stopped and looked
at my life and wondered if I was ever
going to do anything with it." He decided that he could teach himself to
write salable fiction in the same way that
he had learned other skills like carpen-
try and fire fighting. His chief early aim
was financial: he wanted to make sure
that his three young children would not
have to start their adult lives "working
in a factory."

By 1982 Brown had produced three
novels and about 90 stories without
much success, but his breakthrough
came in 1986 when Frederick Barthelme
at the *Mississippi Review* accepted and
published Brown's short story "Facing
the Music." Shannon Ravenel, then
senior editor of Algonquin Press, called
Brown after reading the story. Brown recalled, "she wanted to recommend it for
the Best American Short Stories. And
she asked me if I had enough stories for
a collection. I wrote back and said, 'I've
got a hundred. How many would you
like to see?'" A year later, Algonquin
Press published *Facing the Music*.

JEAN W. CASH
James Madison University

Erik Bledsoe, *Southern Cultures* (Spring
2000); Jean W. Cash, in *Dictionary of Liter-
ary Biography*, vol. 292, ed. Lisa Abney and
Suzanne Disheroon-Green (2004); Susan
Ketchin, ed., *The Christ-Haunted Landscape,
Faith and Doubt in Southern Fiction* (1994);
Dorie LaRue, *Chattahoochee Review* (Spring
1993); Michael S. Manley, in *Delicious
Imaginations: Conversations with Con-
temporary Writers*, ed. Sarah Griffiths and
Kevin J. Kehrwald (1998); Jonathan Miles,
Sports Afield (October 1998); Tom Rankin,
Reckon: The Magazine of Southern Culture
(Fall 1995); Judith Weinraub, *Washington
Post* (9 December 1990).

Brown, Rita Mae

(b. 1944) WRITER AND ACTIVIST.
Rita Mae Brown is a prolific writer of
popular mysteries set in central Virginia
and an early figure in the emergence of
gay and lesbian literature in the United
States. Her ancestors were Virginians, as
she notes that her "father's family came
to Virginia when the earth was cooling."
She was born, however, three miles
north of the Mason-Dixon Line, in
Hanover, Penn., on 28 November 1944.
She grew up as part of a horse culture,
with her mother having "the best eye for
a horse I have ever witnessed." Brown
attended the University of Florida in the
1960s on a scholarship, but participation
in civil rights protests led to her expul-
sion. She won a scholarship to New York
University (NYU), but she recalls being
required to take a remedial speech
course to modify her thick southern accent. Brown majored in English and the
classics at NYU, earned a degree in film
from the New York School of Visual
Arts, and gained her Ph.D. in political
science from the Institute for Policy
Studies in Washington, D.C.

Brown continued her political activism in the late 1960s and early 1970s, drawn into protests against the Vietnam War. She also became active in the feminist movement and gay liberation movement of the 1970s, working with the National Organization for Women (NOW) and cofounding the Student Homophile League. She resigned from NOW when its leader, Betty Friedan, distanced the organization from lesbian activities. *Rubyfruit Jungle* (1973) tells the story of Molly Bolt, a poor young woman from rural Pennsylvania who grows up comfortable with her lesbian sexuality, following her as she moves from her adolescence in Florida to struggles to be a filmmaker in New York, echoing Brown's own path. Brown became a celebrity in the 1970s and 1980s for the gay and lesbian movement. She earned an Emmy nomination while working in Hollywood but realized along the way that she "belongs in the country" and bought a farm in Virginia, where she still lives.

Rita Mae Brown has gone on to "coauthor" with her cat, Sneaky Pie Brown, the Mrs. Murphy series of mystery novels, which include *Wish You Were Here* (1990), *Rest in Pieces* (1992), *Murder at Monticello* (1994), *Pay Dirt* (1995), *Murder, She Meowed* (1996), *Murder on the Prowl* (1998), *Cat on the Scent* (1999), *Sneaky Pie's Cookbook* (1999), *Pawing through the Past* (2000), *Claws and Effect* (2001), *Catch as Cat Can* (2002), *The Tail of the Tip-off* (2003), *Whisker of Evil* (2004), *Cat's Eyewitness* (2005), and *Sour Puss* (2006). The main character of these novels is Mary Minor Haristeen, or "Harry," an amateur detective who solves local crimes with the help of her two cats and Corgi dog, as well as various barnyard animals, all of whom talk among themselves and for the reader. Brown has described her belief in a southern community tradition that draws people together, and she portrays people bringing baskets of food to each other, swapping stories around the post office where Haristeen works, quoting Scripture, and generally engaging in the small-town rituals that once were typical of southern places. Although she resists the title of "southern writer," she militantly asserts her identity as a Virginian, especially prizing its horse culture. Brown is master of the Oak Ridge Foxhunt Club and describes herself as a "huntsman," although her club does not kill foxes. She is an animal welfare activist, having rescued hundreds of cats, dogs, foxes, and hounds. These activities enter prominently in Brown's series of five "Sister" Jane Foxhunting Mysteries, set also in central Virginia.

CHARLES REAGAN WILSON
University of Mississippi

Rita Mae Brown, *Rita Will: Memoir of a Literary Rabble-Rouser* (1997); Blasé DiStefano, *OutSmart* (January 1998).

Brown, Sterling Allen

(1901–1989) TEACHER, POET, LITERARY CRITIC.

More a celebrant of southern culture than a child of its soil, Sterling Allen Brown exalted southern culture and examined the legacy of African Americans in the South through his poetry and essays and, perhaps most markedly, through his long teaching career at Howard University.

Brown was born 1 May 1901, the youngest of six and only son to former slave Sterling Nelson Brown and Adelaide Allen Brown. His father was a minister in the Congregational Church and a professor in the School of Religion at Howard University. An alumna of Fisk University, his mother was a former Fisk jubilee singer and a major influence on her children's appreciation for the arts.

Growing up on the Howard University campus, Brown established relationships with notable scholars of the time, including Jean Toomer, Alain Locke, and W. E. B. Du Bois, and had the benefit of Jessie Redmon Fauset as a high school teacher. Interaction with scholars and writers led to an early appreciation of poetry, history, and culture. Graduation with honors from prestigious Dunbar High School led to a scholarship at Williams College in western Massachusetts. There Brown earned an A.B. degree and his Phi Beta Kappa key. He then entered Harvard in 1922, where he earned the M.A. degree.

A long teaching career followed, starting with an English faculty position at Virginia Seminary in Lynchburg, Va. In the three years he was there, he had two life changing experiences: he met Daisy Turnball, whom he married in 1927, and was introduced to the southern culture that would become his inspiration and the foundation of his writing and teaching for the remainder of his career.

He then taught at Lincoln University in Missouri (1926–28) and Fisk University (1928–29). In 1929 Brown began teaching at Howard University.

His tenure at Howard would span more than 40 years and included semesters spent as a visiting professor at Atlanta University, Vassar College, and New York University.

At Howard, Brown taught the first courses in black literature and became known for his intellectual support of African American culture. According to literary critic Joanne Gabbien, "During the 1930s and 1940s, Brown's studies of the folk experience and culture were the fullest of any in the field." He was one of the first scholars to identify folklore as critical to the black aesthetic and to appreciate it as a form of literature and art. *The Negro in American Fiction* (1937) reveals parallels between the literary experience of African Americans and their real-life experience. Although now-familiar concepts, theories like these made Brown a pioneer in the field of African American criticism. He was able to "tie literature in with life, music, justice, and the struggle for existence."

As a poet, he blended the rhythms of black music and black southern culture. He championed the southern black community, creating folk heroes where caricatures had previously existed. His belief in the voice of the black community extended to his students, who included Ossie Davis, Stokley Carmichael, and Toni Morrison. He challenged them to have confidence in their own voices and to find strength in the experiences of their people.

Sterling Brown's influence is so far-reaching that contemporary theorists believe that "all trails lead, at some point, to Sterling Brown." At the same time, however, Brown's acclaim did not extend far beyond Howard's walls until the black arts movement of the 1960s. In 1979 the Washington, D.C., City Council declared his birthday, 1 May, Sterling A. Brown Day. The next year, Brown published *The Collected Poems of Sterling Brown* and won the 1980 Lenore Marshall Prize as the best book of poetry published. In 1984 he was named poet laureate of the District of Columbia.

JONI JOHNSON WILLIAMS
Georgia State University

Harold Bloom, *Black American Poets and Dramatists of the Harlem Renaissance* (1995); Arna Bontemps and Langston Hughes, *The Book of Negro Folklore* (1958); Sterling Brown, *Phylon* (1953); Joyce Camper, *African American Review* (Fall 1997); Joanne V. Gabbien, *African American Review* (Fall 1997); Ronald Palmer, *African American Review* (1997); Dudley Randall, *The Black Poets* (1972).

Brown, William Wells

(1814?–1884) ANTISLAVERY LECTURER, SLAVE NARRATOR, NOVELIST, DRAMATIST, AND HISTORIAN.

Born into slavery near Lexington, Ky., William Wells Brown is considered the first African American to achieve distinction as a professional man of letters. The son of George Higgins, a white man who never acknowledged the relationship, and a slave mother named Elizabeth, William spent most of his 20 years in slavery in and around St. Louis, Mo., where he worked as a house servant, a field hand, a tavernkeeper's assistant, a hand in the printing house of the abolitionist Elijah P. Lovejoy, a medical office assistant, and a handyman. While in his position as a handyman for a slave trader, William traveled up and down the Mississippi from St. Louis to the infamous New Orleans slave market.

When he returned to his master in 1832, William was put up for sale, which induced him to attempt to escape. This first endeavor failed mainly because William insisted on stealing his mother away with him; both were captured. His mother was soon thereafter sold to a slave trader, and he never saw her again. The following year, he traveled with his new owner, a steamboat operator, to Cincinnati during the last weeks of December. On 1 January 1834 William escaped. Afraid to travel by day, he journeyed through the dark, in the cold, without provisions, from Cincinnati to Cleveland. During this passage William was sheltered by a Quaker couple by the name of Mr. and Mrs. Wells Brown, whose name he later adopted as his own to honor their kindness.

After his escape, William Wells Brown labored on Lake Erie as a steamboatman and a conductor for the Underground Railroad in Buffalo, N.Y. He married Elizabeth Schooner with whom he had two daughters. In 1843 Brown became an antislavery lecturer for the Western New York Anti-Slavery Society. After relocating to Boston, in 1847 Brown wrote his autobiography, *Narrative of William Wells Brown, a Fugitive Slave, Written by Himself*, which earned him international fame. After several years as a lecturer on the antislavery circuit throughout New England, in 1849 Brown traveled to Paris as a delegate to the Peace Congress. Afterward, he continued to England and Ireland promoting his antislavery agenda. During his time in England he penned his travel narrative *Three Years in Europe, People I Have Seen and People I Have Met* (1852), the first of its kind authored by an African American. In 1853 Brown saw his novel *Clotel; or, The President's Daughter* published. The first full-length novel by an African American, *Clotel* tells the story of the daughters and granddaughters of President Thomas Jefferson.

Wary of returning home from his travels because of the fugitive slave law passed in 1850, Brown had his freedom purchased by a group of friends in 1854; thereby he was finally able to return to his native country. In 1858 he published the first drama by an African American, *The Escape; or, A Leap for Freedom* about two slaves who secretly marry. Continuing as an antislavery lecturer until the American Civil War, Brown published three additional versions of *Clotel: Miralda; or, The Beautiful Quadroon* (1861), *Clotelle: A Tale of the Southern States* (1864), and *Clotelle; or, The Colored Heroine* (1867). He also penned two volumes of African American history, *The Black Man: His Antecedents, His Genius, and His Achievements* (1863) and *The Negro in the American Rebellion* (1867).

After his antislavery lecturing days came to an end, Brown entered into the medical profession, opening a doctor's office in Boston in 1864. Brown's final historical book, *The Rising Son*, was published in 1873. In 1880 the accom-plished author published his ultimate autobiography, *My Southern Home; or, The South and Its People*. Brown died on 6 November 1884 in Chelsea, Mass.

DAVID SHANE WALLACE
Louisiana State University

Robert A. Bone, *The Negro Novel in America* (1965); Curtis William Ellison, *William Wells Brown and Martin R. Delany: A Reference Guide* (1978); William Edward Farrison, *William Wells Brown: Author and Reformer* (1969); Vernon Loggins, *The Negro Author: His Development in America to 1900* (1931); Jean F. Yellin, *The Intricate Knot: The Negro in American Literature, 1776–1863* (1971), preface to *Clotel; or, The President's Daughter* (1969).

Burke, James Lee

(b. 1936) WRITER.

A native of Houston, Tex., James Lee Burke spent his early life in Gulf Coast communities along the Texas-Louisiana border. He began college at Southwestern Louisiana Institute and later earned his bachelor's and master's degrees from the University of Missouri. After jobs in the oil industry, as a social worker among the underprivileged in Los Angeles, as a journalist, and in college teaching, he began writing, publishing his first novel, *Half of Paradise*, in 1965. Burke is one of the South's leading mystery writers, twice receiving the Edgar Award for Best Crime Novel, for *Black Cherry Blues* (1990) and *Cimarron Rose* (1998). He has also received Breadloaf and Guggenheim fellowships and a National Endowment for the Arts grant.

Burke transcends the mystery writer category because of his engagement with issues of place and history, as the creator of a distinctive south Louisiana landscape. Dave Robicheaux is the protagonist of 15 Burke novels, and is one of the best-developed characters in contemporary southern popular fiction. Burke writes evocatively of a lush natural landscape, with his writing defined by a lyrical prose; but the landscape is a Gothic one that often holds secrets and bloody deeds. Robicheaux roams the land from New Iberia to New Orleans, dealing with vicious characters and brutal activities. A Vietnam veteran and recovering alcoholic, he is the hard-boiled detective who retains his ethical bearing despite the decadence he sees. His novels have much autobiographical content, as Burke is a recovering alcoholic and both writer and detective have daughters named Alafair (Burke's daughter is herself a mystery writer). Burke has also written four novels featuring Billy Bob Holland, a former Texas Ranger and lawyer who becomes a detective, with stories set in Montana and east Texas.

Burke's writing takes its place as a part of southern literary tradition because he grapples with such issues as violence, race relations, social class divisions, and the South's history. "We live in the most violent society on earth," Burke said in a 1997 interview, and his writing conveys the particular violence of a south Louisiana society with Cajuns, Creoles, African Americans, Italians, and other ethnic groups thrown together in sometimes contentious ways. Burke has said that Robicheaux "is always on the side of those who have

no voice or power." He has written of the Civil War in his novel *White Doves at Morning* (2002), which portrays the drama of battle but also engages issues of racial identity. Southerners are prominent on Burke's list of literary influences on his work, including William Faulkner, Robert Penn Warren, Eudora Welty, Tennessee Williams, and Flannery O'Connor, as well as Ernest Hemingway, James T. Farrell, and Jesuit poet Gerard Manley Hopkins.

Burke's novels are typically best sellers, and two of his works have been made into films. He lives now, with his wife, Pearl, in Missoula, Mont., and New Iberia, La.

CHARLES REAGAN WILSON
University of Mississippi

Greg Langley, *Baton Rouge Advocate* (17 July 2005); Marilyn Stasio, *New York Times* (10 July 2005; 9 July 2006); Avis Weathersbee, *Chicago Sun-Times* (24 July 2005).

Byrd, William, II

(1674–1744) VIRGINIA ARISTOCRAT, LAWYER, POLITICIAN, PLANTER, WRITER, AMATEUR SCIENTIST, AND FOUNDER OF RICHMOND AND PETERSBURG.

Born 28 March 1674, Byrd inherited a large plantation on the James River and the family home, called Westover, from his father, Colonel William Byrd I (1652–1704). Son of a London goldsmith, Colonel Byrd had risen to prominence by inheriting the estate from his uncle and acquiring vast wealth through land speculation, fur trading, and importation of indentured servants and black slaves. Like other wealthy south-

ern colonials, the young Byrd was educated in England, where he developed
many of his talents and tastes. He went
to grammar school in Essex, studied
law at the Middle Temple, was elected
to the Royal Society, attended the theater frequently, and moved in London's
elite social and literary circles. He lived
in England in the years 1681 to 1696,
1697 to 1705, and 1715 to 1726. He married Lucy Parke in 1706, and after her
death in 1716 he courted several wealthy
women and carried on intrigues with
various others before finally marrying
Maria Taylor in 1724.

In Virginia, Byrd devoted his time to
managing his plantations. He enlarged
Westover into a splendid Palladian
mansion with luxurious furnishings,
improved its gardens, and entertained
friends with generous hospitality. He
collected one of the best and largest
libraries in colonial America and read
nearly every day selections in Latin,
Greek, or Hebrew as well as in modern
literature. He also took an active role
in public affairs, as a man of his station
was expected to, serving in the House
of Burgesses briefly and in the Executive
Council from 1708 until his death. He
was the chief member of the joint commission that traveled in 1728 from the
coast to the mountains surveying the
disputed boundary line between Virginia and North Carolina. The manner
of his life was in some ways modeled
after the ideal of the English country
gentleman, and the cosmopolitan Byrd
sometimes described his world in pastoral terms. In continually buying and
selling land, though, he represented a

new southern type divergent from the
English. Though he was a slaveholder,
Byrd disapproved of the institution of
slavery because of its inhumanity and
its fostering of severity in slaveholders,
laziness among whites, and the danger
of bloody insurrections. His attitude
toward New England Puritans blended
admiration for their industriousness
with contempt for their hypocritical
traffic in rum and slaves.

Byrd's writings, marked by urbane
good humor, were diverse. He was
author of a scientific treatise for the
Royal Society, gallant and witty verses,
and *A Discourse Concerning the Plague*
(1721), an anonymous pamphlet rec-
ommending tobacco as a preventive for
plague. He seems to have written part
of *The Careless Husband*, a play he also
directed at a private house in Virginia,
and he contributed to a promotional
tract in German, *New-gefundenes Eden*
(1737). His letters and three portions of
his shorthand diaries have been found
and published. Most important are the
accounts of his travels—*A Progress to
the Mines* (1841), *A Journey to the Land
of Eden* (1928), and two versions of
the dividing-line expedition. Of these,
The Secret History of the Dividing Line,
a travel journal circulated privately
among friends and not published until
1929, is rich in racy humor and satirical
caricatures of the commissioners; the
much longer *History of the Dividing Line*
(1866), evidently intended for London
publication, diminishes the personal
elements and includes political and
natural history. Both versions, from the
vantage point of a Tidewater Virginian,

ridicule the vulgarities of shiftless backwoods Carolinians. Byrd thus inaugurated the southern tradition of literary humor dealing with poor whites.

JUDY JO SMALL
University of North Carolina at Chapel Hill

Kevin Berland, Jan Kristen Gilliam, and Kenneth A. Lockridge, eds., *The Commonplace Book of William Byrd II of Westover* (2002); Richard Beale Davis, in *Major Writers of Early American Literature*, ed. Everett Emerson (1972); Kenneth A. Lockridge, *The Diary and Life of William Byrd II of Virginia, 1674–1744* (1987); Pierre Marambaud, *William Byrd of Westover, 1674–1744* (1971); Margaret Beck Pritchard and Virginia Lascara Sites, *William Byrd II and His Lost History: Engravings of the Americas* (1993); Mark R. Wenger, ed., *The English Travels of Sir John Percival and William Byrd II: The Percival Diary of 1701* (1989); Louis B. Wright, ed., *The Prose Works of William Byrd of Westover* (1966).

Cabell, James Branch

(1879–1958) WRITER.

For literary America, James Branch Cabell played a major role in defining the 1920s. His world view and his tone were appropriate to the sense of loss that many experienced following World War I. As a southerner and no stranger to loss, with "resolute frivolity" he looked intently at the mythic armor that protects the human race. His style was urbane, elegant, sophisticated. Like his heroes, he eschewed realism for the romance, but his romances had a way of making his readers confront a view of mankind as stark as any portrayed by the literary naturalists.

Cabell's prominence as a national figure was greatly aided when his *Jurgen* (1919) was suppressed because of its supposedly salacious content. H. L. Mencken, Theodore Dreiser, and a host of other important figures came to Cabell's defense. Appetite to read the banned book was, of course, intensified, and after the book was exonerated at the trial in New York City in October 1922, Cabell benefited enormously not only through sales for his book but through an eager audience for the steady production of other Cabell titles throughout the decade. His literary prominence was affirmed with the publication in 18 volumes (1927–30) of the Storisende Edition of *The Works of James Branch Cabell*, texts revised with prefaces after the model of Henry James and his New York Edition.

Although Cabell continued to write following that landmark, the 1930s would not similarly be thought of as the James Branch Cabell period. Indeed, in the bleakness of the Great Depression, Cabell's sardonic comedy did not please as it had previously. Nevertheless, Cabell's impact on the Southern Literary Renaissance cannot be denied. In "The Sahara of the Bozarts"(1920), Mencken touted Cabell as the great exception to the vacuity that Virginia's culture had become. Twenty years later, looking back at the 1930s, W. J. Cash underscored in *The Mind of the South* the importance of both Ellen Glasgow and Cabell as harbingers of the flowering of southern literature in the 1930s, and he emphasized how "decisively Southern" Cabell's themes and characters are, finding Cabell's rhetoric an inheritance from southern rhetoric.

Cabell's southern credentials are impeccable. He was born in Richmond. His great-grandfather had been governor of Virginia. Grandfather Cabell had lived next door to Robert E. Lee and served as his physician. The Branches were a prominent Richmond family, linked to other prominent families. Writer Cabell was also a professional genealogist, given to pondering lineages and family skeletons—motifs important in his fiction. He was a brilliant student at the College of William and Mary and knew French and Greek well. As a young man, he traveled in Europe and lived for a time in New York City, but he spent most of his life in Richmond, eventually on Monument Avenue, a setting conducive to his reflection on his southern heritage and the mythic tales he savored from many literatures.

Cabell's greatest contribution is to be found in what he called *The Biography of the Life of Manuel*, Manuel being the great quester from Poictesme (Cabell's invention) whose lineage from the Middle Ages to modern Virginia is central to the 18 volumes in the Storisende Edition. In the realm of comedy and myth, Cabell created a universe akin to the one Faulkner named Yoknapatawpha County. The novels set in contemporary Virginia (they were written first, probably before Cabell realized what his grand design would be) pale beside the more mythic volumes set in Poictesme: *Figures of Earth: A Comedy of Appearances* (1912), *Jurgen: A Comedy of Justice* (1919), *The Silver Stallion: A Comedy of Redemption* (1926), and *Something about Eve: A Comedy of Fig Leaves* (1927). His later works include

the *Nightmare Has Triplets* trilogy (1934, 1935, 1937), the *Heirs and Assigns* trilogy (1938, 1940, and 1942), *Let Me Lie* (1947), and *As I Remember It* (1955).

JOSEPH M. FLORA
University of North Carolina at Chapel Hill

Joe Lee Davis, *James Branch Cabell* (1962); H. L. Mencken, *James Branch Cabell* (1927); M. Thomas Inge and Edgar MacDonald, *James Branch Cabell: Centennial Essays* (1983); Edgar MacDonald, *James Branch Cabell and Richmond-in-Virginia* (1993); James M. Riemer, *From Satire to Subversion: The Fantasies of James Branch Cabell* (1989); Desmond Tarrant, *James Branch Cabell: The Dream and the Reality* (1967); Carl Van Doren, *James Branch Cabell* (1932); Arvin R. Wells, *Jesting Moses: A Study in Cabellian Comedy* (1962).

Cable, George Washington

(1844–1925) WRITER AND CRITIC. During the local-color era Cable wrote of Creole New Orleans, and he has been called the most important southern artist working in the late 19th century, as well as the first modern southern writer. He is praised both for his courageous essays on civil rights, such as *The Silent South* (1885) and *The Negro Question* (1890), and for his early fiction about New Orleans, especially *Old Creole Days* (1879), *The Grandissimes* (1880), and *Madame Delphine* (1881). Cable was not a Creole himself, but he had deep roots in New Orleans. He was born and grew up there, and, after service as a Confederate soldier, he returned to live and work in the city until 1885, when he moved to Massachusetts.

Cable's study of the colonial history

George Washington Cable, late 19th-century critic of southern society (George W. Cable Collection, Manuscript Section, Tulane University Library, New Orleans, Louisiana)

of Louisiana while writing sketches for the *Picayune* revealed "the decline of an aristocracy under the pressure of circumstances," as well as the "length and blackness" of the shadow in the southern garden. In his essay "My Politics," Cable tells how his reading of the Code Noir caused him such "sheer indignation" that he wrote the brutal story of Bras-Coupé, incorporated later as the foundation of *The Grandissimes*. Cable connected the decline of the Creoles to their self-destructive racial pride, and his best work, *The Grandissimes*, makes clear that such racial arrogance has direct application to broader problems of southern history, especially the black-white conflict after 1865. Like the best stories of *Old Creole Days*, *The Grandissimes* balances sympathy for and judgment of New Orleans and the South, but it is stronger because it "contained as plain a protest against the times in which it was written as against the earlier times in which its scenes were set."

Cable continued to write about New Orleans and Louisiana throughout his long career, most notably in *Dr. Sevier* (1884), *The Creoles of Louisiana* (1884), and the Acadian pastoral *Bonaventure* (1888). In all, he published 14 novels and collections of short fiction, with his last novel, *Lovers of Louisiana*, appearing in 1918, just seven years before his death. In his career after *The Grandissimes*, Cable was unable to reconcile his love for the South with his abhorrence of slavery and racism. The result was a split in his career—the polemical essays embody the spirit of reform and the New South, while the romances, beginning with *The Cavalier* (1901), attempt to retrieve an idyllic past, devoid of the problems of racism.

THOMAS J. RICHARDSON
University of Southern Mississippi

Cable's diary, cited in Newton Arvin, introduction to *The Grandissimes* (1957); John Cleman, *George Washington Cable Revisited* (1996); Shirley Ann Grau, foreword to *Old Creole Days* (1961); Gavin Jones, *American Literary History* (Summer 1997); James R. Payne, in *Multicultural Autobiography: American Lives*, ed. James R. Payne (1992); Alice H. Petry, *A Genius in His Way: The Art of Cable's Old Creole Days* (1988); Thomas J. Richardson, ed., *The Grandissimes: Centennial Essays* (1981); Louis D. Rubin Jr., *George W. Cable: The Life and Times of a Southern Heretic* (1969); Merrill Skaggs, *The Folk of Southern Fiction* (1972); Arlin Turner, *George W. Cable: A Biography* (1956).

Caldwell, Erskine

(1903–1987) WRITER.

For all of his life, Erskine Caldwell was fascinated by people—whether they lived in New England, Mexico, Czechoslovakia, Russia, or the American South. And he wrote about people who lived in all of those places. But it was the neglected people of the South who elicited his best work: the novels *Tobacco Road* and *God's Little Acre*, the short-story collection *Kneel to the Rising Sun*, and the documentary *You Have Seen Their Faces*. He was the literary champion of people who had no one else to speak for them.

Born 17 December 1903 near the small community of White Oak, Ga.,

35 miles southwest of Atlanta, Erskine was the only child of Caroline (Carrie) Bell, a schoolteacher, and Ira Sylvester Caldwell, a socially conscious minister in the staunchly conservative Associate Reformed Presbyterian (A.R.P.) Church. Because Ira's duties as a denominational official required frequent moves, Erskine grew up in communities in Georgia, the Carolinas, Florida, and Tennessee. When he was 15, the family settled 30 miles south of Augusta, Ga., in the small town of Wrens, where Ira pastored the A.R.P. Church and where he and Carrie taught high school. Erskine's travels with his father around east central Georgia helping desperately poor tenant farmers made a lasting impression on the teenager and later influenced Erskine's writing incalculably.

Attendance at three colleges failed to result in a degree, but a professor at the University of Virginia awakened in Caldwell a desire to write. He published his first piece, an essay entitled "The Georgia Cracker," shortly before his 23rd birthday. After numerous rejections, he began to place short stories in little magazines, stories that, together with some previously unpublished fiction, would constitute his first collection, *American Earth* (1931). That volume heralded the most creatively productive decade in Caldwell's 60-year career.

In February 1932, despite considerable trepidation on the part of the publisher, *Tobacco Road* came out. Caldwell's novel of starving sharecroppers near Augusta, though applauded by some reviewers, sold poorly—just 500 copies in the year of publication. Only after the appearance of a play based loosely on Caldwell's story did the novel gain wide attention.

The year after *Tobacco Road*'s publication, *God's Little Acre* appeared. Like *Tobacco Road*, Caldwell's novel of the disintegration of a Georgia farm family suffered slow sales—until obscenity charges were brought. The sexual content of the story disgusted some readers, but a federal judge ruled in the novel's favor.

Caldwell's last great work of fiction of the 1930s was published in 1935. *Kneel to the Rising Sun and Other Stories* contains the finest work ever written by one of America's greatest writers. A master of the short short-story, as he had demonstrated in previous tales, Caldwell displayed his skill with that form yet again in stories such as "Candy-Man Beechum" and "The Growing Season." Of more conventional length is the collection's title story, a poignant tale of race and class that is Caldwell's single best work of fiction.

In addition to composing some unforgettable fiction in the 1930s, Caldwell wrote some excellent nonfiction, most notably the narrative of *You Have Seen Their Faces*, a documentary done with the noted photographer Margaret Bourke-White. Together with Bourke-White's pictures, Caldwell's writing presented a powerful portrayal of the South's rural poor, which he hoped would bring greater attention to their plight.

After the great years of the 1930s, the quality of Caldwell's writing declined.

Moreover, his desire to sell his books allowed him to be used by paperback publishers after 1945, a decision that contributed to his reputation's decline among critics. Nonetheless, the 1960s witnessed two thoughtful works of nonfiction: *In Search of Bisco* (1965), an examination of southern race relations, and *Deep South* (1968), at once a moving tribute to his father and a study of the impact of religiosity on the region.

Over the course of a life that lasted for 83 years, Caldwell saw firsthand the lives of countless neglected southerners. Over the course of a career that ran for 60 years, he published 25 novels, nearly 150 short stories, and 12 volumes of nonfiction. Most of that work dealt with the South.

In a region that has produced many exceptional writers, none was more exceptional than Caldwell. He possessed greater firsthand knowledge of the South than any other writer of his generation. No other regional writer of comparable talent showed an interest in the issue of class to equal his. No other white southern writer of the 1930s mounted as sustained an attack against the evil of racism as he.

Caldwell considered himself the people's writer, the champion of the poor, the outcast, and the neglected. His work should not be neglected. It should be read, and his achievement should be honored.

WAYNE MIXON
Augusta State University

Edwin T. Arnold, *Southern Review* (Autumn 2003); Sylvia Jenkins Cook, *Erskine Caldwell and the Fiction of Poverty: The Flesh and the Spirit* (1991); Harvey L. Klevar, *Erskine Caldwell: A Biography* (1993); Scott MacDonald, ed., *Critical Essays on Erskine Caldwell* (1981); Dan B. Miller, *Erskine Caldwell: The Journey from Tobacco Road* (1995); Wayne Mixon, *The People's Writer: Erskine Caldwell and the South* (1995).

Campbell, Will D.

(b. 1924) MINISTER, WRITER, CIVIL RIGHTS ACTIVIST.

In December 2000 when Will D. Campbell received the National Medal for the Humanities, President Clinton referenced the New Testament in his introduction: "Scripture says 'be doers of the word and not hearers only'; Will Campbell is a doer of the word."

Campbell's life bears ample testimony. Born 18 July 1924 in the piney woods of southwestern Mississippi, Campbell spent his early life centered on family and faith. The primordial forces of blood, spirit, and water brought Campbell into the fold of Christian faith at 7 and into the gospel ministry at 16.

Louisiana College was Campbell's introduction to the wider world. His ministerial studies there (1941–43) were interrupted by military service as an army medic in the South Pacific (1943–45). Reading Howard Fast's novel *Freedom Road* transformed Campbell's vision of the South, a view that intensified as he regarded the disparity toward blacks in the army.

After the war in 1946, Campbell and Brenda Fisher, his college sweetheart, married and moved to North Carolina where Campbell completed his studies at Wake Forest College (B.A., 1948). Campbell's decision to attend Yale Divinity School was a momentous one. He embraced both the study and the life-style of an Ivy League graduate student in the early 1950s.

In 1952 Will and Brenda Campbell returned to the South as the "first family" of the Taylor (La.) Baptist Church. Campbell's parish ministry lasted 18 months, long enough to become acquainted with the vocational realities of his calling. Although he believed the gospel sympathetically addressed the rights of local mill workers, congregational problems arose when Campbell attended union meetings.

Convinced that he would find more freedom in a university setting, Campbell became the director of religious life at the University of Mississippi just as the 1954 *Brown v. Board of Education* decision was handed down by the U.S. Supreme Court. Two tense, troubling years later, Campbell left the university to accept a job with the liberal National Council of Churches. In 1956 Campbell became the director of the council's southern office of the Department of Racial and Cultural Relations in Nashville, Tenn. During the next several years he was the "troubleshooter" for the council, traveling around the South to witness the tremendous racial upheaval in southern communities.

Campbell's role in the civil rights movement is well known. He was one of the few who escorted black children to school in Little Rock in 1957. Campbell is also often identified as the only white man allowed to participate in the formation of the Southern Christian Leadership Conference. And he was present at many of the events enshrined today as marker points in the civil rights movement, including sit-ins in Greensboro, N.C., and demonstrations in Birmingham and Nashville.

But by 1963 the exigencies of vocational life within the National Council led Campbell to resign. Experiences within the parish, the university, and the council persuaded Campbell that securing institutional viability is always the bottom line. He became the director of the Committee of Southern Chuchmen, a liberal, loosely organized group of Christians. The committee's journal, *Katallagete*, provided a venue for Campbell to develop his writing.

The publication of *Brother to a Dragonfly* (1977) brought Campbell national exposure and a National Book Award nomination. Campbell portrays the tragic death of his brother, Joe, within the context of the nation's struggle with the legacy of slavery. However, Campbell's first book, *Race and the Renewal of the Church* (1962), remains his best seller and establishes the biblical and theological foundation for later writings.

Arguably the best-known passage of Campbell's writings is found in *Brother to a Dragonfly*. He speaks of his "conversion" to faith, led by two of the "most troubled men I have ever known," his brother, Joe, and a friend, P. D. East. Prodded by East, Campbell realized that he had rejected his own people in his work. Far more significantly, the theological failure of his own beliefs came into focus. His concept of God as loving and accepting disenfranchised blacks had not allowed for God's love and acceptance of poor whites, Klansmen, or "rednecks."

Now nearing 80, Campbell and his wife live on a farm in Mt. Juliet, Tenn. From his log cabin office, Campbell continues his pastoral and priestly duties, baptizing, marrying, burying, and offering shelter for body and soul. He has written 15 volumes, including four children's books. Exploring a wide range of topics anchored in southern life, Campbell's work includes *And Also with You* (1997), the story of Episcopal Bishop Duncan Gray and his role in James Meredith's arrival at Ole Miss; *Providence* (1992), which deals with the forced removal of Native Americans from their tribal lands in Mississippi (1992); *Cecelia's Sin* (1983) and *The Glad River* (1982), which explore faith and community; *The Convention*, a "parable" of a denomination confronting the calling of women to ministry (1988); and, most recently, *Robert G. Clark: Journey to the House: A Black Politician's Story* (2003). The recipient of five honorary doctorates and numerous prestigious literary awards, Campbell remains active as a writer and speaker and, as always, a preacher.

LYNDA WEAVER-WILLIAMS
Virginia Commonwealth University

Thomas L. Connelly, *Will Campbell and the Soul of the South* (1982); Merrill M. Hawkins Jr., *Will Campbell, Radical Prophet of the South* (1997); Susan Ketchin, ed., *The Christ-Haunted Landscape: Faith and Doubt in Southern Fiction* (1995); Mike Letcher, director, *God's Will* (video), University of Alabama Center for Public Television and Radio (1999).

Capote, Truman

(1924–1984) WRITER.

Truman Capote, who was born Truman Streckfus Persons in New Orleans on 30 September 1924, the son of J. A. (Arch) Persons, later took the name of his stepfather. Capote, early determined to be a writer, spent much of his childhood in the lonely pursuit of putting stories down on paper. Following the divorce of his parents, he made his home with relatives in Monroeville, Ala., but in the 1930s went to live with his mother in New York City and later in Connecticut, where he attended high school. Although his formal education ended there, he found a substitute in his reading. After his mother and his stepfather moved back into New York City in the 1940s, Capote took a job as an office boy at the *New Yorker*, the magazine that would eventually publish many of his stories and nonfiction pieces.

Truman Capote achieved overnight fame at the age of 23 with the publication of *Other Voices, Other Rooms* (1948), his first novel. He had already dazzled the New York literary world with his prizewinning stories. A gifted prose stylist—"a fanatic on rhythm and language," as he told one interviewer— he never quite fulfilled his great promise as a writer, though he published a second novel (*The Grass Harp*, 1951) that he later rewrote for the stage, as well as several volumes of short fiction and collections of essays, memoirs, and travel pieces. His early short stories were collected in *A Tree of Night and Other Stories* (1949) and *Breakfast at Tiffany's* (1958), whose centerpiece was the novella that gave the book its title.

Capote's tour de force was *In Cold Blood*, first published serially in the *New Yorker* in 1965 and then as a book; he described it as a new form—the non-fiction novel. A gripping account of the mass murder of a Kansas farm family, it follows the two young killers from the murder scene to their eventual execution five and half years later. *In Cold Blood* was enormously successful and was followed by an equally successful motion picture.

Though his roots were in the South, Truman Capote lived most of his life in New York City. A celebrity himself and a man who cherished the art of conversation, he cultivated the rich and famous of the world and was a frequent guest on network television talk shows. When he died in 1984 during a visit to California, he had still not published his much-talked-about novel *Answered Prayers* (1987). The film *Capote* (2005) portrays Capote's struggles with the writing of *In Cold Blood* and his relationship with the killers he portrayed.

CHARLES EAST
Baton Rouge, Louisiana

Gerald Clarke, *Truman Capote: A Biography* (1988); Malcolm Cowley, ed., *Writers at Work: The Paris Review Interviews* (1958); James Dickey, *Paris Review* (Fall 1985); H. Garson, *Truman Capote: A Study of the Short Fiction* (1992); Lawrence Grobel, *Conversations with Capote* (1985); Marianne M. Moates, *Truman Capote's Southern Years: Stories from a Monroeville Cousin* (1996); George Plimpton, *Truman Capote: In Which Various Friends, Enemies, Acquaintances, and Detractors Recall His Turbulent Career* (1997); Kenneth T. Reed, *Truman Capote* (1981); Marie Rudisill and James C. Simmons, *The Southern Haunting of Truman Capote* (2000); Joseph J. Waldmeir, ed., *Critical Essays on Truman Capote* (1999), ed., *The Critical Response to Truman Capote* (1999).

Cash, W. J.

(1900–1941) JOURNALIST.
Wilbur Joseph Cash was a Piedmont southerner, born in Gaffney, S.C., in 1900, a graduate of Wake Forest College, a journalist for the *Charlotte News*, who died by his own hand in Mexico City in 1941. His influence rests upon a single work, *The Mind of the South*, published by Alfred A. Knopf in 1941, which was an attempt to analyze the relationship between social consciousness and culture in the region. As a prose stylist, Cash was a talented rhetorician, much influenced by H. L. Mencken's slashing, witty, and barbed journalism, but developing his own version, narrower in range of reference and accomplishment, conversational, sentimental, humorous, candid, emotional, and possessed of great impetus; it is a style, like that of Thomas Wolfe, best relished in youth and, indeed, once usually read then. For the book was noticed upon its publication, but only sold a few thousand copies in its first 19 years of life. However, it was put into paperback by Knopf in 1960 and quickly became mandatory reading, especially on northern campuses, when it seemed to offer an explanation for the puzzling society, which the crisis of the civil rights movement was obliged to reform.

Cash was the leading proponent of

the thesis of southern cultural unity and continuity, which he argued was fashioned by climate, physical conditions, frontier violence, clannishness, and Calvinist Protestantism, all of which conspired to create a romantic hedonism, a zeitgeist of anti-intellectualism and prejudice most brutally expressed in racism, the sum of which Cash called the "savage ideal." Having evolved before the Civil War, this unity connects the Old and New South. For Cash, the South's industrial transformation had failed to create the class consciousness and intellectual flexibility appropriate to such a society; thus the sensibility of the savage ideal had remained the master of southern history, which was essentially immobile. Cash himself was a liberal in racial matters by the standards of his time, that is, he had adjusted his views to deprecate the enemies of blacks, but not yet altered his own opinions to sympathize with black culture and personality. Cash's interpretation has proved most appealing to southern liberals who feel pessimistic about and trapped in southern provincial culture (especially its repressive religion) and find an explanation for their fetters in Cash's embittered but vivid portrait. Southern women find little in him of value and African Americans tend to be dismissive, but he retains a loyal following.

MICHAEL O'BRIEN
Jesus College, Cambridge

Bruce Clayton, *W. J. Cash: A Life* (1991); Charles W. Eagles, ed., *The Mind of the South: Fifty Years Later* (1992); Paul D. Escott, ed., *W. J. Cash and the Minds of the South* (1992).

Chappell, Fred

(b. 1936) POET, NOVELIST, SHORT-STORY WRITER, ESSAYIST, BOOK REVIEWER.

Fred Chappell was raised in the paper mill town of Canton, in the mountains of western North Carolina. After earning bachelor's and master's degrees in English from Duke University, he worked for 40 years as an English professor at the University of North Carolina at Greensboro. He lives in Greensboro with his wife, Susan, who appears in many of his poems.

Chappell won international renown in his early 30s with his novel *Dagon* (1968), which received France's Prix du Meilleur Livre Etranger. The book depicts a southern pastor's profound moral and intellectual degeneration. After undertaking a study of residual paganism in American puritanism, Peter Leland murders his wife and plunges into a drunken stupor; he then allows himself to become enslaved to a neighbor girl, who tortures and eventually murders him. Through his suffering and death, however, Leland attains a kind of posthumous redemption. Chappell's other early novels include *It Is Time, Lord* (1963), *The Inkling* (1965), and *The Gaudy Place* (1973).

In 1985 Chappell published *I Am One of You Forever*, the first novel in his popular tetralogy about the Kirkman family. Set in rural western North Carolina, the novel is essentially a story cycle about the farm childhood of Jess Kirkman; often humorous, sometimes poignantly sad, the book derives its power from its combination of magic realism and nonchronological structure. The tetralogy continues with *Brighten the Corner Where You Are* (1989), which narrates one eventful day in the life of Jess's father, Joe Robert; *Farewell, I'm Bound to Leave You* (1996), which focuses on the women in the family; and *Look Back All the Green Valley* (1999), in which Jess has grown up and become a writer with the pen name Fred Chappell.

The long poem *Midquest* (1981) is widely regarded as Chappell's poetic masterpiece. Like Dante's *Comedy*, the poem marks the poet's initiation into middle age; however, whereas Dante investigates the world beyond this one, Chappell remains resolutely focused on this life. The protagonist is "Old Fred," who is more or less Chappell himself. Many of the poem's sections tell stories from his family history; others are lyric reveries. A few take the form of epistles to fellow writers. The poem's overall structure is dazzling, as is its skilled employment of many different verse forms. Explicitly Appalachian in setting, *Midquest* is regarded by many as the greatest long poem of the southern mountains.

Chappell is equally accomplished at incisive brevity, as is demonstrated by *C* (1993), a collection of 100 translated and original epigrams. The same satirical wit that animates most of that book is also present in *Family Gathering* (2000) and *Backsass* (2004). Chappell's other poetry collections include *The World between the Eyes* (1971), *Castle Tzingal* (1984), *Source* (1985), *First and Last Words* (1989), and *Spring Garden: New and Selected Poems* (1995).

Many of Chappell's poetry-related essays and reviews are gathered in *Plow*

Naked (1993) and *A Way of Happening* (1998). His short stories are collected in two volumes, *Moments of Light* (1980) and *More Shapes than One* (1991).

ROBERT M. WEST
Mississippi State University

Patrick Bizzaro, ed., *Dream Garden* (1997); Patrick Bizzaro, ed., *More Lights than One* (2004); John Lang, *Understanding Fred Chappell* (2000).

Cherry, Kelly

(b. 1940) WRITER.

Kelly Cherry was born in Baton Rouge, La., in 1940, daughter of J. Milton (a violinist, composer, and professor of music theory) and Mary (a violinist and writer) Cherry. She attended Mary Washington College, the University of Virginia (where she studied philosophy), and the University of North Carolina at Greensboro. She lives in Halifax, Va., with her husband, fiction writer Burke Davis III.

Grounded in philosophy, Cherry's work in multiple genres constitutes an investigation into the seeking of truth. Abstract notions of truth, morality, love, and emotional and physical fulfillment have remained her focus throughout her career. There is ever-present autobiographical objectivity in her work, and the sense of place (in her poems it is often the South) serves as a mirror through which she sees the complexities of life and, very often, art. The South is a place she seeks to return to and, once there, finds contentment. In the final long ceremonial poem of *Rising Venus* (2002), "To a Young Woman: On the Occasion of Her Graduation from Vanderbilt University," the scene is the university grounds in Nashville before graduation ceremonies are under way. "The mothers and the fathers mill among magnolias," notes the speaker, whom we take to be the poet Kelly Cherry. She recalls some of Vanderbilt's renowned literary figures—Robert Penn Warren, Randall Jarrell, Allen Tate, Cleanth Brooks—and describes the day with tremendous nostalgia: "Blossoms infuse the rain with scent, powerfully." Cherry is likely visiting from Wisconsin, where she served as professor of English for many years; "I miss the South, its exotic perfumes and palette, / The way one moves through the weather here, wearing it / Next to the freed body like chiffon."

Cherry's first novel, *Sick and Full of Burning* (1974), tells the story of the life and relationships of Mary "Tennessee" Settleworth, a newly divorced medical student facing her 30th birthday. In *Augusta Played* (1979), Cherry places equal weight on both male and female points of view to tell the story of a tempestuous relationship between a young flutist and her musicologist husband. The novels *In the Wink of an Eye* (1983) and *The Lost Traveller's Dream* (1984) soon followed. The critically praised *My Life and Dr. Joyce Brothers: A Novel in Stories* was published in 1990, and the story collection *The Society of Friends*, its sequel, was published in 1999. *We Can Still Be Friends*, her most recent novel, was published in 2003. Her writing is formed by the complex world in which we live, by music, by philosophy, and by literature; she explains, "The hidden model for *Augusta Played* is *The Tempest*; the hidden model for *In the*

Wink of an Eye is *A Midsummer Night's Dream*." Her lyrical and texturally rich prose allows her to move with ease from prose into poetry and back again. It is as if one book were always making a way for the next, no matter what the genre. Thematically and lyrically akin but always formally fresh, each new book of prose and poetry extends that developmental passage.

Kelly Cherry's poetry collections include both formal verse and free verse, with *Lovers and Agnostics* appearing in 1975 and *Relativity: A Point of View* in 1977. *Natural Theology* (1988), *God's Loud Hand* (1993), *Death and Transfiguration* (1997), and *Rising Venus* (2002) followed. *Hazard and Prospect* was published in 2007. The citation preceding her receipt of the James G. Hanes Poetry Prize in 1989 by the Fellowship of Southern Writers praised her poetry as "marked by a firm intellectual passion, a reverent desire to possess the genuine thought of our century, historical, philosophical, and scientific, and a species of powerful ironic wit which is allied to rare good humor." In recent years, her work has become even more personal, always sharply depicting the complex nature of human emotions and desires.

Her nonfiction books include *History, Passion, Freedom, Death, and Hope: Prose about Poetry* (2005); *Writing the World*, essays and criticism (1995); and *The Exiled Heart: A Meditative Autobiography* (1991), of which Fred Chappell wrote in a review in *Louisiana Literature*, "The integrity of thought and courage of vision it portrays are qualities that abide in the memory, steadfast as fixed stars. One day this book will come into its own and will be recognized, along with some other works by Kelly Cherry, for the masterwork that it is."

JULIA JOHNSON
University of Southern Mississippi

Fred Chappell, *Mississippi Quarterly* (2004); *Contemporary Authors Online* (2004).

Chesnut, Mary Boykin

(1823–1886) DIARIST AND AUTHOR. Mary Boykin Miller Chesnut was born 31 March 1823 in Stateboro, S.C., eldest child of Mary Boykin and Stephen Decatur Miller, who had served as U.S. congressman and senator and in 1826 was elected governor of South Carolina, as a proponent of nullification. Educated first at home and in Camden schools, Mary Miller was sent at 13 to a French boarding school in Charleston, where she remained for two years broken by a six-month stay on her father's cotton plantation in frontier Mississippi. In 1838 Miller died and Mary returned to Camden. On 23 April 1840 she married James Chesnut Jr. (1815–85), only surviving son of one of South Carolina's largest landowners.

Chesnut spent most of the next 20 years in Camden and at Mulberry, her husband's family plantation. When James was elected to the Senate in 1858, his wife accompanied him to Washington where they began friendships with many politicians who would become the leading figures of the Confederacy, among them Varina and Jefferson Davis. Following Lincoln's election, James Chesnut returned to South Carolina to participate in the drafting of an ordi-

nance of secession and subsequently served in the Provisional Congress of the Confederate States of America. He served as aide to General P. G. T. Beauregard and President Jefferson Davis, and he achieved the rank of general. During the war, Mary accompanied her husband to Charleston, Montgomery, Columbia, and Richmond, her drawing room always serving as a salon for the Confederate elite. From February 1861 to July 1865, she recorded her experiences in a series of diaries, which became the principal source materials for her famous portrait of the Confederacy.

Following the war, the Chesnuts returned to Camden and worked unsuccessfully to extricate themselves from heavy debts. After a first abortive attempt in the 1870s to smooth the diaries into publishable form, Mary Chesnut tried her hand at fiction. She completed but never published three novels, then in the early 1880s expanded and extensively revised her diaries into the book now known as *Mary Chesnut's Civil War* (first published in truncated and poorly edited versions in 1905 and 1949 as *A Diary from Dixie*).

Although unfinished at the time of her death on 22 November 1886, *Mary Chesnut's Civil War* is generally acknowledged today as the finest literary work of the Confederacy. Spiced by the author's sharp intelligence, irreverent wit, and keen sense of irony and metaphorical vision, it uses a diary format to evoke a full, accurate picture of the South in civil war. Chesnut's book, valued as a rich historical source, owes much of its fascination to its juxtaposition of the loves and griefs of individuals against vast social upheaval and much of its power to the contrasts and continuities drawn between the antebellum world and a war-torn country.

ELISABETH MUHLENFELD
Florida State University

Mary A. DeCredico, *Mary Boykin Chesnut: A Confederate Woman's Life* (1996); Elisabeth Muhlenfeld, *Mary Boykin Chesnut: A Biography* (1981); C. Vann Woodward, ed., *Mary Chesnut's Civil War* (1981), with Elisabeth Muhlenfeld, eds., *The Private Mary Chesnut: The Unpublished Civil War Diaries* (1985).

Chesnutt, Charles W.

(1858–1932) WRITER.

Charles Waddell Chesnutt, African American man of letters, was born in Cleveland, Ohio, on 20 June 1858, the son of free blacks who had emigrated from Fayetteville, N.C. When he was eight years old, Chesnutt's parents returned to Fayetteville, where Charles worked part time in the family grocery store and attended a school founded by the Freedmen's Bureau. In 1872 financial necessity forced him to begin a teaching career in Charlotte, N.C. He returned to Fayetteville in 1877, married a year later, and by 1880 had become principal of the Fayetteville State Normal School for Negroes. Meanwhile he continued to pursue private studies of classic English literature, foreign languages, music, and stenography. Despite his successes, he longed for broader opportunities and a chance to develop the literary skills that by 1880 led him toward an author's life. In 1883 he moved his family to Cleveland. There he passed the state bar examination and established his own court reporting firm. Financially prosperous and prominent in civic affairs, he resided in Cleveland for the remainder of his life.

"The Goophered Grapevine," an unusual dialect story that displayed intimate knowledge of black folk culture in the South, was Chesnutt's first nationally recognized work of fiction. Its publication in the August 1887 issue of the *Atlantic Monthly* marked the first time that a short story by an African American had appeared in that prestigious magazine. After subsequent tales in this vein were accepted by other magazines, Chesnutt submitted to Houghton Mifflin a collection of these stories, which was published in 1899 as *The Conjure Woman*. His second collection of short fiction, *The Wife of His Youth and Other Stories of the Color Line* (1899), ranged over a broader area of southern and northern racial experience than any previous writer on African American life had attempted. These two volumes were popular enough to convince Houghton Mifflin to publish Chesnutt's first novel, *The House behind the Cedars*, in 1900. This story of two light-skinned African American siblings who pass for white in the postwar South revealed Chesnutt's sense of the psychological and social dilemmas facing persons of mixed blood in the region. In his second novel, *The Marrow of Tradition* (1901), Chesnutt confronted the causes and effects of the Wilmington, N.C., race riot of 1898. Hoping to write the *Uncle Tom's Cabin* of his generation, Chesnutt made a plea for racial justice that impressed the noted novelist and critic William Dean Howells, who reviewed

The Marrow of Tradition as a work of "great power," though with "more justice than mercy in it." The failure of Chesnutt's second novel to sell widely forced its author to give up his dream of supporting his family as a professional author. In 1905 he published his final novel, *The Colonel's Dream*, a tragic story of an idealist's attempt to revive a depressed North Carolina town through a socioeconomic program much akin to the New South creed of Henry W. Grady and Booker T. Washington. The novel received little critical notice.

In the twilight of his literary career Chesnutt continued to write novels (some of which ultimately found publishers in the late 20th century) and published occasional short stories. His fiction was largely eclipsed in the 1920s by the writers of the Harlem Renaissance. Nevertheless, he was awarded the Spingarn Medal in 1928 by the National Association for the Advancement of Colored People for his pioneering literary work on behalf of African American civil rights and racial understanding. Today Chesnutt is recognized as a major innovator in African American fiction, an important contributor to the deromanticizing trend in post–Civil War southern literature, and a singular voice among turn-of-the-century literary realists who probed the color line in American life.

WILLIAM L. ANDREWS
University of North Carolina at Chapel Hill

William L. Andrews, *The Literary Career of Charles W. Chesnutt* (1980); Frances Richardson Keller, *An American Crusade:*

The Life of Charles Waddell Chesnutt (1978); Joseph R. McElrath Jr., ed., *Critical Essays on Charles Chesnutt* (1999); Henry B. Wonham, *Studies in American Fiction* (Fall 1998).

Chopin, Kate

(1851–1904) WRITER.

Although Katherine O'Flaherty Chopin was a native of St. Louis (born 8 February 1851) and spent barely 14 years in Louisiana, her fiction is identified with the South. At 19, Kate O'Flaherty married Oscar Chopin, a young cotton broker, and moved with him to New Orleans and later to his family home in Cloutierville, La., near the Red River. After Oscar died in 1882, she returned with their six children to St. Louis; but when, eight years later, she began to write, it was the Creoles and 'Cadians of her Louisiana experiences that animated her fiction.

Distinctly unsentimental in her approach, she often relied on popular period motifs, such as the conflict of the Yankee businessman and the Creole, a theme that informs her first novel, *At Fault* (1890), and several of her short stories. These vivid and economical tales, richly flavored with local dialect, provide penetrating views of the heterogeneous culture of south Louisiana. Many of them were collected in *Bayou Folk* (1894) and *A Night in Acadie* (1897). Chopin's second novel also strongly evokes the region, but *The Awakening* (1899) is primarily a lyrical, stunning study of a young woman whose deep personal discontents lead to adultery and suicide. Praised for its craft and damned for its content, the novel was a scandal, and Chopin, always sensitive to her critics, gradually lost confidence in her gift and soon ceased to write.

Chopin died of a brain hemorrhage after a strenuous day at the St. Louis World's Fair, where she had been a regular visitor. She was remembered only as one of the southern local colorists of the 1890s until *The Awakening* was rediscovered in the 1970s as an early masterpiece of American realism and a superb rendering of female experience.

BARBARA C. EWELL
Loyola University

Lynda S. Boren and Sara Davis, eds., *Kate Chopin Reconsidered: Beyond the Bayou* (1992); Barbara C. Ewell, *Kate Chopin* (1986); Per Seyersted, *Kate Chopin: A Critical Biography* (1969); Peggy Skaggs, *Kate Chopin* (1985); Marlene Springer, *Edith Wharton and Kate Chopin: A Reference Guide* (1976); Helen Taylor, *Gender, Race, and Region in the Writings of Grace King, Ruth McEnery Stuart, and Kate Chopin* (1989); Emily Toth, *Kate Chopin* (1990); Nancy Walker, ed., *The Awakening: Kate Chopin* (1993).

Clemens, Samuel Langhorne (Mark Twain)

(1835–1910) WRITER.
Although Samuel Clemens initially tasted fame and employed his pen name in Nevada and California, he traced his "Mark Twain" pseudonym to his pilot days on the Mississippi River, and many features of his writings can also be attributed to that southern background. Clemens was born 30 November 1835 in the border state of Missouri and grew up in Hannibal, but his father was a Virginian and his mother was from a Kentucky family. Sam Clemens became a printer, working in New York, Pennsylvania, Ohio, Illinois, and Missouri before becoming a steamboat pilot. As a pilot posted at the river ports of St. Louis and New Orleans from 1857 until 1861, Clemens glided regularly through the Deep South sugarcane fields of Louisiana and Mississippi.

The South's watershed year of 1861 was momentous for Clemens, who accompanied his brother Orion to the Far West. Subsequently, Clemens moved east to Buffalo and then settled in the New England climate of Nook Farm in Hartford, Conn. His family, too, moved northward—to Fredonia, N.Y., and to Keokuk, Iowa. These shifts resulted in a hybridization, reflected in his literature, of the traditions and atmosphere of the South, the extravagance and energies of the West, and the taboos and commerce of the East. But Louis D. Rubin Jr. has argued persuasively that "the southern experience of Samuel L. Clemens is so thoroughly and deeply imaged in his life and work that one may scarcely read a chapter of any of his books without encountering it," and that in *A Connecticut Yankee* (1889) "the whole ambivalent love-hate relationship of Sam Clemens with the South is dramatized" to indicate "the South's similarity to feudal England."

Mark Twain objected to the South's pretensions. Remembering the grand, absurd village names of his youth, he chose "St. Petersburg" as the name for his fictional river town, trying to catch and satirize those grandiose dreams of splendor. After the Civil War, Twain would blame the historical novels

Samuel Clemens (Mark Twain), one of the nation's best-known novelists, c. 1905
(A. E. Bradley, photographer, Library of Congress [LC-USZ-62-28844], Washington, D.C.)

of Sir Walter Scott for the "romantic juvenilities" and "inflated language and other windy humbuggeries" that still bedeviled the South. Returning to the river for a nostalgic visit in 1882, Clemens was aghast to learn that duels were still being fought by prominent citizens of New Orleans. However, as his steamboat drew into the Louisiana reaches of the Mississippi, he found himself admiring the "greenhouse" lawns and "dense rich foliage and huge, snow-ball blossoms" of the magnolia trees that, along with a "tropical swelter in the air," announced that he was "in the absolute South, now—no modifications, no compromises." On the streets of New Orleans, too, he "found the half-forgotten Southern intonations and elisions as pleasing to my ear as they had formerly been. A Southerner talks music."

This homeland had been a place of grief and disappointment for Twain. In Memphis he had knelt helpless and agonized while his brother Henry died from scalding burns suffered when the steamboat *Pennsylvania* blew up in 1858. Twain also knew firsthand the uncouth, ruffian character of river-town idlers; he portrayed their cruelties in a backward Arkansas town in *The Adventures of Huckleberry Finn*.

Like most southern authors of his generation, Twain felt obliged to explain why he had lived in a land that countenanced human slavery. "In my schoolboy days I had no aversion to slavery," he testified. "I was not aware that there was anything wrong about it. No one arraigned it in my hearing; the local papers said nothing against it; the local pulpit taught us that God approved it." Ultimately, Twain became a great American writer in part because his family had owned slaves, which provided him with an insight into that system of bondage. His finest novel, *The Adventures of Huckleberry Finn* (1885), like Faulkner's *Absalom, Absalom!*, addresses the volatile racial issue that has periodically threatened the unity of a nation. Twain's entrée to the pages of the highbrow *Atlantic Monthly* was

a poignant story inspired by a black woman cook he met at Quarry Farm near Elmira, N.Y. An angry essay of 1901, "The United States of Lyncherdom," castigated Missouri for joining the southern states in resorting to mob violence against accused blacks, though Twain conceded that "the people in the South are made like the people in the North—a vast majority of whom are right-hearted and compassionate."

Twain could also portray an idealized South. One commentator, Arthur Pettit, has observed that in *The Adventures of Tom Sawyer* (1976) Mark Twain transformed antebellum Hannibal "into a Golden Age of prelapsarian innocence and charm." The image of this dozing village rose before Twain's eyes again and again, although *The Tragedy of Pudd'nhead Wilson* (1894) discloses lurking secrets behind the "whitewashed exteriors" of a similar town, Dawson's Landing. Twain's benign movie-reel depiction of the typical downtown district appeared in "Old Times on the Mississippi" (1875), a passage later subsumed in *Life on the Mississippi* (1883); the stir and bustle on Water Street when a black drayman called out "S-t-e-a-m-boat a-comin'!" and the boat came into sight on "the great Mississippi, the majestic, the magnificent Mississippi, rolling its mile-wide tide along, shining in the sun," vividly evoked this scene even for readers who had seen neither that river nor any states bordering it.

Always he acknowledged sincere admiration for amenities of life taken for granted in the South. He lauded its gastronomic delights in *A Tramp Abroad* (1880), listing and praising 20 southern dishes such as "fried chicken, Southern style," "black bass from the Mississippi," "hot corn-pone, with chitlings," "hot hoe-cake," hominy, butter beans, and apple puffs. His mental map of the Quarles farm where he spent his boyhood summers—the main log house, the smokehouse, the slave quarters, the orchard, the tobacco field, the schoolhouse—was re-created for his autobiographical recollections.

Although Twain had a broader and more venturesome approach to fiction than his contemporaries George Washington Cable, Joel Chandler Harris, and Thomas Nelson Page, he is equally indebted with them to the shaping forces of southern culture. His experiments in reproducing black dialect, such as "A True Story," compare favorably with the studied idiom in Harris's *Uncle Remus* (1880) and Page's "Marse Chan" (1884); Jim's patois and Huck's vernacular in *Huckleberry Finn* enriched the form of the American novel forever. In language and in delineation of character, setting, and society, his sketches, short stories, and novels have influenced writers as diverse as Thomas Wolfe, Erskine Caldwell, and William Faulkner. The beneficiary of a tradition of southern frontier humor, Mark Twain multiplied their notable achievements into the richer legacy he bequeathed to modern southern authors.

ALAN GRIBBEN
University of Texas at Austin

Ken Burns, Dayton Duncan, and Geoffrey C. Ward, *Mark Twain: An Illustrated Biography* (2001); Andrew Hoffman, *Inventing Mark Twain: The Lives of Samuel Langhorne Clemens* (1997); Justin Kaplan, *Mr. Clemens and Mark Twain* (1974); Lewis G. Leary, *Southern Excursions: Essays on Mark Twain and Others* (1971); Bruce Michelson, *Mark Twain on the Loose* (1995); Arthur G. Pettit, *Mark Twain and the South* (1974); Ron Powers, *Dangerous Waters: A Biography of the Boy Who Became Mark Twain* (1999); R. Kent Rasmussen, *Mark Twain A to Z: The Essential Reference to His Life and Writings* (1995); Louis D. Rubin Jr., *The Writer in the South* (1972); Thomas A. Tenney, *Mark Twain: A Reference Guide* (1977).

Cohn, David

(1894–1960) NONFICTION AUTHOR.
A prolific nonfiction writer born in the Mississippi Delta, David Cohn was the son of a Polish-born Jewish immigrant who moved to Greenville in the 1880s to become a dry goods merchant. Cohn wrote three memoirs, the last of which, *The Mississippi Delta and the World*, was published long after his death. The changes Cohn made as he moved from *God Shakes Creation* (1935) to *Where I Was Born and Raised* (1947) to the last memoir show the ways Cohn became increasingly concerned with his own place in the racial and class hierarchies of 20th-century Mississippi. His best writing showed his attempts to understand his home region, which he famously described in 1935: "The Mississippi Delta begins in the lobby of the Peabody Hotel in Memphis and ends on Catfish Row in Vicksburg."

God Shakes Creation was in part a memoir, with considerable discussion of Cohn's family and friends in the Greenville area, but above all it was a study of African American life in the Delta. He took the title from a sermon in which an African American preacher described the end of winter in the Mississippi Delta: "De seeds dey sleeps in de ground and de birds dey stops dey singing. Den God shakes creation in de spring." After describing the natural environment of the Delta, and briefly discussing plantation-owning families, Cohn spent most of the book on African Americans' family and sex lives, the medical and folk practices he called "Delta Magic," crime, sharecropping, and religion. Part folkloric with long quotes, part descriptive, part defensive, the book alternated between great respect for what he called African Americans' "joy of living" and a paternalistic sense that sharecroppers were better off in situations where they were secure and knew who was in charge. Cohn wrote of the Delta as neither a problem nor a paradise, but he clearly loved the region's land, people, and complexities.

In 1948 Cohn added 150 pages to *God Shakes Creation* and titled his new book *Where I Was Born and Raised*. The title and new chapters placed Cohn himself more at the center of the book. He wrote as an insider, someone who was "born and raised" in Greenville, but he did not write as a member of a landowning elite, and it was also important that he wrote as an expatriate who had left the Delta and returned only to visit. The main theme of the new chapters was that new technology and the migration of thousands of agricultural workers were creating a new Delta that Cohn found troubling. Thus, the more things changed, the more Cohn, who had never really written as a classic landed paternalist, seemed to admire the way things used

to be. In fact, *Where I Was Born and Raised* seems much more similar in tone to the 1941 *Lanterns on the Levee* by Cohn's friend and fellow Greenville author William Alexander Percy than does *God Shakes Creation*.

In the 1940s and 1950s Cohn wrote several nonfiction books and countless magazine articles for popular audiences on an array of topics he found compelling: marriage, New Orleans architecture, the history of cotton, the effects of the Sears-Roebuck catalog, the automobile, the American military, and the Democratic Party. He wrote with considerable wit and a taste for social criticism. Despite his cosmopolitanism and wide travels, he never chose to condemn or work against racial segregation, usually describing it as a tragedy for the South to solve and critiquing the moral certainty of nonsouthern critics and reformers.

Cohn also showed great interest in American internationalism. He spoke and wrote for the United States to grow more aggressive against world hunger, communism, and especially anti-Semitism. He was a friend and adviser to several Democratic leaders and wrote speeches for, among others, Senators William Fulbright and Adlai Stevenson. A great traveler and observer, Cohn died in Copenhagen in 1960.

TED OWNBY
University of Mississippi

David Cohn, *God Shakes Creation* (1935), *Where I Was Born and Raised* (1948), *Love in America: An Informal Study of Manners and Morals in American Marriage* (1943), *This Is the Story* (1947); David Cohn, *The Mississippi Delta and the World*, ed.

James C. Cobb (1995); James C. Cobb, *The Most Southern Place on Earth: The Mississippi Delta and the Roots of Regional Identity* (1992); James L. Cohn Papers, Special Collections, J. D. Williams Library, University of Mississippi.

Conroy, Pat

(b. 1945) WRITER.

Pat Conroy has spent his career crafting personal trauma and abuse into rich, romantic, and often painfully autobiographical fiction. Along the way, he has become famed nearly as much for his contentious battles and reconciliations with his alma mater and his father as for his artistic and phenomenal commercial accomplishments.

Born in 1945 to Donald N. Conroy, a Marine fighter pilot, and Frances "Peggy" Peek, a native Georgian with an abiding love of Margaret Mitchell's *Gone with the Wind*, Donald Patrick Conroy was the eldest of seven children, nearly all of whom would struggle with the legacy of their domineering father's physical and psychological abuse.

The itinerancy of military life ended for Conroy in Beaufort, S.C., where he spent his final two years of high school. Here, Conroy discovered Thomas Wolfe, the writer to whom his fiction is most indebted. He also excelled in athletics and earned a basketball scholarship to the only school his father would allow him to attend, the Military Institute of South Carolina, popularly known as The Citadel.

Failing to rise above the rank of private, Conroy found far more success with a basketball in his hand than a rifle on his shoulder. As a senior, Conroy started at point guard and received the dubious honor of being named most valuable player for the disappointing 1966–67 season, an experience presented in the memoir, *My Losing Season* (2003).

The Citadel was fertile ground for Conroy. His first book, *The Boo* (1970), was a self-published collection of essays celebrating Lt. Col. Thomas N. Courvoisie, the recently fired assistant commandant of cadets at The Citadel. The publication of *The Lords of Discipline* (1980) drew the ire of the institution, blowing open the secrets of the lightly fictionalized "Carolina Military Academy" with the same voracity—and not dissimilar reaction—with which his other works approached the Conroy family. The novel was awarded the Lillian Smith Book Award in 1981.

Following his graduation in 1967, Conroy returned to Beaufort as a teacher and coach. In the fall of 1969, Conroy met and married Barbara Jones, a Vietnam War widow pregnant with her second child. He also accepted a position at the two-room elementary school on nearby Daufuskie Island, an impoverished African American community that was accessible only by ferry and long-neglected by the school district. Daufuskie became "Yamacraw Island" in *The Water Is Wide* (1973), a memoir that was a modest success and which was adapted as the film *Conrack* (1974).

Conroy followed up the memoir with his first novel, *The Great Santini* (1976), the autobiographical tale of the traumatic abuse suffered by a teenaged boy and his family at the hands of the bullying Marine father. Its publication nearly destroyed both Conroy and his family. He collapsed in a parking lot on his book tour, his father's family quit speaking with him, and his marriage ended, as did his parents'. Peggy Conroy even entered the novel as evidence in her divorce proceedings.

In *The Prince of Tides*, Conroy again turned toward his and his family's tragic history, this time exploring the adult consequences of abuse, particularly in his sister's manic depression and his own history of depression. The novel became a national phenomenon, riding a wave of momentum from instant best seller to Academy Award–nominated film.

Conroy's next novel, *Beach Music* (1995), drew from subjects as disparate as the Holocaust, the Vietnam War, Conroy's first divorce, his time in Rome with his second wife and their children, and the depression and eventual suicide of his youngest brother, Thomas. Highly anticipated and long-delayed, *Beach Music* was another commercial success, if not a critical one.

Throughout the 1990s, Conroy remained in the headlines, vocally and financially supporting attempts to force The Citadel to accept women into its corps of cadets. Ultimately, women were admitted into the institution, and Conroy even received an honorary degree. Likewise, Conroy reconciled with his father: "My father answered my first novel by setting out to prove I was a liar of the first magnitude," he wrote in *Atlanta Magazine* in 1999, shortly after his father's death. "He worked night and day in turning himself into a father even his own children could love."

He has returned to Beaufort and lives on nearby Fripp Island with his third wife, the author Cassandra King. Recently Conroy revealed that he had been engaged with the Margaret Mitchell estate in protracted discussions to write a sequel to *Gone with the Wind*, the novel worshiped by his mother. The negotiations broke off, however, over issues of editorial control.

ANTHONY D. HOEFER JR.
Louisiana State University

John Berendt, *Vanity Fair* (July 1995); Landon C. Burns, *Pat Conroy: A Critical Companion* (1996); Robert W. Hamblin, *Aethlon: Journal of Sport Literature* (Fall 1993); David Toolan, *Commonweal* (February 1991).

Crews, Harry

(b. 1935) WRITER.

A son of tenant farmers, Harry Edward Crews was born 6 June 1935 in Bacon County, Ga. Between his life on the subsistence farm and his full professorship in the University of Florida English Department that had denied him admission as a graduate student, he served in the Marine Corps; attended the University of Florida (B.A., 1960; M.S.Ed., 1962); knocked around the country for 18 months on a motorcycle; taught in a junior high school and a junior college; wrote five-minute daily inspirational stories of achievement for Nelson Boswell, a Florida radio commentator; and passed through the academic ranks at Florida. In 1972 Crews received the Arts and Letters Award from the American Academy and Institute of Arts and Letters.

Harry Crews claims to have written his first novel, a detective story, when he was 13. His first published story, "The Unattached Smile," appeared in 1963; his most recent work, a novel entitled *Celebration*, was published in 1998. In the intervening years he produced 17 books—14 novels, an autobiography, and two collections of essays and stories. In 1989 he was commissioned by the Actors Theatre of Louisville (Ky.) to write *Blood Issue*, a drama, for the 13th Annual Humana Festival of New Plays. Many of his stories first appeared in national magazines, notably *Esquire* and *Playboy*, and he is an example of the prominent place southern writers have long had in those magazines. His stories are rooted in the intersection of biography and history; the biography is poor white, the history is southern. His characters are engaged in a futile struggle to balance the achievement ethic and marketing ethos of modern society against traditional cultural values.

Each of his novels, from *The Gospel Singer* (1968) through *Celebration*, has received mixed reviews. Critics and reviewers seem unable to agree on either the content or significance of Crews's books. Most, however, react strongly to them. He is in the southern Gothic tradition, and each of his novels has been identified by various critics as his best. Crews's comments on his own work suggest that he regards *Naked in Garden Hills* (1969), *The Gypsy's Curse* (1974), and *A Childhood: The Biography of a Place* (1978) as among his best.

A Childhood is a superb ethnography of a rural subsistence community from the perspective of Crews's people.

It details the first five years of his life and traces the consequences of the transition from subsistence farming to a one-crop agricultural and industrial economy. The autobiography shows that Crews's fiction follows the survivors of that culture, whose hermetic seal was broken by the intrusion of the outside world or, more commonly, the outmigration of its inhabitants. *A Childhood* and *A Feast of Snakes* (1976), two of his most widely acclaimed works, may be the best examples of the literary and analytic talents of Harry Crews.

His works illuminate both an internal struggle—heart versus mind—and an eternal struggle—man versus society and culture. His characters, often "freaks," come to appear less unusual as their struggles with each other, place, time, and culture create the story. Crews's work provides important insights into the Americanization of the South and the southernization of America.

His other books are *This Thing Don't Lead to Heaven* (1970), *Karate Is a Thing of the Spirit* (1971), *Car* (1972), *The Hawk Is Dying* (1973), *Blood and Grits* (1979), *Florida Frenzy* (1982), *All We Need of Hell* (1987), *The Knockout Artist* (1988), *Body* (1990), *Scar Lover* (1992), *The Mulching of America* (1995), *Where Does One Go When There's No Place Left to Go?* (1998), and *American Family* (2006).

LARRY W. DEBORD
University of Mississippi

Jeff Abernathy, *Southern Literary Journal* (Fall 2001); Lorene M. Birden, *Arkansas Review* (Fall 1995); Erik Bledsoe, *Perspectives on Harry Crews* (2001); Larry W. DeBord and Gary L. Long, *Southern Quarterly*

(Spring 1982); Joe Dewey, *American Writers*, suppl. 9: *Toni Cade Bambara to Richard Yates* (2002); Timothy Edwards, *Southern Quarterly* (Fall 1998); Matthew Guinn, *After Southern Modernism: Fiction of the Contemporary South* (2000); David K. Jeffrey and Donald R. Noble, *Southern Quarterly* (Winter 1981); Susan Ketchin, *The Christ-Haunted Landscape: Faith and Doubt in Southern Fiction* (1994); Gary L. Long and Larry W. DeBord, *Texas Review* (Fall–Winter 1983) Matthew Teague, *Oxford American* (December–January 1995–96).

Crockett, David (Davy)

(1786–1836) FRONTIERSMAN, POLITICIAN, HUMORIST.

Born on 17 August 1786, in Green County, Tenn., the son of John and Rebecca Hawkins Crockett, this frontiersman, Tennessee and United States congressman, and folk hero was both the historical figure who died at the Alamo and a legendary figure made famous in the media of his day and our own.

Crockett grew up with the new nation and helped it to grow. Although he was elected a lieutenant in the 32nd Militia, served as a justice of the peace, town commissioner of Lawrenceburg, Tenn., and colonel of the 57th Militia Regiment of Lawrence County by 1818, David Crockett was still a relatively unknown backwoods hunter with a talent for storytelling until his election to the Tennessee legislature in 1821 and then to the U.S. House of Representatives in 1827. He promoted himself as a simple, honest country boy, an unassuming hunter and expert marksman, who was literally a "straight-shooter" on all levels. Reelected to a second term in 1829, he

split with President Andrew Jackson on land reform issues and the Indian removal bill. Crockett was defeated for a bid for a third term when he openly and vehemently opposed Jackson's policies, was reelected in 1833, and defeated again in 1835, in part through the combined efforts of Governor Carroll of Tennessee and the president, whom he had labeled "King Andrew I" in print the previous year. This loss encouraged him to explore the possibility of economic and political opportunities in Texas.

His notoriety had also given his legendary image a life of its own. In part, the inventor of his own myth, by 1831 Crockett had become the model for Nimrod Wildfire, the hero of James Kirke Paulding's popular play *The Lion of the West*. In 1834 Crockett published his autobiography, *A Narrative of the Life of David Crockett of the State of Tennessee*, to counteract the outlandish stories printed under his name as the *Sketches and Eccentricities of Colonel David Crockett of West Tennessee* in 1833. A good deal of the information in *Sketches and Eccentricities*, a work that helped to initiate the Old Southwest humor tradition, was, however, supplied by Crockett himself.

The more outrageous stories were soon expanded by anonymous eastern hack writers who spun out tall tales for the Crockett Almanacs (1835–56), one of the most successful series of American comic almanacs ever produced. In the hands of these writers, Davy became a backwoods screamer, and, with the death of the historical Crockett at the Alamo on 6 March 1836, the floodgates of fiction were loosed. Davy could now save the world by wringing the tail off Halley's Comet and flinging it back into outer space or by unfreezing the sun and the earth from their axes, and do both as easily as he could ride his pet alligator up Niagara Falls, tree a ghost, or drink the Gulf of Mexico dry.

Other works published under Crockett's name were *An Account of Col. Crockett's Tour to the North and Down East* (1835), *The Life of Martin Van Buren* (1835), and *Col. Crockett's Exploits and Adventures in Texas* (1836). These works, together with his heroic death, completed an enduring union of history and legend. The image of Crockett in American culture was continued and modified by scores of biographies and "autobiographies" that merged fact and fantasy and most recently resulted in the 1990s fiction of Cameron Judd and David Thompson. This image, however, was also the descendant of the tradition of Davy as the hero of romantic melodrama. His characterization by Paulding as Nimrod Wildfire was carried on through plays and a series of silent and modern films that culminated in the Davys played by Fess Parker, John Wayne, and Billy Bob Thornton and in the Crockett craze of the mid-1950s. This heritage reinforced Crockett's status as a preeminent frontier hero in the American mind.

MICHAEL A. LOFARO
University of Tennessee

Richard Boyd Hauck, *Crockett: A Bio-Bibliography* (1982), reprinted as *Davy Crockett: A Handbook* (1986); Michael A. Lofaro, ed., *Davy Crockett: The Man, the Legend, the Legacy, 1786–1986* (1985); James Atkins Shackford, *David Crockett: The Man and the Legend* (1986).

Crowley, Mart

(b. 1935) WRITER, PRODUCER, ACTOR.

Mart Crowley was born 21 August 1935 in Vicksburg, Miss., where he attended St. Aloysius High School; served as equipment boy for the football team, the Flashes; and donated his time and talent to the Vicksburg Little Theatre. Attracted by the quality of its drama department, he went on to Catholic University of America in Washington, D.C., graduating in 1957. As Ellis Nassour wrote in the Jackson, Miss., newspaper the *Clarion-Ledger*, about Crowley growing up in Vicksburg, "His father operated Crowley's Smoke House. The motto was 'Where All Good Fellows Meet'—for pool, dominoes, cigars, punch-board gambling, a bit of illegal drinking, and the best hamburgers anywhere . . . but movie theatres were [Crowley's] world, where he developed his writer's imagination."

Crowley's most southern play, *A Breeze from the Gulf*, is set in Mississippi with an introductory warning from the playwright that it should not "drip with magnolias." A three-character play, it portrays the familial dysfunction of the Connellys. Psychological violence, drug addiction, and alcohol abuse bring out the worst in parents who strive to love one another and do their best by their son. The horrors of regular trips to Whitfield (Mississippi's psychiatric hospital), free-for-all brawls at Antoine's in "Noo Awlens," and heavy drinking on Bourbon Street are juxtaposed with moments of happiness—always on the Gulf Coast at places like Edgewater and Paradise Point, with the sound of the surf and a touch of the Gulf Coast breeze.

Crowley's career decision was influenced by watching the filming of Tennessee Williams's *Baby Doll* in the Mississippi Delta during the winter of 1955–56 and hanging out with the likes of Elia Kazan, Carroll Baker, Karl Malden, and Eli Wallach at Doe's Eat Place in Greenville. After working on the set of William Inge's *Splendor in the Grass* (1958) with Natalie Wood and Warren Beatty, he was eventually employed as Natalie Wood's assistant, became executive story editor of ABC's *Hart to Hart*, and was named godfather to her children.

Sometimes called "the granddaddy of gay theatre," Crowley is best known for his 1968, long-running play *Boys in the Band*, which opened off Broadway and made theater history by creating sensitive portrayals of a group of gay men attending a birthday party in New York City. Premiering before the Stonewall Riots and before Act Up, Queer Nation, and the Gay Liberation Front, Crowley's play was celebrated by *USA Today*'s David Patrick Stearns as "The *Uncle Tom's Cabin* of homosexual literature."

In Crowley's plays, themes of self-loathing and self-destruction, deep-seated homophobia, and social maladjustment appear with his characters looking for love in all the wrong places as they learn to come to grips with the self, love one another, and achieve meaningful relationships. Crowley's other works include *Remote Asylum* (1970), *For Reasons that Remain Unclear* (1993), and *The Men from the Boys* (2002).

COLBY H. KULLMAN
University of Mississippi

Clive Barnes, *New York Post* (21 June 1996); John M. Clum, *Acting Gay* (1992), *Still Acting Gay* (2000); Ellis Nassour, *Clarion Ledger* (30 June 1996); Vito Russo, *The Celluloid Closet* (1987); Alan Sinfield, *Out on Stage* (1999); Claude J. Summers, *The Gay and Lesbian Literary Heritage* (1997).

Dargan, Olive Tilford

(1869–1968) WRITER.

A daughter of teachers, Olive Tilford Dargan was born 11 January 1869 in Leitchfield, Ky. In 1886 she earned a scholarship to Peabody College. After teaching for several years, Dargan entered Radcliffe in 1893 and continued her classical education while exploring personal questions about the economic disparity of her country. She concluded her education by taking a job as a secretary, realizing firsthand the indifference of wealthy administrators toward their struggling employees. In 1898 she married Pegram Dargan, a poet, and they moved to New York where Dargan launched her writing career.

Dargan released the first collection of her plays, *Semiramis and Other Plays*, in 1904. Two years later she followed with a second collection, *Lords and Lovers* (1906); it was well received and earned money to purchase land in the Blue Ridge Mountains. The writers struggled on their farm near Almond, N.C., and Dargan's writing was stalled while she physically labored to turn the land into a profitable venture. Her correspondence from this time indicated her desire for private space and solitude in which to write, but she also appreciated her new understanding of mountain life and her personal struggle with hard life. Dargan left the farm for England, witnessing for three years the devastating effects of labor strikes on the poor and the political activities of women. These events combined with her interest in socialist works and ideas of economic equality inspired her next publication; *The Mortal Gods and Other Dramas* (1912) illustrated her radical social voice, but her synthesis of political subjects with Shakespearean verse brought mostly negative criticism. After the dismal reception of this volume of plays, Dargan turned to poetry with *Path Flowers and Other Verses* (1914), still receiving mixed reviews. A year later Pegram drowned near Cuba, and she dedicated 1916's *The Cycle's Rim* to him. Composed of Shakespearean sonnets, Dargan's memorial collection earned her several awards. In 1922 she published another book of poems, *Lute and Furrow*, and worked with Frederick Peterson to produce *Flutter of the Gold Leaf*, while shifting her focus to regionally realistic fiction.

Between 1919 and 1924 Dargan published regionalist stories celebrating mountain life in *Atlantic Monthly*. These popular stories were collected in *Highland Annals* (1925). She wrote with the intention to correct misconceptions about the mountain people, refuting stereotypes and especially focusing on portraying strong intelligent women. She revised and reissued the stories in *From My Highest Hill* (1941), accompanied by photographs by Bayard Wootten. Later, construction of the Tennessee Valley Authority's Fontana Dam destroyed the community preserved in Dargan's detailed accounts, leaving only these stories as evidence of a vanishing life-style.

Under the pseudonym Fielding Burke, Dargan published politically themed novels based on radical socialist and feminist ideology. Perhaps her best-known work, *Call Home the Heart* (1932), was inspired by striking textile mill workers in Gastonia, N.C., and earned her the label of proletarian author. Its sequel, *A Stone Came Rolling* (1935), explored the southern church, racism, and the mill strikes in High Point, N.C. Her last novel and self-proclaimed best work, *Sons of the Stranger* (1947), dealt with early American unionism. In a time of rampant communist fears, her publisher feared to draw attention to Dargan's radicalism, and the novel quietly disappeared amid mixed reviews. Its failure inhibited her confidence, and she did not attempt publication again for 11 years. Her return to poetry with *The Spotted Hawk* (1958) won her numerous awards, and her last collection of stories, *Innocent Bigamy* (1962), continued developing her favorite themes. She died 23 January 1968 in an Asheville nursing home.

Badly timed publications can be partially blamed for Dargan's mixed receptions. Her works were generally released into literary atmospheres that misunderstood, dismissed, or disagreed with her art. She promoted communist ideals, desired a classless society, condemned war, and sought the fault in evolution that allowed intelligent beings to oppress fellow humans. Her feminist ideology addressed marriage as an institution between equal partners, challenged idealized motherhood, and explored the conflict between romantic love and political activism in women. The inability to neatly classify Dargan as a regional, proletarian, or feminist writer led to her continued neglect until the Feminist Press reprinted *Call Home the Heart* in 1983. Since then, her reputation and literary standing have slowly been reviving.

KATHY SCHRUM
University of South Carolina

Kathy Cantley Ackerman, *The Heart of the Revolution* (2004), *Olive Tilford Dargan: Recovering a Proletarian Romantic* (1991); Anna Shannon Elfenbein, *From My Highest Hill* (1998).

Davenport, Guy

(1927–2005) WRITER.
Guy Davenport was born and raised in Anderson, S.C., and lived for more than 40 years in Lexington, Ky., where he worked as professor of English at the University of Kentucky, solidly establishing him as a southern writer. Davenport's work, however, bears none of the characteristic emblems of writing from the region. Readers learn nothing of Davenport's personal life or family history from his poems and stories, and none of his work is set in the American South. Several of his stories are set in the hometown of his invented Danish

philosopher, Adriaan Floris van Hovendaal, though Davenport admits to never having visited Denmark, and other fiction is based on the lives and times of the fifth-century Greek philosopher Heraclitus, Franz Kafka, Henry David Thoreau, and Richard Nixon. Details about Davenport's life are conspicuously difficult to locate, as the following exchange from his 2002 *Paris Review* "The Art of Fiction" series interview demonstrates:

> *Interviewer*: Is anyone writing your biography?
> *Davenport*: I have no life.
> *Interviewer*: This from no doubt the only man on earth to have known Ezra Pound, Thomas Merton, and Cormac McCarthy personally!
> *Davenport*: Well, I have no comment about that.

This exchange suggests both modesty and secrecy, but when he claims to have no life, he also insinuates that for the committed artist, the work is the life, and Davenport certainly produced a massive body of work.

The Death of Picasso: New and Selected Writing, which appeared in 2003 from Shoemaker and Hoard, brings together Davenport's fiction and his essays on art and literature. This collection makes for a passable introduction to Davenport's writing, but includes none of his acclaimed translations, poetry, or illustrations. Davenport was a notoriously prodigious writer, but his major poetry can be found in *Flowers and Leaves* (1966) and *Thasos and Ohio* (1986); his major commentary in the books *The Geography of the Imagina-*

tion (1981), *Every Force Evolves a Form* (1987), *The Hunter Gracchus* (1996), and *Objects on a Table* (1998). His short-story collections includes *Tatlin!* (1974), *Da Vinci's Bicycle* (1979), *Eclogues* (1981), *Apples and Pears* (1984), *The Jules Verne Steam Balloon* (1987), *The Drummer of the Eleventh North Devonshire Fusiliers* (1990), *A Table of Green Fields* (1993), and *The Cardiff Team* (1996). In 1996 New Directions published a selection of his paintings and illustrations, edited by his University of Kentucky colleague, Erik Anderson Reece, titled *A Balance of Quinces*.

Davenport was both a classicist and a postmodernist, a poet and scholar, reliant upon equal parts inspiration and intellectual study. In the late 20th-century culture of academic profession-alization and specialization, Davenport wrote with equal authority translations of ancient Greek lyric poets, reviews of critics such as Claude Lévi-Strauss, art criticism, highly inventive poetry and short fiction, novels, and informative critical overviews of John Ruskin and Gertrude Stein. If a label must be ap-plied to the range of writing that came to be Davenport's specialty, it could be called an inquiry into the varied expres-sions of human experience and observa-tion.

In 1990 Davenport won a MacAr-thur "genius" grant, and his numerous other awards include a PEN translation prize for his book *7 Greeks*, an O. Henry Prize for Short Fiction, and a Morton Douwen Zabel Award for Fiction from the American Academy and Institute of Arts and Letters in 1981. After graduat-ing from Duke University with degrees in English and classics, Davenport was a Rhodes scholar in the late 1940s and served in the U.S. Army Airborne Corps from 1950 to 1952. After his military service, he returned to Harvard Univer-sity for a Ph.D., where his thesis on Ezra Pound's *Cantos* was later published as *Cities on Hills*. In all, Davenport wrote or contributed to more than 40 books and published dozens of scholarly articles and book reviews. Guy Daven-port died 4 January 2005 of lung cancer in Lexington, Ky., and is survived by Bonnie Jean Cox, his companion of 40 years.

JESSE GRAVES
University of Tennessee

David Cozy, *Review of Contemporary Fiction* (Fall 2005); Andre Furlani, *Style* (Spring 2002); *Guy Davenport: Postmodern and After* (2007); Wyatt Mason, *Harper's* (April 2004); Lance Olsen, *Journal of Narra-tive Technique* (Spring 1986); John Jeremiah Sullivan, *Paris Review* (Fall 2002).

Davidson, Donald

(1893–1968) WRITER, TEACHER, CRITIC.

Of the 12 writers who, in 1930, pub-lished *I'll Take My Stand: The South and the Agrarian Tradition*, Donald Grady Davidson remained the most firmly committed to "the cause of agrarianism versus industrialism." Not a farmer's but a schoolteacher's son, he was born on 18 August 1893, in the village of Campbellsville, Tenn., near the Alabama border, but spent most of his mature life in Nashville, studying at Vanderbilt Uni-versity before World War I and return-ing there after the war to teach and to write, until his death on 25 April 1968.

Donald Davidson, Vanderbilt Agrarian, late 1940s (Photographic Archives,
Vanderbilt University Library, Nashville, Tennessee)

For a half century he worked as a cultivator in the field of letters, contributing to the Southern Literary Renaissance through his poetry, his criticism, and his active encouragement of talent. He was one of the founders of the *Fugitive* magazine, which in the early 1920s published poetry of such high quality that it quickly gained an international reputation, despite its regional character. As Davidson observed in the final issue of the *Fugitive* in 1925, "the strangest thing in contemporary poetry is that innovation and conservatism exist side by side"; his own poetry reflected his consciousness of the paradox that the traditional culture of the South was in the process of disappearing at the very moment when its highest artistic expression was being achieved.

Like most educated southerners of his generation (and like Thomas Jefferson before them), Davidson was as much a classicist as an agrarian, viewing Greek and Latin as fundamental to civilization, but looking skeptically "on a replica of the parthenon" (in a poem of that title) built in a city park in Nashville, amid the noise and smoke of motors, and asking: "What do they seek, / Who build, but never read, their Greek?" He favored a native southern idealism, of the sort mirrored in such memorable poems as "Sanctuary" and "Hermitage," where he re-created imaginatively the pioneer family farm of his ancestors, and in "Meditation on Literary Fame," where he declared:

Happy the land where men hold dear
Myth which is truest memory,
Prophecy which is poetry.

Davidson was the heir not only of southern agrarianism and classicism, but of southern puritanism (his father came from Blue Stocking Hollow, Tenn.), and he sometimes sounded like a Hebrew prophet in his denunciation of material progress (which he believed to be detrimental to a truly humane culture) and in his praise for the relative poverty and simplicity, even the backwardness, of the South as a region. The latter qualities allowed the oral tradition of storytelling and ballad singing to flourish, laying the basis for literary art to develop naturally (to him, it was no accident that Mississippi was one of the lowest states in the nation in per capita income and one of the richest in talented writers). For Davidson, a strong regional loyalty was essential to a writer's integrity, as he argued persuasively in his essay "Still Rebels, Still Yankees," and he admired those modern writers outside the South who kept a definite identification with their place, such as Robert Frost, William Butler Yeats, and Thomas Hardy. Davidson's own loyalty to the South may have limited his appeal and his reputation outside it, but the genuineness of his convictions was evident in everything he wrote and gave fervor and keenness to both his poetry and his prose. His style was intellectually rigorous and spare, and if his weakness was for didacticism, he was above all a teacher and, in his generation, a great one. A fine poet, an exacting critic, and an able editor, in addition to being an inspiring teacher, Davidson exerted a powerful influence in the creation of a rich modern literature for the South.

First to be mentioned among his many books are *Poems, 1922–1961* (1966); *Still Rebels, Still Yankees and Other Essays* (1957); and *Southern Writers in the Modern World* (1958). *Big Ballad Jamboree: A Novel* captured his appreciation of folk culture, but was not published until 1996.

WILLIAM PRATT
Miami University (Ohio)

John Fair and Thomas Daniel Young, eds., *The Literary Correspondence of Donald Davidson and Allan Tate* (1974); Mark G. Malvasi, *The Unregenerate South: The Agrarian Thought of John Crowe Ransom, Allan Tate, and Donald Davidson* (1997); Thomas D. Young and M. Thomas Inge, *Donald Davidson* (1971), *Donald Davidson: An Essay and a Bibliography* (1965).

Deal, Borden

(1922–1985) WRITER.

Borden Deal was a prolific author who wrote approximately 20 novels and 100 short stories, most of which were set in the American South. Several critics have commented that Deal in his writings chronicled 20th-century southern history as thoroughly and insightfully as in the works of more heralded authors from the South.

Born 12 October 1922 in Pontotoc, Miss., Loyse Youth Deal (nicknamed Borden, which was his father's first name) was reared on his family's farm near New Albany, Miss. His father was a farmer who owned his own land until cotton collapsed as a commodity crop during the Great Depression. The family subsequently relocated to government-sponsored farming projects in Enterprise and Darden, Miss. Borden Deal

attended Macedonia Consolidated High School near Myrtle, Miss.

In 1938, after his father's death, Deal found work in seasonal agriculture, milling, and forest-fire fighting. After a stint as a Department of Labor auditor (1941–42), Deal served in the U.S. Navy (1942–45) as an aviator cadet and radar instructor, based in Ft. Lauderdale, Fla. At war's end, Deal enrolled in the University of Alabama, majoring in English and studying creative writing with Hudson Strode; Deal received a B.A. degree in 1949.

In 1948 Deal's short story "Exodus" was awarded first prize in *Tomorrow* magazine's national college writer's contest and was incorporated into the anthology *Best American Short Stories of 1949*. Deal in 1950 pursued graduate study at Mexico City College, while also writing as a freelance journalist. After returning from Mexico, Deal worked as a correspondent for Association Films in New York City, as a skip tracer for a Birmingham auto finance company, as a telephone solicitor for a New Orleans newspaper, and as a copywriter for two radio stations in Mobile, Ala.

By 1954 Deal was writing full time, and in 1956 his first novel, *Walk through the Valley*, was published. The next year brought the publication of his best-known novel, *Dunbar's Cove*, which explored the Tennessee Valley Authority's impact on the lives of small farmers. Other Deal novels included *The Insolent Breed* (1959), which portrayed the musical culture of rural white southerners; *Dragon's Wine* (1960), which explored the interrelationships of people within a small southern community; *The Tobacco*

Men (1965), which depicted struggles over tobacco between landowners and "nightriders" in late 19th- and early 20th-century Kentucky; and *Interstate* (1970), which was a fictional account of conflicts between environmentalists and developers over the plight of a swamp hosting endangered ivory-billed woodpeckers.

Deal also produced a trilogy of novels—*The Loser* (1964), *The Advocate* (1967), and *The Winner* (1973)—that examined traditional and modern value systems in the New South. Forming another trilogy (which Deal called the Olden Times series) were three other novels—*The Least One* (1967), *The Other Room* (1974), and the overtly autobiographical *There Were Also Strangers* (1985)—that focused on Deal's own youthful experience of growing up in a Depression-era southern farming community.

Deal's short stories were published in numerous magazines and literary journals, including *Saturday Review*, *McCall's*, *Collier's*, *Good Housekeeping*, and *Southwest Review*; in high school and college textbooks; and in such compilations as *Best American Short Stories of 1962* and *Best Detective Stories of the Year*. His most often anthologized story is "Antaeus," which reflects Deal's belief in the healing power of nature and the importance of the urban poor remaining in contact with nature. Additional writings by Deal—poems and reviews—appeared in various periodicals, including the *New York Times Book Review*.

Deal's fiction has been translated into more than 20 languages. In 1963 he received the Alabama Library Association Literary Award, and in 1981 the University of Alabama designated Deal as a "Sesquicentennial Scholar" during that school's 150th anniversary celebration. He participated in the MacDowell Colony and was a member of the Authors Guild, the American PEN, and the Sarasota Writers' Roundtable. Deal's novel *The Insolent Breed* was an inspiration for the 1966 Broadway musical *A Joyful Noise*, while *Dunbar's Cove* was cited by film director Elia Kazan as an influence upon the screenplay for Kazan's 1960 movie *Wild River*.

Deal's two marriages—first to Lillian Slobtotosky and then to author Babs Hodges Deal—both ended in divorce. Borden Deal lived for many years in Florida, where, on 22 January 1985, he died of a heart attack. His manuscripts and other literary materials are at Boston University.

TED OLSON
East Tennessee State University

John C. Calhoun, in *Notes on Mississippi Writers*, vol. 9 (1976); James R. Waddell, *American Novelists since World War II*, ed. James E. Kibler Jr. (1980).

Dickey, James

(1923–1997) WRITER.

A native of Atlanta, Ga., James Lafayette Dickey was born 2 February 1923. A football player in high school and college and an air force combat veteran of World War II, Dickey in his life and his art exhibited a physically aggressive quality matched by few significant poets. He received a bachelor's degree (1949) and a master of arts (1950) from Vanderbilt University, where he was influenced by Monroe K. Spears and was

James Dickey, South Carolina poet and novelist, 1980s (Jim Cleveland, photographer, Public Relations Department, University of Mississippi, Oxford)

surrounded by the Fugitive-Agrarian literary tradition of Donald Davidson, John Crowe Ransom, and Allen Tate. He taught at Rice Institute in Houston and at the University of Florida, served in the air force again during the Korean War, and traveled afterward in Europe. Dickey broke out of academia in 1956 and into the world of advertising, where he was successful in both New York City and Atlanta.

By the end of the decade, however, Dickey grew weary of "selling [his] soul to the devil during the day and buying it back at night." Three national poetry prizes from 1958 to 1959 and a Guggenheim Fellowship in 1961 confirmed his decision to leave advertising and go again to Europe, basing himself in Positina, Italy, from 1962 to 1963. From 1960 to 1964 he published three books of poems: *Into the Stone, Drowning with*

Others, and *Helmets*. When *Buckdancer's Choice* appeared in 1965, Dickey garnered the National Book Award and enormous public notice for being what *Life* magazine called "The Unlikeliest Poet." Dickey was appointed consultant in poetry for the Library of Congress, 1966 to 1968, recognition of a firm national reputation.

By 1969 Dickey had published two books of criticism—*The Suspect in Poetry* and *Babel to Byzantium*—and moved to Columbia, S.C., to teach at the University of South Carolina. The 1970s saw the publication of Dickey's best-selling and increasingly well-regarded novel, *Deliverance*; four books of poetry—*The Zodiac, Tucky the Hunter* (a children's book), *The Strength of Fields*, and *The Eye-Baters, Blood, Victory, Madness, Buckhead, and Mercy*; four books of belles lettres—*Self-*

Interviews, Sorties, Jericho: The South Beheld, and God's Images; two screenplays—Deliverance and The Call of the Wild; and several limited-edition shorter works.

Dickey's southernness is inescapable. He relied frequently on storytelling, often with a typically southern version of exuberance and broad humor, as in "Cherrylog Road" and "The Shark's Parlor." His sense of southern place is strong in poems like "Going Home" and "Hunting Civil War Relics at Nimblewill Creek" and in prose works like Deliverance and Jericho. Family is important, both immediate, as in "The Celebration," "The String," and "Messages," and ancestral, as in "The Escape" and "Dover: Believing in Kings." Racial issues arise rarely in Dickey's work, with "Slave Quarters" the conspicuous exception. Whatever guilt appears in Dickey's poems is most often attached to war, as in "The Firebombing," or to a mysterious, ghostly dread regarding one's sheer existence, as in "The Other," "The String," and perhaps The Zodiac. Religion appears as a curious amalgam of southern fundamentalism and animistic neoromanticism, as in "May Day Sermon," "Approaching Prayer," and "The Heaven of Animals."

More conventionally, Dickey's work embraces bluegrass music (he played 6- and 12-string guitars quite well), espouses athletics as personal and community rituals of a peculiarly southern mystique, and keeps to the middle ground in southern politics and economics. His works show no deep longing for a return of the Old South; rather, he appears comfortable between city and country. Content in the New South suburbs, he called Columbia "a mixture of university town, southern political capital, and military base." The natural scene was important, of course, "the way it balances Appalachia and the Atlantic," but the clichés of southern living were always modified in Dickey's works—and apparently in his life.

ROBERT W. HILL
Clemson University

Matthew Bruccoli and Judith Baughman, eds., *Crux: The Letters of James Dickey* (1999); Richard J. Calhoun, ed., *James Dickey: The Expansive Imagination* (1973); Christopher Dickey, *Summer of Deliverance: A Memoir of Father and Son* (1998); Jim Elledge, *James Dickey: A Bibliography* (1979); Henry Hart, *The World as a Lie: James Dickey* (2000); Robert Kirschten, *James Dickey and the Gentle Ecstasy of Earth: A Reading of the Poems* (1988); Stuart Wright, *James Dickey: A Descriptive Bibliography of First Printings of His Works* (1982).

Dixon, Thomas, Jr.

(1864–1946) WRITER.

Born in the rural North Carolina Piedmont a year before the Civil War ended, Thomas Dixon lived to see the atomic bombing of Hiroshima and the end of World War II. Between 1902 and 1939 he published 22 novels, as well as numerous plays, screenplays, books of sermons, and miscellaneous nonfiction. Educated at Wake Forest and Johns Hopkins, Dixon was a lawyer, state legislator, preacher, novelist, playwright, actor, lecturer, real-estate speculator, and movie producer. Familiar to three presidents and such notables as John D. Rockefeller, he made and lost millions, ending up an invalid court clerk in Raleigh, N.C.

Paradoxically, Dixon is among the most dated and most contemporary of southern writers. In genre an early 19th-century romancer, thematically Dixon argued for three interrelated beliefs still current in southern life: the need for racial purity, the sanctity of the family centered on a traditional wife and mother, and the evil of socialism.

In the Klan trilogy—*The Leopard's Spots* (1902), *The Clansman* (1905), *The Traitor* (1907)—and in *The Sins of the Fathers* (1912), Dixon presents racial conflict as an epic struggle, with the future of civilization at stake. Although Dixon personally condemned slavery and Klan activities after Reconstruction ended, he argued that blacks must be denied political equality because that leads to social equality and miscegenation, thus to the destruction of both family and civilized society. Throughout his work, white southern women are the pillars of family and society, the repositories of all human idealism. *The Foolish Virgin* (1915) and *The Way of a Man* (1919) attack women's suffrage because women outside the home become corrupted; with the sacred vessels shattered, social morality is lost. In his trilogy on socialism—*The One Woman* (1903), *Comrades* (1909), *The Root of Evil* (1911)—he attacks populist socialism expressed in such works as Edward Bellamy's *Looking Backward*, arguing that it is impossible for all classes to be equal in a society. Dixon's last novel, *The Flaming Sword* (1939), written just before he suffered a crippling cerebral hemorrhage, combines the threats of socialism

and racial equality, presenting blacks as communist dupes attempting the overthrow of the United States. Through all his work runs an impassioned defense of conservative religious values.

Young Dixon's religious and political beliefs were melded in a crucible shaped by his region's military defeat and economic depression and by the fiercely independent, Scotch-Irish Presbyterian faith of the North Carolina highlands. As a student reading Darwin, Huxley, and Spencer, he suffered a brief period of religious doubt. But his faith rebounded stronger than ever, and Dixon sought the grandest pulpit he could find. He abandoned a successful Baptist ministry in New York for the larger nondenominational audience that he could reach as a lecturer and, after the success of *The Leopard's Spots*, as a novelist and playwright. With the movie *Birth of a Nation* (based on *The Clansman*), Dixon believed he had found the ideal medium to educate the masses, to bring them to political and religious salvation. Although his work is seldom read today, both in his themes and as a political preacher seeking a national congregation through mass media, Thomas Dixon clearly foreshadowed the politicized television evangelists of the modern South.

JAMES KINNEY
Virginia Commonwealth University

Raymond A. Cook, *Fire from the Flint: The Amazing Careers of Thomas Dixon* (1968), *Thomas Dixon* (1974); F. Garvin Davenport, *Journal of Southern History* (August 1970); Michele K. Gillespie and Randal L. Hall, eds., *Thomas Dixon Jr. and the Birth of Modern America* (2006).

Douglas, Ellen

(b. 1921) WRITER.

When Houghton Mifflin awarded Josephine Haxton a fellowship for her first novel, *A Family's Affairs* (1962), she assumed the pseudonym Ellen Douglas to protect the identity of her maternal aunts, whose lives inspired the plot. Her cover was soon blown when her story "On the Lake" appeared in the *New Yorker* and friends Betty and Hodding Carter recognized the boating accident as a fictionalized version of an incident that had occurred when she was fishing with her sons.

Born Josephine Ayers in Natchez, Miss., on 12 July 1921, Ellen Douglas grew up in small towns in Mississippi, Arkansas, and Louisiana as her family moved to follow her father's civil engineering career. Douglas's literary life was nurtured early on by her mother, who read to her every night, and her paternal grandmother, who wrote children's books. Although her parents lived and breathed the southern segregationist world view, undergirded by a strong Presbyterian faith, Douglas's own world view expanded considerably when she encountered a liberal sociology professor at the University of Mississippi, who directed her honors thesis on tenant farming. Douglas began her studies at Randolph Macon Women's College in Virginia in 1938, but transferred to Ole Miss and graduated in 1942 with a degree in sociology. Books began broadening Douglas's world early on. She devoured Faulkner, Hemingway, and Wolfe in high school and Cash's *The Mind of the South*, Welty's *A Curtain of Green*, and Wright's *Native Son* in college while her first serious boyfriend plied her with texts ranging from *Ten Days that Shook the World* to *The Decline of the West*. Douglas writes vividly of her reading life in the collection, *Witnessing* (2004).

In January 1945 when she married composer and musician Kenneth Haxton, he took her to his fairly liberal and cosmopolitan (for Mississippi) hometown of Greenville, where he managed his family's department store, Nelms and Blum, and collaborated in creating Levee Press, which produced limited editions of works by Faulkner, Welty, and William Alexander Percy. In Greenville they raised three sons, Richard, Ayres, and Brooks, and enjoyed a literary society that included poet Charles Bell, newspaper editor Hodding Carter, historian Shelby Foote, novelist Walker Percy, and literary agent Ben Wasson. During the volatile 1960s when her husband publicly encouraged the peaceful integration of schools, Douglas hosted in their home a historic meeting of black and white women, who advised the welfare department about setting up a daycare center. Shortly after the couple divorced in 1980, Douglas moved to Jackson; she taught as a writer in residence at Northeast Louisiana University, the University of Mississippi, the University of Virginia, and Millsaps College.

Black-white relationships became a very important subject for Douglas, as early as her second book, *Black Cloud, White Cloud* (1963), which included the novella "Hold On," a longer version of her O. Henry prizewinning story, "On the Lake." Drawing inspiration from Faulkner, Douglas planted all of her fiction firmly in Mississippi (her Homochitto derives from Natchez and her Philippi from Greenville), but she used as her models the great 19th-century realists, Flaubert, Dostoevsky, James, and Tolstoy, consciously reacting against the Gothic and mythic elements in Faulkner's work. Douglas admired Eudora Welty, but found her "too idiosyncratic a writer" to serve as an influence; instead she turned to Katherine Anne Porter to validate her own preoccupation with complex family relationships. Douglas's reading of de Beauvoir's *The Second Sex* and Friedan's *The Feminine Mystique* helped shape her views about gender relations, which dominate the plot of her second novel, *Where the Dreams Cross* (1968). A concern with the way America warehouses the elderly and infirm became the subject of her third novel, *Apostles of Light* (1973). Douglas has said that in her fiction she is "always trying to create a world," to make what her favorite aesthetic theorist Susanne Langer would call "a *virtual* world." This concern is as true in her retellings of classic myths and fairy tales, *The Magic Carpet and Other Tales* (1987) illustrated by Walter Anderson, as in her fiction.

Interviewers always seem to press Douglas about how her life relates to her art. And while willing to talk about personal influences in her fiction, she politely but firmly reminds them that where readers see people and places, a writer also sees an artistic "problem": conflicting stories and messy emotions that have to be shaped with the conventions of fiction and worked out within

or against a literary tradition. Interest in her work has increased because of the narrative versatility evidenced in her experimental novels, *The Rock Cried Out* (1979), *A Lifetime Burning* (1982), and *Can't Quit You, Baby* (1988), and in her hybrid collection, *Truth: Four Stories I Am Finally Old Enough to Tell* (1998). Douglas attributes her growing ability to perfectly match form and content in these later works to her reading of metafiction, particularly Milan Kundera's *The Book of Laughter and Forgetting*.

The Rock Cried Out with its embedded narratives focuses on a white youth's naiveté about his family and his community during the 1960s; *A Lifetime Burning*, written in the form of a journal, concerns a wife's misunderstanding of her marriage as well as her own sexuality; and the metafictional *Can't Quit You, Baby* explores a white woman's self-deception in her relationship with her African American maid. Douglas has said that over the years she has "gotten more and more interested in what's true and what isn't true and how impossible it is to recognize the truth or to tell the truth or to read a book and know it's true." By finding just the right form for her books, Ellen Douglas seeks to make her own preoccupation with truth and moral responsibility her readers' as well.

SUZANNE W. JONES
University of Richmond

Ellen Douglas interview with Suzanne Jones at Jackson State University, 19 June 2004; Panthea Reid, ed., *Conversations with Ellen Douglas* (2000); *Southern Quarterly*, special Douglas issue (Summer 1995).

Douglass, Frederick

(1808–1895) REFORMER AND
WRITER.

Frederick Douglass was the most important black American leader of the 19th century. He was born Frederick Augustus Washington Bailey, in Talbot County, on Maryland's Eastern Shore in 1808, the son of a slave woman and, in all likelihood, her white master. Upon his escape from slavery at age 20, Douglass adopted a new surname from the hero of Sir Walter Scott's *The Lady of the Lake*. Douglass immortalized his formative years as a slave in the first of three autobiographies, *Narrative of the Life of Frederick Douglass, an American Slave*, published in 1845. This and two subsequent autobiographies, *My Bondage and My Freedom* (1855) and *The Life and Times of Frederick Douglass* (1881), mark Douglass's greatest contributions to southern culture. Written both as antislavery propaganda and as personal revelation, they are universally regarded as the finest examples of the slave narrative tradition and as classics of American autobiography.

Douglass's public life ranged from his work as an abolitionist in the early 1840s to his attacks on Jim Crow segregation in the 1890s. Douglass lived the bulk of his career in Rochester, N.Y., where for 16 years he edited the most influential black newspaper of the mid-19th century, called successively the *North Star* (1847–51), *Frederick Douglass' Paper* (1851–58), and *Douglass' Monthly* (1859–63). Douglass achieved international fame as an orator with few peers and as a writer of persuasive power. In thousands of speeches and editorials Douglass levied an irresistible indictment against slavery and racism, provided an indomitable voice of hope for his people, embraced antislavery politics, and preached his own brand of American ideals.

Douglass welcomed the Civil War in 1861 as a moral crusade to eradicate the evil of slavery. During the war he labored as a fierce propagandist of the Union cause and emancipation, as a recruiter of black troops, and on two occasions as an adviser to President Abraham Lincoln. Douglass made a major contribution to the intellectual tradition of millennial nationalism, the outlook from which many Americans, North and South, interpreted the Civil War. During Reconstruction and the Gilded Age Douglass's leadership became less activist and more emblematic. He traveled and lectured widely on racial issues, but his most popular topic was "Self-Made Men." By the 1870s Douglass had moved to Washington, D.C., where he edited the newspaper the *New National Era* and became president of the ill-fated Freedmen's Bank. As a stalwart Republican, he was appointed marshal (1877–81) and recorder of deeds (1881–86) for the District of Columbia and chargé d'affaires for Santo Domingo and minister to Haiti (1889–91). Douglass had five children by his first wife, Anna Murray, a free black woman from Baltimore who followed him out of slavery in 1838. Less than two years after Anna died in 1882, the 63-year-old Douglass married Helen Pitts, his white former secretary, an event of considerable controversy. Thus by birth and by his two marriages, Douglass is one of

Frederick Douglass, abolitionist and writer, date unknown (Sophia Smith Collection,
Smith College, Northampton, Mass.)

the South's most famous examples of the region's mixed racial heritage.

Douglass never lost a sense of attachment to the South. "Nothing but an intense love of personal freedom keeps us [fugitive slaves] from the South," Douglass wrote in 1848. He often referred to Maryland as his "own dear native soil." Brilliant, heroic, and complex, Douglass became a symbol of his age and a unique American voice for humanism and social justice. His life and thought will always speak profoundly to the dilemma of being black in America. Douglass died of heart failure in 1895, the year Booker T. Washington rose to national prominence with his Atlanta Exposition speech suggesting black accommodation to racial segregation.

DAVID W. BLIGHT
Yale University

John W. Blassingame et al., *The Frederick Douglass Papers*, 2 vols. (1979–82); David W. Blight, *Frederick Douglass' Civil War: Keeping Faith in Jubilee* (1989); Philip S. Foner, *Life and Writings of Frederick Douglass*, 4 vols. (1955); August Meier, *Negro Thought in America, 1800–1915* (1963); Benjamin Quarles, *Frederick Douglass* (1948).

Dove, Rita

(b. 1952) WRITER.
Rita Frances Dove was born on 28 August 1952, in Akron, Ohio, to Ray A. Dove, the first African American chemist for Goodyear Tire, and Elvira Elizabeth Hord. Rita graduated from high school in 1970 and was awarded the designation of presidential scholar. She then attended Miami University in Oxford, Ohio, receiving her bachelor's degree in English in 1973. After studying modern European literature at Tübingen University, in what was then West Germany, on a Fulbright scholarship, Dove attended the University of Iowa's Writer's Workshop and earned her M.F.A. in 1977. In 1979 she married German writer Fred Viebahn, and in 1983 their daughter was born.

Though she previously published in several literary magazines and journals and produced two chapbooks of poetry, *Ten Poems* (1977) and *The Only Dark Spot in the Sky* (1980), Dove's first major published work was her 1980 volume of poetry, *The Yellow House on the Corner*. In 1983 she published another collection of poetry, *Museum*, which garnered national attention and critical acclaim. Her 1986 collection, *Thomas and Beulah*, won both the Lavin Younger Poet Award, given by the Academy of American Poets, and the 1987 Pulitzer Prize for Poetry, only the second given to an African American. The collection traces the lives of her maternal grandparents from their childhoods in Georgia and Tennessee, through their move north to Akron, Ohio, and on into the 1960s.

Dove served two terms as poet laureate of the United States, from 1993 to 1995, becoming the first African American to serve in the position since it was renamed as such in 1986. She has also served as poet laureate of the Commonwealth of Virginia. In 1999 Dove published *On the Bus with Rosa Parks*, a collection of poetry that honors civil rights workers and their struggle and won the New York Times Notable Book of the Year. Other literary honors received by

Dove include a Guggenheim Fellowship, as well as grants from the National Endowments for the Arts and the Humanities and from the Ohio Arts Council. Dove has taught English at Arizona State University and is currently Commonwealth Professor of English at the University of Virginia in Charlottesville. Additionally, she has served as writer in residence at the Tuskegee Institute and as commissioner of the Schomburg Center for the Preservation of Black Culture at New York's Public library. She has been awarded numerous honorary degrees from American universities, the National Association for the Advancement of Colored People's Great American Artist Award, and the 2001 Duke Ellington Lifetime Achievement Award in the Literary Arts. She also contributed to the Public Broadcasting System documentary on southern literature, *Tell about the South.*

Though Dove was not born in the South, she invokes many of the same themes in her poetry that frequently appear in southern literature, particularly the exploration of the South's history and what its effect was and is on her family, as well as for African Americans more generally. Additionally, many of Dove's poems address issues of segregation, migration, poverty, and domestic work, and her collection *On the Bus with Rosa Parks* memorializes the struggle against racial discrimination that took place primarily in the South.

Dove's other published works include *The Other Side of the House* (1988), *Grace Notes* (1989), *Selected Poems* (1993), *Mother Love: Poems* (1995), and *American Smooth* (2004). In addition to her volumes of poetry, Dove has published a novel, *Through the Ivory Gate* (1992), a collection of short stories, *Fifth Sunday* (1985), and a play, *The Darker Face of the Earth* (1994).

AMY SCHMIDT
University of Mississippi

Harold Bloom, ed., *Writers of English: Lives and Works; Black American Women Poets and Dramatists* (1996); Patricia Yaeger, *Dirt and Desire: Reconstructing Southern Women's Writing, 1930–1990* (2000).

Du Bois, W. E. B.

(1868–1963) WRITER, HISTORIAN, SOCIOLOGIST, AND EDITOR.
William Edward Burghardt Du Bois was born 23 February 1868 in Great Barrington, Mass. A New Englander in thought and conduct, as he put it, he entered the South in 1885, after a promising high school career, to attend Fisk University in Nashville, Tenn. He found the South deeply humiliating. "No one but a Negro," he wrote, "going into the South without previous experience of color caste can have any conception of its barbarism." Nevertheless, Fisk itself was challenging, even exhilarating, and summer teaching in rural counties sealed his attachment to the black masses and his determination to champion their cause. Graduating in 1888, he trained further at Harvard University (Ph.D. 1895) and the University of Berlin. His doctoral dissertation on the suppression of the slave trade was published in 1896. He held positions briefly with the University of Pennsylvania and Wilberforce in Ohio before returning

to the South in 1897 to teach sociology, economics, and history at Atlanta University.

His third book, *The Souls of Black Folk* (1903), was a collection of hauntingly beautiful essays on every important aspect of black culture in the South; perhaps its most famous insight concerned the "double-consciousness" of the black American: "One ever feels his twoness—an American, a Negro; two souls, two thoughts, two unreconciled strivings; two warring ideals in one dark body, whose dogged strength alone keeps it from being torn asunder." With this book he secured preeminence among all African American intellectuals and became the leader of those opposed to the powerful and conservative Booker T. Washington of Tuskegee. His yearly (1897–1914) Atlanta University Studies of black social conditions and a biography of John Brown (1909) added to his reputation.

Increasingly controversial, he moved to New York in 1910 to found and edit the *Crisis*, the monthly magazine of the fledgling NAACP. For 24 years he sustained an assault on all forms of racial injustice, especially in the South. In 1934 he published *Black Reconstruction in America*, a grand Marxist-framed reevaluation of the much-maligned role of blacks in the Civil War and its aftermath. That year he returned to Atlanta University after grave disagreements with the NAACP leadership over strategies during the Depression; Du Bois favored a program of voluntary self-segregation stressing economics that many people found similar to the old program of Booker T. Washington. At Atlanta University he found little support for his projected scheme to organize the study of sociology among black colleges and other institutions in the South. In 1944 he rejoined the NAACP in New York, but soon found himself again at odds with the leadership, this time over his growing interest in radical socialism. He left the NAACP finally in 1948. By this time his attitude toward the South had changed somewhat. Influenced no doubt by the aims of the leftist Southern Negro Youth Congress, he declared in 1948 that "the future of American Negroes is in the South. . . . Here is the magnificent climate; here is the fruitful earth under the beauty of the southern sun; and here . . . is the need of the thinker, the worker, and the dreamer." His socialist activities culminated in his arrest and trial in 1951 as an unregistered agent of a foreign principal; the presiding judge heard the evidence, then directed his acquittal.

Unpopular and even shunned in some quarters, he turned to fiction to express his deepest feelings. In a trilogy set mainly in the South—*The Black Flame (The Ordeal of Mansart)*, 1957; *Mansart Builds a School*, 1959; and *Worlds of Color*, 1961—he told the story of a black southerner, born at the end of Reconstruction, who rises slowly and patiently to the leadership of a small southern school, witnessing in his long lifetime the important events of modern American and world history. In October 1961 Du Bois was admitted to membership in the Communist Party of the United States; that month he left his country to live in Ghana at the invitation of Kwame Nkrumah. In February 1963 he renounced his American citizenship and became a Ghanaian. He had made little progress on the task for which Nkrumah had summoned him, the editing of an *Encyclopedia Africana*, when he died of natural causes 27 August 1963.

ARNOLD RAMPERSAD
Stanford University

Herbert Aptheker, *Annotated Bibliography of the Published Writings of W. E. B. Du Bois* (1973); David Levering Lewis, *W. E. B. Du-Bois: Biography of a Race, 1868–1919* (1993); Arnold Rampersad, *The Art and Imagination of W. E. B. Du Bois* (1976); Raymond Wolters, *Du Bois and His Rivals* (2002); Shamoon Zamir, *Dark Voices: W. E. B. Du Bois and American Thought, 1888–1903* (1995).

Dykeman, Wilma

(1920–2006) WRITER, LECTURER, AND HISTORIAN.

Wilma Dykeman, a native of North Carolina but longtime resident of Tennessee, had a career as a writer, lecturer, and historian that spanned more than 50 years. Beginning with *The French Broad* (1955), a volume in the Rivers in America series, she published numerous books, magazine articles, encyclopedia entries, and newspaper columns. She lectured to civic, religious, and social institutions, with as many as 30 speaking engagements across the nation in some years. In addition, she conducted writers' workshops and taught for several colleges and universities. From 1981 until 2002 she served as state historian for the state of Tennessee.

Dykeman published both fiction and nonfiction, collaborating at various times with her husband, her sons, and others. During the civil rights era, she and her husband, James R. Stokely, worked together to write a book about race relations, *Neither White nor Black* (1957), which won the 1958 Hillman Award for Best Book of the Year on World Peace, Race Relations, or Civil Liberties. Her biographies include *Seeds of Southern Change: The Life of Will Alexander* (1962), coauthored with her husband; *Prophet of Plenty: The First Ninety Years of W. D. Weatherford* (1966); and *Too Many People, Too Little Love—Edna Rankin McKinnon: Pioneer for Birth Control (1974)*. Dykeman was commissioned to write *Tennessee: A Bicentennial History* (1975), a volume in the States of the Nation series commemorating the American Bicentennial. In addition, she wrote history handbooks for the National Park Service, a book about Tennessee women entitled *Tennessee Woman: An Infinite Variety* (1993), and the text for award-winning books of photographs. She is perhaps best known, however, for her novels *The Tall Woman* (1962), *The Far Family* (1966), and *Return the Innocent Earth* (1973), which are recognized as important contributions to Appalachian literature.

In addition to her books, Dykeman published articles and essays in the *New York Times* and wrote columns for the *Knoxville News-Sentinel* newspaper from 1962 to 2000. She contributed to *Encyclopaedia Britannica*, *The Encyclopedia of Tennessee History and Culture*, and numerous other books and periodicals. Selections from her columns and articles were published in two collections of essays, *Look to This Day* (1968) and *Explorations* (1984).

Although some considered Dyke-man a regional (southern and/or Appa-lachian) writer—which she felt has diminished serious evaluation of her work—she said, "I believe that much of the world's best literature is regional, in the largest sense of that word. Dis-covering all that is unique to a place, or a person, and relating that to the universals of human experience may be old-fashioned, but I feel it is one of the challenges of writing." In *An Encyclo-pedia of East Tennessee*, Sam B. Smith identifies three themes in her writings: the history of Tennessee and the state's mountain people; a concern for civil rights and human freedom; and a rever-ence for and affirmation of life, human dignity, and the environment. John Ehle referred to her as the "first lady of Appa-lachia."

Wilma Dykeman was born 20 May 1920, in Asheville, N.C., the daughter of Willard J. and Bonnie (Cole) Dykeman. She attended Asheville-Biltmore Junior College (now University of North Caro-lina at Asheville) and graduated from Northwestern University in 1940 with a degree in speech and drama. She mar-ried James R. Stokely Jr. (of the Stokely canning industry family) not long after-ward. The couple had two sons, Dyke-man Stokely and James R. Stokely III, and lived for many years in Newport, Tenn. Her husband died in 1977, and she died 22 December 2006 in Asheville.

LINDA BEHREND
University of Tennessee

Sandra Ballard, *Appalachian Journal* (Sum-mer 2002); *Iron Mountain Review* (Spring 1989), special issue on Wilma Dykeman;

Scott J. Sebok, *Appalachian Journal* (Sum-mer 2002); Sam B. Smith, in *An Encyclope-dia of East Tennessee*, ed. Jim Stokely and Jeff D. Johnson (1981).

Edgerton, Clyde
(b. 1944) WRITER.
Clyde Edgerton was born 20 May 1944 and lived much of his early life in the Bethesda area of Durham, N.C. In his eight novels he has derived many of the characters and plots from stories and experiences associated with his large extended family. Edgerton especially evokes the religious practices, social customs, family traditions, food, and music of the South as he experienced it. In *The Floatplane Notebooks*, the author reveals something of himself in the character of Mark Oakley, the one in his family to receive a college education and who would become a pilot during the Vietnam War. The author himself had served for five years as a fighter pilot in the air force and, like Mark, Edgerton is also a musician.

Edgerton's first novel, *Raney* (1985), plays on the tensions that arise over matters of religion in the life of Raney and her husband, Charles. In *Walking across Egypt* (1987), religion motivates Mattie Rigsbee's life in a fundamental way, and she cooks generously for her family and acquaintances. The title comes from Edgerton's hymn included at the end of his novel; its music and words infuse Mattie's life. Mattie be-friends Wesley Benfield, an aspiring song writer, and their friendship de-velops further in *Killer Diller* (1991). In his latest novel, *Lunch at the Piccadilly* (2003), the author explores the life and antics of ladies in a retirement home. Overall, Edgerton treats his characters with affection and a pervasive, gentle sense of humor.

THOMAS WARBURTON
University of North Carolina at Chapel Hill

R. Stirling Hennis, Jr., in *Contemporary Fiction Writers of the South*, ed., Joseph M. Flora and Robert Bain (1993).

Ellison, Ralph

(1914–1994) WRITER.
Born on 1 March 1914, in Oklahoma City, Okla., Ralph Waldo Ellison grew up in the black communities of the city's East Side. His father, Lewis Alfred Ellison, died when Ralph was three, leaving his wife, Ida Millsap Ellison, with the arduous task of supporting Ralph and her younger son, Herbert, on the meager wages she earned as a service worker. Ellison left Oklahoma City when he was 19 and left the South when he was 22. Although he lived practically all of his adult life in New York City, the lasting influence of his immersion in southern black folklife and culture is readily evident in the contents of his essays and in both the form and meaning of his fiction.

Between the two world wars, Oklahoma City was one of the South's strongholds for black blues and jazz. From his early childhood through his young adulthood, Ellison was absorbed with blues and jazz and knew several of the city's musicians. He balanced his strong affinity for blues and jazz with his interest and training in classical music. Music was his first love, but his mother provided him with an environment rich also in the other arts. Even as a child he was an avid reader of imaginative literature, and during his school years he excelled as a student, musician, and athlete.

When he graduated from Douglass High School in 1931, he could not afford to attend college. He worked at odd jobs during the next two years, and in 1933, with a music scholarship, he entered Tuskegee Institute in Alabama as a major in classical music. At Tuskegee he sustained his interest in blues and jazz and continued to read widely in various disciplines, especially literature. His chance reading of T. S. Eliot's *The Waste Land* during his sophomore year marked the beginning of his conscious desire to become a professional writer rather than a professional musician.

In the summer of 1936, he went to New York City with the intent of saving enough money by the fall to complete his education at Tuskegee. Failing to do so, he remained in New York, where he studied music and sculpture and the craft of various literary artists. In New York he met Langston Hughes, Richard Wright, and other black writers who encouraged his ambition to become a writer. His job as a researcher for the New York Federal Writers' Project from 1938 to 1942 provided him with his first steady employment since coming to New York.

With experience as editor of *Negro Quarterly*, with a few short publications behind him, and with a Rosenwald Fellowship, in 1944 he concentrated on writing a novel. His first attempt was unsuccessful, and in 1945 he began work on another novel, *Invisible Man*. Except for time he devoted to his wife, Fannie McConnell (he married in 1946), his life from 1945 to the publication of *Invisible Man* in 1952 was spent in polishing his novel, whose content and sophisticated artistry were derived primarily from Ellison's knowledge of music, southern black folklife, American culture, and literature.

Invisible Man was greeted with high critical acclaim. In 1953 it won the National Book Award and the Russwurm Award. By the mid-1960s it had been accepted as an American classic and Ellison as a first-rate American novelist. In 1965 a poll of prominent authors, critics, and editors declared *Invisible Man* to be the most distinguished work of American fiction published since 1945. The publication of his collection of essays, *Shadow and Act* (1964), revealed that he also was an astute essayist and a perceptive critic of literature and music and of southern and American culture in general.

During and after the 1960s, Ellison was a favorite speaker on the lecture circuit. He taught at the University of Chicago, Rutgers, and other institutions, received numerous honorary degrees and awards (including France's Chevalier de l'Ordre des Artes et Lettres and America's Medal of Freedom), and was a favored subject among literary critics and literary and cultural historians in the United States and abroad. Ellison retired in 1980 from New York University after 10 years as a chaired professor in the humanities. From his retirement until his death in 1994 Ellison worked on his long-awaited second novel, *June-*

teenth, which he had begun 40 years earlier. In 1999, although incomplete, the more than 2,000-page manuscript was condensed and posthumously published.

J. LEE GREENE
University of North Carolina at Chapel Hill

Ralph Ellison, *Living with Music: Ralph Ellison's Jazz Writings*, ed. Robert G. O'Meally (2001); John Hersey, ed., *Ralph Ellison: A Collection of Critical Essays* (1974); R. S. Lillard, *American Book Collector* (November 1968); James A. McPherson, *Atlantic Monthly* (December 1970); Carol Polsgrove, *American Book Collector* (November–December 1969).

Evans, Augusta Jane

(1835–1909) WRITER.

Though relatively obscure today, Augusta Jane Evans was one of the most widely read and influential southern writers of the 19th century. In a career that spanned more than 50 years, she produced nine novels, most of which were works of sentimental domestic fiction. Evans's literary reputation rests largely on three books: *Beulah* (1859), *Macaria; or, Altars of Sacrifice* (1864), and *St. Elmo* (1867), the latter of which was the third best-selling novel of the 19th century (following *Uncle Tom's Cabin* and *Ben-Hur*). Despite this popularity, many readers of her day criticized the author's novels for being long-winded, overly sentimental, needlessly obscure, and verbose. Modern scholars tend to concur and also struggle with Evans thematically, as she remained an ardent secessionist and outspoken critic of woman's suffrage throughout her life.

The oldest of eight children, Evans was born to Sarah Howard and Matthew Ryan Evans on 8 May 1835 in Columbus, Ga. The family prospered during Evans's early life, but by 1845 economic depression forced Matt Evans to declare bankruptcy and move the family by covered wagon to Texas. Evans would draw on these experiences when she began at age 15 to work on her first novel, *Inez: A Tale of the Alamo* (1855). Because of ongoing sectional unrest, the Evans clan relocated in 1849 to Mobile, Ala., the city that Augusta Jane would call home for the rest of her life.

Partially in reaction to her first novel's attack on Catholicism, Evans experienced a crisis of faith following its publication. During this time she read heavily in German skepticism and transcendentalism, searching for metaphysical alternatives to Christianity. In the end, she came full circle to a renewed faith in Protestant belief. This tension forms the thematic basis for her highly autobiographical second novel, *Beulah* (1859), featuring a title character who undergoes the same spiritual journey as its author. The book sold well and was largely praised by critics for its great moral worth.

By the time of *Beulah*'s publication, Evans was becoming embroiled in the political conflicts that would define her life and career. The author favored both secession and states' rights and opposed abolition. Evans worked for the Confederacy as a volunteer nurse and by sewing sandbags. Her third novel, *Macaria; or, Altars of Sacrifice* (1864), was a propagandist novel written as a morale booster for her beleaguered region.

The novel portrays an idealized view of both antebellum southern culture and heroic Confederates on the battlefield, including a description of the battle of Manassas based entirely on an account that General P. G. T. Beauregard penned especially for Evans. *Macaria* sold as well in the North as in the South, in spite of the novel's passionate endorsement of the Confederacy. In fact, Union general G. H. Thomas found the book so ubiquitous and dangerous that he banned it and burned all the copies he could confiscate.

Evans's most popular work was also the one that most closely adhered to the conventions of sentimental domestic fiction. *St. Elmo* (1867) tells the story of Edna Earle, who must tame the roguish title character, bringing him into a life of domestic tranquillity and Christian faith. So popular was Evans's fourth novel that its title was borrowed to name more than a dozen towns, several plantations, a girls' school, steamboats, hotels, a punch, brand of cigar, and countless male children born after *St. Elmo*'s publication. Two films—one in 1914, the second in 1923—were made from the book.

After these three major successes, Evans published another five novels at regular intervals throughout her life: *Vashti; or, Until Death Do Us Part* (1869), *Infelice* (1875), *At the Mercy of Tiberius* (1887), *A Speckled Bird* (1902), and *Devota* (1907). All of them garnered relative commercial success, but none matched the sensation that followed the publication of *St. Elmo*.

In looking at Evans's canon, a strange thematic contradiction appears. While the author typically endorses traditional roles for women, she also simultaneously presents independent and empowered female characters. Though the majority of Evans's heroines end their stories married, most do so only after asserting their own intellectual autonomy. Mirroring her fictional heroines, in 1868 Evans married Colonel Lorenzo Madison Wilson, a wealthy widower nearly 30 years her senior. They enjoyed a happy, childless marriage until Wilson's death in 1891. When on 9 May 1909, one day past her 74th birthday, Evans herself died of a heart attack, she was laid to rest in Mobile amid the graves of the Confederate veterans she so admired.

TODD HAGSTETTE
University of South Carolina

William Perry Fidler, *Augusta Evans Wilson, 1835–1909* (1951); Anne Sophie Riepma, *Fire and Fiction: Augusta Jane Evans in Context* (2000); Rebecca Grant Sexton, ed., *A Southern Woman of Letters: The Correspondence of Augusta Jane Evans Wilson* (2002).

Everett, Percival

(b. 1956) WRITER.

Novelist and University of Southern California professor Percival Everett was born in Fort Gordon, Ga., in 1956 but was raised in South Carolina—from age 5 to 16—as the son of a dentist, during which time he became familiar with the racism and police brutality that influence works such as *Watershed* (1996), a novel about a black hydrologist named Robert Hawks who, while uncovering a plot to store anthrax on an Indian reservation, reflects on the revocation of his grandfather's license to practice

medicine after giving testimony about treating a wounded race activist. Everett earned his B.S. from the University of Miami, where he played jazz to support himself through college, after which point he spent years working on a ranch and teaching high-school mathematics. Eventually he attended Brown University's creative writing program where he wrote his first novel, *Suder* (1983). Though he has published nineteen books altogether, he earned the most fame after the publication of *Erasure* (2001), which won the Hurston/Wright Legacy Award.

Arguably his best-known work, *Erasure* arose partly from Everett's personal frustration with his placement in literature as an African American writer, one who endured criticism for purportedly shying away from the realities of racism and what is often inaccurately deemed "the black experience." The novel concerns Thelonious Ellison, a struggling, erudite academic writer who decides, after his latest manuscript receives almost a dozen rejections, to write a parody of the book that critics and talk show hosts have lavished praise. (The novel, by fictitious author Juanita Mae Jenkins, is entitled *We's Lives in Da Ghetto*.) Ellison abandons Greek mythology and poststructuralism—fuel for Everett's actual novels—as inspirational sources to write a satire of Jenkins entitled *My Pafology*, which ironically wins the National Book Award. Despite the recurrent theme of race and class in his novels, however, Everett has often remained adamant about the relationship between his own race and work. When the *New York Times Book Re-*

view, reviewing *American Desert*, called Everett an African American writer, he responded in a letter to the editor that "the color of my skin has little to do with that novel."

Dubbed by the *Washington Post* as "one of the most adventurously experimental of modern American novelists," Everett and his oeuvre refuse identification with any particular genre. Consider his novel *Glyph*. Drastically different from any of his other works, the novel, narrated by the four-year-old prodigy Ralph Townsend, finds pleasure in linguistic theory, such as that of Wittgenstein, whom Everett himself counted as a major influence. This novel, as well, challenges readers' perceptions of race in literature. As the four-year-old Ralph says midway through the novel, "Have you to this point assumed that I am white? In my reading, I discovered that if a character was black, then he at some point was required to comb his Afro hairdo, speak on the street using an obvious, ethnically identifiable idiom [or] live in a certain part of town."

Indeed, Everett inhabits a paradoxical stance—criticizing American culture's preoccupation with race while at the same time engaging and perhaps perpetuating that fascination. In 1989 he made a profound political statement by discontinuing a speech to the South Carolina State Legislature because of the presence of the Confederate flag on top of the statehouse dome. And one of his recent novels, *The History of the African American Race according to Strom Thurmond* (2004), consists of e-mails and memos detailing the origin of a fictitious book proposed by Strom

Thurmond about his role in improving the situations of African Americans, which is eventually picked up by Simon and Schuster and assigned to Everett himself and coauthor James Kincaid as a ghostwriting project.

His works, in addition to those mentioned, include *Walk Me to the Distance* (1985), *Cutting Lisa* (1986), *The Weather and Women Treat Me Fair* (1987), *For Her Dark Skin* (1990), *Zulus* (1990), *The One That Got Away* (1992), *God's Country* (1994), *Big Picture* (1996), *Frenzy* (1997), *Glyph* (1999), *Grand Canyon, Inc.* (2001), *American Desert* (2004), *Damned If I Do* (2004), *My California: Journeys by Great Writers* (contributor) (2004), *Wounded* (2005), and *re:f (gesture)* (2006), a collection of poetry.

BRIAN RAY
University of South Carolina

Forrest Anderson, *Yemassee* (Spring 2004); Shashank Bengali, *Trojan Family Magazine* (Winter 2005); *Callaloo Special Issue: Percival Everett* (Spring 2005), with guest editor James Kincaid.

Faulkner, William

(1897–1962) WRITER.
William Cuthbert Faulkner was born on 25 September 1897, in New Albany, Miss. The great grandson of William Clark Falkner, a southern novelist and Confederate officer, Faulkner was responsible for adding the *u* to his family name—just as he was responsible for transmogrifying his native South into a universal place of the imagination in brilliant novels and stories that have put him first among 20th-century American writers of prose fiction.

Faulkner came to maturity at a time

when Mississippi and the South were changing. He grew up a part of post–Civil War southern culture, which was dominated by memories of the Old South and the war, and yet he experienced also the modernizing forces of the early 20th century in the region. He had romantic instincts, expressed in his early poetry and prose and in his enlistment in the Royal Canadian Air Force in 1918, hoping to be a gallant fighter pilot. He went back to Oxford, Miss., in that same year, though, and pursued work as a writer. Lawyer Phil Stone encouraged him, financially and intellectually, introducing him to the work of modernists such as T. S. Eliot.

Faulkner spent several months in New Orleans in 1925, becoming friends with Sherwood Anderson and other creative talents there, and in July of that year embarked on a walking tour through parts of Europe. With the exception of stints working as a screenwriter in California, he mostly lived thereafter in Mississippi. His first novel, *Soldiers' Pay*, appeared in 1926, followed by *Mosquitoes* in 1927.

All of Faulkner's major novels reflect his southern rootedness. Beginning with *Flags in the Dust* (published as *Sartoris* in 1929), he creates a mythical Mississippi county, Yoknapatawpha, in which his main characters and their families confront not only specifically southern subjects—such as a native Indian population, the Civil War, plantation life, and race relations—but also themes that transcend a regional focus. *Absalom, Absalom!* (1936), perhaps Faulkner's greatest achievement, explicitly conjoins his southernness and his

universality in the partnership of the southerner, Quentin Compson, and the Canadian, Shreve McCannon, Harvard roommates, whose exploration of the southern past provokes questions about the meaning of history itself.

In *The Sound and the Fury* (1929), his first great novel, Faulkner depicts several generations of a southern family, the Compsons, with a sophisticated handling of point of view and human voice that is equal to the greatest work of his European contemporaries. In *As I Lay Dying* (1930), *Light in August* (1932), *The Hamlet* (1940), and *Go Down, Moses* (1942), Faulkner portrays many different kinds and classes of southerners exemplified by the Bundrens, the Snopeses, and the McCaslins; he also conveys penetrating insights into southern Protestantism, miscegenation, and discrimination that again point beyond themselves—especially in the figure of Joe Christmas—to fundamental concerns about the nature of human identity and how it is shaped.

Other leading Faulkner novels include *Pylon* (1935), *The Unvanquished* (1938), *The Wild Palms* (1939), *A Fable* (1954), and his last major work, *The Reivers* (1962). *Sanctuary* (1931) was one of the few Faulkner novels to sell well, and he had abiding financial problems that led to his work in films and as a short-story writer for popular magazines. His accomplished short fiction appears in *Collected Stories* (1950) and *Uncollected Stories* (1979). Despite his critical success, especially in Europe, all of Faulkner's novels were out of print when Malcolm Cowley's edited *Portable Faulkner* appeared in 1946 and led to a

Cover from William Faulkner's 1947 novel (Random House book edition,
Archives and Special Collections, University of Mississippi Library, Oxford)

steadily rising appreciation, and sale, of his work.

In the latter part of his career Faulkner became increasingly aware that he had established his apocryphal county as a counterweight to the actual South, where he had spent most of his life. In *Requiem for a Nun* (1951) he juxtaposed the development of Yoknapatawpha and its town, Jefferson, with the history of Mississippi and its capital, Jackson. In this underrated experimental drama, as well as in his later Snopes novels *The Town* (1957) and *The Mansion* (1959), he directly addressed the issue of the South's changing culture and political structure in the context of world history and national events—as he did at the same time in numerous public letters, speeches, and interviews, especially after receiving the Nobel Prize in 1950.

He died in Mississippi on 6 July 1962.

CARL E. ROLLYSON JR.

Baruch College of the City University of New York

Ann J. Abadie and Doreen Fowler, eds., *Faulkner and the Short Story: Faulkner and Yoknapatawpha, 1990* (1992); John E. Bassett, *William Faulkner: An Annotated Checklist of Criticism* (1972), *William Faulkner: An Annotated Checklist of Recent Criticism* (1983); Joseph Blotner, *William Faulkner: A Biography*, 2 vols. (1974); Louis Daniel Brodsky and Robert W. Hamblin, eds., *Faulkner: A Comprehensive Guide to the Brodsky Collection*, 2 vols. (1982–84); Cleanth Brooks, *William Faulkner: The Yoknapatawpha Country* (1963), *William Faulkner: Toward Yoknapatawpha and Beyond* (1978); James Ferguson, *Faulkner's Short Fiction* (1991); Robert W. Hamlin and Charles A. Peek, *A William Faulkner Encyclopedia* (1999); Donald M. Kartiganer, *Modern Fiction Studies* (Fall 1998); Thomas L. McHaney, *William Faulkner: A Reference Guide* (1976); Michael Millgate, *The Achievement of William Faulkner* (1965); Jay Parini, *One Matchless Time: A Life of William Faulkner* (2004); Daniel J. Singal, *William Faulkner: The Making of a Modernist* (1997); Joel Williamson, *William Faulkner and Southern History* (1993).

Finney, Nikky

(b. 1957) WRITER.

Nikky Finney was born Lynn Carol Finney, in Conway, S.C., on 26 August 1957, the daughter of Ernest A. Finney Jr., an attorney, who became the first African American chief justice of the South Carolina Supreme Court, and Frances (Davenport) Finney, a schoolteacher from Newberry, S.C. She attended St. Jude Catholic School until the mid-1960s, when public schools were integrated. With her older brother she was among the first to integrate Central School in Sumter, S.C. She took the name "Nikky" during her high school years in Sumter.

Finney left Sumter in 1975 to attend Talladega College in Alabama, where she found her calling as a writer. Already as a child she had started keeping a journal, and at the age of 15 she had become interested in the black arts movement. In college she spent her time writing and studying literature, especially that of the African American tradition. During her junior year at Talladega she befriended the poet Nikki Giovanni, who would later play a significant role in her growth as a poet. Finney majored in English in 1979 and won the Whiting Writing Award.

Finney enrolled in the graduate

school at Atlanta University to study African American literature but left the program, which did not allow creative writing components in a thesis. Instead, she joined Pamoja, a writing collective founded by the writer Toni Cade Bambara. From this workshop came Finney's first book of short poems, *On Wings Made of Gauze*, in 1985. The next year she moved to Oakland, Calif., where she made a living from a series of jobs, from photographer to printer to workshop instructor. In 1993 she accepted a position teaching creative writing at the University of Kentucky and moved to Lexington. There she cofounded the Affrilachian Poets, a writing collective of African American writers in the Appalachian region.

In 1995 Finney wrote the script for the Public Broadcasting System documentary *For Posterity's Sake: The Story of Morgan and Marvin Smith*, brothers who were photographers in the 1930s. *Rice*, her second poetry collection, published in Canada in 1995, constitutes an important development in American poetry. The poems are set in coastal Carolina, some during the poet's childhood, when rice, Carolina Gold, was a large export crop. Dealing with race, lost values, womanhood, and abuse, the poetry is in plain lyrical words, and the imagery is powerful and evocative. Finney emphasizes her ancestry and African lineage, celebrates slaves who rebelled, and delights in the Gullah culture of the Lowcountry. PEN American awarded *Rice* the Open Book Award of 1999.

In 1997 she became an associate professor at University of Kentucky, and the same year she published *Heartwood*, a short-story cycle, which is about overcoming racial anger, fears, and prejudice in a small community by relying on the soundness of the "heartwood."

Finney published *The World Is Round*, her third book of poetry, in the fall of 2002. The uncompromising poems deal with racial and engendered provocations, and the imagery invokes all of southern history, but they also breathe life into universal domestic situations. "Hurricane Beulah," the longest section, is a prose poem that celebrates the matriarchal family line by showing a young woman and her grandmother after five hours of the third day at the thrift store.

Finney is a featured poet in the video *Furious Flower II* (2005), a historic gathering of black American poets. She has edited *The Ringing Ear: Black Poets Lean South*, an anthology of 100 African American poets writing about their historical and contemporary connection to the South. Her new collection of poetry is tentatively titled *Head Off and Split*.

JAN NORDBY GRETLUND
University of Southern Denmark

Kwame Dawes, *African American Review Journal* (Summer 1997); Jan Nordby Gretlund, in *American Studies in Scandinavia* 32:8 (2006); Jeraldine Kraver, *Southern Literary Journal* (Spring 2002).

Fitzgerald, Zelda

(1900–1948) WRITER AND PAINTER. Born Zelda Sayre on 24 July 1900, to Minerva and Anthony Sayre, a judge, Zelda Fitzgerald spent most of her childhood in Montgomery, Ala. Though, as an adult, she lived outside the South and for short periods even outside the United States, and she is often neglected as an author, Fitzgerald's published novel, *Save Me the Waltz* (1932), connects and critiques the stereotypes of both the southern belle and the 1920s flapper, placing Fitzgerald within a long tradition of southern women's writing.

In 1918 Zelda Sayre met Francis Scott Fitzgerald at the Montgomery Country Club while Fitzgerald was on leave from the army. Two years later the couple married at St. Patrick's Cathedral in New York. The couple moved and traveled frequently, living in various places, such as Westport, Conn., New York City, St. Paul, Minn., and Baltimore, Md. Beginning in 1921, the Fitzgeralds periodically traveled to Europe and spent short times living in Paris. Later, they also traveled to North Africa and Cuba.

In 1921 Zelda gave birth to their only child, a daughter they named Frances "Scottie" Fitzgerald. After being treated for exhaustion in 1928, Zelda was frequently bedridden, and after collapsing in Paris in 1930, she returned to the United States to live in Montgomery, Ala. Shortly after she moved home, her father died, and Zelda, suffering from a breakdown, was committed to Phipps Psychiatric Clinic of Johns Hopkins University Hospital in Baltimore. This was only the first of a series of stays in institutions. Zelda suffered a third breakdown in 1934 and was committed to Sheppard and Enoch-Pratt Hospital outside Baltimore before transferring to Craig House Clinic in New York later that same year. In 1934 Zelda returned to the Sheppard-Pratt hospital, and two years later she went to the High-

land Hospital for Nervous Disorders in Asheville, N.C., where she returned periodically for treatment. In 1940 F. Scott Fitzgerald died of a heart attack, and Zelda moved in with her mother in Montgomery, where she lived between stays at the Highland Hospital. Zelda died in a fire at the Highland Hospital on 10 March 1948.

Though her husband typically receives the attention of the academy, Zelda Fitzgerald is an artist in her own right. Some critics even speculate that much of her husband's material was the result of her influence. What is certain is that Zelda was featured in multiple art exhibits in both New York City and Baltimore, and she spent much of her time in hospitals writing and painting. Indeed, she was working on a second novel, *Caesar's Things* (unpublished), at the time of her death at the Highland Hospital. Additionally, during her stay at the Phipps Psychiatric Clinic in Baltimore, she completed the first draft of her novel, *Save Me the Waltz*, published in 1932. The novel, which is semiautobiographical, deserves more attention than it has heretofore received. Through the main character, Alabama Beggs, Fitzgerald offers a critique of the stereotypical belle, particularly the focus on physical appearance that it encourages. Illustrating their similar and harmful effects, Fitzgerald connects the stereotype of the belle to that of the flapper and criticizes both the national culture and southern culture, which foster and perpetuate both stereotypes. Though she is rarely taught or studied, Zelda Fitzgerald and her novel provide a unique perspective on what it meant not only to be a woman in the Jazz Age but to be a "southern" woman during that time.

AMY SCHMIDT
University of Mississippi

Koula Svokos Hartnett, *Zelda Fitzgerald and the Failure of the American Dream for Women* (1991); Anne Goodwyn Jones, *Tomorrow Is Another Day: The Woman Writer in the South, 1859–1936* (1981); Marion Meade, *Bobbed Hair and Bathtub Gin: Writers Running Wild in the Twenties* (2004); Carolyn Perry and Mary Louise Weaks, eds., *The History of Southern Women's Literature* (2002); Kathryn Lee Seidel, *The Southern Belle in the American Novel* (1985).

Fletcher, John Gould

(1886–1950) WRITER.

John Gould Fletcher, poet and critic, was affiliated with both early 20th-century modernist writers and the traditionalist Nashville Agrarians. In 1939 he was awarded the Pulitzer Prize for Poetry.

Fletcher was born in Little Rock, Ark., to Adolphine Krause and John G. Fletcher. As a child he was rarely permitted to leave the grounds of the family's mansion and developed a dense imaginative life nurtured by reading Poe, Coleridge, and Goethe. In 1903, following a year at Phillips Andover Academy, John Gould Fletcher enrolled in Harvard. His father's death and an estate settlement allowed Fletcher to leave Harvard without a degree and in 1908 sail for Europe. The family fortune gave the poet an independent income but did not bring him peace. His changeable temperament and explosive rages grew from a bipolar disorder that

first erupted during his college years. By 1913 Fletcher had settled in London, where he associated with Ford Maddox Ford, H. D. (Hilda Doolittle), and Ezra Pound. Pound promoted Fletcher's free-verse experiments to Harriet Monroe of *Poetry* and invited him to join a group of poets that Pound had dubbed *Des Imagiste*. Suspicious of Pound, Fletcher became identified with imagism only when Amy Lowell took over the movement.

In 1914 Fletcher journeyed to America. He enjoyed the critical attention given to his newly published *Irradiations* (1915) and participated in the literary politics associated with the publication of *Some Imagist Poets 1915*. Despite Lowell's urgings, Fletcher returned to England to resume a liaison with the recently divorced Florence Emily Arbuthnot. They married on 5 July 1916.

The end of World War I was a watershed in Fletcher's career. His early poetry as represented in *Irradiations* and *Goblins and Pagodas* (1916) was characterized by heightened emotion and prosodic innovations. Throughout the 1920s he employed mythic themes and visionary language to dramatize the decline of culture in an industrial age. Fletcher's work, which owed much to 19th-century romanticism, placed him at odds with influential modernist writers. His most significant contribution in this mode was the epic *Branches of Adam* (1926), which echoed the prophetic works of William Blake.

In early spring 1927, toward the end of another American sojourn, the expatriate poet met John Crowe Ransom, Donald Davidson, and Allen Tate.

Among the Vanderbilt Fugitives, Tate in particular deferred to Fletcher because of the older poet's acquaintance with T. S. Eliot, and Fletcher for a time treated Tate as an acolyte who could be saved from Eliot's high modernism. Fletcher eagerly enlisted in the Agrarian anti-industrialization cause, but his overwrought, antidemocratic essay on education in the Agrarian symposium, *I'll Take My Stand* (1930), signaled the onset of a depressive crisis. Following a suicide attempt in late 1932 and committal at Royal Bethlehem Hospital, Fletcher permanently left his English family and took up residence in Little Rock.

Fletcher's romantic quest for survivals of lost, agrarian worlds led him to promote the collection of Ozark folk songs and stories. Yet, he remained unsettled. By 1935 he had bitterly seceded from the Agrarians. Fletcher's primary source of stability was the talented writer Charlie May Simon, whom he married 18 January 1936 on the heels of the divorce from his first wife.

Even the awarding of the Pulitzer Prize for his *Selected Poems* (1938) and induction into the National Institute of Arts and Letters did not bring him a new readership. Thus, *The Burning Mountain* (1946), his last and finest collection, was ignored despite including works that expressed a singular perspective through traditional forms. *Arkansas* (1947), a history of the state, remained outside southern historiography. Yet this volume's attention to the role of the natural environment in economic development, to the persistence of folk culture, and to the class tensions underlying political movements distinguished it as an elegant and intuitive portrait.

The knowledge that he was falling into obscurity coupled with worsening arthritis ignited more debilitating bouts with depression. On 10 May 1950, John Gould Fletcher drowned himself in a shallow pond near his home on the western edge of Little Rock.

BEN JOHNSON
Southern Arkansas University

Lucas Carpenter, ed., *The Autobiography of John Gould Fletcher* (1988), *John Gould Fletcher and Southern Modernism* (1990), *Selected Essays of John Gould Fletcher* (1989); Ben F. Johnson, *Fierce Solitude: A Life of John Gould Fletcher* (1994); Leighton Rudolph and Ethel C. Simpson, eds., *Selected Letters of John Gould Fletcher* (1996); Charlie May Simon, *Johnswood* (1953); Edna B. Stephens, *John Gould Fletcher* (1967).

Foote, Horton

(b. 1916) WRITER.

Horton Foote, playwright and award-winning television and motion picture writer, was born in Wharton, Tex., and began his career as an actor. From 1933 to 1935 he studied at the Pasadena Playhouse Theatre and from 1937 to 1939 at an acting school in New York City. He appeared in several Broadway plays in the late 1930s and early 1940s and from 1942 to 1945 managed a production company in Washington, D.C., where he also taught playwriting.

Foote's first play to be produced professionally was *Texas Town*, which opened at the Provincetown Playhouse in New York in 1942. A number of his plays were produced on Broadway, among them *Only the Heart* (1944), *The Chase* (1952), *The Trip to Bountiful* (1953), and *The Traveling Lady* (1954). Much of Foote's best work has been done in television, a medium that he entered when he wrote a teleplay for the Kraft Television Theatre in 1947. His work was frequently seen on *Playhouse 90*, *DuPont Show of the Week*, and other important dramatic series during the so-called golden age of television in the 1950s. His adaptation of Harper Lee's *To Kill a Mockingbird* (1962) earned him an Academy Award for best screenplay based on material from another source.

Foote's other film credits include *Baby, the Rain Must Fall* (1965); *Tender Mercies*, for which Robert Duvall received an Academy Award for best actor; *The Trip to Bountiful* (1985), for which Geraldine Page received an Academy Award for best actress; and *1918* (1985), which starred the writer's daughter, Hallie Foote. He has also done adaptations of stories by southern writers such as Flannery O'Connor (*The Displaced Person*) and William Faulkner (*Old Man, Barn Burning, Tomorrow*).

Most of Horton Foote's plays and films have been set in the fictional town of Harrison, Tex. Foote's strength, as more than one writer has noted, has been his ear for the speech of his part of the country.

CHARLES EAST
Baton Rouge, Louisiana

Paul Grondahl, *Albany (NY) Times Union* (28 April 2006); Daniel Neman, *Richmond Times Dispatch* (28 October 2006); Marjorie Smeltsor, *Southern Quarterly* (Winter 1991); Charles S. Watson, *The History of Southern Drama* (1997), *Studies in American Drama, 1945–Present*, no. 2 (1993).

Foote, Shelby

(1916–2005) WRITER AND HISTORIAN.

If not for Ken and Ric Burns's landmark 1990 Public Broadcasting System (PBS) series *The Civil War*, Shelby Foote would likely be remembered as just a footnote in southern literary history—a noted Civil War historian, the author of six novels, and the best friend of Walker Percy. Although it was the middle of his career before Foote turned to write about the Civil War, the event had always informed and framed his life. He was born in Greenville, Miss., in 1916 into a culture that, even decades after the war ended, preserved that event as its defining cultural memory. Foote's paternal great-grandfather had served as a Confederate colonel, fighting in some of the war's western battles, including Shiloh.

As a young man, Foote had the good fortune of coming under the tutelage of Greenville's poet William Alexander Percy. Foote and Percy's cousin Walker Percy started a lifelong friendship in Greenville that would produce one of the greatest correspondences in American letters.

When Foote graduated from Greenville High School in 1937, he went to the University of North Carolina at Chapel Hill. Two years later, deciding that the college experience was not for him, Foote returned to Greenville to begin his writing career. World War II interrupted his efforts to get a first novel published. In 1940 Foote enlisted as a member of the Mississippi National Guard's Dixie Division, and later that year his unit was federalized. Until the end of 1943 Foote remained stateside as an artillery instructor, but at that point he was sent to the British Isles to be part of the D-Day expeditionary force. With the combat experience he longed for so close at hand, Foote was court-martialed for falsifying the distance he had traveled to see a Belfast girl. By the end of the war, Foote enlisted with the Marines, but he never saw combat.

After World War II Foote returned home to concentrate on his writing. In 1946 he enjoyed his first success, when the *Saturday Evening Post* agreed to publish "Flood Burial." Sure that he had landed as a writer, he immediately quit the job he had at a Greenville radio station. Over the next decade Foote had five novels published: *Tournament* (1949), *Follow Me Down* (1950), *Love in a Dry Season* (1951), *Shiloh* (1952), and *Jordan County* (1954). None sold well, but *Shiloh*, with its deft blending of soldiers' subjective experience and the overall data of the Civil War battle, captured the attention of several publishers. Consequently, Random House in 1954 commissioned Foote to write a history of the Civil War.

Foote arranged trips to battlefields that coincided with the time of year those battles took place, sometimes even sleeping on the fields themselves. He then returned to Memphis to assemble a narrative that was a military account of the most important event in U.S. history and, in its account of the dramas of individual soldiers, a series of set pieces

worthy of Shakespeare. He completed the third volume in 1974.

After writing another novel in 1978 (*September, September*) and then failing to write what he thought was going to be his magnum opus, *Two Gates to the City*, Foote effectively slipped into retirement and out of the public view—until the PBS series. While other experts appeared as many as 16 times in the show, Foote would be used for more than 80 talking spots. In all, his appearances equated to one hour of the 11-hour documentary. Foote's mellifluous southern accent and his vivid anecdotes became the lasting memory of a documentary that reached a PBS record of 40 million people. After the series, Foote became a national icon, sought after by magazines and television shows—and clamored for by Americans who longed to know more about the Civil War. In the year after the show, Foote sold 400,000 volumes of *The Civil War*. A man so steeped in history and tradition, a writer who forsook word processors in favor of a dip pen, had ironically become rich and famous because of a television series.

Foote died on 27 June 2005 and was buried at Memphis's Elmwood Cemetery.

C. STUART CHAPMAN
Washington, D.C.

C. Stuart Chapman, *Shelby Foote: A Writer's Life* (2003); Robert Phillips, *Shelby Foote: Novelist and Historian* (1992); Jay Tolson, ed., *The Correspondence of Shelby Foote and Walker Percy* (1996).

Ford, Jesse Hill

(1928–1996) WRITER.

Jesse Hill Ford was born in Troy, Ala., a medium-sized town southeast of Montgomery, the state capitol, on 28 December 1928. Less than a year later, the Ford family moved to his mother's hometown, Jasper, northwest of Birmingham. In 1932, early in the Depression, Ford's father, a pharmacist, moved the family to Nashville, Tenn., where he bought a house near, but not in, the wealthy enclave of Belle Meade. The Ford house was within walking distance of Belle Meade Plantation, the Belle Meade Country Club, and Parmer Elementary School—a public school that channeled many of its male graduates into nearby Montgomery Bell Academy, a private school for boys. Jesse eventually attended Montgomery Bell, graduating in 1947. He worked at a local Walgreen's Drugstore to help pay tuition.

In the fall of 1947 Ford enrolled in Vanderbilt University. He studied with Donald Davidson and published short stories in a variety of campus magazines. Two years in the navy followed graduation in 1951. From 1953 through 1955 Ford worked on his writing under another Agrarian, Andrew Lytle, in the creative writing program at the University of Florida.

After less than a year in a public relations job in Chicago (1957), Ford left the job and the city and moved to his wife's hometown, Humboldt, in west Tennessee, near Trenton, Peter Taylor's birthplace. There Ford wrote fiction and drama full time. In 1959 two of his short stories were published in *Atlantic Monthly*. In 1960 Ford, writing in Cross Creek, Fla., at the home of Marjorie Kinnan Rawlings, finished a three-act play, *The Conversion of Buster Drumwright*, which was broadcast on CBS television and subsequently chosen for production by the Yale drama workshop.

In 1961 Ford's first novel, *The Mountains of Gilead*, was published, and in the same year he accepted a Fulbright Fellowship to the University of Oslo. He continued to publish short stories in the *Atlantic Monthly*, where Ford developed a close friendship with longtime editor Edward Weeks. Ford's most well-known novel, *The Liberation of Lord Byron Jones*, was published in 1965. The novel was a Book-of-the-Month selection and was excerpted in *Cosmopolitan*. Movie rights were sold the same year, and the novel was nominated for the Pulitzer Prize in 1966. Ford's reputation soared, as did his income. Continuing to live in Humboldt, Ford became a popular lecturer and visiting writer.

Ford's second novel, *The Feast of Saint Barnabas*, was published in 1969. Reviews were disappointing, but the film version of *The Liberation of Lord Byron Jones* (the last feature film directed by William Wyler) premiered in 1970. When the movie was shown in Humboldt, during a period of contentious desegregation, many residents of both races voiced their disapproval of what they took to be disparaging portraits of themselves and the town. Ford, and especially his children, experienced harassment by the community. On the night of 16 November 1970, Ford shot and killed an African American soldier, absent without leave from his post, who had driven onto the Ford property. Ford was charged with murder, tried in Humboldt in late June 1971, and acquitted on 3 July.

Whether the trial and verdict were the cause, a life of wandering soon began. Ford and his wife, Sarah, divorced in 1973. Ford met Lillian Chandler in Spain the same year, and they were married in Nashville in 1975. Although Nashville remained Ford's "permanent" residence, his life turned peripatetic, a constant round of travel for work and for recreation in the Virgin Islands, Mexico, California, and Europe. Ford continued to enjoy popularity as a visiting writer and lecturer.

In 1990 Ford suffered the first of a series of minor strokes. He continued to try to live an active life, but infirmity gradually overcame both flesh and the spirit. He died by his own hand in Nashville in 1996.

MICHAEL P. KREYLING
Vanderbilt University

Wayne Batten, in *The Vanderbilt Tradition: Essays in Honor of Thomas Daniel Young*, ed. Mark Royden Winchell (1991); Donald Davidson, foreword to *The Conversion of Buster Drumwright* (1964); George Garrett, *Southern Quarterly* (Winter–Spring 1995); David Madden, *Southern Review* (Autumn 1990).

Ford, Richard

(b. 1944) WRITER.
Although born in Jackson, Miss., on 16 February 1944, Richard Ford has long resisted the "southern writer" label. Indeed, Ford has spent most of his adult life living outside of the South—in Michigan, New Jersey, Montana, and Maine, to name but a few of the many places that he has called home—and the various locations of his works reflect the writer's nomadic life-style. An astute observer of contemporary society, Ford powerfully depicts the impoverishment of human relationships, as well as the inner emptiness, detachment, and solipsism that characterize so much of life in the dangerous and uncertain postmodern world that is his milieu. His novels, novellas, and short stories dramatize the breakdown of such cultural institutions as marriage, family, and community. His protagonists often typify the sense of dislocation and the nameless longing so pervasive in a highly mobile, present-oriented society in which individuals, having lost a connection to the past, relentlessly pursue connections with others as well as their own elusive identities in the here and now.

Ford's family history would suggest his own early acquaintance with dislocation. When he was only eight years old, his traveling salesman father suffered a heart attack, and the family was forced to move into a hotel run by the boy's maternal grandfather in Little Rock, Ark. The hotel life of permanence amid transience would provide an important formative experience. Just four days after Ford's 16th birthday, his father had a fatal heart attack. Two years later, Ford would begin his peripatetic adult life by enrolling at Michigan State University and majoring in hotel management. He later changed his major to English and, following graduation, taught junior high school, enlisted in the U.S.

Marine Corps (receiving a medical discharge after contracting hepatitis), and attended Washington University Law School for one semester. In 1968 he married Kristina Hensley and decided to pursue a career as a writer. After receiving his M.F.A. degree in creative writing from the University of California at Irvine in 1970, having studied there with Oakley Hall and E. L. Doctorow, he began work on a novel.

Reviewers so often compared his first novel, *A Piece of My Heart* (1976), with its rural Mississippi/Arkansas setting and eccentric characters, to William Faulkner's work that Ford decided never again to write another novel set in his native South. His second novel, *The Ultimate Good Luck* (1981), takes place south of the border in Oaxaca, Mexico. The story focuses on Harry Quinn, an emotionally disabled Vietnam veteran trying to free his ex-girlfriend's cocaine-smuggling brother from prison. Following the publication of that book, Ford, despondent over his mother's death and discouraged by his inability to find a significant readership, decided to quit writing fiction and accepted a job at *Inside Sports* magazine. When the magazine ceased publication after only one year, he began work on his third novel.

The publication of *The Sportswriter* (1986) provided the breakthrough that Ford needed to establish his reputation as a serious writer. This story of New Jersey suburbanite Frank Bascombe's struggle to survive the loss of a son and the loneliness resulting from a painful divorce struck a chord with readers and reviewers alike. Named by *Time* magazine as one of the five best books of the year, the novel was also a PEN/Faulkner finalist. Ford next turned his attention to the Northwest by publishing a critically acclaimed volume of short stories, *Rock Springs* (1987), and a short coming-of-age novel, *Wildlife* (1990). Set mostly against the stark landscape of Montana, those works again deal with the isolation and loneliness resulting from dissolving relationships.

Ford's career reached a new high point with the publication of *Independence Day* (1995), which further develops the narrative of suburban Everyman, Frank Bascombe. In this sequel, Bascombe has turned from a career as a sportswriter to selling real estate. He continues to struggle with the breakup of his family as he strives to adjust to his new life and reconnect with his troubled teenage son. Ford's fifth and most richly developed novel won both the Pulitzer Prize and PEN/Faulkner Award and firmly established him as a major figure among American writers of the post–World War II generation. He has since published *Women with Men* (1997), a collection of three novellas; *A Multitude of Sins* (2002), a volume of short fiction; and a third Frank Bascombe novel, *The Lay of the Land* (2006). With a significant body of work and important literary honors to his credit, Ford's place in the canon of American literature seems secure.

HUEY GUAGLIARDO
Louisiana State University at Eunice

Huey Guagliardo, ed., *Conversations with Richard Ford* (2001), ed., *Perspectives on Richard Ford* (2000); Elinor Ann Walker, *Richard Ford* (2000).

Fox, John, Jr.

(1862–1919) WRITER.

Born in the bluegrass country of central Kentucky during the middle years of the Civil War, John William Fox Jr. was interested in the rural landscape and the conflicts played out upon it. The son of a schoolmaster, Fox graduated from Harvard in 1883. After an abortive attempt at Columbia Law School, he worked variously as a newspaper reporter, tutor, teacher, mine laborer, and war correspondent, marching up San Juan Hill behind Teddy Roosevelt and his Rough Riders during the Spanish-American War. It was in the writing of fiction, however, that Fox found his most enduring vocation, and in the mountainous region along the Virginia-Kentucky border, to which his family relocated in 1890, he found the setting and subjects that would define that writing.

Fox's work is grounded in the conditions and experiences of mountain peoples, and though his writing romanticizes that landscape, the potential coarseness and brutality of it are also perceptively depicted, Fox himself having witnessed hangings and blood feuds and been a participant in early Appalachian volunteer police units. Prefiguring the Agrarians of the 1920s and 1930s, Fox was also intimately concerned with the endurance of rural spaces and the way of life associated with them, as well as the dangers posed to them by outside forces. This concern is readily apparent in his most famous work, the 1908 novel *The Trail of the Lonesome Pine*, whose sophisticated urban protagonist, Jack Hale, comes to the Cumberland Gap in search of coal but soon finds himself entangled in the long-standing local feud between the Falin and Tolliver families, enamored with the daughter of the Tolliver family patriarch, and deeply invested in their world. A dramatic production of the novel, a best seller in its time, is still staged annually in Big Stone Gap, Va., the setting for the novel and Fox's home for much of his adult life.

Tension between the rural and urban was evident in Fox's personal life as well: his single marriage, to Austrian opera singer Fritzi Scheff, lasted less than five years. Though New York City afforded him his start as a writer and his longest-enduring friendship, with fellow writer Richard Harding Davis, it was to the mountain country that he persistently returned. Just pages from completing his final novel, *Erskine Dale: Pioneer*, Fox died from pneumonia on 8 July 1919, at his home in Big Stone Gap.

JACOB SULLINS
Georgia State University

Warren Titus, *John Fox, Jr.* (1971); Darlene Wilson, in *Confronting Appalachian Stereotypes: Back Talk from an American Region*, ed., Dwight Billings, Gurney Norman, and Katherine Ledford (1999); Bill York, *John Fox, Jr., Appalachian Author* (2003).

Fox, William Price

(b. 1926) WRITER.

Born in Waukegan, Ill., on 9 April 1926, William Price Fox grew up in Columbia, S.C. He studied creative writing at the New School of Research in New York City with Caroline Gordon, who encouraged him to publish his first stories and sketches. An author and editor of 14 books, a contributor of personal essays and short stories to such magazines as the *Village Voice, Harper's*, the *Saturday Evening Post*, and *Sports Illustrated*, and a consummate storyteller with a great ear for dialogue, Fox has distinguished himself as a writer of humorous narratives. His comic subject matter and manner echo that of Mark Twain and Flannery O'Connor.

Fox's first book, *Southern Fried* (1962), was a 40-cent paperback with comic caricatures by the *Mad* magazine cartoonist Jack Davis. *Southern Fried* consists of a collection of humorous stories, several of which he had previously published in magazines such as *Cavalier* and the *Village Voice*. The narrator, whom M. Thomas Inge has aptly described as "an urbane, better-educated Sut Lovingood, setting out not to raise hell himself but to record the raucous actions and eccentric behavior of the odd characters who surround him," recounts tales that echo themes, scenarios, and plot patterns that resemble those first popularized in southern antebellum frontier humor. Liars, yarn spinners, bully braggarts, sophisticates, con artists, practical jokers, and hypocrites are all featured in *Southern Fried*. An expanded version of this book, *Southern Fried Plus Six*, was published in 1968.

Fox's other memorable humorous contributions are three novels: *Moonshine Light, Moonshine Bright* (1967), *Ruby Red* (1971), and *Dixiana Moon* (1981). Each of these books employs the picaresque form, a narrative structure especially suitable for the rollicking, sometimes outlandish subject matter they treat. *Moonshine Light, Moonshine Bright* focuses on the humorous escapades of two mischievous adolescent country boys reminiscent of Mark Twain's Tom Sawyer and Huckleberry Finn—Earl Edge and Coley Simms—who spend a summer in a slum section of Columbia, S.C., known as the Bottom, and are trying to obtain money any way they can to purchase their first car. In their rambling misadventures, Earl and Coley encounter bootleggers, loan sharks, sheriffs, a revivalist preacher, and even a murderer. *Ruby Red*, set in Columbia and Nashville, Tenn., is a satire of the country music industry. The novel charts the career of the naive, ambitious, and opportunistic Ruby Jean Jamison, who is determined not only to survive but to prosper. *Dixiana Moon*, the most successful of these three novels, focuses on the escapades of former New York packaging salesman Joe "Bo" Mahaffey, who runs away from his debtors and joins a circus-revival outfit known as the Great Mozingo-Arlo Waters Jubilee Crusade and Famous Life of Christ Show, a scam run by Mahaffey's friend, the affable hustler Buck Brody, and Arlo Waters. The Brody (Mozingo)-Arlo Waters duo, con artists resembling Twain's hilariously hypocritical scheming scoundrels, the Duke and Dauphin in *Huckleberry Finn* and some of Flannery O'Connor's amusing sharpers, have collected a group of religious fanatics.

Fox's other humorous works of note are scripts he wrote in the 1960s for Paul Henning's popular television comedy *The Beverly Hillbillies* and his novel, *Dr. Golf* (1963). The latter, a parody of the popular advice column, is cast in an epistolary format in which the title character offers ridiculous pointers to discouraged golfers. Among Fox's later books are *Chitlin Strut and Other Madrigals* (1983), a work that combines fact and fiction; *How 'bout Them Gamecocks* (1985), which treats the University of South Carolina football; *Golfing in the Carolinas* (1990), which he edited with others and which examines golf courses in North and South Carolina; *Lunatic Wind: Surviving the Storm of the Century* (1992), a docudrama examining the night Hurricane Hugo struck the South Carolina coast; *South Carolina: Off the Beaten Path* (1996), a travel guide to some of the attractions in the Palmetto State such as Patriot's Point in Charleston and Chattooga National Wild and Scenic River; and *Satchel Paige's America* (2005), a book examining an African American baseball legend.

EDWARD J. PIACENTINO
High Point University

George Garrett, in *Dictionary of Literary Biography Yearbook: 1981* (1982); M. Thomas Inge, in *The Companion to Southern Literature: Themes, Genres, Places, People, Movements, and Motifs*, ed. Joseph M. Flora and Lucinda H. MacKethan (2002); Charles Israel, *Kennesaw Review* (Spring 1988); Ed Piacentino, in *The Enduring Legacy of Old Southwest Humor*, ed. Ed Piacentino (2006).

Franklin, John Hope

(b. 1915) HISTORIAN.
Franklin stands in the first rank of professional historians and also in the first rank of those blacks who work actively on behalf of the modern civil rights movement. Born in Rentiesville,

Okla., in 1915, Franklin embodies the ethnic and racial complexities of the South: his family was part Cherokee and part black, and some of its members served as slaves to the Cherokees in the antebellum decades. His father, Buck Franklin, became a successful lawyer in Tulsa and saw his legal offices destroyed in one of the antiblack riots after the Armistice of 1918. Buck Franklin quietly rebuilt his legal practice, for a time actually operating inside a tent, and this experience became vital to the spirit of John Hope Franklin's own protests and achievements.

Given the chance to attend college, young Franklin studied at Fisk (A.B., 1935) and then entered the Harvard graduate program (A.M., 1936, Ph.D., 1941) at a time when there were few black historians in the country. Between 1942 and 1992 he taught at Fisk University, Howard University, Saint Augustine's College, Brooklyn College, the University of Chicago, and Duke University. In the field of civil rights, Franklin was instrumental in integrating the Southern Historical Association, the American Historical Association, and the Mississippi Valley Historical Association (now the Organization of American Historians), all of which he eventually served as president; he also contributed background research for the National Association of Colored People in the campaign to integrate the public schools, culminating successfully in the legal case, *Brown v. Board of Education* (1954).

In the study of black history, Franklin published four major works among scores of edited and special studies: *From Slavery to Freedom: A History of African Americans* (1947; 8th ed., 2000) was an encyclopedic mapping of the path of black progress in America, optimistic in its style; *The Militant South, 1800–1861* (1956) was a bolder, more pessimistic interpretation, which traced both a self-destructive urge among the antebellum southern leaders who produced the Civil War and a continuing tendency to violence after the war; *Reconstruction after the Civil War* (1963) was one of the early efforts to revise the mythic white view of the horrors of Reconstruction, as embodied in historian William A. Dunning's works, and to focus on black participation and achievement in the post–Civil War period; and *Runaway Slaves; Rebels on the Plantation* (with Loren Schweninger, 1999) was a sophisticated quantitative analysis of data concerning slave resistance to oppression, which, like his entire oeuvre, emphasizes at once the glorious idea of equality and the sordid facts of inequality even in the best of southern and national venues.

In 1992 Franklin became emeritus professor of legal history at Duke University, but he in no sense retired, publishing a number of scholarly studies, revising earlier studies, and helping to recruit African American scholars in all fields of study to teach at the school. He remained a public figure of importance, serving in the Clinton administration as chairman of the advisory board to the president's initiative on race. In that post, he took occasion, much as he had when far younger, to lecture federal officials, not excluding President Clinton himself, about the continuing failure of the United States to provide adequate educational or job opportunities for black youth. Through the long decades, Franklin has retained a scholar's dignity and a humanist's respect for the opinions of others while working as diligently as any other activist advocate for racial justice in the South and nation.

JOHN HERBERT ROPER
Emory and Henry College

John Hope Franklin, *Free Negroes in North Carolina, 1790–1860* (1943), with John Whittingham Franklin, *My Life and An Era* (2000); Earle E. Thorpe, *Black Historians: A Critique* (1971); and interviews with Franklin, August Meier, C. Vann Woodward, and LeRoy Graf, typescripts in Southern Historical Collection, University of North Carolina, Chapel Hill.

Franklin, Tom

(b. 1963) WRITER.
Tom Franklin was born on 7 July 1963 in the small town of Dickinson in southwestern Alabama and was raised there until his family moved to Mobile, Ala., in 1981. After graduating from high school that same year, Franklin entered the University of South Alabama in Mobile, where he graduated with a B.A. in English in 1989. Throughout college Franklin worked at a variety of jobs, including a four-year stretch as a heavy-equipment operator in a sandblasting-grit factory, as a clerk at the Mobile Infirmary morgue, and as a construction inspector on a hazardous-waste clean-up crew at a chemical plant. In the fall of 1994 Franklin entered the M.F.A. program at the University of Arkansas, where he revised the short stories that would later be collected in a volume

entitled *Poachers* (1999). By the time he entered Arkansas he had published short stories in both the *Chattahoochee Review* and the *Nebraska Review*.

Franklin graduated from the University of Arkansas in 1998 and has held residencies or taught at various universities, including the University of South Alabama; Bucknell University in Lewisburg, Pa.; Knox College in Galesburg, Ill.; and the University of the South in Sewanee, Tenn. In 2001 Franklin accepted the position of John and Renée Grisham Writer in Residence at the University of Mississippi in Oxford, where he and his wife, the poet Beth Ann Fennelly, have made their home. They both teach in the University of Mississippi's creative writing program.

The title story of Franklin's collection *Poachers* was first published in the *Texas Review* and went on to win the Edgar Allan Poe Award in 1998. The story is set within the swamps of Alabama, along the annually breached banks of the Alabama River, and involves the three Gates brothers, who are caught illegally poaching game. They murder a young and ambitious game warden to conceal their crime, and the local sheriff sends for a legendarily infamous game warden, Frank David, to search out the brothers. He does, tracking them to their home in the swamp and meting out a brutal justice upon them. In other stories in the volume, Franklin draws inspiration from his myriad employments, mining his native Alabama for settings and characters and portraying a world that is distinctly southern and, furthermore, uniquely south Alabaman.

Franklin's next book, *Hell at the Breech* (2003), is a historical novel based on real events that occurred a few miles from Franklin's childhood home. The novel is set in 1897 and follows the vigilante justice that occurs after the accidental murder of an aspiring politician in rural Mitchum Beat, Ala. Friends and relatives of the slain man form a night-riding society, Hell-at-the-Breech, to terrorize the townsfolk they believe are responsible, driving a wedge between people who are perhaps not all that much different to begin with.

Franklin's third book and second novel, *Smonk* (2006), is set in 1911 and follows the one-eyed, dwarflike, goitered, sickly, and excessively violent E. O. Smonk just days before his trial for general mayhem in the town of Old Texas, Ala. He has resolved to kill all the male citizens of Old Texas before they can try him, and he nearly does, but not before he encounters the boyish waif Evavangeline, a 15-year-old female prostitute who is every bit Smonk's violent equal. *Smonk* counts among its themes incest, fratricide, insanity, violence, and the emotional detritus left scattered across the rural South even decades after the Civil War. Violent though *Smonk* is, it is not without the dark comedy that can be compared to that of the humorists of the Old Southwest such as Henry Clay Lewis and Johnson Jones Hooper. The settings and characters throughout Franklin's work remind his readers that while the South was once part of the nation's frontier, there are parts of it that still remain so.

Franklin's highly regarded work has been compared to such Gothic southern authors as Flannery O'Connor, William

Faulkner, Larry Brown, Cormac McCarthy, and Harry Crews. It has appeared
in the *Black Warrior Review*, the *Southern Review*, the *Oxford American, Best
American Mystery Stories of the Century*,
and *New Stories from the South, 1999*.

JAMES G. THOMAS JR.
University of Mississippi

Greg Johnson, *Atlanta Journal-Constitution*
(27 August 2006); Veronica Pike Kennedy,
Birmingham News (Alabama) (3 September
2006); Fredric Koeppel, *Commercial Appeal*
(Memphis, Tenn.) (8 October 2006); Mary
A. McCay, *New Orleans Times-Picayune* (24
September 2006).

Frazier, Charles

(b. 1950) WRITER.

Charles Robinson Frazier was born
4 November 1950 in Asheville, N.C.
He grew up in nearby Andrews and
Franklin, not far from Cold Mountain,
the peak that became a popular tourist
attraction as a result of the phenomenal
success of *Cold Mountain*, Frazier's first
novel.

Son of high school principal C. O.
(Charles Oldridge) and Betty Robinson Frazier, he grew up valuing books
as well as family stories about the life
and history of the mountains he loved
to hike. After earning his B.A. at the
University of North Carolina at Chapel
Hill in 1973, Frazier earned an M.A. in
English at Appalachian State University,
before starting work on his doctorate
at the University of South Carolina.
In graduate school, Frazier met and
married Katherine Beal, an accounting
major. Following their graduations, the
couple taught briefly at the University
of Colorado at Boulder before moving

to Raleigh, where they taught at North
Carolina State University. A daughter,
Annie Elizabeth, was born on 17 August
1985.

Frazier left academic life in 1990 to
devote himself full-time to the writing
of *Cold Mountain* and the care of his
daughter. Although the novel's foundation was the story of W. P. Inman—
Frazier's great-great uncle who had been
wounded, and hospitalized, then walked
away from the war to the mountains
where he was shot in a fight with the
Home Guard—the writing involved a
great deal of research. Frazier wanted
authenticity of language and culture of
the North Carolina mountains in 1865.

When Frazier's long-awaited novel
appeared in 1997, reviewers praised its
historical precision as well as its drama.
At once a best seller, the novel won the
National Book Award. During the next
several years, attention to the novel was
abetted by anticipation of the film version. Directed by Anthony Minghella,
it was released 25 December 2003.
Nominated for several academy awards,
including best film, *Cold Mountain*
did win an Academy Award for Renée
Zellweger in the best supporting actress
category.

No novel depicting the Civil War had
so nearly rivaled the success of *Gone
with the Wind* like Frazier's—though the
war itself had not been Frazier's chief
interest. Above all wanting to capture
the mountain life of that time, he nevertheless portrays realities of the war in
compelling ways, including depiction of
horrific scenes at Petersburg. As Frazier
underscores, the mountain people had
little stake in the economic forces that

caused the war. Men who enlisted were carried along by the spirit of adventure or by the pressure from the community.

In 2002 the phenomenal success of *Cold Mountain* resulted in an $8.25 million advance contract for Frazier's second novel, Random House being the winner of the competition. A meticulous writer, Frazier wrote afternoons and nights for the next four years to meet his deadline. Assured of popular and critical scrutiny, that novel was released in October 2006. Like its predecessor, *Thirteen Moons* is rooted in the South of the 19th century. Epic in scope, it also has many stories to tell and a broad terrain.

If both novels rest under the label of historical fiction, Frazier faced a different challenge for his second novel. The history that shapes *Thirteen Moons* is based on the life of businessman, North Carolina state senator, and self-taught lawyer William Holland Thomas (1805–93), who, as a fatherless child, had been placed under a three-year indenture contract at the trading post in the North Carolina mountains. He became proficient in the Cherokee tongue, and Chief Yonaguska adopted him into his tribe. During debate in Washington, D.C., over Cherokee removal to the Oklahoma territory, Thomas represented the Cherokee and was able to negotiate a "reservation" for the small band. During the Civil War, Thomas recruited two Cherokee companies, along with six companies of whites, and formed Thomas's Legion, with the Cherokee serving mainly as guards rounding up deserters. Although he was pardoned by President Andrew Johnson in 1866, his

mental health deteriorated, and he died in a state asylum. In the novel Thomas becomes Will Cooper, and Frazier makes clear that he takes other liberties with the historical record. Cooper narrates the novel from the asylum and is depicted as an old man wanting to set the record straight, a record that covers much of the 19th century.

For several years the Fraziers lived on a horse farm in northern Wake County, not far from Raleigh. Now they divide their time between a residence in Florida and a summer house outside Asheville, near the mountain life and history central to Frazier's work.

JOSEPH M. FLORA
University of North Carolina at Chapel Hill

Kevin Grauke, *War Literature and the Arts* (2002); John Inscoe, *Appalachian Journal* (Spring 1998).

Gaines, Ernest J.

(b. 1933) WRITER.

Schools stopped at the eighth grade for African Americans in the Louisiana in which Ernest J. Gaines was born, so he joined his mother and stepfather in California in 1948 to complete his education. Prior to that, he had been raised by a crippled aunt, who scooted around her house in a cart with wheels. A precocious boy, young Ernest read to the illiterate people in his community and was targeted, like many of his central characters, to rise above the limitations set upon him by his race and region.

In California, Gaines's stepfather insisted the boy do something besides roaming the streets after school each day, so Ernest went to the library to read. He was homesick for Louisiana and found comfort in the familiar region and characters of William Faulkner, as well as in the peasantry of Turgenev. Still, Faulkner was, as Gaines has said repeatedly, writing about Dilsey in his kitchen rather than her own. There was still a story to be told—by Dilsey herself, and that absent voice apparently inspired the writer in Ernest Gaines to create Miss Jane Pittman, the character who introduced him to a national audience of both readers and television writers.

Prior to *The Autobiography of Miss Jane Pittman* (novel, 1971; made-for-TV-movie, 1974), Gaines wrote a novel, which he burned after it was rejected by the New York publisher he sent it to, and then rewrote it into what became his first book, *Catherine Carmier* (1964). Like *Jane Pittman*, in spite of its title, Gaines's first novel is more about the conflict between the men in the title character's life than it is her story. Indeed, the central conflict of most, if not all, of Gaines's fiction is with African American men struggling to be *men* in a community in which they are called "boy" their whole lives. Asserting their manhood usually results in death or departure, for the Louisiana that would not educate Ernest Gaines also continues to oppress his characters.

Gaines completed his formal education while in California. He began college in Vallejo, where he had lived with his parents, but his studies were interrupted for two years when he was drafted. When he returned from service in the army, he enrolled at San Francisco State College, where he earned his bachelor's degree in 1957. He then went to Stanford on a Wallace Stegner Creative Writing Fellowship. There he rewrote the novel he had burned and thus began his writing career. He eventually returned to Louisiana, where he taught at the University of Southwestern Louisiana (now the University of Louisiana at Lafayette) from 1983 (in addition to a year as a visiting professor in 1981) until his retirement in 2004. He would go back to San Francisco to live during the summer, until his marriage in 1993 to Florida lawyer Dianne Saulney.

Between *Catherine Carmier* and *Autobiography of Miss Jane Pittman*, Gaines published a third novel, *In Love and Dust* (1967), and a collection of short stories, *Bloodline* (1968), which includes the often anthologized "The Sky Is Gray" and "A Long Day in November." After *Jane Pittman*, he published *A Long Day in November* (1971), *In My Father's House* (1978), and *A Gathering of Old Men* (1983), which was also adapted for a television movie (1987) that starred Louis Gossett Jr. and Holly Hunter. His next novel, *A Lesson before Dying* (1993), garnered the kind of attention that *Jane Pittman* had attracted, won the National Book Critics Circle Award for Fiction, and was made into perhaps the best of the film adaptations (though it is still not entirely accurate to the novel), which aired on Home Box Office in 1999 and received the Emmy that year for best movie. His most recent book is a collection of stories and essays called *Mozart and Leadbelly* (2005).

Gaines sets his fiction in his native Louisiana, and he writes about conflicts unique to the region but universally applicable. Besides (and related to) his characters' struggle to assert their manhood in a racist society, Gaines explores the conflict between African Americans and Cajuns, traceable back to when Cajuns were plantation overseers and then given first choice of land when landowners began selling off sections of their large plantations after the Civil War. In these stories, he has told the story he had missed in Faulkner's fiction, the story of the black man living in the Deep South.

MARGARET D. BAUER
East Carolina University

Valerie Melissa Babb, *Ernest Gaines* (1991); Ernest J. Gaines, *Mozart and Leadbelly* (2005); Marcia Gaudet and Carl Wooton, *Porch Talk with Ernest Gaines: Conversations on the Writer's Craft* (1990); John Lowe, ed., *Conversations with Ernest Gaines* (1995).

Gaither, Frances Ormond Jones

(1889–1955) WRITER.

Although Gaither's trilogy of the Old South rivals the work of any other southern writer, she has unfortunately become largely unread and almost forgotten. Her novels stand as some of the most subtle and historically accurate examinations of social relations and plantation culture in the antebellum South.

Gaither was born Frances Ormond Jones on 21 May 1889, in Somerville, Tenn., to a well-off family. Her ancestors included both Yankees-come-South and slaveholders. Gaither graduated from the Industrial Institute and College (now Mississippi University for Women) in 1909, where she studied English under the legendary Pauline

Van de Graaf Orr. While a student, Gaither was already marked as a potential writer, and the yearbook from her senior year includes her poetry and fiction. In 1912 she married Rice Gaither, her childhood sweetheart. The couple settled in New York City in 1929.

Gaither wrote children's books in the 1930s. *The Painted Arrow* (1931) is the story of a young French boy who comes to America. *The Fatal River: The Life and Death of LaSalle* (1931) tells of the explorer's life. *The Scarlet Coat* (1934) follows a fictional French boy who travels with LaSalle and eventually becomes the favorite son of an Indian chief. *Little Miss Capo* (1937), Gaither's last children's book, tells the story of a young girl in 1820 who leaves her native Alabama to enroll in a Monrovian school in North Carolina.

Gaither's adult fiction includes her final three novels: *Follow the Drinking Gourd* (1941), *The Red Cock Crows* (1944), and *Double Muscadine* (1949). A consistent dedication to research and historical accuracy marks Gaither's fiction. Her purpose, however, is not to write history but to search for a narrative emerging from the mass of fact and document, claim and counterclaim.

Follow the Drinking Gourd (1941) traces the development of Hurricane Plantation in Alabama. This is no tale of Tara, and the plantation neither prospers nor founders, though it tends toward the latter. Even masters with good intentions toward "their people" must answer to the demands of bankers for adequate profits and returns on investments. The novel becomes a study of the longing for freedom in every man's heart when an itinerant carpenter, based on a historical figure, begins discreetly informing slaves how they can "follow the Drinking Gourd" north to freedom.

In *The Red Cock Crows* (1944), Gaither explores the fear of insurrection that drove slaveholders to extreme measures in the face of even a rumor of revolt. Shandy Plantation near Scott's Bluff, Miss., seems a veritable paradise, and no white southerner could understand how any slave's heart could harbor discontent, given such kind and indulgent treatment. However, the most trusted slave experiences a vision of himself as a Moses setting his people free and begins to plot an insurrection. In the blood feast that follows revelation of the plan, numerous lynchings and constant calls for violence directed against the slaves express the white population's hysteria and fear. In the end, the privileged daughter of Shandy Plantation leaves the South, though she is the South, to follow a Yankee back North.

Double Muscadine (1949), Gaither's final novel, was the Book-of-the-Month Club main selection for March 1949. Based on a case from Mississippi in the 1850s, the novel explores miscegenation as a fact, and a crime, of the antebellum South. The master of Waverly, a plantation outside Athens, Miss., within a short time brings home both a young wife from Georgia and an attractive mulatto cook. The master's son dies after drinking poisoned tea, and the mulatto stands accused and convicted of this horrible crime. A young backwoods lawyer takes on the case and convinces the High Court to order a new trial. In the course of the new trial, the lawyer reveals the secret habits the master prefers to keep hidden and shows that the crime is not at all straightforward.

After *Double Muscadine*, Gaither wrote no more fiction, though she continued to write book reviews. She died on 28 October 1955 and is buried in Corinth, Miss., her hometown.

SHELDON S. KOHN
Georgia State University

Ronald L. Davis, in *Lives of Mississippi Authors, 1817–1967*, ed. James B. Lloyd (1981); Michael Kreyling, *Inventing Southern Literature* (1998); Robert L. Phillips Jr., in *Southern Writers: A Biographical Dictionary*, ed. Robert Bain, Joseph M. Flora, and Louis D. Rubin Jr. (1979); L. Moody Simms, *Notes on Mississippi Writers* (Fall 1970).

Garrett, George

(b. 1929) WRITER.

Since the appearance of his first poetry collection, *The Reverend Ghost* (1957), George Palmer Garrett has published more than 30 volumes of fiction, nonfiction, poetry, drama, biography, and literary criticism, as well as edited more than 20 anthologies and composed three screenplays. Having published a novel, story collection, and poetry collection on the same day in 1961, Garrett is renowned for his prolific output as much as for his eclectic material and aesthetic innovation. The son of George Palmer Sr., a lawyer, and Rosalie Toomer, Garrett was born on 11 June 1929 in Orlando, Fla., and later attended Sewanee Military Academy and Hill School. He earned a B.A. from Princeton University in 1952, married the musician Susan Parrish Jackson, and fulfilled army service for two years over-seas in Trieste and Austria before re-turning to Princeton for an M.A. degree in English literature. Already publishing stories and poems, Garrett left the uni-versity just before completing a Ph.D. to embark on a teaching career that in-cluded stints at, among others, Wesleyan University, Hollins College, and the University of South Carolina. From 1984 until his retirement in 2000, Garrett was the Henry Hoyns Professor of Creative Writing at University of Virginia. Cur-rently he resides in Charlottesville, Va., and is the state's poet laureate.

Garrett's first novel, *The Finished Man* (1959), is a sobering account of the Ku Klux Klan's involvement in a mid-century Florida senatorial campaign, a story inspired by his father's own legal battles against the Klan. Upon its publi-cation, reviewers hailed Garrett as a new southern writer whose style distinctly contributed to the tradition of modern southern letters, as defined by William Faulkner and Robert Penn Warren. However, Garrett's writing eschews easy regional classification—he has applied his imaginative vision to a variety of landscapes, time periods, and themes, which may account for the lack of sig-nificant, sustained, critical attention his work has received. He is best known for his trilogy of Elizabethan historical novels, beginning with the exploration of the life of Sir Walter Raleigh in *Death of the Fox* (1971), a novel celebrated by critics for its thorough research and metafictive reworking of the genre. Gar-rett's formal and aesthetic innovation, particularly his abandonment of con-ventional plot, found further expression in the two later novels of the trilogy, *The Succession: A Novel of Elizabeth and James* (1983) and *Empire of the Sun* (1990), a fictional investigation of the mysterious death of Christopher Mar-lowe. Princeton University accepted the first two volumes of the trilogy as Gar-rett's dissertation, awarding him a Ph.D. in English in 1985.

Comedy both light and dark abounds in Garrett's fiction and poetry. In the poems of *For a Bitter Sea-son* (1967), Garrett aims his satire at celebrity culture, mocking the hollow images of icons such as Kim Novak and Barbara Steele, as well as the shallow society (including himself as poet) that celebrates them, a theme further ex-plored in his most satiric novel, *The Poi-son Pen* (1986). Even at his most biting, however, Garrett's writing is guided by a unifying vision not unlike that of Flan-nery O'Connor—a Protestant Christian vision certain about the human poten-tial for salvation. Garrett's characters are more often than not sinner-saints strug-gling to find meaning in a fallen world. His antiheroes, such as the manipulative tent revivalist Red Smalley in *Do, Lord, Remember Me* (1963), are characters tormented by their own corruption, an emotional state of being that inevitably leads to their salvation.

Now in his seventh decade, Garrett reflects on the past (his own and those of other southern and nonsouthern writers) in essay collections such as *Going to See the Elephant: Pieces of a Writing Life* (2002), while also continu-ing to explore new thematic and aesthetic territory in creative work such as *Empty Bed Blues* (2006).

L. A. HOFFER
University of Tennessee

Richard A. Betts, *Mississippi Quarterly* (Winter 1991–92); R. H. W. Dillard, *Understanding George Garrett* (1988); Brooke Horvath and Irving Merlin, *George Garrett: The Elizabethan Trilogy* (1998), Monroe K. Spears, *Virginia Quarterly Review* (Spring 1985); Henry Taylor, *Compulsory Figures: Essays on Recent American Poets* (1992); Tom Whalen, *Texas Review* (Winter 1983).

Gautreaux, Tim
(b. 1947) WRITER.

In two novels and two story collections, Tim Gautreaux has conjured up the sights and sounds of his home state with such authority that fellow writer Robert Olen Butler, in a blurb for Gautreaux's novel *The Clearing*, announced: "Hereafter, as with Mississippi and Faulkner, Northern California and Steinbeck, Georgia and O'Connor, when I think of Louisiana, I will hear the voice of Tim Gautreaux."

Born on 19 October 1947 and raised in Morgan City, a port in south-central Louisiana, Timothy Martin Gautreaux is the Catholic son of a tugboat captain. He grew up listening to the men in his family tell stories and, while at Nicholls State University in nearby Thibodaux, he began to put his own words on paper. After graduation with a B.A. in 1969, he enrolled at the University of South Carolina. There, under the direction of writer James Dickey, he composed a volume of poetry for his dissertation, receiving his Ph.D. in English in 1972.

He moved home to teach literature and creative writing at Southeastern Louisiana University, a position he held for 31 years, until his retirement in 2002. Today, although he often cites "retired schoolteacher" as his profession, it is his work outside of the classroom—and not his early poetry, but his more recent fiction—that has brought him national attention.

Gautreaux was 43 years old and had received scores of rejection letters when, in 1991, *Atlantic Monthly* chose his short story "Same Place, Same Things" for publication. ("I'd rather peak late than early," he would tell Robert Birnbaum in hindsight.) This bit of success proved only the beginning. He put out a book of short stories by that same title in 1996, and then a second collection, *Welding with Children*, in 1999. His first novel appeared in between the two story collections. Winner of the Southeastern Booksellers Award, *The Next Step in the Dance* (1998) is the story of a young Louisiana wife who, discontented with marriage and small-town life, flees to California. Her husband follows her out west, intending to win her back and carry her home again. Here, in this married couple's fictional hometown of Tiger Island, many readers have recognized Gautreaux's own Morgan City. Then, in 2003, Gautreaux released what he regards as his best work. *The Clearing*, like *The Next Step in the Dance*, is a redemption tale, but one set in the 1920s. In *The Clearing*, a Pennsylvania businessman discovers his older brother in a swampy, dangerous Louisiana lumber camp, traumatized by service in

World War I and working as constable. The younger brother buys the camp and relocates there, hoping to restore his sibling to good health and to their family.

If Louisiana is southern, then one can argue that Gautreaux is a southern writer. After all, he has lived most of his life in the Bayou State, and he locates most of his fiction there. But often in interviews he shrugs off the label of "southern writer," believing his literary themes are not unique to the South. If anything, he prefers to consider his work akin to the tall tale. This claim has some legitimacy, as his turns of slapstick humor and hyperbole occasionally test the limits of believability. Ultimately, however, his stories are less concerned with literary genre than they are with culture and class. Each is a realistic and cinematic rendering of a way of life that is usually blue-collar, small-town, and Cajun. As a writer, Gautreaux speaks for the mill worker, the train engineer, the local priest, the machine repairman. He makes high art out of the common man's condition.

A recurring character in his fiction is the individual who, through the course of some trial, arrives at a greater awareness of his own humanity and a greater appreciation of his lot in life. The author, for his part, seems to have learned this lesson well and to have embraced his own roots as story worthy. His characters voice the French-touched vernacular of south Louisiana; reviewers have likened his dialogue to that of another writer from the state, Ernest Gaines. Undoubtedly his decision to spend his life in one region has sharpened his ear for conversational language. But

Gautreaux, the retired schoolteacher and late-blossoming writer, explained his talent for dialogue differently when he said, in a 2003 interview, "I taught *Huckleberry Finn* enough times as a college instructor to understand the purposes of the language in the South."

HICKS WOGAN
University of Mississippi

Julie Kane, in *Dictionary of Literary Biography*, vol. 292, ed. Lisa Abney and Suzanne Disheroon-Green (2004); Ed Piacentino, *Southern Literary Journal* (Fall 2005).

Gibbons, Kaye

(b. 1960) WRITER.

While she was a student in Louis Rubin's southern literature class at Chapel Hill, Kaye Gibbons showed him a manuscript of her novel, *Ellen Foster*. Shortly thereafter, in 1987, Rubin's Algonquin Press published the book. Its spare and focused scope reopened the interrogation of what John Crowe Ransom might call the "economy of the household" in southern life. With each following novel, Gibbons continues to chronicle the voice of southern women speaking "in place."

Matriarchal lines root Gibbons's novels. The women here, in the author's words, "remember conversations" and practice a creed of "self-reliance." Ellen Foster (*Ellen Foster*) matures through her own wits as well as in conversations with her friend, Starletta, the Brontë sisters, and a "laughing Middle Ages lady" in the "old stories" given to her by the librarian. Hattie Barnes (*Sights Unseen*, 1995) discovers the means to live with her mother's mental illness, as her mother stares down the men's family relationships that are defined by pride, violence, and power. This self-reliance is a continual touchstone for Gibbons's women, a constant reassertion of the intrinsic value of their social place in the face of history.

In the Gibbons novel, each narrator seems "insulated" in life's domestic spheres; each account feels "overheard." Yet, this is not a self-obsessed, regionalized fiction. Instead, examining Gibbons's *On the Occasion of My Last Afternoon* (1998), Matthew Guinn calls the novelist's project "deconstruction from within." For instance, although one has examined the "official account" of a story in the newspaper or history book, Gibbons gives the reader a way of narrating the South—one that does not simply throw the region back on itself in self-absorption. The narration never feigns to escape place, personal or social history, or even the body. Slowed of narrative momentum, the Gibbons narrator often finds herself in the position of Margaret Birch (*Charms for the Easy Life*, 1993), who, after her grandmother's death, "l(ies) down, rest(s) her head by her (grandmother's) feet, and wait(s) to be found." In this densely textured "waiting," Gibbons delves into the layers of accumulated psychological experience. Here, she engages myths of the unity of that experience. Her "South" geographically breaks into region and neighborhood. Her women are rooted in voices and bodies in which they move through domestic and historical spaces, retell, and disappear. For example, a school counselor challenges Ellen Foster to recall her experiences of poverty and fear. She recounts, "I used

to be (afraid) but I am not now is what I told him. I might get a little nervous but I am never scared. Oh but I do remember when I was scared."

When Gibbons was nine years old, her mother committed suicide. Gibbons herself has faced manic depression, but it is too easy to say that she simply chronicles her own experiences with the disease in her novels, marking some journey toward psychological wholeness. Instead, her characters move from experience to storytelling with this sense of living as distant observers of their own lives. The effect is of a narrator intent on getting all the details right in the face of a generalized and misremembered story line. In *Sights Unseen*, Hattie tells the story of her own naming. While the woman who shares her mother's room in the obstetrics ward joins "the various voices from (her) mother's (psychologically broken) life now in unison, telling her how much joy she could have if she were normal, happy, and sane," Maggie Barnes insists that the child's name be "Hattie" in a defiant stance against the accumulated stubborn and racial angers of the men around her. Each novel's story is obsessively told within these subsumed histories. The force of southern economics and society moves along, the mills and migrant farm workers working in place. This is a reality of which Gibbons's narrators never lose sight. No one would presume to disturb the region's unbroken pastoral appearance. In Margaret Birch's telling of her neighbors' suicide threats, "they would walk fifty miles and jump in some other person's river, but not their own." Similarly, each narrator tells her story with full awareness of that stasis, speaking with a sense of deflected memoir, as she reconstructs these subsumed domestic histories.

Kaye Gibbons was born Bertha Kaye Batts on 5 May 1960 in Nash County, N.C. She continues to write, living with her three daughters in Raleigh, N.C.

GARIN CYCHOLL
University of Illinois-Chicago

Suzanne Disheroon-Green, in *Dictionary of Literary Biography*, vol. 292, ed. Lisa Abney and Suzanne Disheroon-Green (2004); Jan Nordby Gretlund, *South Atlantic Review* (Fall 2000); Matthew Guinn, *After Southern Modernism* (2000).

Gilchrist, Ellen

(b. 1935) WRITER.
Ellen Gilchrist had a newspaper column at the age of 15, which she had to give up when her father once again moved his family out of the South. She would later give up writing again after she married and had her first child. She published her first book of short stories, the genre she is most lauded for, in her mid-40s.

Born in Vicksburg, Miss., to which her family would regularly return for visits, Gilchrist grew up in Indiana, Illinois, and Kentucky. She began her college education at Vanderbilt University in 1953, transferred to the University of Alabama in 1954, then dropped out to get married to Marshall Walker in 1955. She and Walker had three sons, divorcing and remarrying between the second and third (she married and divorced James Nelson Bloodworth during that time, too). In 1963 she divorced Walker again and finished her bachelor's degree

at Millsaps College, where she took classes with Eudora Welty.

In 1968 Gilchrist married Frederick Sidney Kullman of New Orleans, where she resumed newspaper work in 1975 as a contributing editor of the *Vieux Carre Courier*. The next year, she also enrolled in the creative writing M.F.A. program at the University of Arkansas, dividing her time between Fayetteville and New Orleans until she and Kullman divorced in 1981. She settled in Fayetteville, where she still lives, and 20 years later she joined the faculty of the writing program that launched her career.

Although Gilchrist did not complete her M.F.A., during her enrollment in the program Fayetteville's Lost Roads Press published her first collection of poems, *The Land Surveyor's Daughter* (1979), and the university press published her first book of fiction, *In the Land of Dreamy Dreams* (1981). Little, Brown and Company then picked up her first novel, *The Annunciation* (1983), and her American Book Award–winning collection *Victory over Japan* (1984). Since her first book, Gilchrist has continued to publish an average of a book a year— poetry, fiction (including short stories, novellas, novels, and historical fantasy), and nonfiction, which she also regularly publishes in magazines.

In the Land of Dreamy Dreams introduces Rhoda Manning, an admittedly autobiographical character who is paradoxically both spoiled and oppressed by her father. Rhoda would become Gilchrist's most popular recurrent character and the prototype for the protagonists of most of the author's fiction. Other recurring characters include Nora

Jane Whittington, also introduced in the first collection, and Crystal Manning Mallison Weiss, who is introduced by her African American housekeeper and confidante, Traceleen, who narrates several stories in *Victory over Japan*.

The Gilchrist prototype evolves with the author's development of Anna Hand in Gilchrist's second novel, *The Anna Papers* (1988). Gilchrist's characterization of Anna fulfills the promise of her original prototype, Rhoda, who was not able to overcome her conflict with her dominating father and brother or her consequential belief that her value as a woman depends on the opinions of the men in her life. Like her creator, Rhoda is a talented writer with the promise of a career ahead of her, but she drops out of college after eloping and having several children right away. She divorces this husband but continues to focus most of her energy toward finding a mate rather than on writing. In contrast, Anna Hand, also unsuccessful with marriage but not able to have children, is a published author who has set her own priorities and disregards familial obligations when necessary; chooses lovers according to her own desires without regard for whether society or her family would approve of them; and finally, upon discovering that she has cancer, takes her own life rather than succumbing to the disease.

After Anna Hand, Gilchrist's protagonists are divided between manifestations of the original prototype and characters that reflect the evolution. By continuing to create characters with Rhoda's weaknesses, including women of the next two generations, Gilchrist continues to show that overcoming gender strictures continues to be difficult, even into the 21st century. Careers may be more accessible and socially acceptable, but the southern families of these young women continue to emphasize the importance of their daughters finding appropriate husbands and then providing heirs. Even the prototype, in her 60s in recent collections, has begun to echo her father's concern about the consequences of her granddaughters' rebellious natures.

MARGARET D. BAUER
East Carolina University

Margaret Donovan Bauer, *The Fiction of Ellen Gilchrist* (1999), in *The History of Southern Women's Literature*, ed. Carolyn Perry and Mary Louise Weaks (2002); Ellen Gilchrist, *Falling through Space* (2000); Mary McCay, *Ellen Gilchrist* (1990).

Giovanni, Nikki

(b. 1943) POET AND TEACHER.
As a creative voice emerging from the black arts movement of the 1960s, Giovanni received national attention for her powerful, militant poetry. In the following decade, a mellower tone and universal themes gained her a wider audience as her poems were much anthologized. Recognized for its black and feminist themes, Giovanni's poetry and prose contain a southern sense of place and reflect her identification with the values and traditions of the South.

Born Yolande Cornelia Giovanni Jr. in Knoxville, Tenn., on 7 June 1943, she was raised in Cincinnati, Ohio. As part of the Great Migration from the rural South to urban North, Nikki Giovanni's parents, Gus and Yolande (Watson)

Giovanni, both graduates of Knoxville College, escaped segregation and underemployment and worked for the Welfare Department—Yolande as a supervisor and Gus as a social worker.

Giovanni and her sister returned to Knoxville each summer to visit her maternal grandparents, John and Louvenia Watson. Mrs. Watson, a member of the National Association for the Advancement of Colored People (NAACP) and the Colored Women's Federation of Clubs, instilled Giovanni with a sense of social responsibility that inspired her writing and political involvement. Her vivid memories of Knoxville included the unfairness of poll taxes, signs indicating segregated services and entrances, and the prohibition against going to downtown movie theaters and city amusement parks. However, she established a routine of going to the library each day and to church each Sunday. "Don't Worry, There's No Racial Hatred Here" (1996) was inspired by Mount Zion Baptist, Mrs. Watson's church home.

Giovanni moved to Knoxville in 1957 and attended Austin High School, which was desegregated in 1968. She described the bombing of Clinton High School the next year as a personal tragedy, later calling racism boring and frightening. Mrs. Watson involved Giovanni in her charitable, social, and political activities that included taking Sunday dinner to shut-ins. She churned butter and made ice cream, and southern food like string beans, peach butter and biscuits, and fried chicken appear in her poetry and prose.

Admitted to Fisk University in Sep-

tember 1960 after completion of the 11th grade, Giovanni disliked the school's social life. Rebelling against the rules, she left campus without permission to spend Thanksgiving with the Watsons. She was released from the university in 1961 for her bad attitude. Returning to Fisk in 1964, she revitalized the Student Nonviolent Coordinating Committee (SNCC) chapter, edited the literary magazine, and took part in the Fisk Writers' Workshop under John O. Killens. She gradated magna cum laude from Fisk in 1967 with a B.A. in history. Also that year, *Black Feeling, Black Talk*, her first book, was published with help from a Ford Foundation grant, and she organized Cincinnati's first Black Arts Festival. Giovanni enrolled at University of Pennsylvania's School of Social Work and worked in a settlement house until deciding to move to New York City and enter the M.F.A. program at Columbia University's School of Fine Arts in 1968.

She began teaching at Queens College in 1969. Later that year she gave birth to Thomas Watson Giovanni, her only child. Giovanni taught at several institutions including Livingston College of Rutgers University, Ohio State University, and Mount Saint Joseph's College, before finding a permanent place as a University Distinguished Scholar at Virginia Polytechnic Institute in 1987. Beginning in the early 1970s Giovanni received honorary doctorates. Her 22nd was awarded in 2003 from West Virginia University.

Between raising her son, teaching, public speaking, and caring for her aging parents, as well as her involvement in arts and political organizations,

Giovanni published more than 20 books of poetry and prose and 6 books of poetry for children. Many of her poems are placed in the South: "Knoxville, Tennessee," "Each Sunday," "Hampton, Virginia," and "Alabama Poem," while others reference her southern roots via the metaphor of quilts and quilting: "My House," "A Very Simple Wish," "Hands: For Mother's Day," and "Stardate Number 18628.190."

REBECCA TOLLEY-STOKES
East Tennessee State University

Virginia Fowler, *Nikki Giovanni* (1992); Nikki Giovanni, *Gemini: An Extended Autobiographical Statement on My First Twenty-Five Years of Being a Black Poet* (1971); Trudier Harris and Thadious M. Davis, in *Dictionary of Literary Biography*, vol. 41, ed. Trudier Harris and Thadious M. Davis (1985); Tonette Bond Inge, *Southern Women Writers: The New Generation* (1990); Felicia Mitchell, *Her Words: Diverse Voices in Contemporary Appalachian Women's Poetry* (2002).

Glasgow, Ellen

(1873–1945) WRITER.

Ellen Anderson Gholson Glasgow, born in Richmond, Va., on 22 April 1873, published her first novel, *The Descendant*, in 1897, when she was 24 years old. With this novel Glasgow began a literary career encompassing four and a half decades and comprising 20 novels, a collection of poems, one of stories, and a book of literary criticism. Her autobiography, *A Woman Within*, was published posthumously in 1954.

Born into an aristocratic Virginia family, the young Glasgow rebelled against the conventional modes of feminine conduct and thought approved by her caste. Educated at home and through her own energetic readings in philosophy, social and political theory, and European and British literature, she developed a mind with enough strength and resilience to confront the truths of human experience without the sheltering illusions carefully nurtured by the dying southern aristocratic order she saw about her.

Glasgow's strong intellect led her to a conscious channeling of her creative energies toward the making of a substantial body of fiction. The framework of these works was to be, as she stated in 1898, at age 25, "a series of sketches dealing with life in Virginia." As she matured artistically, this early half-formed intention realized itself in a series of novels that constitutes a social history of her native Virginia. The great organizing ideas of her fiction are the conflicts between tradition and change, matter and spirit, the individual and society. The natural bent of her mind taught her that realism and irony were the best tools with which to fashion a new southern fiction to take the place of the sentimental stories of a glorified aristocratic past that dominated the regional fiction of her day. Through her poor white heroes and heroines, she introduced democratic values seldom found in the works of other southern writers outside Mark Twain. From the very beginning of her intellectual and creative life, she rejected Victorian definitions of femininity dominating the social attitudes of her day.

Glasgow produced seven novels of enduring literary merit. *The Deliver-*

*Ellen Glasgow, Virginia author, 1922 (Ellen Glasgow papers [#5771],
University of Virginia Library, Charlottesville)*

ance (1904), the best of her early novels, offers a naturalistic treatment of the class conflicts emerging after the Civil War. Its evocation of the Virginia landscape and tobacco farming invites comparison with Hardy's epics of the soil. In her women's trilogy—*Virginia* (1913), *Life and Gabriella* (1916), and *Barren Ground* (1925)—Glasgow assigns each of her Virginia heroines a fate determined by her response to the patriarchal code of feminine behavior that had formed her, a code that, as Glasgow shows so well in *Barren Ground*, always pitted women against their own biological natures. After *Barren Ground*, which marked her arrival at artistic maturity, Glasgow produced three sparkling comedies of manners—*The Romantic Comedians* (1926), *They Stooped to Folly* (1929), and *The Sheltered Life* (1932), the last the author's finest work. In these novels of urban Virginian life depicting the clash of generations, she again shows her women characters reacting to patriarchal stereotypes limiting their individuality and growth, while at the same time exposing with either comic or satiric irony the limitations these views of women's place on the male characters who hold them.

A popular writer, Glasgow was on the best-seller lists five times. In 1942 she received the Pulitzer Prize for her last published novel, *In This Our Life*, though by this time her powers had declined. Her artistic recognition had reached its height in 1931, when, as the acknowledged doyen of southern letters, she presided over the Southern Writers Conference at the University of Virginia. For many years the victim of heart disease, she died in her sleep at home in Richmond on 21 November 1945.

TONETTE TAYLOR LONG
North Georgia College and State University

Ellen Goodman, *Ellen Glasgow: A Biography* (2003); C. Hugh Holman, *Three Modes of Southern Fiction: Ellen Glasgow, William Faulkner, Thomas Wolfe* (1966); M. Thomas Inge, ed., *Ellen Glasgow: Centennial Essays* (1976); Julius Rowan Raper, *From the Sunken Garden: The Fiction of Ellen Glasgow, 1916–1945* (1980), *Without Shelter:*

The Early Career of Ellen Glasgow (1971); Dorothy M. Scura, ed., *Ellen Glasgow: New Perspectives* (1995).

Godwin, Gail

(b. 1937) WRITER.

Born in Alabama, Gail Godwin became a chronicler of women's struggle for personal fulfillment against social conventions. Godwin was an undergraduate at Peace College in Raleigh, N.C., and graduated from the University of North Carolina at Chapel Hill with a bachelor's degree in journalism and mass communication (1959). Godwin started her career in writing as a newspaper reporter in Miami, Fla., but soon left journalism for graduate school. At the University of Iowa, Godwin completed a master's and Ph.D. in creative writing. Her doctoral thesis, *The Perfectionists*, was published as her first novel in 1970. Godwin quickly established herself as the teller of tales about modern American women in the South.

Godwin's 11 novels and two short-story collections and one nonfiction volume cover an array of emotional subjects and themes while focusing on human interaction. She earned three National Book Award nominations for her novels *The Odd Woman* (1975), *Violet Clay* (1980), and *A Mother and Two Daughters* (1983). Godwin is also the recipient of the Award in Literature from the American Academy and Institute of Arts and Letters as well as a John Simon Guggenheim Fellowship and National Endowment for the Arts grants for both fiction and libretto writing. She also has been awarded honorary degrees from the University of North Carolina at Asheville and the University of North Carolina at Greensboro as well as the Distinguished Alumnae award in 1988 from the University of North Carolina at Chapel Hill.

Her work explores sexuality and spirituality in the lives of contemporary American women living in the South. The often contradictory nature of sexuality and spirituality in women's lives gets revised and reexamined in Godwin's work in fresh and interesting ways. Her consistent use of central female characters reveals the complex choices and issues impacting modern women. Many of her stories chart the struggle of the individual to replace a fractured identity with a sense of wholeness.

A Mother and Two Daughters was on the *New York Times* best-seller list for several weeks, ensuring Godwin's status as a well-known author. The novel traces the experiences of female family members after the death of the father. The complicated relationships among the three women in the family develop throughout the course of the action as each woman deals with her unique personality and life needs within the context of the newly changed family. The changing nature of the American family is a familiar theme in Godwin's other novels, including *A Southern Family* (1987), which chronicles a family's reaction to the murder of several relatives and is told from the perspective of various family members.

Father Melancholy's Daughter (1991) was Godwin's continuing exploration of female emotional journeys but with an added dimension of spirituality and family life. In the novel, the protagonist, Margaret Gower, is the daughter of a minister whose mother left the family during childhood. Margaret's growing into adulthood shifts through individual choices against familial responsibility; she becomes the primary caretaker for her religious and often depressed father. Margaret is in the unenviable position of knowing everything about one parent while her other parent remains a shadowy mystery, because her mother was killed in a car accident shortly after leaving town. The novel juggles questions about parent-child relationships and the role of managing individual needs against family responsibilities. Godwin's interest in spirituality and the story of Margaret Gower was furthered in *Evensong* (1991), in which Gower is now married and a minister herself. These two novels are the strongest examples of Godwin's ability to deal with the overlapping layers of religion, sexuality, and everyday life in accessible and literary fiction.

Her books cover the range of life and death, contrasting the spiritual and the secular, individual independence and social boundedness. Her works feature strong women during moments of life crisis where they are confronted with major changes. Godwin's female characters grapple with the search for their own identities among responsibilities and the freedom to make choices despite the dictates of tradition. Godwin has also co-written 10 musical works with her companion, the late Robert Starer. She has lived in Woodstock, N.Y., since 1976.

MOHANALAKSHMI RAJAKUMAR
University of Florida

Jane Hill, *Gail Godwin* (1992); Lihong Xie, *The Evolving Self in the Novels of Gail Godwin* (1995); Jennifer McMullen, *Southern Quarterly* (Spring 2004); Kerstin W. Shands, *Escaping the Castle of Patriarchy: Patterns of Development in the Novels of Gail Godwin* (1990); Marilynn J. Smith, *Critique* 21:3 (1980); Mary Ann Wimsatt, *Southern Literary Journal* (Spring 1995).

Gordon, Caroline

(1895–1981) WRITER AND CRITIC. Caroline Gordon was as self-consciously southern as a writer can be. She was immensely proud of the Meriwether connection; her mother's family had lived in Todd County, Ky., for generations. Her Meriwether grandfather, a Civil War veteran and tobacco grower, had hired James Maury Morris Gordon to teach his children at home. Gordon married Nancy Meriwether, one of his pupils, and they lived at Merry Mont, the family homeplace, where their three children were born.

Caroline, the Gordons' only daughter, was born 6 October 1895 and grew up hearing her grandparents, dozens of other relatives, and former slaves who were still working as servants talk about the Civil War. She would use this background in several novels.

When her parents and brothers left Merry Mont as her father tried various teaching jobs in the South, Caroline stayed there with her Meriwether grandmother. When Mr. Gordon became a Church of Christ minister, Caroline moved with her parents to several towns. She graduated from Bethany College in Bethany, W.Va., in 1916. She knew she wanted to be a writer but

taught school for a living in West Virginia and Clarksville, Tenn., before she worked on newspapers in Chattanooga. While her duties at the *Chattanooga News* were chiefly editorial, she wrote a story about the Fugitives, a group of young poets at Vanderbilt University in Nashville. When she was visiting her parents in Guthrie, Ky., Robert Penn Warren, whose mother was a friend of Caroline's mother, brought his houseguest and fellow Fugitive at Vanderbilt to call on Caroline. The houseguest was Allen Tate—and it was love at first sight.

Allen and Caroline went to New York City separately in 1924. On 15 May 1925 they were married—Caroline kept her maiden name—and their only child, Nancy, was born in September 1925. Caroline wrote fiction but received no encouragement until she went to work as a secretary to the British writer Ford Madox Ford, who encouraged her to write. Finally, in 1928, while the Tates were in Paris on Allen's Guggenheim Fellowship, she published a short story in *Gyroscope*, a little magazine published in Palo Alto, Calif.

After Paris, the Tates returned to the South and lived in an old house that they named Benfolly, near Clarksville, Tenn., and also near Merry Mont. Gordon's first novel, *Penhally*, which was about the Civil War, was published in 1931. Her next book, *Aleck Maury, Sportsman* (1934), was based on tales of hunting and fishing that her father had told her. She wrote five other novels set in the South: *None Shall Look Back* (1937), *The Garden of Adonis* (1937), *Green Centuries* (1941), *The Women on the Porch* (1944), and *The Forest of* the South (1945), as well as many short stories, including the often-taught "The Captive."

The Tates were divorced in 1945, but soon remarried. Gordon converted to Catholicism in 1947, and the experience affected her writing, especially the novel *The Malefactors*, which appeared in 1956. She regarded this novel as her "big work." The Tates were divorced again, this time for good. Gordon lived in Princeton and commuted to New York to teach writing at Columbia University, City College, and the New School.

She wrote a great deal of criticism at this time, including *How to Read a Novel* (1957) and, with Tate, *The House of Fiction* (1950). *Old Red and Other Stories* appeared in 1963, and *The Glory of Hera*, a novel about Heracles, in 1972.

In 1973, at the age of 78, she moved to Texas to teach writing at the University of Dallas. Five years later she moved to San Cristobal, Mexico, to be near daughter Nancy and her husband, Percy Wood. Caroline Gordon died 11 April 1981 and is buried in Mexico.

ANN WALDRON
Princeton University

Larry Allums, *Southern Quarterly* (Spring 1990); Deborah Core, *Southern Quarterly* (Spring 1990); Robert E. Golden and Mary C. Sullivan, eds., *Flannery O'Connor and Caroline Gordon: A Reference Guide* (1977); Brita Lindberg-Seyersted, ed., *A Literary Friendship: Correspondence between Caroline Gordon and Ford Madox Ford* (1999); Veronica Makowsky, *Caroline Gordon: A Biography* (1989); Darcy A. McLamore, *Southern Quarterly* (Summer 1997); W. J. Stuckey, *Caroline Gordon* (1972); Walter Sullivan, in *Home Ground: Southern Autobiography*, ed. J. Bill Berry (1991); Ann Waldron, *Close Connections: Caroline Gordon and the Southern Renaissance* (1989).

Grau, Shirley Ann

(b. 1929) WRITER.

Although her novels and short stories are often set in southern locations with southern themes, Shirley Ann Grau has managed to transcend the label of a southern or regional writer by making characters that are vivid and multidimensional, thus giving them a universal application. A Pulitzer Prize winner for her 1965 novel *The Keepers of the House*, Grau continues to provide vivid, accurate, and multidimensional complexity to the southern traditions and people she knows best.

Born on 8 July 1929 in New Orleans, La., Shirley Ann Grau was raised in this exotic city, attended private grammar schools in the South, and later completed her bachelor's degree at Tulane University, where she was already recognized as a bright star in the literary world. After graduating Phi Beta Kappa in 1950, she continued her graduate studies at Tulane, where she did not finish her degree but began to publish her first professional stories. Grau married James Kern Feibleman, a professor at Tulane University, in 1955 and had four children.

Shirley Ann Grau has written several compilations of short stories, including *The Black Prince and Other Stories* (1955), *The Wind Shifting West* (1973), and *Nine Women* (1985). *The Black Prince and Other Stories* was highly praised, with Grau being compared to the likes of J. D. Salinger. In this collection of short stories that deals with the lives of both black and white inhabitants in the bayous of the Mississippi, Grau is able to capture the dualities of life in a southern culture: stories of darkness, violence, and death as well as peace, accomplishment, and life through the use of several points of view and elegant, descriptive prose.

Though Grau continued to write and in 1958 published her first novel entitled *The Hard Blue Sky*, which was shortly followed by *The House on Coliseum Street* in 1961, it was not until 1965 that she received critical acclaim for her Pulitzer Prize–winning novel *The Keepers of the House*. This novel deals with three generations of the Howland family, a plantation-owning family in a mythical town in the southern Delta. Grau's character, William Howland, a white plantation owner, takes a black woman, Margaret, as his mistress and housekeeper. Grau chose to address the then-controversial issue of interracial relationships by later revealing that Howland not only took Margaret as his mistress but also made her his wife, much to the dismay of his son-in-law, a segregationist politician. This elaborate tale is presented in a manner that is not philosophical or reflective, but merely addresses the impact of racial prejudice on a family, as well as a community, in a concise and direct manner.

Grau has also written several other novels. She completed *The Condor Passes* in 1971, and *Evidence of Love* was published in 1977. After a long hiatus from writing novels, Grau published *Roadwalkers* in 1994. Although most of her novels have been favorably received, Grau continues to be better known for her contributions of short stories and articles to major journals and magazines.

TRELLA R. WALKER
Georgia State University

Susan S. Kissel, *Moving On: The Heroines of Shirley Ann Grau, Anne Tyler, and Gail Godwin* (1996); Peggy Whitman Prenshaw, ed., *Women Writers of the Contemporary South* (1984); Paul Schlueter, *Shirley Ann Grau* (1981).

Green, Paul

(1894–1981) PLAYWRIGHT.
Paul Green was born 17 March 1894 on a farm in Harnett County, near Lillington, N.C. He worked side by side with the black tenants and hired hands, whom he regarded as part of his larger family. He dramatized this background in his poems, stories, novels, and plays.

In the early 1920s he wrote one-act folk dramas as a student at the University of North Carolina at Chapel Hill. *The No 'Count Boy*, first published in 1924 in *Theatre Arts Magazine*, gave Green his first recognition beyond the South. In 1925 *The No 'Count Boy* won the Belasco Cup competition in New York City. In *The Hawthorn Tree* (1943), Green elaborated on his imaginative concept of the "folk," referring to "the people whose manners, ethics, religious and philosophical ideals are more nearly derived from and controlled by the ways of the outside physical world . . . than by the ways and institutions of men in a specialized society." The success of *The No 'Count Boy* led to the publication of two collections of Paul Green's plays in 1925 and 1926. A longer version of one of these plays, *In Abraham's Bosom*, was awarded a Pulitzer Prize in May 1927. Other Broadway plays were *The Field God* and *The House of Connelly*, subtitled *A Drama of the Old South and the New*. These plays helped establish Paul Green's place among America's leading playwrights.

Instead of writing for what he termed the commercial theater of New York, however, he decided to produce his plays outdoors, amalgamating pageant, music, dance, and poetry into a theater he created and named "symphonic drama." Celebrating events and characters in history as well as nationalistic myths, Green defined symphonic drama in his 1948 "Author's Note" to *The Common Glory* as "that type of drama in which all elements of theatre art are used to sound together—one for all and all for one, a true democracy. The theatre of such a drama is sensitized and charged with a fierce potential of evocation and expressiveness for any moment." The most famous of these symphonic dramas is *The Lost Colony* (1937), the story of Sir Walter Raleigh's dream of settling America in the late 16th century. The play is produced each summer on the North Carolina coast.

Paul Green recognized early the dramatic richness of his native South, championing always his thought that "the greatest sin society can commit is to cause a man to miss his own life."

SHELBY STEPHENSON
University of North Carolina at Pembroke

Agatha Boyd Adams, *Paul Green of Chapel Hill*, ed. Richard Walser (1951); Laurence G. Avery, ed., *A Paul Green Reader* (1998), *A Southern Life: Letters of Paul Green, 1916–1981* (1994); Vincent Kenny, *Paul Green* (1971); Walter S. Lazenby Jr., *Paul Green* (1970); *Paul Green's Celebration of Man, with a Bibliography*, Proceedings of the Sixth Southern Writers' Symposium, Sanford, N.C. (1994); John Herbert Roper, *Paul Green: Playwright of the Real South* (2003).

Greene, Melissa Fay

(b. 1952) JOURNALIST AND NONFICTION WRITER.

Melissa Fay Greene has published many articles as a journalist, but her great success has been with her nonfiction books *Praying for Sheetrock* (1991), *The Temple Bombing* (1996), *Last Man Out* (2003), and *There Is No Me without You* (2006). A native of Macon, Ga., Greene worked for the Savannah office of Georgia Legal Services in 1975, a job that provided her with the inspiration for her first book, *Praying for Sheetrock*. The work exposes the startling corruption of McIntosh County in coastal Georgia.

McIntosh County's only town was Darien, and in the 1970s its black community had no electricity, plumbing, or paved roads. Their language was the rich brogue called Gullah, and Greene's book shows the social history of this poor small town. Here, the most powerful local authority was Sheriff Poppell, who allowed the black community enough petty privileges to keep them "from balking" at the racial inequalities they endured. Poppell himself became a very wealthy man by using his position to gain land from indebted local citizens and money through tourist traps. Eventually, one black man, Thurnell

Alston, emerged as a spokesperson, representing the righteous indignation necessary for positive change. Thurnell was the youngest of fourteen children, and he learned early that Poppell kept the black community hungry in order to control it. Thurnell became a union steward in his 20s when he was the first to question the discrepancies between working conditions of white and black workers. When Poppell shot a man for no good reason in broad daylight, Thurnell Alston led the black community in finally standing against him. Greene's thorough interviewing methods reveal through oral history how "good old boy" southern politics was turned into a civil rights victory.

Greene's second book, *The Temple Bombing*, points out how racism against blacks and Jews was connected in 1950s Georgia. Reform rabbi Jacob M. Rothschild from Pittsburgh was the primary target for the white supremacist bombing in 1958. Rothschild died in 1973, but Greene interviewed his wife Janice about Rothschild's courage and tenacity. At Temple and all over the South, Rothschild spoke out against all forms of racial inequality. Although his congregation hoped he would not stir up conflict, Rothschild believed that it was his duty to speak out for social improvements in Atlanta despite the risks. Greene offers the reader eye-opening historical context for the lingering dangerous racial struggles in the South.

Last Man Out looks at a tragic mine collapse in Nova Scotia in 1958 and explores the crisis dynamics of the miners who survived. However, Greene also focuses on a trip the few survivors took to Jekyll Island in Georgia. The main character in *Last Man Out* is Maurice Ruddick, the only black miner who survived after days of entrapment. Greene tells the story of Ruddick's struggle with racial injustice in Georgia.

Greene's prose often reads like suspense fiction. She consistently employs one historic figure (usually a lesser-known player) who emerges in the leading role in the historic drama. Race also has a great deal to do with Greene's topics. Indeed, readers will typically find that race is significant for the emerging leader whose rise Greene chronicles. Therefore, Greene's works of nonfiction serve not only as historical revelations but also as inspiring stories of individual courage amid prejudice.

RACHEL G. WALL
Georgia State University

Michael P. Johnson, *Nation* (December 1991); Wayne Kalyn, *People Weekly* (June 1996); Nicholas Lemann, *New York Review of Books* (September 1996); Anthony J. Lucas, *Washington Monthly* (August 1996); William S. McFeely, *Times Literary Supplement* (August 1996); Janet Wondra, *Georgia Review* (April 1996).

Grimsley, Jim
(b. 1955) WRITER.
Jim Grimsley—born on 21 September 1955 to a family influenced by poverty and alcoholism—grew up in rural Pollackville, N.C. After attending the University of North Carolina at Chapel Hill, Grimsley moved to Atlanta where, for nearly 20 years, he worked as a secretary in downtown Atlanta's Grady Memorial Hospital. During that time, Grimsley wrote steadily, both drama

and fiction, and built his reputation as a powerful voice in the southern gay literary movement alongside such writers as Dorothy Allison, Allan Gurganus, Randall Kenan, and Blanche McCrary Boyd. As a writer known for his Gothic vision of a harsh, unforgiving South, Grimsley joined the creative writing staff at Emory University in the fall of 1999.

Between 1983 and 1993, 14 of Grimsley's plays were produced and later collected in *Mr. Universe and Other Plays* (1998). *Mr. Universe* (1986), his third full-length play, opened at Atlanta's 7 Stages Theater and went on to productions in New Orleans, Los Angeles, and New York. The play, in which two drag queens decide to take home a bloody, mute bodybuilder whom they have found on a street corner, began Grimsley's role as playwright in residence at 7 Stages. He also served as playwright in residence at About Face Theater in Chicago (1999–2004). Many critics have compared Grimsley's work, with its sharp commentary on violence, sex, and American values, to the early work of Edward Albee.

Grimsley's debut novel, the semi-autobiographical *Winter Birds* (1994), struck American critics as "too dark" in its bitter portrayal of a cruel father and a harsh South. Like Danny, the main character, Grimsley's hemophilia forced him to spend long stretches of his childhood in bed. The novel was discovered at a German book festival, published there in 1992, and picked up in the United States in 1994, a decade after he'd finished it.

His second novel, *Dream Boy* (1995), won the American Library Association's Gay, Lesbian, and Bisexual Book Award for Literature. The dreamlike narrative plays with time, space, and reality against the backdrop of a haunting antebellum South. For his third novel, *My Drowning* (1997), Grimsley was named Georgia Author of the Year. He wrote a fourth novel, *Comfort and Joy* (1999), before shifting his focus from mainstream literature to the fantasy genre that had captured his childhood imagination. Grimsley has written three fantasy novels: *Kirith Kirin* (2000); *Boulevard* (2002), for which he was awarded his second Georgia Author of the Year; and *The Ordinary* (2004). Critics responded positively to his work in this genre, pointing out that the novels, while structured according to the classic epic plot, never sacrifice the complexity and lyrical prose of his earlier work.

Grimsley's work captures the lives of poor southern people—a quiet and intense pain and suffering—without condescension. His vivid, lyrical prose illuminates a South in which poverty and cruelty cast darkness over family life. Winner of a 2005 Academy Award in Literature from the American Academy of Arts and Letters, Grimsley's books have been translated into German, French, Spanish, Portuguese, Dutch, Hebrew, and Japanese. Grimsley lives in Atlanta and is playwright in residence at 7 Stages Theatre. He is the senior resident fellow in the Creative Writing Program at Emory University.

JODY BROOKS
Georgia State University

Kipp Cheng, *American Theatre* (March 1999); Lisa Howorth, *Publisher's Weekly* (November 1999); David R. Jarraway, *Gothic Studies* (April 2000); Ed Madden and Gary Richards, *North Carolina Literary Review* (2000); John L. Myers, *Lambda Book Report: A Review of Contemporary Gay and Lesbian Literature* (September–October 1995).

Grisham, John

(b. 1955) WRITER.

Since his first book was published in 1989, John Grisham has been one of America's most popular novelists. He was born in Jonesboro, Ark., in 1955 and grew up in Arkansas and northern Mississippi. He attended Mississippi State University as an undergraduate and the University of Mississippi Law School, receiving his law degree in 1981. As a young lawyer, he married Renée Jones and began practice in Southaven, Miss. From 1983 to 1990, he was a member of the Mississippi House of Representatives. Intrigued by cases he saw and heard about, he started writing fiction about legal issues.

Grisham's novels set in and near Mississippi show an intriguing dichotomy between an older small-town South in the fictional Ford County and a showy, wealthy, sometimes scary New South. Grisham's books about the edges of Mississippi—Memphis, New Orleans, and the Mississippi Gulf Coast—present a Sun Belt South, marked by new wealth, powerful and often corrupt corporations, organized crime, a powerful federal government, and the facelessness of modern society. Part of the uniqueness

of Grisham's rise to popularity was the juxtaposition of the southern setting of Memphis and organized crime in the extraordinarily popular work, *The Firm*.

It was in the interior of Mississippi, the fictional Ford County, where Grisham deals with traditionally southern settings and issues—racial segregation and white supremacy, face-to-face community life held together through family name, and long traditions. His Ford County novels include his first book, *A Time to Kill* (1989), *The Chamber* (1994), *The Summons* (2002), and *The Last Juror* (2004).

Grisham frequently deals with uncertainties about the law and the temptations of wealth. Many of Grisham's lawyers are young and somewhat rebellious figures. They know the law and use it for the benefit of their clients, but they do so outside the courtroom and sometimes outside conventional structures of the legal system. Some tire of the system and leave it. In some works such as *The Partner*, *The King of Torts*, and the nonfiction work *The Innocent Man*, Grisham takes a dark view of the law as a haven for self-interest. Some of Grisham's more recent books address an issue surely important in Grisham's own life—what to do with extraordinary wealth. In *The Testament*, *The Summons*, and especially *The King of Torts*, large and unexpected amounts of money raise complicated moral and legal issues.

Since moving from Mississippi to Virginia in the late 1990s, Grisham has expanded the range of settings and topics of his work. *A Painted House*, a slowly paced semiautobiographical novel set in 1950s rural Arkansas, discusses childhood, baseball, cotton, Mexican labor, and relative poverty but no legal issues. The first Grisham novel in which the setting is largely irrelevant to the story, *Skipping Christmas*, involves a couple who decide to avoid the typical expectations of Christmas. Other recent novels deal with high school football and CIA intrigue. *The Innocent Man*, Grisham's first nonfiction work, details the life of an Oklahoma man whose conviction for murder was overturned after years of effort and some new evidence.

Grisham's books have become so popular that his book signings are major events. His books frequently become the basis for movies; *A Time to Kill, The Firm, The Pelican Brief, The Client, The Chamber, The Rainmaker, The Runaway Jury, Skipping Christmas*, and *A Painted House* have all become popular movies.

TED OWNBY
University of Mississippi

Martin Arnold, *New York Times* (29 January 1998); Michelle Bearden, *Publishers Weekly* (22 February 1993); Cramer R. Cauthen and Donald G. Alpin III, *Studies in Popular Culture* (October 1996); Martha Duffy, *Time* (8 May 1995); Jennifer Ferranti, *Saturday Evening Post* (March–April 1997); Mary Beth Pringle, *John Grisham: A Critical Companion* (1997).

Grizzard, Lewis

(1946–1994) NEWSPAPER COLUMNIST AND HUMORIST.

Born 20 October 1946 in Fort Benning, Ga., Lewis Grizzard grew up in the small Georgia town of Moreland. His mother and he moved there in 1946 after she divorced his father, who was a professional soldier. Grizzard graduated from the University of Georgia and worked as a sportswriter in Athens and Atlanta, Ga., and in Chicago. He returned to Atlanta as a columnist for the *Atlanta Constitution* in 1978 and became so popular that by 1994 his column had been syndicated to more than 450 newspapers.

The South has a long tradition of newspaper columnists who have recorded the region's folkways and social manners. These columnists have drawn on and contributed to southern traditions of humor and storytelling. Grizzard was among the most successful and insightful contemporary observers of the changing South. From the New South bastion of Atlanta, Grizzard embodied the traditional southern white male's confrontation with modern America.

Grizzard grew up as a small-town boy, and he often wrote of his childhood home and of friends such as Weyman C. Wanamaker ("a great American"), Curtis "Fruit Jar" Hainey (the town drunk), and Hog Phillpot, Cordie Mae Poovey, and Kathy Sue Loudermilk. He told stories of real-life characters, ordinary people whose stories may be offbeat, nostalgic, sentimental, poignant, or tragic. Called the Faulkner of the common man, Grizzard championed his social class of origin—the plain (often poor) whites. Living in the capital of the new southern upper-middle class, he was also an astute observer of southern Yuppies. He chronicled, and sometimes protested, the appearance in Atlanta of "hanging fern" restaurants, singles bars,

BMWs replacing pickup trucks, and the drinking of wine coolers instead of beer.

Grizzard's significance was his assertion of southern distinctiveness and tradition in the face of a changing South. He defended southern traditions in an age when the small towns of his youth have been enveloped by modern cities such as Atlanta. In his books he tried "to keep the South alive and rekindle it." He wrote about country music, trains, pickup trucks, country stores, barbecue, long-necked bottles of beer, fishing, revivals, Sunday schools, saying grace before meals, snuff, pool halls, Vienna sausages, R.C. Cola, MoonPies, juke joints, honky tonks, front porches, dogs, and stock car and dirt-track racing. He was a die-hard University of Georgia football fan, often lambasting rival Georgia Tech. He was defined by his sex—champion of male rights in an age of women's liberation—and his age—a baby boomer who looked back fondly to growing up as part of the Elvis generation.

Lewis Grizzard's books include *Kathy Sue Loudermilk, I Love You* (1979), *Won't You Come Home, Billy Bob Bailey?* (1980), *Don't Sit under the Grits Tree with Anyone Else but Me* (1981), *They Tore Out My Heart and Stomped That Sucker Flat* (1982), *If Love Were Oil, I'd Be about a Quart Low* (1983), *Elvis Is Dead, and I Don't Feel So Good Myself* (1984), *Shoot Low, Boys—They're Ridin' Shetland Ponies* (1985), *My Daddy Was a Pistol and I'm a Son of a Gun* (1986), *Chili Dawgs Always Bark at Night* (1989), *Haven't Understood Anything since 1962 and Other Nekkid Truths* (1992), *Took a Lickin' and Kept on Tickin', and Now I Believe in Miracles* (1993).

CHARLES REAGAN WILSON
University of Mississippi

Peter Applebome, *Dixie Rising: How the South Is Shaping American Values, Politics, and Culture* (1996); David C. Foster, *Atlanta* (October 1986); Chuck Perry, *Don't Fence Me In: An Anecdotal Biography of Lewis Grizzard* (1995); David Treadwell, *Los Angeles Times* (19 June 1986).

Groom, Winston

(b. 1943) WRITER.
Born 23 March 1943 in Washington, D.C., Winston Groom grew up in Mobile, Ala., and attended the University of Alabama, where he was editor of the campus humor magazine, the *Mahout*. After graduation, Groom planned to attend law school and follow his father into the legal profession; instead, he went to Vietnam and served as a captain in the army from 1965 to 1968. After a brief return to Mobile, he accepted a job with the *Washington Star*, where he worked for eight years as a courts and police beat reporter. While at the newspaper he met Willie Morris, then serving as the paper's writer in residence, who encouraged his younger colleague that he had the potential to become a professional novelist. Groom moved to New York to begin a literary career, and though he enjoyed the company of such eminent figures as James Jones, George Plimpton, Kurt Vonnegut, Joseph Heller, Irwin Shaw, and Truman Capote, he spent little time writing. Within a year he returned to the Alabama Gulf Coast to settle down and write full-time about his experiences in

Vietnam and his observations of southern life and southern people. The trajectory of Groom's 14 published works of fiction and nonfiction has thus revealed an eclectic interest in the chronicling of war and of life in the American South.

The publication of Groom's first novel, *Better Times Than These* (1978), an account of the ill-fated company of the Seventh Cavalry in Vietnam, was received with admiration for its authenticity as well as criticized for its use of generalizations that tended toward stereotype. His second novel, *As Summers Die* (1980), addresses moral corruption and southern social politics in 1950s Louisiana and was winner of the Southern Library Association Best Fiction Award. Each of his next three novels—*Only* (1984), *Forrest Gump* (1986), and *Gone the Sun* (1988)—received mixed reviews and illustrated Groom's capacity to write in several diverse fiction genres, but the sensational success of the 1994 film adaptation of *Forrest Gump* would forever change the fortunes of an already respectable career. The character Forrest Gump became a cultural icon and a rerelease of the novel sold more than 1.7 million copies. A sequel to the novel, *Gump and Company* (1995), was followed by *Gumpisms: The Wit and Wisdom of Forrest Gump* (1995), as well as two Forrest Gump cookbooks.

Since the Forrest Gump phenomenon, Groom has primarily published nonfiction, building upon a considerable body of journalism that began with *Conversations with the Enemy: The Story of PFC Robert Garwood* (1983), written with Duncan Spencer and nominated for the Pulitzer Prize. In historical contexts as various as *Shrouds of Glory: From Atlanta to Nashville—The Last Great Campaign of the Civil War* (1994), *A Storm in Flanders: The Ypres Salient, 1914–1918—Tragedy and Triumph on the Western Front* (2002), and *1942: The Year That Tried Men's Souls* (2005), Groom continues to exhibit a penchant for narration that interweaves events on a grand scale while engaging the reader with intimate portraitures through individual diaries and letters. His latest work, *Patriotic Fire: Andrew Jackson and Jean Lafitte at the Battle of New Orleans* (2006), further establishes Groom as a contemporary chronicler of memorable men and the nation's past.

Winston Groom's other books are *Such a Pretty, Pretty Girl* (1999) and *The Crimson Tide: An Illustrated History of Football at the University of Alabama* (2000).

PATRICK BONDS
Louisiana State University

Bill Caton, ed., *Fighting Words: Words on Writing from 21 of the Heart of Dixie's Best Contemporary Authors* (1995); *Contemporary Authors Online* (2006); *Contemporary Novelists* (2001); *Contemporary Southern Writers*, ed. Roger Matuz (1999).

Grooms, Anthony

(b. 1955) WRITER.
Anthony Grooms's work deftly draws complex characters struggling to find their way amid the civil rights movement and its consequences in the ever-changing South.

Born in Charlottesville, Va., Grooms

grew up 20 miles east of there in rural Louisa County. His father, a refrigeration mechanic, and his mother, a textile worker and housewife, had six children. Grooms, the oldest, was 12 when his parents enrolled him in a white public school under Virginia's "Freedom of Choice" program—the state's effort to subvert desegregation. (White politicians expected blacks to be too intimidated to attend white schools.) The experience played a pivotal part in Grooms's life and ultimately his writing.

Grooms attended the College of William and Mary, where he studied theater and speech, writing two plays that were produced at the school. After graduation in 1978, he moved to the Washington, D.C., area, where the novelist Richard Bausch encouraged him to study with him at George Mason University's M.F.A. program in creative writing.

After completing his graduate degree in 1984, Grooms moved to Georgia to teach creative writing and English. His first book was a short collection of poetry, *Ice Poems* (1988), published while he was teaching at the University of Georgia in Athens. *Trouble No More* (1995), a book of short stories, was published by a small California press. Ten years later, the Georgia Center for the Book honored the collection, choosing it for the state's Top 25 Reading List and naming it the 2006 Book All Georgia Reads, a selection resulting in its reprinting. Stories in the collection, several of which are narrated by children, include characters coping with reluctance and the fear of risking their own

relative comfort and safety in exchange for larger social gains achieved through resistance to segregation.

Bombingham (2001), Grooms's first published novel, was received with favorable reviews and honors. It is the story of an African American soldier in the Vietnam War recalling childhood memories of Birmingham's protest marches and bombings, as well as his family's trials and tribulations with faith and illness. Diane Roberts, writing in the *Atlanta Journal-Constitution*, said that "most Americans see the civil rights movement in cartoon simplicity. Of course, the reality of Birmingham in the early 1960s was not quite so black and white. Grooms gets at the heart of the horror in a terse, unsentimental, almost surgical first novel, a coming-of-age story where maturity is gained only through the most bitter suffering." *Bombingham* earned Grooms his second Lillian Smith Book Award (the first coming for *Trouble No More*), a citation that recognizes books for their messages of social and racial justice; it also was a finalist for the Hurston/Wright Legacy Award.

A professor of creative writing at Kennesaw State University northwest of Atlanta, Grooms recently completed a novel that centers on a lynching in Georgia in the late 1940s. He spent five months in 2001 teaching in Ghana and is working on a book of poems that grew out of the experience. In 2006 Grooms spent four months as a Fulbright lecturer in Stockholm, Sweden, where he researched a novel based on a community of African American expatriates that began there in the 1960s, many of whom had deserted from the U.S. military during the Vietnam War.

JOE SAMUEL STARNES
Saint Joseph's University

Pearl A. McHaney, foreword to *Trouble No More* (2005); Don O'Briant, *Atlanta Journal-Constitution* (19 July 1992).

Gurganus, Allan

(b. 1947) WRITER.
Allan Gurganus, one of the most memorable personalities in contemporary southern literature, was born in Rocky Mount, N.C., on 11 June 1947, to a family he describes as "shabbily genteel." That essence, of the aspiring-yet-earthbound, has proved to be a magnetic trait in his fiction as well, because Gurganus's work has won both popular and critical acclaim.

Gurganus's literary training began in an unlikely place: the United States Navy, aboard the USS *Yorktown*. Working as a naval cartographer during the Vietnam War, Gurganus spent his internment on the sea devouring more than a thousand books stowed in the ship's library. Later, his formal education included studying under such accomplished writers as Grace Paley, Stanley Elkin, and John Cheever, the latter at the prestigious Iowa Writers' Workshop. It was Cheever who launched Gurganus's publishing career by sending "Minor Heroism," without the author's knowledge, to the *New Yorker*.

From that first publication in 1974, Gurganus's bibliography to date is concise but well honored. His first book, *Oldest Living Confederate Widow Tells*

All, published in 1989, was awarded the Sue Kaufman Prize for Best First Work of Fiction and spent eight months on the *New York Times* best-seller list. *White People* (1991), a collection of short stories accrued over a 20-year period, won Gurganus the Los Angeles Times Book Prize for Fiction and the Southern Book Award for Fiction from the Southern Book Critics Circle, was a finalist for the PEN/Faulkner Award, and also was a *New York Times* Notable Book. Gurganus's second novel, *Plays Well with Others* (1997), earned him the National Magazine Prize, and *The Practical Heart: Four Novellas* (2001) won the Lambda Literary Award for excellence in gay and lesbian literature. Among other journals, his fiction has appeared in the *Paris Review*, the *Atlantic*, *GRANTA*, and *Harper's Magazine*.

Oldest Living Confederate Widow Tells All, Gurganus's debut novel, typifies his work in all but its length. An epochal 718 pages, the story is a recounting of Lucy Marsden, a Civil War widow nearing the end of her life in the modern day. Driving Lucy's narrative is a strong need to account for her husband's life, her life, and the lives of all whom she has loved and mythologized. Throughout, *Widow*'s story excels in voice, flourishing with diverse personalities that engender a fertile language— a defining characteristic of Gurganus's fiction. From pedophiles (as in the short story "Art History") to white-guilt-laden insurance salesmen ("Blessed Assurance") to the myriad slaves, children, coots, and witches channeled doubly through the voice of a 99-year-old

Civil War widow (*Widow*), Gurganus discovers the music locked inside each character's epistemology and native tongue. For better or for worse, these voices often wax (sometimes darkly) with unabashed, bighearted humanism, but remain rooted by their sense of accountability: accountability for personal actions, for the past, for the social present.

Off the page, this thematic emphasis is no abstraction for Gurganus, but a definite practice. He has been a steady figure in the gay community, frequently lecturing, supporting AIDS awareness, and cofounding the organization Writers against Jesse Helms (a North Carolina Senator known for his opposition to AIDS research and lesbian, gay, bisexual, and transgender rights). His story "Minor Heroism" holds the distinction of featuring the first gay character to be published in the *New Yorker*.

Allan Gurganus currently spends his time between homes in Chapel Hill, N.C., and New York City. His peregrinations have led him to the U.S. Navy, to teaching positions at Stanford, Duke, the Iowa Writers' Workshop, and Sarah Lawrence, and, early in his career, a brief stint as a painter at the Pennsylvania School of Fine Arts. Along with other southern writers, such as Eudora Welty, visual art figures into Gurganus's creative process. He has illustrated three chapbooks of his own work and is responsible for the calligraphy on the cover of *Widow*. One medium informs the other, evident in the visual vibrancy of his prose, winning him accolades from the outset of his career more than

30 years ago. And if—as Gurganus has often quipped—life for a writer begins at 40, then we can expect a lifetime of his work yet to come.

BRANDON WICKS
George Mason University

Will Blythe, ed., *Why I Write: Thoughts on the Craft of Fiction* (1998); Naomi Epel, ed., *Writers Dreaming: Twenty-six Writers Talk about Their Dreams and the Creative Process* (1993); Dwight Garner, *Salon.com* (December 1997); Susan Ketchin, *The Christ-Haunted Landscape: Faith and Doubt in Southern Fiction* (1994); James Wilcox, *New York Times* (13 August 1989).

Haley, Alex

(1921–1992) WRITER.

Alexander Murray Palmer Haley was born in Ithaca, N.Y., on 11 August 1921, but his family joined relatives in Henning, Tenn., while Haley was still an infant. As a child in Henning, Haley listened to the familial stories of an African ancestor who was kidnapped from Africa and struggled against enslavement and acculturation in the American South. Haley carried these stories with him for decades until they provided the inspiration for the literary and cultural phenomenon of *Roots: The Saga of an American Family* (1976).

The Haley family moved in 1929 from Henning to Normal, Ala., where Haley's father taught agriculture at Normal Institute and his mother taught grade school. Haley joined the U.S. Coast Guard in 1939, and he served for the next 20 years. He developed his skills as a writer by penning letters, sketches of Coast Guard life, and

Alex Haley, best-selling author of Roots, 1980s
(Robert Jordan, photographer, University of Mississippi, Oxford)

articles. Recognizing his talent, the Coast Guard appointed him chief journalist, and when Haley retired from the service in 1959, he was determined to become a professional writer.

He led a penurious existence in New York until *Playboy* hired him to inaugurate its interview section in 1962. Haley interviewed various artists, athletes, and political figures, including Miles Davis, Cassius Clay, and Malcolm X. His interview with Malcolm X led to a joint literary endeavor in which Haley ghostwrote *The Autobiography of Malcolm X* (1965). The enduring popular and academic success of the autobiography testifies to the effective blend of Haley's literary talent with Malcolm X's experiences.

This project seems to have stirred Haley's desire to understand more about his own American experience, and he launched himself into the monumen-

tal project of researching and writing a family chronicle beginning with the African ancestor whose memory survived in his family's oral tradition. Drawing on hints from this tradition, Haley traced his ancestry through numerous archives and libraries to the Mandingo village of Juffure in West Africa, where a youth named Kunta Kinte had been kidnapped in 1767. Haley spent 12 years researching and writing *Roots*, and he spared no efforts in his attempt at realism. He even traveled in the hold of a cargo ship from Africa to the United States in his attempt to re-create the horrors of the middle passage as accurately as possible.

A historical novel that Haley described as a mixture of fact and feeling, *Roots* chronicles seven generations of his family history. The first half of the novel relates life in Juffure, Kunta Kinte's kidnapping, and his life in slavery, while the remainder of the novel presents the experience of subsequent generations in slavery and freedom. *Roots* emphasizes the crosscurrents of resistance and acculturation that mark the African American experience. As the cultural distance from Africa increases with time, the oral tradition that passed from one generation to the next provides the tenuous but enduring link to the family's African roots. The novel concludes with Haley's autobiographical account of how he drew on family lore to retrace two centuries of family history to Kunta Kinte.

Roots was an immediate success, selling more than a million copies in its original hardback publication and millions more over the years as a paperback. It was a *New York Times* best seller for months and has been translated into dozens of languages. Haley won the National Book Award and a Pulitzer Prize in 1976. The NAACP awarded him a Spingarn Medal in 1977, and the U.S. Senate passed a resolution honoring his work. When ABC released a 12-hour miniseries based on the novel, Haley's work reached an unprecedented audience. With 130 million viewers watching the eight-part series, *Roots* proved to be the most successful television production to date, and its sequel, *Roots: The Next Generation* (1979), enjoyed similar success.

The accolades and popularity, however, were accompanied by less enthusiastic responses as well. Critics have taken issue with the historical accuracy of some elements, and Haley was sued for plagiarism by both Harold Cour-

lander, who won, and Margaret Walker, who did not. Neither the questions of accuracy nor the charges of plagiarism tempered the popularity of *Roots*. Haley's work is broadly credited with stimulating an American dialogue about slavery as well as producing a widespread interest in family history and genealogy. He was working on several projects when he died of a heart attack in 1992, and David Stevens completed both *Alex Haley's Queen* (1993) and *Mama Flora's Family* (1998).

ANDREW B. LEITER
Wake Forest University

Harold Bloom, ed., *Alex Haley and Malcolm X's the Autobiography of Malcolm X* (1996); Mary Kemp Davis, in *Contemporary Fiction Writers of the South: A Bio-Bibliographical Sourcebook*, ed. Joseph M. Flora and Robert Bain (1993); Leslie Fishbein, in *Why Docudrama? Fact-Fiction on Film and TV*, ed. Alan Rosenthal (1999); Marilyn Kern-Foxworth, in *Dictionary of Literary Biography*, vol. 41, ed. Trudier Harris and Thadious M. Davis (1985); David Chioni Moore, *Resources for American Literary Study* (1996).

Hannah, Barry

(b. 1942) WRITER.

Born in Meridian, Miss., in 1942, Barry Hannah holds degrees from Mississippi College (B.A., 1964) and the University of Arkansas (M.A., 1966, and M.F.A., 1967). With the exception of a one-year stint (1980) in Hollywood working as a writer for filmmaker Robert Altman, Hannah has supported his writing habit by teaching at various colleges and universities: Clemson University (literature and fiction) 1967–73; Middlebury College (writer in residence) 1974–75; University of Alabama, Tuscaloosa (literature and fiction) 1975–80; University of Iowa (writer in residence) 1981; University of Mississippi (writer in residence) 1982; University of Montana (writer in residence) 1982–83; University of Mississippi (writer in residence) 1984–85 and 1987 to the present. As writer in residence, he has worked with such contemporary writers as Cynthia Shearer, Donna Tartt, and the late Larry Brown.

Hannah has published eight novels: *Geronimo Rex* (1972), *Nightwatchmen* (1973), *Ray* (1981), *The Tennis Handsome* (1983), *Hey, Jack!* (1987), *Boomerang* (1989), *Never Die* (1991), and *Yonder Stands Your Orphan* (2001); and four short-story collections: *Airships* (1978), *Captain Maximus* (1985), *Bats out of Hell* (1993), and *High Lonesome* (1996).

Hannah's first published novel, *Geronimo Rex*, earned him a nomination for the National Book Award and won the William Faulkner Prize for Writing. He won the Arnold Gingrich Short Fiction Award for *Airships* (1978), an Award for Literature from the American Institute of Arts and Letters (1979), and the William Faulkner Award for Literature from the William Faulkner Foundation in Rennes, France, for *Bats out of Hell* (1997). In 1996 Hannah received a Pulitzer Prize nomination for *High Lonesome*. He has also received a Guggenheim Fellowship and the Robert Penn Warren Lifetime Achievement Award. He has been elected to the Fellowship of Southern Writers, and in 2003 he won the PEN/Malamud Award for Excellence in the Short Story.

Hannah's prose exhibits much of the same linguistic pyrotechnics as the prose of his fellow southerner and near contemporary Lewis Nordan, but Hannah's work is much darker. Most of Hannah's most memorable characters, and there are many of them, are defeated and somewhat self-loathing. The narrator of *Tennis Handsome* seems to sum up their collective lot when he says, "Affection and esteem can bear hard on a man who is convinced he's worthless." And the narrator of "Power and Light," the screen treatment (published as the final work in *Captain Maximus*) Hannah wrote at the behest of Robert Altman, describes the actions of Fritz Walls, another character in the work: "He gathers the hose, but he hates it. He hates his wristwatch when he looks at it, despises the cigarette he's lighting."

The anger in Hannah's work is not limited to characters; places suffer too. Ray, the eponymous narrator of Hannah's third novel, says:

> Ohio is silly.
> Ken, my nephew, once asked me as we were going to sleep after some snapper fishing in Destin, Florida: "Promise me something, Uncle Ray?"
> "What?"
> "That when I die, I won't be from Ohio."

The narrator in "Fly, Ride, Penetrate, Loiter," in *Captain Maximus* observes, "There is a poison in Tuscaloosa that draws souls toward the low middle."

Ray, Hannah's third novel, is his most experimental, most complex, and most fragmented work. It weaves together material introduced in short stories in *Airships*, material concerning Confederate general J. E. B. Stuart, and material concerning Vietnam into the nightmarish background against which we see the life of Dr. Ray Forrest disintegrate. Form follows theme, and as Ray disintegrates, the chapters he is narrating become shorter and more fragmented.

As messed up as he is, Ray is the figure of the modern educated South, haunted by both its past and its present; therefore, it is good to know that Hannah is at work on the manuscript of *Long, Last, Happy*. In it "a busted doctor, Ray Forrest, becomes a lay preacher amidst a series of church, mosque, temple, and cathedral burnings, in which his own nephew is involved."

JAMES A. PERKINS
Westminster College

Jeff Chapman, Christopher Giroux, and Brigham Navins, eds., *Contemporary Literary Criticism* (1996); Mark J. Charney, *Barry Hannah* (1992); Lacey Galbraith, *Paris Review* (Winter 2004); Barry Hannah, *Playboy* (August 2007); David Madden, in *Southern Writers at Century's End*, ed. Jeffrey J. Folks and James A. Perkins (1997); Jason Mitchell, in *Contemporary Southern Writers*, ed. Roger Matuz (1999); Ruth D. Weston, *Barry Hannah, Postmodern Romantic* (1998).

Hardwick, Elizabeth

(b. 1916) WRITER AND SOCIAL CRITIC.

In 1962, 10 years before the Equal Rights Amendment was proposed, Elizabeth Hardwick took women's work from home to the front pages of the *New York Review of Books*, a magazine she founded that focuses on literature, culture, and current affairs.

A social commentator, literary critic, novelist, and short-story writer, Hardwick was born in Lexington, Ky., to Eugene and Mary Ramsey Hardwick. One of 11 children, Hardwick distinguished herself by earning A.B. and M.A. degrees at the University of Kentucky. Leaving Lexington in 1939, she moved to New York and studied at Columbia University for the next two years.

Although she spent her earliest days as a writer in Kentucky, Hardwick did not consider herself a southern writer. She once told an interviewer that her aim was to be a "New York Jewish intellectual." She explores place and sensibility in her first novel, *The Ghostly Lover*, in 1945. Focusing on a young Kentucky woman's adjustment to life in New York, the novel is set in New York City and Hardwick's native South. In 1947 Hardwick was awarded a Guggenheim Fellowship for fiction. After *The Ghostly Lover* was published, an editor of the *Partisan Review* invited her to become a contributor. This invitation marked what would become a prolific career in literary criticism with submissions to publications like the *New Yorker*, *Sewanee Review*, the *New Republic*, and *Harper's*.

In 1949 Hardwick married poet Robert Lowell and traveled throughout Europe and the United States. Their domestic travel, which facilitated Lowell's teaching career at the University of Iowa, University of Cincinnati, and the University of Indiana, landed them in Boston in 1954. Hardwick published her second novel, *The Simple Truth*, in 1955, and it also received mixed reviews. Hardwick and Lowell's only child, daughter Harriet Winslow Lowell, was born in Boston in 1957.

The family relocated to New York in 1960, and Hardwick once more became active on the scene of social and literary criticism. In 1962 she joined with like-minded writers and social critics, Jason and Barbara Epstein, Robert Silvers, and A. Whitney Ellsworth to establish the *New York Review of Books*. The first issue appeared during the publishing strike in the winter of 1963. As advisory editor, Hardwick had two pieces in the first issue, which also featured a letter to readers that stated that the *New York Review of Books* was created not only to "fill the gap" created by the strike that affected the book review offices of the *New York Times* and the *Herald Tribune* but also "to take the opportunity . . . to publish the sort of literary journal which . . . is needed in America." Hardwick continues to serve as an advisory editor.

Hardwick's marriage to Lowell ended in 1972. She published her third novel, *Sleepless Nights*, in 1979 and won public and critical praise for what is considered her most inspiring work. Noted for its evocative, lyrical prose and nominated for the National Book Critics Circle Award, *Sleepless Nights* is a collection of autobiographical vignettes that relate a woman's looking back over her life, including a broken marriage and time spent in Kentucky, Boston, and Manhattan.

A recipient of a Gold Medal from the American Academy of Arts and Letters, Hardwick is also the author of a Herman Melville biography (2000) and four collections of essays, *A View of My Own: Essays on Literature and Society* (1962), *Seduction and Betrayal: Women and Literature* (1974), *Bartleby in Manhattan* (1986), and *Sight Readings: American Fictions* (1998). A collection of her papers (1934–91) is held at the Harry Ransom Humanities Research Center at the University of Texas at Austin. She resides in Manhattan and Maine.

JONI JOHNSON WILLIAMS
Georgia State University

Louis Harap, *In the Mainstream: The Jewish Presence in Twentieth-Century American Literature, 1950s–1980s* (1987); Elizabeth Hardwick, *A View of My Own: Essays on Literature and Society* (1962); Elizabeth Hardwick, *New York Times Book Review* (1979); Elizabeth Hardwick, *New York Review of Books* (2006); Harry Ransom Humanities Research Center, *Elizabeth Hardwick* (2006); James Kibler, *American Novelists since World War II* (1980); Robert Lowell, *New York Review of Books* (1963).

Harington, Donald

(b. 1935) WRITER.

Donald Harington was born 22 December 1935 in Little Rock, Ark., the son of Conrad Fred and Jimmie (Walker) Harington. As a boy he spent summer vacations with his grandparents in the Arkansas Ozarks, listening to people swapping stories in their general store and absorbing the language and culture of the region. That language remained in his imagination after he lost his hearing to meningitis at the age of 12. He calls himself an Arkansawyer but his novels, while celebrating the rural Ozarks, engage the reader with a combination of ribald humor, lyricism, and postmodern technical artistry that transcends regional boundaries.

Harington received a B.A. in 1956 and an M.F.A. in art in 1958 from the University of Arkansas. He married Nita Harrison 20 July 1957, and the couple had three daughters. The marriage ended in divorce. He received an M.A. in art history from Boston University in 1959 and did doctoral work at Harvard University. For the next 25 years Harington wrote novels rooted in the Arkansas Ozarks while he taught at Bennett College in North Carolina, Windham College in Vermont, the University of Missouri at Rolla, the University of Pittsburgh, and South Dakota State University. He married Kim McClish on 8 October 1983, and the couple collaborated on a book, *Let Us Build Us a City: Eleven Lost Towns* (1986). In 1986 he returned to the University of Arkansas, where he is professor of art history and has been recognized for excellence in teaching. He and his wife live in Fayetteville.

Harington's work has been highly appreciated by other writers. Among the general public his following, though not large, is enthusiastic and loyal. His books have sold steadily enough that two publishers have issued reprint editions of his work. He has received several local and regional literary prizes, the Porter Prize in 1987 and the Heasley Prize at Lyon College in 1998. In 2002 *Southern Quarterly* published a special issue on Donald Harington. In 2003 the Fellowship of Southern Writers awarded

him the Robert Penn Warren Award for Fiction. In 2006 the *Oxford American* presented him its first Lifetime Award for Southern Literature.

Harington has resisted being defined as an Arkansas author, however, or even as a southern writer. He includes William Styron and Vladimir Nabokov along with folklorist Vance Randolph among influences on his work. Like William Faulkner's works, Harington's contain characters, places, and incidents that recur in successive novels, particularly those set in the Ozark village of Stay More, introduced in *Lightning Bug*. One of these is entitled *The Cockroaches of Stay More*.

He uses some of the conventions of postmodernist fiction, but with a difference. Sometimes he blurs the boundaries between author and story, throws real-life people together with his characters, or moves characters between the narrative itself and stories it contains. "My work is not metafictional in the sense of escaping the bounds of ordinary storytelling. I have always considered storytelling the most important thing," Harington explained. "I've played around with tense shifts and metaphysical devices simply to give the story greater impact and to make the reader an important participant in the story."

ETHEL C. SIMPSON
University of Arkansas

Ed Gray, *Wall Street Journal* (11 March 2006); Izzy Grinspan, *Believer Magazine* (February 2006); *Southern Quarterly* (Winter 2002), special issue on Donald Harington.

Harper, Frances Ellen Watkins

(1825–1911) WRITER AND REFORMER.
Born Frances Ellen Watkins on 24 September 1825 in Baltimore, Md., Harper
was the only child of free parents, who
both passed away when she was only
three years old. Harper then went to live
with her aunt and her uncle, William
Watkins, an educator and abolitionist,
and attended William Wilson's Academy
for Negro Youth, a school for free blacks
that was owned by Watkins. At age 13,
Harper's formal education ended, and
she began to hire out for domestic work.
In 1845 she published her first book of
poetry, *Forest Leaves*, and though no
copy of the volume exists today, scholars
speculate that some of the poems may
have been reprinted in later volumes.

After the Fugitive Slave Act passed
in 1850, allowing for free blacks in slave
states to be sold into slavery, Harper
moved to Columbus, Ohio, to teach at
Union Seminary, becoming the first
female professor of the school. Wanting
to be more active in the abolitionist
cause, Harper moved to Little York, Pa.,
a town on the Underground Railroad.
In 1854 she became the first woman to
be a full-time lecturer for the Maine
Anti-Slavery Society, and her employment as such precipitated invitations
from other groups. That same year, she
published *Poems on Miscellaneous Subjects*, which sold so many copies that 20
editions were printed during Harper's
lifetime. Additionally, during this time,
Harper traveled widely in New England,
the Midwest, and Canada, speaking
to garner support for the abolitionist
movement. She also published abolitionist essays in a number of journals,
and her short story, "The Two Offers"
(1859), is the first published short story
written by an African American woman.

In 1860 Frances married Fenton
Harper and moved to his farm in
Columbus, Ohio, where she gave birth
to their only child, Mary. After Fenton's
death, in 1864, Harper began lecturing
again, and after the Civil War, she traveled through the South twice between
1867 and 1871, teaching emancipated
slaves. Her experiences in the Reconstruction South led Harper to become
concerned with the condition of emancipated women and to write her only
novel, *Iola Leroy; or, Shadows Uplifted*
(1892), which was praised by critics for
the ways it addresses issues of racial
equality during Reconstruction. Heralded as one of the founders of black
feminist thought, Harper saw the connections between gender and race and
worked to end both racism and sexism.
She particularly advocated economic
independence for black women and
encouraged them to redefine notions of
"true womanhood."

Working for both women's and
African Americans' suffrage, Harper
cofounded and was an officer of the National Association of Colored Women.
Additionally, she was a member of the
American Equal Rights Association and
director of the American Association of
Colored Youth. Harper also participated
in a number of other organizations,
working for issues such as temperance.

On 20 February 1911, after a long
period of health problems, Harper died
of heart disease. Though she lived most

of her adult life outside of the South, Harper made lasting contributions to the genre of southern literature. In *Iola Leroy* and *Sketches of Southern Life* (1870), she voices concerns of African American women in the South, and she depicts slaves as active agents in their emancipation and frees them from prominent stereotypes of the day. She also contributes to a tradition of protest literature among African American writers. Indeed, Harper's poetry inspired many young poets of the 1960s to employ their creative writing in protesting segregation.

Other works by Harper include *Moses: A Story of the Nile* (1868), *Sowing and Reaping: A Temperance Story* (1867), *Trial and Triumph* (1888), *Atlanta Offering* (1895), *Martyr of Alabama and Other Poems* (1895), *Poems* (1895), and *Eventide* (1854), which was published under the pseudonym, Effie Afton.

AMY SCHMIDT
University of Mississippi

Harold Bloom, ed., *Writers of English: Lives and Works; Black American Women Poets and Dramatists* (1996); Susanne B. Dietzel, in *The History of Southern Women's Literature*, ed. Carolyn Perry and Mary Louise Weaks (2002); Brenda Wilkinson, *Black Stars: African American Women Writers* (2000).

Harris, George Washington

(1814–1869) WRITER.
Harris was born in Allegheny City, Pa., but his parents were probably North Carolinians. At five he was taken to Knoxville, Tenn., by his married half brother, Samuel Bell, who opened a metalworking shop. Harris received little formal education, was early apprenticed, and by his late teens had served as captain for a Tennessee River steamboat. In 1835 he married Mary Emiline Nance, tried large-scale farming in Blount County, Tenn., and lost his land, a slave, and even household goods. By 1843 he was back in Knoxville operating a metalworking and jewelry shop.

While living on his farm Harris had already begun to contribute to local newspapers, and during the next decade he practiced a variety of literary forms and published in the internationally circulated sporting magazine, the *New York Spirit of the Times*. During 1843 Harris published, under the pen name "Mr. Free," four formal letters describing rural customs, sports, and hunts. Presented from a gentlemanly perspective, the Tennessee backwoods is evoked in versions of pastoral. In 1845, in "The Knob Dance," Harris created a fictional account of a ritual frolic presented in the comic dialect of a narrator whose extravagance and sense of community are richly expressive of deep patterns of the folk culture. Action and language celebrate freedom, intensity, and the joys of the body.

In 1854, again in the *Spirit*, Harris expanded his comic depiction of southern backwoods life with the creation of his vital, intense, "nat'ral born durn'd fool," Sut Lovingood, a Tennessee youth who declares his brains are "mos' ove the time onhook'd," recounting his family background in a comic, grotesque fable of conflict with his father and flight from home. Throughout the 1850s Harris created a variety of adventures for his character, many revised and included in *Sut Lovingood's Yarns* in 1867.

Although Harris's achievement is complex, two areas stand out. Harris peoples his backwoods with self-assertive characters and develops Sut as an arresting seer. Sut's folk speech, metaphorically rich and presented in painstakingly detailed dialect, is an unsurpassed creative distillation of the American comic vernacular. Inseparable from this aesthetic achievement and embodied in it is a set of unique, uninhibited southern social and political ideas.

Harris's topics cluster around the prankster's search for excitement, the family and community, the reduction of authority figures—sheriffs, judges, preachers, and fathers—and the complexities of relations between the sexes. Some episodes convey the responses of the insular community to outsiders, such as blacks, Jews, Catholics, Mormons, and Yankees. Harris's first political targets were Tennesseans, but later he similarly treated many national figures, including James Buchanan, John C. Frémont, Abraham Lincoln, and numerous abolitionists. Other targets were "strong-minded women," philosophers, and utopian theorizers. His reductive satires express dramatically the narrowest fears and hatreds of his community.

Writers such as Mark Twain, William Faulkner, and Flannery O'Connor have praised Harris's characterization and language. Critics' responses have been from "Rabelaisian" to "repellent." Clearly, Harris's range extends from vituperative satire to the ambiguities of grotesque realism and, finally, to the celebratory mode of folk humor.

MILTON RICKELS
University of Southwestern Louisiana

James E. Caron and M. Thomas Inge, eds., *Sut Lovingood's Nat'ral Born Yarnspinner: Essays on George Washington Harris* (1996); George Washington Harris, *High Times and Hard Times*, ed. M. Thomas Inge (1967), *Sut Lovingood: Yarns Spun by a "Nat'ral Born Durn'd Fool"* (1867); Milton Rickels, *George Washington Harris* (1965).

Harris, Joel Chandler

(1848–1908) WRITER.

Harris, the illegitimate son of Mary Harris and an Irish laborer, was born on 9 December 1848, near Eatonton, Ga. His death from nephritis came in Atlanta on 3 July 1908.

Harris's formal schooling was spotty, but he read widely in world, English, and American literature, with Goldsmith's *The Vicar of Wakefield* being his favorite book. His major training came at the hands of Joseph Addison Turner, who edited the *Countryman*, a weekly newspaper published at the middle Georgia plantation Turnwold. From 1862 to 1866 young Harris worked on the paper, read from Turner's library, and listened to the speech and tales of the plantation blacks. It was his beginning as a writer.

Harris worked for several other newspapers before joining the staff of the *Atlanta Constitution* in 1876 as associate editor. Here he began publishing his famous Uncle Remus stories, using the black dialect he had heard on the plantation. His fame soon spread nationally because of the Uncle Remus tales, and three major Remus books followed: *Uncle Remus: His Songs and His Sayings* (1880), *Nights with Uncle Remus* (1883), and *Uncle Remus and His Friends* (1892). Numerous other volumes of the tales were published both during his lifetime and posthumously.

Diverse in taste and talents, Harris also wrote six children's books, all set on a Georgia plantation, and several novelettes and novels—most importantly, *Sister Jane: Her Friends and Acquaintances* (1896), a novel that depicts antebellum Georgia, and *Gabriel Tolliver: A Story of Reconstruction* (1902), his major long work. Other ventures into long narrative include an autobiographical novel, *On the Plantation* (1892), the setting of which is Turnwold. Adept at the short story, Harris produced five collections, the main ones being *Mingo, and Other Sketches in Black and White* (1884) and *Free Joe and Other Georgia Sketches* (1887). And with his son Julian he established *Uncle Remus's Magazine* in 1907.

Although Harris disavowed regionalism in art ("My idea is that truth is more important than sectionalism, and that literature that can be labeled Northern, Southern, Western, or Eastern, is not worth labeling at all"), his writings are unsurpassed in reflecting the southern environment. His short stories are born of the Georgia soil, his novels echo the strains of the Civil War South, his editorials for the *Constitution* deal with southern social and political issues, and, of course, his famed Uncle Remus tales capture the diction and dialect of the plantation blacks while presenting genuine folk legends. Enlivened with gentle humor and irony, Harris's portraits of Georgia blacks and his faithful handling of the folktales constitute his major contributions to southern and American literature. His was a southern voice with a national range.

DAVID B. KESTERSON
North Texas State University

R. Bruce Bickley Jr., *Joel Chandler Harris* (1978), with Karen L. Bickley and Thomas H. English, *Joel Chandler Harris: A Reference Guide* (1978); Walter M. Brasch, *Brer Rabbit, Uncle Remus, and the "Cornfield Journalist": The Tale of Joel Chandler Harris* (2000); Stephen Davis, *Georgia Historical Quarterly* (Spring 1990); John C. Inscoe, *Georgia Historical Quarterly* (Fall 1992); Arthur Hobson Quinn, *American Fiction: An Historical and Critical Survey* (1936); Bernard Wolfe, *Commentary* (July 1949).

Harris, Thomas

(b. 1940) WRITER.

Few writers have been able to develop and sustain the type of anticipation that Thomas Harris creates, especially considering the relatively long time periods between his publications. In the modern age of multibook contracts, Harris remains devoted to the perfection of his works, spending an average of nearly eight years between books. Born in Jackson, Tenn., in 1940, Thomas Harris was the only child of William Thomas Harris Jr., an electrical engineer with the Tennessee Valley Authority, and Polly Harris, a high school chemistry and biology teacher. When Harris was still a baby, the family moved to Rich, Miss., where his father ran a small farm. Though a personable and well-liked man, William Harris was an unsuccessful farmer, and the family went through a period of financial troubles. In high school, Thomas went to live with his aunt in Cleveland, Miss. After graduating, Harris opted not to attend nearby Delta State University or the University of Mississippi in Oxford, deciding instead to move to Waco, Tex., and attend Baylor University.

At Baylor, Harris first embarked on his writing career. As a student he wrote crime pieces for the *Waco News Tribune* and eventually landed his first full-time job there as a crime reporter. His co-workers remember his precise attention to detail and a stylistic tendency to make his subjects come alive, something unique for a young crime reporter. At this time Harris was also sending fiction stories to fantasy magazines like *True* and *Argosy*, his first attempts at mixing the sometimes surreal real-life with his own imagination. The year before his graduation in 1964, Harris married a fellow student, Harriet, and they had one daughter, Anne. When Anne was still a small child, Thomas and Harriet divorced, and he traveled through Europe for a few years.

When he returned to the United States, Harris worked at the Associated Press in New York from 1968 to 1974, first as a general reporter and then as a night editor. In 1973 Harris and two other AP reporters, Sam Maull and Dick Riley, came up with the idea of writing a thriller based on the May 1972 massacre of 23 people at the Tel Aviv airport by PLO-trained terrorists and the PLO attack at the Munich Olympics that September. After splitting the advance and researching for the book together,

Harris bought out his partners and finished the book himself. The result, *Black Sunday*, was published in 1975. Though the book was not a tremendous success, it was turned into a movie directed by John Frankenheimer in 1977. The profits from *Black Sunday* allowed Harris to focus on his writing full time.

Harris's second novel, *Red Dragon*, was published six years later. This novel marks the birth of Harris's most enduring character, Dr. Hannibal Lecter, though he plays only a minor role. The novel was adapted to film in 1986 under the title *Manhunter* but was remade in 2002 under its original title. Harris sold the paperback rights to *Red Dragon* for $1 million and had the financial security he needed to produce his masterpiece, *The Silence of the Lambs* (1988). This novel has sold more than 12 million copies worldwide and inspired the wildly successful movie of the same name. The movie, starring Anthony Hopkins as Dr. Lecter, won five Academy Awards, including awards for best actor, best actress, and best picture. Harris followed *The Silence of the Lambs* with *Hannibal* in 1999, finally giving full spotlight to his most famous character. Though not received nearly as well as *Silence*, *Hannibal* was a financial success and was also adapted to film in 2001. Harris's fifth novel, *Hannibal Rising*, was published in 2006 and provides Dr. Hannibal Lecter's history.

Perhaps because Thomas Harris himself is reluctant to give interviews, his novels have taken on a life of their own. Compared favorably to the mystery and thriller novels of Bram Stoker, Conan Doyle, Wilkie Collins, and Edgar Allan

Poe, Harris's reinvention of the crime thriller is one of the rare instances of an author creating texts that function as both popular thrillers and sophisticated literature.

DANIEL WALDEN
University of Mississippi

Mokoto Rich, *New York Times* (19 September 2006); David Sexton, *The Strange World of Thomas Harris* (2001) .

Haxton, Brooks

(b. 1950) POET AND TRANSLATOR. Brooks Haxton can attribute at least some of his love of language and his ear for its rhythms to his lineage: his mother is the novelist Josephine Haxton, who publishes her fiction under the pen name Ellen Douglas, and his father is the composer and writer Kenneth Haxton. The youngest of their three sons, Brooks is one of the most acclaimed American poets at work today. In a career spanning the past 30 years he has published six acclaimed collections of poetry and several books of translations that showcase both his wide-reaching interests and his prodigious gifts with the English language.

Haxton was born on 1 December 1950, in the river town of Greenville, Miss., and his work often touches, to some extent, on his childhood and adolescence, while moving between the worlds of personal memory and world history with ease, often even blurring the line. His roots run deep in Mississippi. Haxton has said that he began writing poetry during junior high school in Greenville, when the town was in the midst of school integration, and

he and his friends became interested in the protest songs of Bob Dylan.

Haxton graduated from Beloit College in 1972 and later received an M.A. from Syracuse University. His first volume was the book-length narrative poem *The Lay of Eleanor and Irene* (1985). In his second book, *Dominion* (1986), he provides a clear snapshot of his favored working modes—the long or semilong poem concerned with a specific moment (sometimes only seconds) of the poet's life and shorter poems that recount various moments as he interacts with the greater universe.

Haxton is masterful at both forms. Whereas the longer poems have an almost lulling hypnotic effect in their cadence and rhythm, the shorter poems reverberate with the power of the vaguely familiar. In later books like *Traveling Company* (1989), Haxton is able to delve into even the minutia of everyday life.

In Haxton's later work, such as the long poem "What If the Old Love Should Return" from *Nakedness, Death, and the Number Zero* (2001), a preoccupation with loneliness and emptiness seems to creep forward, yet in the course of the later poetry Haxton produces talisman after talisman to keep such clouds at bay. Haxton may tackle a variety of subjects and tones, but he always seems to return to the lone voice of the poet imparting somewhat quiet and understated (but revealing) truths. From his observations of the natural world to the insights he brings to the interplay of human relationships, Haxton continually shows both a deep sympathy and a deft touch for all the modes of human interaction. In both ornate and plain language he can produce a wealth of poetic effects like few other modern poets.

Besides his own poetry, Haxton is also a respected translator. His love for Greek and other cultures and languages often comes through in his own published poetry, but he has also published several works of translation, including translations of Greek poetry, the philosopher Heraclitus, and Victor Hugo. His largest translation project has been a selection of Else Lasker-Schuler, the German Jewish poet, and he has also collaborated with Ken Frieden on translations of poems from the Hebrew.

Haxton has received fellowships, grants, and awards for his work from the Academy of American Poets, the D.C. Commission on the Arts, the Ingram Merrill Foundation, and the National Endowment for the Arts. He has taught at Syracuse University for several years. He is married to the physician Frances Haxton and has one son, Issac, and twin daughters, Miriam and Lillie.

J. E. PITTS
University of Mississippi

Dorothy Abbott, ed., *Mississippi Writers: Reflections on Childhood and Youth*, vol. 3: *Poetry* (1988); Brooks Haxton, *The Lay of Eleanor and Irene* (1985), *Dominion* (1986), *Traveling Company* (1989), *Nakedness, Death and the Number Zero* (2001).

Hellman, Lillian

(1905–1984) WRITER.

Lillian Florence Hellman was born of Jewish heritage in New Orleans, La., on 20 June 1905, the only child of Julia Newhouse and Max Bernard Hellman.

During childhood, she divided her time between New York, where her father's job took him when she was quite young, and New Orleans, attending schools in both cities. Between 1922 and 1924 she attended New York University but left before her senior year to work as a manuscript reader for publisher Horace Liveright. On 31 December 1925 she married Arthur Kober, a theatrical press agent, and spent the ensuing four years reading scripts for New York producers, writing book reviews for the *New York Herald Tribune*, and traveling. In the fall of 1930 she and Kober moved to Hollywood, where he worked as a scriptwriter for Paramount and she as a manuscript reader for Metro-Goldwyn-Mayer and where, in November 1930, she met Dashiell Hammett, a successful and popular writer. In March 1931 Hellman moved back to New York and shortly thereafter divorced Arthur Kober and began her 30-year relationship with Hammett.

After writing a few short stories and discovering that was not to be her literary mode, Hellman collaborated with critic Louis Kronenberger on a play, *Dear Queen*, which was completed in 1932 but never produced. In November 1934 *The Children's Hour* opened on Broadway and was both a hit and a sensation, at least partially because it introduced the topic of lesbianism to the American stage. Its success sent its author back to Hollywood, where she adapted *Dark Angel* from a novel by Guy Bolton and did a sanitized film version of *The Children's Hour* entitled *These Three*. For the next 30 years she continued to write for both the stage and screen, doing movie versions of Sidney Kingsley's *Dead End* (1937) and of Horton Foote's novel *The Chase* (1966), as well as of her own plays *The Little Foxes* (1941) and *The Searching Wind* (1944), in addition to a documentary, *North Star* (1943).

Her other plays included *Another Part of the Forest* (1946), *The Autumn Garden* (1951), and *Toys in the Attic* (1960). The last play and *Watch on the Rhine* each won a New York Drama Critics' Circle Award for best American play of the year. Hellman also adapted a number of works for the Broadway stage.

Having grown disillusioned with Broadway, Hellman turned in the 1960s from writing plays and began a series of autobiographical memoirs, which included *An Unfinished Woman* (1969), *Pentimento* (1973), and *Scoundrel Time* (1976), the last her account of the McCarthy years after World War II, her blacklisting in Hollywood, and her appearance before the House Un-American Activities Committee.

Although only four of Hellman's plays—*The Little Foxes, Another Part of the Forest, Autumn Garden*, and *Toys in the Attic*—have southern settings and southern characters (some based on her family), they are among her best writing. In a 1939 interview about *The Little Foxes*, probably her most enduring work, she indicated that she chose the South as a setting "because it fitted the period I wanted for dramatic purposes and because it is a part of the world whose atmosphere I personally am familiar with as a Southerner. I also wanted a certain naive or innocent

quality in some of my characters which I could find in the South but which would have been quite out of place in any other American setting." And late in her life, when she had lived in the Northeast for some 55 years, she admitted that she still considered herself a southerner, despite the fact that at age 11 she had moved North: "I came from a family of Southerners. It wasn't simply that I was brought up and down from the South. I came from a family, on both sides, who had been Southerners for a great many generations."

JACKSON R. BRYER
University of Maryland

Timothy D. Adams, *Telling Lies in Modern American Autobiography* (1990); Thomas C. Austenfeld, *American Women Writers and the Nazis: Ethics and Politics in Boyle, Porter, Stafford, and Hellman* (2001); Margaret Booker, *Lillian Hellman and August Wilson: Dramatizing a New American Identity* (2003); Mark W. Estrin, *Lillian Hellman: Plays, Films, Memoirs: A Reference Guide* (1980); Doris V. Falk, *Lillian Hellman* (1978); Katherine Lederer, *Lillian Hellman* (1979); Richard Moody, *Lillian Hellman: Playwright* (1972).

Henley, Beth

(b. 1952) PLAYWRIGHT.

Beth Henley was born Elizabeth Becker Henley in Jackson, Miss., on 8 May 1952 to Charles Boyce Henley, an attorney, and Elizabeth Josephine Henley, who was active in Jackson-area theater. She was educated in the public school system in Jackson, and after graduating from Murrah High School, she went on to attend Southern Methodist University in Dallas, Tex., where she earned a

B.F.A. and wrote her first play, a one-act comedy set in New Orleans titled *Am I Blue.*

After spending a year doing graduate work at the University of Illinois, Henley moved west to Los Angeles, where she aspired to find work in the movie industry. There she wrote what is generally considered to be her greatest work, *Crimes of the Heart* (1979)—a dark, yet comic, three-act play set "five years after Hurricane Camille" that depicts the three McGrath sisters of Hazlehurst, Miss., who reunite when the youngest of the sisters, Babe, attempts to murder her overbearing husband. When asked why she shot him, Babe simply states, "'Cause I didn't like his looks. I just didn't like his looks." The play found its initial audience when a friend of Henley's entered it in the Great American Play Contest sponsored by the Actors Theatre of Louisville. *Crimes of the Heart* was the co-winner of the contest in 1979.

On 4 November 1981 *Crimes of the Heart* debuted on Broadway to much critical acclaim. That year it was nominated for three Tony Awards, won the Pulitzer Prize for Drama, and won the New York Drama Circle Award for Best American Play. In 1986 Henley wrote the screenplay for *Crimes of the Heart*, starring Diane Keeton, Sissy Spacek, and Jessica Lange. The film garnered three Academy Award nominations (one for Henley for best screenplay based on material from another medium) and two Golden Globe nominations. Spacek won the Golden Globe Award and the New York Film Critics Circle Award for Best Actress for her role as Babe.

Henley has written numerous plays since her success with *Crimes of the Heart*, many of which are set in the South, specifically Mississippi and Louisiana, including *The Wake of Jamey Foster* (1983), *The Miss Firecracker Contest* (1985), *The Lucky Spot* (1987), *Abundance* (1991), and *The Debutante Ball* (1991). *Crimes of the Heart* is widely accepted as the most southern of her plays. Her continuing status as a "southern" playwright has been called into question with the location and themes of many of her later plays existing outside the geographic and thematic world of what is often considered the "southern" milieu (e.g., the Wyoming frontier, the shores of Lake Michigan, and a futuristic Los Angeles; and feminism, postmodernism, and eroticism), but *Crimes of the Heart* has been repeatedly and favorably compared with the southern Gothic humor of Flannery O'Connor and Eudora Welty, and it is commonly considered as much a part of the southern dramatic canon as is Tennessee Williams's seminal drama *Cat on a Hot Tin Roof*. Henley currently lives in Los Angeles.

JAMES G. THOMAS JR.
University of Mississippi

Robert J. Andreach, ed., *Understanding Beth Henley* (2006); Julia Ann Fesmire, ed., *Beth Henley: A Casebook* (2002); Gene A. Plunka, *The Plays of Beth Henley: A Critical Study* (2005); Frank Rich, *New York Times* (5 November 1981); June Schlueter, *Modern American Drama: The Female Canon* (1990).

Heyward, DuBose

(1885–1940) WRITER.
Edwin DuBose Heyward achieved
enduring fame for his creation of a
black character immortalized in George
Gershwin's opera *Porgy* (1935). Heyward
was born in Charleston on 31 August
1885 to Edward Watkins and Janie
Screven DuBose Heyward, and as a descendant of a signer of the Declaration
of Independence, he was in the Charleston aristocracy. Economic losses from
the Civil War plagued the family, however, and the death of Heyward's father
when Heyward was two compounded
family woes. He abandoned formal education at age 14 to work in a hardware
store. At 18 he was stricken with polio.
At 20 he suffered from typhoid and then
worked for a time as a wharf checker.
A pleurisy attack in 1906 resulted in an
18-month recuperation in Arizona. In
1906 he entered an insurance and real-
estate partnership. Exhausted by over-
work and a second pleurisy attack, in
1917 he sought refuge in Hendersonville,
N.C., where he took up painting, wrote
stories, and bought a summer cottage.

In Charleston Heyward became
friends with northern writers Hervey
Allen and John Bennett. Under their influence, he began to write poetry. In the
fall of 1920 the trio founded the Poetry
Society of South Carolina. As secretary
of the society, Heyward edited its year-
books until 1924. *Carolina Chansons*,
his first volume of poems, with Allen,
appeared in 1922.

Invited to MacDowell Colony for
the summers of 1922 and 1923, Heyward met playwright Dorothy Hartzell

Kuhns. They married on 22 September
1923. (A daughter, Jennifer, was born
in 1930.) In 1924 Heyward gave up his
business and committed himself full
time to writing and to lecturing on
southern literature. *Porgy* (1925), his first
novel, was based on Heyward's appreciation for black life and speech on the
wharves of Charleston. He and his wife
adapted the novel for the stage, where
it had a highly successful run. Heyward
later wrote the libretto for the opera.
The couple also dramatized Heyward's
Mamba's Daughters, another depiction
of black life in Charleston.

Continuing to work in fiction,
poetry, and drama, Heyward also wrote
the movie treatments for *The Emperor
Jones* and *The Good Earth*. His realistic
and compassionate portrayal of blacks
won him praise and censure. He died on
16 June 1940, in Tryon, N.C.

JOSEPH M. FLORA
*University of North Carolina at
Chapel Hill*

Frank Durham, *DuBose Heyward: The
Man Who Wrote "Porgy"* (1954), *DuBose
Heyward's Use of Folklore in His Negro
Fiction* (1961); Alpert Hollis, *The Life and
Times of Porgy and Bess* (1990); James M.
Hutchisson, *Dubose Heyward: A Charleston
Gentleman and the World of "Porgy and
Bess"* (2000).

Holland, Endesha Ida Mae

(1944–2006) ACTIVIST, EDUCATOR,
PLAYWRIGHT, AND MEMOIRIST.
Endesha Ida Mae Holland was born
29 August 1944 in Greenwood, Miss.,
to Ida Mae Holland, a midwife. Raised
with her three older siblings, Simon Jr.,

Bud, and Jean, she came of age during an era when racism imposed a climate of fear and restriction on the lives of black southerners, and her own childhood reflected these difficult circumstances.

Holland grew up in the county where Emmett Till was murdered in 1955. Only three years younger than Till, Holland and her peers recognized the impact of this event on their sense of place in a racially polarized world. Holland and her family worked seasonally in the cotton fields of Leflore County to generate income for the family. A white man raped her, at age 11, while she was babysitting for his daughter.

At age 13, Holland quit school and sought employment to help provide for her mother and siblings. For the next several years she worked as a prostitute and served time on a prison farm for shoplifting. Holland gave birth to her only child, Cedric, in 1961, only months after being released from the prison farm. She married Cedric's father, Ike, in 1963 and was divorced in 1966. After her first marriage, Holland married and divorced two more times.

Following a chance encounter with Bob Moses in 1962, Holland gave up prostitution and devoted herself to the civil rights movement as a volunteer for the Student Nonviolent Coordinating Committee (SNCC) in Greenwood. Holland traveled extensively promoting civil rights outside of the South between 1962 and 1965. She was arrested on several occasions as a result of her SNCC activities in Mississippi and served time in Parchman, Mississippi's notoriously tough state penitentiary. She became the target of violence in her hometown of Greenwood when her home was firebombed in 1965. Her beloved mother was a casualty of this attack, burned to death in the flames.

In the summer of 1965, five months after her mother's death, Holland left Mississippi and traveled north. Through the help of the activist community, she entered the University of Minnesota, where she studied playwriting. As a student, Holland remained active in black issues, and she helped establish the school's department for African American studies. She also founded Women Helping Offenders, a program designed to provide aid to women in prison. Holland received three degrees from the University of Minnesota: her B.A. in African American Studies in 1979, her M.A. in 1984, and her doctorate in 1986. She taught at the State University of New York at Buffalo as a professor of American Studies and Women's Studies, before moving to the University of Southern California in Los Angeles as playwright in residence and a professor.

In 1991 Holland won recognition as a gifted playwright. Her two-act, autobiographical drama *From the Mississippi Delta*, which she revised from the earlier *The Second Doctor Lady*, was produced in London before playing off-Broadway. *The Second Doctor Lady* won Holland the Lorraine Hansberry Award for Best Play in 1981, and in 1991 *From the Mississippi Delta* was awarded the Helen Hayes Award for Best Non-Resident Play. The play includes some of the more harrowing moments from Holland's own life, including her rape, and has been acknowledged as an intense and inspirational work. Commenting on the dramatization of her life and her triumph over poverty and immorality, Holland in an interview with Glenn Collins of the *New York Times* said that today's "young people need to know that they can do wrong things and yet still change and grow." Six years after the first production of her play, Holland published *From the Mississippi Delta* (1997) as a memoir. Like the play, her book won rave reviews and was nominated for a Pulitzer Prize. On 18 October 1991, the city of Greenwood, Miss., declared Dr. Endesha Ida Mae Holland Day to celebrate her contributions to Greenwood's culture and history. Holland retired from the University of Southern California in 2003 and died in Santa Monica on 25 January 2006 after a 15-year battle with ataxia, a degenerative neurological condition.

FRANCES ABBOTT
University of Mississippi

Endesha Ida Mae Holland, *From the Mississippi Delta: A Memoir* (1997); Michael L. Lablanc, ed., *Contemporary Black Biography*, vol. 3 (1991); Emily J. McMurray, ed., *Contemporary Theatre, Film, and Television*, vol. 11 (1992).

Holman, C. Hugh

(1914–1981) CRITIC AND TEACHER. A native of Cross Anchor, S.C., Clarence Hugh Holman was the son of David Marion and Jessie Pearl Davis Holman. He earned two baccalaureates at Presbyterian College: a B.S. magna cum laude in chemistry in 1936, an A.B. cum laude in English in 1939. In 1949 he received his Ph.D. in English from the University of North Carolina at Chapel Hill.

His dissertation was entitled "William Gilmore Simms's Theory and Practice of Historical Fiction." In 1938 he married Verna Virginia McCleod with whom he had a son and daughter.

Holman spent his entire professional career at one or the other of his alma maters. From 1936 to 1946 he served Presbyterian College variously as director of public relations, director of radio programs, faculty member, and academic dean. Beginning at Chapel Hill in 1946 as a graduate student, Holman held almost every academic position conceivable from instructor to professor, Kenan Professor, department chair, dean of the graduate school, provost, and special assistant to the chancellor. Elected to Phi Beta Kappa in 1946, Holman received numerous awards including a Guggenheim Fellowship (1967) and honorary degrees from Presbyterian College (1963) and Clemson University (1968). In 1980 he was elected a fellow of the American Academy of Arts and Sciences.

Holman published some 70 essays, many of which were reworked to appear in one or another of the 26 books he wrote, co-wrote, or edited. He revised and co-wrote with W. J. Thrall and Addison Hibbard the second, third, and fourth editions of the widely used *A Handbook to Literature*, and with Louis D. Rubin Jr. he was founding co-editor of the *Southern Literary Journal*.

Holman's most characteristic work was his research into and criticism of southern prose fiction. This work established him as one of the primary scholars who defined, explained, and in the best sense promoted the renascence of southern literary studies that has flourished since the middle of the 20th century. This work falls into two broad categories: one contains those books and essays that focus on a single author. The other contains his studies that treat more broadly major themes and currents in southern fiction.

Although Holman wrote about a variety of southern novelists, on no one did he expend more effort or do more to enhance the reputation of than Thomas Wolfe. His work includes the monograph *Thomas Wolfe* (1960), *The Thomas Wolfe Reader* (1962), *The Letters of Thomas Wolfe*, with Sue Fields Ross (1968), and *The Loneliness at the Core: Studies in Thomas Wolfe* (1975), a collection of eight essays published earlier. This latter work was very important in securing Wolfe a prominent position in the American literary canon. At least as important is Holman's *The Short Novels of Thomas Wolfe* (1961), an edition of five works originally written as novellas but whose integrity of form (with one exception) was lost in subsequent publication. Holman's collection demonstrates that Wolfe's reputation for self-indulgent formlessness was as much the creation of his editors as it was the result of his creative instincts.

Holman's more thematically focused writing is found in such works as *Three Modes of Southern Fiction* (1966), *The Roots of Southern Writing* (1972), *The Immoderate Past: The Southern Writer and History* (1977), and *Windows on the World: Essays on American Social Fiction* (1979). The essays in these collections look at issues such as the differences between broadly defined areas of southern culture (the Tidewater, the Appalachian, the Deep South) and the writers each produced; or the meaning of history to southern writers (in contrast to those from other regions) as one moves from a William Gilmore Simms to a Robert Penn Warren. Holman's method is to focus insightfully on the particular examples that illuminate the similarities and distinctions he sees.

C. Hugh Holman was a southern scholar-critic of the highest distinction who, by all accounts, was a superb teacher. It is especially fitting that the dedication to *The History of Southern Literature* (1985) reads: "This book is dedicated to the memory of C. Hugh Holman by its editors who were also his friends and his beneficiaries."

LADELL PAYNE
Randolph-Macon College

Lewis Leary, in *The Dictionary of North Carolina Biography* (1988).

Hood, Mary

(b. 1946) WRITER.
Before turning to the full-time writing of fiction, Mary Hood was once employed as a painter of portraits, animals, and rural scenes, a fitting occupation for a writer whose work is defined by a deeply nuanced sense of character and place. Refusing simple narrative structures and distinctions, her stories are peopled by figures of startling emotional depth, small-town characters whose struggles and survival she infuses with an intricate subtlety and meaning. In lieu of local color, Hood writes in universal shades.

Born 16 September 1946 in the

coastal Georgia town of Brunswick, Hood and her family lived in various locations around the state before settling in Cherokee County in 1976. This area, and particularly Victoria, a rural community now almost entirely covered over by the combination of the Army Corps of Engineer–constructed Lake Allatoona and the persistent urban sprawl from north Atlanta, figures prominently in Hood's early stories. The dedication of her first collection, *How Far She Went*, evidences the significance of her connection to this setting: "For Little Victoria, big enough." The book, published in 1984, won the Southern Review/Louisiana State University Short Fiction Award and the Flannery O'Connor Award for Short Fiction. In her second collection, 1987's *And Venus Is Blue*, Hood continues to engage with particular expressions of personal identity, development, and loss, expressions often accompanied by a dark awareness of the kind of disappearing rural kinships and networks that Victoria epitomized. Stories such as "Something Good for Ginnie," which won the National Magazine Award for Fiction in 1986, highlight the effects of this disappearance: independence replaced with isolation, wildlife displaced by mechanization, and, perhaps most important, meaningful communion degraded to baser communications. The collection garnered further awards for Hood, such as the Townsend Prize for Fiction and the Lillian Smith Award, and was followed in 1995 by the novel *Familiar Heat*, an elaborate story of the multidimensional nature of love set in a small fishing village on the Florida coast.

Hood has taught creative writing at a number of colleges and universities in the South, including the University of Mississippi (where she was the John and Renée Grisham Writer in Residence), the University of Georgia, and Berry College. She currently lives and works in Commerce, Ga.

JACOB SULLINS
Georgia State University

David Aiken, in *Southern Writers at Century's End*, ed. Jeffrey J. Folks and James A. Perkins (1997); Joy A. Farmer, *Studies in Short Fiction* (Winter 1996).

Hooper, Johnson Jones

(1815–1862) WRITER AND NEWSPAPER EDITOR.

Johnson Jones Hooper was born 9 June 1815 in Wilmington, N.C., into a distinguished Tidewater family that could claim descent from William Hooper II, a Harvard graduate who served North Carolina as delegate to the Continental Congress and signed the Declaration of Independence. Although Hooper never attended college, he was ably tutored at home and exposed daily to the inner workings of the newspaper trade in his father's editorial offices at the *Cape-Fear Recorder*. In 1835 he moved south to join his brother George and to study law in his established practice in the frontier town of La Fayette, Ala. Here he was admitted to the local bar and in 1840 was temporarily deputized as an assistant census marshal for Tallapoosa County.

Although Hooper practiced law intermittently throughout his professional career, he was not long in revealing his serious interests in politics and journalism by accepting the editor's post on La Fayette's *East Alabamian,* the weekly newspaper of the local Whig Party, whose platform Hooper staunchly supported. It was here in the summer of 1843 that he drew on his earlier experiences to publish the comical "Taking the Census in Alabama." William T. Porter reprinted the piece in the *Spirit of the Times* on 9 September 1843, giving Hooper's gifts as a literary comedian national circulation and launching his reputation in the field of American humorous literature. Porter actively encouraged Hooper to continue with his humorous writing and helped him to arrange a publishing contract with the Philadelphia firm of Cary and Hart for his best-known work, *Some Adventures of Captain Simon Suggs, Late of the Tallapoosa Volunteers,* published in 1845. Its immediate and resounding success firmly established Hooper's position in the front ranks of contemporary southwestern humorists, including Augustus Baldwin Longstreet, William Tappan Thompson, and Thomas Bangs Thorpe. Though it would later become something of a political embarrassment, Hooper's name became synonymous with his title character, a shrewd, brazen, picaresque rogue whose outrageous schemes for self-advancement are presented in the form of a burlesque campaign biography that satirized the reverential treatment of General Andrew Jackson. Despite Suggs's conscienceless opportunism, he remains an engaging character who succeeds because his rare insight into human nature allows him to take advantage of the hypocrisy and avarice of his compatriots. By 1856 *Simon Suggs* had gone through 11 print-

ings, and over the same span Hooper would publish over 50 other stories and sporting sketches in the *Spirit of the Times.*

By the end of 1849 Hooper had gained national fame as a frontier humorist and regional renown as an accomplished lawyer and celebrated newspaper editor. In August he became editor of the newly formed *Chambers County Tribune* and in November was elected solicitor for Alabama's Ninth Judicial Circuit. He capped the year's success in December with the publication of his second volume of humorous sketches, *A Ride with Old Kit Kuncker,* reissued in a revised and expanded version for his third book, *The Widow Rugby's Husband* (1851). In 1854 Hooper moved to the state capital in Montgomery to edit the *Mail,* an "independent" newspaper that provided him with the perfect platform for his gifts as political essayist. The quantity of his humorous writing declined over the next few years as he became more seriously involved in the political controversies of the period, especially those surrounding slavery and southern independence. By 1859 Hooper had become a fiery, outspoken supporter of southern rights, and after Lincoln's election he used his editorial voice on the *Mail* to advocate secession in the strongest possible terms. Elected as the secretary to the Provisional Confederate Congress in 1861, Hooper moved with his family to Richmond when the capital was relocated there from Montgomery and was reassigned as the editor for the records of the Provisional Congress. His career was cut short when he died of lung disease on 7 June 1862. Hooper was buried in the Shockhoe Hill cemetery in Richmond.

JACOB RIVERS
University of South Carolina at Columbia

Hening Cohen and William B. Dillingham, eds., *Humor of the Old Southwest* (1975); Nancy Snell Griffith, *Humor of the Old Southwest: An Annotated Bibliography of Primary and Secondary Sources* (1989); W. Stanley Hoole, *Alias Simon Suggs: The Life and Times of Johnson Jones Hooper* (1952); Paul Somers, *Johnson J. Hooper* (1984); Norris Yates, in *Southern Writers: A Biographical Dictionary*, ed. Robert Bain, Joseph M. Flora, and Louis D. Rubin Jr. (1979).

Hubbell, Jay Broadus

(1885–1979) CRITIC AND TEACHER. Jay Broadus Hubbell was born in Smyth County, Va., on 8 May 1885. He went east to earn his B.A. at Richmond College (now the University of Richmond) in 1905, his A.M. at Harvard in 1908, and his Ph.D. at Columbia in 1922. Between his B.A. and A.M. Hubbell taught Latin and Greek at Bethel College in Russellville, Ky., and between his A.M. and Ph.D. he taught at the University of North Carolina at Chapel Hill (1908–9), at Wake Forest (1911–14), where he was eventually promoted to associate professor, and at Southern Methodist University (1915–27), where he rose to Lilly Professor of English and head of the department. There he founded the journal *Southwest Review* in 1924. He was visiting professor of American literature at the University of Vienna in 1949 and 1950 and Fulbright Professor of Ameri-

can Literature and Civilization at the University of Athens in 1953.

In 1927 Hubbell moved from Southern Methodist University to Duke University, where he was professor of American literature until his retirement in 1954. After retirement, Hubbell held visiting professor appointments at Virginia, Clemson, Columbia, Texas Tech, and Kentucky. It was at Duke that Hubbell made his lasting mark on the profession. He was instrumental in bringing American literature into parity with British literature inside the major professional organization, the Modern Language Association. Hubbell was principal founder of the journal *American Literature* in 1929 and served on its editorial board until his retirement from Duke. The result of his work was to raise the profile of American literature in the academy. Hubbell's professed purpose was to replace the conventional and gentlemanly books then prevailing in the field of American literature with work on a par with British literary history and criticism. After Hubbell retired, Duke University honored his achievement by establishing the Jay B. Hubbell Center for American Literary Historiography in 1976.

Hubbell's scholarly contributions mirror the geography of his education: a Virginian by birth and tradition, he was educated in the headquarters of the Puritan tradition of American literary culture (Cambridge, Mass.) and of the urban antitype to the agrarian South (New York City). His edition of John Pendleton Kennedy's novel *Swallow Barn*—which begins with a New Yorker visiting kin for the first time in the Old

Dominion—must have seemed partly déjà vu to Hubbell. His two-volume anthology of American literature, *American Life in American Literature*, appeared the same year as *Gone with the Wind* and *Absalom, Absalom!* Hubbell found room for Timrod's "Ode" and Robert E. Lee's field dispatches in the same volume with Melville, Hawthorne, and Lincoln. In other words, in the early years of the southern drive for distinctiveness, led formidably by the Vanderbilt Agrarians, Hubbell took a national rather than regional view. *The South in American Literature, 1609–1900* (1955) will always be recognized as Hubbell's monumental achievement. The work of a career, this project argues that southerners are and have always been Americans, not regional anomalies to be understood by their own autochthonous vocabulary.

After retiring from Duke University, Hubbell continued to live and work in Durham, N.C. He died in Durham on 13 February 1979 at the age of 93.

MICHAEL P. KREYLING
Vanderbilt University

Clarence Gohdes, *University of Mississippi Studies in English* (1980).

Humphreys, Josephine

(b. 1945) WRITER.

The contemporary South Carolina author Josephine Humphreys portrays southern families and environments under stress in all four of her novels. In her 1988 essay "A Disappearing Subject Called the South," she remarks that the South's literature has been changed by the rapid transformation of the region's geography. A woman's nightmarish trip to an urban supermarket in her first novel, *Dreams of Sleep* (1984), hints at the modern household's distance from nature. Humphreys continues to grieve for endangered landscapes in her latest work, *Nowhere Else on Earth* (2000), which re-creates a North Carolina Lumbee Indian settlement under siege during the Civil War. Although the sense of loss is strong, outsider characters bring a measure of hope to threatened communities in each of Humphreys's books.

Born in Charleston, S.C., on 2 February 1945, Josephine Trenholm Humphreys graduated Phi Beta Kappa from Duke University, where William Blackburn and Reynolds Price were her mentors. She earned a master's degree at Yale and enrolled in the doctoral program at the University of Texas at Austin but did not complete her dissertation. After her marriage to Thomas A. Hutcheson, an attorney, she returned to Charleston, where the couple's two sons were born. Humphreys taught English at the city's Baptist College from 1970 to 1977, when she resigned to concentrate on writing.

Iris Moon, a babysitter for the dysfunctional Reese family in *Dreams of Sleep*, is the first of several young characters who serve a redemptive function in Humphreys's fiction. The teenager's name suggests the author's fascination with legends and fairy tales, another constant in her work. Like the unhappy Alice Reese in *Dreams of Sleep*, Helen Odom of *Rich in Love* (1988) feels confined by her home and marriage, underscoring Humphreys's conviction that "there is a great deal of sadness in women's lives that really has no outlet."

Alfred Uhry wrote the screenplay for a successful movie adaptation of *Rich in Love* in 1992. Humphreys's themes of escape and infidelity are prominent, too, in *The Fireman's Fair* (1991), which is narrated from the point of view of an attorney who flees the confines of the legal profession and his upscale Charleston milieu. Set on a coastal island after a hurricane, her third novel underscores the possibilities of new beginnings in a makeshift family. In contrast to the contemporary settings of the first three books, the late 19th-century scenes of *Nowhere Else on Earth* involved Humphreys in meticulous historical research. Interracial friendships, a motif in her earlier work, are prominent in this new plot as the aptly named protagonist, Rhoda Strong, develops alliances beyond her Lumbee tribe.

Humphreys told an interviewer that her concept of southernness was transformed by the legendary Rhoda, Queen of Scuffletown. She would like to write another historical novel about the South, although she says she might decide to set her next novel in the present. A rare negative review of *Nowhere Else on Earth* suggested that Humphreys was at her best with the "sassy sophistications" of the first three books. An admirer of Walker Percy, Humphreys is a graceful stylist and a close observer of southern society, whether her fiction is located in suburban Charleston or in a 1860s forest. She was selected for membership in the Fellowship of Southern Writers, which awarded her the Hillsdale Prize for Fiction in 1993. Humphreys's many other honors include a Guggenheim Fellowship, a Lyndhurst Foundation stipend, and the PEN American Center's Ernest Hemingway Foundation Award. A popular reader on her book tours, she is also a frequent speaker on college campuses, including Duke University, where many of her letters and manuscripts are housed.

JOAN WYLIE HALL
University of Mississippi

Elizabeth A. Ford, in *Southern Writers at Century's End*, ed. Jeffrey J. Folks and James A. Perkins (1997); Joan Wylie Hall, in *Dictionary of Literary Biography*, vol. 292, ed. Lisa Abney and Suzanne Disheroon-Green (2004); Dannye Romine Powell, in *Parting the Curtains: Interviews with Southern Writers*, ed. Dannye Romine Powell (1994); Elinor Ann Walker, in *The History of Southern Women's Literature*, ed. Carolyn Perry and Mary Louise Weaks (2002).

Hurston, Zora Neale

(ca. 1901–1960) WRITER AND FOLKLORIST.

Born either in 1891 or 1901—the latter is normally given as the date of birth, but recent studies suggest an earlier date—in the all-black town of Eatonville, Fla., Hurston became a distinguished novelist, folklorist, and anthropologist. She was next to the youngest of eight children, born the daughter of a Baptist minister who was mayor of Eatonville. Her mother died when Hurston was nine, and she left home at 14 to join a traveling show. She later attended Howard University, where she studied under Alain Locke and Lorenzo Dow Turner, and she earned an A.B. degree from Barnard College in 1928, working with Franz Boas. She became a well-known figure among the New York intellectuals of the Harlem Renaissance in the mid-1920s and then devoted the years 1927 to 1932 to field research in Florida, Alabama, Louisiana, and the Bahamas. *Mules and Men* (1935) was a collection of black music, games, oral lore, and religious practices. *Tell My Horse* (1938) was a similar collection of folklore from Jamaica and Haiti.

Hurston published four novels—*Jonah's Gourd Vine* (1934), *Their Eyes Were Watching God* (1937), *Moses, Man of the Mountain* (1939), and *Seraph on the Sewanee* (1948). Her autobiography, *Dust Tracks on a Road*, appeared in 1948. Married and divorced twice, she worked for the WPA Federal Theatre project in New York (1935–36) and for the Federal Writers' Project in Florida (1938). She taught briefly at Bethune-Cookman College in Daytona Beach, Fla. (1934), and at North Carolina College in Durham (1939), and she received Rosenwald (1934) and Guggenheim fellowships (1936–37).

Hurston was noteworthy for her portrayal of the strength of black life in the South. In her essay "The Pet Negro System," she assured her readers that not all black southerners fit the illiterate sharecropper stereotype fostered by the northern media. She pointed to the seldom-noted black professionals who, like herself, remained in the South because they liked some things about it. Most educated blacks, Hurston insisted, preferred not to live up North because they came to realize that there was "segregation and discrimination up there, too, with none of the human touches of the South." One of the "human touches"

to which Hurston referred was the "pet Negro system" itself, a southern practice that afforded special privileges to blacks who met standards set by their white benefactors. The system survived, she said, because it reinforced the white southerner's sense of superiority. Clearly, it was not a desirable substitute for social, economic, and political equality, but Hurston's portrayal of the system indicated her affirmative attitude toward the region, despite its dubious customs.

Hurston had faith in individual initiative, confidence in the strength of black culture, and strong trust in the ultimate goodwill of southern white people, all of which influenced her perceptions of significant racial issues. When she saw blacks suffering hardships, she refused to acknowledge that racism was a major contributing factor, probably because she never let racism stop her. Hurston's biographer, Robert E. Hemenway, notes that "in her later life she came to interpret all attempts to emphasize black suffering . . . as the politics of deprivation, implying a tragedy of color in Afro-American life."

After working for years as a maid in Miami, Hurston suffered a stroke in early 1959 and, alone and indigent, died in the Saint Lucie County Welfare Home, Fort Pierce, Fla., 28 January 1960. Alice Walker has led a recent "rediscovery" of Hurston, whose works have become an inspiration for black women writers.

ELVIN HOLT
University of Kentucky

Valerie Boyd, *Wrapped in Rainbows: The Life of Zora Neale Hurston* (2002); Robert E. Hemenway, *Zora Neale Hurston: A Literary Biography* (1977); Zora Neale Hurston, *I Love Myself*, ed. Alice Walker (1979); Carla Kaplan, ed., *Zora Neale Hurston: A Life in Letters* (2002); Alice Walker, *In Search of Our Mothers' Gardens* (1983).

Jackson, Blyden

(1910–2000) LITERARY SCHOLAR
AND TEACHER.

Blyden Jackson was a path-breaking scholar of African American literature in the South and a teacher and mentor at universities across the region. Born in Paducah, Ky., in 1910, Jackson was the grandson of former slaves, but both of his grandfathers went on to become clergy in the African Methodist Episcopal Church. His father was a school principal and his mother a librarian. Jackson grew up in Louisville, Ky., earned an undergraduate degree at Wilberforce University in 1930, and entered graduate school at Columbia University. Jackson did not earn his degree there but lived in Harlem and observed the final phases of the Harlem Renaissance. He received a master's degree (1938) and his doctorate (1952) from the University of Michigan. After teaching in the Louisville public schools, Jackson joined the Fisk University faculty in 1945. He also taught and later served as dean of the Graduate School at Southern University in Baton Rouge. He joined the faculty at the University of North Carolina in 1969, later serving in administrative posts there as well. Jackson was married to Roberta

Bowles Hodges Jackson, who taught in the School of Education at Chapel Hill and became the first African American woman to achieve tenure there.

Jackson published more than 50 articles, often exploring the novels, poetry, and drama of African American writers. In addition to one novel, *Operation Burning Candle* (1973), his books include *Black Poetry in America: Two Essays in Historical Interpretation* (1974), *The Waiting Years: Essays on American Negro Literature* (1976), and *A History of Afro-American Literature: The Long Beginning, 1746–1895* (1989). He was an editor of a seminal work of literary scholarship, *The History of Southern Literature*, a volume that helped incorporate more fully than before African American literature into studies of southern literature.

CHARLES REAGAN WILSON
University of Mississippi

Roberta H. Jackson and Blyden Jackson Papers, 1955–1991, Southern Historical Collection, University of North Carolina at Chapel Hill.

Jarrell, Randall

(1914–1965) WRITER AND CRITIC.
Born in Nashville, Tenn., Randall Jarrell grew up there and around Los Angeles, Calif. He earned two degrees from Vanderbilt University: a B.A. in psychology (with a minor in philosophy) and an M.A. in English. During World War II he served stateside in the army air forces. He taught at various colleges and universities before and after the war; his longest affiliation was with the Woman's College of the University of North

Carolina (now UNC at Greensboro). From 1956 to 1958 he was consultant in poetry to the Library of Congress. Possibly the most influential poetry book reviewer in 20th-century America, he died in Chapel Hill, N.C., after being struck by an automobile.

Jarrell published seven poetry collections. Shortly after appearing in New Directions' *Five Young American Poets* (1940), he produced his first book, *Blood for a Stranger* (1942); that was followed by *Little Friend, Little Friend* (1945), *Losses* (1948), and *The Seven-League Crutches* (1951). His *Selected Poems* (1955) consolidates and reshapes that early oeuvre: he added two new poems, reprinted very little of his first book, and organized the whole selection topically rather than chronologically. *The Woman at the Washington Zoo* (1960) juxtaposes Jarrell's own poems with a dozen of his translations, chiefly from Rilke; it won a National Book Award. Jarrell's last volume of poetry was *The Lost World* (1965), an often autobiographical book that his friend Robert Lowell deemed his best.

Jarrell's most famous poem is uncharacteristically brief, and also unusually startling. "The Death of the Ball Turret Gunner" is only five lines long; the titular gunner gives a shorthand account of his life that concludes with a grisly evocation of his death. Jarrell's best poems are typically much more leisurely and contemplative. Several examine women's lives: "A Girl in the Library" ponders the half-asleep title character's ignorance and inexperience, while "The Woman at the Washington Zoo," "Next Day," and "The Player Piano" all give voice to older women disappointed with their failure to live life fully. Jarrell also wrote memorable poems based on the visual arts, such as "The Knight, Death, and the Devil" (inspired by Albrecht Dürer), "The Bronze David of Donatello," "In Galleries," and "The Old and the New Masters."

Two collections of his criticism, *Poetry and the Age* (1953) and *A Sad Heart at the Supermarket* (1962), appeared during his lifetime; later came *The Third Book of Criticism* (1969) and *Kipling, Auden & Co.* (1980). Although Jarrell did write on other subjects, his standing as a critic is based primarily on his writing about poetry. He could be cruel, but he could also be a compelling advocate: his assessments of Walt Whitman, Robert Frost, and William Carlos Williams did much to solidify those poets' reputations. His broader essays, such as "The Obscurity of the Poet," present a rare combination of learning, wit, and passion.

Although best known as a poet and a critic, Jarrell was also the author of a widely admired novel, *Pictures from an Institution* (1954). An academic satire, the novel is set at Benton College, a fictitious college for women. At the book's heart is Gertrude Johnson, a mean-spirited novelist who serves a brief appointment to teach creative writing and who plans to write a satirical novel based on her experiences. The unnamed narrator, who also teaches at Benton, resembles Jarrell so closely as to be virtually indistinguishable from him, and the novel's witty style recalls that of the author's liveliest criticism.

Posthumous editions of Jarrell's work

include *Complete Poems* (1969); *Randall Jarrell's Letters* (1985), edited by Mary Jarrell, his second wife; *Selected Poems* (1990), edited by William H. Pritchard; and *No Other Book: Selected Essays* (1999), edited by Brad Leithauser.

ROBERT M. WEST
Mississippi State University

J. A. Bryant Jr., *Understanding Randall Jarrell* (1986); William Harmon, in *The History of Southern Literature*, ed. Louis D. Rubin Jr. et al. (1985); William H. Pritchard, *Randall Jarrell: A Literary Life* (1990).

Jefferson, Thomas

(1743–1826) U.S. PRESIDENT, WRITER, PLANTER, SCIENTIST, ARCHITECT.

Thomas Jefferson was born on the edge of the frontier in colonial Virginia. He went on to acquire as fine an education as America offered, graduating from the College of William and Mary in 1726. He studied law under George Wythe and practiced at the bar until the Revolution. He was elected to the Virginia House of Burgesses in 1769. Already the inheritor of large landholdings, he increased his property greatly through the dowry of his wife, Martha Wayles Skelton, whom he married in 1772. They had two daughters who survived to maturity.

In 1774 Jefferson drew political attention with his pamphlet *A Summary View of the Rights of British America*, the best remonstrance against the king and defense of colonial rights that had yet been seen. He carefully controlled his writing style so that any literate reader might follow his argument. Then, in 1776, Jefferson—now a member of the Continental Congress—was chosen to write the Declaration of Independence. It is his masterpiece and America's fundamental political document. In succeeding years he was elected governor of the state of Virginia and member of Congress and was appointed minister to France. From 1790 to 1793 he served under Washington as the first secretary of state.

Jefferson's only book, *Notes on the State of Virginia*, in which he recorded the milieu of early America, was published in 1785. Jefferson was an advocate of the scientific method, and his book included efforts to classify botanical, geological, and paleontological specimens. He showed the confident Enlightenment belief that science could promote progress. His collection and classification of items reflected the practical need of a farmer to know the environment, as well as simply the desire to satisfy his curiosity. He agonized over the question of slavery (he held many slaves), echoing most of the persistent stereotyping of blacks so noticeably American. Controversies over Jefferson's relationship with his slave, Sally Hemings, have reverberated from his time to the contemporary era. Yet he was a true Enlightenment man, also voicing—as in the Declaration—the finest of ideals concerning justice, religious freedom, and equality.

He was paternalistic, not only at home but in his attitudes toward Indians, blacks, women, and commoners. Thus, his long political service was noblesse oblige. He was elected third president of the United States in 1801 (a second term followed). While president, he arranged the Louisiana Purchase (1803), doubling the size of the nation.

Always busy, he designed his mansion, Monticello, the Virginia capitol at Richmond, and, late in life, the University of Virginia. He designed an Episcopal chapel in Charlottesville, dozens of Virginia country homes, simple and functional courthouses, and even jails in Cumberland and Nelson counties. He accumulated an architectural library of 50 titles in French, Italian, German, and English. His architectural achievement was to adapt classical forms to Virginian and southern needs.

Jefferson personified character, vision, grace, scholarship, and leadership—the qualities of the early southern gentleman that are part of his legacy. Students of southern culture look to him as the exemplar of major themes, ideals, and achievements of the region as well as the nation.

WILLIAM K. BOTTORFF
University of Toledo

R. B. Bernstein, *Thomas Jefferson* (2003); Julian P. Boyd et al., eds., *The Papers of Thomas Jefferson* (1950–); Fiske Kimball, ed., *Thomas Jefferson, Architect: Original Designs in the Coolidge Collection of the Massachusetts Historical Society, with an Essay and Notes* (1968); Dumas Malone, *Jefferson and His Time*, 6 vols. (1948–81).

Johnson, James Weldon

(1871–1938) WRITER AND CIVIL RIGHTS LEADER.

James Weldon Johnson, the renaissance man of the New Negro Renaissance of the 1920s, was born James William Johnson on 17 June 1871 in Jacksonville, Fla., the son of a schoolteacher and a headwaiter in a luxury hotel. In Johnson's middle-class family, he was encouraged to excel academically and develop his talents musically. Johnson's parents sent him to Atlanta in the fall of 1887 to enter Atlanta University's high school. In 1890 he enrolled in Atlanta University. During his college years he met Booker T. Washington and Paul Laurence Dunbar, taught school in rural Henry County, Ga., and won an oratory contest. After graduation in 1894, he was appointed principal of Stanton School, the largest African American public school in Florida.

In Jacksonville, Johnson founded a short-lived African American daily newspaper, passed the Florida state bar, and composed music with his brother, Rosamond. In 1900 James wrote the lyrics to "Lift Every Voice and Sing" (with music by Rosamond) for a local commemoration of Lincoln's birthday. The poem and song would become famous as "The Negro National Anthem." Increasingly successful musical collaboration between the brothers led them to move to New York City in 1902 to form with Bob Cole, a song writer and performer, a popular Broadway songwriting team, responsible for creating a number of hits. Despite the commercial success of the team, however, Johnson decided in 1905 to pursue a diplomatic career. The following year he was appointed U.S. Consul to Puerto Cabello, Venezuela's second largest port, by President Theodore Roosevelt. During his consular appointment he published poetry, such as "O Black and Unknown Bards," and worked on a novel, *The Autobiography of an Ex-Colored Man*.

In 1910 Johnson married Grace Elizabeth Nail of New York City, while on leave from his consular post. In 1912 *The Autobiography of an Ex-Colored Man* was published anonymously in Boston to scant critical attention. The story of a light-skinned African American who dreams of artistic success as a black man but settles for material success by passing into the white world, Johnson's novel anticipated the probing of black consciousness noted in the fiction of the New Negro Renaissance. The 1 January 1913 edition of the *New York Times* published Johnson's "Fifty Years," a 41-stanza celebration in verse of the 50th anniversary of the Emancipation Proclamation. Later in the year he resigned from the diplomatic corps after the election of President Woodrow Wilson.

Resettling in Harlem in the fall of 1914, Johnson became the lead editorial writer for the *New York Age*, the oldest African American newspaper in the city, a post he held for the next decade. Joining the National Association for the Advancement of Colored People (NAACP) in 1915, he was elected the first African American field secretary of the organization the following year. During his 14-year tenure as field secretary, the NAACP expanded dramatically, lobbied forcefully against lynching, and demanded the nation address the injustices of racial discrimination. Despite his exhausting duties as the leading black civil rights exponent of his generation, Johnson's literary genius flourished. In the 1920s influential New York commercial publishers vied to bring out his writing in a variety of genres. In 1922 he compiled *The Book of American Negro Poetry*, the first anthology of African American verse published by a major American commercial press. In 1925 he edited *The Book of American Negro Spirituals*. Two years later his landmark volume of poetry, *God's Trombones: Seven Negro Sermons in Verse*, appeared, winning considerable critical praise and the Harmon Award for Poetry. In the same year *The Autobiography of an Ex-Colored Man* was reissued with the celebrated author's name firmly linked to the text. In 1930 came *Black Manhattan*, a history of African Americans in New York, and a long satirical poem, *Saint Peter Relates an Incident of the Resurrection Day*, in a limited private edition.

Johnson accepted the Adam K. Spence Chair of Creative Literature and Writing at Fisk University in 1931. He published his memoir, *Along This Way*, in 1933, and a year later, *Negro Americans, What Now?*, a collection of essays championing integration. A groundbreaking visiting professorship at New York University in 1934 led to his lecturing at a wide range of colleges and universities over the next three years. Johnson died in 1938 of injuries sustained in an automobile accident. He was the most versatile African American literary artist of the early 20th century.

WILLIAM L. ANDREWS
University of North Carolina at Chapel Hill

William L. Andrews, ed., *James Weldon Johnson: Writings* (2004); Robert E. Fleming, *James Weldon Johnson* (1987); Eugene Levy, *James Weldon Johnson: Black Leader, Black Voice* (1973).

Johnston, Mary

(1870–1936) WRITER.

Now neglected by literary critics, Mary Johnston was once a best-selling and highly respected author, publishing 23 novels, a drama titled *The Goddess of Reason* (1907), and a history called *Pioneers of the South* (1918), as well as numerous stories and essays. Her novels passed through several stages of development as Johnston's beliefs became involved with her fiction, and her initial following dwindled and died away after her death. Her works offer a compelling vision of the social and political conflicts of the early 1900s, exploring class conflicts, religious struggles, and mystical awareness. Heavy in historical details, Johnston's novels, 15 of which are set in Virginia, are as significant for their preservation of southern culture and history as they are advanced in ideology.

Johnston was born in Buchanan, Va., on 21 November 1870. She was a sickly child and spent the majority of her youth in solitude. She used her time to read excessively, exploring a wide range of authors and subjects in her father's library; her favorites included Shakespeare, Dickens, Scott, James, and, most notably, Whitman. In 1886 the Johnston family moved to Birmingham, Ala. After her mother's death in 1889, Johnston took over household management and forged a strong relationship with her father. His business ventures moved the family to New York in 1892, where Johnston began writing during periods of extended illness. When the Panic of 1895 devastated the Johnston's economic

security, she began writing with a serious purpose.

Johnston's first novel, *Prisoners of Hope* (1898), was successful enough for her to continue writing with support from Houghton Mifflin. It was her first historical adventure romance, and she wrote in this style until 1906. Her second novel, *To Have and to Hold* (1900), brought her widespread fame and financial security, earning her nearly a staggering $50,000 in its first year. Serialized in the *Atlantic Monthly* in 1899, it became the best-selling novel of 1900 and the work for which Johnston is now remembered. She followed it with *Audrey* (1902) and *Sir Mortimer* (1904), continuing to develop the strongest aspects of her writing: her meticulous attention to historical details, her vivid nature imagery, and a growing understanding of human character.

Johnston's next three novels shifted away from the typical romance plot in favor of more serious subjects and intense realism. Dedicated to her father and set in Virginia, *Lewis Rand* (1908) introduced the reconciliation theme that would become vitally important in her later works. Johnston had been raised in an environment steeped in the lore of the Civil War, and her historical curiosity combined with her father's Confederate service to fuel her next two works: *The Long Roll* (1911) and *Cease Firing* (1912).

Johnston's popularity faded as she turned her novels into vehicles for causes such as women's suffrage, socialism, and religious toleration. *Hagar* (1913) surprised her readers with its emphasis on its suffrage message instead of its story line, and *The Witch* (1914), *The Fortunes of Garin* (1915), and *The Wanderers* (1917) quickly followed in a similar vein. The metaphysical novels, *Foes* (1918), *Michael Forth* (1919), and the sometimes incoherent *Sweet Rocket* (1920), produced disappointing results. Her next novels attempted to recapture her original audience with a return to historical fiction. *Silver Cross* (1921), *1492* (1922), *Croatan* (1923), *The Slave Ship* (1924), and *The Great Valley* (1926) all varied widely in setting but were joined by a subordinate mystical message. With *The Exile* (1927), she returned to her blatant mysticism, apparently coming to terms with the idea that her interests were not those of her contemporary literary public. After a period of short-story publication, she produced the simple romance novel *Hunting Shirt* (1931) and a structurally faulty biographical sketch in *Miss Delicia Allen* (1932). Her last novel, *Drury Randall* (1934), was perhaps her most skillful synthesis of philosophy, fiction, and talented prose, but it failed to revive her career. She died on 9 May 1936, misunderstood and unremembered for her true talent.

KATHY SCHRUM
University of South Carolina

C. Ronald Cella, *Mary Johnston* (1981); Gayle Melton Hartley, *The Novels of Mary Johnston: A Critical Study* (1972).

Jones, Madison

(b. 1925) WRITER.

Madison Jones is a central figure in southern literature, but paradoxically not well known. He writes about conflicts between the native and the alien, tradition and progress, and innocence and experience, and shares the general Old South regret at the loss of inherited values.

Madison Jones grew up in rural Tennessee, served in Korea, and has degrees from Vanderbilt and University of Florida. He taught at University of Miami, Ohio; the University of Tennessee; and is Auburn University Writer in Residence, Emeritus. He was inducted into the Fellowship of Southern Writers in 1989.

He is the author of 11 novels: *The Innocent* (1957); *Forest of the Night* (1960); *A Buried Land* (1963); *An Exile* (1967, made into the film *I Walk the Line*); *A Cry of Absence* (1971); *Passage through Gehenna* (1978); *Season of the Strangler* (1982, a short-story cycle); *Last Things* (1989); *To the Winds* (1996); and *Nashville 1864: The Dying of the Light* (1997), winner of the prestigious T. S. Eliot Award for Creative Writing 1998. His most recent novel, *Herod's Wife*, appeared in 2003; during the writing of the novel, Jones converted to Catholicism.

Madison Jones is the only writer of the Nashville Agrarian movement still alive today. He is a product of Vanderbilt's conservative environmentalism, which he in his youth combined with a good deal of T. S. Eliot's thinking and made his mental heritage. His teachers were Donald Davidson and Andrew Lytle. His English-language teacher was the Old Testament, and his master artists were Nathaniel Hawthorne and

Flannery O'Connor. Jones remained transfixed, however, in the shadow of the success of William Faulkner, Robert Penn Warren, William Styron, and the many other literary giants of his youth. Neither his novels nor John Frankenheimer's movie of *An Exile* have brought Jones popular recognition in his own country. Jones also remains almost unknown abroad, in spite of several excellent translations of individual novels.

Madison Jones is not a deeply religious writer like his friends Flannery O'Connor and Marion Montgomery, but in all his fiction Jones has written about the presence of good and evil in man in a classic Greek sense. Jones has been preoccupied with the presence of the past in our present and its influence on our modern "vacuum" lives. It was for his lasting topics and preoccupations that Jones was singled out for praise by literary critics, such as Ashley Brown, George Garrett, Lewis P. Simpson, Monroe K. Spears, Allen Tate, and Robert Penn Warren, who saw Jones as an important transitional figure between the generation born at the turn of the century and the southern writers of today. Jones succeeded in finding his own "language," characters, and images to create and re-create his own existence, time, and experience. According to testimony by contemporary writers, his achievement has become an example and "a lesson in the possibility of the immediate." This proved especially true for Madison Smartt Bell (named for Madison Jones), Larry Brown, William Hoffman, and Lee Smith.

Madison Jones's influence on the early Cormac McCarthy is obvious, and there are others who have been influenced by his settings, ideas, and style. Larry Brown in *Joe* to be sure, but also William Gay in *Provinces of Night*, Robert Morgan in *Gap Creek*, Charles Frazier in *Cold Mountain*, and Ron Rash in *One Foot in Eden*. It is "an echo in the reader's mind" of something we should not forget, something dark, sinister, inexplicably evil, and basically tragic, relentless, very much of the mountains, and at times of the isolated rural areas in the South. It is found in Jones's *Forest of the Night*, *An Exile*, *A Buried Land*, and *Passage through Gehenna*, besides in individual characters in all his novels.

Madison Jones has a dark view of human experience, but also self-knowledge, humility, and compassion. He has succeeded in finding his own voice and has created an emphatically moral world that transcends its southern particulars and has become a universal legacy. "Mortuary of Eternal Rest," a section of Jones's work in progress, was published in *American Studies in Scandinavia* during the fall of 2006.

JAN NORDBY GRETLUND
University of Southern Denmark

Chattahoochee Review (Fall 1996), special issue on Madison Jones; Jan Nordby Gretlund, ed., *Madison Jones' Garden of Innocence* (2005).

Kenan, Randall
(b. 1968) WRITER.
Though born in Brooklyn, N.Y., 12 March 1968, Randall Kenan grew up in Chinquapin, a small Duplin County town in southeastern North Carolina, which became the fictional Tims Creek

in his novel, *A Visitation of Spirits*, and story collection, *Let the Dead Bury Their Dead*. As a student at the University of North Carolina at Chapel Hill, he changed his major from physics to creative writing and literature, graduated with honors in 1985, and spent four years doing editorial work for publisher A. A. Knopf. His first novel garnered critical praise and catapulted him into national attention, leading to teaching stints at Vassar, Duke, Columbia, Sarah Lawrence, the University of Mississippi, the University of Memphis, and then back to his alma mater, where he settled and was promoted to full professor in 2006. During those teaching years he published *James Baldwin: Author* (1994), the text for a photography book, *A Time Not Here* (1997), and after years of travel across the United States, a collection of 200 interviews with black Americans, *Walking on Water* (1999).

His fiction shares with that of Toni Morrison a thematic mixture of reality and fantasy and with Faulkner a predilection for recurring characters who grow and change but are centered in the historically racially complex rural South. Characters from his first novel recur in later stories. The MacElwaine and Cross families are scheduled to reappear 20 years later in his forthcoming novel, *The Fire and the Baptism*. Their stories are tangled not only by proximity but by sexual liaisons that have crossed and recrossed the color line.

Although he has said there are 36 million ways "to be black," Kenan accepts being tagged both a black writer and a southern writer, categories to which he adds the further dimension of homosexuality, though he has said he does not want to write merely "polemical fiction." His black, white, gay, and straight characters confront a contemporary South undergoing rapid change. As his first novel included a detailed description of an old-fashioned country hog-killing by friends and neighbors, a current project, *Swine Dreams*, will explore today's huge hog-killing industry in North Carolina. His forthcoming novel focuses on two kidnappers—one black, one white—and what has happened to both since their original crime in 1970.

Like Morrison, Kenan makes use of folktales, oral history, superstition, and the supernatural, and his stories often barely conceal both real ghosts and haunting memories. His lyrical language has been highly praised not only in his fiction but in essays and biography, as well as in interviews that portray very diverse black Americans at the end of the 20th century. Dubbed by Terry McMillan "our black García Márquez," Kenan has not only explored black culture as it has been modified by video, computer technology, and affirmative action in major cities but also continues to return to that community of poor, rural families he knew best when growing up in Chinquapin—population then under 1,000.

DORIS BETTS
University of North Carolina at Chapel Hill

Doris Betts, in *Southern Writers at Century's End*, ed. Jeffrey J. Folks and James A. Perkins (1997); Trudier Harris-Lopez, *The Power of the Porch: The Storyteller's Craft in Zora Neale Hurston, Gloria Naylor, and*

Randall Kenan (1996), *South of Tradition: Essays on African American Literature* (2002); Sharon P. Holland, *Raising the Dead*, (2002); George Hovis, *Southern Literary Journal* (Spring 2004); Robert McRuer, *Critical Essays: Gay and Lesbian Writers of Color*, ed. Emmanuel Nelson (1993).

Kennedy, John Pendleton

(1795–1870) WRITER.

Descendant of a Tidewater Virginia clan, Kennedy was born in Baltimore, Md. He studied law with an uncle after receiving his formal education at a local academy and at Baltimore College. Following his admission to the bar in 1816, he practiced law rather aimlessly while writing essays and satirical pieces. In 1820 he began a political career as a member of the Maryland House of Delegates. Returning to creative writing, Kennedy published *Swallow Barn* (1832), a pioneer contribution to plantation literature that enjoyed moderate success. Capitalizing on a genre made popular by James Fenimore Cooper, Kennedy published his best work, *Horse-Shoe Robinson*, in 1835. An American historical romance, it was an early contribution to the legend of the southern role in the Revolution. Appearing in 1838, Kennedy's *Rob of the Bowl* was a tale of religious and political rivalries in 17th-century Maryland. His budding career as a romancer ended with his election to the U.S. House of Representatives in 1838. Kennedy subordinated his creative work to his political and business interests for the remainder of his life. His last major literary work was *Memoirs of the Life of William Wirt* (1849).

As Kennedy grew to manhood during the early years of the 19th century, he saw his native Baltimore change from village to thriving commercial town—its atmosphere becoming distinctly less southern. Such changes wrought their effect upon Kennedy. His ties to the South were strong, but his commitments to the border state he lived in led him to fear the rise of southern sectionalism and to embrace a nationalistic point of view.

Kennedy's place in southern letters rests on *Swallow Barn*, *Horse-Shoe Robinson*, and *Rob of the Bowl*. Of the three romances, *Swallow Barn* proved to be the most important in reflecting an image of a self-conscious South. Though the book cataloged all that seemed good in the plantation world, it also satirized the provinciality of a closed Virginia society. Despite his somewhat sympathetic depiction of slavery in *Swallow Barn*, Kennedy was convinced that the institution kept Virginia and the rest of the South from enjoying the benefits of commercial and industrial expansion. He portrayed Virginians after the Revolution living in a dream world that slavery and sectionalism would turn into a nightmare.

L. MOODY SIMMS JR.
Illinois State University

Charles H. Bohner, *John Pendleton Kennedy: Gentleman from Baltimore* (1961); Jay B. Hubbell, *The South in American Literature, 1607–1900* (1954); Joseph V. Ridgely, *John Pendleton Kennedy* (1966).

King, Florence

(b. 1936) WRITER.

In one of her best-known books, the semiautobiographical *Confessions of a*

Failed Southern Lady, Florence King writes, "a pretty girl was supposed to be a melody, not a misanthrope." These are fitting words for a writer whose career has encompassed providing an ironic look at American, especially, southern institutions. Although King has referred to herself as a misanthrope, even using that name in her column for the *National Review*, the term is not entirely accurate. King is far too engaged with the various characters she creates simply to hate or distrust them.

Born 5 January 1936 in Washington, D.C., King spent much of her childhood in Virginia. The daughter of Herbert Frederick and Louise Rudding King, she has written that her father's English heritage and her grandmother's obsession with being a southern lady were strong influences in her life. King graduated from American University in Washington, D.C., where she received a B.A. in history. She attended graduate school at the University of Mississippi but did not complete a degree. King held a number of jobs before turning to writing as a full-time career, including teaching history and working as a file clerk. In the 1960s she worked as a feature writer for the *Raleigh News and Observer*.

King's early work includes pulp fiction and erotica under pseudonyms. Her first book published under her own name was *Southern Ladies and Gentlemen* (1975), a collection of essays about southern culture, the first of which is tellingly entitled "Build a Fence around the South and You'd Have One Big Madhouse." In this essay the narrator wonders why she has become part of a drunken midnight kidnapping escapade while in graduate school in Mississippi. Her answer to the question of how a sane young woman could get into such a situation: "I was not sane, I was a Southerner."

King's most popular work, *Confessions of a Failed Southern Lady* (1985), continues in the same vein. In this fictionalized autobiography, King writes of her grandmother's obsession with raising girls in her family to be ladies. Having failed with King's mother, a cigarette smoking, foul-mouthed tomboy, she "looked around the family for a malleable girl who would heed her advice, a surrogate daughter cast in the traditional mold, someone delicate and fragile in both body and spirit, a true exemplar of Southern womanhood. Someone, in other words, either sick or crazy."

In her column "the Misanthrope's Corner," written for the *National Review* from 1990 to 2002, she widens her attack on inanity from the South to the nation at large. These columns have been collected in an anthology entitled STET, *Damnit!* (2002).

Other works by King include *Wasp, Where Is Thy Sting?* (1976), *The Barbarian Princess* (under pseudonym Laura Buchanan, 1977), *He: An Irreverent Look at the American Male* (1978), *When Sisterhood Was in Flower* (1982), *Reflections in a Jaundiced Eye* (1989), *Lump It or Leave It* (1991), *With Charity toward None: A Fond Look at Misanthropy* (1992), *Satan's Child: A Survivor Tells Her Story to Help Others* (under pseudonym Laura Buchanan, 1994).

Although works such as *Confessions*

of a Failed Southern Lady are best read in their entirety, A Florence King Reader (1995) provides an excellent sampling of King's work. Her "Author's Note" provides King's assessment of her own literary canon. In preparation for editing the Reader, she read her first three books and found: "In each book I sabotaged my observer status by inserting myself into the text and going off on personal tangents." King notes, "One of the values of an anthology is supposed to be the opportunity it gives readers to see how a writer has 'grown' over the years. Well, tough titty. I refuse to publish anything unless it's the best that I can make it, so I have cut, revised, edited and in general rewritten the excerpts [from the first three books] to bring them up to my present standards." Editing her early work was not a chore, King writes, "I love it. Some women primp; I rewrite. Polishing and tightening my prose is my idea of good clean narcissistic fun."

Since 2002 King has been retired and lives in Fredericksburg, Va.

ANNE E. ROWE
Florida State University

Florence King, The Florence King Reader (1995).

King, Grace

(1852–1932) WRITER.

Grace Elizabeth King was born in New Orleans, La., into a genteel family reduced to poverty following the Civil War. The city of New Orleans became the stage in her work, as she supplied a voice for the post–Civil War South in the face of the failure of Reconstruction and, according to biographer Robert Bush, her "grand theme." Yet King was no apologist. Much of her fiction depicts female characters who are forced to confront a white patriarchal society, and, as a woman writer, she ultimately achieved literary success in a male-dominated literary establishment.

Like her New Orleans contemporary George Washington Cable, King was critical of the mistreatment of African Americans in the South and portrayed a culturally variegated society in New Orleans. She is often remembered as part of the thriving local-color tradition of the 1880s, but the relevance of her work over a century later suggests a complexity beyond exotic descriptions of New Orleans. Her aesthetic approach recalls the works of the French realists Flaubert and Maupassant, and the literary and intellectual community in which she involved herself included William Dean Howells, Charles Dudley Warner, and Samuel Clemens.

King's father, William Woodson King, was a member of a successful law practice in New Orleans prior to the Civil War. When she was nine, the King family fled occupied New Orleans to an outlying plantation within Confederate lines. After the South's defeat, the family, like many of the antebellum elite, returned to New Orleans impoverished. King received a French Creole education as a child in New Orleans. This experience exposed her to the French literary tradition, and her writing would be influenced by these models, rather than English ones. Though her family experienced economic hardships after the war, she was still able to move in the elite circles of New Orleans society where she met Charles Dudley Warner, who encouraged King and backed her in the process of publishing her first story, "Monsieur Motte," in the *New Princeton Review*. She slowly began to achieve literary acclaim both in the South and in and around the Hartford intellectual scene that included Howells and Clemens. Her publications were featured in *Harper's Magazine* and *Century Magazine*. In 1891 King's success allowed her to travel abroad to Paris, where she frequented the same salons as Paul Desjardins and functioned as an unofficial literary ambassador from the former French colony. She returned in 1892 to live with her family in New Orleans and began the most productive period of her career.

Throughout the year of 1893 King published a series of short fiction pieces in *Century* that would eventually become the collection entitled *Balcony Stories*. "Little Convent Girl" and "La Grande Demoiselle" are two noteworthy pieces from this collection and often serve as examples of King's work in anthologies of southern literature. In addition to her literary pursuits, King also published *New Orleans, the Place and the People* (1895), a historical account of 18th- and 19th-century Creole society. She dedicated the book to the famous Louisiana historian and close friend Charles Gayarre, who passed away shortly before the book's publication. Gayarre's death marked the beginning of a series of deaths among King's close friends and family members and a period in which her productivity declined. *The Pleasant Ways of St. Medard* (1916) received critical recognition

but little commercial success. In light of literary history, however, the novel remains an interesting example of early experimental fiction. In her latter years, King continued to live in New Orleans and nurtured some of the next generation's writers, including Sherwood Anderson and Lyle Saxon. She also served as a Louisiana literary and historical icon until her death in 1932.

ROBERT RAE
University of Mississippi

Violet Harrington Bryan, *The Myth of New Orleans in Literature: Dialogues of Race and Gender* (1993); Robert Bush, *Grace King of New Orleans: A Selection of Her Writings* (1973); Anna Shannon Elfenbein, *Women on the Color Line: Evolving Stereotypes and the Writings of George Washington Cable, Grace King, Kate Chopin* (1994); Anne Goodwyn Jones and Susan Van D. Elden Donaldson, eds., *Haunted Bodies: Gender and Southern Texts* (1997).

Kingsolver, Barbara

(b. 1955) WRITER AND ACTIVIST. Although some of her most commercially successful fiction is not set in Kentucky, Barbara Kingsolver is perhaps one of the best known Kentucky authors of contemporary southern and southwestern literature. Born in Annapolis, Md., Kingsolver moved to Carlisle in Nicholas County, Ky., at the age of two. While growing up in this rural environment, Kingsolver was influenced by the work of Flannery O'Connor, Eudora Welty, Carson McCullers, and William Faulkner, among others, as well as her father's profession as a doctor and her parents' love of the arts, distaste for materialism, and philanthropic spirit. As a result, Kingsolver developed an interest in science and the humanities, as well as a propensity for social activism.

Kingsolver entered Depauw University on a music scholarship, but changed her focus to biology and English. After living abroad, Kingsolver graduated in 1977 and settled in Tucson, Ariz., in 1979 after intending only a short trip. She earned a master's degree in ecology and evolutionary biology from the University of Arizona in 1981. Kingsolver also worked toward a Ph.D., but left academia to pursue a paid writing position, as well as freelance writing opportunities in publications such as *Virginia Quarterly Review*, *Cosmopolitan*, *Nation*, and *Tucson Weekly*, among others.

Kingsolver's freelance work allowed her to draw the influences of her childhood and formal education into her writing. She infused her poetry and short stories with a deep sense of place, a feeling of community, an understanding of science, and a respect for nature, all of which have continued to permeate her work, whether she writes about the South, the West, or Africa. Reading Kentuckian Bobbie Ann Mason's *Shiloh and Other Stories* (1982) encouraged Kingsolver to find literary merit in her rural upbringing. Time spent reading, telling stories, and roaming the countryside, as well as the disparity of wealth in east-central Kentucky and racial segregation became important to her work. A coauthored piece about a Kentucky labor strike in the *Progressive* resulted in Kingsolver's first national exposure as a writer.

Kingsolver's first novel, *The Bean Trees* (1988), a *New York Times* Notable Book, made her a celebrated author. In it she depicts Taylor Greer's journey from Kentucky to the West in search of identity; rather than succumbing to early marriage and motherhood, Taylor finds renewal in community with an abused Native American child, elderly neighbors, and Guatemalan refugees. Taylor's involvement in the sanctuary movement for undocumented aliens and her unique idea of family reflect Kingsolver's own engagement with liberal causes as both a writer and an activist. The beginning of a prolific career, *The Bean Trees* speaks from a female perspective to highlight issues such as childcare, friendship, and human rights.

A national best seller chosen for Oprah Winfrey's book club, as well as one of the *New York Times* Best Books of 1998, *The Poisonwood Bible* is likely Kingsolver's best-known book. Set in the Congo, where she lived for two years during childhood while her parents' worked for a public health agency, this novel tells the story of Nathan Price, a Baptist minister, from the perspectives of his wife and daughters. Kingsolver's commitment to social justice becomes apparent as she portrays decades of violence in the Congo, as well as the inner workings of the Price family. *The Poisonwood Bible* has received overwhelming acclaim: the National Book Prize of South Africa, the Patterson Fiction Prize, the American Booksellers Book of the Year Award, runner-up for the Pulitzer Prize for Fiction, finalist for the British Orange Prize, and finalist for the PEN/Faulkner Award.

As a result of the impending success of *The Poisonwood Bible* in 1997, Barbara

Kingsolver established the Bellwether Prize for Fiction to recognize literature that promotes social change. Given biannually, the award helps Kingsolver insure a place for socially conscious writing in America. In 2000 Kingsolver was awarded the National Humanities Medal for activism.

Kingsolver's most recent novel, *Prodigal Summer* (2000), takes her readers back to Kentucky, as well as to Virginia and West Virginia, for an exploration of the earth through her characters' intimate connection to place.

Other Kingsolver works include *Holding the Line* (1989), *Homeland* (1989), *Animal Dreams* (1990), *Another America* (1992), *Pigs in Heaven* (1993), *High Tide in Tucson* (1995), and *Small Wonder* (2002).

NICOLE DREWITZ-CROCKETT
University of Tennessee

Mary Jean DeMarr, *Barbara Kingsolver: A Critical Companion* (1999); Wade Hall, *The Kentucky Anthology* (2005); Mary Ellen Snodgrass, *Barbara Kingsolver: A Literary Companion* (2004); Linda Wagner-Martin, *Barbara Kingsolver* (2004); Gioia Woods, in *Dictionary of Literary Biography*, ed. Richard H. Cracroft (1999); Charlotte M. Wright, *Updating the Literary West* (1997).

Knight, Etheridge

(1931–1991) POET.
The third of seven children, Etheridge Knight was born on 19 April 1931 in Corinth, Miss. After dropping out of school in the eighth grade, he enlisted in the army in 1947 and saw active combat duty as a medical technician in Korea, where he received a shrapnel wound and began to abuse heroin and alcohol, addictions with which he would struggle for much of his life. Discharged from the military in 1957, Knight turned to a life of wandering and theft until his 1960 arrest in Indiana for robbery. During his time in Indiana State Prison, Knight began to write and submit poetry, and, with the encouragement of black arts movement writers such as Gwendolyn Brooks and Sonia Sanchez, who would become his first wife, he crafted the pieces that became his first collection, *Poems from Prison*. Published just before his parole, in 1968, the book launched Knight's career as a poet and included a number of the poems which would become his most well known, such as "The Idea of Ancestry" and "Hard Rock Returns to Prison from the Hospital for the Criminal Insane."

Confinement, whether physical, emotional, or psychological, is a pervasive theme in much of Knight's work, yet time and again he returns to the possibilities of resistance to such forces through family and community, as well as through "poeting," Knight's term for the finding and cultivating of a personal identity and voice. Though he has been associated with the black arts movement, Knight's writing does not demonstrate the overt militancy that characterizes that aesthetic, tending to foreground personal voice and experience over political concerns. Throughout the 1970s and 1980s, Knight continued to refine and expand his vision, producing several collections, including *Belly Song and Other Poems* (1973), which was nominated for the National Book Award and the Pulitzer Prize. He was also awarded two grants from the

National Endowment for the Arts and a Guggenheim Fellowship, and served as writer in residence at a number of universities, beginning with the University of Pittsburgh in 1968.

Etheridge Knight died of lung cancer on 10 March 1991, in Indianapolis, Ind. Since his death, the annual Etheridge Knight Festival of the Arts has been established in Indianapolis to honor Knight's legacy and pay tribute to the work of various writers and artists.

JACOB SULLINS
Georgia State University

Etheridge Knight, *Born of a Woman: New and Selected Poems* (1980); Sanford Pinsker, *Conversations with Contemporary American Writers* (1985); Cassie Premo, in *The Oxford Companion to African American Literature*, ed. William L. Andrews, Francis Smith Foster, and Trudier Harris (1997).

Komunyakaa, Yusef

(b. 1947) WRITER.
Born in racially segregated Bogalusa, La., in 1947, Yusef Komunyakaa began his writing career in Vietnam, while he was a soldier in the U.S. Army and a correspondent and managing editor of the newspaper, the *Southern Cross*. Armed with Donald Allen's groundbreaking anthology of experimental verse, *New American Poetry*, Komunyakaa began to see poetry as a complex organization of visual and rhythmic impulses, although he did not write poetry during his tour of duty (1969–70). After leaving military service Komunyakaa earned a B.A. from the University of Colorado (1975), an M.A. from Colorado State (1979), and an M.F.A. from the University of California at Irvine

(1980). He published two chapbooks, *Dedications and Other Darkhorses* (1977) and *Lost in the Bonewheel Factory* (1979), during graduate school, before returning to New Orleans to serve as poet in the schools (1984–85).

Komunyakaa first came to national prominence with *Copacetic* (1984), which showcases his tendency to infuse his poems with surrealist imagery and jazz-blues rhythms, distinctive features he has continued to develop throughout his writing career. Musicians have been immensely important to Komunyakaa's aesthetics, and in his collection of essays, *Blue Notes* (2000), the poet tells of his early fascination with the sounds of Miles Davis, Thelonius Monk, and John Coltrane, among others, and how such music signaled a new "kind of freedom" that allowed him "to make vivid excursions into [his] creative universe." Komunyakaa's use of a vernacular voice, grounded in everyday speech patterns, rooted in the blues, and tinged with irony, his hip language, and syncopated rhythms, have earned him praise as one of the most innovative and stylistic poets of his generation. His blues-inspired poems, featuring down-and-out loners, victims of heartache, betrayal, and oppression, *wunmonije* witchdoctors, and juju men, place Komunyakaa's work firmly in the tradition of Langston Hughes, Sterling Brown, Amiri Baraka, Michael Harper, and Cornelius Eady. A prolific writer, Komunyakaa worked on three books at a time, producing *I Apologize for the Eyes in My Head* (1986), for which he won the San Francisco Poetry Center Award, *Toys in a Field* (1986), and *Dien*

Cai Dau (1988). Each received increasingly enthusiastic reviews. In *Dien Cai Dau*, which means "crazy" in Vietnamese, Komunyakaa makes a major contribution to Vietnam literature. Written from the perspective of a shadowy, anonymous, African American soldier, these spare poems carry immense emotional weight. Night patrols, tunnel rats, ambushes, and frontal assaults meld with days off in camp, desperate recreations with Saigon bar girls, getting "high on Buddha grass," and temporary escapes at the officer's club. The book contains perhaps Komunyakaa's signature poem, "Facing It," where the poet stands at the Vietnam memorial and sees a woman "in the black mirror . . . / trying to erase names: / No, she's brushing a boy's hair."

Magic City (1992) is set in the childhood home of the poet, Bogalusa, La., and in these poems Komunyakaa explores the journey of the black masculine self. Capturing the lush evocative sounds of the Louisiana nightscape, these poems resound with memory, personal and collective, with pain and sadness, with what has been called "the dark tenor of Komunyakaa's rhetorical music." For *Neon Vernacular: New and Selected Poetry* (1993), he won the Pulitzer Prize as well as the Kingsley Tufts Poetry Award from Claremont Graduate University, cementing his place in the canon of contemporary American poets. Komunyakaa was a National Book Critics Circle Award finalist for *Thieves of Paradise* (1998), a collection that intermingled his previous poetic voices of the experiential African American male, the Vietnam vet, and the black child in Bogalusa. Garrett Hongo has spoken of this pluralistic quality in Komunyakaa's poetic world, its containing of traditions "as diverse as Spanish surrealism, the Harlem Literary Renaissance, Modern jazz eclecticism, North Beach San Francisco Beat Poetry, and the trickster roles in Yoruba poem-dramas." Recently, Komunyakaa has published *Beyond the Pleasure Dome: New and Selected Poetry* (2001), *Talking Dirty to the Gods* (2001), and *Taboo* (2004). He also edited the anthology *Poetry 180: A Turning Back to Poetry* (2003), recorded the spoken-word compact disc *The Best Cigarette* (1997), and translated *Gilgamesh* (2006).

RANDALL S. WILHELM
University of Tennessee

Muna Asali *New England Review* (Winter 1994); Vicente F. Gotera, *Callaloo* (Spring 1989); Garrett Hongo, *Thieves of Paradise* (1997); Yusef Komunyakaa, *Blue Notes: Essays, Interviews, and Commentaries* (2000).

Lanier, Sidney

(1842–1881) WRITER AND MUSICIAN. Sidney Clopton Lanier, once considered one of America's premier southern writers, was born 3 February 1842 in Macon, Ga. Lanier was of French Huguenot descent on his father's side and Scotch-Irish on his mother's. His father, Robert Sampson Lanier, was a lawyer in Macon, but an even greater impact on Sidney was his father's descent from a line of musicians. His mother, Mary Jane Lanier, was a strict Presbyterian and raised Sidney, along with siblings Clifford and Gertrude, according to the rigid doctrines of the church. The Lanier children were schooled in southern hospitality and encouraged to appreciate music, literature, and nature as well as the God who created them.

Lanier entered Oglethorpe University in Midway, Ga., in 1857, at age 15. At Oglethorpe, he was influenced by James Woodrow, a professor of science and former student of Louis Agassiz at Harvard. Lanier began to explore a concept that stayed with him throughout his life: the value of the relationship of science to poetry and religion. He graduated in July 1860 at the head of his class. Following graduation and a year tutoring in English at Oglethorpe, Lanier developed a plan to study in a German university as a means of eventually becoming a professor in an American university. However, loyalty to his state in the Civil War interrupted his plans and changed the course of his life.

Lanier enlisted in the Confederate cause on 10 July 1861 by joining the Macon Volunteers. He saw action in several battles, including the Seven Days fighting around Richmond, Va., in 1862. While stationed at Fort Boykin in 1863, Lanier began writing his novel *Tiger-Lilies* (1867), recounting the summer before the war spent at his uncle's hotel in the mountains of east Tennessee and his experiences as a soldier in the war. After he was transferred in August 1864 to Wilmington, N.C., and became a signal officer on the blockade runners, his ship was captured and Lanier was imprisoned at Point Lookout, Md. Held prisoner for four months, he never fully recovered from the rigors of his prison experience.

Lanier eventually returned to Macon to practice law with his father. In 1867 he married Mary Day of Macon. That same year, *Tiger-Lilies* was published and brought Lanier critical praise and recognition but little money. The marriage produced four sons, but the Lanier home was hampered by poverty and by Sidney's tuberculosis. In 1873 the family settled in Baltimore, Md., where Lanier found solace in music, playing first flute in the Peabody Orchestra.

Lanier became a published poet in 1875 when *Lippincott's Magazine* published "Corn." It was followed by "Symphony" and "Florida" in 1876. These works appeared in his first volume entitled *Poems* (1877), the only volume of his poetry published in his lifetime. His best-known and critically acclaimed work, "The Marshes of Glynn," was published in 1878 and exemplified his exploration of the interrelationship of music and poetry.

Lanier's interest in Anglo-Saxon and Elizabethan poetry was apparent in works such as "Marsh Song—At Sunset" and "A Ballad of Trees and the Master." In 1878 he began teaching Shakespeare at Baltimore's Peabody Institute and the following year became a lecturer in English literature at Johns Hopkins University. Lanier contributed to critical scholarship through *The Science of English Verse* (1880) and the posthumously published *The English Novel and the Principle of Its Development* (1883).

Lanier died of tuberculosis on 7 September 1881, in the North Carolina mountains shortly after writing the poem "Sunrise." Accomplished musician and inspired poet, he produced some of the South's most melodic verse, evident in poems such as "The Song of the Chattahoochee." He is buried in the Greenmont Cemetery in Baltimore.

CHRISTIAN L. FAUGHT
University of Tennessee

Lincoln Lorenz, *The Life of Sidney Lanier* (1935); Edwin Mims, *Sidney Lanier* (1968); Edd Winfield Parks, *Sidney Lanier: The Man, the Poet, the Critic* (1968); L. Moody Sims Jr., in *Southern Writers: A Biographical Dictionary*, ed. Robert Bain, Joseph M. Fora, and Louis D. Rubin Jr. (1979); Aubrey Harrison Starke, *Sidney Lanier: A Biographical and Critical Study* (1964).

Lee, Harper

(b. 1926) NOVELIST.
Harper Lee, the author of the Pulitzer Prize–winning novel *To Kill a Mockingbird* (1960), remains one of the South's most celebrated yet most elusive authors. She was born Nelle Harper Lee in Monroeville, Ala., on 28 April 1926 to Amasa Coleman Lee and Frances Finch Lee. Her father, Amasa, would serve as inspiration for the father-lawyer character of Atticus Finch in *Mockingbird*, and it is widely considered that several other characters in her famous novel are based on herself, her family members, her friends, and her Monroeville neighbors. Lee, like Scout, the young daughter of Atticus Finch and narrator of *To Kill a Mockingbird*, was also a tomboy and the daughter of a small-town attorney in Alabama, and Lee's lifelong friend Truman Capote is commonly thought to be the model for Scout's young cousin Dill. Incidentally, the character of Ida Bell in Capote's first novel, *Other Voices, Other Rooms* (1948),

is based on Lee as a child, and his best-selling nonfiction novel, *In Cold Blood* (1965), is dedicated to her.

Lee grew up in Monroeville, and after finishing high school there she enrolled at the all-female Huntingdon College in Montgomery. In 1945, after only one year at Huntingdon, Lee transferred to the University of Alabama in Tuscaloosa, where she wrote for several student publications, and in 1947 she enrolled in the University of Alabama Law School, spending one year abroad as an exchange student at Oxford University in England.

Lee returned to Alabama after her year overseas, but instead of completing the requirements necessary to earn her law degree, she opted to move to New York to pursue a career as a writer. While in New York she worked as a reservations clerk in an airlines office, hoping to save enough money to quit and work at writing full time. One Christmas her closest friends, Michael Brown, a writer, and his wife, Joy Williams Brown, a dancer, gave her a present of a one-year salary to write. Lee accepted the money as a loan, quit her job, and began writing essays and short stories. She presented the manuscripts to an agent who, because of the difficulty in marketing essays and short stories, suggested she turn to the writing of long fiction. Lee incorporated two of her short stories into a long manuscript that became *To Kill a Mockingbird*—a story about the Depression-era arrest, trial, and defense of a black man, Tom Robinson, who lives in a small southern town and is falsely accused of raping a white woman. The book became an instant best seller, was translated into numerous foreign languages, and won the Pulitzer Prize in 1961. In 1962 Gregory Peck starred in the film version of the novel and won an Academy Award for best actor for his role as Atticus Finch. During filming of the movie, Peck and Lee began an enduring friendship. Horton Foote, another close friend of Lee's, won an Academy Award for writing an adapted screenplay.

After publication of *To Kill a Mockingbird*, Lee moved back to Monroeville and began work on a second novel, a project that she ultimately abandoned. Today Lee still lives in Monroeville, the town of her birth, but since the publication of *Mockingbird* she has consistently refused to grant interviews or accept speaking engagements. *To Kill a Mockingbird* is her only published book, yet it sells roughly 1 million copies a year, 30 million copies worldwide to date, and is among the most beloved works in American literature.

JAMES G. THOMAS JR.
University of Mississippi

Ginia Bellafante, *New York Times* (30 January 2006); Harold Bloom, ed., *Harper Lee's "To Kill a Mockingbird"* (1995); Claudia Durst Johnson, *"To Kill a Mockingbird": Threatening Boundaries* (1995); Don Lee Keith, *Delta Review* (Spring 1966); Thomas Mallon, *New Yorker* (May 29, 2006); Charles J. Shields, *Mockingbird: A Portrait of Harper Lee* (2006).

Lewis, Henry Clay

(1825–1850) PHYSICIAN AND HUMORIST.

Like several other newspaper humorists of the Old Southwest—Francis James Robinson, Orlando Benedict Mayer, and Marcus Lafayette Byrn—Lewis was a frontier doctor and a writer by avocation. Born in Charleston, S.C., on 26 June 1825, Lewis, who graduated from the Louisville Medical Institute in 1846, practiced medicine, first in Yazoo City, Miss., and then in rural Madison Parish on the Tensas River in northeastern Louisiana, and in late 1848 in Richmond, La., the county seat of Madison Parish. Many of Lewis's patients were planters and their slaves, farmers, swampers, and hunters—the real-life inspiration for some of the characters he featured in his humorous sketches.

Lewis's reputation as a humorist derives from a few sketches that, beginning in 1845 with "Cupping on the Sternum," began appearing in William T. Porter's weekly New York sporting paper, the *Spirit of the Times*, and a single book, *Odd Leaves from the Life a Louisiana "Swamp Doctor"* (1850), which he published pseudonymously as Madison Tensas, M.D., and which consists of 22 sketches, many of them partly autobiographical and drawing on his experiences as a medical apprentice, medical student, and backwoods physician. The persona Madison Tensas, an old swamp doctor, recounts retrospectively his experiences, including some self-deprecating ones that make him look foolish, immature, and even reprehensible and cruel.

Lewis's humor, often dark and sinister, focuses on what Hennig Cohen and William B. Dillingham call the "underside of comedy," the grotesque and shockingly disgusting, the outlandish and horrifying, sometimes reminiscent of the grim subject matter of Edgar Allan Poe. Sketches in *Odd Leaves* such as "Valerian and the Panther," depicting a young boy having three of his fingers nearly bitten off when he tries to steal a plug from his sleeping father's mouth, and "The Indefatigable Bear Hunter," portraying a backwoodsman whose leg had to be amputated after a confrontation with a bear and the leg's wooden replacement, which the hunter subsequently uses as a weapon to bludgeon another bear, represent Lewis's brand of realistic sardonic humor.

Subversive and antisentimental, Lewis's humorous sketches sometimes defy limits and boundaries, going well beyond conventions of the acceptable and proper. In his rollicking mock-oral sketch "A Tight Race Considerin'," arguably one of Lewis's most amusing and daring pieces, a son relates to Tensas how he deceptively and deliberately fabricated a horse race between Mrs. Hibbs, his mother who always loved racehorses, and a circuit-riding parson, whose steed is a former racehorse. In the story's graphic conclusion, Mrs. Hibbs wins the race, having stripped off most of her clothes to lighten her horse's load and therefore veritably stark naked, the horse pitching her "like a lam for the sacryfise" through the church meeting house's window and into the midst of the embarrassed congregation.

Lewis's anticonventional and transgressive mode of humor is also exemplified in his depiction of women and African American slaves who, in selected sketches, transcend the narrow boundaries of gender and race portraiture. Besides the example of the immodest and unconventional behavior of Mrs. Hibbs in "A Tight Race Considerin'," Lewis, in "A Curious Widow," further destabilizes male dominance and misogyny by having a practical and cruel joke instigated by Tensas and some of his fellow medical students in which they sew the deformed and horrifying face of an albino cadaver to an oil cloth and place it in their room for the widow to find, a prank intended to terrify her that goes awry. When she expectedly finds the package containing the face, she laughs hysterically and verbally berates them into humiliation. Several of Lewis's sketches exhibit human dimensions of African American slaves and thereby counter and challenge racial stereotypes that emphasize black inferiority.

A celebrator of the unconventional, grotesque, and unsavory, Henry Clay Lewis, as Richard Boyd Hauck has accurately noted, is a "native absurdist who thrived upon the absurd ambivalence of the comic-horrible life," which makes him one of the most complex and intriguing of the South's antebellum humorists. Equally important, Lewis is a precursor of the brand of comic grotesquery prevalent in modern southern literature in selected works of Erskine Caldwell, William Faulkner, Flannery O'Connor, Harry Crews, Barry Hannah, Dorothy Allison, and others.

EDWARD J. PIACENTINO
High Point University

John Q. Anderson, *Louisiana Swamp Doctor: The Life and Writings of Henry Clay Lewis* (1962); Hennig Cohen and William B. Dillingham, eds., *The Humor of the Old Southwest* (1994); Richard Boyd Hauck,

A Cheerful Nihilism: Confidence and "The Absurd" in American Humorous Fiction (1971); Gretchen Martin, *Southern Literary Journal* (Spring 2005); Ed Piacentino, in *Humor of the Old South*, ed. M. Thomas Inge and Edward J. Piacentino (2001).

Longstreet, Augustus Baldwin

(1790–1870) WRITER.

Longstreet is remembered today for his collection of humorous stories, *Georgia Scenes* (1835). A native of Augusta, Ga., he earned a degree from Yale University in 1813, studied law in Litchfield, Conn., and returned to his home state. He later attained professional success as a lawyer, a superior court judge, a proprietor and editor of a newspaper (the *State Rights Sentinel*, which he used as a forum for his political views, especially for a defense of slavery and nullification), a Methodist minister, and president of four institutions of higher learning (Emory College in Georgia, Centenary College in Louisiana, the University of Mississippi, and the University of South Carolina).

His experiences as a lawyer and judge in Georgia furnished Longstreet with an opportunity to observe southerners of every social class, and he made use of these people as characters for *Georgia Scenes*. Ostensibly related by two refined narrators—Hall, a country gentleman, and Baldwin, an urbane judge—the 19 sketches are populated by crackers, dirt eaters, crafty horse traders, and other indigenous southern types. The clash of the narrators' values and highly literate writing styles with the values and vernacular speech of the rural people that Hall and Baldwin

encounter is the basis for much of the humor of the volume.

Walter Blair called *Georgia Scenes* "the first and most influential book of Southwestern humor." Longstreet's themes and techniques foreshadowed those in the works of the antebellum humorists, such as Johnson Jones Hooper and George Washington Harris, who followed in this tradition, a tradition that attracted Mark Twain during his writing career. In his use of the South and its people to create a sense of place in fiction, Longstreet opened new territory later traveled by the local colorists of the postbellum period, such as Richard Malcolm Johnston and Thomas Nelson Page, and by writers of the 20th century, from William Faulkner to Eudora Welty.

Georgia Scenes is also important as social history. In it Longstreet wished to depict representative "Characters, Incidents . . . in the First Half Century of the Republic" in his state, because he realized that complex social and economic forces had already begun altering the mores and daily activities there. In the book, for example, the narrator Hall described in detail a no-holds-barred Georgia fight, a backwoods shooting match, and the brutal sport of gander pulling; the narrator Baldwin contrasted the attitudes and popular tastes of the time with those of his youth. For the most part, Longstreet projected an optimistic view of the narrowing of the gulf between wealthy planters and poor whites, but he recognized that both classes would lose something of their unique life-styles in the process. Perhaps the most notable aspect of *Georgia*

Scenes is Longstreet's generally objective portrayal of southern poor whites, a group frequently viewed with complete disdain by other antebellum writers.

MARK A. KELLER
Middle Georgia College

Kimball King, *Augustus Baldwin Longstreet* (1984); James B. Meriwether, *Mississippi Quarterly* (Fall 1982); John Donald Wade, *Augustus Baldwin Longstreet: A Study in the Development of Culture in the South* (1924, 1969).

Lumpkin, Grace

(1891–1980) WRITER.

Born in Milledgeville, Ga., to wealthy, conservative parents, Grace Lumpkin was an activist writer whose early works were well received by the Communist Party. Lumpkin's proletariat works include *To Make My Bread* (1932), *A Sign for Cain* (1935), *The Wedding* (1939), and *Full Circle* (1962). She grew up and resided in Georgia and South Carolina before moving to New York in the mid-1920s. Her first novel, *To Make My Bread*, is a tale of the hardships endured by Appalachian peoples and the social injustices they experienced. With this publication, she found herself lauded by communists for her commentary on American culture during the Great Depression.

Initially a social realist and communist sympathizer, Lumpkin found herself increasingly distancing herself from ties she made with New York City literary circles after McCarthyism took hold. Her 10-year marriage to Mike Intrator also spurred her political backpedaling, as Intrator's standing with the party was questionable. After testifying to the U.S. Senate subcommittee, where she informed on her former communist associates, Grace returned to Columbia, S.C. There she fully embraced an anticommunist sentiment, which is revealed in the writings and speeches she produced until her death in 1980.

MISTY DAWN CARMICHAEL
Georgia State University

Barbara Foley, *Radical Representations: Politics and Form in U.S. Proletarian Fiction, 1929–1941* (1993); Jacquelyn Dowd Hall, *Journal of Southern History* (February 2003); Sherry Linkon and Bill Mullen, eds., *Radical Revisions: Rereading 1930s Culture* (1996).

Lumpkin, Katherine Du Pre

(1897–1988) WRITER AND ACTIVIST.

Born on 22 December 1897 in Macon, Ga., to Annette and William Lumpkin, a Confederate Civil War veteran and lawyer, Katherine Du Pre Lumpkin grew up in a household that adamantly embraced the ideology of the Lost Cause. Her memoir, *The Making of a Southerner* (1946), portrays a southern tradition that she herself was very much a part of, and as such, it provides unique insights into the perspectives of white, southern, elite families, detailing the system of slavery, the hardships of the Civil War and Reconstruction, and the rationale behind Jim Crow from their point of view. After illustrating this mentality and how it affected her childhood, Lumpkin then describes how she, as an individual, came to question and then to ultimately reject the mythology of the Lost Cause, which served to buttress southern hierarchies of gender, race, and class.

In Richland County, S.C., where she and her family moved to farm when she was 11 years old, Lumpkin came into close contact with economically exploited working-class whites. Her contact in South Carolina with white poverty ignited what would later become her critical stance toward the ideology she was taught as a child. Additionally, her education played a large role in facilitating her thoughtful analysis of oppression in the South. From 1912 to 1915, Lumpkin attended Brenau College, in Gainesville, Ga., where she earned a bachelor's degree before attending Columbia University to study sociology. After earning a master's degree from Columbia, Lumpkin moved to the University of Wisconsin and earned a doctorate in economics in 1928. While receiving her postgraduate education outside of the region, Lumpkin periodically returned to the South, and for a time she worked as the national student secretary for the southern region of the YWCA, an interracial organization that further challenged many of the biases and taboos Lumpkin learned as a child.

After earning her doctorate, Lumpkin lived most of her adult life in the northeastern United States, and she taught economics and social science at several women's colleges, including Mount Holyoke and Smith. Much of her academic research and writing deals with labor issues and social reform, and Lumpkin herself spent periods of time working in mills and factories in order to inform this research. She used her position as a social scientist to argue against white supremacy, the devalued status of women, and economic exploitation in the United States.

Lumpkin's memoir, *The Making of a Southerner*, remains an essential work for anyone seeking to understand the ways in which white supremacy was justified and accepted by elite white southerners as well as the roles white women played in this process. As such, her memoir is often compared to Lillian Smith's *Killers of the Dream* as it not only provides insight into this process but also details the difficulties of rejecting an ideology that was so thoroughly ingrained.

AMY SCHMIDT
University of Mississippi

Darlene Clark Hine, *The Making of a Southerner* (1991); Fred Hobson, *But Now I See: The White Southern Racial Conversion Narrative* (1999); Carolyn Perry and Mary Louise Weaks, eds., *The History of Southern Women's Literature* (2002).

Lytle, Andrew

(1902–1995) WRITER, CRITIC, EDITOR, AND TEACHER.
Born in Murfreesboro, Tenn., Andrew Lytle attended Vanderbilt University, where he associated with the Fugitive poets. When his Vanderbilt teachers John Crowe Ransom and Donald Davidson helped organize the Agrarian symposium, *I'll Take My Stand* (1930), Lyle contributed a spirited defense of the yeoman farmer, "The Hind Tit," which reveals the milieu for much of his later fiction, the disappearing folk culture of middle Tennessee. Like fellow Agrarians Allen Tate and Robert Penn Warren, who wrote Civil War biographies early in their careers, Lytle

published *Bedford Forrest and His Critter Company* in 1931. Utilizing detailed research of Civil War battleground strategy, it contrasted weaknesses within the Confederate high command with the military skills of Forrest and the strength of "the plain folk" who supported him. Between the 1930s and 1980s, in many social and political essays collected in *From Eden to Babylon* (1990), Lytle continued to examine the South's legacy of defeat and to criticize the values of an urban-industrial society. Influenced by his study of religion and history, Lytle associated the disintegration of southern tradition with the spiritual decline of Western culture, "the gradual fall from a belief in a divine order of the universe into a belief in history, that is man judging man as the final authority of meaning in life."

The last of the Agrarians to die, Lytle became the South's most articulate defender of traditional values. A celebrated raconteur, described by Robert Penn Warren as "the perfect teller of tales," he lived much of his life in a family log home in Monteagle, Tenn., where he entertained many well-known southern writers including Warren, Tate, Eudora Welty, Katherine Anne Porter, Cleanth Brooks, and Peter Taylor. An influential teacher of prominent American writers including Flannery O'Connor, Lytle established writing programs at the University of Florida and the University of the South, where he was editor of the *Sewanee Review*.

Andrew Lytle's most important contribution to American letters was as an artist whose short stories and novels reflect the aesthetic position of his favorite and often-quoted poet, William Butler Yeats: "We make out of the quarrel with others, rhetoric, but of the quarrel with ourselves, poetry." Carefully distinguishing between the voice of the cultural critic and that of the artist, Lytle wrote dramatic, not didactic, fiction: "In 'The Hind Tit' I took a position. . . . An artist cannot take such a position. It was like closing a door." In *The Long Night* (1936) a boy's private need to avenge his father's murder is dissolved in the public violence of the Civil War. Through its examination of pride and an often-violent code of honor, this novel explores a darker side of southern tradition. At the *Moon's Inn* (1941), the story of Hernando De Soto's unsuccessful effort to conquer the wilderness of Spanish Florida, places Lytle's agrarian beliefs within the context of Western imperialism and the destructive emergence of what he calls "the autonomous mind." *A Name for Evil* (1947), a Gothic study of obsession and egotism, describes the failure of that mind to regenerate the traditional southern agricultural life that Lytle vigorously defended in his early agrarian essays. *The Velvet Horn* (1957), Lytle's last and finest novel, dramatizes the disintegration of the old order, but through a complex religious and mythic structure influenced by Lytle's reading of Carl Jung and Erich Neumann, it also suggests the possibility of renewal. Stating that his original intention was to "do a long piece of fiction on a society that was dead," Lytle discovered that "out of death comes life." *A Wake for the Living* (1975), a family and social memoir, reveals the source of many ideas and characters in Lytle's fiction while it joins past and present in a predominately comic celebration of life.

Stories: Alchemy and Others (1984) contains most of Lytle's short fiction, including "Jericho, Jericho, Jericho," an often-anthologized rendering of the moment of death. Lytle's literary essays on writers ranging from Tolstoy and Flaubert to Henry Miller and William Styron are collected in *Southerners and Europeans* (1988). *Kristin* (1992) provides a final summary of Lytle's understanding of fiction through a close examination of Sigrid Undset's Nobel Prize–winning trilogy, *Kristin Lavransdatter*.

THOMAS M. CARLSON
University of the South

M. E. Bradford, ed., *The Form Discovered: Essays on the Achievement of Andrew Lytle* (1973), *From Eden to Babylon: The Social and Political Essays of Andrew Nelson Lytle* (1990); Mark Lucas, *The Southern Vision of Andrew Lytle* (1986); Stuart Wright, *Andrew Nelson Lytle: A Bibliography, 1920–1982* (1982).

Madden, David

(b. 1933) WRITER, TEACHER, AND CRITIC.
David Madden is one of the most prolific and eclectic writers alive today. His body of work includes nine published novels (including a serial), two short-story collections, almost 100 published short stories, 52 critical works and textbooks, 11 plays, a screenplay (*Cassandra Singing*, unproduced), as well as numerous articles, essays, and interviews. However, as Madden says in a new interview at the end of the first full-length scholarly work on his career, *David Madden: A Writer for All Genres*, he has never been as famous as he dreamed of being as an usher of the Bijou movie theater.

Jerry David Madden grew up in Knoxville, Tenn. At 14, he had a literary agent and, before graduating high school, won a playwriting contest. His *Call Herman in to Supper* was performed at the University of Tennessee. He joined the Merchant Marine after high school and the army at 20. Two years later, in 1955, he went to Iowa State Teacher's College. He met his wife, Roberta, and they were married the following year. They have one son, Blake. Madden finished his M.A. in creative writing at San Francisco State in 1958, and his thesis became his first published book in 1961, *The Beautiful Greed*. Beginning in 1960, he taught at several colleges and universities before moving to Baton Rouge and Louisiana State University in 1968, where he has remained since.

Madden grew up listening to his grandmother's and other relatives' stories in the Tennessee mountains. His work often deals with the relationship between audience and storyteller, and he has opened essays and novels the same way a respected storyteller might, knowing exactly how to capture his audience, "Did I ever tell you about the time. . . ?" Another way Madden's early immersion in the Appalachian and southern oral traditions impacts his literary work is his tendency to revisit stories from different angles and to revise published work—for instance, his second book, *Cassandra Singing* (1969), is also a play and screenplay. Madden's writing exists inside a tension created between the oral and literary traditions. He has called this tension a schizophrenia, which he thinks impacts the writing of many southern writers.

Madden emphasizes language, the craft or art of writing, rather than theme or subject matter alone. This approach is demonstrated in his experimental courses and the innovative textbooks he has edited, including *Revising Fiction* and his Pocketful series.

Madden's *Brothers in Confidence*, originally published in 1972, was brought out in a new edition in 2000. *The Shadow Knows*, a book of short stories, won a National Council on the Arts Award judged by Walker Percy and Hortense Calisher. His stories have appeared in *Best American Short Stories* twice. He received a National Endowment for the Arts Prize in 1970 and a Rockefeller grant in 1969 on the recommendation of Robert Penn Warren and Saul Bellow. *Bijou* (1974), which tells the story of Lucius Hutchfield, an usher at the Bijou Theater, was a Book-of-the-Month Club selection and was followed by a sequel of sorts, *Pleasure-Dome*, published in 1979. Between them, *The Suicide's Wife* was published in 1978 and made into a CBS movie starring Angie Dickinson.

Two of Madden's books have been nominated for Pulitzer Prizes: *The Suicide's Wife* and *Sharpshooter: A Novel of the Civil War*, his most recent published novel, in 1996. While researching *Sharpshooter*, Madden was stunned to find that there was no one central location for Civil War materials. He founded the United States Civil War Center at LSU in 1992 and acted as director until 1999.

David Madden still lives in Baton Rouge with his wife, Roberta. He is now Donald and Velvia Crumbley Professor of Creative Writing at LSU and is finishing his novel *London Bridge Is Falling Down*, set in London during the plague and fire of 1666.

EMILIE STAAT
Louisiana State University

A. B. Crowder, ed., *Writing in the Southern Tradition: Interviews with Five Contemporary Authors* (1990); Randy Hendricks and James A. Perkins, eds., *David Madden: A Writer for All Genres* (2006); William Parrill, ed., *The Long Haul: Conversations with Southern Writers* (1994); Sanford Pinsker, ed., *Conversations with Contemporary American Writers* (1985).

Marion, Jeff Daniel

(b. 1940) WRITER AND EDITOR. Jeff Daniel Marion—poet, essayist, teacher, and highly influential editor—was born 7 July 1940 in Rogersville, a small town in northeastern Tennessee. For 35 years he was an English professor at Carson-Newman College, in Jefferson City, Tenn., where he also served as Distinguished Poet in Residence and director of the Appalachian Center. Marion has made the people and landscape of this area the core of his subject matter, transcribing local flora and fauna into lyrics of praise for the mystery and solace of nature, as in his poems "By the Banks of the Holston" and "Brakeshoe Spring," and giving voice to his forebears in many of his poems, such as the sequence of "Detroit Days" poems, his long poem "Barsha Buchanan," and an elegy for his father, "The Man Who Made Color." Readers of Marion's work encounter a language closely attuned to the worldly and the natural, but rendered with a spiritual reverence and sensibility. Scholars have linked this nondogmatic religious tendency to the American transcendentalists and Buddhist mystics, noting as well the deeply Christian roots of language in the poet's native Appalachia. One aspect of this mysticism comes in the voice of an unexpected speaker from another place and time whom Marion calls "the Chinese poet," a counterpart who occasionally finds himself in the circumstances of Marion's life and gives presence to the universality of human feelings and experiences.

A definitive selection of his work, titled *Ebbing and Flowing Springs: New and Selected Poems and Prose, 1976– 2001*, appeared in 2002. Marion's other books include the poetry collections *Out in the Country, Back Home* (1976), *Tight Lines* (1981), *Vigils: Selected Poems* (1990), *Lost and Found* (1994), *The Chinese Poet Awakens* (1999), and *Letters Home* (2001), as well as the children's book *Hello, Crow* (1992). He is also the author of four chapbooks and a number of essays on poetry and photography (his other artistic passion), and he edited the book *Kinfolks and Other Selected Poems* by Kentucky poet Ann Cobb. Marion's work as an editor, beginning in 1975 with *The Small Farm* and ending with his retirement and the final issue of *Mossy Creek Reader*, brought attention to many young writers from the Appalachian region. The field of Appalachian literature is noted for its

sense of community, and Marion has distinguished himself within that tradition of generosity to young and developing writers through his teaching and editorial work.

In 1994 Marion was the subject of the annual Appalachian Literature Festival at Emory and Henry College, and the spring 1995 issue of *Iron Mountain Review* featured Marion's poetry and prose, along with an interview conducted by the poet's son, novelist Stephen Marion (author of the 2002 novel *Hollow Ground*), and several essays on Marion's body of work. In 2003 a special issue of the journal *Appalachian Heritage* was devoted to Jeff Daniel Marion's writing and life, including essays by John Lang and Marianne Worthington. In 1978 Marion was awarded the first literary fellowship from the Tennessee Arts Council, and he served as Copenhaver Scholar in Residence at Roanoke College in 1998. Most recently Marion's volume of selected writings, *Ebbing and Flowing Springs*, was selected as "Appalachian Book of the Year" by the Appalachian Writers' Association, and he was honored with the Knoxville Writers' Guild's Lifetime Achievement Award in 2006. Marion currently lives and writes in Knoxville, Tenn., with his wife, the poet and editor Linda Parsons Marion.

JESSE GRAVES
University of Tennessee

Don Johnson, *Iron Mountain Review* (Spring 1995); John Lang, *Appalachian Heritage* (Fall 2003); Dan Leidig, *Appalachian Journal* (Spring 1983); Guy Owen, *Southern Poetry Review* (1977); Lynn Powell, *Iron Mountain Review* (Spring 1995); Lynne P.

Shackelford, *Contemporary Poets, Dramatists, Essayists, and Novelists of the South: A Bio-Bibliographical Sourcebook* (1994); Marianne Worthington, *Appalachian Heritage* (Fall 2003).

Marlette, Doug

(1949–2007) WRITER AND CARTOONIST.

Douglas N. Marlette was born in Greensboro, N.C., into a military family. At various points during his life, he lived in Florida, Mississippi, and New York City. As a child he liked to draw. In his book *In Your Face* (1991), he remarks that his second-grade teacher encouraged him to take classes in art. He also notes that in elementary school he reveled in comic strips from "Peanuts" to "Li'l Abner" and that his interest in comics spilled over into classroom mischief, such as drawing over photographs of important public people in order to make them humorous. At Florida State University in Tallahassee, Marlette produced editorial cartoons for the student newspaper on topics that ranged from coeducational dormitories to the war in Vietnam. After graduation, he started to draw and write political cartoons for the *Charlotte Observer* in North Carolina. In 1987 he joined the *Atlanta Journal-Constitution*, and in 1989 he moved to New York to work for *Newsday*. He began to work for the *Tallahassee Democrat* in 2002 and the *Tulsa World* in 2006. His work appeared in *Time*, *Newsweek*, the *New York Times*, the *Washington Post*, and various other venues.

Marlette gained considerable renown for his trenchant editorial-page cartoons and also for his comic strip *Kudzu*, both of which were widely syndicated. His cartoons, which often treated political topics, were perhaps inevitably controversial. After the 11 September 2001 attacks on the World Trade Center in New York City and the Pentagon in Washington, D.C.—which prompted the United States to invade Afghanistan—Marlette drew a cartoon depicting a man in Middle Eastern clothes driving a truck that carried a nuclear bomb, with the caption: "What Would Mohammed Drive?" Because of the cartoon, Marlette received furious e-mails and death threats. In an article published in the *Tallahassee Democrat* in December 2002, he defends the cartoon by observing that it parodies the debates by Christian evangelicals over "What Would Jesus Drive?" He notes that he received similar threats for cartoons attacking what he saw as the falsehood of the Jim and Tammy Bakker Christian televangelist empire. He also notes that he has been attacked for defending the rights of minorities, including Muslims and African Americans.

To indicate the nature of the attacks on the Bakker cartoons and for ones lampooning Jerry Falwell, he titled another article, published in the *Columbia Journalism Review* in 2003, "I Was a Tool of Satan." His subtitle, "An Equal-Opportunity Offender Maps the Dark Turn of Intolerance," humorously suggests the issues addressed in response to various criticisms of his work. In this article, he notes that the Mohammed drawing was aimed not at Islam but at its distortion by Arab fanatics. In addition, he observes that few people are less tolerant than those demanding tolerance, and he defends his cartoons as expressions of free speech.

The *Kudzu* comic strip, according to Marlette's *In Your Face*, had its origins in his feelings about his failures as a teenager. The strip originally consisted of the young character Kudzu Dubose, his mother, his friend Maurice, the belle Veranda Tadsworth, various pets, and the preacher Will B. Dunne. Marlette later added other characters, with humorous names such as Nasal T. Lardbottom, to the strip. *Kudzu*, which was less controversial than the cartoons, ran in the magazine the *Christian Century*. It was made into a successful musical that was produced at Duke University as well as at Ford's Theatre in Washington, D.C.

Marlette also published two semiautobiographical novels, *The Bridge* (2001) and *Magic Time* (2006). *The Bridge* is, for the most part, narrated in the first person by its central character Pick Cantrell, who describes his dismissal from a New York City publication and his return to the South. The present time of *Magic Time*, which takes its title from an old roadhouse, is 1991, but the novel centers on the historical events of Freedom Summer 1964, when three youthful civil rights workers—Michael Schwermer, Andrew Goodman, and James Chaney—were killed in Mississippi by the Ku Klux Klan.

Marlette, who published 19 books, received many awards for his work. He won the 1988 Pulitzer Prize for Editorial Cartoons; he received the National Headliners Award for Consistently Outstanding Editorial Cartoons three times; and he collected numerous simi-

lar honors. *The Bridge* was named the Best Novel of 2002 by the Southeastern Booksellers Association.

MARY ANN WIMSATT
University of South Carolina

Mason, Bobbie Ann
(b. 1940) WRITER.

Bobbie Ann Mason was born in Mayfield, Ky., to a farm family headed by her parents, Wilburn A. and Christianna Lee Mason. The rolling countryside of western Kentucky serves as the touchstone for much of her personal life and the setting for the majority of her fiction, located in and around the imagined community of Hopewell, Ky. The people Mason knew and observed growing up in the rural South populate her fiction—working-class white Americans whose lives are dictated by forces beyond their control: the weather, the factory owner, the bank. Critical response to Mason's work ranges from praise for her ability to capture through spare prose and images of popular culture the patterns of meaning in her characters' lives, to critiques of her fictional world's emotional and spiritual barrenness.

Before writing so closely about home, Mason first left it. After graduation from Mayfield High School in 1958 and then from the University of Kentucky in 1963, she went to New York City, where she worked briefly as a journalist for *Movie Life* before earning advanced degrees from the State University of New York at Binghamton (M.A. in English, 1966) and the University of Connecticut (Ph.D. in English, 1972). She then moved with her husband,

Roger Rawlings, to Pennsylvania, where both taught at Mansfield State College. Mason published her dissertation in 1974 as *Nabokov's Garden: A Guide to Ada*, and she quickly followed that volume of literary criticism with *The Girl Sleuth* (1975), an examination of the detective fiction she had read growing up. She left her teaching position in 1979 to devote full energy to writing fiction.

The 18 February 1980 issue of the *New Yorker* includes her first published short story, "Offerings." Her first collection, *Shiloh and Other Stories* (1982), followed within a few years and received the PEN/Hemingway Award. The title story, "Shiloh," is among Mason's most regularly anthologized and is significant for its investigation of a male character's sense of powerlessness in the face of his life's changed circumstances. In 1985 Mason published her first novel, *In Country*, an exploration of the legacy of the Vietnam War for a generation of Americans who cannot even remember it, teenagers like the protagonist Samantha Hughes, whose father died in the conflict, leaving her only the letters and diaries he penned in the midst of a war he understood no better than she does. Mason has followed her early successes with a steady stream of publications, including *Spence + Lila* (1988), *Love Life* (1989), *Midnight Magic* (1998), and *Zigzagging down a Wild Trail* (2001).

Mason and her husband moved to central Kentucky in 1990, initiating a second phase of her career trained more tightly on the personal resonances between the author and her place. *Feather Crowns* (1993), recipient of the Southern

Book Award for Fiction, is a long historical novel set at the turn into the 20th century that initially appears as a wide departure from the author's characteristic focus on life in the present, yet the novel actually revisits and expands upon themes present in her earlier work: the felt or denied power of individuals to control their lives, the search for meaning in the routine of everyday existence, and the struggle to live into a womanhood at odds with cultural prescriptions for it. Her work takes a more deeply and immediately personal turn with *Clear Springs: A Memoir* (1999), a episodic account of Mason's life that inevitably leads her deep into her Kentucky roots, most particularly into her mother's life.

Despite Mason's abiding connection to Kentucky, readers should be wary of finding in her work more of the traditional "sense of place" they have been trained by paradigms of southern literature to recognize. Mason's fiction and nonfiction about her home is anything but classically nostalgic; deep within it runs an ambivalence about the much-touted agrarian life-style that adds up realistically to debt, mud, and disdain from people with lawns well manicured by hired help. If Mason's social realism (alternately termed "grit lit," "dirty realism," and "K-mart realism" by critics) speaks a message, it has much more to do with respecting the lives of her characters and understanding their choices than it does with any neo-agrarian condemnation of their television watching or indictment of their decisions to sell out to bland subdivisions. Mason's South is not one that needs saving from itself, but it is one in which change is

MASON, BOBBIE ANN   359

a constant. Surviving that change becomes her characters' central preoccupation.

KATHRYN MCKEE
University of Mississippi

Paula Gallant Eckard, *Maternal Body and Voice in Toni Morrison, Bobbie Ann Mason, and Lee Smith* (2002); Matthew Guinn, *After Southern Modernism: Fiction of the Contemporary South* (2000); Joanna Price, *Understanding Bobbie Ann Mason* (2000); Albert Wilhelm, *Bobbie Ann Mason: A Study of the Short Fiction* (1998).

McCarthy, Cormac

(b. 1933) WRITER.

In a 40-year literary career Cormac McCarthy has transformed himself from a little-known southern writer to a popular western writer, and done it, furthermore, without actually changing much more than his address and fictional settings. Born Charles McCarthy (he renamed himself Cormac in adulthood) in Rhode Island on 20 July 1933, he was raised in Knoxville, Tenn., where he lived, off and on, until 1976. There and in the surrounding countryside he set his first four novels, beginning with *The Orchard Keeper* (1965). That book was a remarkable debut, particularly coming from a writer who had drifted rather aimlessly in and out of the University of Tennessee (he never did graduate), the air force, and a marriage, leaving only a sparse trail of literary achievement. In its lyricism and its willingness to contemplate the dark corners of the southern landscape and the human heart, it reminded many reviewers of William Faulkner, whose death just three years

earlier had indeed created a literary vacancy that many young southern writers were striving to fill. With this novel about an east Tennessee mountain boy and his two father figures, McCarthy became one of the leading candidates.

McCarthy defined his relationship to Faulkner, and to the southern literary tradition generally, in three more east Tennessee novels, *Outer Dark* (1968), *Child of God* (1973), and *Suttree* (1979). His characters (poor whites, small farmers, scions of old families) and situations (incest, murder, the self-destructive grief of a young southern aristocrat) would have looked familiar to any Faulkner fan. But McCarthy reworked this material, draining it of even such slender humanistic affirmation as Faulkner had allowed. These grim novels are brightened only by the stunning, incandescent lyricism of their prose, jarringly contrasting with the depravity it discloses.

By the time the last of them appeared, McCarthy had left Knoxville for El Paso, Tex., where he began reinventing himself as a western writer. *Blood Meridian; or, The Evening Redness in the West* (1985), the violent story of a Tennessee boy who learns to be an Indian fighter on the Texas-Mexico border of the 1840s, was his first effort in the new genre. It fared about as well as McCarthy's previous books: a handful of admirers hailed it as a masterpiece, but few copies were sold. McCarthy had always subsisted, very modestly, on a series of grants and prizes, most notably the "genius grant" awarded by the MacArthur Foundation in 1981. When in

1992 he granted his first interview, to promote his forthcoming book, Richard Woodward of the *New York Times* found him cooking on a hot plate, doing the wash at a Laundromat, and cutting his own hair.

His circumstances changed dramatically after the publication of that next book, *All the Pretty Horses* (1992), an appealing highbrow western about two teenaged cowboys on a horseback adventure in Mexico. Though not without violence and tragedy, it was his sunniest novel, and the hero, John Grady Cole, easily his most likable protagonist. Too, its way was paved by a brilliantly orchestrated publicity campaign, courtesy of his new publisher, Alfred A. Knopf. Suddenly everyone knew who McCarthy was, belatedly regretted his long years of neglect, and rushed to make up for it. *All the Pretty Horses* won the National Book Award and went into more than 20 hardcover printings. Almost overnight McCarthy became perhaps the best-known serious writer in the country. But nothing indicated that stardom had turned his head. He followed his success with two much darker cowboy novels, *The Crossing* (1994) and *Cities of the Plain* (1998), completing what he called "The Border Trilogy." Neither sold quite so well as their predecessor. But that success continued to bear fruit: *All the Pretty Horses* was made into a high profile Hollywood movie, and two dramatic works McCarthy had written in the 1970s, the stage play *The Stonemason* and the screenplay *The Gardener's Son*, were unearthed and published to take advantage of his new fame.

After *Cities on the Plain* McCarthy remained mostly silent and out of sight, hard at work on *No Country for Old Men* (2005), his ninth novel. Another violent story of the southwestern border, this one is set in our own time and concerns a young hunter caught up in the illegal drug trade. McCarthy now lives in Santa Fe, N.M., with his third wife and their young child. Though he is in his 70s, it seems too soon to sum up a career that could yield several more books. But it is safe to say that he will keep his reputation as a lyrical and exacting prose stylist and an uncompromising adherent to his own difficult vision.

JOHN GRAMMER
University of the South

Vereen Bell, *The Achievement of Cormac McCarthy* (1988); Robert L. Jarrett, *Cormac McCarthy* (1997); Edwin T. Arnold and Dianne C. Luce, eds., *Perspectives on Cormac McCarthy* (1999).

McCorkle, Jill

(b. 1958) WRITER.

In 1984 Jill McCorkle arrived on the national literary scene in a most unconventional way. That year, Algonquin Books, a newly formed press in Chapel Hill, gambled on the young writer and brought out her first and second novels simultaneously. The move paid off, earning attention for the publisher and for the author, who was only 26. Reviews of the two books, *The Cheer Leader* and *July 7th*, were positive. S. Keith Graham called the dual release "the literary equivalent of a rebel yell," while Annie Gottlieb introduced the barely-out-of-college McCorkle this way: "One suspects the author of *The Cheer Leader* might be a born novelist; with *July 7th*, she is also a full-grown one."

This latter bit of acclaim should have pleased but not shocked the writer, who already had 20 years of experience behind her. Born 7 July 1958 (her birthday begat the title of her second book) in Lumberton, N.C., the daughter of a postal-worker father and a medical-secretary mother, Jill Collins McCorkle took to writing at an early age. She sold her first story when she was seven, to her mother for a quarter. And in the summer after second grade, her father brought home a large wooden crate which Jill claimed as her writing room. So encouraged by her parents, she entered the University of North Carolina at Chapel Hill, where three teachers recognized and nurtured her talents: writers Lee Smith and Max Steele and literary scholar Louis Rubin Jr., the last of whom would go on to found Algonquin Books. McCorkle followed her B.A. in 1980 with an M.A. in writing one year later from Hollins College.

Since her first two novels, she has penned three more: *Tending to Virginia* (1987), *Ferris Beach* (1990), and *Carolina Moon* (1997). As well, she has published three collections of short stories: *Crash Diet* (1992), *Final Vinyl Days* (1998), and *Creatures of Habit* (2001). Five of these six offerings were tabbed as New York Times Notable Books of the Year and, for her body of work, McCorkle has received the North Carolina Award for Literature and the Dos Passos Prize for Excellence in Literature. She has reviewed books, too, for the *Washington Post*, the *New York Times Book Review*, the *Atlanta Journal-Constitution*, and other newspapers.

A Jill McCorkle story reads like an exercise in character; its narrative is driven by the protagonist's evolution. In a 1990 essay, the author wrote that "by the ripe age of adolescence . . . our emotional baggage is already fully packed. [*We spend*] the rest of our lives *unpacking*, sorting and choosing, what to treasure, what to alter, what to throw off the nearest cliff never to look at again." It is no surprise, then, that many of her characters are young adults—often young women—who wrestle with insecurities and pursue an idealized version of life and love, before they eventually recognize and accept truth. McCorkle gives these characters not only her focus but also a voice. She often writes in the first person, handing the narrative over to her protagonists. Barbara Bennett points out that, in *July 7th* alone, the author "employs no fewer than twenty voices." Reviewers have praised her for these southern voices (much of her work is set in her native North Carolina), for her comic sensibility, and for the way she uses pop culture in her fiction, but perhaps her chief virtue as a writer is her empathy. As McCorkle herself came of age, she was writing, and even now she seems able to inhabit the emotional terrain of adolescence. She locates her characters at their most vulnerable, and she celebrates those moments in which their lives change.

McCorkle lives in Chapel Hill, N.C. and is a professor at North Carolina State University. She is also on the faculty of the Bennington College M.F.A. program in Vermont.

HICKS WOGAN
University of Mississippi

Barbara Bennett, *Understanding Jill Mc-Corkle* (2000); Annie Gottlieb, *New York Times Book Review* (7 October 1984); S. Keith Graham, *Atlanta Journal-Constitution Book Review* (30 September 1990); C. R. McCord, *Southern Quarterly* 36, no. 3 (1998).

McCullers, Carson

(1917–1967) WRITER.

Born and raised in Columbus, Ga., Carson McCullers published her first novel in 1940, following the most important decade in the history of southern letters. She extended the tradition of the Southern Literary Renaissance by employing the modern South as symbolic setting in all of her major fiction. More importantly, her work uses the harsh symbolism of southern life to re-create the universal failures and anxieties of modern America.

In *The Heart Is a Lonely Hunter* (1940), her allegorical structure—the complex solar system of grotesque "lonely hearts" in complementary orbits—is perfectly balanced by an intensely realistic documentation of the social conditions discovered in a southern mill city during the Depression. It remains her finest effort. *Reflections in a Golden Eye* (1941), her second novel, is an example of the modern Gothic; McCullers's tale of bizarre sexuality on a peacetime army base demonstrates considerable versatility and artistic daring. *The Ballad of the Sad Café* (1941) is a more traditional work in the Gothic mode. The distancing effect of the balladeer-narrator allows the bizarre characters and strange events to be unified in one of the most intriguing novellas in modern southern fiction.

After a long silence caused by physical and psychological problems during the war, McCullers re-created some of the literary and popular success of her first novel in *The Member of the Wedding* (1946). This smaller portrait of the mill city again probes social relationships and individual feelings through the symbolic use of the alienated adolescent. It is a narrower achievement, though one that was more accessible for a popular audience in the stage (1951) and screen (1952) versions, which made the author famous and financially secure.

McCullers worked for more than a decade on *Clock without Hands* (1961), her last novel. Unfortunately, her long and debilitating illness made the successful completion of the book impossible. The novel's weak characterization and stereotyped action cannot create a structure strong enough to make order of the complicated changes transforming the South in the days of integration.

Like many southern writers, Carson McCullers developed an ambivalent attitude toward her native land; in her eventual northern expatriation, she cut herself off from the southern roots, yet she never developed others to replace them. Her achievement was still a considerable contribution to the fiction of the Southern Literary Renaissance.

JOSEPH R. MILLICHAP
Western Kentucky University

Virginia Spencer Carr, *The Lonely Hunter: A Biography of Carson McCullers* (1975); Virginia Spencer Carr and Joseph R. Millichap, in *American Women Writers: Bibliographical Essays* (1983); Beverly Clark and Melvin Friedman, eds., *Critical Essays on Carson McCullers* (1996), *Understanding Carson McCullers* (1990); Judith G. James, *Wunderkind: The Reputation of Carson McCullers, 1940–1990* (1995).

Mencken, H. L.

(1880–1956) EDITOR, ESSAYIST, AND CRITIC.

Henry Louis Mencken was a writer of enormous national influence who also played a leading role in southern intellectual life of the 1920s. A native of Baltimore, he became a contributor to the *Smart Set* and the *American Mercury*. As such, he was, Walter Lippmann wrote, "the most powerful personal influence on this whole generation of educated people." In particular, he conducted a crusade against American provincialism, puritanism, and prudery—all of which he believed he found, to a degree larger than elsewhere, in the states below the Potomac and Ohio. Mencken shocked southerners when he published a severe indictment of southern culture, "The Sahara of the Bozart," which first appeared in 1917 in the *New York Evening Mail* and was reprinted in his book, *Prejudices, Second Series* (1920). In his essay he charged that the South was "almost as sterile, artistically, intellectually, culturally, as the Sahara Desert." "In all that gargantuan paradise of the fourth-rate," he contended, "there is not a single picture gallery worth going into, or a single orchestra capable of playing the nine symphonies of Beethoven, or a single opera-house, or a single theater devoted to decent plays." Most southern poetry and prose was drivel, he charged, and "when you come to critics, musical composers, painters, sculptors, architects and the like, you will have to give it up, for there is not even a bad one between the Potomac mud-flats and the Gulf." Nor, Mencken added, a historian, sociologist, philosopher, theologian, or scientist.

The essay, written in characteristic Menckenian hyperbole, suggested that the condition of the modern South was especially lamentable because the antebellum South, particularly Virginia, had been the seat of American civilization. Mencken attributed the decline of southern culture to the "poor whites" who, he charged, had seized control of the South after the Civil War. Particularly to blame were the preachers and the politicians. What the South needed, he maintained, was a return to influence of a remnant of the old aristocracy.

Mencken's "Sahara" and other essays on the "godawful South" attracted widespread attention in Dixie in the decade that followed. Traditional southerners denounced him as a "modern Attila," a "miserable and uninformed wretch," a "bitter, prejudiced and ignorant critic of a great people." But other southerners such as James Branch Cabell, Howard W. Odum, Gerald W. Johnson, Paul Green, Thomas Wolfe, and Wilbur J. Cash declared their agreement with the substance of the indictment.

The Southern Literary Renaissance

followed Mencken's "Sahara," and literary historians have suggested that Mencken shocked young southern writers into an awareness of southern literary poverty and thus played a seminal role in the revival of southern letters. But as important as Mencken's effect on southern literature was his effect on the general intellectual climate of the "progressive" South. Menckenism became, as the 1920s progressed, a cultural force, a school of thought for iconoclastic southerners. Not all young southerners accepted him: Donald Davidson, Allen Tate, and other southern Agrarians challenged him with particular vigor. In the mid-1930s Mencken lost interest in the South, as the South lost interest in him. Nevertheless, his impact on southern letters, even if more indirect, was felt for many years.

FRED HOBSON

University of North Carolina at Chapel Hill

Carl Bode, *Mencken* (1969); Vincent Fitzpatrick, *H. L. Mencken* (1989); Fred Hobson, *Serpent in Eden: H. L. Mencken and the South* (1974); Edward A. Martin, ed., *In Defense of Marion Bloom: The Love of Marion Bloom and H. L. Mencken* (1996); William H. Nolte, *H. L. Mencken, Literary Critic* (1966); Terry Teachout, *The Skeptic: A Life of H. L. Mencken* (2002); W. H. A. Williams, *H. L. Mencken Revisited* (1998).

Miller, Jim Wayne

(1936–1996) WRITER AND TEACHER. Born in 1936 in mountainous Buncombe County, N.C., Jim Wayne Miller was one of the leaders of the Appalachian literature movement that began in the 1960s, and the Brier, the third-person speaker of much of Miller's late poetry, has been seen as the prototypical Appalachian. Reared on the family farm, Miller did his undergraduate work at Berea College and, after a stint teaching high school, enrolled at Vanderbilt University, where he earned a Ph.D. in German and American literature in 1965. From 1963 until his death of lung cancer in 1996, Miller taught at Western Kentucky University in Bowling Green. He frequently lectured and led writing workshops throughout Appalachia. He was married to Mary Ellen Yates, with whom he had three children.

Miller credited Berea, which had as its mission the education of mountain youth, with awakening him to the significance of his Appalachian heritage. Conversely, he cited the German poets whom he read and translated as being important intellectual and artistic influences. As this dualism suggests, Miller's life and work were characterized by social and cultural disparity. He was keenly aware of how the contradictions in his own experiences epitomized the conflicts facing many Appalachians, who were exchanging their traditional, relatively isolated, agricultural life-style for full membership in mainstream American—even global—culture. Throughout Miller's writing, the pain of lost tradition is in tension with the inevitability of change and the desirability of expanded horizons. Complicating this tension is the fact that even without social change, loss is unavoidable, as death and dispute take their toll on individuals no matter where they reside.

Miller's earliest poetry struggles with the death of family members, particularly his grandfather. *Copperhead Cane* (1964) is a series of elegiac sonnets about his grandfather's death. Although Miller would soon reject this tight formal structure, the astonishingly skillful use of image and metaphor that would characterize his oeuvre is evident in this volume. In "Family Reunion," the third section of *Dialogue with a Dead Man* (1974), the speaker moves beyond the immediate family to the extended family and community, and the poems suggest that, through memory, the living are reunited with the dead.

Between these two deeply personal volumes, Miller published *The More Things Change the More They Stay the Same* (1971). He cast this overtly political book in the mold of traditional folk balladry and the social justice songs of the Appalachian coal fields. These poems deal with strip mining, the civil rights movement, and Vietnam, drawing the conclusion that protesting 1960s youths who offended their middle-class fathers carried on the tradition of social protest espoused by those fathers when they went on strike.

Although Miller would continue to write first-person poetry, such as his exploration of an unhappy marriage in *Nostalgia for 70* (1986), with his 1980 volume *The Mountains Have Come Closer* Miller introduced the third-person speaker who would dominate the remainder of his poetry—the Brier. The Brier takes his name from derogatory jokes about Appalachians who migrated to work in the industrial cities of the Midwest. Miller's Brier has many faces—ruralite, out-migrant, craftsman, street preacher, eye doctor, college professor—and he functions both as Appalachian Everyman and as Miller's alter ego. Through him, Miller comes to terms with the twin thieves, social change and death.

Using spatial metaphors of geography, the natural world, and the home, Brier eloquently articulates the loss of family, community, and landscape. However, while tearing down an old barn, Brier realizes that a new life can be built out of defunct traditions, and as a street preacher in "Brier Sermon," he urges listeners to be "born again" to the importance of heritage. Yet Miller resists narrowly sentimentalizing or idealizing the past. In "The Brier Opens a Mountain Vision Center," from *Brier, His Book* (1988), the Brier wants to combat provincialism or seeing "ridge to ridge" rather than having global awareness and seeing "ocean to ocean."

Sometimes Miller's Brier is a trickster, a gentle descendant of that most beloved deviant of southern and southern Appalachian literature, Sut Lovingood. Miller was as noted for humor and satire as he was for metaphor, and he resurrects Sut himself in the essay ". . . And Ladies of the Club," which criticizes the canonical reductivism and anti-Appalachian bias of southern literary studies. Miller attempted to rectify these biases in publications such as the coedited anthology *Appalachia Inside Out* (1995) and numerous other anthologies and works of nonfiction.

THERESA LLOYD
East Tennessee State University

L. Elisabeth Beattie, *Conversations with Kentucky Writers* (1996); Rita Sims Quillen, *Looking for Native Ground: Contemporary Appalachian Poetry* (1989); James Still and Jim Wayne Miller, *Iron Mountain Review* (Spring 1988); J. W. Williamson, *Appalachian Journal* (Spring 1979).

Milligan, Jason

(b. 1961) WRITER.

Born in Texas and raised in Oxford, Miss., and a graduate of the University of Mississippi (B.F.A. in theatre arts), Milligan has explored an array of southern themes in many of his plays, ranging from period family dramas set in Mississippi (*. . . And the Rain Came to Mayfield* and *Homecoming Bride*) to slices of small-town southern life (*Key Lime Pie, Spit in Yazoo City, Can't Buy Me Love, Lullaby, Instincts*, and *The Prettiest Girl in Lafayette County*). He has also dramatized the effects of violence during the civil rights movement of the 1960s (*Willy Wallace Chats with the Kids*) and examined the lonely lives of military spouses in 1950s Texas (*Navy Wife*).

When Milligan was 12 years old his mother enrolled him in a photography course sponsored by the Oxford Park Commission. This was the beginning of his lifelong interest in the arts. Milligan recalled: "Our photography teacher started us out taking still pictures and eventually let us try our hand at movies with an old Super 8 mm camera. A year later, my friends and I were on our own, making 12-minute James Bond movies in and about Oxford with a home movie camera and editing them with a Sears home movie editing machine."

He began writing while working as an acting apprentice at the Actors Theatre of Louisville, Ky., in 1983.

Milligan's many plays have been performed in numerous productions all across the United States, as well as in Canada and Europe. Presentations of his newer pieces have featured such well-known actors as Burt Reynolds, Peter Falk, Charles Durning, Dan Lauria, Joe Mantegna, Christian Slater, George Segal, Tony Danza, Jean Smart, Fred Savage, and Ron Pearlman. Thirty-five of his plays are now published by Samuel French, Inc.

In addition, Milligan has written or co-written six collections of original monologues for Samuel French: *Both Sides of the Story, Next!, His and Hers, Going Solo, Actors Write for Actors*, and *Encore* (the latter two coauthored with Deborah Cowles Scott and Robert Spera). These works contain countless colorful southern characters.

Collaborating with Mary Hanes, Milligan served as cocreator, writer, and producer of the television series *Hope Island*, a critically acclaimed family drama aired on PAX-TV. Other film and television work includes the screenplay for *Museum of Love*, directed by Christian Slater for Showtime for its Academy Award–winning series of original films, *Directed By*.

Since 1995 Milligan has served as writer for the Walt Disney Company, for whom he has written literally thousands of scripts, concepts, media events, press releases, speeches, industrials, stage shows, and storytelling theatre pieces for Disney theme parks and other Disney business units around the world.

Milligan is busy writing the book for an original contemporary country western musical comedy, tentatively titled *Cowboy Up*, with collaborators Michael Barnard, Carolyn Gardner, and Bret Simmons.

COLBY KULLMAN
University of Mississippi

Mitchell, Margaret

(1900–1949) WRITER.

Margaret Mitchell was as proud of her long-established Atlanta family as she was of *Gone with the Wind*. She wrote in 1941: "I know of few other Atlanta people who can claim that their families have been associated as long and intimately, and sometimes prominently, with the birth and growth and history of this city."

Mitchell was educated in Atlanta schools and at Smith College. After her mother died in the flu epidemic of 1919, Mitchell returned from Smith to Atlanta to keep house for her father and her brother. She made her debut in 1920 and in 1922 married Berrien Kinnard Upshaw. The marriage lasted barely three months.

In December 1922 Mitchell found a job on the staff of the *Atlanta Journal Sunday Magazine*. On the *Journal* she worked with such writers as Erskine Caldwell and Frances Newman. On 4 July 1925 she married John Robert Marsh, public relations officer of the Georgia Power Company, and in 1926 resigned her job because of ill health. She tried writing short stories but found no market for them, and they were eventually destroyed. Discouraged, she turned to the composition of a long novel for her own amusement during an extended recuperation.

Most of *Gone with the Wind* was completed by 1929. It was still incomplete, however, when in April of 1935 she somewhat quixotically allowed Harold Latham (on a scouting trip for the Macmillan Company) to see the manuscript. Macmillan's almost immediate acceptance was followed by months of checking for historical accuracy, filling gaps in the story, and rewriting. The book was a best seller the day it was published, 30 June 1936, and dominated its author's life thereafter.

For the next 13 years Mitchell nursed an aging father and, later, an invalid husband, enthusiastically did war work, and maintained a massive amount of correspondence relating to *Gone with the Wind*. She wrote no more fiction and emerged from private life only occasionally, most notably for the premiere of the film *Gone with the Wind* in Atlanta 15 December 1939.

Accident prone throughout her life, she met her death in an accident on 11 August 1949. Crossing Peachtree Street with her husband, she was struck by a speeding taxicab. She died five days later and was buried in Atlanta's Oakland Cemetery.

RICHARD HARWELL
Athens, Georgia

Anne Edwards, *The Road to Tara* (1983); Finis Farr, *Margaret Mitchell of Atlanta* (1965); Richard Harwell, ed., *Margaret Mitchell's "Gone with the Wind" Letters, 1936–1949* (1976); Darden Asbury Pyron, *Recasting: "Gone with the Wind" in American Culture* (1983), *Southern Daughter: The Life of Margaret Mitchell and the Making of*

"Gone with the Wind" (2004); collection of over 50,000 items of Miss Mitchell's correspondence, reviews of Gone with the Wind, magazine and newspaper articles, pictures, and other memorabilia is in the Manuscript Department of the University of Georgia Libraries, Athens.

Moody, Anne

(b. 1940) ACTIVIST AND WRITER. The oldest of nine children, Anne Moody was born on 15 September 1940 to Fred and Elmire Moody in Wilkinson County, Miss. Her parents were sharecroppers, and most of Moody's childhood was spent on a plantation. Experiencing racism at an early age, Moody attended segregated schools and did domestic work to help support her family.

In 1961 Moody attended Natchez Junior College on a basketball scholarship, and while there, she became involved with several civil rights groups, including the Congress of Racial Equality (CORE), the Student Non-Violent Coordinating Committee (SNCC), and the National Association for the Advancement of Colored People (NAACP). When Moody transferred to Tougaloo College in Jackson, Miss., where she would receive a bachelor of science degree in 1964, she became even more active in the struggle for civil rights in Mississippi.

Working for CORE, she canvassed the neighborhoods of Canton, Miss., to register African American voters and was often threatened and harassed for doing so. Like those of many other civil rights activists, Moody's family was repeatedly threatened by police and others because of Moody's involvement in the movement. Her mother was harassed, her brother threatened, her uncle beaten, and another relative shot and killed. Despite the sometimes dire consequences and the pervasive climate of fear, Moody stayed committed to the movement, marching on Washington, D.C., with Martin Luther King Jr. and helping to organize a student march in Jackson to protest the acquittal of Byron de la Beckwith for the murder of Medgar Evers.

Her most famous form of involvement in the movement, however, was on 28 May 1963, when Moody participated in the Woolworth's lunch counter sit-in in Jackson, Miss. The media attention garnered by the sit-in sparked numerous other direct action, nonviolent protests and helped to launch the Jackson movement. Eventually, like many others, Moody became disillusioned with the movement and of the internal divisions within it. She had a short marriage to Austin Stratus, with whom she had a child, Sascha, but the two divorced in 1967. Later Moody moved to New York and then back south, in the 1990s, where she lives today.

Coming of Age in Mississippi (1968) is Moody's own account of her childhood, her involvement in the civil rights movement, and the racial discrimination she experienced during both. The autobiography is considered a classic of civil rights literature and has received national attention and critical acclaim. *Coming of Age in Mississippi* won the Brotherhood Award from the National Council of Christians and Jews and the Best Book of the Year Award from the

National Library Association. Moody also published a collection of short stories, *Mr. Death* (1975), and won a silver medal for her short story, "New Hopes for the Seventies," from *Mademoiselle* magazine.

AMY SCHMIDT
University of Mississippi

John Dittmer, *Local People: The Struggle for Civil Rights in Mississippi* (1994); Charles M. Payne, *I've Got the Light of Freedom: The Organizing Tradition and the Mississippi Freedom Struggle* (1995); Carolyn Perry and Mary Louise Weaks, eds., *The History of Southern Women's Literature* (2002).

Morgan, Robert

(b. 1944) WRITER.

Born 3 October 1944, Robert Ray Morgan grew up in the mountains of North Carolina, and although he is now a half century and several hundred miles removed from that existence, his writings remain rooted in his old homeplace. The poetry he has written and published has earned him a nickname, "the poet laureate of Appalachia," while his fiction has found an audience far beyond his rocky native soil. In 1997 he told the *Carolina Quarterly*: "My ties to western North Carolina are so deep I doubt that I will ever escape them. My first sixteen years were spent on one particular piece of ground, and that seems to be the landscape that most nurtures my imagination."

Yet leave the mountains he did, at the age of 16, to study engineering and applied mathematics at North Carolina State University. He never received a science degree, instead deciding to transfer to the University of North Carolina at Chapel Hill and pursue his love of English. He took a B.A. degree in 1965, followed by an M.F.A. in 1968 from University of North Carolina at Greensboro. He divided his time among writing, farming, and house painting until, in 1971, he was offered and accepted a position in the English department at Cornell University. Today he continues to live in Ithaca, N.Y., to teach at Cornell, and to write.

His first works were short stories, but since 1969 he has composed poems regularly, placing many of them with top journals. His most recent book of poetry is *The Strange Attractor* (2003). In the 1980s he turned again to fiction and, to date, he has published several collections of short stories and five novels. His novels, in particular, have swelled his readership. Three of them—*The Truest Pleasure, Gap Creek*, and *This Rock*—unfold in the early decades of the 20th century. Strong Appalachian woman Ginny Peace narrates *The Truest Pleasure*, a love story that in 1995 was named the *Publishers Weekly* Best Book of the Year. Morgan opted for a female voice in his next novel as well: *Gap Creek* (1999). The tale of young Julie Harmon's battle to survive in an incessantly cruel natural world, it won Morgan his most important admirer. Talk show host Oprah Winfrey selected the novel for her book club and featured the author on an episode of her show that, when it aired, made *Gap Creek* a best seller. More than 2 million copies of the book have been sold thus far. On the heels of such a huge success came *This Rock* (2001), a Cain and Abel tale of the blood feud of two brothers.

As part of an effort to highlight the story itself, Morgan writes prose that is spare—so spare, in fact, that his narrative-based novels resemble the transcripts of oral history interviews. Reviewing *Gap Creek*, Dwight Garner wrote: "At their finest, his stripped-down and almost primitive sentences burn with the raw, lonesome pathos of Hank Williams's best songs." But if short on lush language, his fiction is not lacking for content or conflict. His stories are the stuff of an Appalachia real or imagined—violence, visions, moonshine, gambling, the wilderness; and pushing against these elements are men and women who, in their daily lives, work as hard as they love. With great detail the author describes acts of physical labor, and it is through these descriptions that Morgan communicates both the difficulty of life in a harsh environment and the towering triumph of survival. In a review of *This Rock*, Katharine Whittemore claimed that "Morgan's trademark is sheer relentlessness." In his final products, though, writing is made to look easy. Morgan draws on his North Carolina roots to create evocative poetry and tell dynamic stories. His is an understanding of language and the human condition that he tries to impart to his students at Cornell, too. In an interview with the *Carolina Quarterly*, he said: "I tell students they will know they are getting somewhere when an idea, a scene, is so painful they can just barely bring themselves to write about it. A writer has to touch quick, and draw blood."

HICKS WOGAN
University of Mississippi

Cecelia Conway, in *Dictionary of Literary Biography*, vol. 292, ed. Lisa Abney and Suzanne Disheroon-Green (2004); Dwight Garner, *New York Times Book Review* (10 October 1999); Robert West, *Carolina Quarterly* (Fall 1997); Katharine Whittemore, *New York Times Book Review* (14 October 2001).

Morris, Willie

(1934–1999) WRITER.

Willie Morris, Mississippi-born journalist, editor, essayist, and novelist, continued the long-standing tradition of the southern man of letters as explainer of the South to the rest of the nation, to itself, and to himself. Seeing the South as "the nation writ large," he probed the complexities of the region and of the country.

When he was six months old, Morris's family moved from Jackson, where he was born in 1934, to Yazoo, Miss., which, Morris said, "Gave me much of whatever sensibility I now possess." At 17, told by his father "to get the hell out of Mississippi," he entered the University of Texas. As editor of the *Daily Texan*, he battled both the oil and gas interests of Texas and the university's board of regents before graduating and becoming a Rhodes scholar. After earning the B.A. and M.A. degrees at New College, Oxford University, he returned to Austin in 1960 to edit the liberal *Texas Observer*.

Hired as an editor at *Harper's Magazine* in 1963, Morris became editor in chief in 1967. He made *Harper's* probably the most significant magazine in America during a time of fundamental change. In 1965, on the 100th anniversary of Appomattox, his special supplement, *The South Today*, sought to "illuminate for non-Southerners the interaction of North and South, and make it more clear that the assignation of regional guilt or failure is each day becoming a more subtle and complex question" and to provoke for southerners an "awareness of the moral nuances of their own society."

After resigning from *Harper's* in 1971, he settled in Bridgehampton, Long Island. In 1980, perhaps drawn by that "chord of homecoming" that he sensed to be "one of the very threads of my existence as a Southern American of the Twentieth Century," Morris became writer in residence at the University of Mississippi. Since 1971 Morris published, among others, the children's classics *Good Old Boy: A Delta Boyhood* (1971) and *My Dog Skip* (1995), which was made into a 2000 movie; the novel *The Last of the Southern Girls* (1973); and the autobiography *New York Days* (1993), the sequel to his seminal autobiography *North toward Home* (1967). In his last years, he married editor Joanne Prichard and moved to Jackson, Miss., where he died.

In all his works, Morris reveals himself "still a son of that bedeviled and mystifying and exasperating region, and sen[sing] in the experience of it something of immense value and significance to the Great Republic." That sense, reconciling in Willie Morris's writings "the old warring impulse of one's sensibility to be both Southern and American," brought Dan Wakefield to write, "In the deepest sense we all live in Yazoo.

Mr. Morris' triumph is that he has made us understand that."

WILLIAM MOSS
Clemson University

Jack Bales, *Willie Morris: An Extensive Annotated Bibliography and a Biography* (2006); Larry L. King, *In Search of Willie Morris: The Mercurial Life of a Legendary Writer and Editor* (2006); Willie Morris, *North toward Home* (1967), *Terrains of the Heart and Other Essays on Home* (1981), *Yazoo: Integration in a Deep-Southern Town* (1971); Dan Wakefield, *New York Times Book Review* (16 May 1971).

Morrison, Toni

(b. 1931) WRITER.

Toni Morrison, whose given name was Chloe Antony Wofford, was born in Lorain, Ohio, into a family where parents and grandparents with southern roots taught her about African American myths and folklore, a fact that would later influence her writing. She was educated at Howard University and at Cornell, from which she received a master's degree in English. She married Harold Morrison in 1958 and had two sons with him. The couple divorced in 1964. After working as an editor for textbooks and trade books, she began a series of university teaching appointments that culminated in her being named the Robert F. Goheen professor at Princeton University in 1989.

Morrison had in the meantime begun to publish novels, beginning with *The Bluest Eye* (1970). The novel is told largely from the vantage point of Claudia MacTeer, who in adulthood muses over the fate of her childhood friend Pecola Breedlove. The fondness of Pecola's mother for the blue-eyed daughter of her employer makes Pecola wish for blue eyes and eventually believe that she has them. After being raped by her father and losing the baby, Pecola goes insane.

Morrison's next novel, *Sula* (1973), centers on the title character and her friend Nel, who marries, rears children, and lives a conventional life until the promiscuous Sula makes love to Nel's husband, causing him to leave his wife. Nel, though alienated, manages to assist Sula while she is dying. Afterward, Nel realizes that she has missed Sula's friendship more than she has her husband.

Morrison's third novel, *Song of Solomon* (1977), is narrated from the perspective of Macon or "Milkman" Dead, whose search for his African American and Indian heritage leads him from Michigan to Virginia. Critics hailed *Song of Solomon*, and it was named a Book-of-the-Month Club selection.

She next wrote *Tar Baby* (1981) in which for the first time white characters play leading roles. Valerian Street and his wife, Margaret, spend a great deal of time on a Caribbean island with their longtime servants, Sydney and Ondine Childs. Valerian has educated the Childs's niece and adopted daughter, Jardine, in Paris, where she is a sought-after fashion model. When Jardine visits her relatives, she meets Son, an intruder on the island, who falls in love with her. They try to live in Florida and New York City, but Jardine eventually returns to

Paris. For Son, Jardine is the "tar baby" of folklore who entraps him in a relationship from which he cannot escape. After publishing *Tar Baby*, Morrison was featured on the cover of *Newsweek* magazine, further indicating she had become a major American novelist.

Beloved (1987), perhaps Morrison's best-known novel, treats slavery and its consequences. Sethe escapes from slavery with her three children, but when the slave catcher finds her, she murders her youngest child rather than have her grow up as a slave, burying her under a tombstone simply marked "Beloved." Later Sethe gives birth to a daughter, Denver, and becomes friendly with Paul D, a former slave. Suddenly a young woman with skin like a baby's appears, finds Sethe, and moves in with her and Denver. Eventually Sethe realizes that the woman, who calls herself Beloved, is the baby she had murdered, now grown to maturity. She explains to Beloved about the murder, while accepting and loving her. Beloved, however, betrays Sethe by making love to Paul D and becoming pregnant by him. Near the end of the novel, when Denver's white employer comes to pick her up, Sethe rushes at him to murder him because she fears he has come for Beloved. Denver wrestles Sethe to the ground, Beloved vanishes, and Paul D comes back into Sethe's life.

In addition, Morrison has written the novels *Jazz* (1992), *Paradise* (1997), and *Love* (2003); a play, *Dreaming Emmett* (1986), about the 1950s murder of an African American boy; *Playing in the Dark: Whiteness and the Literary*

Imagination (1993); and several children's books with her son, Slade. One of America's most celebrated authors, she won the Pulitzer Prize in 1988 for *Beloved* and, in 1993, the Nobel Prize for Literature. In 1996 she was awarded the National Book Foundation Medal for Distinguished Contributions to American Literature.

MARY ANN WIMSATT
University of South Carolina

Elizabeth Ann Beaulieu, *The Toni Morrison Encyclopedia* (2003); J. Brooks Bouson, *Quiet As It's Kept: Shame, Trauma, and Race in the Novels of Toni Morrison* (2000); John N. Duval, *The Identifying Fictions of Toni Morrison: Modernist Authenticity and Postmodern Blackness* (2000); Barbara Kramer, *Toni Morrison: Nobel Prize-Winning Author* (1996); Linden Peach, *Toni Morrison* (2000).

Murfree, Mary Noailles (Charles Egbert Craddock)

(1850–1922) WRITER.

Mary Noailles Murfree was born into upper-class society near Murfreesboro, Tenn., in 1850 at the family home Grantland, an estate that was eventually destroyed in the Civil War battle of Stones River in 1862. At the age of four, Murfree was stricken with fever, an illness that left her with partial paralysis and slight permanent lameness. As a child she spent 15 consecutive summers visiting the family cottage Crag-Wilde, in Beersheba Springs in the Cumberland Mountains, where she first came into contact with the various Appalachian "types" she would make famous through her adult fiction.

After the Civil War, Murfree was sent to prestigious boarding schools in both Nashville and Philadelphia. Upon her return to Murfreesboro, between the ages of 19 and 24, with the support of her father, she began to write seriously about three interwoven themes that would dominate her fiction throughout her career: the politics of social interchange, the romance and tragedy of the Civil War around Grantland, and the allure of the unspoiled mountaineers and the mysterious Appalachian landscape of the Cumberlands.

In an early, unpublished manuscript containing a mixture of Civil War and mountaineer characters entitled *Alleghany Winds and Waters*, Murfree created an exaggerated masculine type named Egbert Craddock. Appending Charles to this name, Murfree fashioned her own nom de plume as a means of entering the burgeoning field of local-color writing that dominated the literary scene in America in the years following the Civil War. After she assumed the masculine identity, Murfree's first published story, "The Dancin' Party at Harrison's Cove," appeared in the *Atlantic Monthly* for May 1878 and won instant acclaim for its rugged author Craddock, who most readers assumed merely recounted the adventures Craddock himself had personally witnessed or experienced firsthand as an indigenous native of this mountain region. Over the next six years, Murfree sold seven more "mountaineer" stories to the *Atlantic*. In 1884, on her editor Thomas Bailey Aldrich's recommendation, Houghton Mifflin published these eight stories in book form as *In the Tennessee Mountains*. Murfree, or rather "Craddock," became an overnight literary sensation, ranked among the best of local-color writers such as Johnson J. Hooper, George Washington Cable, and Bret Harte. In her eight stories, Murfree, informed by her childhood at Beersheba, codified a cast of specific mountain types for generations of readers and writers to come. In stories such as "The Dancin' Party," "Over on the T'other Mountain," and "The Romance of Sunrise Rock," Murfree melds the documentary style of realism with romantic sentimentality to create a unique world, the mountaineers serving as a pure culture retaining ancient manners and customs unadulterated by the materialism and corruption of industrial America.

Like most local-color writing, Murfree's work contrasts the simple mountaineers who speak in dialect and are often shown trapped in various states of backwardness such as illiteracy, superstition, clannishness, and violence with a more sophisticated, urbane narrator who enters the region temporarily and offers commentary on the mores and customs of these isolated people. Murfree's narrators, although cognizant of their own superiority, nevertheless tend to sympathize with the mountain folk.

Despite the stereotypes, all the stories share the theme of a common humanity, that regardless of birth, education, or degree of refinement human nature is the same everywhere. Murfree published her Civil War novel of Grantland, *Where the Battle Was Fought*, in 1884. It was followed by *The Prophet of the Great Smoky Mountains* a year later to enthusiastic audiences and critical acclaim. Murfree continued to write her mountain tales, publishing 15 more stories in major periodicals between 1885 and 1920, but she also ventured into other genres, such as such as juvenile literature and historical romance, as the local-color vogue waned. Among the more successful of these works are *The Story of Old Fort Loudon* (1887), *The Fair Mississippian* (1908), and *The Story of Diciehurst* (1914). Although Murfree would write 25 novels over the course of her career, she would never regain her previous celebrity. Her first published mountaineer stories, with their emphasis on rugged characters in a pristine natural world, remain her most enduring and influential contribution to American fiction.

RANDALL S. WILHELM
University of Tennessee

Richard Cary, *Mary N. Murfree* (1960); Edd Winfield Parks, *Charles Egbert Craddock* (1941); Emily Satterwhite, *American Literature* (March 2006).

Murray, Albert

(b. 1916) WRITER.
Born in the town of Nokomis in south Alabama 12 May 1916 and raised by adoptive working-class parents in Magazine Point, just outside of Mobile, Albert Murray uses his upbringing in the Deep South as a backdrop for his fiction and for much of his theorizing about music and African American culture. Murray's freewheeling 1971 memoir *South to a Very Old Place*, which the author has referred to as a "nonfiction novel" and an epilogue to his fiction, considers the prospect that not only can one go home again, but one must

do so in order to take account of whom he has become. The book, like much of Murray's work, explores racial tensions in America, but it tends to emphasize the richness and individualism of African American life and defies sociological stereotypes of the period that depict African Americans living in helpless subjugation. Although he may be best known as America's foremost philosopher of the blues, a musical idiom he traces from its origins in *Stomping the Blues* (1976), and gives it consideration as a form of literary quest in *The Hero and the Blues* (1973), Murray also enjoys a reputation as a novelist, scholar, and cultural contrarian and remains an unregenerate modernist, claiming as his aesthetic mentors not only Basie, Ellington, and Armstrong but also Joyce, Malraux, Mann, Hemingway, and Faulkner. It may give further insight into the person of Albert Murray to note what Duke Ellington said when Murray's first novel, *Train Whistle Guitar* (1974), was published: "He doesn't have to look it up. . . . If you want to know, look him up. He is the unsquarest person I know."

Murray published the fourth installment in his chronicle of the life of Scooter, his fictional persona and sometime alter ego, in 2005, just short of his 90th birthday. The story of Scooter (who also goes by Jack the Rabbit and Jack the Bear and never really receives a formal name) began in 1974 with Murray's most acclaimed novel, *Train Whistle Guitar*, winner of the Lillian Smith Award for Southern Fiction, and continues through the novels *The Spyglass Tree* (1991) and *The Seven League*

Boots (1996). Though he did not publish his first book until he was 54 years old, Murray enjoyed a flurry of productivity in the early 1970s, which saw the publication of four books in four years, including *The Omni-Americans: New Perspectives on Black Experience and American Culture* (1970), a controversial book that proposes that black and white experience in America is so deeply intertwined as to form a composite, and any attempts at separation comes at the expense of both cultures.

Murray began a lifelong friendship with the great American novelist Ralph Ellison while both were students at the Tuskegee Institute, resulting in a long correspondence that is one of Murray's most enduring claims on literary history. A selection of their voluminous exchange of letters resulted in *Trading Twelves: The Selected Letters of Ralph Ellison and Albert Murray* (2000), which spans the entire decade between 1950 and 1960 and which Murray co-edited. Murray served for 20 years in the U.S. Air Force, retiring with the rank of major, after which he turned with full energy to a writing career. His other books include the essay collections *The Blue Devils of Nada* (1996) and *From the Briarpatch File* (2001), a biography titled *Good Morning Blues: The Autobiography of Count Basie as Told to Albert Murray* (1986), and a slim volume of verse riffs titled *Conjugations and Reiterations* (2001). Murray has held academic positions at Colgate, Columbia, Emory, and the Universities of Missouri and Massachusetts. He lives in New York City with his wife, Mozele, and their daughter

Michele, to whom every Albert Murray book is dedicated.

JESSE GRAVES
University of Tennessee

Warren Carson, *African American Review* (Summer 1993); Stanley Crouch, *Notes of a Hanging Judge* (1990); Henry Louis Gates Jr., *The New Yorker* (April 8,1996); Roberta S. Maguire, ed., *Conversations with Albert Murray*, (1997); Sanford Pinsker, *Virginia Quarterly Review* (Autumn 1996); Charles H. Rowell, *Callaloo* (Spring 1997).

Newman, Frances

(1883–1928) WRITER.

On 13 September 1883, in Atlanta, Ga., Frances Newman was born, the fifth and final child of Frances Alexander Percy and William Tuslow Newman, a Confederate Civil War veteran and U.S. district judge. Newman attended public schools in Atlanta before she went to boarding schools in both Washington, D.C., and New York. Though she attended Agnes Scott College for only a year, she was well versed in at least seven languages and thoroughly understood the mechanics of style. After leaving Agnes Scott, Newman began working as a librarian, which led her to Florida State College for Women in Tallahassee and then back to Atlanta, where she worked for the Carnegie Library and then for the Georgia Institute of Technology. After her mother's death in 1922, Newman stayed primarily in Atlanta, though she frequently traveled to western Europe and the northeastern United States. In Atlanta she supported herself as well as her household, which included her childhood mammy, Susan Long, and her nephew, Louis Rucker, whom she adopted after his mother died.

Newman came to the attention of the American literary establishment when she began publishing critical essays and book reviews in the Richmond, Va., literary magazine, *Reviewer*, as well as in various New York newspapers. Though some of her contemporaries, such as F. Scott Fitzgerald, felt attacked by her reviews, Newman was praised by others, such as H. L. Mencken, who dubbed her one of the "violets" in what he otherwise thought was "the Sahara of the Bozart." In 1924 Newman published a short story, "Rachel and Her Children," which won the O. Henry Prize. That same year, she edited and translated a collection of short stories, *The Short Story's Mutations: From Petronius to Paul Morand*. Newman spent the summer of 1926 at the McDowell Colony in Peterborough, N.H., working on her first novel, *The Hard-Boiled Virgin* (1926). The novel went through eight editions in just six months and scandalized not only Atlanta but also Boston, where it was banned. Writing in the same unique style, which nearly defies a label but is comparable to modernist writing of her day, Newman published her second novel, *Dead Lovers Are Faithful Lovers*, in 1928.

In the midst of her work on a second collection of translated stories, *Six Moral Tales from Jules Laforgue* (1928), Newman was found dead in her New York hotel room on 22 October 1928. Though numerous papers proclaimed her death a suicide or an accidental overdose, others believed that her death may have been because of a cerebral hemorrhage, resulting from an inflammation of her optic nerve. The cause of her death is still debated.

Though Newman lived most of her life in Atlanta and defined herself as a southerner, she astutely criticizes southern gender norms in her writing. Through her characterizations of southern, upper-class, white women, Newman satires stereotypes and ideals, such as the belle and lady. Because of her unflinching yet ambivalent portrayals of life in the South, and because of her treatment of women's bodies and sexuality, Newman and her works often elicited extreme responses from her contemporaries, and they continue to do so among present-day readers and scholars.

AMY SCHMIDT
University of Mississippi

Anne Goodwyn Jones, *Tomorrow Is Another Day: The Woman Writer in the South, 1859–1936* (1981); Kathryn Lee Seidel, *The Southern Belle in the American Novel* (1985); Miriam J. Shillingsburg, in *The History of Southern Women's Literature*, ed. Carolyn Perry and Mary Louise Weaks (2002).

Nordan, Lewis

(b. 1939) WRITER.

A native of Forest, Miss., Lewis Nordan suffered the early loss of his father, Lemuel Alonzo Nordan, and in 1942 moved with his mother, Sarah Hightower (later married to Gilbert R. Bayles), to Itta Benna, Miss., the small town in the Delta that would inspire his fictional Arrow Catcher, the locale for the majority of his stories and novels.

After serving in the navy for two years (1958–60), Nordan attended Millsaps College in Jackson, Miss., from which he graduated in 1963. He pursued graduate studies at Mississippi State University (M.A., 1966), and later at Auburn University, where he received his Ph.D. in 1973 with a dissertation on William Shakespeare. After holding diverse jobs in Florida and Arkansas, in 1983 Nordan joined the University of Pittsburgh as a professor of creative writing, a position he held until his retirement.

One of the most original voices in the contemporary South, Nordan revisits often in his fiction the experience of growing up amid the tensions and contradictions that troubled the South of the forties and fifties, as seen through the eyes of Sugar Mecklin, the author's literary alter ego. He began writing at a relatively late age: "I was a storyteller long before I became a writer. Everyone in my family is a storyteller, though none of the others are writers." His first short-story collection, *Welcome to the Arrow Catcher Fair*, appeared in 1983, and was followed by *The All-Girl Football Team* in 1986. Both collections revealed Nordan's profound sense of place, as well as his complicity with the southern literary tradition, and were widely acclaimed by reviewers. Fifteen of the stories from those books were later collected in *Sugar among the Freaks* (1996). Nordan's first novel, *Music of the Swamp* (1991), is a cycle of stories that traces Sugar Mecklin's coming of age in the Delta, a territory that emerges as a primeval landscape full of wonder and magic, but also "filled up with death."

Likewise, death is also at the heart of his second novel, *Wolf Whistle* (1993), a re-creation of the 1955 lynching of Emmett Till, one of the events that acted as a catalyst for the civil rights movement. The murder of the black teenager from Chicago took place in Money, Miss., and the subsequent trial of the two whites who were formally indicted, and eventually acquitted, was held in Sumner, near Itta Benna. Nordan was deeply affected by the whole affair, and the images of Emmett Till's corpse became a lifelong obsession for the writer: "Those helpless feet and legs, upside down, almost comic, have haunted me all my life." *The Sharpshooter Blues*, his third novel, appeared in 1995, to be followed in 1997 by his fourth and last novel to date, *Lightning Song*, which abandons temporarily the Delta to go to a "kind of hilly country." In 2000 Nordan published his fictional memoirs, *Boy with a Loaded Gun*, a humorous mixture of fact and imagination though which the writer comes to terms with the personal drama of the loss of two sons and the fight against severe alcoholism.

Lewis Nordan belongs in the school of the southern grotesque as represented, for example, by Flannery O'Connor, a writer with whom Nordan has been recurrently related, although O'Connor's overwhelming sense of religion is absent in his fiction. Nordan has also been related to Latin American magical realists such as Gabriel García Márquez, with whom he shares a similar perception of the world as marvelous and uncanny. In fact, Nordan's Mississippi looks more on the Caribbean Sea than on the Deep South, and the writer's aesthetic response to the land and its people has been defined as "magical grotesque," for it combines elements of both literary modes. Arrow Catcher appears as a god-forsaken, islandlike territory lost in the waterways of the Delta, as if it were but another isle of the Caribbean, and becomes the recipient of influx arriving from the ocean, like the dolphins, porpoises, and myriad other creatures that find hospitable refuge in the salty waters of the swamp. Lewis Nordan's fictional universe is a region of wonders, at once comic and tragic, inhabited by deformed beings who strive to reconcile themselves with the essential loneliness of man, which is indeed the central motif that unifies his fiction.

MANUEL BRONCANO
University of León

Blake Maher, *Southern Quarterly* (Fall 1995); James R. Nicosia, *Southern Studies* (Spring 1993); Jack Sullivan, *New York Times Book Review* (2 January 1994).

O'Connor, Flannery

(1925–1964) WRITER.

Flannery O'Connor was born a Roman Catholic in Savannah, Ga., on 25 March 1925. She attended parochial school there until 1938 when her father's disseminated lupus was diagnosed and the family moved to Milledgeville, Ga., the home of the author's maternal grandparents. O'Connor attended high school in Milledgeville and went on to that town's Georgia State College for Women, where she majored in English and social science. Her father died in 1941. Upon her graduation from college in 1945 she received a Rinehart

Fellowship to the Writers' Workshop of the University of Iowa. She received an M.F.A. from Iowa in 1947, a year after her first story had appeared in *Accent*. From Iowa she went to Yaddo, where she started her first novel, *Wise Blood*. She met Robert and Sally Fitzgerald while in New York and moved in with them in Ridgefield, Conn., in 1949.

In 1950 her own disseminated lupus was diagnosed, and she moved to her mother's farm, Andalusia, just outside Milledgeville. She finished *Wise Blood* there and published the book with Harcourt, Brace in 1952. Her collection of short stories, *A Good Man Is Hard to Find*, came out in 1955; her second novel, *The Violent Bear It Away*, in 1960. She died on 3 August 1964, a year before her last collection of stories, *Everything That Rises Must Converge*, appeared. Her other posthumous publications are *Mystery and Manners* (1969), *The Complete Stories* (1971), and *The Habit of Being: Letters of Flannery O'Connor* (1979).

O'Connor worked with the traditional themes and characters of the South. But because of her specifically religious view, she seemed to find new meaning in them as she focused on postlapsarian existence. Her grotesques usually reflect some spiritual shortcoming with their physical handicaps. Her southern children are as deeply into sin as her adults; her adults are as helpless in this life as her children. And the vanity of aristocratic backgrounds is a trap for the sinner. To her, the land, traditionally a symbol of well-being in southern literature, is one more sign of the foolish accumulation of earthly stores that gets no one into heaven. The industrialization of the South that Faulkner symbolized so well with the car of *The Reivers* came to be just another sign of human vanity as Hazel Motes of *Wise Blood* established "The Church without Christ" in a broken-down Essex, a vehicle that ends up in the kudzu of a Georgia pasture. O'Connor even discovered religious implications in polite southern conversation. Her rednecks and aristocrats alike point inadvertently to a godless world as they make casual statements such as "a good man is hard to find" or "the life you save may be your own."

Religion, of course, has long been a concern of southern writers; but probably no successful writer of the region has treated it as specifically and as thoroughly as O'Connor. Her considerable talent lay in rendering scenes with vivid accuracy, allowing them to reflect, almost invariably, the emptiness of existence in worlds—southern and otherwise—without Christ.

G. W. KOON
Clemson University

Robert H. Brinkmeyer Jr., *The Art and Vision of Flannery O'Connor* (1989); Anthony DiRenzo, *American Gargoyles: Flannery O'Connor and the Medieval Grotesque* (1993); Stephen G. Driggers, Robert J. Dunn, and Sarah Gordon, *The Manuscripts of Flannery O'Connor at Georgia College* (1989), *Flannery O'Connor: An Introduction* (1991); Paul Eli, *The Life You Save May Be Your Own: An American Pilgrimage* (2003); Sally Fitzgerald, ed., *The Habit of Being: Letters of Flannery O'Connor* (1979); Katherine Hemple Prown, *Revising Flannery O'Connor: Southern Literary Culture* and the Problem of Female (2001); Brian A. Ragen, *A Wreck on the Road to Damascus: Innocence, Guilt, and Conversion in Flannery O'Connor* (1989); Sura Roth, *Flannery O'Connor: New Perspectives* (1996).

Owen, Guy

(1925–1981) WRITER AND CRITIC.
Guy Owen was from the Cape Fear region of North Carolina, and he spent the majority of his life within the state. He earned all of his degrees, from bachelor to doctorate, at the University of North Carolina at Chapel Hill. He served in the army in World War II for three years in the European theater of combat. He taught at Davidson and Elon colleges and Stetson University for short periods before taking up a position at North Carolina State University, then North Carolina State College, in 1962, where he would spend the remainder of his career as an associate professor of English. He was the recipient of a Bread Loaf scholarship in 1960, the Henry Bellamann Foundation Literary Award in 1964, and a Yaddo Fellowship in 1968.

Owen was both an acclaimed southern novelist and poet in addition to being a critic. Even though all of his novels were set in the tobacco country of North Carolina, Owen never considered himself a "regional" writer. Such a label is too restrictive and might be too dismissive to describe his body of work. *Season of Fear* (1960), his first novel, was written and published while he was living in Florida and working at Stetson. His most famous novel, *The Ballad of the Flim-Flam Man*, was a lighthearted book about a confidence man and a soldier who was absent without leave, namely Mordecai Jones and Curley Treadaway. Owen and his readers were enamored of the characters; Owen wrote another novel featuring the pair of tricksters, *The Flim-Flam Man and the Apprentice Grifter* (1972) and also featured them in the collection of short stories entitled *The Flim-Flam Man and Other Stories* (1980). *Ballad* was made into a film titled *The Flim-Flam Man* in 1967 starring George C. Scott and Michael Sarrazin. His novel *Journey for Joedel* (1970) was nominated for the Pulitzer in 1971 and received the Sir Walter Raleigh Award, which is given to the best piece of fiction by a writer who hails from North Carolina. His poetry was widely published in journals and collections and also received awards. In 1969 his collection *The White Stallion and Other Poems* received the Roanoke-Chowan Cup for North Carolinian poetry. Much of his poetry might be classified as "nature poetry," as it focuses on various aspects of nature and the natural landscape of his beloved North Carolina. His criticism, like his other writings, was occasionally light-hearted and witty, but always insightful. His articles appeared in such journals as *College English*, *English Journal*, and *South Atlantic Review*, among others.

A champion of southern literature, Owen coedited the *North Carolina Folklore Journal* from 1966 to 1972 with Richard Walser for four years and Leonida Betts for two. While still at Stetson in 1958, he founded *Impetus*, a poetry journal that was renamed the *Southern Poetry Review* after he returned to North Carolina and brought it with him. He was the editor of this journal for 19 years, from 1958 to 1977. A prize is given in his name every year by the journal to a single-poem entry. Owen was also the editor and coeditor of a number of poetry and essay collections, among which are *New Southern Poetry: Selected Poems from Southern Poetry Review* and *Contemporary Poets of North Carolina.*

Most of his papers are housed at the University of North Carolina at Chapel Hill and North Carolina State University. Included in these collections are professional correspondences, drafts of poems, stories, critical essays, and novels, many of which have never been published, as well as newspaper clippings and press releases. The collection at N.C. State also features a copy of the screenplay of *The Flim-Flam Man* and materials from the film's premiere. Both collections are open to public research.

ANNA SMITH
University of Mississippi

Guy Owen, *South Atlantic Review* (May 1978), *College English* (May 1957, November 1961), *Modern Language Notes* (February 1958); Guy Owen and Mary C. Williams, eds., *New Southern Poetry: Selected Poems from Southern Poetry Review*, (1974), *Contemporary Poets of North Carolina* (1977).

Page, Thomas Nelson

(1853–1922) WRITER.
Thomas Nelson Page, author of short stories, novels, essays, and poetry, is best known for his role as literary spokesman for the glories of the Old South. Born in Hanover County, Va., in 1853 and only 12 years old when the Civil War ended, Page, writing in the planta-

tion genre of John Pendleton Kennedy and others, created of the antebellum South a mythical, would-be land of noble gentlemen and ladies and contented slaves, a society ordered by the laws of chivalry.

A descendant of the prominent but no longer wealthy Nelson and Page families, and a native of Virginia, Page attended Washington College and later studied at the University of Virginia for a legal career. Page married in 1886, and his wife died two years later. He practiced law in Richmond from 1876 until 1893, when he moved with his second wife, the former Florence Lathrop Field, to Washington. Although Page became active in the social life of the capital and later served six years as ambassador to Italy under Woodrow Wilson, he continued in his writing to depict Virginia and the passing of the old order there. His works, set for the most part in the South, composed 18 volumes when they were published in a collected edition in 1912.

In Ole Virginia (1887) was Page's first collection of short stories treating the antebellum South. Other works dealt with later periods in southern history. For example, *Red Rock* (1898) was a sympathetic portrait of the South during Reconstruction, and *John Marvel, Assistant* (1909) depicted the New South of the early 20th century. Page was consistently a proponent of the southern way of life, and in such stories as "Marse Chan" in *In Ole Virginia* his finest sketches were realized. In this story, told by a faithful ex-slave, of a young southerner who died for the southern cause and who placed duty and honor above all personal gain, Page postulates a kind of heroism that seemed to be missing from modern life. Page's South, of course, was finer than any real place could ever be, but he satisfied the nostalgia of his readers for what might have been—a place where heroic men and women adhered to a code of perfect honor. Only in the 20th century would Ellen Glasgow and, later, the writers of the Southern Literary Renaissance dispel the romantic image of the Old South so carefully fashioned by Thomas Nelson Page.

ANNE E. ROWE
Florida State University

Theodore Gross, *Thomas Nelson Page* (1967); Kimball King, introduction to Thomas Nelson Page, *In Ole Virginia; or, Marse Chan and Other Stories* (1969).

Percy, Walker

(1916–1990) WRITER.

Percy was a novelist, cultural critic, and lay philosopher who occupies a unique position in post–World War II southern literature. Born into a distinguished and prominent southern family, Percy spent his childhood in Birmingham, Ala. His father committed suicide in 1929, and after his mother died in a car accident in 1932 Percy was raised in Greenville, Miss., by his father's cousin, William Alexander Percy (author of *Lanterns on the Levee*). In Greenville he met and formed a lifelong friendship with novelist-historian Shelby Foote. Both attended the University of North Carolina at Chapel Hill, where Percy earned a B.S. in chemistry. He received an M.D. from Columbia's College of Physicians and Surgeons in 1941 but subsequently contracted tuberculosis while working as a pathologist at Bellevue Hospital in New York. While recuperating, he read deeply in European existentialist writers such as Camus, Sartre, Heidegger, Kierkegaard, and Marcel, and also the Russian writers Tolstoy, Dostoevsky, and Chekhov. He also undertook a serious study of linguistics, especially semiotics, and of the Christian theological and philosophical traditions. Convinced by his reading that science cannot explain the predicament of individual man *qua* man, he abandoned medicine as a career in favor of becoming a writer.

After recuperating, Percy returned to the South and married Mary Bernice Townsend ("Bunt") in New Orleans in 1946. In the following year, both newlyweds converted to Roman Catholicism and soon established permanent residence in Covington, La. Percy's writing career followed two tracks. He first began to publish philosophical essays, mostly on the phenomena of language, in scholarly journals, while at the same time learning the craft of novel writing. His first published novel, *The Moviegoer* (1961), won the National Book Award. Five more novels followed: *The Last Gentleman* (1966), *Love in the Ruins: The Adventures of a Bad Catholic at a Time Near the End of the World* (1971), *Lancelot* (1977), *The Second Coming* (1980), and *The Thanatos Syndrome* (1987)—and two collections of essays, *The Message in the Bottle: How Queer Man Is, How Queer Language Is, and What One Has to Do with the Other* (1975) and *Signposts in A Strange Land* (1991), edited by Patrick Samway and published posthumously. He also pub-

Walker Percy, Louisiana novelist, 1983 (Jerry Bauer, photographer,
Farrar, Straus and Giroux photo, New York)

lished a nonfiction work: *Lost in the Cosmos: The Last Self-Help Book* (1983).

Percy's uniqueness as a post–World War II southern writer stems from two interwoven qualities of his writing: first, his transformation of traditional southern themes within a universal philosophical and religious perspective; and, second, his application of phenomenological techniques to novel writing. While his novels are set within a New South upper-middle-class social milieu, Percy recast this milieu as a postapocalypse dystopia inhabited by loners who are alienated from their own being, from each other, and from God. All of his protagonists are highly self-conscious southern males afflicted with angst and Augustan longing, unable to find meaning in themselves or their sham world of pseudoaristocrats, intellectual poseurs and ironists, and crass consumers. Percy subjects the familiar southern values of personal honor, stoicism, nostalgia for the past, and family loyalty—all values Percy thoroughly imbibed as a youth—to biting satire. He exposes the despair at the heart of this culture, sometimes humorously, as in *Love in the Ruins*, and sometimes savagely, as in *Lancelot* and *The Thanatos Syndrome*. In addition, with his brilliant sensitivity to ordinary language, he strips away the mythos of southern storytelling to reveal the desperate state of language in the 20th century, its degeneration into abstraction and a Gnostic incoherence that threatens meaning within the entire social order. In Percy's view, it is "not the Bomb but the beastliness"—the "loss of the creature" and the descent in barbarism—that most threatens his characters.

Combining a phenomenological approach to writing with his deep knowledge of science, philosophy, and linguistics, Percy's writings diagnose a spiritual malaise that is both southern and universal, that reaches from the French Quarter to Auschwitz, from former slave quarters refurbished into upscale condos to the slavery of modern consumerism. Yet Percy always presents these profound concerns through the trials of an individual caught in a particular "predicament" or existential crisis, a character on a journey through the ruins of an affluent modern South that has become a microcosm of all the spiritual ills of technological society. Still, Percy counterbalances despair with hope, a hope manifested in his saving humor, his empathy with its alienated characters, and his faith in their ability to rediscover their humanity through humility, compassion, and love with another creature.

JOHN F. DESMOND
Whitman College

Gary M. Ciuba, *Walker Percy: Books of Revelations* (1991); Robert Coles, *Walker Percy: An American Search* (1978); John F. Desmond, *Walker Percy's Search for Community* (2004); Paul Ellie, *The Life You Save May be Your Own: An American Pilgrimage* (2003); David Horace Harwell, *Walker Percy Remembered: A Portrait in the Words of Those Who Knew Him* (2006); Lewis A. Lawson and Victor Kramer, eds., *Conversations with Walker Percy* (1985), *More Conversations with Walker Percy* (1993); Patrick Samway, *Walker Percy: A Life* (1997); Jay Tolson, *Pilgrim in the Ruins: A Life of Walker Percy* (1992), ed., *The Correspondence of Shelby Foote and Walker Percy* (1997).

Percy, William Alexander

(1885–1942) WRITER.

William Alexander Percy was born on 14 May 1885 into one of the wealthiest and most politically powerful families of the Mississippi Delta. Although he was more proud of his poetry than his prose, his best-remembered work remains *Lanterns on the Levee: Recollections of a Planter's Son* (1941), a memoir that also serves as an impassioned defense of southern aristocratic virtues. He also left his mark on southern literature by instilling a deep appreciation of literature in his adopted son, Walker Percy.

The grandson of a Confederate hero and the son of a U.S senator, Will Percy sought initially to avoid a life of public service, spending much of his youth and early adulthood preparing for a literary career. He was educated in his childhood at home and then later at the University of the South in Sewanee, Tenn., where he returned as an instructor for a year.

Percy was the author of three volumes of poetry, *Sappho in Levkas, and Other Poems* (1915), *In April Once, and Other Poems* (1920), and *Enzio's Kingdom, and Other Poems* (1924). Although his poetry was collected in two editions, *Selected Poems* (1930) and *Collected Poems* (1944), his verse has remained out of print since shortly after his death.

Preferring the cosmopolitan life to that of a small southern town, Percy spent many of his summers vacationing among the wealthy American and European expatriates in the stylishly decadent Italian resort communities of Taormina and Capri. Yet, at his father Leroy Percy's insistence, the younger Percy, who had reluctantly studied law at Harvard, returned to Greenville to practice law with his father and assist him in his failed campaign for reelection to the U.S. Senate. After serving with distinction in World War I, he lived the remainder of his life in Greenville, practicing law, managing Trail Lake, the family's 3,000-acre cotton plantation, and serving as a civic and cultural leader for the community. During the Mississippi River's catastrophic flood of

1927, he was quickly named the director of the area's emergency relief efforts (he was already county director of the Red Cross), only to see his efforts to evacuate African American refugees undermined by his father, whose powerful planter friends were desperate to keep the displaced agricultural laborers from leaving the Delta. He recruited a young progressive editor, Hodding Carter, to run Greenville's newspaper, and with Carter launched scathing attacks against the Ku Klux Klan, which never were able to establish a strong base in Percy's part of the Delta. In 1931, when his three young cousins, among them a 13-year-old Walker Percy, were orphaned (their father committed suicide two years earlier and their mother died under mysterious circumstances in a one-car accident), he took the boys in and raised them as his own.

Lanterns on the Levee: Reflections of a Planter's Son (1941), Percy's only prose work, may be the most fully developed and articulate defense of southern noblesse oblige ever penned. Contemporary readers may balk at Percy's paternalistic views on class and race relations, which include an apologia for the sharecropping system and a description of poor whites in the region as "the most unprepossessing [breed] on the broad face of the ill-populated earth," but *Lanterns* offers a rare glimpse into a receding world view that shaped the South we have inherited today. In much the same vein as *The Education of Henry Adams*, Percy presents a self-consciously anachronistic, highly ironic autobiographical persona that is alienated by its outmoded aristocratic sensibilities and ill-suited to the corrupt and chaotic world of modernity. Despite these gestures of identification with the old order, however, *Lanterns* also hints at the author's profound ambivalence regarding traditional notions of masculinity and his own sexuality and is replete with homoerotic imagery that points suggestively, if also obliquely, to a private life that was radically at odds with the provincial values of the small town South.

After years of struggling with clinical depression, Will Percy died of cancer on 21 January 1942 at the age of 56. His adopted son Walker Percy would write of him, "he was the most extraordinary man I have ever known."

JAMES H. WATKINS
Berry College

John M. Barry, *Rising Tide: The Great Mississippi Flood of 1927 and How It Changed America* (1997); Scott Romine, *Southern Quarterly* (Fall 1996); Bertram Wyatt-Brown, *The House of Percy: Honor, Melancholy, and Imagination in a Southern Family* (1994).

Peterkin, Julia Mood

(1880–1961) WRITER.

Julia Mood Peterkin was a southern writer best known for her sympathetic portrayals of black folklife in the South Carolina Lowcountry, where she was born 31 October 1880. Her novel *Scarlet Sister Mary* won the Pulitzer Prize for Literature in 1929.

Early reviewers focused on her depiction of black culture rather than on her literary techniques. Black intellectuals in particular, such as Countee Cullen, Langston Hughes, Paul Robe-son, and Walter White, praised her avoidance of the racist stereotypes common at the time among white writers, North and South. W. E. B. Du Bois said of her, "She is a Southern white woman, but she has the eye and the ear to see beauty and know truth."

Scholars continue to find in her delineation of the world view of a black community and in her depiction of its Creole language—Gullah—a near-native sensitivity and richness of texture. She may, in fact, be regarded as a native speaker of the language. Raised by a Gullah-speaking nurse after the death of her mother, she wrote, "I learned to speak Gullah before I learned to speak English."

Folklorists have praised Peterkin's "primary knowledge" of African American folk culture. Her explanation was that "I have lived among the Negroes. I like them. They are my friends, and I have learned so much from them."

The literary establishment, after its initial enthusiasm, ignored her writings for more than a generation. Not until the late 1970s were the literary aspects of her work—its scope and themes, characterization and narrative techniques—examined. Now literary scholars rank her fiction high and recognize that she, like Joyce and Faulkner, was more interested in individual human beings in timeless and universal struggles than in local color. Although many of the incidents in her books she had personally witnessed on her plantation, Lang Syne (near Orangeburg, S.C.), the physical setting—Sandy Island, Heaven's Gate Church, and "Blue Brook" (Brookgreen) plantation—is often the Waccamaw region of Georgetown County, her summer home.

Peterkin's narrative technique grew out of the southern storytelling tradition (with the Gullah necessarily simplified to accommodate the limitations of her readers). She did not attempt, as did Hemingway, Dos Passos, Faulkner, and many of her other contemporaries, to borrow experimental styles from such modern European masters as Joyce. Unlike those of most writers, her male and female characters are equally well drawn and credible. Her vivid characterization owes much more to reality and the burdens of the immoderate past than to literary influences. There are no literary counterparts to her God-haunted but courageous and compassionate black heroes and heroines—Scarlet Sister Mary, Black April, Cricket, Maum Hannah, and Killdee Pinesett, whom a modern critic calls "one of the most moving, one of the most admirable characters in modern fiction."

Among her most important works are the mythic *Green Thursday* (1924), a story cycle like *Go Down, Moses* and *Dubliners*; her classical tragedy *Black April* (1927), which has been called "perhaps her most powerful work of fiction"; her feminist comedy *Scarlet Sister Mary* (1928), whose sexually demanding heroine not merely endures but prevails over all men and circumstances; her lyrical but disappointing *Bright Skin* (1932); and her magisterial work of nonfiction, *Roll, Jordan, Roll* (1933).

CHARLES JOYNER
University of South Carolina at Coastal Campus

Thomas H. Landess, *Julia Peterkin* (1976); Noel Polk, in *South Carolina Women Writers*, ed. James B. Meriwether (1979); Susan Miller Williams, *A Devil and a Good Woman, Too* (1997).

Phillips, Jayne Anne

(b. 1952) WRITER.

Born to a close knit family in the small town of Buckhannon, W.Va., in July 1952, Jayne Anne Phillips was urged by her mother, a teacher, to read and write. Phillips graduated from West Virginia University (B.A., 1974) and the University of Iowa (M.F.A., 1978), where she wrote her first story collection, *Sweethearts* (1976). During the mid-1970s, she left West Virginia for California, embarking on a cross-country trip that would greatly influence her fiction, known for its lost, lonely souls and its struggling survivors. Her most recent novel, *MotherKind* (2000), is the story of a multigenerational family struggle, birth and death under the same roof.

Phillips's first commercial success came with a story collection titled *Black Tickets* (1979). A combination of brief character studies, monologues by damaged outcasts, and family dramas, the stories in *Black Tickets* capture the themes of personal and sexual alienation, family tension, and the unsuccessful quest for the American dream. Critics responded positively to this collection, noting that Phillips captures a familial love that endures even after a family's collapse.

Five years after *Black Tickets*, Phillips published her first novel, *Machine Dreams* (1984), which chronicles the lives and fortunes of a southern family in the years between World War II and the Vietnam War. The family slowly disintegrates; both family and society descend into chaos as the American Dream dissolves. Phillips's second novel, *Shelter* (1994), set in a West Virginia girls' camp in the summer of 1963, has been described as dark and beautifully disturbing. Her themes (loss of innocence, family secrets, sexual and psychological abuse) find their place in the Appalachian woods that are haunted, like much of her writing, by Christianity.

Jayne Anne Phillips's characters are more or less ordinary people, families of survivors who are trying to love each other after circumstances have been drastically, sometimes violently, altered. Phillips's South is a place where familial love unexpectedly persists, a place where there is terror in the commonplace. Hope is rarely found in this world of sex, violence, loneliness, and illness; and when it is, it seems out of place. For her strong sense of place and depictions of society's misfits, Phillips has been compared to Eudora Welty and Flannery O'Connor. For her use of point of view, she has been influenced by William Faulkner. In a prose style that draws attention to her love of language, Phillips creates characters who continue on, despite adversity.

Phillips's works have been translated and published in 12 languages. She is the recipient of a Guggenheim Fellowship and two National Endowment for the Arts Fellowships. Currently, she is professor of English and director of the M.F.A. program at Rutgers-Newark, the State University of New Jersey. She and her husband, physician Mark Stockman, have three sons. Other works by Jayne Anne Phillips include *Counting* (1978), *How Mickey Made It* (1981), *The Secret Country* (1982), and *Fast Lanes* (1984).

JODY BROOKS
Georgia State University

Richard Godden, *Journal of American Studies* (August 2002); Sarah Anne Johnston, *Conversations with American Women Writers* (2004); Bonnie Lyons and Bill Oliver, eds., *Passion and Craft: Conversations with Notable Writers* (1998); Carol S. Manning, *Female Tradition in Southern Literature* (1993); Sue Willis Meredith, *Appalachian Journal: A Regional Studies Review* (Fall 1996); Jayne Anne Phillips, in *Why I Write: Thoughts on the Craft of Fiction*, ed. Will Blythe (1998); Kate Rhodes, *Women's Studies* (July–August 2002); Sarah Robertson, *European Journal of American Culture* (2001).

Poe, Edgar Allan

(1809–1849) WRITER.

The South's most renowned literary artist of the 19th century spent most of his productive years as a struggling journalist in large northern cities. Born on 19 January 1809, in Boston, Mass., Poe was the second child of David and Elizabeth Arnold Poe, both active theatrical performers on the East Coast of the United States. His father mysteriously disappeared in 1810, and after his mother's subsequent death, in December 1811, he became the foster son of John Allan, a prominent Richmond, Va., tobacco merchant who gave Poe many childhood advantages. In 1826 he attended the University of Virginia, leaving after only a few months to join the U.S.

Army. His first volume of poems, entitled *Tamerlane and Other Poems*, was privately published in 1827; a second volume, *Al Aaraaf, Tamerlane, and Minor Poems*, appeared in 1829, shortly after he was honorably discharged from the army. Aided by his foster father, he entered West Point in 1830 as a cadet, but was soon discharged for failing to heed regulations. Beginning in 1829, influential writers and journalists like John Neal and John P. Kennedy began to support his efforts to attain literary prominence. *Poems*, a third volume of poetry, was published in 1831.

Thoroughly trained in the classics and in the rhetoric and aesthetics of the Scottish commonsense school of philosophers, Poe was, according to the critic Robert D. Jacobs, indeed a southerner by temperament and inclination. Many of his formative years were spent in the southern cities of Richmond and Baltimore, the latter being the home of his blood relatives. Choosing a literary career after the death of his foster father, Poe began to contribute critical reviews to the Richmond *Southern Literary Messenger* in 1835 and later became its editor for two years. He married Virginia Clemm, his cousin who was less than 14 years old, in 1836. Until his death in 1849, Poe worked tirelessly as an editor and a reviewer, composing at the same time poetry, fiction, reviews, and essays of the highest literary excellence. He contributed to several noted American periodicals and newspapers; and in October 1845 he edited and briefly owned his own magazine, *Broadway Journal*.

Poe published his only major long piece, *The Narrative of A. Gordon Pym*, in 1838 and a short-story collection, *Tales of the Grotesque and Arabesque*, in 1839. His poem "The Raven," printed in the *New York Evening Mirror* on 29 January 1845, brought him considerable recognition. *Tales*, a second collection of short stories, and a third volume of poems, *The Raven and Other Poems*, appeared in 1845. After the death of his wife in January 1847, he continued to write and to pursue his ambition of owning his own magazine. In early October of 1849, while traveling to New York to marry Sarah Royster Shelton, a widowed former sweetheart, Poe stopped in Baltimore, where he was later found ill on a city street. He died in a Baltimore hospital on 7 October 1849. His unexpected death was noted by nearly every significant newspaper and magazine in the eastern United States.

A controversial figure, Poe has been the subject of much speculative analysis. Generally, his biographers conclude that his instability as a person was in part due to the pressure of being a journalist. Although periodically he experienced poverty and the ill effects of poor health, Poe managed to perfect a variety of literary forms. He absorbed the current wave of romantic thought, which in his day brought significant changes in literary theory and practice. His classical bent, along with his background in Scottish philosophy and aesthetics, contributed to his theory of unity of effect and to his ideas about the short poem. He and Nathaniel Hawthorne introduced the ambiguities of symbolism in their Gothic tales, and Poe is credited with defining the short story as a distinct literary form. His attempts to formulate an objective method for writing poetry had some impact upon the French symbolist poets of the later decades of the 19th century. In the area of popular literature, he is said to have fathered the modern detective story and some forms of science fiction.

Poe believed his art—all art—should be evaluated by international, rather than national or regional, standards, but he was, nonetheless, frequently identified at the time with the South. He did not defend his region's politics or social customs, like other antebellum southern writers, but his lyricism was common to southern poets. Raised a Virginian, Poe sometimes posed as the southern gentleman, even if transcending regionalism in his work.

J. LASLEY DAMERON
Memphis State University

Benjamin F. Fisher, *Poe and His Times: The Artist and His Milieu* (1990); James A. Harrison, ed., *The Complete Works of Edgar Allan Poe* (1902); Robert D. Jacobs, *Poe: Journalist and Critic* (1969); Jeffrey Meyers, *Edgar A. Poe: His Life and Legacy* (1992); Arthur H. Quinn, *Edgar Allan Poe: A Critical Biography* (1941); Kenneth Silverman, *Edgar A. Poe: Mournful and Never-Ending Remembrance* (1991).

Porter, Katherine Anne

(1890–1980) WRITER.
Porter was born in Indian Creek, Tex., on 15 May 1890, the fourth of five children born to Harrison Boone and Mary Alice Porter. Her mother's death before she was two and her father's ineffectuality as a provider led to her being brought up in poverty by her severely puritanical grandmother. Porter was so deeply affected by these events—the deprivation, the social embarrassment of being perceived, she thought, as "poor white trash," her father's emotional unreliability, and her grandmother's relentless prohibitions on her behavior—that throughout her life she reacted against or simply denied this early unhappiness.

Porter began at an early age to rely on a vivid imagination to create a life—and soon a past—more palatable to her than what she experienced. She fabricated so many stories about herself, and was so persuasive in doing so, that biographers endlessly recorded "facts" that had never been true. Porter's imagination also contributed significantly to the richness of her finest stories, in which (through protagonists who were personae for herself) she described her family as once aristocratic, living in a plantation home with still-loyal former slaves, longing for more prosperous days. In writing such stories as "Old Mortality" and "The Old Order," Porter was like other southern writers who found the imagined past much more congenial than the troubled present. In a recurring character such as Miranda, Porter conveyed her sense of herself as a child of the "lost (Civil) War" and explored the historical, familial matrix out of which she had emerged.

Although Porter's stories are sometimes set in the South and the pasts remembered are often linked to southern history, Porter's larger themes are not uniquely southern. She was concerned with the universal issue of how human beings create myths about themselves that keep them from recognizing and responding to one another's needs—with how, indeed, the immersion in myth can lead human beings, through blindness, to be accomplices in evil. The children in her stories gradually learn the falsehood of adult myths and, in doing so, find their own loneliness confirmed. Porter's personal ambivalence toward these matters—her oscillation between human involvements as crippling and isolation as a kind of death—suggests the remarkable candor of her stories, whose power often resides precisely in their delineation of human failures.

In later years, public recognition of Porter's achievements included honorary degrees, Guggenheim Fellowships, Fulbright and Ford Foundation grants, the O. Henry Memorial Award, and the Pulitzer Prize. Although her only novel, *Ship of Fools* (1962), was considered a failure because of its heavy-handed ironies, Porter's place in American fiction was already secure. In the subtlety, precision, and insight of her best work, she had proved herself a genius of the short story.

Porter's major works include *Flowering Judas and Other Stories* (1930), *Pale Horse, Pale Rider: Three Short Novels* (1939), *The Leaning Tower and Other Stories* (1944), *The Old Order: Stories of the South* (1944), *The Days Before* (1952), *A Defense of Circe* (1955), *Ship of Fools* (1962), *Holiday* (1962), *The Collected Stories of Katherine Anne Porter* (1965), and *The Collected Essays and Occasional Writings of Katherine Anne Porter* (1970).

GAIL L. MORTIMER
University of Texas at El Paso

Jane Krause DeMouy, *Katherine Anne Porter's Women: The Eye of Her Fiction* (1983); Joan Givner, *Katherine Anne Porter: A Life* (1982); Myron M. Liberman, *Katherine Anne Porter's Fiction* (1971); William L. Nance, *Katherine Anne Porter and the Art of Rejection* (1964); Janis P. Stout, *Katherine Anne Porter: A Sense of the Times* (1995); Darlene Harbour Unrue, *Katherine Anne Porter: The Life of an Artist* (2005).

Portis, Charles

(b. 1933) WRITER.

Charles McColl Portis was born in El Dorado, Ark., 28 December 1933, the son of Samuel Palmer, a schoolteacher and administrator, and Alice (Waddell) Portis, the daughter of a Methodist minister. Portis, author of five novels, has been favorably compared with Mark Twain as a comic genius. His fiction has characteristics of classic Old Southwest humor, in which a naive or inexperienced narrator tells about a journey to "the wilds"—in Portis's case, including New York City and various places in Central America—where he or she meets colorful characters who provide the material for the narrator's observations about life and death, political or moral questions, and language. Portis has perfect pitch in rendering contemporary American language across region, class, and economic status. Especially, his work represents a very high order of storytelling, weaving countless details and digressions to bring into view a pattern that delights and astonishes the reader.

Charles Portis grew up in small towns in southern Arkansas and got his high school education at Hamburg. From 1952 to 1955 he was in the U.S. Marine Corps and served in the Korean War. After being discharged, he studied journalism at the University of Arkansas. He worked on the *Traveler*, the university newspaper, and on the *Northwest Arkansas Times*.

He was hired by the *Memphis Commercial Appeal* after he graduated in May 1958, but early in 1959 he returned to Arkansas to work at the *Arkansas Gazette* in Little Rock in the golden era of publisher J. N. Heiskell and editors Harry Ashmore and Bob Douglas. Two years later he moved to the *New York Herald Tribune*, where his assignments included civil rights stories in the South. He was chief of the *Tribune*'s London bureau in 1963–64. Portis then returned again to Arkansas and began writing fiction. As Ray Midge, the narrator of *The Dog of the South*, says, "A lot of people leave Arkansas and most of them come back sooner or later. They can't quite achieve escape velocity."

His first novel, *Norwood* (1966), is a great American picaresque. Norwood Pratt sets out from Texas to deliver two cars for Grady Fring, the Kredit King, to New York City. En route he encounters, along with the woman he takes home to be his wife, the world's smallest perfect fat man, Joann the Wonder Hen, and other unique characters. The deadpan

narrative style was repeated in *True Grit* (1968), in which the elderly narrator, Mattie Ross, recounts her girlhood adventure when, accompanied by the notorious U.S. marshal Rooster Cogburn, she avenged her father's murder. *True Grit* was made into a movie in 1969 starring John Wayne.

Roy Blount Jr. has written that "no one should die without having read *The Dog of the South*." *Dog* (1979) is ostensibly another travel story, following Ray Midge as he goes to Honduras in pursuit of a newspaper copy editor who has run off with his wife and his car. *Masters of Atlantis* (1985) satirizes New Age delusions and secret societies and is embellished with more travel sequences and weird characters. The blurb on the reprint calls it Portis's "brilliant white comedy." His gift for wordplay is fully exercised in the jargon of Gnomonism. In *Gringos* (1991) the narrator is Jimmy Burns, an expatriate drifter living in Mexico in a gringo community of hippies and runaways, a fallen-away doctor, a couple investigating flying saucers and the Mayan ruins, and a failed archaeological expedition. Burns is a more vigorous character than Midge or Norwood, yet in the end, Burns does not go anywhere either.

Portis, on the other hand, keeps moving. Recognizing a renewed public and critical enthusiasm for his work, Overlook Press reissued all of Portis's books in paperback, beginning in the late 1990s. Short pieces have appeared in magazines, including the *Oxford American* and the *Atlantic Monthly*, which in 1999 published a story, "Combinations of Jacksons," of a boy's life in the small south Arkansas towns where Portis grew up. In 2006 Portis was living in Little Rock, steadfastly inaccessible to almost all interviewers.

ETHEL C. SIMPSON
University of Arkansas

Ron Rosenbaum, *New York Observer* (24 May 1999).

Price, Reynolds

(b. 1933) WRITER.

Reynolds Price was born on 1 February 1933 in the farmhouse his grandfather built in Macon, N.C., 10 miles south of the border with Virginia, in the shadow of the Roanoke River.

Price's bibliography includes more than a dozen novels, a series of plays, short-story and essay collections, volumes of poetry, a medical memoir, a children's book, a *Time Magazine* cover story examining Jesus, an interpretation of the gospels of Mark and John, an introduction to a popular picture book commemorating the front porch, and collaboration with James Taylor on the hit song "Copperline" (1991).

Price's academic and literary career is a story of success eclipsing success. He graduated from Broughton High School in Raleigh and was awarded the Angier Duke Scholarship to study at Duke University. During his senior year, Price sat in on Eudora Welty's guest lecture entitled "Place in Fiction." Recognizing his talent, Welty passed on Price's work to her agent.

After graduating from Duke summa cum laude, Price traveled to Oxford as a Rhodes scholar and began work on

A Long and Happy Life (1962). Set in North Carolina, the story follows its rural character, Rosacoke Mustian, as she seeks to fulfill the promise of the novel's title. Welty's praise, "His is a first-rate talent," graces the cover of the original Atheneum edition. As proof of Price's talent, the novel won the William Faulkner Award.

Early critics of *A Long and Happy Life* attempted to make connections to Faulkner. Yet Price resisted comparison to the Mississippian. When interviewers ask Price to discuss Faulkner's influence on his work, he is likely to redirect them across the Atlantic to Milton and Tolstoy or point to other American authors, including Welty, Ernest Hemingway, and Mark Twain. According to Price, his stories are situated in the South because he was born, raised, and educated there. His status as a southern writer is a geographical accident, compounded by his love for storytelling in place.

Price continued to tell stories about the South in *The Surface of the Earth* (1975). Now included in *A Great Circle: The Mayfield Trilogy* (2001), the novel drew infamous criticism from Richard Gilman, a drama and literary critic who reviewed the book for the *New York Times*. Calling Price's novel "a mastodon," he bemoaned its exploration of two families from a passé literary region—the South. Welty came to her friend's defense, writing a letter to the editor that questioned how Price "could benefit by cutting off any source of wisdom that he was heir to." Gilman shot back, calling Welty's rhetoric "pompous" and "flaccid" and reiterating his main

394 PRICE, REYNOLDS

point—"'Southern Fiction' as a distinctive presence in our literary consciousness is past its great period."

Clearly, Price did not agree with Gilman's grim prognosis. In 1984 he began writing *Kate Vaiden* (1986), again situating his female narrator in North Carolina and Virginia. In the midst of drafting the novel, doctors discovered what Price has called a "lethal eel" inside his spinal cord, a malignant tumor that would soon make him a paraplegic. His medical memoir, *A Whole New Life* (1994), details Price's experience with the impersonal touch of modern medicine. It also serves as an example of the absurdity of classifying Price's work as purely southern. Like his fictional works, his memoir is set in the South. Yet the story of his treatment at Duke Hospital is not bound by regional literary elements but by experience.

Upon recovery, Price rose from the ashes of his old self a reenergized writer. His latest novel, *The Good Priest's Son* (2005), combines religion, North Carolina, and 9/11. Thus, Price's work continues to serve as an example for southern writers who wish to draw from the region's realities and, in spite of critics, confirm the lasting and distinctive presence of southern literature, without being restrained by traditional expectations.

KAREN LEE GENTRY
Georgia State University

Richard Gilman and Eudora Welty, *New York Times* (29 June and 20 July 1975); Jefferson Humphries, ed., *Conversations with Reynolds Price* (1991); Reynolds Price, *A Long and Happy Life* (1962), *Out on the Porch* (1992), *A Whole New Life* (1994), *Three Gospels* (1996), *Time Magazine: Jesus of Nazareth Then and Now* (1999), *A Great Circle: The Mayfield Trilogy* (2001), *The Good Priest's Son* (2005); Constance Rooke, *Reynolds Price* (1983); James A. Schiff, ed., *Critical Essays on Reynolds Price* (1998), *Understanding Reynolds Price* (1996).

Randolph, Vance

(1892–1980) FOLKLORIST.
Vance Randolph's academic training was in psychology (M.A., Clark University, 1915), and Randolph described himself most often as a "hack writer." To be sure, for many years he supported himself by writing, often under a pseudonym, pulp fiction and nonfiction on a vast range of subjects. The shelf of books resulting from his long lifetime's work in the Arkansas and Missouri Ozarks, however, is responsible for his continuing reputation as one of the nation's premier regional folklorists. Driven by an encyclopedic, curious mind, he collected all facets of Ozark lore. His works on the region's speech offer unparalleled insight and are the foundation of all subsequent scholarship in this field.

Randolph was born in Pittsburg, Kan., just west of the Ozarks, but he lived his adult life in small towns in Missouri (Pineville, Galena) and Arkansas (Eureka Springs, Fayetteville), where he assiduously sought out and perpetuated in print and on recordings the sayings, doings, singings, and believings of his Ozark neighbors. His first books, *The Ozarks: An American Survival of Primitive Society* (1931) and *Ozark Mountain Folks* (1932), are long out of print, but remain notable excellent examples of what later were called folklife studies. His methods and definitions were often in advance of their time—he included, for example, discographical references to "hillbilly" records in his four-volume folk song collection *Ozark Folksongs* (1946–50) at a time when many scholars found such recordings unworthy of notice.

Randolph first achieved renown as a student of dialect when H. L. Mencken lavishly praised his numerous article-length studies published beginning in 1926 in two American Dialect Society periodicals, *American Speech* and *Dialect Notes*. His major work in this area, *Down in the Holler: A Gallery of Ozark Folk Speech* (1953), gathered material from more than 30 years of study and observation and covered Ozark grammar, pronunciation, archaisms, taboos and euphemisms, and wisecracks, along with the use of the dialect in fiction. The book also provided an extensive, scholarly glossary. Like others working on Ozark dialect until recent years, he frequently identified archaisms that could also be found in Renaissance-era English literature, but he kept any ideas about the "Elizabethan" character of Ozark speech in perspective with its other qualities, unlike his peers. Along with his massive folk song collection, the 1940s saw the publication of Randolph's major study of folk belief, *Ozark Superstitions* (1947). In the 1950s Randolph published five volumes of folktales, including *We Always Lie to Strangers: Tall Tales from the Ozarks*. A collection of jokes, *Hot Springs and Hell* (1965), and Randolph's huge bibliographic work, *Ozark Folklore: A Bibliog-*

raphy (1972), were followed by his classic collection of bawdy humor, *Pissing in the Snow* (1976). Taken together, Randolph's many publications provide a detailed and sympathetic portrait of Ozark traditional life and speech. Academic folklorists honored Randolph in 1978 by electing him a Fellow of the American Folklore Society.

ROBERT COCHRAN
University of Arkansas

Robert Cochran, *Vance Randolph: An Ozark Life* (1995); Vance Randolph, *The Ozarks: A Bibliography* (1972); Vance Randolph and George P. Wilson, *Down in the Holler: A Gallery of Ozark Folkspeech.* (1953).

Ransom, John Crowe

(1888–1974) WRITER AND CRITIC. John Crowe Ransom was born 30 April 1888 in Pulaski, Tenn., the third of five children of Methodist minister John James Ransom and his wife, Ella Crowe Ransom. John Crowe attended the Bowen preparatory school in Nashville, completing a rigorous program in classical languages, English, history, mathematics, and German. Entering Vanderbilt University at 15, he continued his classical studies. He was a Rhodes scholar at University College, Oxford, from 1910 to 1912, reading widely in classics and philosophy. In 1914 Ransom accepted an instructorship in English at Vanderbilt, where he immediately began the method of teaching that, through texts written in the late 1930s and early 1940s by his former students Cleanth Brooks and Robert Penn Warren (the "New Critics"), was to dominate the teaching of literature in American colleges and universities for nearly 30

John Crowe Ransom, Vanderbilt Agrarian, 1927 (Photographic Archives,
Vanderbilt University Library, Nashville, Tennessee)

years: close analysis of individual texts with emphasis on the uses of language.

Except for army service during World War I, followed by a term at the University of Grenoble, Ransom remained in the English department at Vanderbilt until 1937 (teaching many summer sessions in other colleges and programs). His first volume of poetry, *Poems about God*, appeared in 1919.

In the fall of 1919 Ransom began meeting with the group that would, in 1922, begin to publish the *Fugitive*, a magazine whose name signified flight from "the high-caste Brahmins of the Old South" (according to Ransom's foreword). Ransom, an already-published poet and a respected teacher, was sought out for advice and judgment by such younger members of the group as Donald Davidson and Allen Tate (and later Warren, Andrew Lytle, Jesse Wills, and others). The *Fugitive*, which lasted 19 issues, from 1922 to 1925, and expired not for lack of funds but for want of an editor, published the bulk of Ransom's mature poetry, collected in the volumes *Grace after Meat* (1924) and *Chills and Fever* (1924). In 1927 *Two Gentlemen in Bonds* was published, containing some of Ransom's best poems: "Dead Boy," "Blue Girls," "Janet Waking," "Vision by Sweetwater," "Antique Harvesters," and "The Equilibrists."

In *God without Thunder* (1930), Ransom proposed that new rationalistic theologies were destructive of man's religious sense, for they destroyed his respect for the mysterious universe and elevated "science," which analyzes and uses "nature" rather than fearing and loving it. Ransom's religious ideas were coordinate with his defense of the South in "Reconstructed but Unregenerate," his essay for *I'll Take My Stand* (1930), and other essays about the South in contemporary society, such as "The South Defends Its Heritage" and "The South—Old or New?" For the former Fugitives and others who published *I'll Take My Stand*, the respect and love for nature associated with farming, especially family subsistence farming, were intimately bound up with the best social values of the culture— filial piety, kindliness, good manners, respect for the past, contemplativeness, and appreciation not only of the natural world but of art.

The publicity focused upon *I'll Take My Stand* and a series of debates related to it made the agrarian position a focal point for discussion of broad cultural values of American society. In an essay for a 1936 collection, *Who Owns America? A New Declaration of Independence* (edited by Herbert Agar and Allen Tate), Ransom retreated from the extreme agrarian position, acknowledging that the South must accept industrialization in order to preserve economic autonomy. By 1940, in the *Kenyon Review*, Ransom had called the agrarian ideal a "fantasy," thus making public and final his defection from the economic position he had defended a decade before. The espousal of humane values—including respect for the mysteries—was not recanted, but became the center of Ransom's poetic theory in *The World's Body* (1938), *The New Criticism* (1941), and later essays.

Ransom accepted a teaching position at Kenyon College in Gambier, Ohio, in 1937 and founded the *Kenyon Review* two years later. During Ransom's editorship of the *Kenyon Review* (1939–59), he published important works by such southern writers as Andrew Lytle, Randall Jarrell, Caroline Gordon, and Flannery O'Connor. Although Ransom had left the South and had abandoned the agrarian program, he remained a staunch spokesman for the aesthetic and ethical values formulated in the essays and poems of his Vanderbilt period. He died 2 July 1974, in Gambier, Ohio.

SUZANNE FERGUSON
Ohio State University

Mark G. Malvasi, *The Unregenerate South: The Agrarian Thought of John Crowe Ransom, Allen Tate, and Donald Davidson* (1997); Kieran Quinlan, *John Crowe Ransom's Secular Faith* (1989); Louis D. Rubin Jr., in *The New Criticism and After*, ed. Thomas Daniel Young (1976); John L. Stewart, *John Crowe Ransom* (1962); Thomas Daniel Young, *Gentleman in a Dustcoat: A Biography of John Crowe Ransom* (1976).

Rash, Ron

(b. 1953) WRITER.

Born in Chester, S.C., in 1953, Ron Rash grew up in Boiling Springs, N.C., and traces his Welsh ancestry to the hardscrabble mountain farms of Madison and Watauga counties, an Appalachian landscape that provides the scene for much of his writing. Rash earned degrees from Gardner Webb College and Clemson University before beginning to write and publish in journals such as the *Southern Poetry Review*, *Foot (Hill) Notes*, and the *Kennesaw Review*. From the beginning, his work has been characterized by a knowledge of and reverence for the southern Appalachian mountain region, for its customs, folklore, superstitions, and familial and communal histories. His first collection of stories, *The Night the New Jesus Fell to Earth* (1994), is a Fred Chappell–like sequence of tales told by three narrators all coping with the loss by fire of the only café in Cliffside, N.C. By turns satirical and poignant, *The Night the New Jesus Fell to Earth* differs in tone from Rash's poetry, which tends toward the elegiac and somber and is infused with the dark vision of Irish poets such as Seamus Heaney and Patrick Kavanaugh.

Rash's early work won several awards, including an National Endowment for the Arts Poetry Fellowship (1994) and the Sherwood Anderson Prize (1996), but with *Eureka Mill* (1998), Rash announced himself as a poignant new voice in American poetry. Through a sequence of 40 poems, Rash relates the story of his grandparents' move off the family farm to join other dispossessed families in the textile mills of the South Carolina Piedmont. Rash's poetry is highly narrative, driven through the use of precise images and evocative metaphors, structured through multiple speakers capturing the disjunction, isolation, and anger of Appalachian farmers bereft of their land and turned into clonelike cogs in a capitalist machine. *Among the Believers* (2000) features poems by speakers from western North Carolina whose experiences embody the harsh beauty and violent past of the region. Ceremonial rites such as foot washing, baptisms, and serpent handling blend with

Civil War–era violence and a host of bodies strewn throughout, victims of flood, matricide, bad luck, murder, and even of the wilderness itself. In *Raising the Dead* (2002), Rash stakes claim to the Appalachian underwater world of Jocassee Valley (the Cherokee word for "place of the lost") in northwestern South Carolina, which was flooded for hydroelectric power in the 1960s. In these evocative poems, mountain residents speak with dignity of a lost world, a place of intense belonging filled with mystery, beauty, and death.

Rash continued to write stories, publishing *Casualties* in 2000, but with the enthusiastic reception of his first novel, *One Foot in Eden* (2002), he was catapulted into the forefront of contemporary southern writers, winning the Appalachian Book of the Year. Set in Jocassee Valley and told in five sections each narrated by a specific character, *One Foot in Eden* tells the story of Billy Holcombe and his wife, Amy, who, unable to produce a child, commit crimes in their desperation and find themselves enmeshed in a fateful web of seduction and murder. His second novel, *Saints at the River* (2004), won the Southern Book Critics Circle Fiction Award and tells the story of Maggie Glenn's return to her mountain home in Tamassee, S.C., to photograph the battle of forces surrounding the drowning of a young girl in one of the most sensitive ecological areas in the region. In *The World Made Straight* (2006), which won the Sir Walter Raleigh Award, Rash returns to themes originally explored in his poetry, specifically the Civil War massacre of "Bloody Madison" County, where mem-

bers of a Confederate force massacred 13 Union sympathizers. In this novel, past and present, victim and victimizer, family and country, and duty and survival all cohere in a poetic intensity that evokes Rash's larger concerns regarding the preciousness of hope, the fragility of dreams, and the moral responsibility we all must face. Rash has continued to earn honors, winning the James Still Award from the Fellowship of Southern Writers (2005) and the O. Henry Prize for his short story "Speckled Trout" (2005). He currently holds the Parris Chair of Appalachian Studies at Western Carolina University.

RANDALL S. WILHELM
University of Tennessee

Joyce Compton Brown, *Appalachian Heritage* (Fall 2002); Anna Dunlap Higgins, *North Carolina Literary Review* (2004); John Lang, ed., *Iron Mountain Review: Ron Rash Issue* (Spring 2004).

Ray, Janisse

(b. 1962) ENVIRONMENTAL ACTIVIST AND WRITER.

From the beginning, Janisse Ray has had an agenda for her published work. Although she writes about many topics other than the environment, her quest to preserve nature is paramount. In fact, Ray's first and most momentous book, *Ecology of a Cracker Childhood* (1999), alternates chapters about the author's own family and upbringing with chapters on naturalism. For instance, a story about the writer playing school with her siblings in a neighborhood junkyard is followed by a story about the plight of the red cockaded woodpecker. Ray admits that she knew no one would read a book about "a damn pine tree," so she weaves the naturalist descriptions together with beautiful passages concerning the human species. This structure works together perfectly because it seems modeled after an ideal ecosystem where people and nature interconnect harmoniously.

Janisse Ray was born 2 February 1962. She grew up in Baxley, Ga., with her siblings and both her parents, who survived on just a few thousand dollars a year. Ray's thinking often differed from her father's fundamentalist ideas, but she continually honored her parents through her writing. Ray attended North Georgia College and State University in Dahlonega, Ga., before earning her M.F.A in creative writing from the University of Montana in 1997. In her writing classes, Ray learned that publishing a book would make a difference, and shorter publications would not. With the publication of *Ecology of a Cracker Childhood* in 1999, Ray has definitely made a difference with her autobiographical and nature "stories."

Readers discover Janisse Ray's agenda through her nature writing but also get to know the author as a person in all of her works. In *Ecology*, readers learn about the mental illness in her family, which understandably brought constant anxiety, yet Ray's parents appear to be wonderful people despite health and financial problems. Ray's personal saga continues in *Wild Card Quilt: Taking a Chance on Home* (2003), which tells about the years when Ray moved back to the "old homeplace" in Baxley, Ga., with her son. Ray's introduction says she "was looking for

wholeness" but instead she discovered "an erosion of human bonds—both to each other and to the land." This book has even more of the human element of ecology than her first, and much of it reads like a novel. Ray's research and nature writing pursuits gave her several adventures, including a wild night of riding in a boat with sexy alligator hunters. Ray does take a chance on place, family, and romantic love in *Wild Card Quilt*, and perhaps this book is her best so far in revealing how people make choices that can destroy or nurture relationships and the environment.

Ray's *Pinhook: Finding Wholeness in a Fragmented Land* (2005) is unique in its particular environmental focus and in its activist tone. If readers want to learn specifically how to get involved in curbing development and deforestation, this is a good literary source. As usual, Ray's writing style makes *Pinhook* read like good fiction; however, the point is clear that people who care need to join forces and make positive changes. The positive change that many people have already made in Georgia and Florida is to allow more natural habitat by providing a corridor called Pinhook Swamp. This book takes some of the key lessons and suggestions that *Ecology* offered and gives specific examples of ideal solutions to environmental problems. This specific example in the South shows how individuals, volunteer and government organizations, and multiple states have put funding and effort into reclaiming wildness.

RACHEL G. WALL
Georgia State University

Josephine Humphries, in *Friendship and Sympathy: Communities of Southern Women Writers*, ed. Rosemary M. Magee (1992); Jay Watson, *Mississippi Quarterly* (Fall 2002); Susan Miller Williams, *Women's Review of Books* (July 2003).

Reed, Ishmael

(b. 1938) WRITER AND EDITOR.
One of the great literary iconoclasts and satirists of his generation, Ishmael Reed has been revered and reviled by various literary critics since his extraordinary debut novel in 1967, *The Freelance Pallbearers*, which dazzled readers with its stylistic innovations and satirical look at power and race relations. The *Nation* magazine called Reed "the brightest contributor to American satire since Mark Twain."

Born in Chattanooga, Tenn., in 1938, Reed grew up in the industrial haunts of Buffalo, N.Y., where he became actively involved in community issues as a young correspondent for the *Empire Star*, an African American weekly publication, and briefly attended the University of Buffalo. After losing his host position at a local radio station because he interviewed Malcolm X, Reed moved to New York City in 1962, where he helped to launch the underground *East Village Other* publication and became one of the early shapers and participants in the black arts movement.

Author of more than 20 novels and collections of essays, plays, poetry, and memoir, Reed moved to the East Bay area in California in the late 1960s, where he became a member of the creative writing faculty at the University of California at Berkeley, a fixture in the Oakland literary scene, and a prominent critic in the early multicultural movements.

Acclaimed for its extraordinary gift of language, unyielding parodies, and stylistic and nonlinear innovations, Reed's singular work has expressed a literary hybrid that he referred to as the "Neo-HooDoo Aesthetic," which he introduced in his second novel, *Yellow Back Radio Broke-Down*, a postmodernist western published in 1969. With cunning insight into the vagaries and hypocrisy of his times, Reed has let few subjects escape his biting satirical escapades. His novel *Flight to Canada*, which Edmund Wilson called "the best work of black fiction since *Invisible Man*," excoriated slave narratives, as well as Harriet Beecher Stowe's *Uncle Tom's Cabin*. Other novels took on the president of the United States, corporate America, the cultural elite, Christian fundamentalists, and academia. His detective farce, *Mumbo Jumbo*, was set in New Orleans.

Along with his varied literary accomplishments, Reed has become legendary for his unusual role in supporting the works of other writers, as well as working with young authors. He was one of the founders of the Before Columbus Foundation, which presents the annual American Book Awards. In 2004 the *Los Angeles Times* awarded Reed the Robert Kirsch Award for Lifetime Achievement, citing not only his numerous works of fiction, nonfiction, and poetry, but his commitment to publishing a wide array of voices as a former book publisher and serving as editor of critically acclaimed anthologies that sought to widen the traditional canons of literature, including *From Totems to Hip Hop: A Multicultural Anthology of Poetry across America.*

Along with a Lila Wallace Fellowship and a MacArthur Foundation Fellowship, Reed has been a finalist for the Pulitzer Prize for Fiction and twice a finalist for the National Book Award in both fiction and poetry.

JEFF BIGGERS
Illinois

Chester J. Fontenot, *Black American Literature Forum* (Spring 1978); Sämi Ludwig, *African American Review* (Fall 1998); Barry Saunders, *News and Observer* (Raleigh, N.C.) (20 May 2006); Neil Schmitz, *Twentieth Century Literature* (April 1974); Kenneth Womack, *MELUS* (Winter 2001).

Reed, John Shelton

(b. 1942) WRITER, TEACHER, AND SCHOLAR.

The person whom novelist Lee Smith has described as "hysterically funny and the most astute observer of the South that we have" was born on 8 January 1942 in New York City, a circumstance he admits he could not avoid. John Shelton Reed's mother came from Rochester, N.Y., and his family line included many "mountain Republicans" who were accustomed to standing on their own ground. For Reed, who would become a renowned commentator on the South, one might say that iconoclasm was bred in the bone.

Raised in Kingsport, Tenn., Reed went to the Massachusetts Institute of Technology with the intent of becoming a statistician. As a student there, in the words of writer Doris Betts, "[he] first found himself called upon to define how the South was distinctive, then to defend it." Reed has often pointed to Lord Acton's observation that exile is the cradle of nationalism, and seeing himself self-consciously as a southerner for the first time, he changed majors, his studies culminating in a Ph.D. in sociology from Columbia (1969).

Reed's dissertation, which became *The Enduring South* (1972), argued that southern culture was more plastic, resilient, and redoubtable than was commonly believed. His ideas went against the thinking of scholars such as C. Vann Woodward, who believed that the advent of the bulldozer effectively spelled the end of regional cultural distinctiveness. Over the years, in a series of published studies, Reed would develop the notion that southerners might be viewed through the same lens as other American ethnic groups. In his words, "When it worked, it was really interesting. When it didn't, that was interesting, too." Reed's central insight helped to explain how the themes of localism, religiosity, and violence within southern culture might be understood as "plausible responses for a minority group, surrounded by a culture which is viewed as powerful, hostile, and unresponsive." His analysis also helped to explain something as counterintuitive as the blossoming of southern culture in a massively transformed region and the paradoxical ascendancy of regional consciousness and the decline of "traditional" southern values.

As remarkable as Reed's ideas was the method of their delivery. Sociology is a field reputationally rife with social liberals and opaque prose; John Reed proved exceptional on both counts. As a sociologist with a flair for writing, John Reed's work has been appreciated by both writers and academicians. He was inducted into the Fellowship of Southern Writers in 2000. His insistence that academic writing should be jargon free and intelligible to ordinary readers influenced the tone of the *Southern Cultures*, a journal that he founded in 1992. His style has inspirited a generation of scholars. In gathering data about the region, Reed's polls went directly to the subjects and laid emphasis on self-perception that went beyond roseate sociological theory.

A flavor of Reed's evolving and far-ranging exploration of the South can be sampled across his essay collections, *Whistling Dixie* (1990), *My Tears Spoiled My Aim* (1993), *Kicking Back* (1995), and *Minding the South* (2003). He has written about the free play between southern social types and stereotypes, the vestiges of agrarianism, and the vicissitudes of Confederate emblems in publications ranging from *Science* to *Southern Living*. Some of Reed's witticisms are so well known that they stand as truisms of southern identity (e.g., "[Atlanta] represents what a quarter of a million Confederates died to prevent"). He has been honored as a Fulbright lecturer, an National Endowment for the Humanities fellow, and a Guggenheim fellow.

Reed has charted the finer points of Anglo-Catholicism, in keeping with what he has described as a "long-term love affair" with England. He has been invited to teach at Oxford and Cambridge universities, and at the University of London, and now regularly travels to England. His peripatetic life-style has continued following his retirement as a professor of sociology at the University of North Carolina at Chapel Hill. Most recently he has offered a late entry into the field of country music, with characteristic humor, available in the Music Issue of *Southern Cultures*. He continues to lecture on facets of southern studies, both in the United States and abroad.

BRYAN GIEMZA
Wake Forest University

John Shelton Reed, *The Enduring South: Subcultural Persistence in Mass Society* (1972), *Minding the South* (2003), *My Tears Spoiled My Aim and Other Reflections on Southern Culture* (1993), *One South: An Ethnic Approach to Regional Culture* (1982), *Whistling Dixie: Dispatches from the South* (1990), *Surveying the South: Studies in Regional Sociology* (1993); "The South According to John Shelton Reed" (special issue), *Southern Cultures* (Spring 2001).

Richard, Mark

(b. 1955) WRITER.
Known for his award-winning short stories and a novel that reads like a long dream, Mark Richard is of Cajun-Creole-French descent. He was born in Lake Charles, La., on 9 November 1955 and grew up in Texas and Virginia. He arrived on the literary scene in 1989 with a startling book of short stories published by Alfred A. Knopf entitled *The Ice at the Bottom of the World*. Full of strange and tender moments, the book won the 1990 PEN/Ernest Hemingway Foundation Award. This publication was the culmination of years of travel, a formal education at

Washington and Lee University, and work at various off-the-radar jobs that gave Richard vivid material for his often surreal fiction.

Richard became the youngest radio announcer in the United States at wysr-am in Franklin, Va., at the age of 13. He later spent time working as an aerial photographer and a naval correspondent and logged three years as a commercial fisherman. These were formative years for Richard. During them he absorbed the strangeness of the world, and that strangeness served as inspiration for some of the most grotesque American fiction of the late 20th century.

Although his settings are often harrowing and menacing, he puts the resolution into the hands of the most innocent and seemingly least powerful—the children. They are usually lost or searching or, in some cases, simply orphans. One of his most anthologized short stories is "The Birds for Christmas," which centers around two orphan boys who want to do nothing on Christmas Eve but watch Alfred Hitchcock's *The Birds* on a black-and-white television in a charity ward. Another story, "Strays," relates the adventures of two poor brothers and their Uncle Trash, who descends on their house in the midst of a bleary bender. In Richard's fictional world adults are often the enemies that bring about serious problems, and they are to be avoided or forgotten, but the children in his stories possess the wisdom, end up solving the problems, and, more importantly, survive and endure.

Richard's only novel to date, *Fishboy* (1993), is an expansion of a short story from his first book. The novel follows a boy who escapes the physical abuse of his childhood by jumping a fishing trawler manned by what may be the worst crew of seafaring renegades in all of literature. He chases survival until he meets his end by being boiled in a pot and turning into the ghost he has always wanted to be. Besides its dreamlike characters and plot, and the fever pitch that propels the book, the novel is also humorous—a current in Richard's work that is often overlooked.

Richard's third book, *Charity* (1998), is a second volume of short stories. The stories bring to mind the best of minimalist short-story masters such as Barry Hannah or Frederick Barthelme, yet only Richard could have a young boy spend a story conversing on and off with Death, who has come to call wearing a white dinner jacket and white pants, nibbles fortune cookies, and confesses to the boy that he is a "people person." Not even in the best of Flannery O'Connor (whom Richard is often compared to) does Death take on such a physical (and believable) presence.

Richard's characters often waver between hope and outright disaster, but hope often springs eternal. His characters are outcasts, yet Richard finds that there is a place for them in the world, too, and that they may receive an even greater reward than the most socially upright and adjusted. In believing the kind of stories that Richard tells, his readers end up believing in the greater story that we all share—that of the human condition and what we might yet make of it.

J. E. PITTS
University of Mississippi

Roger Matuz, ed., *Contemporary Southern Writers* (1999); Mark Richard, *The Ice at the Bottom of the World* (1989), *Fishboy* (1993), *Charity* (1998).

Roberts, Elizabeth Madox

(1881–1941) WRITER.

Catapulted to national acclaim with her first published novel, *The Time of Man* (1926), Elizabeth Madox Roberts produced seven novels, two poetry collections, and two volumes of short stories during her relatively brief career, but reception of her work suffered from critical comparisons to her wildly successful debut. Known primarily as a novelist of rural Kentucky life, Roberts declared from age eight that she wished to be a poet. While studying at the University of Chicago (Ph.B., 1921), she met *Poetry* editor Harriet Monroe, who became an early champion of her work and awarded her *Poetry*'s John Reed Memorial Prize in 1928.

Elizabeth Madox Roberts was born 30 October 1881 in Perryville, Ky., the second of eight children. As a young child, she moved with her family to Springfield, Ky., where her father, a former Confederate soldier, worked as a surveyor, farmer, and schoolmaster, and where young Elizabeth, who would be plagued by lifelong health problems, was to spend most of her life. The Kentucky pioneer tales she heard from her family, including stories of ancestors going west with Daniel Boone, find voice in her novels, particularly *The Great Meadow* (1930), in which Boone appears as a character. In 1900 Roberts entered the State College of Kentucky (now the University of Kentucky), but

poor health and poverty soon forced her to return to Springfield, where she taught school. In 1915 she published her first book, *In the Great Steep's Garden*, a poetry collection that described flora for tourists and foreshadowed the future influence of nature in her writing. In 1917, at age 36, Roberts left teaching and returned to college at the University of Chicago. Her second poetry collection, *Under the Tree*, followed in 1922.

Returning to Springfield after graduation, she turned her poetic instincts to the novel, a medium in which she hoped to exert more originality. *The Time of Man* superbly weaves Kentucky folklore together with Roberts's spiritual philosophy. Ellen Chesser, a poor itinerant farmer yearning for love and permanence, evokes Homer's *Odyssey* and reflects Roberts's own captivation with the presence of the natural world and the power of the spirit. *The Time of Man* earned praise from Sherwood Anderson and Ford Madox Ford, who called it "the most beautiful individual piece of writing that has yet come out of America."

Though none of her future novels achieved the same level of critical or popular success as *The Time of Man*, they featured similar heroines, like Theodosia Bell in *My Heart and My Flesh* (1927) and Diony Hall in *The Great Meadow* (1930), who confront and overcome financial and emotional obstacles, ultimately resolving them in favor of their own strength of spirit and awareness of the importance of inner knowledge. Though her work in the early 1930s, such as *The Haunted Mirror* (1932) and *He Sent Forth a Raven* (1935), reflects alternative influences, *Black Is My Truelove's Hair* (1938) marked a return to her regional focus on rural Kentucky and themes of the natural world and the life of the mind. Roberts was diagnosed with Hodgkin's disease in 1936 and published only two more books before her death: *Song in the Meadow* (1940), a compendium of songs and poems in the tradition of Whitman, and *Not by Strange Gods* (1941), a short-story collection compared by critics to Welty's *A Curtain of Green*. Both books affirmed her gifts as a storyteller of poetic realism and a chronicler of rural life in Kentucky.

JANE CARR
University of Virginia

J. Donald Adams, *Virginia Quarterly Review* (January 1936); Louis Auchincloss, *Pioneers and Caretakers: A Study of Nine American Women Novelists* (1965); Alison D. Goeller, in *Dictionary of Literary Biography*, vol. 9, ed. James J. Martine (1981); Frederick P. W. McDowell, *Elizabeth Madox Roberts* (1963); Edd Winfield Parks, *American Literature* (November 1957); Blair Rouse, *American Literature* (November 1965); Earl H. Rovit, *Herald to Chaos: The Novels of Elizabeth Madox Roberts* (1960); Elaine Showalter, *College English* (May 1971); Lewis Simpson, *The Fable of the Southern Writer* (1994); Linda Tate, *Resources for American Literary Study* (1992); Mark Van Doren, *English Journal* (September 1932).

Rubin, Louis D., Jr.

(b. 1923) CRITIC AND WRITER.
For his entire career as a critic, essayist, editor, novelist, publisher, and teacher, Louis Decimus Rubin Jr. has championed the recognition of an authentically southern literature. In *The History of Southern Literature* (1985), Rubin affirms the existence of southernness in literature and literary history: "The facts are that there existed in the past, and there continues to exist today, an entity within American society known as the South, and that for better or for worse the habit of viewing one's experience in terms of one's relationship to that entity is still a meaningful characteristic of both writers and readers who are or have been part of it." One of the most influential contemporary critics in southern literature, Rubin founded Algonquin Books of Chapel Hill, N.C., in 1982, in order to encourage, promote, and showcase talented young southern writers. Over the course of his career, Rubin has published more than 20 volumes of both fiction and nonfiction and edited many more.

Rubin was born 19 November 1923 in Charleston, S.C. After serving in the U.S. Army during World War II, he attended the College of Charleston (1940–42), Yale University (1943–44), and the University of Richmond in 1946, from which he received a B.A. in history. He earned his M.A. from Johns Hopkins University (1949), and while working on his Ph.D. at Johns Hopkins, established his literary reputation by coediting, with R. D. Jacobs, *Southern Renascence: The Literature of the Modern South* (1953). He further established himself as a major southern literary figure by publishing *Thomas Wolfe: The Weather of His Youth* (1955).

Before choosing an academic career, Rubin worked as a journalist for both newspapers and the Associated Press. He also served as editor for several literary magazines, including the *Hopkins Review* (1949–53) and the *Provincial* (1956–57). In 1957 he began teaching at Hollins College, a post that he would keep for 10 years. While at Hollins, he founded the *Hollins Critic* (1963) and taught many talented students, including Lee Smith and Annie Dillard. He moved to the University of North Carolina at Chapel Hill in 1967, remaining there until his retirement in 1989. While there, he taught such writers as Kaye Gibbons and Jill McCorkle as well as cofounding the *Southern Literary Journal* with Hugh Holman in 1968. He was also deeply involved in his Algonquin Books as well as publishing his own critical works.

Rubin has received a *Sewanee Review* Fellowship (1953), a Guggenheim Fellowship (1956), an American Council of Learned Societies Fellowship (1964), the Distinguished Virginian Award (1972), the Jules F. Landry Award, Louisiana State University Press (1978), membership in South Carolina Academy of Authors (1987), the O. Max Gardner Medal (1989), the R. Hunt Parker Memorial Award for lifetime contributions to the literary heritage of North Carolina, and numerous honorary degrees.

Other Rubin works include *The Faraway Country: Writers of the Modern South* (1966), *The Curious Death of the Novel: Essays in American Literature* (1967), *George W. Cable: The Life and Times of a Southern Heretic* (1969), *The Writer in the South* (1972), *Black Poetry in America: Two Essays in Interpretation* (1974), *William Elliot Shoots a Bear: Essays on the Southern Literary Imagi-*

nation (1976), *The Wary Fugitives: Four Poets and the South* (1978), *The Edge of the Swamp: A Study in the Literature and Society of the Old South* (1989), *Small Craft Advisory: A Book about the Building of a Boat* (1991), *The Mockingbird in the Gum Tree: A Literary Gallimaufry* (1991), *A Memory of Trains: The Boll Weevil and Others* (2000), and *An Honorable Estate: My Time in the Working Press* (2001).

CHRISTIAN L. FAUGHT
University of Tennessee

Contemporary Authors Online (2002); George Core, *Southern Review* (Autumn 2002); Fred Hobson, *Southern Review* (Autumn 2002); Michael Kreyling, *Inventing Southern Literature* (1998); Renee Lautenbach, ed., *Directory of American Scholars*, vol. 2 (1974); Shannon Ravenel, *Southern Review* (Autumn 2002); Louis D. Rubin Jr., *The History of Southern Literature* (1985); Lewis P. Simpson, *Southern Review* (Autumn 2002).

Rutledge, Archibald Hamilton

(1883–1973) WRITER.
Although born into South Carolina's aristocracy—an ancestor signed the Declaration of Independence—Rutledge maintained modest ways throughout his long life.

After passing his early years at his family's Hampton Plantation, he entered Porter Military Academy in Charleston, where he began writing poetry and essays. At 16 he enrolled at Union College in New York, from which he graduated in 1904. Following stints in sales and journalism, he taught at Mercersburg Academy in Pennsylvania. Acclaimed for his nature writing, poetry, and devotional literature, Rutledge was named South Carolina's first poet laureate in 1934.

Leaving Pennsylvania in 1937, he returned to Hampton Plantation, laboring to restore its 18th-century grandeur and writing prolifically. During his career, Rutledge authored nearly 60 books (*Life's Extras*, *My Colonel and His Lady*, and *Home by the River* are among his best-loved titles) and more than a thousand articles and poems that appeared in such publications as the *Saturday Evening Post*, *Field and Stream*, *Reader's Digest*, *Good Housekeeping*, *Georgia Review*, and *Virginia Quarterly*. At his death in 1973, the twice-widowed Rutledge was deeply mourned.

Currently his books are little read outside South Carolina. While his devotional writings still inspire readers, and his meditations on southern landscapes are vividly detailed, the racial attitudes that surface in some of his works belong to a bygone era. Nonetheless, the lyrical beauty that Rutledge's poetry and prose exude in depicting his beloved native state attests to his unquestionable literary gifts.

HARRY MCBRAYER BAYNE
Brewton-Parker College

Jim Casada, *Hunting and Home in the Southern Heartland: The Best of Archibald Rutledge* (1992); Archibald Rutledge, *Deep River: The Complete Poems of Archibald Rutledge* (1960), *Home by the River* (1941); Mary B. Wheeler and Genon H. Neblett, *Hidden Glory: The Life and Times of Hampton Plantation, Legend of the South Santee* (1983).

Sanders, Dori

(b. 1934) WRITER AND FARMER.
The granddaughter of a free slave, Dori Sanders was born in Filbert, S.C., in York County during the time of racial segregation. She, along with her nine brothers and sisters, was raised on her family's peach farm. The Sanders farm is well known in this region because in 1915 Dori's father, an elementary school principal, purchased the 81 acre land, becoming the county's first African American farmland owner. Not only did this farm provide for his family throughout his lifetime, but it is still the place Dori calls home.

The Sanderses led a rather sophisticated life-style for a rural farm family. Both Dori's mother and father were piano players, and Dori's mother trained all of the children to sing a cappella. Because of her father's career as a teacher, education—and literature in particular—was always of great importance to the Sanderses. Dori was an avid reader and enjoyed reading classical texts by authors such as Homer and Hawthorne. This love of literature developed into a passion for storytelling for Dori and her siblings. The Sanders children would go to a place they called the "storytelling rock" and spend hours creating stories that were about either adventure or family. Many of the stories created during her youth at the "storytelling rock" were incorporated into the novels she wrote as an adult.

Content with life on the farm, Dori spent her summers working on the farm and her winters working in a hotel in Maryland. During her time at the Maryland hotel she began to write. In an attempt to preserve her family's history, Sanders wrote short stories about farming for her nieces and nephews. After reading some of Sanders's work, her supervisor at the hotel convinced her to submit her writing for publication. Because of his persistence, Sanders submitted her first novel to a publisher, but it was rejected with the advice that she should write about subjects that were familiar to her. This advice led to the success of her first book, *Clover*.

Clover (1990) is set in a small African American rural community in South Carolina in the integrated New South. The main character, a 10-year-old African American girl named Clover Hill, is forced to live with Sara Kate, her white stepmother, after her father is killed in a car accident. The relationship between Clover and Sara Kate undergoes a number of challenges, primarily rooted in their racial difference, yet in the end, the two develop an affinity for each other. *Clover* received rave reviews, many of which compliment Sanders on her handling of race relations in the text. It also became a best seller, received the Lillian Smith Award (1990), has been translated in numerous languages, and was made into a film in 1997.

Sanders's second novel, *Her Own Place* (1993), also set in South Carolina, begins during World War II and ends in the 1980s. The main character, Mae Lee Barnes, is forced to become the sole provider for her five children after her husband returns home from the war and decides to leave the family. In addition to having to raise her children alone, Mae Lee purchases a farm and encounters many struggles; yet in the end, she

is the heroine of the text. *Her Own Place* received critical acclaim for its depiction of female struggle and empowerment and race relations.

Sanders has also gained renown for her nonfiction books. *Dori Sanders' Country Cooking: Recipes and Stories from the Family Farm Stand* (1995), her third book, is a collection of family recipes coupled with narrative that describes the history of each dish, and *Promise Land: A Farmer Remembers* (2005) chronicles the history of the struggles her family endured as a result of living in the Jim Crow South.

Her induction into the South Carolina Academy of Authors in 2000 is indicative of the importance of Sanders to her community. Today, she is still a committed farmer and can be found selling her peaches in Filbert during the summer. During the off-season, she spends her time writing and traveling across the country to speak and do readings.

LAKISHA ODLUM
University of Maryland, College Park

Nicholyn Hutchinson, in *Contemporary African American Novelists*, ed. Samuel S. Nelson (1999); Leonard D. Moore, *African American Review* (Spring 1995).

Scott, Evelyn

(1893–1963) WRITER.
Evelyn Scott was born Elsie Dunn in Clarksville, Tenn., on 17 January 1893 to Maude Thomas and Seely Dunn. Her mother was from a well-to-do Clarksville family, and her father, though born in New Orleans, was from Yankee parentage. Two of her great-uncles had fought for the Union in the Civil War,

and she admitted later in life that the fact that there were no great Civil War heroes in her mother's family was a cause of humiliation to her as a young child.

In 1901 Elsie and her family moved to New Orleans to be near her father's family, who was providing them with financial support. As a girl, Elsie struggled to reconcile the sophistication and propriety required by her southern upbringing with her family's faltering fortunes. She became the youngest to ever enroll in the all-female Sophie Newcomb College of Tulane University while in her mid-teens, though she never graduated. Soon after enrolling she left Sophie Newcomb, and the pressure from her mother to present herself with the pretensions of southern aristocracy led her to rebellion. As she writes in her second memoir, *Battleground in Tennessee*, "I was not a beautiful child, but neither was I stupid, except as I reacted with blind impressionableness to demands made by southern custom upon the vanity of womanhood." But no longer was Elsie willing to adhere to those demands, and she found expression through writing. She published a short story in the *Times-Picayune* under the pseudonym of Hiram Hagan Beck, wrote a now-lost novel about a young girl and her friendship with a prostitute, and brought embarrassment to her family when she published an editorial letter in the *Times-Picayune* advocating legalizing prostitution as a means to curb social diseases. By the time she was 17, Elsie was the secretary of the Louisiana Woman's Suffrage Party and was actively casting off the southern mores

and traditions that she was expected to blindly accept.

In 1913 Elsie began a romantic relationship with the married Frederick Creighton Wellman, dean of Tulane's School of Tropical Medicine. That December the love-struck couple changed their names, Elsie to Evelyn Scott and Wellman to Cyril Kay Scott, and absconded from New Orleans, with Brazil as their final destination. Once there, Evelyn gave birth to her only child, a son they named Creighton Scott. They lived in Brazil for six years in relative poverty, an experience Evelyn wrote about in her first memoir, *Escapade*.

After returning to the States, the Scotts settled in New York City's Greenwich Village. Between 1920 and 1941 she published two volumes of poetry, four children's books, a play, two memoirs, more than three dozen short stories, and several novels. Her first novel was *The Narrow House* (1921); *Narcissus* (1922) and *The Golden Door* (1925) completed the trilogy—a trio of books that explores themes of southern familial and hierarchical dysfunction through stream-of-consciousness prose. Her next three novels, *Migrations* (1927), *The Wave* (1929), and *Calendar of Sin* (1931), composed another trilogy, one that deals with a century of change between the antebellum South up to 1914. Scott used much of her own family history for the novels, and *The Wave* achieved much popular and critical success. Experimental in structure, *The Wave* employs a kaleidoscope of vignettes recounting the stories of countless characters—northern, southern, black, white, male, and female—swept up in the horror of the Civil War. In *The Wave*, Scott illustrates how each individual character (northern and southern alike) maintains his or her system of beliefs in the face of the intense suffering caused by them. The novel remained popular for more than two decades, and it is considered to be partially responsible for the flood of sprawling Civil War books that soon followed its publication, culminating in Margaret Mitchell's 1936 classic *Gone with the Wind*.

Scott divorced Cyril Kay Scott in 1928 and married British author John Metcalfe in 1930. She continued to write, but she never again achieved the success she did with *The Wave*. In 1941 she published her last novel, *The Shadow of the Hawk*. The last years of her life were spent in financial straits, illness, and paranoia. On 3 August 1963 Evelyn Scott died from heart disease and lung cancer.

JAMES G. THOMAS JR.
University of Mississippi

D. A. Callard, *Pretty Good for a Woman: The Enigmas of Evelyn Scott* (1985); Evelyn Scott, *Battleground in Tennessee* (1937; 1980), *Escapade* (1923, 1995); Dorothy M. Scura and Paul C. Jones, eds., *Evelyn Scott: Recovering a Lost Modernist* (2001); Mary Wheeling White, *Fighting the Current: The Life and Work of Evelyn Scott* (1998).

Seay, James
(b. 1939) POET.
James Seay was born in Panola County, Miss., in 1939. His father was a heavy-equipment operator and supervised land development projects, and his mother was a homemaker. Seay's work is solidly grounded in the South, and he has spent his career as a poet recounting both his own history and the stories and people of the region. In his seminal work *The History of Southern Literature*, Louis Rubin states that James Seay was the best poet of his generation at recounting those stories.

Even though in his later work his lines turn more lyrical, the narrative thread has always been strong in Seay. His work is rare in that it portrays the stories of both the Old South and the New South with equal ease. In many of his poems he takes on the mantle of both observer and participant to impart a sort of secret double wisdom to the reader. His poems have become a model for other modern southern poets such as Dave Smith and David Bottoms, who have both publicly stated that Seay influenced their own development as poets. His work, put simply, is a unique poetic record of the modern South.

After earning a B.A. degree at the University of Mississippi in 1964 and an M.A. from the Virginia Military Institute in 1966, Seay taught at Virginia Military Institute, Alabama, Vanderbilt, and the University of North Carolina at Chapel Hill, where he is currently on the faculty and was head of the creative writing program from 1987 to 1997. He was married to the southern novelist Lee Smith from 1967 to 1982, and their marriage produced two children. Seay's first two books, *Let Not Your Hart* and *Water Tables*, were published in the early 1970s by Wesleyan University Press, arguably America's most prestigious publisher of poetry. Both books are lush testimonials to Seay's strong gifts as a storyteller.

Let Not Your Hart (1970) contains some of Seay's most direct and revealing work; Seay himself has said that he was operating on "raw energy, with very little formal schooling in poetry." The raw energy works. The book shifts back and forth between three poles—intense self-examination, odes to nature, and southern anecdotes—and is reminiscent of the early work of James Dickey and Richard Wilbur, two American poets Seay has long admired. The book is also ripe with mystery, whether it is the car junkyard revealed as a "Valley of Dry Bones" or the seemingly random thoughts that Seay has while in a train sleeping car in "Line Composed a Few Miles below Princeton Junction."

His second book, *Water Tables* (1974), turns to an even greener world where every interaction with nature has profound meaning for the speaker (and the reader). The water imagery in the book is a recurrent theme. In poems like "Patching up the Past with Water" and "On the Island," water or one of its forms is a constant companion, whether it is life-giving water or the driftwood of rivers that dissolve into the rivers of memory.

Seay's third collection, *The Light as They Found It* (1990), is considered by most critics to be his most mature, developed work. Exploring the themes of family, community, and nature, Seay is fully realized as a sort of southern Everyman who both exists in the world fully formed and still needs to explore the smaller bits and pieces that make

up the whole. His musical ear is fully defined in this book, also, in lines such as "This morning the light lay across the table / in a way that lifted / from the shallow of a favored bowl the tincture / of petals I floated there / half without a plan over the course of a year / I had hoped long lost."

His most recent collection of poetry, *Open Field, Understory: New and Selected Poems* (1997), provides a selection from the scope of his career and also continues the themes he has always explored: family, memory, and human interaction with the natural world.

J. E. PITTS
University of Mississippi

Dorothy Abbott, ed., *Mississippi Writers: Reflections of Childhood and Youth*, vol. 3: *Poetry* (1988); Joseph M. Flora and Amber Vogel, eds., *Southern Writers: A New Biographical Dictionary* (2006); Roger Matuz, ed., *Contemporary Southern Writers* (1999); Louis Rubin, *The History of Southern Literature* (1985); James Seay, *Let Not Your Hart* (1970), *Water Tables* (1974), *The Light as They Found It* (1990), *Open Field, Understory* (1997); Ernest Suarez, *Southbound: Interviews with Southern Poets* (1999).

Settle, Mary Lee

(1918–2005) WRITER.

Mary Lee Settle's life was as colorful as is her fiction. As a young woman, she dropped out of Sweet Briar College to pursue acting, tested for the role of Scarlett O'Hara in *Gone with the Wind*, worked as a fashion model in New York City, served in the British Women's Auxiliary Air Force during World War II, and worked as an assistant editor at

Harper's before deciding to become a serious writer. Not content to remain literarily or physically in one place, she wrote about varied locales, including England, Spain, Hong Kong, Africa, Greece, Italy, and Turkey, and lived in several of these countries for extended periods of time.

Mary Lee Settle was born in Charleston, W.Va., on 29 July 1918, and although she also lived in Kentucky and in Florida during portions of her childhood, her best-known fiction links her solidly with West Virginia. Settle's work has garnered relatively little critical interest to date, but the scholars who recognize the significance of the writer's achievement focus primarily on her *Beulah Quintet* (1956–82), a series of five novels written and published over a period of 26 years, the actual texts spanning two countries and 300 years. Settle has often been compared with William Faulkner because of both her treatment of history and the sense of place she evokes in her work; her Yoknapatawpha is the Beulah Valley, and her Jefferson is Canona, W.Va., modeled on the city of Charleston, W.Va., where she spent the majority of her teen years. With a few exceptions, Settle's fiction is set in either Canona or the Beulah Valley: *The Love Eaters* (1954), *The Kiss of Kin* (1955), *The Clam Shell* (1971), *Charley Bland* (1989), and *The Beulah Quintet* are all set in Canona or the surrounding area, and some of these works even share the same characters.

Scholars are sometimes reluctant to refer to Settle as a southern writer, even though her best-known work, *The Beulah Quintet*, takes as subject matter many of those themes traditionally regarded as southern: preoccupation with history, sense of place, the lasting effects of slavery, importance of family, and so on. When asked about her regional identity, Settle sometimes referred to herself as "southern," but in other instances she argued that her native West Virginia is a region distinctly separate from the remainder of the United States; West Virginians are "mountain people," she claimed.

Clearly, Settle's work was shaped by place and through certain childhood experiences and recollections connected with her coming of age in the coal-mining Allegheny region. Her father owned a coal mine in Kentucky, and her mother's family was associated with the coal business; and, when Settle was 10, her family lived with her grandmother in Cedar Grove, W.Va., where Settle observed the life-style of the coal miner about whom she would write decades later. When asked how growing up in coal country influenced her writing, Settle explained that she considered *The Beulah Quintet* to be "payback" for her family's profiting from coal while maintaining a respectable distance from mining operation.

Over a period of 51 years, Mary Lee Settle produced 14 novels, four nonfiction works, three books for children, and numerous periodical articles and short stories. She was the recipient of many prizes and honors, including two Guggenheim Fellowships (1958 and 1960) and the National Book Award for Fiction (1978); in addition, she founded the PEN/Faulkner Award for Fiction and helped establish the Fellowship of

Southern Writers. Often referred to as a "writer's writer," Settle never gained a popular following, and although her first two novels were received favorably by critics when they appeared in 1954 and 1955, Settle was virtually unknown when she won the National Book Award for *Blood Tie* in 1978. When she died from lung cancer at 87 in Ivy, Va., she was at work on a new book; her last, *Spanish Recognitions*, had been published the previous year.

WENDY PEARCE MILLER
Marian College

Cynthia H. Amorese, *Commonwealth* (January 1981); Edward L. Galligan, *Sewanee Review* (1996); George Garrett, *Understanding Mary Lee Settle* (1988); Brian Rosenberg, *Mary Lee Settle's Beulah Quintet: The Price of Freedom* (1991); Jane Gentry Vance, in *American Women Writing Fiction: Memory, Identity, Family, Space*, ed. Mickey Pearlman (1989); Jane Harris Woodside, *Now and Then* (1992).

Simms, William Gilmore

(1806–1870) WRITER.

William Gilmore Simms was born in Charleston, S.C., and lived much of his life in or near it, making frequent visits to northern publishing centers and to the Gulf Coast and the southern mountains. His extensive knowledge of southern regions influenced novels and tales set in the Lowcountry, such as *The Yemassee* (1835), *The Partisan* (1835), and *The Golden Christmas* (1852), which trace the development of the region from the colonial era through the Revolution and into the antebellum period. Simms also published border and mountain romances like *Richard Hurdis*

(1838) and *Voltmeier* (1869), set in the antebellum backwoods South.

To a greater extent, perhaps, than any other 19th-century southern author, he gave a comprehensive picture of his region in its historical and cultural diversity—of the Lowcountry with its class hierarchy, its agrarian economy, its increasingly conservative politics, and its keen sectional self-consciousness; of the Gulf South, both civilized and violent, part plantation, part frontier; and of the Appalachian Mountain South in its pioneer phase. His writing exhibits qualities that mark southern literature from its beginnings: a sense of time and history, a love of southern landscape, a respect for southern social institutions, and a firm belief in class stratification and enlightened upper-class rule. In addition to fiction, poetry, drama, orations, and literary criticism, he wrote a history and a geography of South Carolina and biographies of Francis Marion, Captain John Smith, the Chevalier Bayard, and Nathanael Greene. At the beginning and near the end of his career, he edited several South Carolina newspapers, and in the 1840s and 1850s he served as editor of important southern journals, among them the *Magnolia*, the *Southern and Western*, and the proslavery *Southern Quarterly Review*, which gave voice to sectional issues.

The embodiment of southern letters, Simms was also an influential spokesman for what he saw as the region's social and political concerns. A unionist in the 1832 nullification controversy, in the 1840s he supported the intensely nationalistic Young America group, which pushed for American freedom from British literary models. Active in politics, he served in the South Carolina legislature from 1844 to 1846, conferred with prominent planters like James Henry Hammond about southern agricultural policies, conducted a copious correspondence with fire-eating Beverley Tucker of Virginia about slavery and secession, and helped develop the proslavery argument. As his southern nationalism mounted in the 1840s and 1850s, he supported the annexation of Texas and advocated the creation of a southern empire in the Caribbean. When the Civil War broke out, he served as adviser to several southern politicians and made elaborate proposals for Confederate military defenses. During the war, he wrote little of literary importance save the lively backwoods novel *Paddy McGann* (1863); after it, he ruined his health by the incessant writing and editing chores he took on to support his impoverished family. Energetic and often humorous, his work is important for its sweeping picture of the colonial and antebellum South in its regional diversity and also for its representation of continuing southern literary and intellectual issues.

MARY ANN WIMSATT
University of South Carolina

John C. Guilds, ed., *Long Years of Neglect: The Work and Reputation of William Gilmore Simms* (1988), *Simms: A Literary Life* (1992); John C. Guilds and Caroline Collins, eds., *William Gilmore Simms and the American Frontier* (1997); C. Hugh Holman, *The Roots of Southern Writing: Essays on the Literature of the American South* (1972); James E. Kibler Jr., *The Poetry of William Gilmore Simms: An Introduction and Bibliography* (1978), with Keen Butterworth, *William Gilmore Simms: A Reference Guide* (1980); Mary C. Simms Oliphant et al., eds., *The Letters of William Gilmore Simms* (1952–56).

Simpson, Lewis P.
(1916–2005) WRITER.

Lewis Pearson Simpson, whom Eugene D. Genovese and Elizabeth Fox-Genovese have called "our premiere interpreter of southern letters," was born on 18 July 1916 in Jacksboro, Tex., a point along the line at which the Old South intersects the frontier West. The early influence of these cultures in transition helped to shape the mind that, "more than [that of] any other critic, has penetrated the nature of southern society."

From 1933 through 1935 Simpson attended the North Texas Agricultural College at Arlington, Tex., now the University of Texas at Arlington, and earned a bachelor's degree in 1938 and a master's degree the following year at the University of Texas at Austin. After serving as a communications instructor in the U.S. Navy Air Corps from 1942 through 1944, he returned to the University of Texas, earning a Ph.D. in American literature and American history—the precursor of the present degree in American civilization—in 1948. Later that year he joined the English faculty at Louisiana State University, where he taught until his retirement in 1987.

On campus, Simpson almost invariably wore a seersucker suit, bow tie, and a belt with an enormous cowboy buckle, further testimony to his being a product—like Katherine Anne Porter—of the cultural fault line where the South met the West. In the same vein, on the wall of his cramped, book-choked office at LSU hung a framed picture of William Faulkner by J. R. Cofield and another of a span of mules. Less predictable was a portrait of Satanta, the Kiowa chief who had led the Jacksboro Raid of 1871. Simpson had grown up with his grandmother's stories of Indian incursions across the Red River, and these became a vital constituent of his intellectual life.

Such ironies of dress and decor are also symbolic of the tension that defined Simpson's lifework, the exploration of the line at which the South of the medieval tradition met the South of modernism. In the intersection of tradition and modernity, he has discovered an explanation for southern distinctiveness. The dissonance produced by the simultaneous but incompatible presence of a belief in the region as a new Eden—a land of redemption—and the existence of chattel slavery as its defining characteristic rendered the vision of the New World Adam a hideous sham. The southerner's consequent sense of guilt and alienation, Simpson has shown, gives to him a special relationship to history, at once revering and despising the region's past. His writings demonstrate how southern men and women of letters have been alienated from the larger Republic of Letters by their perceived need to defend the institution of slavery, or, in a later generation, to defend their ancestors who supported the South's "peculiar institution," while at the same time remaining conscious of the fact that if the South was indeed the new Garden of Eden, it was a garden tended by slaves.

Simpson's primary articulation of this thesis is to be found in three volumes of collected literary essays—*The Man of Letters in New England and the South* (1973), *The Brazen Face of History: Studies in the Literary Consciousness of America* (1980), and *The Fable of the Southern Writer* (1994)—and in two published lecture series, *The Dispossessed Garden: Pastoral and History in Southern Literature* (1975) and *Mind and the American Civil War: A Meditation on Lost Causes* (1989), the first from the Mercer University Lamar Memorial Lectures and the second from the Walter Lynwood Fleming Lecture Series in Southern History at Louisiana State University.

Also of vital importance to the life of southern letters was his role in the revival, in 1965, of the *Southern Review*. With Donald Stanford, also of the English Department at LSU, Simpson began the new series of the literary quarterly originally edited by Cleanth Brooks and Robert Penn Warren. As Simpson later wrote, the new editors "aspired to locate the second series in a literary context approximately similar to the one that the first had claimed," that is, "the magazine continues to reflect a cosmopolitan diversity in its authorship and at the same time to assent its context in the national and the southern literary expression."

Lewis P. Simpson died at Baton Rouge on 17 April 2005 and is buried at Roselawn Memorial Park.

THOMAS W. CUTRER
Arizona State University West

Gerald Kennedy and Daniel Mark Fogel, eds., *American Letters and the Historical Consciousness: Essays in Honor of Lewis P. Simpson* (1988); Lewis P. Simpson, *Southern Review* (October 1990).

Smith, Dave

(b. 1942) POET.

"I was southern before I became a poet," Dave Smith writes in the introduction to his collection of essays entitled *Hunting Men: Reflections on a Life in American Poetry*. A prolific and accomplished figure in American poetry, Smith was born in Portsmouth, Va., and grew up there in the suburbs near Norfolk. He attended the University of Virginia and, after graduation in 1965, returned to the eastern shores of the state when he moved to Poquoson, a small fishing village that the salt-of-the-earth locals called Bull Island, to teach high school English and French and coach football. The place left a distinct mark on him— *Bull Island* would be the title of his first publication, a chapbook of poetry in 1970. His second book of poems, *The Fisherman's Whore* (1974), and his novel, *Onliness* (1981), also are set there. "No place is more home to me than Poquoson," Smith writes. Smith's round-trip journey to the stately flagship Jeffersonian university and then back to the blue-collar tidewater fishing village had a significant impact on him, inciting a push and pull between the life of the mind and the life of grit. Smith writes, "Even now I but dimly understand how the opposition of Poquoson and Charlottesville forecast the long, unresolvable struggle of the physical and intellectual in my poems."

He left Poquoson after two years for graduate school in Illinois and then three years service in the air force where he reached the rank of staff sergeant. After that, he followed an academic path that took him to Ohio, Michigan, Missouri, Utah, New York, Florida, back to Virginia, Louisiana, and, most recently, Maryland, where he is the Elliot Coleman Professor of Poetry and chairman of the Writing Seminars at the Johns Hopkins University. Although he has moved often in his itinerant career, he frequently returns to Virginia in his poems (and did so for eight years, teaching at Virginia Commonwealth University from 1982 to 1990). He has published 20 books of poetry, including two that were finalists for the Pulitzer Prize for Poetry: *Goshawk, Antelope* (1979) and *Dream Flights* (1981). Other notable books include *Cumberland Station* (1977), *In the House of the Judge* (1983), and *Gray Soldiers* (1984). He has three books that include new and selected poems: *The Roundhouse Voices* (1985), *Night Pleasures* (1992), and *The Wick of Memory* (2000).

As might be expected of a former football coach and staff sergeant, Smith's poems are written in concrete language and images—a reviewer in the *New York Times* recently called it a "tough, knotty style"—but he still delves deeply into emotions attached to places and people. His relationships with family and friends and the homes where they have lived are frequent topics of Smith's vast body of work. His father, who was killed in a car wreck when Smith was only 17, his grandfathers, and his wife of 40 years, Dee, all play significant roles in his poetry and essays, as do his children and grandchildren. Memory, or the inaccuracy of it, is another subject of much of Smith's work, as he describes, "the gulf between memory's version of events and imagination's." Although he is very much a southern poet, his settings are not of the mule-and-plow variety so common in the region's literature, but most often take place in suburbs of the New South. And his work is by no means limited to Virginia settings: *Goshawk, Antelope* was inspired by his time in the West, and he has written a number of poems about Louisiana, where he lived for more than a decade.

Hunting Men, published in December 2006, is an insightful collection of his essays spanning southern and American poetry, as well as personal essays about his life and his relationships to people, places, and poetry. His large body of work to some extent has been a lifelong search for the mythical place called home. Smith writes, "Poetry has taught me, finally, that home is only inside my head, streets I walked, swamps I smelled, waters I lolled in."

JOE SAMUEL STARNES
Saint Joseph's University

Mark Johnson, *Southern Literary Journal* (Fall 2005); Dave Smith, *Hunting Men: Reflections on a Life in American Poetry* (December 2006); John Taylor, *Poetry* (November 2001).

Smith, Lee

(b. 1944) WRITER.

Lee Marshall Smith, born in the town of Grundy in southwestern Virginia, is the author of 12 novels and three collections of short stories. A voracious reader as a child, she found her focus as a writer at Hollins College, where she studied with Louis Rubin and such classmates as Annie Dillard and Henry Taylor and met her first husband, the poet James Seay. Her early novels—*The Last Day the Dogbushes Bloomed* (1968), *Something in the Wind* (1971), and *Fancy Strut* (1973)—were not commercially successful, but did reveal her keen interest in analyzing female lives, early experimentation with narrative form, and use of humor in storytelling. Her fourth novel, *Black Mountain Breakdown* (1980), was a turning point in its presentation of the conflicted female protagonist and especially in its rich portrayal of the history and people of her native Grundy, qualities that would be important in the success of her novels *Oral History* (1983) and *Fair and Tender Ladies* (1988).

Oral History was published to general acclaim and remains among the best of her explorations of female identity in an Appalachian setting. The book was praised for its vivid presentation of the hollers and mountains where the Cantrell clan lived, for its use of multiple narrators to tell the mythic story of the family over four generations, and for its strong, even if limited in freedom, female characters. *Family Linen* (1985) also revealed Smith's ability to use multiple voices to explore a family mystery that highlights female characters. In *Fair and Tender Ladies* (1988), her favorite novel, Smith turned to an older narrative form—the epistolary novel—for her story of Ivy Rowe, an uneducated mountain woman whose letters written, over a lifetime, convey in lyrical prose her struggles with family expectations and her own sexuality. The first-person perspective of the letters offers the reader deep insight into a character who, through her writing voice, defines herself positively. In addition, the novel emphasizes Smith's concern for a cherished land despoiled by outsiders.

In *The Devil's Dream* (1992), a historical novel about the rise of country music, Smith uses country music "as a metaphor for finding one's voice as a woman." Although Smith's novels—including *The Devil's Dream*—convey a general distrust of institutionalized religion, at the end of *Saving Grace* (1995), Florida Grace Shepherd, who has rebelled against the snake-handling Pentecostal religion of her family, returns to her mountain home and church. *The Last Girls* (2002) again uses multiple narrators, but this time to reinvent an experience she had as a college student traveling with college friends on a raft down the Mississippi. Although the setting is not Appalachia, the book echoes earlier novels in portraying women's voices and female bonding, the interconnections of past and present, and the continuing exploration of how women can "navigate" life's challenges. Smith's most recent novel is *On Agate Hill* (2006).

Smith's strength and diversity as a short-story writer are illustrated in three collections of short stories—*Cakewalk* (1981), *Me and My Baby View the Eclipse* (1990), and *News of the Spirit* (1997). In a labor of love, she edited *Sitting on the Courthouse Bench: An Oral History of Grundy, Virginia* (2000), a collection of remembrances researched and written by high school students. Stage adaptations of *Family Linen*, *Oral History*, and *The Devil's Dream* have been successful, as well as the play *Good Ol' Girls*, which combines vignettes of the work of Smith and her former student Jill McCorkle.

Smith is grouped with the new southern regional writers who do not define themselves through a shared Civil War past or racial guilt, but locate their fictions in a contemporary world. Because of her emphasis on the folklore, myth, and landscape of a particular place, it has been argued that she is more accurately described as an Appalachian rather than southern writer. Influenced by writers such as Eudora Welty, William Faulkner, Flannery O'Connor, and James Still, Smith has become a major influence on a new generation of writers through her successful books and long teaching career. She lives in Hillsborough, N.C.

KATHERINE H. JAMES
Barton College

Dorothy Combs Hill, *Lee Smith* (1992); Rebecca Smith, *Gender Dynamics in the Fiction of Lee Smith: Examining Language and Narrative Strategies* (1997); Shelby Stephenson, ed., *Pembroke Magazine* (2001); Linda Tate, ed., *Conversations with Lee Smith* (2001).

Smith, Lillian

(1897–1966) WRITER AND SOCIAL CRITIC.
Internationally acclaimed as author of the controversial novel *Strange Fruit* (1944) and the autobiographical critique of southern culture *Killers of the Dream* (1949), Lillian Eugenia Smith was the

most outspoken white southern writer in areas of economic, racial, and sexual discrimination during the 1930s and 1940s. When other southern liberals—Ralph McGill, Hodding Carter, Virginius Dabney, and Jonathan Daniels—were charting a cautious course on racial change, Smith boldly and persistently called for an end to racial segregation. Furthermore, her work for social justice continued throughout her life. In 1955 she wrote *Now Is the Time*, urging support for the Supreme Court's decision on school desegregation. Her last published book, *Our Faces, Our Words* (1964), reflects her personal knowledge and experience with the young black and white civil rights activists of the 1950s and 1960s.

Lillian Smith was born 12 December 1897, the seventh of nine children of Anne Hester Simpson and Calvin Warren Smith, and grew up in Jasper, Fla., where her father was a prominent business and civic leader. Some of the richness of that childhood is portrayed in *Memory of a Large Christmas* (1962). Her life as the daughter of upper-class whites in the small-town Deep South ended rather abruptly when her father lost his turpentine mills in 1915 and moved the family to their summer home near Clayton, Ga. Financially on her own, Smith attended the nearby Piedmont College one year, was principal of a two-room mountain school, and helped her parents manage a hotel before she was able to pursue her interest in music. During the school terms of 1916–17 and 1919–22 she studied piano at Peabody Conservatory in Baltimore, spending summers working in the family's summer lodge and teaching music at Laurel Falls Camp for Girls, opened by her father in 1920.

In the fall of 1922 Smith accepted a three-year position as director of music at Virginia School in Huchow, China. But her ambitions for a career in music ended when her parents' ill health necessitated her return to direct Laurel Falls Camp. Under her direction from 1925 through 1948, the camp became an outstanding innovative educational institution, known for its instruction in the arts, music, theater, and modern psychology. It was also a laboratory for many of the ideas informing Smith's analysis of southern culture, especially her understanding of the effects of child-rearing practices on adult racial and sexual relationships.

Through the camp, Smith also met Paula Snelling and began the lifelong relationship that encouraged and sustained her writing career. From 1936 to 1946 Smith and Snelling coedited a magazine, first called *Pseudopodia*, then *North Georgia Review*, and finally *South Today*, which quickly achieved acclaim as a forum for liberal opinion in the region.

A record-breaking best seller, *Strange Fruit* was translated into 15 languages, banned for obscenity in Boston, and produced as a Broadway play. But *Killers of the Dream*, an even more insightful exploration of the interrelationship of race, class, and gender in southern society, brought strong criticism from more moderate southerners. Though widely reviewed, none of her subsequent works achieved the popularity or financial success of her first novel.

Her more philosophical works, *The Journey* (1954) and *One Hour* (1959), demonstrate the extent to which Smith's concerns extended beyond race relations to encompass all aspects of human relationships in the modern world. In *The Journey* she wrote, "I went in search of an image of the human being I could be proud of." *One Hour*, Smith's response to the McCarthy era, is a complex psychological novel about the inevitable destruction unleashed in a community when the reality and power of the irrational are unacknowledged in human life.

Two collections of her work have been published posthumously: *From the Mountain* (1972), a selection of pieces from the magazine, edited by Helen White and Redding Sugg, and *The Winner Names the Age* (1978), selected speeches and essays, edited by Michelle Cliff with an introduction by Paula Snelling.

MARGARET ROSE GLADNEY
University of Alabama

Louise Blackwell and Frances Clay, *Lillian Smith* (1971); John Egerton, *Speak Now against the Day: The Generation before the Civil Rights Movement in the South* (1994); Margaret Rose Gladney, *How Am I to Be Heard? Letters of Lillian Smith* (1993), *Southern Studies* (Fall 1983); Fred Hobson, *Tell about the South: The Southern Rage to Explain* (1983); Anne C. Loveland, *Lillian Smith: A Southerner Confronting the South* (1986); Darlene O'Dell, *Sites of Southern Memory: The Autobiographies of Katharine Du Pre Lumpkin, Lillian Smith, and Pauli Murray* (2001); Jo Ann Robinson, in *Notable*

American Women: The Modern Period, ed. Barbara Sicherman and Carl Hurd Green (1980).

Southworth, E. D. E. N.
(1819–1899) WRITER.

A deserted wife who started writing to support her children, Emma Dorothy Eliza Nevitte Southworth became one of the most popular writers in 19th-century America. During her writing career of 40 years, she produced more than 50 novels, most of which were serialized in periodicals and later printed in book form. As a southern woman writer, Southworth adopted popular genres of her age: the domestic novel and the plantation novel. Despite charges of sentimentality and conventionality, her works are subtle and subversive enough to empower women and criticize slavery under the pretense of moralizing womanhood and defending the South.

Southworth was born 26 December 1819 in Washington, D.C. She was the first child of Charles L. Nevitte and Susannah Wailes, who was 30 years younger than her husband. Nevitte died when Southworth was four, and Mrs. Nevitte married Joshua L. Henshaw two years later. Southworth was educated in her stepfather's school, discovering her intellectual ability and fascination with books and stories. After graduation, she taught in the public schools of Washington, D.C., until she married Frederick H. Southworth and moved to Wisconsin in 1840. The marriage did not last long. Four years later, a pregnant Southworth returned to Washington, D.C., with only her son,

Richmond. Not much is known about her marriage, but her husband seemed to be an irresponsible man who did not provide for his family. He eventually abandoned them and went to Brazil in 1844. After her daughter, Lottie, was born, Southworth had to find a job to support her children. She started teaching again but turned to writing for more money.

Her first story, "The Irish Refugee," was published in the *Baltimore Saturday Visitor* in 1846. Her first novel, *Retribution*, was serialized in the *National Era* in 1849 and published as a book by Harper the same year. The popularity of *Retribution* and subsequent novels eased her financial burden, but the best phase of her writing career began after the 1856 contract with Robert Bonner, editor of the *New York Ledger*. Bonner provided Southworth not only financial security but also emotional support for the next 30 years. Her most popular and enduring novel, *The Hidden Hand*, was written during this period. First serialized in 1859, it was so immensely popular that the *New York Ledger* republished it twice before it finally allowed the book publication in 1888. The adventures of its class- and gender-crossing heroine, Capitola Le Noir, widely appealed to the public. *The Hidden Hand* was also made into a play and staged in both America and Britain. It is Southworth's only novel available in modern reprint.

Southworth's female protagonists are strong and independent, whether they are rejected brides, unloved or deserted wives, discarded daughters, or lost heiresses. Her male and African American characters are not so well developed. Although her genre is limited and her plots seem melodramatic and formulaic, her works address various social issues such as women's role in society, slavery, political corruption, and temperance. The realists and naturalists in the late 19th century denounced Southworth's works as too sentimental. Since the mid-20th century, however, feminists and revisionists have argued that her works could conform to social conventions and criticize them at the same time.

JEE EUN KIM
University of Southern Mississippi

Nina Baym, *Woman's Fiction: A Guide to Novels by and about Women in America, 1820–70* (1978); Joanne Dobson, *American Quarterly* (Summer 1986); Joanne Dobson and Amy E. Hudock, in *American Women Prose Writers, 1820–1870,* ed. Amy E. Hudock and Katharine Rodier (2001); Ann M. Ingram, *American Transcendental Quarterly* (December 1999); Paul Christian Jones, *Unwelcome Voices: Subversive Fiction in the Antebellum South* (2005); Mary Kelley, *Private Woman, Public Stage: Literary Domesticity in Nineteenth-Century America* (1984).

Spencer, Elizabeth

(b. 1921) WRITER.
Elizabeth Spencer was born on 19 July 1921, in Carrollton, an old Mississippi town of 500 people on the eastern edge of the Delta. At an early age, she escaped social and familial strictures by riding her horse to her uncle Joe McCain's plantation at Teoc, 13 miles away. This distancing freed her to observe the inhabitants of Carrollton, their mores and foibles, observations she would later

put down in her memoir, *Landscapes of the Heart* (1998), and use well in all her writings.

Spencer's roots go deep. Both sides of her family settled in Carroll County as early as the 1830s. Her mother's family, the McCains, were big readers, and her mother read to her often from her library that included Greek and Roman myths, the Arthurian legends, and the Bible. The McCains talked about characters as if they were part of the family. "It was a shame," they might say, "that Fantine [in *Les Misérables*] had to sell all her hair and teeth." Because her brother, James Luther Spencer Jr., was seven years her senior, Spencer kept herself company early on by writing adventure stories.

Spencer's father, James Luther Spencer, was business-minded and a strict Presbyterian. He neither encouraged nor supported Elizabeth's writing aspirations. Nevertheless, Spencer majored in English at Belhaven College in Jackson, Miss.

Her senior year, as president of the literary society, Spencer invited Eudora Welty to be their guest. It was a short distance for Welty to walk, just across Pinehurst Street, but momentous for Spencer, strengthening her desire to be a writer. In her foreword to *The Stories of Elizabeth Spencer* (1983), Welty describes Spencer's grace, her dark blue eyes by which you knew she was "a jump ahead of you," and says, "the main thing about her was blazingly clear—this girl was serious. She was indeed already a writer."

Spencer attended graduate school at Vanderbilt University, studying under the Fugitive poet Donald Davidson. Upon receiving a master's degree in English, she taught briefly, worked as a reporter, and saved $500, enough to sustain her for a year while she wrote her first novel, *Fire in the Morning* (1948). Before the manuscript was completed, Davidson found a publisher for her at Dodd Mead. On the book's meager royalties, she hopped a freighter to France and traveled in Germany and Italy. Soon after, she returned to Italy on a Guggenheim Fellowship.

Her sojourns in Italy would prove provident. Achieving distance as learned in her youth, she was able to write about the night in Carrollton when the Spencers' maid, Laura Henley, showed up at their back door brutally beaten. It would become the subject of the novel *The Voice at the Back Door* (1956). Italy would be the setting for her most famous work, *Light in the Piazza* (1960), and its companion, *Knights and Dragons* (1965). Written in about a month, *Light in the Piazza* became a popular movie and in 2005 a highly acclaimed Broadway musical. In a romance that rivaled fiction, it was in Italy also that she met a dashing gentleman from Cornwall, England, John Rusher, whom she married in 1956.

Spencer's settings and themes changed as she and Rusher traveled around, settling in various places, from Florence, Italy, to Montreal, Canada, and finally to Chapel Hill, N.C. In *No Place for an Angel* (1967) she examines the emptiness in the lives of the rich and powerful, and the settings are far-flung,

Washington, D.C., and Key West among them. In *The Snare* (1972), set in New Orleans, the protagonist, Julia, becomes caught up in the evil underbelly of that city. Conscientious objectors to the Vietnam War who escaped to Canada are the subject of *The Night Travelers* (1991), set in North Carolina and Montreal. Though her male characters are dominant in her early fiction, her female protagonists, such as Nancy in "Ship Island," prove equally compelling when pushing against social, familial, or cultural expectations.

Award-winning author of nine novels, five collections of short stories, an exquisite memoir, and a play, Elizabeth Spencer has mastered all these forms. Because she is cosmopolitan, her themes universal, her mind original and versatile, categorizing her is a happy impossibility.

MARION BARNWELL
Jackson, Mississippi

Peggy Whitman Prenshaw, *Elizabeth Spencer* (1985), ed., *Conversations with Elizabeth Spencer* (1991); Terry Roberts, *Self and Community in the Fiction of Elizabeth Spencer* (1994); Elizabeth Spencer, *Landscapes of the Heart* (1998).

Stanford, Frank

(1948–1978) POET.
In the span of his short career, Frank Stanford established himself as one of America's most promising young poets, receiving praise from the likes of Allen Ginsberg and Alan Dugan. His unique poetry successfully fuses the southern literary tradition of Twain and Faulkner with Beat poetics and international influences such as magic realism. Despite these innovations he now receives little critical attention, and unfortunately much of his work is out of print.

Stanford was born on 1 August 1948 at Emery Memorial Home, a Catholic charity for unwed mothers in Richton, Miss. Dorothy Gilbert Alter soon adopted him, marrying wealthy Memphis contractor A. F. Stanford four years later. Stanford's family lived in the city until 1959, but he passed his summers in worker camps along the Mississippi River, where his adoptive father oversaw levee maintenance. Stanford's early poetry, especially *The Singing Knives* (1971), mythologizes these youthful experiences, crafting a brutal but aesthetic southern dreamscape filled with knife fights, cottonmouths, and long days of fishing. Surreal adolescent adventures like "The Gospel Bird" and "The Snake Doctors" establish a central thread of violence that runs through Stanford's entire body of work. Many of the recurring characters in Stanford's poetry are based on the children of black laborers he befriended at the levee camps, relationships that also provided him with a rich regional lexicon.

In 1959 Stanford's family moved to Mountain Home, Ark. His adoptive father died in 1963, and Stanford subsequently enrolled at a Benedictine preparatory school, Subiaco Academy. Stanford began writing poetry in earnest during these high school years. After graduating from Subiaco in 1966 Stanford enrolled at the University of Arkansas to study civil engineering, but he soon turned to English and poetry. A

Frank Stanford, poet (Ginny Stanford, photographer)

talented young writer, he gained admittance to the university's graduate poetry workshop in the spring of his sophomore year.

Stanford never took a degree, though, and began a tumultuous adulthood after leaving the university in 1971. He married his first wife, Linda Mencin, that same year. The poet spent much of 1972 and 1973 traveling around the United States with the publisher Irving Broughton, interviewing authors for a documentary film. Stanford and Mencin divorced soon after, and in 1974 he married the painter Ginny Crouch. They settled in Rogers, Ark., where he worked as a land surveyor. In 1975 Stanford and Broughton collaborated on the award-winning experimental film *It Wasn't a Dream, It Was a Flood*. Like much of his poetry, this film is loosely autobiographical. Stanford founded Lost Roads Publishers a year later with fellow poet C. D. Wright.

Between 1971 and 1978 Stanford published seven small-press chapbooks, in addition to poems in leading magazines and literary journals such as *Esquire* and the *Iowa Review*. During this prolific period, the violent themes of Stanford's early poetry gave way to complex treatments of death. In poems like "Death and the Arkansas River," published in *Constant Stranger* (1976), death becomes a tangible entity, a personification directly engaged by Stanford. This fascination with mortality proved sadly prophetic. In Fayetteville on 3 June 1978, Stanford took his life, shooting himself three times with a revolver. He was only 29 years old.

Stanford's out-of-print volumes include *The Singing Knives, Shade* (1973), *Ladies from Hell* (1974), *Field Talk* (1975), *Arkansas Bench Stone* (1975) *Constant Stranger, Crib Death* (1979), and *You* (1979). *The Light the Dead See* (1991), a volume of selected poems edited by Leon Stokesbury, is more readily available, as are a collection of Stanford's stories, *Conditions Uncertain and Likely to Pass Away* (1990), and a republication of his 20,000 line epic, *The Battlefield Where the Moon Says I Love You* (1977, 2000).

STEVEN KNEPPER
University of Virginia

Murray Blaine Shugars, "What the Moon Says: Frank Stanford's Quest for Poetic Identity" (Ph.D. dissertation, Purdue University, 2000); C. D. Wright, *Oxford American* (Winter 2006).

Steinke, Darcey

(b. 1964) WRITER AND TEACHER. The daughter of a Lutheran minister and a former beauty queen, Darcey Steinke explores questions of religion and morality, spirituality and sensuality through her blunt and fearless writing. Whether through fiction about sexual predators and gay priests or nonfiction about rock 'n' roll icons and cult leaders, Steinke attempts to rouse the interest and emotions—whether positive or negative—of her readers.

Darcey Steinke was born in Roanoke, Va., in 1964. She contributes her lifelong love of language to two distinct factors of her childhood: a minister for a father (as well as five uncles) and a severe stutter. While listening to her father practice and deliver his sermons, she had to write notes to communicate with other people. All this, she has said in interviews, led her to appreciate and adore the written word, first as a reader, then as a writer. Without the freedom to speak her mind, she resorted to writing it out.

After graduating from Cave Spring High School in Roanoke, Steinke attended Baltimore's Goucher College. She returned to her native state for a master's degree from the University of Virginia as a Henry Hoyns Fellow. During this time, Doubleday gave Steinke a $10,000 advance to complete her first novel. While working with editor Jackie Kennedy Onassis, Steinke finished her M.F.A. and moved west to serve as a Wallace Stegner Fellow at Stanford University's Creative Writing Program.

In 1989 Steinke published *Up through the Water*, which the *New York Times* cited as a Notable Book of the Year. Set off the coast of North Carolina, the novel marked Steinke, in the minds of several critics, as a promising young author. Three years later, Steinke's second novel, *Suicide Blonde*, capitalized on her earlier success and on controversy surrounding the frank sexuality of the novel and a scathing critique in the *New Yorker* magazine. Against the backdrop of San Francisco's Mission District, Steinke wrote about the possibilities of salvation within a world of decadence and depravity. The book sold almost 100,000 copies.

Despite studying and chronicling the wilder side of life, Steinke's personal life began to follow a more traditional route. While in San Francisco, she met and married literary agent Michael Hornburg. By 1996 they had a daughter,

Abbie, and had relocated to New York City.

Jesus Saves, Steinke's third novel and another *New York Times* Notable Book of the Year, explored a theme of degeneracy and deliverance similar to that in *Suicide Blonde* but through the lens of the southern Gothic. Again, religion and sex mixed as the lives of a kidnapped girl and the daughter of a lackluster Lutheran pastor intertwined. Published almost in tandem with *Jesus Saves*, *Joyful Noise: The New Testament Revisited*, coedited with novelist Rick Moody, was a collection of essays written by young artists and authors about religion and spirituality. Two years later Steinke continued her religious exposition by contributing the introduction to a small-format edition of *The Gospel according to John*.

During the 1998–99 academic year, Steinke served as the John and Renée Grisham Writer-in-Residence at the University of Mississippi. While in Oxford, Steinke worked on two distinct novels. The first, *Milk*, published in 2005, was a short erotic work, which Steinke has described as "a cross between *The Story of O* and St. John of the Cross's *Dark Night of the Soul*." The other, *The Great Disappointment*, was a lengthy and as-yet-unpublished historical novel about her ancestor, William Miller, an apocalyptic religious leader whose teachings contributed to the founding of the Seventh-Day Adventist Church. In 2000 Steinke served as the first writer in residence at the Kratz Center for Creative Writing at her alma mater, Goucher College.

Currently, Steinke, now divorced,

lives with her daughter in Brooklyn and teaches creative writing at the New School. In addition to her novels, her short fiction has appeared in the anthologies *That's What I Like*, *The Wild Women Reader*, and *Sounds of Writing* and journals such as the *Literary Review*, *Story*, and *Bomb*. She is also a frequent contributor to the magazine *Spin* and numerous newspapers. Her memoir, *Easter Everywhere*, was published in 2007.

JAY TODD
Southeastern Louisiana University

Leonard Gill, *Memphis Flyer* (1 March 1999); Susan Gossling, *Goucher Quarterly* (Summer 2000); Mike Hudson, *Roanoke Times* (22 April 2001); Beth Macy, *Roanoke Times* (8 March 2005); Darcey Steinke, *Boston Review* (February–March 2005).

Still, James

(1906–2001) WRITER.

James Still was born 16 July 1906 and was reared in Chambers County, Ala. Virtually all of Still's writings, though, were set in the eastern Kentucky hills, where he moved in 1932. Still's published writings include his acclaimed novel *River of Earth* (1940), award-winning short stories, poetry, children's books, and folklore collections.

At an early age Still developed a passion for reading, despite a scarcity of books in his parents' house. He was also fascinated by the speech of his rural neighbors. Listening as a youth to stories told by veterans of the Civil War, Still developed a romanticized view of the Confederacy. When an adolescent, however, he witnessed a public hanging and a Ku Klux Klan cross burning, and he subsequently denounced capital punishment and racism.

In the mid-1920s Still left Alabama for Lincoln Memorial University (LMU), located in Harrogate, Tenn., near Cumberland Gap. After earning an A.B. degree at LMU in 1929, Still attended Vanderbilt University, where he studied with several people associated with Vanderbilt's Fugitive-Agrarian literary circle. Receiving the M.A. degree in literature from Vanderbilt in 1930, Still enrolled at the University of Illinois, where in 1931 he received the B.S. degree in library science.

Still's classmates at LMU and Vanderbilt included Jesse Stuart and Don West. In 1932 Still visited West at a summer Bible school the latter was running in Knott County, Ky. Impressed by that locality's natural beauty and its people, Still accepted a librarian position at the Hindman Settlement School, in Hindman, Ky. Having previously published two scholarly articles and two poems, Still began to write prolifically after arriving in Hindman, producing poems and short stories that explored aspects of Appalachian regional folklife. Soon, his writings were appearing in such leading national periodicals as *Atlantic*, *Esquire*, *Nation*, *New Republic*, *New York Times*, *Poetry*, and *Sewanee Review*. In 1937 Viking Press issued the first of three books by Still that today form the basis of that author's literary reputation: the poetry volume *Hounds on the Mountain*. The other two volumes— *River of Earth* and the short-story collection *On Troublesome Creek* (1941)— were published after Still decided, in 1939, to move 11 miles from Hindman into a remote 100-year-old log house in order to devote more time to his writing.

While *Hounds on the Mountain* was generally well received, *River of Earth* garnered glowing reviews from literary critics, though the book soon fell into neglect nationally, as scholars and readers alike favored Steinbeck's *The Grapes of Wrath* as the most significant novel of the American Depression-era experience (the 1978 republication of *River of Earth* by the University Press of Kentucky ultimately secured for Still's novel an enduring place in Appalachian literature). Witnessing firsthand the plight of Depression-era Kentucky coal miners, Still became committed to writing a book that depicted the changes wrought by industrialization on the traditional Appalachian way of life. Noted for its lyrical prose (a literary approximation of Appalachian folk speech), the resulting novel, *River of Earth*, is today generally considered Still's masterpiece.

A number of Still's short stories were published in leading national periodicals during the 1930s before being incorporated into *On Troublesome Creek* (1941). Select stories from that period as well as later short fiction appeared in *Pattern of a Man* (1976) and *The Run for the Elbertas* (1980). Still's short stories were anthologized in *O. Henry Memorial Prize Stories* (in 1939 and 1941) and *Best American Short Stories* (in 1946, 1950, and 1952).

Still's other literary works include the novel *Sporty Creek* (1977), the poetry collections *The Wolfpen Poems* (1986) and *From the Mountain, from the Valley: New and Collected Poems* (2001),

and a number of books for children. Of ethnographic interest is Still's study of Appalachian verbal folklore, *The Wolfpen Notebooks* (1991).

In recent years, numerous authors, including Wendell Berry, Fred Chappell, Wilma Dykeman, Silas House, Gurney Norman, and Lee Smith, have publicly acknowledged Still's influence.

TED OLSON
East Tennessee State University

Carol B. Boggess, *Dissertation Abstracts International* (Summer 1996); Ted Olson and Kathy H. Olson, eds., *James Still: Critical Essays on the Dean of Appalachian Literature* (2007).

Street, James

(1903–1954) WRITER, JOURNALIST, AND MINISTER.

James Howell Street, an American novelist, journalist, short-story writer, essayist, pseudohistorian, and Baptist minister, was born on 15 October 1903 in the sawmill village of Lumberton, Miss., to John Camillus Street, a liberal Irish Catholic lawyer, and his Scots-Irish Calvinist mother, William Thompson Scott, an unusual but true name. While Street never considered himself a literary writer, he acquired international recognition for his work in fiction, which relied heavily upon his thorough understanding of southern culture and folklore. Street's literary corpus includes 17 novels and 35 short stories. A majority of his novels became best sellers, and *The Biscuit Eater* (1939), *Tap Roots* (1942), and *Good-bye, My Lady* (1954) were later adapted into successful film versions.

As a teenager, Street accepted journalist positions for newspapers in Laurel and Hattiesburg, Miss. In 1923 he married Lucy Nash O'Briant and decided to follow his father-in-law's occupational footsteps by becoming a Baptist minister, attending Southwest Baptist Theological Seminary and Howard College. While he was in the ministry, Lucy gave birth to their three children, James Jr., John, and Ann, but soon after their births Street grew unsatisfied with pastoral work and settled on returning to journalism and novel construction.

Street worked as a feature writer for newspapers in Memphis, Nashville, and Atlanta, until he was offered a position as a reporter for William Randolph Hearst's *New York American*, where he covered such high-profile national events as the Scottsboro trial and the kidnapping of Charles A. Lindbergh's son. While working for Hearst, Street published his first book, *Look Away! A Dixie Notebook* (1936). Additionally, he was contracted to write a history of the New York City Police Department, but he never completed the obligation. In 1940 he returned to Mississippi and settled the family in Natchez, but five years later relocated again to Chapel Hill, N.C., because Street wanted his two war-veteran sons and daughter to attend the University of North Carolina. Street assisted with the establishment of the University of North Carolina's school of journalism, and while living in Chapel Hill he continued to write fiction. Afflicted by glaucoma, Street took to dictating his books, in which the daily routine consisted of dictating for three hours, then turning attention to editing the day's work. In his spare time,

he was known to have many hobbies, which included raising cacti and collecting recordings of American ballads, walking sticks, books, and pipes. He was an avid gardener, painter, and cook, and he loved dogs, hunting, and electric trains. On 28 September 1954, Street died of a sudden heart attack in Chapel Hill.

Street wrote sequence novels, a single sociological novel, dog stories, and nonfiction travel and historical texts. Throughout the 1940s and early 1950s, Street composed a five-novel sequence series of historical fiction regarding the progress of the Dabney family in Lebanon, Miss., spanning the late 18th century to the late 19th century. The Dabney Pentology comprised *Oh, Promised Land* (1940), *Tap Roots* (1942), *By Valor and Arms* (1944), *Tomorrow We Reap* (1949), and *Mingo Dabney* (1950), which primarily revolved around issues concerning race and honor in the South. Street wrote two semi-autobiographical novels classified as works in his "preacher" sequence, *The Gauntlet* (1945) and *The High Calling* (1951); *In My Father's House* (1941), his sociological novel, was said by Street to be his best work. *The Biscuit Eater* (1939), arguably his most famous work, and *Good-bye, My Lady* (1954) were two stories concerning country boys and dogs. Street wrote two nonfiction travel narratives, *Look Away! A Dixie Notebook* (1936) and *James Street's South* (1955), and his nonfiction historical pieces consist of *The Revolutionary War* (1954) and *The Civil War* (1953).

PETER J. MORRONE
University of Mississippi

James L. Cox, *Mississippi Almanac* (1997); Josephine Frazier, *James Street: A Bio-Bibliography* (1958); Lindsay Roberts, *James Street: A Biography* (1999).

Stribling, T. S.

(1881–1965) WRITER.

A prolific writer, the author of 14 novels, a collection of detective stories, an autobiography, and the practitioner in many genres—moral stories for Sunday school publications, adventure and science fiction stories for the pulps, romance novels, detective fiction, book reviews, drama, memoirs, and novels of iconoclastic social realism, the most notable being those set in the South—Thomas Sigismund Stribling, whose father had been a Union soldier from Tennessee during the Civil War and whose mother's family had lived in northern Alabama and fought for the Confederacy, was born in Clifton, Tenn., on 4 March 1881. Stribling's divided heritage would provide him with a rich fund of material for his southern novels, especially his fictional trilogy of the 1930s.

During the 1920s and 1930s, Stribling made his most important contributions to southern letters. His first three novels—*Birthright* (1922), *Teeftallow* (1926), and *Bright Metal* (1928)—are iconoclastic, emphatically presenting themes and subject matter emulating the popular "revolt-from-the-village" movement, principally popularized in Sinclair Lewis's best seller, *Main Street* (1920). Like *Main Street*, these three novels—all set in middle Tennessee—present graphically disparaging portraits of small-town life, unmasking many undesirable aspects of the southern provincial experience—hypocrisy, bigotry, narrow-mindedness, violence, political chicanery, and religious fanaticism, among others. *Birthright*, one of the first American novels to present a realistic and sympathetic treatment of African American life in the South, was widely praised by African Americans, including Charles W. Chesnutt, William Stanley Braithwaite, Jessie Fauset, Nella Larson, James Weldon Johnson, and George E. Haynes.

Stribling's greatest literary achievement, his most significant contribution to modern southern literature, and the work for which he is principally remembered today was his trilogy of the South—*The Forge* (1931), *The Store* (1932), and *Unfinished Cathedral* (1934). Like his three Tennessee novels of the 1920s, the trilogy, set principally in Florence, Ala., and its environs, is an iconoclastic work. Covering a period from the eve of the Civil War to the economic boom era of the 1920s and featuring three generations of a southern family, the Vaidens, Stribling's trilogy focuses on key changes in the southern social fabric, showing particularly the demise of the Old South plantation aristocracy and its world and the rise of a greedy and conscienceless mercantile class of the New South, which favor materialistic and social values over human ones, with the chief victims being African Americans, some of whom have biological ties to their exploiters. *The Store*, the author's best-selling single novel, was awarded the Pulitzer Prize for Fiction in 1933, Stribling's most prestigious literary accolade. Stribling's final book, his autobiography *Laughing Stock*, begun in 1940, was posthumously published in 1982.

As a critical social realist, a seminal and influential force in southern literature of the second and third decades of the 20th century, T. S. Stribling, despite being condemned to oblivion by the Fugitive-Agrarians at the height of his career in the 1930s, was a forerunner of the Southern Literary Renaissance who left a rich fund of usable material that he used first and that more-talented modern southern writers would mine and transform into higher forms of art. William Faulkner, the principal beneficiary of Stribling's legacy, treats a similar pattern of southern social history in chronicling the rise and fall of Thomas Sutpen in *Absalom, Absalom!* (1936); in his own trilogy—*The Hamlet, The Town*, and *The Mansion*—Faulkner creates in the character of Flem Snopes, a rapacious and unscrupulously opportunistic individual similar to Stribling's Militiades Vaiden, the central figure of his own trilogy; and in *Go Down, Moses* (1942) Faulkner depicts realistically some of same social problems stemming from miscegenation and incest that Stribling previously explored in the trilogy. Erskine Caldwell, who showcased the deprived and unsavory lives of poor whites; Thomas Wolfe, who treated critically the debilitating environments of small mountain towns on their inhabitants; and Robert Penn Warren, who, his most famous novel *All the King's Men* (1946), featured in Willie Stark an unprincipled, power-wielding, self-made man who rises to political power and succumbs to politi-

cal graft, offer further manifestations of Stribling's literary legacy.

EDWARD J. PIACENTINO
High Point University

Wilton Eckley, *T. S. Stribling* (1975); Edward J. Piacentino, *T. S. Stribling: Pioneer Realist in Modern Southern Literature* (1988), *Southern Literary Journal* (Fall 1990); Kenneth W. Vickers, *T. S. Stribling: A Life of the Tennessee Novelist* (2004).

Stuart, Jesse Hilton

(1906–1984) WRITER.

One of seven children, Jesse Stuart was born 8 August 1906 in a log cabin in W-Hollow near Greenup in the northeast corner of Kentucky. After attending Plum Grove school and completing high school in Greenup, Stuart graduated from Lincoln Memorial University (B.A., 1929) in Harrogate, Tenn., and did graduate work at Vanderbilt (1931–32) and George Peabody College in Nashville, Tenn. Stuart led a busy and productive life, writing nearly 50 books, serving as a teacher and administrator in local schools, and farming in his beloved W-Hollow. He died on 17 February 1984 and was buried in Plum Grove Cemetery near W-Hollow, his lifelong home.

Stuart spent more than 50 years exploring his native locale and making good use of local characters and incidents. One of Appalachia's most prolific writers, Stuart portrayed southern mountain and hill people to a reading audience that was becoming interested in Appalachians as distinct cultural types. His W-Hollow stories, published in collections from *Head O' W-Hollow* (1936) and *Men of the Mountains* (1941) to *Thirty-Two Votes before Breakfast* (1974), depict elemental experiences of life—births, deaths, funerals, weddings, elections, and marital and intergenerational relationships. His poetry, collected in several volumes from *Man with a Bull-Tongue Plow* (1934) to *Hold April* (1962), also celebrates the youth, men, and women of W-Hollow.

Many of Stuart's novels mirror a youth's (usually a narrator's) growing awareness of himself, an awareness shaped by the conflicting demands of a small nuclear family and the larger society that surrounds it. In *Trees of Heaven* (1940), young Tarvin Bushman sees the virtues of both the town and the hill way of life and is prepared at the end of the novel to try to merge the best qualities of the two. The young boy Sid, the outsider in the Tussie clan in *Taps for Private Tussie* (1943), gains knowledge of the Tussies and appreciation for "book-learning" and formal education. David Stoneking, in *Daughter of the Legend* (1965), has been part of the Melungeon culture and will presumably carry that culture beyond the setting of Sanctuary Mountain.

Stuart's own struggles in growing up and coming to a broader and deeper view of life are recorded in *Beyond Dark Hills* (1938). His efforts to educate youth are told in *The Thread That Runs So True* (1949) and *To Teach, To Love* (1970). His recuperation from a nearly fatal heart attack is described in *The Year of My Rebirth* (1956).

Stuart's last book, *The Kingdom Within* (1979), recounts an out-of-body experience in which Shan Powderjay, Stuart's fictional alter ego, attends his own funeral along with all of Stuart's "head children"—the fictional characters he created.

DONALD H. CUNNINGHAM
Texas Tech University

J. R. LeMaster and Mary Washington Clarke, eds., *Jesse Stuart: Essays on His Work* (1977); H. Edward Richardson, *Jesse: The Biography of an American Writer—Jesse Hilton Stuart* (1984).

Stuart, Mary Routh (Ruth) McEnery

(1852–1917) WRITER.
Mary Routh (later Ruth) McEnery Stuart wrote local-color fiction and verse drawn from her experiences in Arkansas and Louisiana. She achieved critical recognition and financial success and, after falling into obscurity during the mid-20th century, was rediscovered by feminist and social literary critics.

Routh McEnery was born 21 May 1852 (the year stated on her marriage license, although she might have been born as early as 1849). Her parents were Mary Routh Stirling and James McEnery, at that time the mayor of Marksville, La., where Routh was born. In addition to their farming interests in central Louisiana, the McEnerys were prominent in Louisiana politics. Some time before 1860, the family moved to New Orleans, where she grew up in the culturally and racially diverse Louisiana atmosphere of many of her stories. She taught at the Loquet-LeRoy Institute for young women in New Orleans. In 1879, when she was 27 (or 30), she married Alfred Oden Stuart, an Arkansas widower. The couple lived in Washington,

Ark., where A. O. Stuart was a farmer and a partner in the mercantile establishment of Stuart and Holman.

Alfred Stuart died in 1883, three years after the birth of their son, Stirling. Mary Routh then returned with her son to her family home in New Orleans and began to support herself as a writer. Her first story "Uncle Mingo's Speculations" was published in February 1888 in *New Princeton Review*. "Lamentations of Jeremiah Johnson" followed in May 1888 in *Harper's New Monthly Magazine*. Encouraged by these early successes, she moved to New York. She also discarded the family spelling of her name for the more familiar "Ruth."

In 1893 Harper and Brothers published *A Golden Wedding and Other Tales*, a collection of 11 of her short stories and two poems previously published in magazines. "The Woman's Exchange of Simpkinsville" is set in an imaginary Arkansas town modeled after Washington. After the success of this story, she set others in Simpkinsville and elaborated a cast of recurring characters. She became a regular writer for *Harper's*, and in the early 1890s was occasionally a substitute editor in the Harper publishing house. Between 1888 and 1917, Stuart published more than 75 stories, in addition to dialect verse. She traveled as far west as Denver reading her poems and stories in public performance. Her work regularly appeared in national publications, including *Harper's Bazaar, Harper's New Monthly Magazine, Century Magazine, New Princeton Review, Delineator*, the *Outlook*, and *Lippincott's Magazine*. It

was collected in more than two dozen volumes, including *Carlotta's Intended and Other Tales* (1894), *In Simpkinsville: Character Tales* (1897), *Napoleon Jackson, the Gentleman of the Plush Rocker* (1902), and *Daddy Do-Funny's Wisdom Jingles* (1913).

Her only child, Stirling, died in 1905, and Stuart's health declined, along with her literary output. At about that time, literary taste moved away from Stuart's sentimental and idealized South. Nevertheless, in 1915 Tulane University in New Orleans awarded her an honorary degree of doctor of letters. Stuart died in New York 6 May 1917 and was buried in New Orleans.

Stuart's fiction depicts the white "plain folk" of rural Arkansas, the immigrants and aristocrats of New Orleans, and African Americans in New Orleans and central Louisiana. She describes the environment and cultural, religious, and social values. She was considered a master at reproducing southern dialect, especially African American. Black people in her stories are treated sympathetically, and some of them, like Sheba and the old man in "An Arkansas Prophet," are among her most interesting characters.

Toward the end of the 20th century, women's studies programs introduced Stuart into the curriculum. In 1983 the University of Arkansas Press published *Simpkinsville and Vicinity: Arkansas Stories of Ruth McEnery Stuart*. The sentimentality and condescension in her work were overlooked, and she was praised for creating strong female characters who overcome widowhood, poverty, and shattered hopes, and who quietly subvert the mores of their culture. Her gentle satire of the narrow conventions of southern life is a foretaste of humorists like Eudora Welty and Anne Tyler.

ETHEL C. SIMPSON
University of Arkansas

Ruth McEnery Stuart, *Simpkinsville and Vicinity: Arkansas Stories of Ruth McEnery Stuart*, ed. Ethel C. Simpson (1999); Helen Taylor, *Gender, Race, and Region in the Writings of Grace King, Ruth McEnery Stuart, and Kate Chopin* (1989).

Styron, William
(1925–2006) WRITER.

Born and raised in Newport News, Va., William Styron received his preparatory education at Christchurch School, in rural Tidewater, and his college education in North Carolina, first at Davidson College and then at Duke. His earliest work was written at Duke under the tutelage of William Blackburn. After graduation in 1947 Styron left the South, and he subsequently pursued his career in Europe and New York.

Styron's decision to live and to write outside the South has perhaps fueled critical disagreement over how closely his fiction should be linked to a regional context. With the publication of *Lie Down in Darkness* in 1951, some critics noted a strong thematic, technical, and stylistic indebtedness to southern writers, especially William Faulkner and Robert Penn Warren. But the dominant thrust of Styron criticism has been to weigh rather lightly these regional influences, concentrating instead on the universal dimensions of his themes and identifying broader contemporary ideas, from existentialism to the French nouveau roman.

Few who have read the entire corpus of Styron's work, however, would deny that important southern perspectives exist in his fiction. Much of the power of *Lie Down in Darkness* derives from the novel's highly evocative rendering of its suburban Tidewater country club setting, and Styron's strongly delineated characters are grotesque distortions of the conventional character stereotypes of the southern gentleman, southern lady, and southern belle. Though Styron consciously moved his setting from Virginia to Europe in *Set This House on Fire* (1960), the novel's primary characters remain southerners, and they re-create the tragic narrative, sitting in a boat on the Ashley River a few miles from one of the South's oldest and most legendary cities. Styron returned triumphantly to his Virginia fictional terrain in *The Confessions of Nat Turner* (1967), a narrative of the infamous and bloody slave uprising, which enlists the Old Dominion's hallowed plantation tradition as part of a provocative and unflinching analysis of black rage. In *Sophie's Choice* (1970) the horrors of Auschwitz and of a fatally destructive relationship between a Polish concentration camp survivor and her brilliant but insane Jewish lover are filtered, much like the action of *Set This House on Fire*, through a point of view that is both intensely personal and southern.

William Styron did not share the historical perspective of an earlier genera-

William Styron, Virginia author, 1982 (Nancy Crampton, photographer, Random House, New York)

tion of southern writers like Faulkner in which individual failure is inextricably linked to the failure of community or culture. It would be a mistake, however, to underestimate the importance of the South, and particularly of his native state, in his novels. Though Styron deftly inverts their romantic associations, the traditional staples of the southern novel—the plantation, the cavalier figure, and the idea of gentility—occupy an important place in his oeuvre. From *Lie Down in Darkness* to the loosely autobiographical sketches of *A Tidewater Morning* (1993), Styron's fiction provides ample evidence to support the assertion, advanced in one of the essays composing *This Quiet Dust* (1982), that the Old Dominion so "vividly and poi-gnantly" recalled in the author's novels and stories "worked on me a lasting effect" and "made me in large measure the writer that I am."

William Styron died 1 November 2006.

RITCHIE D. WATSON
Randolph-Macon College

Daniel W. Ross, ed., *The Critical Response to William Styron* (1995); James L. W. West, *William Styron: A Life* (1998).

Sullivan, Walter

(1924–2006) CRITIC AND WRITER.
A native of Nashville, Tenn., Walter Sullivan was graduated from Vanderbilt University in 1947 following his service in the U.S. Marine Corps as a lieuten-ant during World War II. In 1949 he earned an M.F.A. from the University of Iowa and returned to Vanderbilt, where he taught with great distinction for 51 years. Sullivan began his writing career as a novelist with the publication of *Sojourn of a Stranger* (1957), a historical novel set in antebellum middle Tennes-see, and nearly 50 years later concluded it with his memoir, *Nothing Gold Can Stay* (2006). During the nearly 60 years that Sullivan published, he wrote in many modes—short fiction, textbook, literary criticism, and personal essays (especially reminiscence and tribute), as well as novels. He made himself into a man of letters who could write well in nearly any form of prose. He was best known as a critic, and his criticism has a philosophical and religious dimen-sion that marks it distinctively as his own—original, not derivative. "Death by Melancholy" (1970), his best-known and most representative essay, contains these wise and eloquent words: "As writers, we have fallen victim to our own excesses, and a deep melancholy now grips our lives. We see that our new god, art, has failed us."

Sullivan's brilliance as a lecturer and teacher went hand in glove with his critical voice and manner. He was a man of uncommon grace, great panache, and unforgettable style both in person and on the page.

The bare-bones record of his pub-lications yields three novels, including *The Long, Long Love* (1959) and *A Time to Dance* (1995), both of which are set in 20th-century Nashville; three books of critical essays that are by no means ran-dom collections; *Allen Tate: A Recollec-tion* (1988); and many stories, of which there is unfortunately not a book-length selection. He edited two highly regarded books: *A Band of Prophets: The Vander-bilt Agrarians after Fifty Years* (1982), in collaboration with William C. Havard, and *The War the Women Lived* (1995), a collection of memoirs written by southern women about the vast range of their experience of the Civil War. His work in periodical form—short stories, essays, and reviews—chiefly appeared in the *Southern Review* and the *Sewanee Review*. His first two novels were pub-lished by Henry Holt; thereafter the Louisiana State University Press, which reprinted the novels, published his work. Finally, a book dedicated to him, *Place in American Fiction* (2004), and his *Nothing Gold Can Stay* (2006) were published by the University of Missouri Press.

Sullivan was a founding member of the Fellowship of Southern Writers and served as its chancellor from 2001 through the spring of 2004. He directed the Vanderbilt Literary Symposium for many years. He was a Ford Foundation fellow, a Sewanee Review fellow, and a Lamar lecturer at Mercer University. His Lamar lectures were published as *A Requiem for the Renascence: The State of Fiction in the Modern South* (1976). In addition to Mercer, Sullivan lectured at a wide variety of colleges and universities. He was named an outstanding educator in America in 1973.

His literary friends and acquaintances include a distinguished roll call of writers in and out of the South: John Crowe Ransom, Donald Davidson, Andrew Lytle, Allen Tate, Robert Penn Warren, Eudora Welty, Cleanth Brooks, Lewis Simpson, Elizabeth Spencer, Walker Percy, Flannery O'Connor, William Hoffman, C. Hugh Holman, Louis D. Rubin Jr., George Garrett, Wendell Berry, and Fred Chappell, southerners all; and Malcolm Cowley, Paul Engle, Robert B. Heilman, Donald Davie, Wallace Stegner, Robert Lowell, and Denis Donoghue.

Although occasionally stereotyped as a late Agrarian and a southern conservative, Sullivan was more nearly what Lewis P. Simpson and Mark Winchell have deemed a Catholic modernist. His criticism was devoted in considerable part to such Catholic writers as James Joyce, Evelyn Waugh, Graham Greene, Jacques Barzun, and J. F. Powers. He should be remembered as a good fiction writer, a superb and highly original critic, an eminently readable memoir-

ist, and as a man of letters and teacher whose unmistakable stamp has made an enduring mark on our age, on the South and its literature, and on the profession of letters.

ROBERT BENSON
GEORGE CORE
University of the South

Harold McSween, *Mississippi Quarterly* (Winter 1990–91); Walter Sullivan, *In Praise of Blood Sports and Other Essays* (1990), *Death by Melancholy: Essays on Modern Southern Fiction* (1972); Mark Royden Winchell, *Hollins Critic* (February 1990).

Tate, Allen

(1899–1979) WRITER AND CRITIC. The most cosmopolitan of major modern southern writers, [John Orley] Allen Tate was a prime exemplar of his own theory that the highest artistic achievements come from a combination of native and foreign influences. He was born on 10 November 1899 in Winchester, Ky., a town in the heart of the Bluegrass country. Family loyalty first led him away from home, for he followed his elder brothers to Vanderbilt University in Nashville and there encountered the writers who were to determine the course of his life. John Crowe Ransom and Donald Davidson were his teachers, Robert Penn Warren was a younger fellow student, and all became colleagues in the *Fugitive* magazine, which began appearing in 1922 while Tate was still an undergraduate.

By 1930 Tate had produced the centerpiece of modern southern poetry, the "Ode to the Confederate Dead," using techniques of imagery and deliberate fragmentation learned from for-

Allen Tate, Tennessee poet, early 1920s (Photographic Archives,
Vanderbilt University Library, Nashville, Tennessee)

eign poetry to portray the experience of a native southerner who felt cut off from the traditional society he wished to memorialize. His theme in this masterful poem, as in the equally masterful literary essays he wrote and in his only novel, *The Fathers* (1938), was the decline, not simply of southern tradition, but of the whole tradition of Western civilization, which he came to see as the result of the loss of religious faith. "Modern man suffering from unbelief," he wrote near the end of his illustrious career, was what all his writing was about.

Tate was by education and conviction a Renaissance man, a classical Christian humanist, but by force of circumstance he became a modernist, trapped unwillingly in what he called "the squirrel cage of modern sensibility," a "provincialism of time" (more constrictive than the old provincialism of place), where solipsism, or uniquely personal intuition, was the sole alternative to scientific determinism, or positivism, as the measure of truth and value. His theory was that traditional society, where people were bound into community by ties of family, locale, and religion, had been replaced by industrial society, in which the only ties were economic and political; the southern writer's vantage point, living in a place where the agrarian community was still alive, if rapidly vanishing, made him an eyewitness to the change from traditional to industrial society, which in other places was already an accomplished fact.

Tate's definition of the Fugitive was "quite simply a Poet: the Wanderer, or even the Wandering Jew, the man who carries the secret wisdom about the world." He lived out this definition himself, as he went from Nashville to New York, where he became part of another group of writers, less regionally aligned, that included Hart Crane, Malcolm Cowley, and e. e. cummings; then to Paris on a Guggenheim Fellowship, where he spent some time in the circle of Gertrude Stein, with Ernest Hemingway, Scott Fitzgerald, and Archibald MacLeish; then back to Southwestern College in Memphis, where he taught, to Princeton University, to the Library of Congress, as its first consultant in poetry, to the University of the South, where he edited the *Sewanee Review* for a few distinguished years; and finally to the University of Minnesota, where he became Regents Professor of English. His career had taken him far away from the South and earned him an international reputation and many honors, including the Bollingen Prize for Poetry and the presidency of the National Institute of Arts and Letters, but he had always remained a southerner as well as a Fugitive. At the end of his life he returned to Tennessee, where he died, in Nashville, on 9 February 1979.

Southerner, American, and internationalist in turn, Tate retained his regional identity all his life, nowhere more convincingly than in his late poem, "The Swimmers," where he recalled his Kentucky boyhood in an elegant series of terza rima stanzas that are a triumphant blend of the local and the universal. He wrote and edited many notable books; much of his best work can be found in *Collected Poems, 1919–1976* (1977); *Essays of Four Decades* (1968); and *Memories and Opinions, 1926–1974* (1975).

WILLIAM PRATT
Miami University (Ohio)

Ferman Bishop, *Allen Tate* (1967); William Doreski, *The Years of Our Friendship: Robert Lowell and Allen Tate* (1990); John M. Dunaway, ed., *Exiles and Fugitives: The Letters of Jacques and Raissa Maritain, Allen Tate, and Caroline Gordon* (1992); George Hemphill, *Allen Tate* (1964); Mark G. Malvasi, *The Unregenerate South: The Agrarian Thought of John Crowe Ransom, Allen Tate, and Donald Davidson* (1997); Radcliffe Squires, ed., *Allen Tate and His Work: Critical Evaluations* (1972); Thomas A. Underwood, *Allen Tate: Orphan of the South* (2000); Thomas Daniel Young and John Hindle, eds., *The Republic of Letters in America: The Correspondence of John Peale Bishop and Allen Tate* (1981).

Taylor, Peter

(1917–1994) WRITER.

Peter Taylor, the first southern writer to produce fiction of Jamesian subtlety and complexity scrutinizing the urban upper class of the Upper South, drew from a background perfect for his task. He was born in Trenton, a west Tennessee courthouse cotton town, in 1917. His father, Hillsman Taylor, sprang from a line of west Tennessee lawyers and political figures; and his mother, Katherine Taylor, was a daughter of the most famous political family in the state. Adding to that rich heritage was the varied social exposure of Peter Taylor's childhood and youth. When he was seven, the family moved to Nashville, where his father worked as a corporation lawyer amid the highest circles of the region. After just two years, the family moved again, this time to St. Louis, where Hillsman Taylor was president of an insurance company. A victim of the Great Depression and betrayed by his business partner, Hillsman Taylor was forced to start over again in Memphis, where Peter Taylor was sent for the first time to a large public school. Thus the future writer had experienced the old small-town South, the security and privilege of the New South, the grand echelons of the central city of middle America, and finally ruin, and then recovery in a city on the border of the Deep South.

Taylor's literary exposure was as remarkable as his social experience. The protégé first of Allen Tate at Southwestern College (now Rhodes College) and then of John Crowe Ransom at both Vanderbilt and Kenyon College, Taylor encountered at Kenyon a group of northern literary students who would later be significant on the New York literary scene. Foremost among them was Taylor's roommate and closest friend, the poet Robert Lowell. After graduation, Taylor studied under Robert Penn Warren and Cleanth Brooks at Louisiana State University.

Taylor left graduate school after just a few months, having placed three accomplished short stories in Brooks and Warren's *Southern Review*. Drafted into the army, he spent the first half of World War II stateside. Shortly after he married Eleanor Ross, a young North Carolina poet studying at Vanderbilt, he was shipped to England. During the rest of the war, while never seeing combat, he produced other distinguished stories.

Returning home in 1946, he began a peripatetic academic career that gave him time for his writing and covered stints at the University of North Carolina at Greensboro, Indiana University, Kenyon College, Ohio State University, Harvard University, and, finally for the longest period, the University of Virginia. In 1948 his first volume of short fiction, *A Long Fourth and Other Stories*, was published with an introduction by Robert Penn Warren, and Taylor also began an association with the *New Yorker* that lasted several decades.

Taylor's early *Southern Review* stories had attracted the attention of literary people, and one of these works, "The Fancy Woman," was selected for the *Best Short Stories* volume for 1942. Over the next thirty years, he published a novel and several other collections that drew the praise of critics and earned the respect of his literary peers—culminating in *The Collected Stories of Peter Taylor* in 1969. He also worked intermittently at writing plays.

After a period in his middle 50s, marked by abandonment of fiction, concentration upon one-act plays and verse narratives, and a serious heart attack, he experienced a second fictional flowering. In the pages of the *New Yorker*, which had rejected his efforts for several years, he published two of his greatest stories, "In the Miro District" (1977) and "The Old Forest" (1979). The two collections to which these stories gave their titles brought more critical attention to

Taylor than he had ever enjoyed. This growing public recognition led to his winning the Pulitzer Prize for his 1986 novel *A Summons to Memphis*. Shortly before the novel appeared, he suffered a serious stroke, and the last eight years of his life were marked by failing health. He continued to write and produced a final collection of short fiction and a novel, *In the Tennessee Country*, in his last two years. He died on 2 November 1994 in Charlottesville and was buried at Sewanee, Tenn.

HUBERT MCALEXANDER
University of Georgia

Hubert H. McAlexander, in *Critical Essays on Peter Taylor* (1993), *Peter Taylor: A Writer's Life* (2001); Stuart Wright, *Peter Taylor: A Descriptive Bibliography, 1934–87* (1988).

Thorpe, Thomas Bangs

(1815–1878) WRITER AND EDITOR. Born 1 March 1815 in Westfield, Mass., Thomas Bangs Thorpe grew up in Albany and New York City. As a teenager, he studied painting under John Quidor, whose influence can also be seen in the comic writing for which Thorpe is still remembered. In September 1837 Thorpe traveled overland to south Louisiana to visit Wesleyan University classmates when poor health prevented him from finishing his degree. He was immediately drawn to the frontier scenes and characters that became his principal subjects. Thorpe lived in Louisiana until 1854, active as the editor of six newspapers and as a Whig politician. In New Orleans with Union forces from 1862 to 1864, he was in charge of food distribution and sanitation and was also elected to the state constitutional convention. Returning to New York City, he continued to paint and write. He was appointed a weigher in the custom house, where he became caught up in the corruption for which that institution was infamous. Thorpe died of Bright's disease on 20 September 1878.

Thorpe first displayed his literary genius in a mock-heroic sketch entitled "Tom Owen, the Bee-Hunter," which was printed in the 27 July 1839 issue of the *New York Spirit of the Times*. The piece describes an idiosyncratic backwoodsman and local hero from East Feliciana Parish, where Thorpe had been visiting a planter. Widely reprinted, "Tom Owen" helped the *Spirit* become known as a repository for humorous and sporting writing by amateurs from the South. Thorpe continued to contribute to the *Spirit* humorous sketches as well as factual accounts of wild game and hunting practices on the southwestern frontier.

Thorpe's greatest comic achievement is "The Big Bear of Arkansas," published in the *Spirit* on 27 March 1841. While traveling by steamboat, an urbane narrator meets the backwoods raconteur, Jim Doggett (aka The Big Bear), who proceeds first to mock his pretensions and then to monopolize his attention with a tall tale about extraordinary adventures with "an unhuntable bear." The yarn is characterized by its skilled use of dialect, mythic overtones, and scatological humor. William Faulkner is among those southern writers who have publicly acknowledged its power.

As editor of the *Concordia Intelligencer*, published across the river from Natchez in Vidalia, La., Thorpe wrote "Letters from the Far West," an occasional series under the pseudonym P.O.F. that was closely followed and received much comment in local newspapers. The 12 letters burlesque reports sent by Matthew Field to the *New Orleans Picayune* about the 1843–44 western hunting expedition of a Scottish nobleman. Thorpe peoples his letters with Native Americans, a Mexican, a black man, and the naturalist John James Audubon. The humor of physical discomfort suggests some of Sut Lovingood's pranks. For unknown reasons, Thorpe chose not to include "Letters from the Far West" in either of the two popular collections of his backwoods sketches—*The Mysteries of the Backwoods* (1846) and *The Hive of the "Bee-Hunter"* (1854).

Throughout his life, Thorpe continued to search for profitable venues for his writing. For example, in 1846 and 1847 he published two books recounting the U.S. Army's adventures in the Mexican War and followed these with a brief campaign biography called *The Taylor Anecdote Book* (1848), which did not lead to the preferment he hoped. Probably as a response to *Uncle Tom's Cabin*, he published *The Master's House: A Tale of Southern Life* (1854). Set on a Louisiana plantation, it opposes both slavery and dueling. By the time of his death, Thorpe had published more than 150 articles in such national publications as *Appleton's Journal*, *Harper's New Monthly Magazine*, and the *Knickerbocker Magazine*. Although lacking in literary merit, these pieces contributed to shaping Americans' knowledge of the natural scenery, the flora and fauna, and the distinctive inhabitants of the antebellum southwestern frontier.

DAVID C. ESTES
Loyola University

David C. Estes, ed., *A New Collection of Thomas Bangs Thorpe's Sketches of the Old Southwest* (1989); Milton Rickels, *Thomas Bangs Thorpe: Humorist of the Old Southwest* (1962).

Timrod, Henry

(1828–1867) POET.

Henry Timrod is known as "The Poet Laureate of the Confederacy." That title may be a decoy for Timrod's real gifts. He wrote stirring poems celebrating the South during the Civil War, but he also possessed a versatile talent like few other poets of his time. Often in or out of favor, his work has undergone a new appreciation in the past few years.

Timrod was born in Charleston, S.C., on 8 December 1828, the only son of William Henry Timrod and Thyrza Prince. William Timrod was a bookbinder who regularly entertained local writers in his shop, but he died when Henry was 10 years old.

Timrod received a secondary education in languages, history, and mathematics at the Classical School overseen by Christopher Cotes in Charleston. The most important contact of his life was made during this time when he befriended fellow student Paul Hamilton Hayne, who, after Timrod's death, shepherded the definitive edition of his poems into print in 1873. Timrod first began to write poetry at the Cotes school, and he continued his writing at the University of Georgia, but a complete formal education eluded him. He was able to attend the university for only three semesters before financial difficulties and health problems forced him to withdraw. Back in Charleston, he studied law and tutored at plantations before turning full time to writing. Timrod's only book publication came in 1859 when Ticknor and Fields of Boston brought out a slim volume entitled *Poems*, consisting of his magazine and newspaper publications. The book sold respectably in Charleston.

The great shift in his work occurred with the advent of the Civil War. Timrod was a somewhat conventional romantic poet, with Tennyson and Wordsworth as models, yet with the outbreak of war he came into his own. His emotions took flight; he spoke longingly in his work of the birth of "a nation among nations." By a strange twist, the formation of the Confederate States gave him subject matter to finally match his abilities.

Timrod enlisted twice, but he was discharged both times because of ill health. He married Katie Goodwin in February 1864, but the happiness was not to last. Even the birth of a son, William, on Christmas Eve 1864 could not stave off the darkness brought on by the war.

In January 1864 he had become editor and part owner of the *Columbia Daily South Carolinian*, but the Federal army sacked and burned Columbia in February 1865, and the newspaper office was leveled. Timrod went into hiding. Upon returning to Columbia, he was unemployed and penniless. He and his wife had to move in with his sister Emily, and later they sold her furniture and silver in order to survive. He never again wrote an important poem. His son, William, died in October 1865, and the tuberculosis that had shadowed Timrod throughout his life returned. He died on 7 October 1867.

Timrod could do many things well in poetry. Still one of the best nature poets of the South, his nature poems are underrated when compared with those of Longfellow or William Cullen Bryant, but that side of his output has also been diminished by his pro-Confederacy poems. Those poems are powerful—it is easy to see in retrospect how his heroic odes inspired hundreds, perhaps thousands, of young southern men to voluntarily conscript.

But war has two sides, a beginning and an end, and his elegies may be his lasting legacy. "The Magnolia Cemetery Ode" is perhaps his best poem. It has all of Timrod's trademarks: a controlled but still musical cadence, respect for simple men who do heroic things, and a restrained command of language and poetic form.

While searching for reasons for the tragedy that swirled around him and also engulfed his countryside, Timrod left behind some of the most beautiful verses written by a southerner. To consider him just a drum-beating Confederate patriot is to overlook his other gifts. He may rank behind Poe and Lanier in terms of popularity among readers, but he belongs in the first rank of 19th-century southern poets. Certainly, whenever the literature of the

Civil War is examined, his work must be taken into account.

J. E. PITTS
University of Mississippi

Susan Disheroon-Green, *Voices of the American South* (2005); Joseph M. Flora and Amber Vogel, *Southern Writers: A New Biographical Dictionary* (2006); Claud B. Green, *Dictionary of Literary Biography*, vol. 3, ed. Joel Myerson (1979); James D. Hart, *Oxford Companion to American Literature* (1995); Edd Winfield Parks, *The Collected Poems of Henry Timrod* (1965).

Toole, John Kennedy

(1937–1969) NOVELIST.
In the world of southern fiction, there are many novelists' works and characters that overshadow their creators, but perhaps none does so as completely as John Kennedy Toole's novel *A Confederacy of Dunces* and its protagonist Ignatius J. Reilly. Toole's relative celebrity is a result of his tragically short life and his posthumous and legendary publication of *Dunces*, but today Reilly is considered an icon representing the real-life inhabitants of the French Quarter (to their equal pride and discontent). No other novel in contemporary popular literature so accurately represents, as Walker Percy writes in his foreword to the book, "the particularities of New Orleans, its back streets, its out-of-the-way neighborhoods, [and] its odd speech." Reilly is a "slob extraordinary, a mad Oliver Hardy, a fat Don Quixote, a perverse Thomas Aquinas rolled into one—who is in violent revolt against the entire modern age." Ignatius is eccentric and delusional, intellectual and contemptuous,

and, most precisely, a reflection of his inventor.

John Kennedy Toole was born in New Orleans on 17 December 1937, the only child of John and Thelma Ducoing (pronounced *Dewcoin*) Toole, and raised in the Uptown area of the city. He was educated in the New Orleans Parish public school system, an odd educational choice considering the Tooles were practicing Roman Catholics and that parochial schools, which were generally superior to public schools, were prevalent across town. Nevertheless, Toole excelled in his studies and graduated from high school at age 16. He went on to graduate with honors from Tulane University in 1958 and earned a master's degree from Columbia University in New York in 1959.

The summer of 1959 found Toole teaching English at Southwestern Louisiana Institute (now the University of Louisiana at Lafayette), but he soon desired to return to New York and begin doctoral studies at Columbia. In 1960 he took a teaching position at Hunter College for Women in New York and substitute-taught night classes at City College while working on his doctorate. Toole was called up for military service in 1961 and sent to Puerto Rico; there he began work on his classic novel about New Orleans and its inhabitants, *A Confederacy of Dunces*. He completed his military service and returned to the city that had captured his heart and his imagination. There he took a job teaching at St. Mary's Dominican College (Loyola University's sister school) and finished his novel.

In 1964 Toole sent *A Confederacy of Dunces* "over the transom" to Simon and Schuster in New York, where it promptly landed in the slush pile. Jean Marks, the assistant to senior editor Robert Gottlieb, retrieved the novel and recommended it to Gottlieb as having promise. That year Gottlieb and Toole actively reworked the book, with Gottlieb ultimately abandoning the project, saying to Toole in a December 1964 letter that "it isn't *really* about anything. And that's something no one can do anything about." Simon and Schuster returned Toole his unpublished manuscript in 1965.

During the last years of Toole's life he lived in his parents' home, depressed and increasingly paranoid. He believed there were various plots to steal his novel and that electronic devices read his mind. He ceased teaching classes at Dominican and turned to alcohol. On 26 March 1969 John Kennedy Toole's nervous breakdown reached a pinnacle, and he took his own life by carbon-monoxide poisoning in Biloxi, Miss.

For the next five years Thelma Toole sent *A Confederacy of Dunces* to seven publishing houses across the United States. All seven rejected it. In July 1976 Thelma Toole, still convinced that her son's novel was a work of genius, read an article in the *Times-Picayune* about a National Book Award winner named Walker Percy, who was teaching creative writing at Loyola. It was then that she decided she would hound the writer until he agreed to read her son's novel, sure that he would serve as an instrument toward its publication. By Thanksgiving Percy was still successfully avoiding Thelma Toole, but she, ever determined, showed up at his Loyola office and personally handed him the manuscript. Grudgingly he accepted it, and after reading it, he enthusiastically agreed with its merit. *A Confederacy of Dunces* was published in 1980 by Louisiana State University Press, with Walker Percy writing the foreword. Toole was posthumously awarded the Pulitzer Prize in 1981.

Today, in New Orleans, a bronze statue of Ignatius J. Reilly stands in front of the Chateau Sonesta Hotel on Canal Street, the former D. H. Holmes department store and the setting for the opening scene of *A Confederacy of Dunces*.

JAMES G. THOMAS JR.
University of Mississippi

Joel L. Fletcher, *Ken and Thelma: The Story of "A Confederacy of Dunces"* (2005); Rene Pol Nevils and Deborah George Hardy, *Ignatius Rising: The Life of John Kennedy Toole* (2005).

Toomer, Jean

(1894–1967) WRITER.
The only child of Nina Pinchback and Nathan Toomer, Nathan Eugene Toomer, also known as Jean Toomer, was born in the Washington, D.C., home of his grandparents, Nina Emily Hethorne and P. B. S. Pinchback. Born into a socially and politically prominent family—Pinchback was the first black lieutenant governor of Louisiana during Reconstruction—Toomer enjoyed the advantages and privileges of a middle-class family.

Toomer received his primary and secondary education in the public schools of the District of Columbia. After graduating from M Street High School (now known as Paul Laurence Dunbar High) in 1914, Toomer studied scientific agriculture at the University of Wisconsin, sociology at the University of Chicago, and law at the City College of New York. Toomer's range of interests was impressive, but it revealed not so much the possibilities of an expansive intellect as the workings of an anxious mind in search of what he would later call an "intelligible scheme." The chaotic years between 1914 and 1919, described by Toomer as the "years of wandering," were not completely devoid of order. During this period, Toomer experimented with writing and discovered such writers as Walt Whitman, George Bernard Shaw, and Waldo Frank. These writers exercised an extraordinary influence over Toomer: from Whitman, Toomer sensed the potentialities of ordinary speech; from Shaw, he discovered the didactic uses of art; in Frank, he found a friend and mentor who was instrumental in publishing the single work on which his reputation as an imaginative artist rests—*Cane* (1923).

A collection of verse, prose, and drama, *Cane* was the outcome of a two-month sojourn in the fall of 1921 in Sparta, Ga., where Toomer was acting principal of the Sparta Normal and Industrial Institute. Toomer responded passionately to the black folk culture, whose dissolution is the subject of *Cane*. Toomer's sensual portrayal of black life, his emphasis on black folk culture, and his experimentation with jazz forms and imagist techniques forged new artistic possibilities for the writers of the New Negro Movement.

Toomer's southern sojourn had personal as well as artistic consequences. Long in search of a sense of wholeness, the young author of *Cane* achieved a unity of art and being while in the South never matched by his conversion to Quakerism, his involvement in Dianectics, and, most important of all, his work as a teacher of the psychological theories of George I. Gurdjieff. Gurdjieff's theories did not impart to the large body of fiction, verse, and drama written after 1923 the depth of feeling and the complexity of thought so characteristic of *Cane*. This fact explains why so much of the writing after *Cane* remains unpublished and why Toomer died in Doylestown, Pa., in obscurity and isolation.

RUDOLPH P. BYRD
Los Angeles, California

Brian Joseph Benson and Mabel Mayle Dillard, *Jean Toomer* (1980); Rudolph P. Byrd, *Jean Toomer's Years with Gurdjieff: Portrait of an Artist, 1923–1936* (1990); Robert B. Jones, *Jean Toomer and the Prison-House of Thought: A Phenomenology of the Spirit* (1993); Nellie Y. McKay, *Jean Toomer, Artist: A Study of His Literary Life and Work, 1894–1936* (1984); Therman B. O'Daniel, ed., *Jean Toomer: A Critical Evaluation* (1988); Charles W. Scruggs, *Jean Toomer and the Terrors of American History* (1998); Darwin Turner, *In a Minor Chord: Three Afro-American Writers and Their Search for Identity* (1971).

Trethewey, Natasha

(b. 1966) POET.
Winner of the 2007 Pulitzer Prize for Poetry, Natasha Trethewey uses poetry to reimagine the southern past. At a time when interracial marriage was illegal in Mississippi, Trethewey was born in Gulfport, Miss., in 1966 to a father who was white and a mother who was black. Her poetry uses this personal experience to inform her evocation of a biracial South that she claims and whose meanings she explores. She grew up in Decatur, Ga., but spent summers with her grandmother in Mississippi and New Orleans, both of which figure prominently in her work.

Trethewey earned a bachelor's degree in English and creative writing at the University of Georgia, a master's degree in English and creative writing at Hollins University, and a M.F.A. in poetry from the University of Massachusetts. She taught at Auburn University before moving to teach at Emory University.

Trethewey's poetry engages southern issues of race, class, and gender. Her first book, *Domestic Work* (2000), begins with a poem, "Gesture of a Woman-in-Process," that portrays two women, surrounded by:

"their dailiness:
clotheslines sagged with linens,
    a patch of greens and yams,
buckets of peas for shelling."

This image evokes a rural, African American experience, and Trethewey uses photographic images in her work to position women and blacks as central figures of southern history.

Bellocq's Ophelia (2002), Trethewey's second book of poetry, has been described by Rafael Campo as a "novella-in-verse." She imagines the inner life of a mixed-race prostitute photographed by E. J. Bellocq in the Storyville red-light district in early 20th century New Orleans. The central character is Ophelia, a mulatto from Mississippi who moves to New Orleans and eventually becomes a prostitute in a "fancy house," documenting her life by writing letters and keeping a diary. Bellocq teaches her to become a photographer, and she uses her ability to represent others through the camera as a form of empowerment that suggests what Katherine Henninger calls "the possibility of resistance and transformation," which are always important in Trethewey's poetry.

"Southern Pastoral" is a 2002 sonnet that portrays a recurring dream of being photographed with the Fugitive poets, in the very un-Agrarian Atlanta. The towering urban skyline of the city is hidden by the photographer (assisted by Robert Penn Warren), who focuses instead on "a lush pasture, green, full of soft-eyed cows." The Fugitives offer the dreamer a glass of bourbon, but she fears that if she accepts it she must accept traditional expectations of women and blacks. "Say Race," the photographer intones, and the dreamer seems "in / blackface again when the flash freezes us." Trethewey is the dreamer, in effect, who presents her postmodern playful reversal of southern role playing—she is the poet commanding, in the end, a new vision of the South that goes beyond an Agrarian vision.

Native Guard (2006) engages the specifics of that ultimate symbol of southern distinctiveness, the Civil War. Off the coast of Trethewey's native Gulfport, Ship Island once held a fort that had been a Union prison housing Confederate prisoners. The second regiment of the Louisiana Native Guards—one of the Union's first black units—protected the fort. In the title poem of the book, Trethewey enters the mind of a former slave stationed at the fort who writes letters for the illiterate and invalid Confederate prisoners of war and his fellow Union soldiers. He comes, in her portrayal, to hold a valuable memory of the Civil War experience that has been unacknowledged by historical plaques and official recognition. Other poems in the book explore her childhood as the daughter of an interracial marriage. The racial past pervades poems honoring her mother and also the overlooked history of her South.

CHARLES REAGAN WILSON
University of Mississippi

Rafael Campo, *Prairie Schooner* (Winter 2003); Katherine Henninger, *Ordering the Façade: Photography and Contemporary Southern Women's Writing* (2007).

Tyler, Anne
(b. 1941) WRITER AND SCREENWRITER.

Baltimore, Md., has been the home of the Pulitzer Prize–winning, best-selling southern author Anne Tyler since 1967 when her family made Baltimore its permanent residence. Although she was born 25 October 1941 in Minneapolis, Minn., and spent much of her childhood in various Quaker communities in the Midwest and North Carolina, Tyler has embraced the city of Baltimore and used it as the backdrop for the majority of her writings throughout the years. Her characters often exhibit the gentility of their southern upbringing, while maintaining elements of the urban life-style they experience as residents of Baltimore.

Tyler completed her bachelor's degree at Duke University in 1961 and went on to complete her graduate studies at Columbia University in 1962. She met her future husband, Taghi Modarressi, whom she married at the age of 21; they have two children, Tezh and Mitra.

Anne Tyler has written many novels, most of which are set in the city of Baltimore. She is known for presenting stories written about mundane, everyday life through characters whose insight and personal reflection give sustenance to their very existence. Her character's positions in family and community often demonstrate the depths of despair as a result of trial and tragedy.

Tyler's contribution to the world of literary novels began in 1964, when she wrote *If Morning Ever Comes*, which was soon followed by *The Tin Can Tree* in 1965; in 1970 she wrote *A Slipping-Down Life*. Tyler then produced a steady stream of novels—*The Clock Winder* (1972), *Celestial Navigation* (1974), *Searching for Caleb* (1976), *Earthly Possessions* (1977), and *Morgan's Passing* (1980). Tyler's beginning works were seen as a demonstration of her promise as a writer, but *Morgan's Passing* was labeled her "breakout" novel. Although she was recognized with several awards for previous writing, for *Morgan's Passing* alone she received a nomination for both the National Book Critics Circle Award for Fiction and the American Book Award for Paperback Fiction, and won the Janet Heidinger Kafka Prize.

Her next novel, *Dinner at the Home-sick Restaurant*, was published in 1982. Using multiple points of view, this novel gave poignant insight into the complexities of family issues. *Dinner at the Homesick Restaurant* received another nomination for the National Book Critics Circle Award for Fiction, was a nominee for the Pulitzer Prize for Fiction, and was chosen for the PEN/Faulkner Award for Fiction.

Her renowned novel *The Accidental Tourist* was written in 1985 and received the National Book Critics Circle Award for Fiction and another Pulitzer Prize nomination. *Breathing Lessons* was written in 1988 and received the Pulitzer Prize. Her subsequent novels are *Saint Maybe* (1991), *A Ladder of Years* (1995), *A Patchwork Planet* (1998), *Back When We Were Grownups* (2001), *The Amateur Marriage* (2004), and *Digging to America* (2006). She is also the author of a children's book, *Tumble Tower* (1993), which was illustrated by her daughter, Mitra. Tyler has had two books adapted to film—*The Accidental Tourist*, starring Kathleen Turner and William Hurt, released by Warner Brothers in 1988, and *Back When We Were Grownups*, a Hallmark Hall of Fame presentation on CBS in 2004. Also, with Robert W. Lenski, she wrote the screenplay for *Breathing Lessons* in 1994.

TRELLA R. WALKER
Georgia State University

Robert William Croft, *Anne Tyler: A Bio-Bibliography* (1995); Susan S. Kissel, *Moving On: The Heroines of Shirley Ann Grau, Anne Tyler, and Gail Godwin* (1996); Bethanne Kelly Patrick, *Writer* (2004).

Alice Walker, author of The Color Purple, *1976 (William R. Ferris Collection, Southern Folklife Collection, Wilson Library, University of North Carolina at Chapel Hill)*

Walker, Alice

(b. 1944) WRITER.

Alice Walker's *The Color Purple* is saturated with the atmosphere of the South, the rural Georgia farmland of her childhood. Walker, who has written more than 29 books of poetry, fiction, biography, and essays, finds strength and inspiration in the land and the people: "You look at old photographs of Southern blacks and you see it—a fearlessness, a real determination and proof of a moral center that is absolutely bedrock to the land. I think there's hope in the South, not in the North."

Alice Walker was born in 1944 in Eatonton, Ga., the youngest of eight children. Her parents were poor sharecroppers. As a child, she read what books she could get, kept notebooks, and listened to the stories her relatives told. She attended Spelman College in Atlanta and graduated from Sarah Lawrence College in Bronxville, N.Y., where her writing was discovered by her teacher Muriel Rukeyser, who admired the manuscript that Alice had slipped under her door. Rukeyser sent the poems to her own editor at Harcourt Brace, and this first collection of Walker's poetry, *Once*, was published in 1965. From 1966 through 1974 Walker lived in Georgia and Mississippi and devoted herself to voter registration, Project Head Start, and writing. She married Mel Leventhal, a Brooklyn attorney who shared her dedication to civil rights in his work on school desegregation cases. Their daughter, Rebecca, was born in 1969. After they left the South, Walker and Leventhal lived for a while in a Brooklyn brownstone, and then separated. Alice Walker now lives in rural northern California, which she chose primarily for the silence that would allow her to "hear" her fictional characters.

Alice Walker is the literary heir of Zora Neale Hurston and Flannery O'Connor. Walker has visited O'Connor's home in Milledgeville, Ga., and Hurston's grave in Eatonville, Fla., to pay homage. Walker's novels *The Third Life of Grange Copeland* (1977), *Meridian* (1976), and *The Color Purple* (1982) and short stories *In Love and Trouble* (1973) and *You Can't Keep a Good Woman Down* (1980) capture and explore her experiences of the South. She draws on her memories and her family's tales of Georgia ancestors in creating the portraits of rural black women in *The Color Purple*. Their speech is pure dialect—colloquial, poetic, and moving. Walker's poems too are filled with the rich landscape and atmosphere of the South.

Consciousness of the South has always been central to Alice Walker. The flowers and fruits in her California garden recall her mother's garden back in Georgia, a place so important to Walker that it became the inspiration for her collection of essays entitled *In Search of Our Mother's Gardens: Womanist Prose* (1983). Her mother's creativity was a compelling example to Alice Walker as well as a constant source of beauty amid the poverty of rural Georgia. Her mother died in 1993 at the age of 80. The headstone reads "Loving Soul, Great Spirit."

Among her many accomplishments and honors, Alice Walker has been Fannie Hurst Professor of Literature at Brandeis University and a contributing editor to *Ms. Magazine*. In her writing and teaching she continually stresses the importance of black women writers. She edited a Zora Neale Hurston reader and wrote a biography of Langston Hughes for children. In 1984 Walker launched Wild Trees Press in Navarro, Calif., and until 1988 published the work of unknown writers. The film version of *The Color Purple* was released in 1985 to much acclaim. In 2004 the musical version of *The Color Purple* premiered in Chicago, and it opened on Broadway in 2005. Alice Walker continues to champion vital issues such as female genital mutilation, which is central in her 1992 novel, *Possessing the Secret of Joy*. Alice Walker's literary awards include the Rosenthal Award of the National Institute of Arts and Letters, the Lillian Smith Award for her second book of poems, *Revolutionary Petunias* (1972), and the American Book Award and the Pulitzer Prize for Fiction for *The Color Purple* (1983).

ELIZABETH GAFFNEY
Westchester Community College, State University of New York

David Bradley, *New York Times Magazine* (January 1984); Robert Towers, *New York Review of Books* (12 August 1982); Alice Walker, *Atlanta Constitution* (19 April 1983); Evelyn C. White, *Alice Walker: A Life* (2004).

Walker, Margaret

(1913–1998) WRITER AND TEACHER.
Margaret Walker played an active role in American arts and letters for at least seven decades. She was a distinguished

Margaret Walker, Mississippi writer, 1976 (William R. Ferris Collection,
Southern Folklife Collection, Wilson Library, University of North Carolina at Chapel Hill)

poet, respected essayist, groundbreaking novelist, and award-winning educator. Her final collection of poetry, *This Is My Century*, accurately describes the wide range of themes and issues encompassed in her work. The 20th century became Margaret Walker's century, as she "saw it grow from darkness into dawn" ("This Is My Century"). Her writings demonstrate vestiges of the Harlem Renaissance of the 1920s and 1930s, traces of the black arts movement of the 1960s and 1970s, and markings of what some would deem as the womanist renaissance of the 1980s.

While Walker wrote across literary genres, she is most accomplished as a poet. She began publishing poetry in local vehicles at the age of 12 and gained her first appearance in a national publication by age 19, when "I Want to Write" appeared in *Crisis* under the editorship of W. E. B. Du Bois. Just a few years later, at age 22, "For My People" was printed in the November 1937 issue of *Poetry: A Magazine of Verse* and launched her career as a poet. In 1940 Walker collected 26 poems under the title *For My People* as her master's thesis, and it was published as a collection in 1942. She produced four other significant collections of poetry: *The Ballad of the Free* (1966), *Prophets for a New Day* (1970), *October Journey* (1973), and *This Is My Century: New and Collected Poems* (1989). *Prophets for a New Day* celebrates the civil rights movement, *October Journey* (1973) takes its name from a piece written in honor of her husband, whom she met in the month of October and who died in the month of October after 37 years of marriage. *This Is*

My Century: New and Collected Poems (1989), her last collection, presents 100 pieces of poetry—37 of which had never appeared in print.

Walker chose to write in only three forms: (1) narratives as stories or ballads, (2) lyrical songs and sonnets, and (3) the long line of free verse punctuated with a short line. Within these three forms she pays attention to an assortment of issues and themes. At times she elegizes the South, as in "Southern Songs," where she longs to have her "body bathed again by southern souls" and to "rest unbroken in the fields of southern earth." In other pieces she memorializes the acts of cultural heroes, such as Paul Lawrence Dunbar, Harriet Tubman, Mary McCleod Bethune, and Owen Dodson, and she struggles to place her own life and work within a collective black American experience in pieces such as the legendary "For My People," "A Litany of Black History for Black People," "A Litany from the Dark People," and "They Have Put Us on Hold." What remains constant through each thrust is Walker's ability to capture everyday experiences of the common and the legendary with effective cadences and striking imagery.

Many of these same characteristics are visible in her singular novel, *Jubilee* (1966). Walker labored over *Jubilee* from 1934 to 1966 and constructed it as a fictional tribute to the life of her maternal grandmother, Margaret Duggans Ware Brown, who was born into slavery. Readers are able to follow the biracial protagonist, Vyry, through enslavement and Reconstruction and closely follow her ascent out of the pit of slavery.

Jubilee won the 1966 Houghton Mifflin's Literary Fellowship Award, and Walker saw the novel go through 40 printings, sell more than 2 million copies, be published in 7 foreign countries, and even adapted as an opera. Walker unsuccessfully sued Alex Haley for copyright infringement of *Jubilee* with his publication of *Roots*.

Margaret Walker was successful in gaining publishing opportunities for diverse forms of writing, and in 1988 she published a psychobiography of Richard Wright, *Daemonic Genius*, which grew out of their long and tumultuous friendship. In 1990 she published *How I Wrote Jubilee and Other Essays on Life and Literature*. And, in 1997, with the help of Maryemma Graham, she published a final collection of speeches and essays, *On Being Female, Black, and Free*. In the last decade of her life, Walker won countless Mississippi and national awards honoring her work, not the least of which includes the National Book Award for Lifetime Achievements (1993).

ETHEL YOUNG-MINOR
University of Mississippi

Amiri Baraka, "Obituary: Margaret Walker Alexander," *Nation* (4 January 1999); Maryemma Graham, ed., *Conversations with Margaret Walker* (2002); Margaret Walker, *This Is My Century* (1989).

Warren, Robert Penn

(1905–1989) WRITER.

Described by Allen Tate as the most gifted person he had ever known, Robert Penn Warren excelled in every area in which his literary interest took him. Pulitzer Prize–winning novelist and poet, literary critic, social historian, biographer, editor and essayist, creator of plays and short stories, insightful cowriter of pedagogical guides to understanding literature and rhetoric, Warren created a large body of work that reflected the major themes and concerns of the southern writer.

Born in 1905 in Guthrie, Ky., Warren entered Vanderbilt University at age 16 in 1921. By 1923 he was a member of the Nashville Fugitive group, and in 1930 he contributed to that group's Agrarian manifesto, *I'll Take My Stand*. During the interim he had graduated summa cum laude from Vanderbilt, earned a master of arts degree in English at the University of California at Berkeley, and spent two years as a Rhodes scholar at Oxford.

Warren's first published book, *John Brown: The Making of a Martyr* (1929), reflected his early interest in history, especially the tragic social and historic events that produced the 20th-century South. During the 1930s he taught at both Vanderbilt and Louisiana State University, collaborated on *An Approach to Literature* (with Cleanth Brooks and John T. Purser), wrote *Thirty-six Poems*, helped found the *Southern Review*, collaborated again with Brooks on *Understanding Poetry*, and published his first novel, *Night Rider*.

Warren's early work typifies the range of his interest in poetry, fiction, and criticism. The intelligence he and Brooks brought to bear on textual analysis in *Understanding Poetry* and its sequels shows through precept and example the major tenets of the New Criticism that had such a formative influence on American letters during the middle of this century.

The 1940s saw Warren move from Louisiana State University to the University of Minnesota and publish more poetry, criticism, novels, and short fiction. The most critically acclaimed of these was the Pulitzer Prize–winning *All the King's Men* (1946), a novel that is almost a case study in characteristic southern literary concerns. Based on the career of Huey P. Long, it considers such themes as man and change in history, the difficulty of self-knowledge, human responsibility, free will, problems of "ends justifying means," and the southern social condition. It also demonstrates the southerner's characteristic concern with time and its meaning, his fascination with the power of rhetoric, and his propensity toward violence. His other major fiction includes *At Heaven's Gate* (1943), *World Enough and Time* (1950), *Band of Angels* (1955), *The Cave* (1959), *Wilderness* (1961), *Flood* (1964), *Meet Me in the Green Glen* (1971), and *A Place to Come To* (1977).

In 1950 Warren accepted a professorship at Yale, where he served until retirement. He became the only person ever to receive a Pulitzer Prize for both fiction and poetry when he received the award again in 1957 for *Promises: Poems 1954–1956*. In this and his subsequent poetry, Warren treated personally the same themes of original sin, self-knowledge, love, and human possibilities he presented more objectively in his fiction. His meditations on history—*Brother to Dragons* (1953), *The Legacy of the Civil War* (1961), and *Jefferson Davis Gets His Citizenship*

Back (1980)—deal with the same philosophical concerns.

Warren's creative energies continued to sustain him, and he continued to garner honors—a National Book Award, two Guggenheim Fellowships, a MacArthur Foundation Fellowship, the Bollingen Prize for Poetry, the National Medal for Literature, and even, for *Now and Then* (1978), a third Pulitzer Prize. In 1986 he was named the nation's first poet laureate.

LADELL PAYNE
Randolph-Macon College

Joseph L. Blotner, *Robert Penn Warren: A Biography* (1997); Leonard Casper, *Robert Penn Warren: The Dark and Bloody Ground* (1960); Neil Nakadate, *Robert Penn Warren: A Reference Guide* (1977), *Robert Penn Warren: Critical Perspectives* (1981); Hugh M. Ruppersburg, *Robert Penn Warren and the American Imagination* (1990); Marshall Walker, *Robert Penn Warren: A Vision Earned* (1979); Robert Penn Warren, *All the King's Men: Restored Edition* (2001).

Washington, Booker T.

(1856–1915) EDUCATOR.

Booker Taliaferro Washington was the foremost black educator of the late 19th and early 20th centuries. He also had a major influence on southern race relations and was the dominant figure in black public affairs from 1895 until his death in 1915. Born a slave on a small farm in the Virginia backcountry, he moved with his family after emancipation to work in the salt furnaces and coal mines of West Virginia. After a secondary education at Hampton Institute, he taught an upgraded school and experimented briefly with the study of law and the ministry, but a teaching position at Hampton decided his future career. In 1881 he founded Tuskegee Normal and Industrial Institute on the Hampton model in the Black Belt of Alabama.

Although Washington offered little that was innovative in industrial education, which both northern philanthropic foundations and southern leaders were already promoting, he became its chief black exemplar and spokesman. In his advocacy of Tuskegee Institute and its educational method, Washington revealed the political adroitness and accommodationist philosophy that were to characterize his career in the wider arena of race leadership. He convinced southern white employers and governors that Tuskegee offered an education that would keep blacks "down on the farm" and in the trades. To prospective northern donors and particularly the new self-made millionaires such as Rockefeller and Carnegie, he promised the inculcation of the Protestant work ethic. To blacks living within the limited horizons of the post-Reconstruction South, Washington held out industrial education as the means of escape from the web of sharecropping and debt and the achievement of attainable, petit-bourgeois goals of self-employment, landownership, and small business. Washington cultivated local white approval and secured a small state appropriation, but it was northern donations that made Tuskegee Institute by 1900 the best supported black educational intuition in the country.

The Atlanta Compromise Address, delivered before the Cotton States Ex-

position in 1895, enlarged Washington's influence into the arena of race relations and black leadership. Washington offered black acquiescence in disfranchisement and social segregation if whites would encourage black progress in economic and educational opportunity. Hailed as a sage by whites of both sections, Washington further consolidated his influence by his widely read autobiography *Up from Slavery* (1901), the founding of the National Negro Business League in 1900, his celebrated dinner at the White House in 1901, and control of patronage politics as chief black adviser to Presidents Theodore Roosevelt and William Howard Taft.

Washington kept his white following by conservative policies and moderate utterances, but he faced growing black and white liberal opposition in the Niagara Movement (1905–9) and the NAACP (1909–), groups demanding civil rights and encouraging protest in response to white aggressions such as lynchings, disfranchisement, and segregation laws. Washington successfully fended off these critics, often by underhanded means. At the same time, however, he tried to translate his own personal success into black advancement through secret sponsorship of civil rights suits, serving on the boards of Fisk and Howard universities and directing philanthropic aid to these and other black colleges. His speaking tours and private persuasion tried to equalize public educational opportunities and to reduce racial violence. These efforts were generally unsuccessful, and the year of Washington's death marked the beginning of the Great Migration from the rural South to the urban North. Washington's racial philosophy, pragmatically adjusted to the limiting conditions of his own era, did not survive the change.

LOUIS R. HARLAN
University of Maryland

W. Fitzhugh Brundage, ed., *Booker T. Washington and Black Progress: "Up from Slavery" 100 Years Later* (2003); Louis R. Harlan, *Booker T. Washington*, 2 vols. (1972, 1983), *Booker T. Washington in Perspective: Essays of Louis R. Harlan*, ed. Raymond W. Smock (1988); *The Booker T. Washington Papers*, 14 vols. (1972–89); August Meyer, *Negro Thought in America, 1880–1915* (1963).

Watkins, Samuel Rush

(1839–1901) MEMOIRIST.

Sam Watkins was a common Confederate foot soldier who fought through the bloodiest battles of the Civil War, from Robert E. Lee's first campaign in September 1861 through his capture as a prisoner of war in Memphis just before Lee's surrender in April 1865, and lived to tell about his experiences in one of the most engaging and witty memoirs of the war, *"Company Aytch"; or, A Side Show of the Big Show* (1882). Born on a farm near Columbia, Tenn., on 26 July 1839 and educated at nearby Jackson College, Watson joined the local enthusiastic volunteers for the Confederate army just as hostilities were about to begin and helped organize Company H of the 1st Tennessee Infantry Regiment. By the time the war was over, of the original 3,150 members of the 1st Tennessee, only 125 men survived; Sam Watkins was one of them. He returned home to nurse his wounds, marry, father eight children, and in 1881 begin to contribute sketches about his experiences to the local newspaper, the *Columbia Herald*, and to several Civil War magazines. Most of his sketches were collected into a book published the following year as *"Company Aytch."*

Watkins's memoir is distinguished from hundreds of other such accounts by his comic style and engaging personality. He had a way with words and invested his narrative with a skillful degree of literary artistry. His uses of irony, humor, metaphor, imagery, fable, and description compare favorably with such authors as Stephen Crane, Ambrose Bierce, and Mark Twain among his contemporaries. In fact, it appears likely that the younger Crane, inexperienced in battle and the ways of war, may have read and borrowed from Watkins in his classic novel *The Red Badge of Courage* (1895). Watkins's book has never been long out of print. Civil War historian and novelist Shelby Foote once noted, "Sam Watkins is by far my favorite Civil War memorialist," and documentary filmmaker Ken Burns called the book "a memoir of staggering significance, wit, and beauty." Watkins deserves to be read alongside the fictional accounts of the war because of his talent as a writer and the authenticity of his experience in one of the worst conflicts in human history.

M. THOMAS INGE
Randolph-Macon College

Sam Watkins, *"Company Aytch"; or, A Sideshow of the Big Show and Other Sketches*, ed. M. Thomas Inge (1999); Andrew C. Higgins, *Mississippi Quarterly* (Winter 2004–05).

Eudora Welty, 1977 (William R. Ferris Collection, Southern Folklife Collection, Wilson Library, University of North Carolina at Chapel Hill)

Welty, Eudora

(1909–2001) WRITER.

Eudora Welty was born 13 April 1909 in Jackson, Miss., the daughter of parents from Ohio and West Virginia. Educated in the Jackson public schools, she went to college for two years at the Mississippi State College for Women and completed her formal education at the University of Wisconsin. After some courses in journalism at Columbia University, she returned home in 1932 after the death of her father.

She had been writing all along—as student newspapers and annuals attest—but upon returning to Mississippi from New York City, she began writing in earnest. She wrote a society column for the *Memphis Commercial Appeal*, and in downtown Jackson she worked at a radio station at the top of the Lamar Life building, which her father had been instrumental in developing. Most importantly, during the mid-1930s she traveled for the Works Progress Administration throughout Mississippi backwoods, mostly taking pictures of rural peoples, black and white, engaging them in conversation, and learning what she could of their lives. This time was prodigiously formative of her imagination, as she later attested in her writings and interviews, and as her several books of photographs amply document.

During this formative period, she brought together a collection of these photographs and the stories based on them (calling the book *Black Saturday*), which she tried to sell to New York publishers, who were not interested. She also began selling her stories to smaller literary journals throughout the country. Her developing reputation led her to the literary agent Diarmuid Russell, son of the Irish poet A. E., whom Welty admired. She and Russell became lifelong friends; he gave her advice and helped her to sell her stories to more influential national magazines.

Her first book, *A Curtain of Green* (1941), is a collection of many of the stories she had written over the previous years. It was followed immediately by a novella, *The Robber Bridegroom* (1942), *The Wide Net* (stories, 1943), *Delta Wedding* (novel, 1946), *The Golden Apples* (story cycle, 1948), *The Ponder Heart* (novella, 1954), *The Bride of the Innisfallen* (stories, 1955), *The Optimist's Daughter* (novel, 1968), *Losing Battles* (novel, 1970), *One Writer's Beginnings* (autobiography, 1984), and several collections of photographs. *The Optimist's Daughter* won the Pulitzer Prize.

Often taken as a sort of female Faulkner, she is nothing of the sort. When asked about Faulkner's "presence" on the Mississippi literary landscape, she generally responded modestly, "It was like living near a mountain," without even hinting that what most often lives near a mountain is another mountain. Part of critics' trouble with her over the years is that they mistook the surface geniality and "southernness" of her work as her subject, when in fact she used that geniality and those conventions of southern life as a lens to examine precisely many of those conventions, especially family relations, about which very few have written with more insight, more trenchancy, or more love.

Though rooted in Jackson, she traveled widely, in Europe and throughout the United States, especially in her later years, when she was the grande dame of American letters—and continued to be, as she often put it, "underfoot locally" as a beloved celebrity in Jackson. She was invited to dozens of universities to give readings, to teach, and to receive honorary degrees. She died in July 2001.

NOEL POLK
Mississippi State University

Michael Kreyling, *Author and Agent: Eudora Welty and Diarmuid Russell* (1991); Suzanne Marrs, *Eudora Welty: A Biography* (2005); Noel Polk, *Eudora Welty A Bibliography of Her Work* (1994).

Wilcox, James

(b. 1949) WRITER.
James Wilcox creates in his novels a vivid world populated by small-town characters of the modern South who are hilarious in their eccentricities while irresistibly endearing in their human imperfections and struggles.

Wilcox's parents were both classical musicians who relocated to Hammond,

La., from Wisconsin after World War II, shortly before Wilcox was born. His father, a Methodist, was born in England and came to the United States when he was five; his Polish mother was Catholic, the church in which Wilcox was raised. Although he does not describe himself as a musical prodigy, Wilcox was a talented cellist and played in the Baton Rouge Symphony in high school. After graduation he headed north, attending Yale University where he studied under both Robert Penn Warren and Harold Bloom and began to write fiction. After completing his studies at Yale in 1971, he moved to New York where, with Warren's help, he found a job in publishing, rising from an editorial assistant position to associate editor in seven years.

At the age of 29, Wilcox walked away from publishing to devote himself to writing full time. After working diligently for three years, including a dire stretch that found him typing mailing labels for an attorney to support himself, Wilcox got his first big break when the *New Yorker* published his short story "Mr. Ray" in January 1981. It was the first of many of his works to be set in Tula Springs, a fictionalized town between Baton Rouge and the Mississippi state line (a geography much like his native Hammond).

Buoyed by this publication, he wrote the novel *Modern Baptists* (1983). It is primarily the story of Bobby Pickens, most often referred to as "Mr. Pickens," a 41-year-old bachelor and somewhat hapless assistant manager of Sonny Boy Bargain Store in Tula Springs. A sparkling review that ran on the front page of the *New York Times Book Review* hailed him as a "comic genius."

His next three novels, *North Gladiola* (1985), *Miss Undine's Living Room* (1987), and *Sort of Rich* (1989), continue the setting of Tula Springs, a quirky hamlet that captures the absurdities of small southern towns with great detail. It is the kind of place where the character Mrs. Coco in *North Gladiola* vows not to buy any "more bargain makeup from that roadside stand by the snake ranch." While critics draw the obvious comparisons between Tula Springs and the wholly developed world of Faulkner's Yoknapatawpha County, the settings are vastly different. Wilcox's work is very much rooted in the New South, a place where residents are often transients, such as a Korean doctoral student or a New Yorker who served in the Peace Corps, and where characters eat at a restaurant known as Dick's China Nights.

Polite Sex (1991) was Wilcox's first novel not set in Tula Springs, although it did feature a cast of characters from there living in New York. Wilcox's next novel, his sixth in a decade, was *Guest of a Sinner* (1993), also set in New York but absent the cast of characters from Tula Springs.

Wilcox's novels came with less frequency after that. *Plain and Normal* (1998) again featured characters from Tula Springs living in New York, this time centered on a character dealing with his homosexuality. *Heavenly Days* (2003), Wilcox's most recent work, was his first book to be based in Tula Springs in 14 years; it is the story of Lou Jones, a former college professor with a Ph.D. in music who spends her days working as a receptionist at a fundamentalist-owned "makeover franchise."

Complex plots that are not easily summarized on a book jacket are a key trait of Wilcox's fiction; another is his depiction of women, often the central characters in his novels. In an interview in 1997, he credits having three sisters as helping him to understand and write about the opposite sex.

Although he lived more than 30 years in New York, Wilcox has returned to Louisiana, where holds the Robert Penn Warren Professorship at Louisiana State University in Baton Rouge.

JOE SAMUEL STARNES
Saint Joseph's University

John Lowe, *Mississippi Quarterly* (Fall 1999); Charles Pastoor, *Renascence* (Spring 2006); James B. Stewart, *New Yorker* (27 June 1994).

Williams, Ben Ames

(1889–1953) WRITER.

Known as the prolific, versatile, and best-selling author of short stories and novels, Ben Ames Williams was the author of more than 400 published short stories and dedicated his later career to writing mystery novels, thrillers, and historical fiction. His most widely read novel, *Leave Her to Heaven* (1944), a story of obsessive love and murder, was translated into seven languages, made into a motion picture starring Gene Tierney and Vincent Price, and recommended by the *Harvard Law Review* to prospective students as a book "of value in preparation for the study of law" for its portrayal of the murder trial. His most substantial best seller at 1,500

pages, *House Divided* (1947), was the culmination of two decades of meticulous research on the Civil War, chronicling the psychological and emotional toll of war on the Currain family, whose close family friend in the book, General James Longstreet, was a real person and Williams's great-uncle.

A grandson of Welsh immigrants, Ben Ames Williams was born 7 March 1889 in Macon, Miss. While he was still an infant, his family relocated to Jackson, Ohio, where he cultivated a childhood love for books and worked for the *Jackson Standard Journal*, edited and owned by his father, Daniel Webster Williams. After high school study in Cardiff, Wales, where his father was U.S. consul, Williams attended Dartmouth College (A.B., 1910) and he returned to the life of a newsman, taking a position as a reporter with the *Boston American*. His first story, "The Wings of Lias," was published in *Smith's Magazine* in 1915. Two years later, after achieving wide publication in "pulp" magazines, Williams began a career-long association with the *Saturday Evening Post*, which published more than 135 of his stories and articles during his career. Williams's influences included Maupassant, O. Henry, Kipling, and Balzac, and his move from "pulp" publications like *Smith's* to "slick" magazines like the *Saturday Evening Post* allowed him to indulge in greater complexities of place and characterization for a more erudite audience.

Though a difficult period for him as a writer, Williams's years as a newspaperman were productive personally; in 1912 he married Florence Talpey, a native of Maine and a graduate of Wellesley, who, like Williams, had lived abroad as a child. Their marriage began Williams's relationship with the quiet idiosyncrasies of rural Maine, a setting in many of his later stories and novels, notably the popular "Fraternity" stories, located in the imaginary town of the same name. In 1919 his short story "They Grind Exceeding Small" was among 15 stories chosen for the first O. Henry Prize collection, and his first novel, *All the Brothers Were Valiant*, was published.

Though predominantly a writer of popular tastes, Williams's predilection for historical research prompted his work in 1949 on a controversial updated edition of Mary Boykin Chesnut's *A Diary from Dixie*, one of the most important sources for *House Divided*. His lack of scholarly acumen was alternately hailed by reviewers and lamented by academic critics, but Williams's work on the edition signaled his unwavering immersion in Civil War history, borne out in his final work, *The Unconquered* (1953), a sequel to *House Divided* completed just before Williams's fatal heart attack during a curling match. These two historical novels, moving from Virginia and North Carolina during the Civil War to Reconstruction-era New Orleans, constitute the heart of Williams's literary engagement with the South. Beyond the strong ties between his historical fiction and his southern heritage, Williams remains known primarily for his ability to convey psychological depth and demand moral rigor, as well as his prolific output; he published at least one book each year

during the 1920s. Williams's other important novels include *Splendor* (1927), *The Strumpet Sea* (1938), *Come Spring* (1940), *Time of Peace* (1942), and *Owen Glen* (1950). Beyond his longtime relationship with the *Saturday Evening Post*, Williams also published short stories frequently in *Collier's* and edited *Letters from Fraternity* (1931) and *Amateurs at War: The American Soldier in Action* (1943).

JANE CARR
University of Virginia

Richard Cary, *Colby Library Quarterly* (September 1963, December 1973); Mary Boykin Chesnut, *A Diary from Dixie*, ed. Ben Ames Williams; *Harvard Law Review* (April 1945); *New York Times* (5 February 1953); Henry T. Shanks, *Journal of Southern History* (May 1950); Wendell Holmes Stephenson, *American Historical Review* (April 1950); Philip Stevick, in *Dictionary of Literary Biography*, vol. 102, ed. Bobby Ellen Kimbel (1991); John W. Wilson, *College English* (March 1949).

Williams, Tennessee

(1911–1983) PLAYWRIGHT.
Tennessee [Thomas Lanier] Williams was born in Columbus, Miss., in 1911. His mother was the daughter of an Episcopal minister. His father, from Tennessee, had among his ancestors Sidney Lanier and Tennessee's first governor and first senator. A traveling salesman, he was home very little; and his wife and children, Williams and his older sister Rose, lived with his wife's parents. When he was still very young, the family moved to Clarksdale, Miss., where they lived for several years. Around 1919 Williams's father moved his family to St.

Louis, thus taking his children out of a traditional southern environment to a big-city life, in which at least part of the time they lived in apartments in relatively poor neighborhoods.

The nostalgia for a southern past reflected in plays such as his first two successes, *The Glass Menagerie* (1945) and *A Streetcar Named Desire* (1947), is in part clearly a product of Williams's bitter dislike of the new environment and his fond memories, perhaps exaggerated, of the old. Williams himself is reflected in Tom Wingfield in *Menagerie*, who, like Williams, became a wanderer because of his unhappiness with his home environment, and in Blanche DuBois in *Streetcar*, who, like Williams, bitterly misses her gracious past and finds the modern world alien and forbidding. *Streetcar* and a later play, *Cat on a Hot Tin Roof* (1955), won the Pulitzer Prize. After *The Night of the Iguana* (1962), his plays failed to be popular successes, but he continued to write and be produced. All his major plays are set in the South and concern southerners, except *Iguana* (Mexico) and the expressionistic *Camino Real* (1953, set in Central America).

His southerners represent a wide variety: most importantly, Tom's mother, Amanda, in *Menagerie*, a genteel southerner displaced in St. Louis; Blanche and her sister, Stella, fallen aristocrats in lower-class New Orleans; Stella's husband, Stanley Kowalski, and his friends, born to the neighborhood; an upper-class New Orleans family in *Suddenly Last Summer* (1956); transplanted Sicilians in a Gulf Coast town in *The Rose Tattoo* (1951); middle-class, small-town southerners and Latin American "invaders" in the early 20th century in *Summer and Smoke* (1948); a corrupt southern politician in *Sweet Bird of Youth* (1959); and poor white southerners risen to money and power in *Cat on a Hot Tin Roof*. Oddly, however, his plays include almost no blacks and none prominently.

The most important dramatist to come out of the South, Williams provided innumerable insights into southern life and character, conveying authenticity to southerner and non-southerner alike. Like Chekhov, his dramatic master, Williams's best plays go beyond the world of their origin to achieve portraits of human nature and human situations that are of universal interest and validity.

Despite a nervous collapse, alcoholism, drug dependence, and scant critical acclaim, Williams continued to write in his Key West, Fla., home until his death, at 71, in a New York hotel room. Ironically, and against his stated wishes, he was buried in Calvary Cemetery in St. Louis, the city he claimed to despise. "He came into the theater bringing his poetry," dramatist Arthur Miller said in his final tribute, "his hardened edge of romantic adoration of the lost and the beautiful."

JACOB ADLER
Purdue University

Kenneth Holditch and Richard F. Leavitt, *Tennessee Williams and the South* (2002); Esther Jackson, *The Broken World of Tennessee Williams* (1965); Brenda Murphy, *Tennessee Williams and Elia Kazan: A Collaboration in the Theatre* (1992); Jac Tharpe, ed., *Tennessee Williams: A Tribute* (1977); Nancy

Tischler, *Tennessee Williams: Rebellious Puritan* (1961); Tennessee Williams, *Five O'clock Angel: Letters of Tennessee Williams to Maria St. Just, 1948–1982* (1990), *Notebooks*, ed. Margaret Bradham Thornton (2007).

Wolfe, Thomas

(1900–1938) WRITER.

His parentage and the time and place of Thomas Wolfe's birth created the cultural tug and pull underlying most of his writing. His father's Pennsylvania roots and his mother's close ties to the southern highlands were the first of many opposing forces that shaped Wolfe and were to be the subject matter of his plays and novels.

Born in a place (Asheville, N.C.) still suffering from the ravages of the Civil War and Reconstruction, Wolfe not only sensed the brighter prospects of the North but felt the clash of power and ideas that kept largely pro-Union western North Carolina and pro-Confederacy eastern North Carolina from solving scores of problems facing the state. "The Men of Old Catawba" explores some of the cultural differences dividing his native state.

Much of western North Carolina remained poverty-stricken long after other areas of the state had begun to recover from the war. Yet amid the poverty still evident in Asheville were signs of fabulous wealth, such as the building of the Biltmore House. Thousands of tourists crowding into such expensive quarters as Grove Park Inn began to vie with one another for choice lots in Asheville and surrounding towns. A boom in building seemed to point the way out of poverty and toward power for Ashevillians and their mountain neighbors. Wolfe's mother lodged many of the tourists in her boardinghouse, the Old Kentucky Home, and bought, swapped, and sold lots with such zeal and success that she became one of Asheville's wealthiest women. Asheville was thus aswirl with diverse groups of people and ideas when Wolfe was growing up there.

Beginning with *Welcome to Our City*, a play Wolfe wrote while at Harvard (1920–23), and continuing with *Look Homeward, Angel* (1929) and parts of *You Can't Go Home Again* (1940), Wolfe chronicled Asheville's hectic rush toward becoming a tourist mecca, and he reached back in *The Mountains* (1970), *The Hills Beyond* (1941), and *The Web and the Rock* (1939) to trace the patterns of migration, religious beliefs, political notions, and educational values linked to Asheville's southern highlands heritage, which was largely Scotch-Irish with an admixture of German, English, African, and Indian stock.

The time and place of Wolfe's collegiate education also helped to shape him and to provide materials for his plays and novels. When Wolfe attended the University of North Carolina, champions of the ideas and goals of the New South held important posts and were working to solve the economic, educational, and health problems of the state and region. Progressive teaching was in the air, but Wolfe still clung to many of the agrarian values of his maternal forebears, a position made clear in his sympathetic portrayal of Nebraska Crane in *You Can't Go Home Again*.

Thomas Wolfe and his mother at her boarding house, the Old Kentucky Home, Asheville, N.C., 1937
(Thomas Wolfe Collection, Pack Memorial Public Library, Asheville, North Carolina)

Still another shaping experience at Chapel Hill was his study of Hegelian philosophy under Horace Williams, who reinforced Wolfe's tendency to see opposite positions. As the late C. Hugh Holman showed many years ago, this philosophic training informs the picture Wolfe painted of the South and North and provides vital clues to understanding Wolfe and his surrogate protagonists, Eugene Gant and George Webber.

His graduate studies at Harvard, his subsequent teaching and writing career in New York City, and his European travels led Wolfe to see the provincialism of his youth, but at the same time the golden visions of the North inspired by his father's stories were growing tarnished. During the years following the 1929 stock market crash, Wolfe saw both the common man's suffering and his heroic will to endure and thus turned from his Joycean dream of winning love, fortune, and fame to work toward achieving a dream of America he had had in France.

He would celebrate America, become its bard, speak as its prophet, embrace both the South and the North, and assume the mantle of Whitman. But Wolfe came to this bardic role with some limitations: he had not lost the mountaineer's penchant for deflating the social claims of plantation aristocrats, he excessively despised the money-grubbing proclivities of Snopesian people escaping from hard times, he too eagerly defined and described his world in Hegelian terms, and he had not overcome racial prejudice. Still, his achievement as a writer was enormous: one of his contemporaries, William Faulkner, ranked Wolfe as one of the nation's greatest writers.

JOHN L. IDOL JR.
Clemson University

David Donald, *Look Homeward: A Life of Thomas Wolfe* (1987); Leslie A. Field, comp., *Thomas Wolfe: Three Decades of Criticism* (1968); C. Hugh Holman, in *South: Modern Southern Literature in Its Cultural Setting*, ed. Louis D. Rubin Jr., and Robert Jacobs (1961); Louis D. Rubin Jr., *Thomas Wolfe: The Weather of His Youth* (1955); Floyd C. Watkins, *Thomas Wolfe's Characters: Portraits from Life* (1957).

Wolfe, Tom

(b. 1931) WRITER.

Tom Wolfe's wildly distinctive prose has been defining American decades and roiling the nation's literary landscape for more than 40 years. A native Virginian turned Upper East Side New Yorker, he has maintained his congenial southern accent and dandy white suits while his skewering, breathless voice on the page—first in the advent of New Journalism and then in vast novels rooted in contemporary realism—has become so very unmistakable that it has acquired its own adjective: *Wolfean*.

Born in Richmond, he was named after his father, an agronomist and editor of the *Southern Planter*. He is of no relation to writer Thomas Wolfe, although the North Carolinian's fluid style made a vivid impression. "He was one of the first novelists that I read," he told an interviewer. "I was just swept away by the sort of thing that he did. I was always convinced, incidentally, that Thomas Wolfe was kin to me, and it was very hard for my parents to convince me that he wasn't."

Wolfe attended Washington and Lee University, where he was one of the founders of the literary magazine *Shenandoah*, and graduated in 1951. He went on to earn a Ph.D. in American studies from Yale University in 1957. He worked as a reporter for three years for the *Springfield (Mass.) Union* and three years for the *Washington Post* before joining the *New York Herald Tribune* in 1962.

At Washington and Lee, where a coat and tie was mandatory, he developed his taste for fancy dress, saying he "took great delight in wearing black or maroon shirts, silver-blue ties and powder-gray camel's hair coats." As many in the rebellious 1960s shucked traditional dress codes, Wolfe became more formal, donning the white suits he is famous for in the sartorial style he has called "counterbohemian."

He got his first national magazine assignment for *Esquire* in 1963, and it proved to be a formative moment, not only for Wolfe but also for the movement that would be known as New Journalism. After doing extensive reporting on custom-built cars in California, he suffered writer's block and told his editor that he was unable to complete the assignment. His editor told him to type up his notes and send them in for another writer to finish the piece. In one night Wolfe banged out 49 pages in a stream-of-consciousness style and delivered it to *Esquire*. Editors decided to run it as it was, and the flamboyant Wolfean style was born.

His first book took the name of that article: *The Kandy-Kolored Tangerine-Flake Streamline Baby* (1965), a collection of 22 journalistic essays. Three years later his publisher issued two of his books on the same day: *The Electric Kool-Aid Acid Test*, a look into Ken Kesey's LSD-loaded band of Merry Pranksters, and *The Pump House Gang*, his second collection of essays. Both books became best sellers.

Three more nonfiction works followed in the 1970s, including two that were illustrated with Wolfe's drawings, and an anthology he edited entitled *The New Journalism* (1973). His journalistic work introduced several famous phrases into print, most notably "the me decade," a pithy description of the seventies.

In 1979 *The Right Stuff*, an entertaining examination of the early years of the U.S. space program, appeared to rave reviews and won the National Book Award for Nonfiction. It was made into a blockbuster 1983 movie that was nominated for eight Academy Awards.

Wolfe published three more journalistic works in the early 1980s before turning to fiction. *The Bonfire of the Vanities* (1987), his first novel, was written with regular deadlines every two weeks and serialized in 25 issues of *Rolling Stone* magazine spanning from 1984 to 1985. He rewrote it extensively for book form. It is the quintessential New York 1980s novel, an epic tale of race and greed amid the clash of the city's haves and have-nots centering on a hit-and-run car accident in the Bronx.

Wolfe worked on his second novel for more than a decade. *A Man in Full* (1998) is set alternately in Atlanta and the San Francisco Bay area, and, like his first novel, it delves into issues of wealth, race, and class. It was a finalist for the National Book Award for Fiction. *I Am Charlotte Simmons* (2005) also takes place in the South, exploring the hedonistic revelries and sexual habits of students at the fictional Dupont University set in North Carolina. All three of Wolfe's novels were received with wildly varying reviews, ranging from raving praise to stinging criticism, and all spent extended appearances on best-seller lists.

JOE SAMUEL STARNES
Saint Joseph's University

Dorothy Scura, ed., *Conversations with Tom Wolfe* (1990); Tom Wolfe, *Hooking Up* (2000).

Woodward, C. Vann

(1908–1999) HISTORIAN.
Born 13 November 1908 in Vanndale, Ark., to Hugh Allison and Bess Vann Woodward, Comer Vann Woodward was the most influential historian of the 20th-century South. Educated at Emory University (Ph.B., philosophy, 1930), Columbia University (A.M., political science, 1933), and the University of North Carolina at Chapel Hill (Ph.D., 1937), Woodward did not come to the discipline of history by a straight line but rather through a succession of student and teaching careers in the humanities, which course produced an undying interest in creative literature that kept him in the company of great writers, from Robert Penn Warren and Cleanth Brooks to John Updike. After briefly teaching English at Georgia Institute of Technology, he entered the study of history in 1934, was one of the attendees at the first meeting of the Southern Historical Association in that year, and subsequently taught at the University of Florida, Scripps College, the University of Virginia, Johns Hopkins University, and Yale University, where he became Sterling Professor of History and kept an office until late in the 20th century. Yale University has established a chair in history in honor of Woodward and his son Peter Vincent, a student of political science who, like the historian's wife, Glenn Boyd Macleod, and a number of close friends, succumbed to cancer at an early age.

Woodward showed an unusual blend of activism and detachment, of aristocratic provenance and fascination with the masses, of great privilege conferred by family and friends and iconoclastic rebelliousness, of professional specialization and an eclectic training. Evoking irony in his writings, he also lived a life of considerable irony, demonstrating what David Minter has called "deep reciprocities" between experiences of his personal life and the history he wrote.

Growing up in Arkansas during a period of racial violence and of grinding regional poverty, Woodward was nurtured by a family of devout Methodists committed to moderate social reform. Forsaking their path, he left an Arkadelphia Methodist college for Emory University, studying philosophy there with Leroy Loemker, who taught him German existentialism and demonstrated to him a life that successfully combined scholarly excellence with social activism. After brief seasons teaching literature at Georgia Institute of Technology and studying political science at Columbia University, Woodward entered the University of North Carolina, studying with Howard Kennedy Beale; there he developed a historical interpretation based on class analysis and economic determinism, writing a dissertation that became his first book and his only biography, a celebration of Georgia populism entitled *Tom Watson: Agrarian Rebel* (1938). In subsequent years, during World War II, he began to integrate his understanding of creative literature with this economic history, producing his most enduring scholarship, *Origins of the New South, 1877–1913* (1951), and his most influential study, *The Strange Career of Jim Crow* (1955; subsequent revisions to 1974), which the Reverend Martin Luther King Jr. called "the Bible of the civil rights movement." In his provocative biography and in his magisterial 1951 study of the region, he established certain themes of interpretation that set historians onto new paths of exploration—and considerable and continuing debate. In these works, and in all later works, he said there was a sharp discontinuity, or break, in southern history caused by the Civil War, with a new group of more bourgeois leaders replacing the old agrarian elite; he also insisted that certain aspects of race relations, especially the legal de jure segregation called Jim Crow, were essentially New South and products of neither Reconstruction nor the Old South. In all these works, too, among many other things, he tried to use the tools of irony in his style of writing to belittle those with power and authority and to uplift those, especially black and white allies in the rural countryside, who sought radical economic redress of social injustice.

After distinguishing himself as a professor at Johns Hopkins University and as a visiting professor at Oxford University, he became Sterling Professor at Yale University in 1961. At both Johns Hopkins and Yale, he directed excellent graduate students, three of whom earned the Pulitzer Prize, one of whom became director of the National Endowment for the Humanities, and all of whom made their own impact on the study of southern history. At Yale

he became an essayist and an editor, turning out the collections of poignant essays, *The Burden of Southern History* (1960) and *American Counterpoint: Slavery and Racism in the North-South Dialogue* (1971), while editing the Pulitzer Prize–winning *Mary Chesnut's Civil War* (1981). He continued to travel to conferences and to work with young scholars, and he continued to turn out essays both provoking and graceful, a number of which were collected usefully in an interesting set, *The Future of the Past* (1989).

His work received the Bancroft and Sydnor awards; and he served as president of the Southern Historical Association, which he worked mightily to integrate; the American Historical Association; and the Organization of American Historians. Inside the profession, his interpretation of history, a subtle melding of lyric determinants, has been criticized for underestimating the force of racism and understating the longevity of segregation; and many others have scored him for overvaluing the reformism inherent in agrarian movements at the turn of the century. Although he paid attention to women in history in ways unprecedented by the scholars who went before him, it is likely a fair judgment that he failed to appreciate the variety of roles played by women in the South. While his judgments in such controversies may finally be ruled incorrect in every instance by subsequent scholars, he, like Charles Beard whom he so admired, will be long remembered as the starting point for the major debates in the discipline of history. Outside the profession, his essays, especially *The Strange Career of Jim Crow* and those in *The Burden of Southern History*, attracted and held the attention of nonspecialist readers and thinkers who appreciated his grace, wit, commitment to moral change, and his insistence that *southern intellectual* and *southern reformist* were not oxymorons.

JOHN HERBERT ROPER
Emory and Henry College

John Herbert Roper, ed., *C. Vann Woodward: A Southern Historian and His Critics* (1997), *C. Vann Woodward, Southerner* (1987), *Journal of Southern History* 67 (2001); C. Vann Woodward, *Thinking Back* (1985), ed., *Responses of the Presidents to Charges of Misconduct* (1974); C. Vann Woodward Papers, Manuscript Division, Library of Yale University, New Haven, Conn.; Glenn Weddington Rainey Papers, Manuscript Collections, Library of Emory University, Atlanta, Ga.; interviews: Woodward, Leroy Loemker, John Hope Franklin, Bennett Harrison Wall, Manning J. Dauer, William G. Carleton, Glenn Weddington Rainey, August Meier, Georgia Watson Craven, J. William Fulbright, and Bola Martin, typescript and corr., Roper Papers of the Southern Historical Collection (SHC) of the Library of the University of North Carolina, Chapel Hill; interview, Charles Crowe with Woodward, tape recording, SHC.

Wright, Richard

(1908–1960) WRITER.

Born near Natchez, Miss., on 4 September 1908, Richard Wright, like the famous protagonist of his first novel, was a native son. The child of a sharecropper who deserted the family in 1914, young Richard moved with his mother during his early years from one to another of the extended family's homes in Arkansas and Jackson, Miss., living in Memphis after he completed the ninth grade. Poverty and the fear and hate typifying post-Reconstruction racial relations in the Lower South, more than the sustaining power of black culture or education in segregated schools, prepared him to be an author. If he omitted from his autobiographical record his experience with middle-class values in his mother's family, or the effect of the motions and rituals of the black world, there was psychological truth in his record of nativity as written in *Black Boy* (1945).

In "The Ethics of Living Jim Crow," published in a Works Progress Administration writer's anthology, *American Stuff* (1937), which first appeared in the year he moved from Chicago to New York City, Wright revealed the dynamics of his life's work as an author. Caste, he says, prescribed his public behavior; but though he knew its requirements, he would not accede. *Uncle Tom's Children* (1938, and expanded 1940), the collection of novellas with which Wright won his first literary success, indicates by an irony of its title the goal southern whites had for southern blacks. The stories are united by the theme of collective response to racist terror, as the children of Uncle Tom refuse to accept the popular stereotype.

Lawd Today was the first example of Richard Wright's extension of southern learning to life in the migrant black communities of the North, but this apprentice novel was not published until 1963. *Native Son* (1940) first carried his insights to a large and appreciative audience. A Guggenheim Fellowship to complete the novel, its selection by the

Richard Wright, Mississippi-born writer who became an expatriate in France, c. 1940
(Archives and Special Collections, University of Mississippi Library, Oxford)

Book-of-the-Month Club, and its arrival within weeks at the top of the best-seller list attested to the appearance of a major American author. In the compelling character of Bigger Thomas, Wright creates a complex symbol of a rising awareness that no risk is too great in order to become master of one's own life. By creating sympathy for Bigger's violent actions, Wright carries the tradition of protest to new lengths.

Wright's next book, *12 Million Black Voices* (1941), presents a folk history extending from slavery's middle passage through the development of an Afro-American culture in the South and the hope of a black nation as a result of migration north. On the other hand, *Black Boy*, an ostensible autobiography representing the birth of the artist, necessarily suppresses the importance of group experience in order to focus on the power of the individual sensibility. Wright forged his identity among his people on southern ground but sought room to write by passage into modern life, symbolized by northern cities. This strategy becomes even clearer in the second part of the autobiography, published as *American Hunger* in 1977.

In time Wright found that Jim Crow knew no regional boundaries. Chicago and then New York constrained him as much as had Mississippi. So in 1946 he moved with his wife, Ellen Poplar, whom he had married in 1941, and their daughter to Paris. Suggestions have been made that the self-imposed exile, which was to last until Wright's death in 1960, sapped his creativity; yet he created two novels concerning American racial relations and politics even after his exile. *The Outsider*, presenting an existentialist antihero living in Chicago and New York, appeared in 1953, and *The Long Dream*, a comprehensive reimagining of coming-of-age in Mississippi, appeared in 1958. Other fiction from the exile years includes *Savage Holiday* (1954), an experiment in raceless fiction, and the collection of stories, old and new, posthumously published as *Eight Men* (1961). This record of production hardly suggests flagging creativity.

Even more important to Wright's career, however, was the energy he found in exile to undertake four studies on a global scale. *Black Power* (1954) relates observations on his travels in the Gold Coast shortly before it became the nation of Ghana; *The Color Curtain* (1956) reports on the anticolonial positions developed at the conference in Bandung; *Pagan Spain* (1957) records a trip into a culture Wright viewed as a survival of premodern Europe; and *White Man Listen!* (1957) collects essays on race in America and the European colonies.

Despite the apparent departure from the experience of the American South in these later works, continuity exists between the original treatments of Jim Crow and the commentary on historical change in Africa and Asia. The prevailing subject remains race relations between whites and blacks, but beyond that is the more profound connection Wright saw in the special history of "colored" peoples. To be black in America, he believed, was to be marched forcibly into the pain of the modern world. As a representative black American, Wright already had lived the historical experience that awaited the Third World. By the power of literary imagination, Wright with matchless skill drew forth the significance of his southern education for world citizenship.

JOHN M. REILLY
State University of New York at Albany

Charles T. Davis and Michel Fabre, *Richard Wright: A Primary Bibliography* (1982); Michel Fabre, *The Unfinished Quest of Richard Wright* (1973); Eugene E. Miller, *Voice of a Native Son: The Poetics of Richard Wright* (1990); John M. Reilly, in *Black American Writers: Bibliographical Essays*, ed. M. Thomas Inge and Maurice Duke (1978); Hazel Rowley, *Richard Wright: The Life and Times* (2002).

Yarbrough, Steve

(b. 1956) WRITER.

Since the beginning of Steve Yarbrough's writing career, he has written about the place he was born and raised—the Mississippi Delta. Born in the mid-Delta town of Indianola, Miss., on 29 August 1956, he began writing short stories in high school. While his love of reading took him places far beyond the borders of the Mississippi Delta, he has consistently used the Delta as the setting for his work.

Yarbrough was not the first to write about his Delta hometown. In 1937 John Dollard wrote on race relations within the town in his *Caste and Class in a Southern Town*. Soon after, Hortense Powdermaker used Indianola—"Cottonville"—as the setting for her 1939 ethnographic study of an African American Delta community, *After Freedom*. Somewhat more recently,

Willard B. Gatewood Jr. included in his book, *Theodore Roosevelt and the Art of Controversy: Episodes from the White House Years* (1970), a chapter entitled "The Indianola Post Office Affair." It is from this "post office affair" that Yarbrough draws inspiration for his critically acclaimed novel *Visible Spirits* (2001). The setting for the novel is the fictional town of Loring, Miss., and the plot is a fictionalized account of the historical events surrounding Minnie Cox, the 1902 African American Indianola postmaster whom white townsfolk threatened with violence to protest the power blacks held in the South. The actual event led to President Theodore Roosevelt stepping in and shutting down the Indianola post office, while continuing Cox's salary.

In his next novel, *Prisoners of War* (2004), also set in Loring, Yarbrough fictionalizes the true story of World War II German prisoners of war imprisoned in camps located throughout Mississippi, 10 of which were located in the Delta. The novel earned Yarbrough the distinction of being named one of five PEN/Faulkner Award finalists in 2005.

Yarbrough earned B.A. and M.A. degrees from the University of Mississippi and an M.F.A. in creative writing from the University of Arkansas. He spent the next four years teaching at Virginia Polytechnic Institute and State University. In 1988 Yarbrough left the South to join the English department at California State University, Fresno, but his writing has remained focused on the Mississippi of his youth. Yet, despite the historical nature of Yarbrough's *Visible Spirits* and *Prisoners of War*, the majority of his work deals with the modern Mississippi Delta, often illuminating its social and cultural stasis. *The End of California* (2006) tells the tale of a man returning to the Mississippi Delta after having left the area following his high school graduation. He returns to find a Delta much like the one he left years ago: a place where racial hostilities are evident, cotton is still big money, and Sunday is sacred. However, Yarbrough's residents of the Delta now visit on cell phones, drink Starbucks coffee, and do Google searches. Much like Faulkner's Yoknapatawpha County, Yarbrough's Loring wrestles with its own identity, resisting change yet helpless to prevent it.

Yarbrough's other works include the collections of short stories *Family Men* (1990), *Mississippi History* (1994), and *Veneer* (1998), and his only novel set in Indianola, *The Oxygen Man* (1999). His stories have appeared in a Pushcart Prize anthology and in *Best American Mystery Stories 1998*, and his awards include the Mississippi Authors Award, the California Book Award, and the 2000 Mississippi Institute of Arts and Letters Award for Fiction. He served as the John and Renée Grisham Writer in Residence at the University of Mississippi in 1999–2000.

JAMES G. THOMAS JR.
University of Mississippi

Suzanne Berne, *New York Times Book Review* (6 November 1994); Linda A. McMurtrey, *Clarion-Ledger* (25 September 1994); Steve Yarbrough, *Oxford American*, no. 16 (1997).

Yerby, Frank
(1916–1991) WRITER.

Frank Garvin Yerby, one of the most popular novelists to set tales in the Old South, was born in Augusta, Ga., on 5 September 1916. He completed degrees at Paine College (A.B., 1937) and Fisk University (M.A., 1938) and did graduate work at the University of Chicago. A black man, Yerby published several excellent short stories from 1944 to 1946 dealing with racial themes. Although he won a major award for his short fiction, Yerby's fame and fortune rest on his widely popular romance novels, the first of which was published in 1946 and sold more than 2 million copies. Like many of his novels to follow, *The Foxes of Harrow* was set in the antebellum South and tapped public interest in the Old South that had been fostered by the phenomenal success of Margaret Mitchell's *Gone with the Wind* (1936).

Yerby's southern romances, including such titles as *A Woman Called Fancy* (1951), *Benton's Row* (1954), and *Griffin's Way* (1962), dominated popular fiction set in the Old South for nearly two decades. His works were meticulously researched and included a wealth of elaborate and surprisingly accurate period detail in such areas as costuming, architecture, southern society, and even slave life. One critic termed *Fair Oaks* (1957) a "primer in black history."

The novels were primarily romantic glimpses of the planter elite and were aimed at a predominantly white, female audience. This led many critics to condemn his work as potboiler fiction, and others have often charged that he ignored racial issues. Yerby once countered the latter charge by saying that the novelist does not have the right to "inflict on the public his private ideas on politics, religion or race." In most respects the charges were unfair, for Yerby managed to influence the ideas and values of far more readers through historical romance than could possibly have been reached by other forms of fiction. This point is demonstrated by Yerby's own career, for he did attempt a few novels with racial themes. These included *The Old Gods Laugh* (1964) and *The Dahomian* (1971), both of which sold poorly in comparison to his plantation novels.

Yet Frank Yerby's impact was not in the area of popular and accurate history. His importance rests on his fostering of public interest in the antebellum South and his fiction's impact on extending the romantic ideal of the South as one great plantation. Besides Mitchell's *Gone with the Wind* and Kyle Onstott's *Mandingo* (1957), the novels of Frank Yerby did more to standardize the plantation fiction genre than did the works of any other author. Apart from his careful attention to historic detail, Yerby's major contribution to the fictional portrayal of the Old South was an entrance into the bedrooms of the planters. His incredibly successful fiction helped to solidify the popular impression of the antebellum South as a land of "moonlight and magnolias," of aristocratic life-styles, of beautiful belles, and of dashing and handsome young gentlemen.

CHRISTOPHER D. GEIST
Bowling Green State University

James L. Hill, in *Perspectives of Black Popular Culture* (1990); Jack Temple Kirby, *Media-Made Dixie: The South in the American Imagination* (1978); Jack B. Moore, *Journal of Popular Culture* (Spring 1975); Frank Yerby, *Harper's* (October 1959).

Young, Al

(b. 1939) WRITER AND EDITOR.

Appointed in 2005 as the second poet laureate in the state of California, Mississippi native Al Young has fashioned an extraordinarily prolific and varied writing career since the publication of his first collection of poems, *Dancing*, in 1969. A poet, novelist, memoirist, and essayist, and a performer as well as a screenwriter and editor, Young has often been considered one of the finest chroniclers of the American musical experience. *Kinds of Blue*, his landmark "musical memoir," wonderfully charted Young's coming of age through the blues, jazz, soul, and rhythm and blues hits of his times.

The son of a navy shipman, Young was born in Ocean Springs, Miss., in 1939, where he spent the first years of his life. His family relocated to Detroit, where Young became active in music and literary circles and briefly attended the University of Michigan. Transferring to the San Francisco area in 1961, where he has been based ever since, Young published stories and poems in various magazines, did a stint as a disc jockey, graduated from the University of California at Berkeley with a degree in Spanish in 1969, and then set off on a peripatetic career as a creative writing teacher and lecturer.

His first novel, *Snakes*, won the American Library Association Notable Book of the Year Citation in 1970. Over the next three decades, Young authored four other novels, eight collections of poetry, and several works of narrative nonfiction, memoir and essays, including *Bodies and Soul*, another musical chronicle that received an American Book Award. Young's work has been noted for its originality, language play, rhythm, humor, and insight. Young's southern roots, especially in music, rarely veer too far from his work. In his novel, *Seduction by Light*, a former Mississippi entertainer deals with the travails of life in Beverly Hills in a comic look at southern California.

As the cofounder of pioneering multicultural journals, such as *Yardbird* and *Quilt*, coeditor of several notable anthologies, including *Califia: California Poetry* and *The Literature from California* (2 vols.), and California poet laureate for 2005–7, Young has maintained his reputation as an African American mentor for multigenerational voices of literature in California and the rest of the country.

JEFF BIGGERS
Illinois

Dorothy Abbott, ed., *Mississippi Writers: Reflections of Childhood and Youth*, vol. 1: *Fiction* (1985); James P. Draper, ed., *Black Literature Criticism*, vol. 3 (1992).

Young, Stark

(1881–1963) WRITER AND CRITIC. Born in Como, Miss., on 11 October 1881, Stark Young, a versatile figure in the Southern Literary Renaissance, devoted his life entirely to the arts and achieved widespread recognition for his contributions as teacher, poet, playwright, director, drama critic, fiction writer, essayist, translator, and painter. His parents were both descended from distinguished families who emigrated from the British Isles in the 17th and early 18th centuries.

Young's feelings and attitudes were powerfully influenced by the southern ways of living in Como and Oxford, Miss., to which his father moved after his second marriage. Young attended elementary school in Como and received his baccalaureate from the University of Mississippi. In 1902 he was awarded the master of arts degree from Columbia University. He taught English at the University of Mississippi, the University of Texas, and Amherst College, and began publishing poetry, plays, and aesthetic criticism.

After moving to New York in 1921, Young entered a period of intense activity in the theater. He became drama critic for the *New Republic* and a member of its editorial board as well as that of *Theatre Arts*. Soon he was recognized as the leading New York critic. He associated himself with the Provincetown Players and the Theatre Guild. His own plays, *The Saint* (1925) and *The Colonnade* (1924), both dealing with southern themes and reflecting Young's southern values, were well received. As early as 1923 he began to assemble from his drama criticism several volumes treating virtually every aspect of the theater: *The Flower in Drama* (1923), *Glamour* (1925), *Theatre Practice* (1926), and *The Theatre* (1927).

While still involved in drama criticism, Young turned to fiction. He published *Heaven Trees* (1926), *The Torches Flare* (1928), and *River House* (1929). In 1930 he wrote the concluding essay, "Not in Defense, but in Memoriam," for *I'll Take My Stand*, supporting the manifesto of the Nashville Agrarians. In all of these works, as in others like *The Three Fountains* (1924), *Encaustics* (1926), *The Street of the Islands* (1930), and *Feliciana* (1935), Young's object was to identify those elements of life in the Old South that should be preserved in subsequent generations. His final novel, *So Red the Rose* (1934), was the most complete and powerful statement of his position. Although critical of the urban, industrial, highly competitive life in the North, Young had no desire to resurrect the southern civilization that had perished in the Civil War. Consistently, he defended the traditional values of the individual, the family, and the community, values that ultimately derived from classical humanism and the art of Western society.

By 1940 Young believed that the New York theater had declined notably from the promise and achievements of the 1920s and early 1930s. When changes at the *New Republic* rendered his position there less congenial, he began to think of retirement; and in 1947, after writing more than a thousand essays during the previous 40 years, he resigned. In 1959 he suffered a stroke from which he never fully recovered. He died 6 January 1963.

JOHN PILKINGTON
University of Mississippi

Thomas L. Connelly, *Tennessee Historical Quarterly* (March 1963); John Pilkington, *Stark Young* (1985), ed., *Stark Young, A Life in the Arts: Letters, 1900–1962* (1975).

Young, Thomas Daniel

(1919–1997) WRITER, CRITIC, AND SCHOLAR.

Born too late to have been part of the Southern Literary Renaissance of the 1920s and 1930s or a major figure in the New Critical revolution of the 1940s and 1950s, Thomas Daniel Young was nevertheless instrumental in establishing the institution of southern literature for the post–World War II generation. From *The Literature of the South*, a vastly influential textbook he edited with Richmond Croom Beatty and Floyd C. Watkins in 1952, to *The History of Southern Literature*, a magisterial volume that he and four colleagues collectively edited in 1985, Young never forgot that all criticism worthy of the name performs a pedagogical function.

Born and raised in the small town of Louisville, Miss., he enrolled at Mississippi Southern College in Hattiesburg in 1919 with the intention of following his father into medicine. Upon discovering a greater love and aptitude for the study of literature, he completed a B.S. in English in 1941. After service in the U.S. Air Force in World War II, he took an M.A. degree from the University of Mississippi in 1948 and a Ph.D. from Vanderbilt in 1950. He taught at a number of colleges and universities over the course of his career, ultimately retiring from Vanderbilt in 1985.

Almost all of Young's published scholarship (25 books and more than

50 major articles, along with countless book reviews, professional papers, and public lectures) was devoted to southern literature, principally to writers associated with Vanderbilt University. In 1965 he and M. Thomas Inge published *Donald Davidson: An Essay and a Bibliography*. Then, in 1968, he and Inge coauthored the first book-length critical study of Davidson's life and work. Finally, in 1974 Young and John Tyree Fain coedited *The Literary Correspondence of Donald Davidson and Allen Tate*. Over the next 13 years, Young would edit two more volumes of Tate's letters. In 1981 he and John Hindle published *The Republic of Letters in America: The Correspondence of John Peale Bishop and Allen Tate*, and in 1987 he and Elizabeth Sarcone edited *The Correspondence of Andrew Lytle and Allen Tate*.

Despite the usefulness of these volumes, Young is best known for having written or edited eight books on John Crowe Ransom. In particular, *Gentleman in a Dustcoat: A Biography of John Crowe Ransom* (1976) is a significant contribution to the art of literary biography. In addition to presenting the relevant facts of Ransom's life, Young makes sense of his subject's often elliptical poetry and criticism, while establishing his permanent importance in the literary history of the 20th century. In an era when literary fashion seemed to be reacting against virtually everything that Ransom represented, Young resolutely stood against the tide.

As a critic, Young was responsible for no revolutionary new theories. His vocation was to make difficult texts more accessible rather than less so. A student of modern southern fiction might well begin with *The Past in the Present* (1981). In discussing representative novels by Faulkner, Warren, Welty, O'Connor, Percy, and Barth, Young demonstrates the decline of tradition as an animating force in southern culture. Unlike other areas of the country, where such a decline might be taken in stride, the South has felt the loss of tradition as a palpable absence.

If anything, Young's *Selected Essays* (1990) are even better. His comparison of Robert Frost and John Crowe Ransom fosters a greater appreciation of these two very different poets, while his contrast of the critical theories of Ransom and Cleanth Brooks demonstrates the genuine intellectual diversity that existed among the southern New Critics. Even his one nonsouthern essay ("The Little Houses against the Great") concerns a controversy involving the New Critics. In debating whether Ezra Pound deserved the Bollingen Prize for *The Pisan Cantos* while under indictment for treason, the literary world divided itself between those who believed in the autonomy of art and those who stressed the social responsibilities of the artist. In his life and work, Thomas Daniel Young remained committed to the first of these principles, while never losing sight of the second.

MARK WINCHELL
Clemson University

Mark Royden Winchell, ed., *The Vanderbilt Tradition: Essays in Honor of Thomas Daniel Young* (1991); Thomas Daniel Young, *Fabulous Provinces* (1988).

INDEX

Page numbers in boldface refer to articles.

Brown, H. Rap, 24

Brown, Henry Box, 19

Brown, Larry, 77, 137, 145, **198–201**, 275, 306, 336; *Big Bad Love*, 14, 199; *Billy Ray's Farm*, 199; *Dirty Work*, 198–99; *Facing the Music*, 198, 201; *Father and Son*, 198–99; *Fay*, 14, 198; *Joe*, 14, 198–99, 336; *The Miracle of Catfish*, 199; *On Fire*, 199; *The Rabbit Factory*, 198

Brown, Mary Ward, 145

Brown, Rita Mae, **201–2**; *Catch as Cat Can*, 202; *Cat on the Scent*, 202; *Cat's Eyewitness*, 202; *Claws and Effect*, 202; *Murder at Monticello*, 202; *Murder on the Prowl*, 202; *Murder, She Meowed*, 202; *Pawing through the Past*, 202; *Pay Dirt*, 202; *Rest in Pieces*, 202; *Rubyfruit Jungle*, 80, 202; *Sneaky Pie's Cookbook*, 202; *Sour Puss*, 202; *The Tail of the Tip-off*, 202; *Whisker of Evil*, 202; *Wish You Were Here*, 202

Brown, Robert R., 142

Brown, Rosellen, 55

Brown, Sterling A., 12, 20, **202–4**, 344; "The Blues as Folk Poetry," 47; *Collected Poems*, 204; "Ma Rainey," 46, 47; *The Negro in American Fiction*, 203; *Southern Road*, 20, 47; "Tin Roof Blues," 47

Brown, William Wells, 19, 22, 36, **204–5**; *Black Man*, 205; *Clotel*, 24, 78, 205; *Clotelle*, 205; *Escape*, 21, 205; *Miralda*, 205; *My Southern Home*, 205; *Narrative of William Wells Brown*, 3, 204; *Negro in the American Revolution*, 205; *Rising Son*, 205; *Three Years in Europe*, 205

Bruynoghe, Yannick, 48

Buck, Pearl, 31

Burke, James Lee, **205–6**; *Black Cherry Blues*, 205; *Cimarron Rose*, 205; *Half of Paradise*, 205; *Jolie Blon's Bounce*, 63; *A Morning for Flamingoes*, 63; *The Neon Rain*, 63; *White Doves at Morning*, 206

Burroughs, Franklin, 100

Burroughs, John, 97

Bush, Robert, 340

Butler, Robert Olen, 83, 129, 281

Butterfield, Paul, 49

Byrd, William, II, 1, 28, **206–8**; *Careless Husband*, 207; *Discourse Concerning the Plague*, 207; *History of the Dividing Line*, 15, 30, 35, 70, 86, 137, 160, 207–8; *A Journey to the Land of Eden*, 207; *New-gefundenes Eden*, 207; *A Progress to the Mines*, 30, 207; *The Secret History of the Dividing Line*, 86, 207–8

Cabell, James Branch, 7, **208–9**, 364; *As I Remember It*, 209; *The Biography of the Life of Manuel*, 209; *Figures of Earth*, 209; *Heirs and Assigns*, 209; *Jurgen*, 208, 209; *Let Me Lie*, 209; *Nightmare Has Triplets*, 209; *The Silver Stallion*, 209; *Something about Eve*, 209; *The Works of James Branch Cabell*, 208

Cable, George Washington, 6, 57–58, 65, **209–11**, 226, 340, 375; *Bonaventure*, 211; *The Cavalier*, 57, 211; *The Creoles of Louisiana*, 211; *Dr. Sevier*, 211; *The Grandissimes*, 78, 138, 149, 209, 211; *Lovers of Louisiana*, 211; *Madame Delphine*, 209; *The Negro Question*, 209; *Old Creole Days*, 138, 209, 211; *The Silent South*, 209

Caldwell, Erskine, 8, 15, 28, 142, **211–13**, 226, 349, 368, 433; *American Earth*, 212; *Deep South*, 213; *God's Little Acre*, 90, 211–12; *In Search of Bisco*, 213; *Journeyman*, 90; *Kneel to the Rising Sun*, 211–12; *Tobacco Road*, 90, 120, 121, 211–12; *You Have Seen Their Faces*, 161, 211–12

Caldwell Theater (New Orleans), 153

Calhoun, John C., 41

Campbell, Bebe Moore, 53

Campbell, Will D., **213–15**; *And Also with You*, 215; *Brother to a Dragonfly*, 38, 214; *Cecelia's Sin*, 215; *The Convention*, 215; *The Glad River*, 215; *Providence*, 215; *Race and the Renewal of the Church*, 214; *Robert G. Clark*, 215

Camuto, Christopher, 100

Cao, Lan, 129

Capen, Nahum, 192

Capote, Truman, 12, 81, 142, 179, **215–16**, 347; *Answered Prayers*, 216; *Breakfast at Tiffany's*, 215; *The Grass Harp*, 215; *In Cold Blood*, 216, 347; *Other Voices, Other Rooms*, 80, 215, 347; *A Tree of Night*, 215

Carolina Playmakers, 153, 156

Carpentier, Alejo, 126

Carruthers, William, 3, 105–6

Carter, Charles David, 94

Carter, Hodding, 14, 99, 244, 386, 421

Cash, Jean W., 43

Cash, W. J., **216–17**, 364; *The Mind of the South*, 12, 208, 216–17, 244

Cassill, R. V., 53

Caudill, Harry, 31

Cawein, Madison, 7

Chaffin, Lillie D., 31

Chappell, Fred, 13, 114, 191, **217–18**, 219–20, 430, 439; *Bloodfire*, 32; *Brighten the Corner Where You Are*, 218; *C*, 218; *Castle Tzingal*, 218; *Dagon*, 217; *Family Gathering*, 218; *Farewell, I'm Bound to Leave You*, 218; *First and Last Words*, 218; *The Gaudy Place*, 217; *I Am One of You Forever*, 32, 217; *The Inkling*, 217; *It Is Time, Lord*, 217; *Look Back All the Green Valley*, 218; *Midquest*, 218; *Plow Naked*, 218; *River: A Poem*, 32; *Source*, 218; *Spring Garden*, 218; *A Way of Happening*, 218; *The World between the Eyes*, 32, 218

Cheney, Brainard, 10

Cherry, Kelly, **218–20**; *Augusta Played*, 219; *Death and Transfiguration*, 219; *God's Loud Hand*, 219; *Hazard and Prospect*, 219; *History, Passion, Freedom, Death, and Hope*, 219; *In the Wink of an Eye*, 219; *The Lost Traveller's Dream*, 219; *Lovers and Agnostics*, 219; *My Life and Dr. Joyce Brothers*, 219; *Natural Theology*, 219; *Relativity: A Point of View*, 219; *Rising Venus*, 218–19; *Sick and Full of Burning*, 219; *Society of Friends*, 219; *We Can Still Be Friends*, 219

Chesnut, Mary Boykin, 35, 42–43, 57, **220–**

21; *A Diary*, 464; *Mary Chesnut's Civil War*, 35, 220–21, 471

Chesnutt, Charles W., 6, 19, 65, **221–22**, 432; *Colonel's Dream*, 222; *Conjure Woman*, 22, 89, 221; *House behind the Cedars*, 23, 78, 221; *Marrow of Tradition*, 221; *Wife of His Youth*, 221

Childress, Alice, 21–22, 157

Childress, Mark, 54–55

Chivers, Thomas Holley, 4

Choi, Susan, 83, 129

Chopin, Kate, 6, 139, **222–23**; *At Fault*, 222; *The Awakening*, 72, 77, 222–23; *Bayou Folk*, 222; *A Night in Acadie*, 222

Civil rights, **52–56**, 214, 251, 272–73, 300–301, 320, 369, 421, 452

Civil War, 5, 8, 27, 35, 40, **56–60**, 94, 113, 135, 191, 220, 246, 265–66, 275–76, 291, 340, 346, 352–53, 374, 416, 445, 450, 459, 463–64

Clark, Thomas D., 159, 160

Cleage, Pearl, 25

Clemens, Samuel Langhorne (Mark Twain), 27, 30, 58, 64, 65, 67–69, 91–92, 142, 179, 192, **223–26**, 271, 287, 312, 350; *Adventures of Huckleberry Finn*, 5, 37, 67–68, 79, 88, 143–44, 225, 226; *Adventures of Tom Sawyer*, 37, 68, 225; *A Connecticut Yankee in King Arthur's Court*, 223; "Dandy Frightening the Squatter," 88; "Jim Smiley and His Jumping Frog," 5, 88; *Life on the Mississippi*, 37, 68, 98, 161; *Roughing It*, 88; *Tragedy of Pudd'nhead Wilson*, 79, 225; *A Tramp Abroad*, 225–26

Cliff, Michelle, 422

Cobb, Ann, 356

Cobb, William, 54

Cofer, Judith Ortiz, 115

Cohen, Octavus Roy, 62

Cohn, David, **226–28**; *God Shakes Creation*, 226–27; *The Mississippi Delta and the World*, 226; *Where I Was Born and Raised*, 226, 227

Cohn, Deborah, 84

Dupuy, Eliza Ann, 117

Dykeman, Wilma, **251–52**, 430; *Explorations*, 251; *The Far Family*, 251; *The French Broad*, 251; *Look to This Day*, 251; *Neither White nor Black*, 251; *Prophet of Plenty*, 251; *Return the Innocent Earth*, 251; *Seeds of Southern Change*, 251; *The Tall Woman*, 31, 251; *Tennessee: A Bicentennial History*, 251; *Tennessee Woman*, 251; *Too Many People, Too Little Love*, 251

Early, Jubal, 40

East, P. D., 214

Edgerton, Clyde, 137, 145, 191, **252–53**; *The Floatplane Notebooks*, 252; *Killer Diller*, 252; *Lunch at the Piccadilly*, 252–53; *Raney*, 252; *Walking across Egypt*, 14, 252

Edmonds, Randolph, 21

Edwards, David "Honeyboy," 46, 51

Edwards, Harry Stillwell, 6

Egerton, John, 129

Elliott, Stephen, 108

Elliott, William Yandell, 73, 108

Ellis, Joseph J., 39

Ellison, Ralph, 107, **253–54**, 376; *Invisible Man*, 13, 23, 24, 36, 48, 90, 144, 254; *Juneteenth*, 254; "Richard Wright's Blues," 48; *Shadow and Act*, 254; *Trading Twelves*, 376

Emerson, Claudia, 114

Equiano, Oladuah, 19

Erdrich, Louise, 95

Evans, Augusta Jane, 3, 148–49, **254–56**; *At the Mercy of Tiberius*, 255; *Beulah*, 254, 255; *Devota*, 255; *Inez*, 255; *Infelice*, 255; *Macaria; or, Altars of Sacrifice*, 57, 135, 254, 255; *St. Elmo*, 77, 149, 254, 255; *A Speckled Bird*, 255; *Vashti; or, Until Death Do Us Part*, 255

Evans, Walker, 161, 163

Everett, Percival, **256–57**; *American Desert*, 257; *Big Picture*, 257; *Cutting Lisa*, 257; *Damned If I Do*, 257; *Erasure*, 256; *For Her Dark Skin*, 257; *Frenzy*, 257;

Glyph, 257; *God's Country*, 257; *Grand Canyon, Inc.*, 257; *The History of the African American Race according to Strom Thurmond*, 257; *My California*, 257; *The One That Got Away*, 257; *re:f (gesture)*, 257; *Suder*, 256; *Walk Me to the Distance*, 257; *Watershed*, 256; *The Weather and Women Treat Me Fair*, 257; *Wounded*, 257; *Zulus*, 257

Fabre, Michel, 43

Fain, John Tyree, 480

Fairbain, Ann, 52

Fast, Howard, 213

Faulkner, John, 120

Faulkner, William, 5, 8–9, 12, 15–16, 33, 43, 56, 60–61, 65, 68–69, 76–77, 95, 102, 107, 110, 127, 129, 139, 140–42, 183–84, 189–90, 199, 206, 226, 244–45, **257–60**, 269, 274–75, 277, 280, 312, 336–37, 341, 349–50, 360, 389, 394, 414, 417, 420, 433, 436–37, 444, 461, 468, 476, 480; *Absalom, Absalom!*, 58, 76, 105, 126, 149–50, 179–80, 225, 258, 433; "Afternoon of a Cow," 89; *As I Lay Dying*, 89, 149, 258; "The Bear," 28, 69, 99; *Collected Stories*, 258; *A Fable*, 258; *Flags in the Dust*, 258; *Go Down, Moses*, 99, 258, 433; *The Hamlet*, 28, 89, 258, 433; *Intruder in the Dust*, 61, 259; *Knight's Gambit*, 61; *Light in August*, 78, 149–50, 258; *The Mansion*, 28, 260, 433; *Mosquitoes*, 258; "Pantaloon in Black," 79; *Pylon*, 258; *The Reivers*, 68, 78, 89, 258, 380; *Requiem for a Nun*, 260; *Sanctuary*, 28, 60, 78, 89, 143, 149, 258; *Sartoris*, 47, 76, 258; *Soldiers' Pay*, 47, 258; *The Sound and the Fury*, 71–72, 76, 144, 173, 180, 258; *The Town*, 28, 260, 433; *Uncollected Stories*, 258; *The Unvanquished*, 58, 77, 258; *The Wild Palms*, 258

Fauset, Jessie Redmon, 203, 432

Faust, Drew Gilpin, 41

Federal Theater Project, 155, 328

Federal Writers Project, 176, 253, 328

Fellman, Michael, 40

Southern Literary Journal, 321, 408

Southern Literary Messenger, 4, 56, 108, 109, 110, 390

Southern Literary Renaissance, 7–8, 10, 14, 82, 110, 127, 130, 139, 141, 183, 186, 196–97, 208, 238, 363, 364–65, 383, 433

Southern Nature Project, 100

Southern Poetry Review, 116, 381–82

Southern Review, 2, 103, 107–8, 110, 116, 175, 198, 417, 456

Southworth, E. D. E. N., **422–23**; The Hidden Hand, 423; Retribution, 423; Shannondale, 117; Virginia and Magdalene, 117

Spears, Monroe K., 240

Spencer, Anne, 20

Spencer, Duncan, 300

Spencer, Elizabeth, 13, **423–25**, 439; Fire in the Morning, 424; Knights and Dragons, 424; Landscapes of the Heart, 424; Light in the Piazza, 424; The Night Travelers, 425; No Place for an Angel, 242–25; The Snare, 425; Stories, 424; The Voice at the Back Door, 424

Spirit of the Times, 4, 65, 87, 311, 324, 348

Springer Opera House (Columbus, Ga.), 153

Sprinkle, Patricia, 61–62

Stallings, Lawrence, 10

Stanford, Donald, 417

Stanford, Frank, **425–27**; Arkansas Bench Stone, 427; The Battlefield Where the Moon Says I Love You, 427; Conditions Uncertain and Likely to Pass Away, 427; Constant Stranger, 427; Crib Death, 427; Field Talk, 427; It Wasn't a Dream, It Was a Flood, 427; Ladies from Hell, 427; The Light the Dead See, 427; Shade, 427; The Singing Knives, 425, 427; You, 427

Starr, Alfred, 73

Steadman, Mark, Jr., 5

Steele, Max, 362

Steinke, Darcey, **427–29**; Easter Everywhere, 429; The Gospel according to John, 428; The Great Disappointment,

428; Jesus Saves, 428; Joyful Noise: The New Testament Revisited, 428; Milk, 428; Suicide Blonde, 428; Up through the Water, 428

Stephens, Alexander, 41

Stern, Steven, 145

Stevens, David, 305

Stevenson, Alec, 73

Stewart, Randall, 12

Still, James, 10, 32, 113, 420, **429–30**; From the Mountain, from the Valley, 430; Hounds on the Mountain, 31, 429–30; On Troublesome Creek, 31, 429; Pattern of a Man, 430; River of Earth, 31, 429–30; Run for the Elbertas, 430; Sporty Creek, 430; Wolfpen Notebooks, 430; Wolfpen Poems, 430

Stockley, Grif, 63

Stokely, James R., 251

Stone, Ruth, 114

Stovall, Floyd, 12

Stowe, Harriet Beecher, 106, 117, 254, 402, 444

Straight, Susan, 52–53

Street, James, **430–32**; Biscuit Eater, 430–31; By Valor and Arms, 431; Civil War, 431; Gauntlet, 431; Good-bye, My Lady, 430, 431; High Calling, 431; In My Father's House, 431; James Street's South, 431; Look Away!, 431; Mingo Dabney, 431; Oh, Promised Land, 431; Revolutionary War, 431; Tap Roots, 430, 431; Tomorrow We Reap, 431

Stribling, T. S., 10, 62, 197, **432–33**; Best Dr. Poggioli Detective Stories, 62; Birthright, 432; Bright Metal, 432; The Forge, 432; Laughing Stock, 433; The Store, 62, 432; Teeftallow, 432; Unfinished Cathedral, 432

Strode, Hudson, 239

Stuart, Dabney, 13

Stuart, Jesse, 8, 28, 31, 113–14, 429, **433–34**; Beyond Dark Hills, 434; Daughter of the Legend, 434; Head O' W-Hollow, 433; Hold April, 434; The Kingdom Within,